60,001+
best baby
names

DIANE STAFFORD

Copyright © 2008, 2011 by Diane Stafford
Cover and internal design © 2011 by Sourcebooks, Inc.
Cover design by Krista Joy Johnson/Sourcebooks
Cover photo © Anatoliy Samara/iStockphoto

This publication is designed to provide accurate and authoritative information in regard to the subject matter covered. It is sold with the understanding that the publisher is not engaged in rendering legal, accounting, or other professional service. If legal advice or other expert assistance is required, the services of a competent professional person should be sought.—*From a Declaration of Principles Jointly Adopted by a Committee of the American Bar Association and a Committee of Publishers and Associations*

All brand names and product names used in this book are trademarks, registered trademarks, or trade names of their respective holders. Sourcebooks, Inc., is not associated with any product or vendor in this book.

Published by Sourcebooks, Inc.
P.O. Box 4410, Naperville, Illinois 60567-4410
(630) 961-3900
Fax: (630) 961-2168
www.sourcebooks.com

Library of Congress Cataloging-in-Publication Data

Stafford, Diane.
  60,001 best baby names / Diane Stafford.
    p. cm.
  Includes bibliographical references.
  1. Names, Personal—Dictionaries. I. Title. II. Title: Sixty thousand and one best baby names. III. Title: Sixty thousand one best baby names.
  CS2377.S57332 2011
  929.4'4—dc23

2011021586

Printed and bound in Canada.
WC 10 9 8 7 6 5 4 3 2 1

I dedicate this book to:
My wonderful and perfect husband, Greg.
My sweet and beautiful daughter, Jenny.
My lovely, personality-plus stepchildren: Matthew, Laura, Patrick, Molly, and Cita.
And the children who make me smile every time I see them: Ben, London, Liam, Ethan,
Patrick, Amanda, Mateo, Josie, Romano, Isabella, Joey, Liliana, Eamon, and Joaquin.
You give me sweetness, hugs, laughs, and the best conversations ever.
All of you are pure magic.

Contents

Acknowledgments

Sincere thanks to Ed Knappman of New England Publishing Associates for giving me the chance to write this book—and to Elizabeth Frost Knappman, literary agent and friend, who made my professional dreams come true again and again (fourteen books and still going strong).

Thank you to literary agent Roger Williams of Publish or Perish Agency, whose sense of humor, expertise, and direction keep me writing and publishing.

Thanks, too, to Sourcebooks' Dominique Raccah, Shana Drehs, Hillel Black, Emily Williams, Bethany Brown, Kelly Barrales-Saylor, Dan Bulla, Samantha Raue, Morgan Hrejsa, and Kristin Esch for their work on *60,001+ Best Baby Names*.

Thanks to my dear friends Chris Slovacek, Dana and Clarence Chandler, Rachel Capote, David Nordin, Melinda Munoz, Tessie Patterson, Renee Redden, Donna Pate, Dinah Anderson, Brent Richardson, Katrina Munoz, Greg Graber, Dylan Rigdon, Mark Bottini, Frances Munoz, Vera Harrison, Angie and Bobby Quinones, Margie Munoz, and Lupe Munoz.

Thanks to my dear family in Texas: Allen, Christina, Austin, Xanthe, Camilla, Richard, Gina, Curtis, Cameron, Lindsay, Josh, Ella, Britt, and Renee.

From the bottom of my heart, I thank my loving husband, Greg Munoz, with whom I'm having the time of my life.

Introduction

Why Names Matter So Much

Your name is important. Whether you liked it growing up or loathed it, your name was significant. People used it often or they didn't. People couldn't pronounce it or spell it right—or they could. Friends always remembered it—or they couldn't seem to place your name—*ever*.

All of these factors figure into the satisfaction rating you would give your name. So now that you're going to name your own baby, you want to know how that happened. Why are some people so lah-de-dah happy with their names while others despise the names they were given at birth, even to the point of going to court and paying to have them changed?

Indeed, a name can affect the ebb and flow of your entire existence. That's exactly why parents-to-be often give the baby-naming process numerous hours of list-perusing, head-scratching, and poll-taking.

Most people express satisfaction with their names if their names are mainstream, such as Michael, David, and Sam, or Lisa, Kathryn, and Christina. But it's common to see huge drops in satisfaction when we enter the realm of unusual names. A third of those with odd names will say they hated the name during childhood, but later "grew into" the name and now enjoy it. Another third with odd names report that they enjoyed having a different kind of name. The final third hated their names while they were children and still hate their names years later in adulthood. The latter group often think of their names as the albatross around their necks—the miserable excuse for a name that caused them grief and pain.

One woman named Charmaine says she didn't like her name because people always misspelled it and made fun of her. Every time she met someone, she heard, "Don't squeeze the Charmin!" She also faced a common problem that people with unusual names encounter: you can't ever buy personalized necklaces, key chains, or pens.

The irony is that some kids with plain names envy the girl or boy with the unusual name. (I remember knowing a girl in elementary school whose name was Romaine, and I thought she had the coolest name on earth.)

For a kid who feels "stuck" with an albatross name, however, life can be long and bumpy. While people with better names seem to glide through social encounters effortlessly, the name-challenged types are more likely to stumble and bumble their way through the jungle.

If you have any doubt, note the baby-naming efforts of a person who grew up as Nyleen or Hortense, Huelett or Drakeston: you'll probably find that this individual will have offspring named John or Ann. One woman named Daphne-Jade says she wanted her daughter's name to be beautiful and unique but not freakish. "I didn't want her to have a lot of stress like I did with my name."

Sure, you just want your child to love his or her name. You want the name to fall off everyone's lips, making your kid happy and loved. You want that tot to grow up to excel in sports and academics and careers and relationships, and you want to see that name on a team roster, marquee, or at least an Academy Award or Pulitzer Prize.

So can a name pave the way to success and happiness? Psychologists tell us that having a name that's a good fit can make a person feel more self-confident. Conversely, your child's self-esteem may suffer if he winces every time someone laughs at his name.

What's the significance of all this for you, the parent-in-waiting? You are dead-on right in thinking that finding the "right" name constitutes a major responsibility. This occasion is momentous enough to merit lots of discussion and lots of thumbing through this book until you finally hit on it—The Right Name.

You're looking for a name that resonates, one that's memorable and perfect—but not frighteningly memorable or overly perfect. You're looking for a name that is absolutely sure to have a positive effect on your little tyke's life.

Names Send Messages

Are you more likely to trust a Michael or a Donovan? An Erica or a Mary? A Crash or a Blake?

We know that most employers prefer middle-of-the-road names to crazy, quirky ones. Their bias tells them that maybe parents who give wild names to their babies don't have the genetic potential for brilliance that some other people may have. Of course, this isn't necessarily true—but it's a common perception. Of course, if the employer is interviewing for a screenwriter or creative think tank, a Quentin or a Hazel might get his attention, while he might not be interested in a Mary or John.

Many employers freely admit that they form opinions based on names—and even throw away a résumé if the name has a negative connotation. "If I'm interviewing for a position of financial responsibility," says one human resources director, "why would I want to talk to a woman whose name is Fluffy Petunia? I can't take her seriously."

Wait a minute here. You didn't choose your name, right? It's not your fault—your parents gave it to you. As a newborn, you had no vote or voice.

True. But that doesn't change the fact that people react to names—in positive and negative and even neutral ways.

Same Name, Different Experience

Your own individual experiences affect how you feel about your name, and the same will be true for your child.

One girl tells of loving her name, which is Grace. "My sisters were named Honor and Faith, and we all liked our names."

But another girl named Grace hates the name, saying, "Thanks, Mom and Dad, for giving me the most boring name known to mankind." This Grace is an example of a person who blames all her disappointments on the all-wrong name her parents gave her. "If I had just been Samantha or Roxanne, my life would have been better."

You may decide you just can't win when you name a baby. The question is, does that child make the name? Or does the name shape the child?

Warm, Fuzzy Names

Most people want to give their kids names they will love. That's why many of us can't let the process go. For the whole nine months we fret and falter, marvel and malinger, worry and wonder. Then when we hear that John Travolta and Kelly Preston have named their new baby Benjamin, and we nod and say, "*Nice*—I like that name." All parents are looking for a good fit like that one—a name that just feels right.

We warm to some names; they're just fun to say. A girl named Chloe says that people love to say her name. They meet her and after that when they see her they always say, "Hi, Chloe" or "Hey, there's Chloe," as if they just enjoy saying the name.

Some names feel more comfortable than others. For example, one man who works at a call center experimented with using different names on the phone on different days. He says he got good responses when he used the names Chris, Kevin, Michael, and Brad. But he got a terrific response when he switched to Chad. Callers would reply, "Hey, Chad!" in an upbeat tone. So he started using Chad all the time, and the response was 100 percent positive. He was amazed. If he changed to another name and returned to Chad, the exchange was always the best with Chad.

What Makes a Name Problematic?

What kinds of names cause problems? Those that people can't pronounce or spell, or those that resemble other, more familiar names.

Many women in particular report that they dislike having a name that is often mistaken for something that sounds similar. For example, a girl named Callie says people always think she is saying "Kelly" or "Kaley," and it drives her crazy because she has to set the record straight time after time.

Another woman named Chelsa always gets asked if her name is actually Chelsea. "People act like I don't really know what my own name is!" she says.

Too much cuteness isn't a good idea, either. One woman named her twins To-dae and Tamara (pronounced "tomorrow"), and found that the reaction she got most often was laughter. Such names can put undue stress on your child.

Another potential minefield is giving your child a name like Pilot or High Tea or Cupcake. Such a non-name becomes a bona fide name when you register it on the birth certificate. But you also give your child the legacy of explaining it lifelong.

A girl named Jam says that people never believe she is telling the truth when she tells them her name. "They look at me like I'm a loser for walking around with a nickname like that, or they start telling jokes about preserves and jellies."

The Unpredictability of Pop Culture

You can't predict when you might accidentally select a baby name that later becomes "huge" via the media. And when it happens, it's not always a good thing. One woman named Phoebe says that when she meets people, they always say, "Oh my God, like on *Friends*!"

Certain names experience heydays, while others fall out of favor. Today's Angelina Jolie and Jessica Alba are beauty icons, so no one is surprised to hear of babies named Angelina and Jessica. The same thing happened in the fifties when Debbie Reynolds was America's sweetheart. Suddenly little Deborahs were running around everywhere.

We can also pinpoint names that were never cool for even a minute because the name sounded heavy or unattractive. For example, can you really imagine a beautiful Bertha? Or Ethel? They're out there, but the names have some heavy, heavy baggage.

Do be aware that if you choose a name that's hot, the chances are good that your daughter will be Ashley S. in preschool because she will be in a classroom with others named Ashley. Same goes for Jake and Emma, Nick and Emily—any name in the top 100 is fair game.

A Name That Makes Your Baby Smile

Your first gift to your baby boy or baby girl is a name. Make it one that is meaningful to you, and it will probably turn out to be a good fit.

Use this book to make a list of the names you love. Ask your spouse to do the same. Then when you look at the lists and there are no names you both like, start over and come up with a list of names that you can both embrace.

A good name is a treasure. Odds are, you will never love a name more than you love the one you give your baby.

Living with an Unusual Name

At nineteen, Xanthe Shirley, my niece and a sophomore at Texas A&M University, offers her excellent perspective on what it was like to grow up with a unique name:

"My attitude toward my name ranged from rejection to acceptance, and I finally embraced it," says Xanthe, whose name is pronounced X-anth.

"In elementary school, it was rough having a bizarre name because no one could pronounce it. Little kids had a hard time saying Xanthe, let alone remembering it, and since bluntness is the norm for children, classmates would always tell me how weird my name was. That alone was very heartbreaking for me because I just wanted to fit in. Teachers also had trouble pronouncing it. After a month or so they finally got it, but the time in between was difficult because I was a shy kid so I absolutely hated having to correct a teacher. Another thing that bothered me was that I could never find pencils or key chains in the store with my name on them, and for some reason that was always a big defeat for me. When I was in second grade, I recall looking at all the cool miniature bicycle license plates with names on them, but no Xanthe, of course. I remember thinking, 'Why can't I have a normal name, like Erin?' I went through a phase of longing for a common name, but that didn't last very long.

"I soon began to accept that my name was different and that people would always have trouble pronouncing it at first. I realized that just because my name was odd, it didn't mean that people automatically thought I was an odd person, which was the silly notion I had when I was a child. My introduction speech telling how my name was spelled, what it meant, and why my parents picked it became my routine, and no longer bothered me. I even enjoyed it a little. I had come to appreciate the interest that sparked when people learned my name, and I saw that my friends with 'normal' names like Ashley or Brittany didn't get this attention.

"In junior high and high school I began to embrace my name. It made me different and set me apart, but that had become a good thing. I was the only Xanthe at my school and in the whole community, and that made me feel very special. My friends even embraced it. When we had substitute teachers, they butchered my name, but the whole class would correct him or her. They were proud to have a friend whose name started with an X.

"Now that I'm in college, I feel extremely fortunate to have a name that is not common. Acquaintances recognize me, and professors actually remember me. In interviews, my name and its history serve as an immediate icebreaker.

"I would definitely say that my name has shaped me into the person I am. Xanthe means 'golden' in Greek, and I have always tried to live up to that. I think the situations I have gone through because of my name have helped me become more humble, patient, and respectful of others. As of now, I can say that I would not give my child a mainstream name because of the positive impact that my strange name has had on me."

part one

Tips for Naming Your Baby

Name Quiz

What's Your Baby-Naming Style?

Take this revealing little quiz to see what you and your spouse know about names. This is a good way to determine whether your final name choice is likely to please you and your child one year from now (as well as ten years down the road).

No one walks into the baby-naming arena free of biases. In truth, we all have names we don't like simply because we sat by someone in school named Bathsheba and she popped her gum the whole livelong day, which made us loathe that name "just because."

So, just for fun, see how you fare on the following quiz. This will tell you what kind of slant and awareness you bring to the baby-naming table.

1. On a scale of 1 to 10, how important was your name in your own development of confidence and sense of self?

2. Do you believe that a name influences a child's life insofar as popularity, achievement, and self-confidence?

3. How would you rate your satisfaction with your own name, from 1 to 10 (with 10 meaning that you always loved it)?

4. What do you want in a name for your baby—one that's safe, fun, respectable, bizarre, or exciting?

5. What's one thing that always bothered you about your name?

6. What's something nobody knows about how you feel about your name?

7. Did you have to grow into your name or did you like it early on?

8. Do you believe certain names are so lightweight or weird that they make teachers and potential employers dismiss those individuals before they even meet them?

9. Can you remember the names of the most popular boy and girl in your high school?

10. Do you think it matters when a child has a name he or she has to explain, repeat, or pronounce for other people?

Check it out. Your answers reveal the following:

1. 7 to 10: Give yourself 10 points for an elevated awareness of a name's importance in forming a person.
2. Yes: Give yourself 10 points. No: give yourself 0 points.
3. 7 to 10: 0 points. 1 to 6: 10 points. (People who have always been comfortable with their names often don't fully understand how an odd, hard-to-pronounce name can affect someone.)
4. If you answered "bizarre" or "exciting," give yourself 0 points. If you answered "safe," "fun," or "respectable," you get 10 points.
5. If you have an answer for this question, you get 10 points for elevated awareness of the importance of a name. Otherwise, you get 0.
6. If you have always kept your feelings secret about your name, you may have "issues" when it comes to baby naming, so you get 0 points. If you answered that you have no secrets about your name, you get 10 points.
7. If you said that you had to grow into your name, you get 10 points because this indicates you went through the pain of having a name that didn't feel comfortable or right. If you always liked your name, you also get 10 points because you know how great it feels to have a name that fits.
8. Yes: You get 10 points. No: Wrong answer—studies prove that employers and teachers sometimes prejudge people in a negative way when their names are odd or spelled differently than usual. So you get 0 points.
9. Yes: You get 10 points because this indicates a high level of name awareness. No: You get 0 points because you weren't paying enough attention to names.
10. Yes: You get 10 points. No: You get 0 points—it does matter. Having to explain a name or pronounce it all the time turns out to be a bit of a liability for a child—a small setback.

Score of 90–100: You will do a fantastic job naming your baby! You bring to the table both an interest in names and an awareness of what counts.

Score of 80–89: You have better-than-average knowledge on what counts in baby naming. You should do well in finding the right name for your child.

Score of 70–79: You may want to read the naming tips in this book to improve your understanding of the importance of names.

Score of 69 or fewer: Take a deep breath, read the naming tips in this book, and then toss out all those names on your list that your family tells you sound way too scary, over-the-top, or unpronounceable. Be good to that baby. Choose a nice name or he or she will exact payback (not sleeping through the night for two or three years).

Caveats and Trends in Baby Naming

Name game caveats:
*   You don't have to please relatives, alive or dead.
*   You don't have to mimic celebs to have a star of your own.
*   You don't have to give your son the name Lawyer or Judge to make him look in those career directions.
*   You don't have to call your daughter Star or Glitz for her to understand that you want her to shine.
*   You don't have to avoid the names of people you disliked in school.
*   You do need to remember that a name can shape personality, career, and self-esteem.

Trends in naming:
*   Combine two names to form a new one.
*   Find a name you think will work if your child chooses a serious career.
*   Use your maiden name for a first name.
*   Honor a relative by using his or her name as a middle name.
*   Make up a name by checking out street names, TV credits, astrological signs, and chemistry charts.

Ten Great Tips for Naming Your Baby

1. Check to see if a name works well with your last name.

You don't want a tongue twister or a rhyme, but you do want the first, middle, and last names to sound great together. Try not to pair a first name ending in a vowel with a last name that starts with a vowel, like Ava Amazon—it's hard to say. Puns aren't good, either. Ima Hogg probably never liked her name. And I'm not so sure how King Solomon liked his.

2. Be aware of the spin off of an ultra-cool name.

The Emmas of recent years wound up being Emma S. and Emma R. in first grade because there were several girls with the same name. Somewhere down the line (around teen years), you can expect to hear complaints from your child, who will ask, "Why did you give me the same name eighty million other kids have?"

3. Know what will happen if your baby has an unusual name.

An odd name takes a bit of swagger to pull off. If that's in your genes, you're probably safe in calling your girl Rio or your boy Renzo. But remember it's a double whammy if you have a hard-to-say last name. That's a big load—two hard names to spell.

Plus, a unique name may lead to supersized bullying. Peers might be more likely to taunt Camaro and Denim, while everyday, ordinary Jake and Michael get a pass.

Ask yourself how your child will like having the name Willow or Lake, Bark or Destiny. Will she feel special? Will he feel silly?

4. Think a long time before you give your child a family name that sounds dated.

Your kid won't enjoy being an Ethel or Mortimer in a classroom filled with kids named Emily, Josh, Amber, Lindsay, Madison, Chloe, Marissa, and Harry. Names like Durwood and Drusilla got ditched for good reasons. There are lots of old-fashioned names that still sound good today—think Charlotte, Eleanor, Henry, William. Just think carefully when browsing through the family tree.

5. Know that namesakes have identity problems.

A child who is named after a parent won't like being called Junior or Little Allen. On the other hand, Trey, for a third-named boy, may get a kick out of having a historical name.

The real downside is personal ID confusion. Ask anyone who has been in that position what he had to deal with in regard to credit ratings and such. Unraveling mix-ups becomes your part-time job.

Shrinks tell us that giving a child his very own name is a better start in life than making him your mini-me. Tradition and heritage are fine things, but most kids won't appreciate the gesture until they're much older.

6. Make the family name your baby's middle name.

If you prefer mainstream names, but you want some touch of history in your baby's name, use a family name as a middle name. That way you get it in there—but the child doesn't have to use it if he doesn't like it.

7. Don't overplay the meaning of a name.

If you love a name but dislike its meaning, don't let that keep you from using it. A name's meaning doesn't have to weigh heavily in your choosing process. That kind of baggage is unlikely to affect your child's life.

8. Consider initials, shortened versions, and the length of the name.

Kids at school won't fail to notice that your child's initials are S.C.U.M. And the name you don't want shortened will get shortened.

The main thing is to avoid giving your child a name that puts a target on his back. A boy named Sue or a girl named Mack may hate you for being so unaware of the repercussions.

California mom Molly Rigdon also recommends giving your child a name with few letters so that when your child starts school, it's easy to learn to spell and write. "These things don't come to mind until you're helping your five-year-old Liliana write her name." Jill or Kate would have been easier.

9. See how it sounds when you say it.

Try typical parent language: "Hannibal Hayes, have you done your homework?" Check to see if you like how the words roll off your tongue. Sing "Hush Little Baby" and see if Abigail Anne sounds sweet. Think of a name that will make your child smile when the teacher calls it out on the first day of fifth grade.

10. Keep your name choice a big secret.

So you and your spouse finally have a name! Congratulations! I hope you love it. Now don't tell anyone. Otherwise, you can bet you will get a landslide of other options from well-meaning relatives. Or they might even start using the name to refer to your unborn child, and if you change the name, that will be unfortunate.

✳ ✳ ✳

More than anything else, just go with the name that feels right to you. That precious infant is going to be the best thing that ever happened to you—so choose a name you'll love to sing and say every single day of your life.

Note to Readers

Find within the text the most popular names of 2010 for boys and girls designated by ✪.

Find within the text the top twin names of 2010 for boys and girls designated by ➊.

part two

How Names Shape Our Lives

Here, twenty-one people share their thoughts on their names:

Camilla Shirley Pierce, homemaker and mother, Houston: "Although I was named for a beloved great aunt, I always felt that carrying around such an unusual name was not great. When I was a child, no one could pronounce it or spell it. It was a source of embarrassment and aggravation. Now, at age sixty-five, when people read my name they still mispronounce it, and I always feel like saying, 'How hard can it be? I could pronounce it at age three!'"

David Nordin, consultant: "I always liked my name because it had more character than other names. David has Biblical history, and it's more elegant and regal than your average name. On the flip side, my odd middle name caused me years of embarrassment. Teachers would call out that name during roll call, and people would laugh and make fun of me … As soon as I was grown, I had it legally changed. Parents should never name their kids anything that could make them objects of ridicule."

Clarence Raymond Chandler, President of Marshall & Winston, Inc., in Midland, Texas: "I was named after my dad's favorite brother, who was a great guy I admired. I was raised in south Texas (Benavides), where my friends were named Roberto, José, Ricardo, Jesus, and Francisco, so being a George, Bill, Jerry, Charles, or Roger never really came up on my 'wish list.' I was content! Today, technology has caused the minor inconvenience of not being able to find enough room on forms to print out my long name, much less my signature." Chandler adds: "I had it easy compared to my dad, who was born in an era when children were named after famous people; he got incessant ribbing, not to mention playground fights, when he was growing up, because his challenge was answering to Napoleon Bonaparte Chandler, which is right up there with the ranks of Johnny Cash's 'how do you do, my name is Sue.' In school, it was common knowledge that you only picked on him once, or you had a real dogfight on your hands. To avoid 'you gotta be kidding' comments, he adopted the name 'Nap' Chandler. He was a great dad, patriot, WWII veteran, ethical businessman, champion for the little guy, and a loving and tough SOB—he was my hero!"

Jennifer Wright, psychiatrist in Atlanta, Georgia: "I've always liked my name. Some of my best friends have been named Jennifer also, and I think it suits our personalities. The benefit of having a 'common' name is that I never have difficulty finding personalized items. Plus, I like the nicknames 'Jen' and 'Jenny.'"

Kristina Kaczmarek Holt, graphic artist: "I have always liked my name because it was unique. I had never come across a Kristina with a 'K' until I was a teenager, and then it was usually a Kristy or Kristine. I liked the sound of my first and last name together (the two Ks)—that seemed to work. My name was a heck of a thing to learn to spell in kindergarten, but it was all mine. They used to tape your name to those thick green pencils you learned to write with, and I was always sharpening my pencil down into my name. It wasn't until I recently had a child of my own (Noah) that my dad told me where he got my name. I assumed he picked it because it was a Polish name, and his family was half Polish. But, instead, he named me after a woman who was especially nice to him when he was young, who must have made a strong impression, because the name stuck with him until I was born."

Homemaker Dana Huggins Chandler: "I like to be just a little different from everyone else around me, so I always loved my name. There are now many people named Dana, but most don't have the same pronunciation. My name rhymes with Anna and Lana. I always tell people I was named after my dad—Dan—which isn't true, but it does help people remember how to pronounce my name."

Houston TV anchor Dominique Sachse: "Considering you can't pick your name at birth, I'm quite pleased with the one my parents chose for me. I think it has a level of sophistication, and it's unique and European, which I am. I've never considered changing it, shortening it, or going by a nickname. It's a name I feel I've had to live up to."

Cari LaGrange, Internet business owner: "I liked my name growing up, but like most kids, I went through a phase when I wished I could change it, the way girls with straight hair want curly hair and vice versa. Thankfully, my name and its spelling were unique in the town where I grew up, so there was no other girl by my name to compare my identity to."

Jane Vitrano, homemaker in Midland, Texas: "My mother named my sister Linda and me Jane because she hated her own name, Lula Mae, and said she would never want her daughters to have anything but plain names—and no middle names."

Donna Pate, technical writer: "I was neutral about my name. It was okay but not too exciting or interesting. At least it didn't lend itself to juvenile humor. There was the chance of being labeled 'Prima Donna,' but that was beyond the vocabulary of most kids. I liked my name better after I learned what it meant, but that wasn't until I was an adult."

Natasha Graf, editor, New York: "My name is pretty special because I was named after a very important woman in my father's life. When I was young and wanted to be like every other girl with an American name, I didn't always like my name because it was unusual at the time, being Russian and all. However, when my father shared with me who I was named after, I came to love it because I feel like I am connected to her somehow. She was a professor at my father's college, and she spoke seven languages—a brilliant woman who had emigrated from Russia. She was his mentor—the first really intellectual person he met during college, and they stayed friends after he went to medical school. It was not an affair—more a meeting of the minds. They wrote to each other. He saved every letter she wrote, and he let me read them. It was so interesting to see my father as a young person through these letters. She died before I was born, before my father was married. I wish I could have met her; I wonder what she would have thought of me. As you can tell, I wouldn't want my name to be anything else."

JoAnn Roberson, counselor, Edna, Texas: "I didn't like my name because it reminded me of a boy's name—Joe. My dad said they were going to name me Jacquelyn, but an uncle said that was too long a name for a little baby, and I would never learn to spell it. I always wished that was my name."

Trey Speegle, former art director for *US Weekly*, New York City: "I've always appreciated my name, although when I was very young and wanted to fit in, I wished I had a more normal name, like Chris, or a cool name, like Skip. My great-grandmother named me; I was born on her birthday, April 13, and I was her thirteenth great-grandson. Her son (my grandfather) was John Hugh Speegle Sr., and my father is John Hugh Speegle Jr., so she named me Trey John—'the third' John."

Angela Theresa Clark, co-owner of Court Record Research, Inc.: "My mother named me Angela Theresa after two of her favorite Carmelite nuns. I was known as Theresa until sixth grade, when I tired of telling teachers that I didn't go by Angela and just surrendered to being called that. I thought it was stupid to be named something so close to the word 'angel.' Angels are imaginary, soft, and I saw them as easy prey. I was also afraid people might think I was angelic. I thought I had to be tough in my family, with five brothers and two big (mean) older sisters (ha!). I was tomboyish, and Theresa just fit better. Some family members still call me Theresa, although it doesn't fit me anymore because now I'm softer and much more vulnerable. I love my name."

Spiker Davis, dentist, Houston, Texas: "I really liked my name because people always remembered it, and there's no one to get confused with. Also, with a last name like Davis (seventh most common name in the U.S.), you need something to separate you from the crowd."

Cristy Ann Hayes, journalist and mother of two: "My name became a primary focus when I was young and searching for a sense of self, like other preteens. I was disappointed when people would ask what Cristy was short for, and I had to reply 'nothing.' I would wish my mom had taken more time to give me a name as substantial as Christina or Christian. My name also worked well as a taunt for my brother, who insisted I was the only one of the three siblings whose name didn't start with W, so I was not part of the family. Will and Wendy could be rascals that way. My mom thought it was clever to give my name an unconventional spelling, so I have, my entire life, had to take special care in spelling my name, and often people will add an h. My driver's license is incorrect because of this, and many of my in-laws still spell it wrong. But after years of frustration regarding the spelling, I now appreciate the measuring tool it has become for me, showing how attuned someone is to me. I hold in high regard those who actually take the time to recognize the unique spelling and write it correctly. I believe it says something about one's character and approach to life when you take care to get a name right!"

Frank Vitrano, retired petroleum engineer in Midland, Texas: "I was born in Waco, Texas, of a Sicilian father, and I was named for my grandfather, Frank Anthony, which is the Italian custom for the firstborn son. You get your grandfather's name."

Jennifer Colwell, commercial property management, Midland, Texas: "Since I'm in my fifties, there were not very many Jennifers when I was growing up, and I always loved my name. I thought it was pretty and considered it an asset."

Christopher (Chris) Fleming, teacher and consultant, Houston, Texas: "Growing up, I hated my name, Christopher Anne. I was called Christopher Columbus, was sent a draft notice, and was labeled 'effeminate' on an aptitude test in high school. I finally told my mother how much I had hated my name, and she was surprised. In my opinion, parents should choose a name that indicates the child's sex (not one that's androgynous), and that's easy to spell. I don't think it's good to give a baby a name that's bizarre or made up from several words."

Wendy Schnakenberg Corson, EMT, Oklahoma: "I have always hated my name. There were never any other Wendys, and if there were, they certainly weren't popular. My parents said they also liked the name Robin, which is a name I love; I told them how mad I was that they chose such a terrible name for me. Also, my middle name, Anne, is just boring. I was never teased about my name, so I suppose that is a positive. But, of course, kids had my last name—Schnakenberg—to tease me with!"

part three

Choosing Names That Project Success

You think names don't have socioeconomic impact? Well, think again. A survey conducted by Barclays Bank (in the UK) reveals that people with certain names actually earn more money than folks with "lesser" names. In fact, those most likely to bring home a six-figure income are men named David, John, and Michael.

When Barclays's analysts looked at sixty thousand of their high-end customers whose annual salaries topped £100,000 ($180,000), Susans topped the list of female wage earners, and close behind were Elizabeths, Sarahs, and Janes. Other femmes who brought in big bucks were named Alison, Helen, and Patricia.

Remember, though, that these were names that parents gave their kids in the '60s. Making projections based on lists of favored names for 2011, what we'll probably see topping the earners' chart forty years from now are Emmas and Isabellas, Ethans and Jacobs. Note that all these names sound conventional and trustworthy—nothing quirky, trendy, or fanciful. So if you want your offspring to support you when you're quasi-senile, choose substance over flash.

In his bestselling *Freakonomics*, author Steven D. Levitt observes that names first become entrenched with affluent families and then trickle down into lower income strata in subsequent years. So if a CEO names his twins Graham and Taylor, lower income parents will soon take up the Graham-Taylor banner. By the same token, the names Maddox and Zahara (kids of super-hot, mega-rich Angelina Jolie) resonate with star-watchers and gain momentum accordingly.

Sure, we like glitz, we love glamour, and we're fools for snob appeal. But this particular penchant wars with common sense, which tells us that quirky names give children dubious legacies.

Just like clothing, hairstyle, and grooming, a name makes an impression and often leads to unfair assumptions. That's why savvy business types sometimes go so far as to change their names simply to have a better shot at affluence; "Caprice" becomes "Jane," "Panama" morphs into "Mark," and "Canyon" snags Wall Street success as "James."

In the same way that we attribute good qualities to attractive people before we know them, people with "good" names may get a free pass just by virtue of having been named well. Maybe we simply perceive that people named Elizabeth and David are more substantial, and that paves their way to greater success and wealth than Terrell, Brandy, Fifi, or Fluffy.

Names make statements. Images of success come with names like Elizabeth and Michael, Madison and Ethan, whereas people take less seriously the Roxies, Bambis, Roccos, and Bucks of this world.

Lessons learned:
* Don't give your child a name that conveys undesirable qualities.
* Do give your child a name that implies success, attractiveness, depth, intelligence, and compassion.
* Do ask yourself what kind of impression a name will make on people your child comes in contact with.
* Don't choose haphazardly because "that's my favorite sitcom star" or "I like the sound of it" or "that was my aunt's name."

So while you're going through the rigors of baby-naming, why not factor in future earning potential? Ponder who will make more money: Will or Rip? Anna or Lotus? Sonny or Daniel? DeeDee or Sarah?

Sure, weighing a name's financial ramifications goes against the grain because most parents select sentimentally—they "love" a name, want to honor a relative, or think the name is unique, classic, or cool and trendy.

But good names can indeed provide an edge. You absolutely *can* choose a name that will help your child make friends more easily, have more confidence, have fewer psychological hang ups, be happier and more successful, and perhaps become the richest guy or girl on the block.

According to the Barclays survey, the top ten high-earning boys' names were:

1. David	6. Andrew
2. John	7. Richard
3. Michael	8. Robert
4. Peter	9. Mark
5. Paul	10. Stephen

And the survey yielded these top ten high-earning girls' names:

1. Susan	6. Patricia
2. Elizabeth	7. Jacqueline
3. Sarah	8. Alison
4. Jane	9. Anne
5. Helen	10. Nicola

part four

222 Fun Lists

Future Landscapers

Boys	*Girls*
Acre	Amaryllis
Arbor	Apple
Ash	Berry
Bamboo	Bouquet
Bark	Eucalyptus
Bougain	Fig
Boxwood	Flower
Branch	Gladiola
Brown	Ivy
Cedar	Juniper
Douglas	Kumquat
Fir	Lemon
Grape	Lily
Green	Orchid
Hedge	Pansy
Longwood	Petunia
Pine	Rose
Plum	Tree
Redwood	Twiggy
Spruce	Water
Woody	Wreath
Zen	

Future Jewelry Designers

Boys	*Girls*
Art	Artismo
Brash	Bracelet
Chain	Caliste
Clay	Champagne
Diamo	Diamond
Festoon	Flourish
Garland	Glamour
Golden	Glow
Hue	Jolie
Jon-Michel	Legend
Rich	Midnight
Salsa	Minim
Sandreene	Ornate
Shine	Pear
Silver	Ribbon
Trey	Sparkle
Twitch	Stella
Vintage	Touch
	Twinkle
	Vase
	Whimsy

Future Surfwear Business Tycoons

Boys	Girls
Arch	Aqua
Beach	Becca
Board	Bunny
Break	Butter
Bronze	Cocoa
Catch	Day
Casz	Drama
Crash	Fluff
Dude	Horizon
Dune	Kiki
Dylan	Missy
Eric	Moonbeam
Fritter	Sandy
Grit	Savor
Mammoth	Season
Midas	Sky
Move	Starry
Shore	Summer
Smooth	Sunny
Tyler	Sunshine
Wave	Tanna
	Tanny

Future Pro Athletes

Boys	Girls
Arliss	Brett
Atari	Cat
DeShawn	Charde
Devarick	Danesha
Jamin	DeWanna
Jamone	Ebony
Jerime	Eshaya
Kemba	Fabiana
Khary	Iziana
LaDainian	Kasey
LaMichael	Keeley
LeBron	Manya
Marquand	McCall
Martrez	Mistie
Marviel	Roneeka
Montavious	Sandrine
Ruvell	Selmone
Taurean	Yelena
Trumaine	

Achievers

Jewish/Hebrew Names

Boys	Girls	Boys	Girls
Andrew	Addison	Aaron	Anne
Butler	Emma	Abe	Claire
Chason	Blythe	Barry	Esther
Dennis	Bonnie	Benjamin	Golda
Doug	Brittney	Daniel	Hannah
Ewan	Camille	David	Ilana
Gavin	Christina	Eli	Jenny
Hank	Cindy	Esau	Johanna
Jeff	Delisa	Ethan	Judith
John	Emerey	Gabriel	Leah
Kaufman	Emma	Ira	Lena
Keane	Erin	Isaac	Lillian
Kent	Gaynor	Jake	Linda
Kevin	Gina	Jay	Mary
Mitchell	Hollyn	Joshua	Miriam
Norton	Janiqua	Levi	Naomi
Patton	Jessalyn	Marvin	Rachel
Rance	Leanne	Milton	Rebekah
Robert	Mallory	Nathan	Ruth
Schultz	Phoebe	Sam	Sadie
Scott	Rebecca	Saul	Sarah
Skip	Roxanne	Sheldon	Shara
Teague	Shae	Solomon	Sophie
Thorne	Taylor	Stanley	Sylvia
Usher	Tonya		Tovah

Future "Most Dependable"

Boys	Girls
Aaron	Amica
Alton	Amy
Barry	Bethany
Brent	Carrie
Chris	Chandra
Clint	Deb
Cole	Elle
Demarris	Heather
Derek	Hope
Devin	Juliet
Elmer	Larsen
Forrest	Lemuela
Gary	Lynn
Hunter	Olena
Jack	Otilie
Jeston	Penthea
Keller	Randie
Leo	Siaka
Mack	Sofie
Manny	Trella
Overton	Tucker
Radu	Varina
Scott	Weslee
Werner	Ximena
Will	Zore

Charmers

Boys	Girls
Brad	Ajana
Bret	Bead
Chance	Bridget
David	Chandi
Deryn	Coco
Devean	Dancy
Duncan	Denise
Fernando	Dionne
Jaret	Gidget
Jase	Ginzi
Jeremy	Halea
Kobe	Jen
LeBron	Joanna
Lorenzo	Kimana
Luke	Laya
Nissan	Maryann
Rasheed	Mia
Rob	Nicolae
Russ	Rita
Sage	Robin
Santino	Roxy
Slater	Shauna
Tolbert	Sierra
Tolfe	Tanisha
Viggo	Torry

Celebrity Names

Boys

Antonio
Ashton
Ben
Booker
Brad
Burt
Casey
Casper
Damon
Denzel
Fabrice
Fernando
Goran
Griffin
Hudson
Keenan
Kiefer
Liam
Marc
Matthew
Mel
Patrick
Russell
Ryan
Tom

Girls

Charlize
Demi
Drea
Drew
Fiona
Halle
Isabella
Jennifer
Jessica
Julia
Kate
Lara
Liv
Natasha
Oprah
Portia
Reese
Renee
Rosanna
Sela
Selma
Sheena
Simone
Thora
Uma

What Celebrities Name Their Babies

Boys

Abel James *(Amy Poehler and Will Arnett)*

Aleph *(Natalie Portman and Benjamin Millepied)*

Bear Blu *(Alicia Silverstone and Christopher Jarecki)*

Benjamin *(John Travolta and Kelly Preston)*

Bowen Christopher *(Drew and Brittany Brees)*

Caspar *(Claudia Schiffer and Matthew Vaughn)*

Denim *(Toni Braxton and Keri Lewis)*

Diezel *(Toni Braxton and Keri Lewis)*

Draco *(Danica McKellar)*

Egypt Daoud *(Alicia Keys and Swizz Beatz)*

Ever *(Alanis Morissette)*

Giacomo *(Sting and Trudie Styler)*

Gideon Scott *(Neil Patrick Harris and David Burtka)*

Henry Tadeusz *(Colin Farrell and Alicja Bachleda)*

Julian Fuego *(Robin Thicke and Paula Patton)*

Liam Aaron *(Tori Spelling and Dean McDermott)*

Louis *(Sandra Bullock)*

Knox *(Angelina Jolie and Brad Pitt)*

Mason Dash *(Kourtney Kardashian and Scott Disick)*

Moroccan *(Mariah Carey and Nick Cannon)*

Seven *(Erykah Badu and Andre 3000)*

Sparrow James Midnight *(Nicole Richie and Joel Madden)*

Zion *(Lauryn Hill and Rohan Marley)*

Zuma Nesta Rock *(Gwen Stefani and Gavin Rossdale)*

What Celebrities Name Their Babies

Girls

Adalynn Rose (*Chris and Deanna Daughtry*)

Aviana Olea (*Amy Adams and Darren Le Gallo*)

Beatrix Carlin (*Jodie Sweetin and Morty Coyle*)

Billie Beatrice (*Rebecca Gayheart and Eric Dane*)

Bryn (*Bethenny Frankel and Jason Hoppy*)

Cosima Violet (*Claudia Schiffer and Matthew Vaughn*)

Dakota Jefferson Holiday (*Big Kenny and Christiev*)

Faith Margaret (*Nicole Kidman and Keith Urban*)

Genevieve Marie (*Jimmie and Chandra Johnson*)

Gia Francesca (*Mario Lopez and Courtney Mazza*)

Grace Margaret (*Mark Wahlberg and Rhea Durham*)

Harper Grace (*Neil Patrick Harris and David Burtka*)

Harlow Winter Kate (*Nicole Richie and Joel Madden*)

Honor (*Jessica Alba and Cash Warren*)

India Pearl (*Harvey Weinstein and Georgina Chapman*)

Liberty Grace (*Joey Lawrence and Chandie Yawn-Nelson*)

Locklyn Kyla (*Vince Vaughn and Kyla Weber*)

Monroe (*Mariah Carey and Nick Cannon*)

Raquel Blue (*Joe Don Rooney and Tiffany Fallon*)

Seraphina Rose (*Jennifer Garner and Ben Affleck*)

Stella Doreen (*Tori Spelling and Dean McDermott*)

Sunday Rose (*Nicole Kidman and Keith Urban*)

Sunny (*Adam and Jackie Sandler*)

Tabitha Hodge (*Jason Priestley and Naomi Lowde*)

Vivienne (*Angelina Jolie and Brad Pitt*)

Pistols, Wild Things, and Pieces-of-Work

Boys

Ajay
Alec
Brush
Corbin
Cuca
Demetrie
Derant
Drake
Dyron
Enrico
Erold
Flint
Harold
Kin
Lynus
Mandrake
Mashawn
Rockney
Sean
Shamone
Slim
Steve
Storm
TeRez
Teshombe

Girls

Ambelu
Aundrea
Brynne
Callie
Caralyn
Cawana
Charner
Concetta
Dandra
Dorshea
Dracy
Emmagene
Harley-Jane
Heydee
Jacquier
Kisha
Krysia
Mallory
Mireya
Moti
Nevelyn
Pariann
Sharell
Tangie
Trenna

Future Fashionistas

Names That Are So Over

Boys	Girls	Boys	Girls
Ant	Anoushka	Al	Bertie
Barkan	Ardythe	Bob	Betty
Blevin	Austene	Dennis	Carla
Calum	Chiara	Donald	Delores
Clarke	Corianna	Douglas	Edith
Clay	Divine	Ernie	Faye
Dario	Dori	Frank	Frances
Harding	Elkie	Garland	Gail
Kamal	Emge	Gary	Hilary
Jean-Luc	Evette	Glanville	Judy
Kelvin	Fabulia	Harold	Loretta
Kenji	Joonypur	Harvey	Louise
Kirklin	Kisha	Jaden	Marilyn
Laranz	Mare	Jason	Maureen
Lear	Misti	Jerry	Minnie
Leon	Roquina	Juwon	Myrna
Massimo	Sasa	Ken	Nancy
Mustafa	Selia	Leon	Nina
Rage	Shawnda	Marvin	Priscilla
Rainier	Shaytella	Morey	Stacy
Robin	Siva	Oscar	Tiffany
Ruben	Tammy	Ottis	Tracy
Tayshaun	Tanis	Randy	Veronica
Wash	Tirsa	Rick	Wanda
Worth	Viviana	Todd	Winona

Future Truck Drivers

Boys

Butch
Carl
Cash
Derlin
Derrell
Earl
Hal
Harlan
Henry
Herb
Hugh
Joe-Eddy
Johnny
Lonnie
Mace
Marvin
Milton
Nate
Norman
Otis
Otto
Revill
Rylance
Scatman
Sorlie

Girls

Clara
Cora
Davette
Edna
Ethelene
Flo
Gretchen
Irma
Jody
Lacresha
Lataisha
Latrice
Makula
Nadine
Nerline
Pearlie
Sherlene
Sonequa
Sue
Usha
Vatoya
Veva
Virgia
Wanda
Zennida

Future Computer Techies

Boys

Alcazar
Alexandre
Boleslav
Brian
Challen
Cornel
Dan
Dickey
Don
Emeril
Gray
Gurinder
Jayon
Jensen
Jim
Lon
Marshall
Matthieu
Ned
Randolph
Saginaw
Timothy
Todd
Warren
Zero

Girls

Anna
Arye
Brana
Devane
Eva-Marie
Gert
Glenne
Jules
Kala
Kate
Keira
Kim
Kitty
Margot
Megan
Nell
Rachel
Ramonda
Ravada
Shannon
Skylar
Sonora
Stephanie
Talisa
Tania

Burdensome Names

Boys	Girls
Ambrose	Alfre
Ankoma	Antigone
Archibald	Bathsheba
Bartholomew	Chastity
Boaz	Clotilde
Bouvier	Columbine
Cord	Cornelia
Dakarai	Cricket
Durwood	Edna
Gershom	Elspeth
Godfrey	Flannery
Hercules	Henrietta
Humphrey	Indiana
Ignatius	Keturah
Kalunga	Majidah
Lafayette	Millicent
Lazarus	Minerva
Marmaduke	Muriel
Mortimer	Priscilla
Percy	Prudence
Reginald	Purity
Thelonius	Thomasina
Vladimar	Ursula
Wolfgang	Zona
Zacharias	Zuwena

Names Derived from Literature

Boys	Girls
Ahab	Alice
Ali Baba	Austen
Boswell	Bronte
Cervantes	Browning
Chaucer	Cale
Cummings	Charlotte
Cyrano	Colette
Dickens	Daisy
Don Quixote	Godiva
Dryden	Grisham
Emerson	Harper
Foster	Jane
Grimm	Kipling
Hunter	Lara
Keats	McMurtry
Lowell	Meg
Milton	Melanie
Norman	Millay
Pope	Patricia
Rhett	Sadie
Sherman	Scarlett
Spenser	Scout
Swift	Simone
Wordsworth	Stella
Yeats	Whittier

Nerd/Dork/Wallflower Names

Barney
Bruce
Cheryl
Chester
Dabney
Dudley
Durwood
Edgar
Edward
Elwood
Emory
Engelbert
Estes
Ethelbert
Eugene
Eustace
Ewan
Fagan
Fairfax
Gomer
Pembroke
Percy
Priscilla
Ted
Warren

Future Gymnasts

Boys	Girls
Antone	Berit
Bendell	Chaley
Bourne	Colleen
Brandon	Dimitra
Cam	Emma
Chad	Erica
Costa	Fabiana
Costello	Goldie
Eric	Grisham
Fahren	Jamie
Harve	Marissa
Kifney	Mary Lou
Lohan	Nadia
Markie	Nasha
Plato	Natasha
Roddick	Olympia
Ryan	Oxana
Silver	Pamela
Taber	Shannon
Tony	Shonna
Varden	Summer
Wash	Tynisha
Whip	Winter
Zatuichi	Zina
Zhano	Zooey

Place Names

Mr. Perfect and Ms. Perfect

Boys	Girls	Boys	Girls
Aberdeen	Asia	Alex	Alexandra
Albany	Bali	Anthony	Allison
Aleppo	Bonn	Ben	Bailey
Alps	Cairo	Blake	Brittney
America	Cambay	Brent	Celeste
Beaumont	Capri	Christian	Christiane
Bexley	China	Christopher	Courtney
Billings	Dallas	Clint	Danielle
Bradford	Dayton	Fletcher	Elizabeth
Carson	Easter	Giancarlo	Hollyn
Cuba	Egypt	Harrison	Jennifer
Cyprus	Flanders	Hunter	Jill
Dodge	Georgia	James	Leah
Elam	India	Joaquin	Lexi
Gobi	Indiana	Justin	Marissa
Gwent	Ireland	Kirk	Meredith
Hollywood	Jordan	Kyle	Merit
Hull	Kansas	Monty	Mia
Logan	Kentucky	Reese	Miranda
Macon	Kenya	Riley	Natalie
Orlando	Lansing	Robert	Nia
Rainier	Odessa	Rory	Riley
Sydney	Persia	Ryan	Shara
Texas	Savannah	Wells	Sloan
Yukon	Venice	Zack	Trina

Future Cops

Boys	Girls
Arlen	Anne
Artie	Becky
Bold	Bristol
Bruno	Carni
Buck	Cricket
Cody	Darla
Doug	Darlyn
Frank	Donella
Gary	Holly
George	Jana
Gray	Janet
Guard	Jessie
Justice	Kathy
Ken	Kim
Ladden	Kyla
Law	Lori
Mace	Lydia
Mark	Marg
Matt	Micah
Mike	Moira
Rocko	Paige
Seno	Raquel
Stu	Serena
Tom	Tiawanna
Wayne	Tully

Future Televangelists

Boys	Girls
Abbott	Alma
Adam	Amanze
Aleksey	April
Alf	Ariel
Brendon	Athena
Carl	Autumn
Cedric	Beate
Ceph	Bernadette
Coley	Blynthia
Cordell	Capricia
Cornelius	Cherlyn
Darius	Danyelle
Dayne	Darice
Dayton	Dinah
Deangelo	Eunicetine
Erfan	Irma
Felix	Jardene
Hamilton	Karolyn
Hardman	Palmira
Hardy	Sharonda
Jim	Sondra
Malcolm	Tabitha
Sean	Tammy
Sumpter	Trish
Wyatt	Valorie

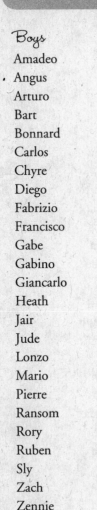

Tomorrow's Justin Timberlake and Gwen Stefani

Future Politicians

Boys	Girls	Boys	Girls
Amadeo	Adora	Ave	Amarosa
Angus	Becca	Bradlee	Annaca
Arturo	Blondelle	Brew	Ceidy
Bart	Bonita	Chant	Consuell
Bonnard	Breanna	Colt	Danal
Carlos	Caitlin	Deshan	Donna
Chyre	Dyana	Elmo	Erica
Diego	Emma	Gagan	Floweret
Fabrizio	Grace	Hec	Ganine
Francisco	Janelle	Hermanse	Heidel
Gabe	Jasmine	Howie	Hillario
Gabino	Julia	Jerrell	Jillianeo
Giancarlo	Kiki	Kib	Kanique
Heath	Liliana	Lobby	Kishey
Jair	Lily	Mazime	Lanetta
Jude	Lisa	Nixon	Luzey
Lonzo	Lourdes	Ogery	Mavis
Mario	Marva	Owelie	Monda
Pierre	Maryann	Real	Ranika
Ransom	Natalie	Rich	Sabrine
Rory	Nicole	Silverio	Shawna
Ruben	Renee	Theodorist	Starret
Sly	Roxanne	Ty	Vernissha
Zach	Shae	Wilbret	Veronica
Zennie	Shyla	Zekel	Yania

Names for Daredevils

Names That Make Kids Feel Weird

Boys	Girls	Boys	Girls
Andre	Alyx	Arno	Breezy
Avery	Anatasia	Bloo	Charm
Beau	Ardythe	Butler	Chastity
Blevin	Austin	Car	Cherish
Colombo	Bead	Delete	Delite
Dagan	Della	Elmo	Fashion
Emrys	Elkie	Elmore	Glory
Fernando	Emge	Ervin	Harmony
Fico	Kiera	Excell	Lake
Fitz	Kita	Fabio	Leaf
Geronimo	L'Ann	Fable	Liberty
Hector	LaSonya	Fergus	Michelin
Hughey	Latona	Fife	Misty
LeBron	Lena	Forester	Oceana
Matt	Mare	Geronimo	Panther
Mustafa	Paradise	Gomer	Peace
Nissan	Priss	Maverick	Pity
Owen	Raven	Oswald	Precious
Rick	Rocket	Paris	Promise
Rossano	Seneca	Prince	Purity
Santino	Swan	Rebel	Rain
Sergio	Tirsa	Stone	Sweetpea
Slater	Yelana	Stormy	Tree
Tassos	Zabrina	Welcome	True
Tayshaun	Ziz	Ziggy	Vixen

Bad-to-the-Bone, Death Row Names

Boys	Girls
Adolph	Aileen Carol
Clydell	Ana
David	Andrea
Excell	Antoinette
Henry Lee	Betty
Jeffrey	Blanche
Jemarr	Caroline
Jessie	Christa Gail
John	Darlie Lynn
John Wayne	Debra
Leonard	Delores
Mack	Faye
Markum	Frances
Napoleon	Gail Kirsey
Randy	Jaqueline
Reginald	Karla Faye
Richard	Kerry
Ricky	Latasha
Robert	Maria
Rodolfo	Marilyn
Speck	Mary Ellen
Stanley	Maureen
Ted	Nadine
Timothy	Pamela
Toronto	Vernice
Windell	

High-Spirited Kids

Boys	Girls
Ace	Armey
Demeet	Bianca
Dezi	Brandi
Dino	Chris
Eddie	Dottie
Grasshopper	Fawn
Jaquan	Gia
Jarrup	Jama
Jehan	Kawana
Jerome	KayKay
Jovan	Kendra
Kayotae	Latoya
Kerry	Mandy
Lance	Pammy
Levi	Rochelle
Mikey	Sheilia
Rambabu	Sherin
Rocky	Suzy
Rosheon	Tara
Tajuan	Tonie
Thad	Tyna
Tony	Vicki
Troy	Vida
Vito	Yvette
Willie	Zorina

Future TV Anchors

Boys

Audon
Carland
Carr
Chaffee
Chazz
Cornel
Doran
Gavin
Judson
Karcher
Kwame
Landon
Long
Lundy
Montgomery
Ran
Roly
Ronan
Sammon
Seaton
Seth
Tassilo
Taye
Trev
Vane

Girls

Bai
Calliope
Cerah
Dominique
Grisham
Jorja
Julia
Kaley
Kanye
Kelly
Lea
Livia
Marianela
Meloni
Meryl
Pfeiffer
Phia
Shanahan
Sheanne
Star
Taft
Tana
Tessa
Tru
Wyoming

Names for Playful Personalities

Babe
Bebe
Bliss
Bunny
Buzzie
Chica
Dusky
Fluffy
Happy
Jandy
Jinx
Lily
Merrilee
Miranda
Pal
Pixie
Poppy
Precious
Queenie
Rabbit
Schmoopie
Skip
Sunny
Trixie
Viveca

Names for Vegetarians

Old-Fashioned Names That Are Cute Again

Boys	Girls	Boys	Girls
A'Dhron	Alula	Atticus	Abby
Binyon	Analisa	Barney	Alma
Biondi	Anita	Casper	Annette
Bruce	Beatrice	Charlie	Arden
Clyde	Bonita	Chester	Arlene
Dorian	Cassie	Clem	Ava
Germain	Connie	Curtis	Belle
Jerrell	Daphne	Dexter	Betsy
Jovan	Detra	Duane	Beulah
Kemper	Donnette	Duke	Corinna
Kent	Fara-Lynn	Elmer	Ethel
Lari	Gerrita	Gill	Flo
Loring	Jaslynne	Harvey	Hazel
Marquis	Jeannie	Homer	Inez
Nolan	Jenette	Luke	Irene
Norm	Jini	Mitchell	Isabel
Ocy	Jolyn	Monty	Kay
Rex	Joyce	Mort	Kyra
Rhys	Justine	Myron	Laverne
Riquee	Kelsi	Ned	Loretta
Rumford	Kimber	Norm	Lorraine
Silas	Rita	Oscar	Lydia
Todd	Sarita	Stanley	Mabel
Trav	Talonna	Wilbur	Polly
Vince	Zhyra	Wyatt	Trudy

Future Inventors

Boys	Girls
Arnold	Amira
Brody	Cate
Cain	Clea
Chew	Connery
Clever	Crisiant
Deems	Cyd
Dov	Delfina
Gif	Drea
Grail	Fia
Hadwin	Gaudi
Halston	Greer
Inder	Isolde
Isaac	JoBeth
John	Joie
Jute	Juanita
Kelvis	LaTanya
Kobi	Madelon
Laphonso	Nicollette
Lee	Novela
Lucan	Olwen
Marvell	Pandora
Ola	Rhonwen
Pirney	Robin
Thanos	Romola
Tinker	Wendy

Names for Smart Kids

Boys	Girls
Adam	Allene
Allen	Beth
Barry	Carolyn
Benjamin	Carrie
Brent	Colby
Byron	Dana
Clarence	Dominique
Curtis	Donna
David	Elizabeth
Eric	Jamie
Gray	Jennifer
Guy	Karen
Hillel	Kathleen
Jack	Kristina
Kent	Leticia
Laurens	Maude
Martin	Micheline
Maximilian	Natasha
Peter	Page
Philip	Shannon
Richard	Shari
Russell	Shaune
Scott	Suzanne
Trevor	Tessie
William	Zoann

Future Models

Future Doctors

Boys	Girls	Boys	Girls
Adebayo	Alessandra	Bryant	Ann
Alim	Anise	Charles	Athena
Anka	Bovary	Dimitri	Brenda
Canyon	Camara	Frazier	Bryce
Carswell	Carles	George	Catrice
Dagan	Cinda	Herbert	Claire
Daly	Donella	James	Dana
Eaves	Estelle	John	Donna
Fabron	Heather	Judd	Elaine
Faldo	Imogene	Lister	Elizabeth
Faxan	Gabi	Mark	Freda
Flea	Grazia	Martin	Greta
Franchot	Jonica	Mason	Jane
Friso	Katrine	Murray	Jennifer
Gabor	Lily	Newell	Linda
Hagan	Lizzie	Nick	Lydia
Jory	Madchen	Niles	Lynn
Kipp	Majandra	Peter	Marianne
Tyee	Mirren	Philip	Mary
Tymon	Monet	Ralph	Maureen
Umar	Paulina	Randall	Miriam
Vachel	Rue	Reagan	Sarah
Walmond	Rylance	Rell	Suzanne
Yudel	Sloan	Russell	Tina
Xenos	Zim	Sabin	Victoria

Last Names as First Names

Boys	Girls
Afton	Abery
Besley	Briley
Bevil	Campbell
Bolin	Childers
Brandt	Cortland
Cawley	Fields
Chatwin	Garson
Coben	Gilmore
Corbitt	Gray
Deagan	Harrison
Given	Holiday
Greer	Keaton
Halliwell	Jennings
Hutter	Lancaster
Kentlee	Lane
Laskey	Mackenzie
Mackeane	Maclaine
Orton	O'Brien
Prescott	Pace
Rollins	Payton
Stadler	Pfeiffer
Tomlin	Rainey
Trivett	Reeve
Vane	Somers
Wingate	Taylor

Future Republicans

Boys	Girls
Alan	Angie
Ambrose	Barbara
Ari	Bo
Arnold	Condoleezza
Bill	Diane
Calvin	Elaine
Charlton	Erika
Colin	Gale
David	Heather
Dennis	Jeane
Gary	Jenna
Gerald	Jennette
J.C.	Jill
Jack	Katherine
Mitt	Laura
Newt	Lilibet
Norm	Linda
Orrin	Lindsey
Richard	Lynne
Rudy	Mary
Rush	Michelle
Sean	Mona
Spiro	Nancy
Tony	Peggy
Trent	Tammy

Future Democrats

Boys

Al
Barack
Bill
Blythe
Bob
Carter
Delano
Evan
Harry
Howard
Jesse
Joseph
Kent
Lloyd
Lyndon
Max
Michael
Robert
Thomas
Tim
Theodore
Walter
Warren
Wesley
Zell

Girls

Barbara
Bess
Carol
Chelsea
Claudia
Debbie
Donna
Edith
Eleanor
Geraldine
Gloria
Jacqueline
Janeane
Janet
Joycelyn
Kim
Madeleine
Molly
Patricia
Rosalynn
Ruth
Sandra
Susan
Teresa
Tipper

Patriotic Names

America
Amerigo
Asia
Blue
Cherokee
Cheyenne
Columbus
Eagle
Flag
Free
Liberty
Librada
Lincoln
Loyalty
Nation
Pacifika
Patriot
Peace
Red
Sailor
Salute
Spirit
Starr
Utopia
Victory

Overpowering Names		Soap Opera Names	
Boys	*Girls*	*Boys*	*Girls*
Abbott	Antoinette	Blake	Allura
Axelrod	Aunjanue	Carson	Amanda
Baldridge	Bjork	Cyrano	Amber
Balthazar	Calista	Dag	Bianca
Domenico	Colemand	Dante	Brandy
Don Quixote	Deja-Marie	Dario	Brisa
Dontrell	Gwyneth	Dax	Candy
Esmond	Illeana	Dean	Carmen
Gabbana	Ione	Deone	Charmaine
Galbraith	Jowannah	Destin	Cocoa
Huntley	Kallioppe	Diego	Dakota
Hyde	Karalenae	Dom	Desiree
Kensington	Madonna	Duke	Fawn
Lothario	Mariangela	Fabio	Madonna
Montague	Oprah	Harley	Monica
Napoleon	Penelope	Keller	Renee
Ottway	Perabo	Maximilian	Salome
Pluto	Philomena	Rico	Samantha
Quintavius	Russo	Rip	Sasha
Reginald	Sahara	Romeo	Simone
Rochester	Siphronia	Ryan	Tatiana
Ronford	Stockard	Sebastian	Tawny
Roosevelt	Teah	Shiloh	Tish
Thor	Thora	Thor	Treece
Wyclef	Winifred	Wells	Yolie

Future Olympians

Boys	Girls
Aaron	Amanda
Alexei	Carly
Andre	Chris
Apolo	Dorothy
Bart	Fanny
Bruce	Jill
Dan	Joanna
David	Katarina
Derek	Kelly
Dwight	Kerri
Gary	Kimberly
Greg	Kristi
Jeremy	Mariel
Justin	Mia
Matthew	Michelle
Michael	Misty
Paul	Nadia
Phil	Nancy
Rulon	Natalie
Scott	Peggy
Shawn	Sarah
Steven	Sasha
Timothy	Sonja
Todd	Tristan
Tyler	

Future Lawyers

Boys	Girls
Atticus	Ann
Bryan	Brianna
Caleb	Campbell
Carlson	Carlisle
Dick	Charlotte
Gary	Dana
Jack	Emily
Jacob	Haley
John	Joanna
Josh	Kate
Lawrence	Kendra
Noble	Lane
Preston	Madison
Price	Mariel
Quinn	Mason
Reese	Meg
Roark	Parker
Robert	Rachel
Rush	Sally
Rusty	Sarah
Ryder	Serena
Samuel	Sloan
Sander	Taylor
Sandford	Tekla
Tom	Terese

Future Cowboys and Cowgirls

Future Nobel Prize Winners

Cowboys	Cowgirls	Boys	Girls
Austin	Abilene	Archer	Alva
Beau	Angeline	Baruch	Barbara
Chaparro	Annie	Boyd	Bertha
Cody	Arizona	Cordell	Betty
Cole	Cassidy	Dario	Christiane
Cooper	Cheyenne	Desmond	Dorothy
Dallas	Conroe	Emil	Emily
Dobie	Cydell	Giulio	Gabriela
Doc	Dacey	Hamilton	Gerty
Dustin	Daisy	Jacinto	Grazia
Earp	Dakota	Kenichi	Irene
Emmett	Denton	Kenzaburo	Jane
Gene	Dixie	Linus	Jody
Jesse	Dobie	Niels	Mairead
Jimmydee	Dusty	Peyton	Marie
Justin	Harlee	Renato	Nadine
Kyle	Jessie	Roald	Pearl
Maverick	Johanna	Romain	Rigoberta
Rusty	Luella	Seamus	Rita
Shane	Montana	Simon	Rosalyn
Stetson	Oakley	Sinclair	Selma
Sudbury	Rosita	Susumu	Shirin
Sutter	Ruby	Sydney	Sigrid
Wadell	Sierra	Werner	Teresa
Wyatt	Suellen	Winston	Toni

TV Character Names

Boys	Girls
Aidan	Blossom
Balki	Calleigh
Cory	Carla
Dante	Daphne
Elliot	Dharma
Elvin	Elaine
Gil	Fran
Grady	Jeannie
Gunther	Krissie
Jack	Laverne
Jordan	Lorelai
Kramer	Lucy
Maxwell	Mallory
Niles	Marissa
Odafin	Meadow
Raymond	Miranda
Ricky	Phoebe
Sam	Prue
Simon	Rayanne
Vinnie	Rhoda
Wilson	Rudy
	Scully
	Sidney
	Tabitha
	Topanga

Architects

Boys	Girls
Aaron	Adrianna
Alan	Alana
Alexander	Annie
Art	Beata
Ed	Candace
Jack	Deandra
Jay	Diana
Lawrence	Ernestine
Liam	Fawn
Paul	Fortune
Rafael	Grace
Robert	Hannah
Ron	Janna
Royce	Joann
Sage	Justine
Sam	Katy
Sebastian	Kelly
Seth	Landa
Shaw	Marianne
Smith	Olga
Sterling	Penelope
Taylor	Queen
Theo	Stella
Victor	Susannah
Walt	Treece

Unforgettable Names

Allegra
Aura
Bai
Cocoa
Hyacinth
Jumbe
King
Lake
Leelee
Lindberg
Madonna
Momo
Montague
Pink
Prince
Rivers
Santeene
Schmoopie
Spirit
Sting
Symphony
Talent
Tame
Trocky
Wyclef

Future Chefs

Boys

Alton
Baker
Basil
Bobby
Cary
Charlie
Cook
Coriander
Delmonico
Dweezil
Emeril
Francis
George
Herb
Hiroyuki
Jamie
Lawson
Martin
Rick
Tamarind
Tarragon
Ted
Tyler
Wolfgang

Girls

Angelica
Betty
Candy
Caraway
Cassia
Ceci
Cicely
Crescent
Debbie
Genievre
Ginger
Honey
Ina
Jenny
Julia
Marjolaine
Martha
Nigella
Poppy
Rosemary
Saffron
Sandra
Sarriette
Seattle
Verbena

Season/Weather Names

Autumn
Cloudy
Dusky
Easter
Equinox
Fog
Frosty
Grey
Holly
Misty
Noel
Rain
Rainbow
Season
Sky
Snow
Soleil
Spring
Storm
Summer
Sunny
Sunshine
Typhoon
Windy
Winter

Scary/Creepy Names

Boys	Girls
Bigram	Adelaide
Brick	Agnes
Bruno	Arlette
Butcher	Beatrix
Delete	Crispy
Dweezil	Denz
Elmo	Earlene
Graven	Edna
Gruver	Hortense
Horatio	Lakeesha
Izzy	Nunu
Modred	Nyleen
Nada	Peta
Napoleon	Phyllida
Narcissus	Quinceanos
Nellie	Randelle
Neptune	Scylla
Nero	Sharama
Percival	Swoosie
Pontius	Tashanee
Seymour	Uzbek
Sindbad	Winnie
Sisyphus	Wyetta
Socrates	Zeb
Zero	Zulemita

Boys	Girls	
Allen	Addison	Ajax
Austin	Anabelle	Alala
Benjamin	Annie	Argus
Cal	Ashley	Aries
Cameron	Ava	Bacchus
Chad	Belle	Bran
Cooper	Catrice	Cadmus
Dax	Dominique	Cressida
Dylan	Eden	Evander
Ethan	Gina	Galatea
Fletcher	Jade	Gawain
Gus	Jennifer	Gemini
Hudson	Jessica	Kalliope
Ian	Jinx	Lake
Jan-Erik	Jolie	Lancelot
Jude	Jordan	Merlin
Julian	Liz	Nestor
Kyle	Marisol	Ocean
Logan	Miranda	Penelope
Owen	Natasha	Phoenix
Riley	Petra	Tane
Ryan	Rachel	Terra
Sebastian	Renee	Thor
Shiloh	Sheyn	Venus
Will	Trista	Zeus

Macho Men	Sweetie-Pies	Names for Popular Kids	
		Boys	*Girls*
Bucko	Alicia	Britt	Ava
Butch	Angie	Cam	Britney
Buzz	Annabelle	Cody	Clancy
Cal	Bay	Dylan	Coby
Cash	Brook	Ethan	Coco
Duke	Darcy	Evan	Emma
Esteban	Dolce	Fletch	Gina
Evander	Dove	Gino	Lauren
Hud	Faith	Gus	Lexi
Hugo	Goldie	Heath	Lily
Jock	Greta	Hunter	Lindsay
Judd	Honey	Ian	Lola
Mack	Jenny	Jake	London
Ram	Julianna	Jason	Lyla
Rebel	Kate	Jeremy	Mackenzie
Reem	Laurel	Jerod	Madison
Rip	Lisa	Joshua	Morgan
Rocco	Marina	Julian	Nicole
Sam	Robin	Justin	Piper
Santiago	Rosa	Kyle	Reese
Spike	Roseanne	London	Samantha
Stone	Sarah-Jessica	Max	Skye
Trocky	Tammy	Morgan	Sophie
Waylon	Wylie	Nick	Tara
Zoom	Yolie	Tyler	Taylor

Future Artists

World's Strangest Names

Boys

Ballard
Blaze
Ceron
Eduardo
Francesco
Francoise
Frederic
Gansta
Graham
Hector
Jean-Claude
Jose
Laurent
Lionel
Maximilian
Michael
Octavio
Oscar
Paulo
Pash
Pedro
Ronnie
Sancho
Sebastian
Stephan

Girls

Alexis
Ashantia
Azure
Caramia
Chantal
DeeDee
Emelle
Eve
Janice
Jenna
Kavita
Lace
Lanee
Lavonne
Margina
Mary-Catherine
Michaele
Mona
Neva
Prema
Regine
Sisteene
Skyler
Tallulah
Zora

Adjanys
Bego
Blue
Bucko
Bukola
Car
Dix
Dweezil
Edju
Idarah
Kermit
Kiwa
Lovella
Moon Unit
Nimrod
Oak
Obey
Pity
Rudow
Swell
Tiago
Tilla
Zap
Zip
Zone

Future Workaholics		Wimpy Names	Girly-Girl Names
Boys	*Girls*	Babe	Bebe
Aneel	Abigail	Barney	Bubbles
Archie	Andrea	Bobo	Buffy
Bill	Belva	Brownie	Bunny
Charles	Bette	Brucie	Cherry
D.J.	Brenda	Byrd	Cinderella
David	Carleton	Chubby	Cinnamon
Douglas	Carol	Clydell	Cookie
Edward	Catherine	Corky	Darlie
Franklin	Christa	Denny	Debbie-Jean
Fred	Clara	Dewey	Deedee
Ivan	Dale	Dudley	Dolly
James	Dawn	Dusty	Fluffy
Jerry	Emma	Dwight	Melrose
Lawrence	Judith	Feo	Poppy
Louis	Lucille	Fergie	Posy
Matthew	Macy	Fuddy	Precious
Michael	Marjorie	Perry	Primrose
Miles	Mary Kay	Skeeter	Princess
Pierre	Meg	Skippy	Prissy
Promod	Muriel	Spanky	Sissy
Roger	Nadia	Terry	Sugar
Seth	Oprah	Timmy	Sweetpea
Ted	Shelly	Tippy	Tippie
Thomas	Shirley	Wendell	Trixiebelle
Vernon	Valentina		
William			

Exotic Names

Names Teachers Can't Pronounce

Boys

Desiderio
Destin
Diego
Enrique
Enzo
Esme
Francesco
Franco
Frederic
Gabriel
Gaston
Genaro
Giancarlo
Hamlet
Hansel
Hawke
Heinz
Helio
Hermes
Honorato
Jacques
Janus
Javier
Jean-Paul
Johann

Girls

Cherokee
Cheyenne
Chiara
Kia
Kimone
Lakesha
Lani
Laurent
Pax
Pepita
Phaedra
Philomena
Phyllida
Quanda
Rania
Rasheeda
Rhiannon
Saffron
Santana
Sasha
Sequoia
Sheba
Shoshana
Simone
Solange

Boys

Artemus
Declan
Dionysus
Flody
Gyth
Hamif
Hermes
Hieronymos
Honorato
Iago
Ignatius
Ioannis
Isidro
Jetal
Jovan
Larrmyne
Mihow
Mischa
Moey
Raoul
Revin
Sladkey
Slavek
Takeya

Girls

Aisha
Aleithea
Camilla
Carenleigh
Chesskwana
Deighan
Falesyia
Gisbelle
Gresia
Madchen
Maromisa
Mayghaen
Meyka
Naeemah
Nissie
Nunibelle
Rhonwen
Ruthemma
Sade
Shaleina
Sharrona
Shawneequa
Tanyav
Tierah
Twyla

Names for Sports Fanatics

Boys	Girls
A.J.	Annika
Al	Cammi
Barry	Carol
Dick	Chamique
Eddie	Charlotte
Edwin	Cheryl
Elgin	Chris
Gale	Donna
Gordie	Florence
Honus	Glenna Collett
Jack	Hazel
Lawrence	Ingrid
Mario	Janet
Maurice	Jeannie
O.J.	Julie
Oscar	Lisa
Otto	Manon
Rafer	Mickey
Roberto	Paula
Rocky	Senda
Rogers	Sheryl
Sammy	Steffi
Satchel	Susan
Willie	Tamara
	Tracy

Names for Future Authors

Boys	Girls
Albert	Alice
Antoine	Amy
Anton	Anais
Bertolt	Bobbi Ann
Conrad	Djuna
Derek	Doris
Ernest	Edith
Fenimore	Eudora
Isaac	Flannery
Italo	Harper
James	Helen
Jean-Paul	Isabel
John	Jamaica
Jorge	Judy
Kurt	Kate
Miguel	Louisa May
Raymond	Maeve
Samuel	Margaret
T.S.	Marguerite
Thomas	Maryse
Umberto	Sandra
Upton	Simone
Vladimir	Virginia
William	Willa
	Zora

Hippie-Sounding Names	Joe Schmoe	Plain Jane
Apple	Bill	Annabelle
Breezy	Bob	Betty
Cloud	Buddy	Carol
Dune	Claude	Cindy
Free	Ed	Dana
Gypsy	Floyd	Dawn
Happy	Fred	Doris
Maverick	Guy	Edith
Oceana	Henry	Jane
Peace	Jack	Janet
Peaches	Joe	Jill
Rain	John	Martha
Rainbow	Kevin	Mary
River	Larry	Nancy
Sea	Lloyd	Norma
Serenity	Mark	Patty
Sierra	Max	Pauline
Spring	Paul	Sally
Star	Ralph	Sarah
Summer	Rick	Shirley
Sunny	Sam	Sue
Tree	Scott	Thelma
True	Tom	Velma
Willow	Wally	Vera
Winner	Wayne	Wilda

Names That Spawn Nasty Nicknames

Androgynous

Boys

Adolf
Aldred
Alec
Alfonso
Apple
Ash
Asher
Ashley
Ashton
Babe
Boris
Bucky
Butler
Byrd
Clement
Dominic
Farley
Farnham
Farr
Ferdinand
Flabia
Harry
Haywood
Jericho
Titus

Girls

Christopher
Cocoa
Dusky-Dream
Earlene
Feather
Fortune
Gay
Harriet
Haute
Hedy
Hermione
Hodge
Hortense
Lesbia
Monica
Rainey
Romona
Ruta
Scarlett
Sesame
Sigrun
Sweetpea
Taffy
Teddi
Winifred

Androgynous

Andy/Andi
Bailey
Cameron
Carol, Carroll
Chris
Corey
Dakota
Dale, Dell
Darcy
Darryl
Dylan
Gail/Gale
Jamie
Jean, Gene
Jordan
Kat
Kelly
Kerry/Carrie
Lane
Lee
Leslie
Morgan
Pat
Shawn, Sean
Terry

Names That Sound Presidential

Boys	Girls
Abraham	Andrea
Adam	Ann
Adlai	Carolyn
Andrew	Claire
Benjamin	Elizabeth
Blake	Ella
Calvin	Emily
Charles	Emma
Daniel	Evan
Dwight	Helen
Earnest	Hillary
George	Isabel
Hamilton	Julia
Hampton	Kay
Harrison	Kelly
Henry	Kyle
Hudson	Lauren
James	Madison
John	Mia
Reagan	Miriam
Robert	Parker
Roger	Rachel
Ronald	Rose
Winston	Stella
Zachary	Taylor

Names for Future Poets

Boys	Girls
Billy	Adrienne
Carl	Amy
Charles	Anne
David	Audre
Dylan	Barbara
Edgar Allan	Brigit
Ezra	Christina
Gary	Denise
Gerard	Dorothy
Henry David	Edna
John	Elizabeth
Kahlil	Emily
Langston	Gertrude
Ogden	Gwendolyn
Pablo	Hilda
Percy	Jorie
Philip	Louise
Ralph Waldo	Marge
Robert	Marianne
Seamus	Maxine
Sherman	Maya
Stanley	Nikki
Tennyson	Rita
Theodore	Sara
William	Sylvia

60,001+ best baby names

Comfy Names		Over-the-Top Names to Avoid	
Boys	**Girls**	**Boys**	**Girls**
Allen	Allison	Achilles	Aphrodite
Ben	Amber	Adonis	Asp
Brent	Annie	Amadeus	Bijou
Brian	Ashley	Aristotle	Birdie
Casey	Becca	Attila	Blaze
Chad	Callie	Bark	Bless
Daniel	Carrie	Beauregard	Blossom
Dave	Danielle	Brando	Blush
Ethan	Diane	Caesar	Butter
Gavin	Emily	Eagle	Chantilly
Jack	Hailey	Goliath	Chastity
Jake	Heather	Hamlet	Cher
Jason	Isabel	Jock	Cleopatra
Jesse	Jessica	Lancelot	Desire
Josh	Jordan	Laramie	Fantasia
Justin	Justine	Lobo	Fashion
Logan	Kim	Lord	Fawn
Matt	Lauren	Lothario	Fluffy
Max	Liz	Rambo	Honesty
Mike	Maggie	Rip	Jezebel
Nicholas	Nicole	Rocco	Loyalty
Rob	Rachel	Rod	Ophelia
Ryan	Samantha	Stormy	Psyche
Sam	Sarah	Sylvester	Purity
Tyler	Selena	Titan	Tempest

Colors

Future Country-Western Singers

Boys	Girls	Boys	Girls
Amarillo	Amber	Alan	Allison
Auburn	Azura	Billy Ray	Anne
Brinley	Bionda	Brad	Barbara
Brown	Blanche	Buck	Brenda
Cyan	Burgundy	Cash	Carlene
Forest	Carmine	Chance	Cristy
Hazel	Cerise	Charley	Dolly
Hunter	Ciara	Chet	Emily
Jet	Crimson	Clay	Faith
Kuper	Crystal	Clint	Jo Dee
Laban	Cyanetta	Conway	Kitty
Loden	Fuchsia	Dwight	LeAnn
Odhran	Henna	Garth	Lee Ann
Phoenix	Indigo	George	Loretta
Red	Iona	Hank	Martie
Ross	Jade	Kenny	Martina
Rudd	Jetta	Lyle	Maybelle
Russet	Kelly	Merle	Natalie
Rusty	Lavender	Tex	Pam
Sable	Melina	Tim	Patsy
Sand	Peridot	Toby	Reba
Slate	Saffron	Travis	Shania
Stone	Scarlet	Vince	Tamara
Tyrian	Sienna	Waylon	Trisha
Umber	Xanthe	Willie	Wynonna

Brand-Name Babies

Old Maids and Grumpy Old Men

Boys

(Uncle) Ben
(Mercedes) Benz
Brooks (Brothers)
Calvin (Klein)
Carter (Carter's babyclothes)
Duncan (Hines)
Gianni (Versace)
Giorgio (Armani)
Hamlet (Cigars)
Hiram (Walker)
Hugo (Boss)
Isaac (Mizrahi)
Jack (Daniels)
Jimmy (Dean)
John (Deere)
Johnnie (Walker)
Kenneth (Cole)
Merrill (Lynch)
Morton (Salt)
Samuel (Adams)
Scott (Tissue)
T.J. (Maxx)
Thomas (Cooke)
Todd (Oldham)
Tommy (Hilfiger)

Girls

Anna (Sui)
Anne (Klein)
Betsey (Johnson)
Betty (Crocker)
Campbell (Soup)
Charmin (bath tissue)
Cristal (champagne)
(Little) Debbie
Donna (Karan)
Elizabeth (Arden)
Ellen (Tracy)
Fanta
Gloria (Vanderbilt)
Harley (Davidson)
(Aunt) Jemima
Kimberly (Clark)
Lexus
Liz (Claiborne)
Mercedes (Benz)
Sara (Lee)
Stella (Artois)

Grumpy Old Men

Adolf
Ambrose
Amos
Clifford
Cyrus
Diedrich
Ebenezer
Edwin
Elmer
Engelbert
Felix
Gaylord
Godfrey
Gomer
Henry
Herb
Leander
Lester
Maurice
Maynard
Mortimer
Oscar
Otis
Percival
Sigmund

Old Maids

Amelia
Baptista
Bertha
Clemence
Clotilde
Corliss
Eldora
Ernestine
Estelle
Geraldine
Gladys
Heloise
Hildegard
Hortense
Mabel
Matilda
Maude
Mavis
Mildred
Millicent
Phyllis
Solange
Thelma
Winifred
Zelda

Boys	Girls		
Bob	Ceil	Aaron	Allegra
Brent	Celeste	Antonin	Aria
Buddy	Connie	Antonio Lucio	Baird
Chalmers	Darla	Belle	Bongo
Davey	Fay	Dimitri	Cadence
Deke	Fern	Domenico	Canon
Dewey	Florence	Elisabetta	Chantal
Dick	Gayle	Felix	Citare
Duane	Ingrid	Francesca	Giritha
Fabian	Jo-Dee	Franz Peter	Gloria
Gareth	Kay	Fryderyk Franciszek	Harmony
Gene	Lauralee	George	Harper
Howard	Leeanne	Johann Sebastian	Kalliope
Irv	Leonora	Joseph	Kyrie
Leonard	Luna	Leo	Lydia
Myron	Marge	Ludwig	Lyra
Newt	Marisol	Maria	Melody
Ronnie	Mitzi	Melinda	Nicola
Rosco	Myrtle	Paul	Octavia
Sal	Pearl	Rebecca	Odele
Sanford	Ruth	Wolfgang Amadeus	Pitch
Skip	Shirley		Sonata
Terrance	Trudy		Tune
Ward	Velma		Viola
Wyatt	Yvonne		Whistler

Eccentric Names

Antigone
Balfour
Bark
Beetle
Bird
Chantilly
Cloudy
Echo
Ecstasy
Flirt
Free
Fudge
Galatea
Gawain
Goliath
Lady
LaRue
Lazarus
Obedience
Orson
Oz
Rambo
Stoli
Webb
Zeus

International Treasure Names

Alexandria (Lighthouse)

Amazon (rainforest, Brazil)

Artemis/Artemesia/ Artemia (Temple, Sardis)

Asmara (capital of Eritrea)

(Magna) Carta

Damascus (capital of Syria)

Delphi

Dover (Cliffs)

Easter (Island)

Euphrates (River)

Giza (pyramid)

Hope (Diamond)

Limoges (French China)

Niagara (Falls)

Nicosia (capital city of Cyprus)

(city of) Olympia

Petra (Ancient City, Jordan)

(The Colossus of) Rhodes

Saffron (Spice)

Santorini (Greece)

Sistine (Chapel, Vatican City)

Names from Works of Art

Adam (Michelangelo)

Ambroise Vollard
  (Picasso)

Beatrice (Tiepelo)

Cana (Gerard David)

Cindy (Robert Longo)

Danae (Gustav Klimt)

David (Donatello,
  also Michelangelo)

Fanny (Chuck Close)

Francesco Clemente

Pinxit (Francesco)

Clemente

Hyacinth
  (Alphonse Mucha)

Irene (Renoir)

Jackie (Andy Warhol)

Jacob (Gaugin)

Jeremiah (Rembrandt)

Joseph Roulin
  (Van Gogh)

Madonna
  (Sanzio Raffaello)

Magdalen (La Tour)

Marcus Aurelius
  (unknown)

Marie (Rubens)
  (sculpture)

Mona Lisa
  (Leonardo da Vinci)

Olympia (Manet)

Salome (Beardsley)

Sarah Bernhardt
  (Nadar)

Theresa (Bernini)

Venus (Botticelli)

Names from John Hughes Movies

Boys	Girls
Andrew	Allison
Blane	Amanda
Brian	Andie
Bryce	Brenda
Cameron	Caroline
Chet	Claire
Ferris	Kristy
Jake	Lisa
Richard	Samantha
Ted	Sloane

Names Resurrected from the Past

Boys
Atticus
Charlie
Dexter
Gill
Mitchell
Monty
Oscar
Stanley
Wilbur
Wyatt

Girls
Annette
Ava
Belle
Hazel
Inez
Isabel
Kyra
Lydia
Polly
Trudy

Names this Author Loves

People often ask me which names I like because they think a baby-name book author knows inside secrets about names. While that isn't the case, I do have some favorites, and here they are:

Boys

Anthony	Julian	Jinx
Ben	Marcus	Jules
Beckham	McAfee	Lana
Cannon	Renzo	Layla
Carlo	Riley	Leah
Cody	Ryan	Loibeth
Damian	Russ	Maggie
Dax	Shane	Merit
Duke	Shiloh	Monet
Dylan	Stellan	Natalie
Eli	Zack	Reagan
Ethan		Savannah
Fletcher	**Girls**	Scout
Gabriel	Ava	Shay
Gavin	Bella	Simone
Gianni	Clancy	Sophie
Gus	Delayna	Stella
Haden	Donalee	Taffin
Hudson	Eden	Teague
Javier	Ginger	Theo
Joaquin	Jade	Yancy
Jude	Jennifer	
	Jill	

Arabic/Islamic Names

Boys	Girls
Abdul-Jabbar	Aisha
Ahmad, Ahmed	Almira
Ali	Asma
Amir	Bathsira
Dawud	Cala
Fariol	Dhelal
Ghassan	Fatima
Habib	Habibah
Hakim, Hakeem	Hadil
Hamid	Hajar, Hagir
Hasan	Hayfa
Ibrahim	Ihab
Jabir, Jabbar	Jamila
Jamal	Kalila
Kamal, Kamil	Karima
Kareem	Laila
Khalid	Leila
Mahmud	Malak
Muhammad, Mohammad	Nada
	Nima
Nuri	Rashidah
Rafi	Rida
Rashid	Sabah
Salim	Salima
Sharif	Zulema
Yasir	

Biblical and Saintly Names

Boys	Girls
Abel	Anna
Adam	Bathsheba
Benjamin	Deborah
Daniel	Delilah
David	Dinah
Elijah	Esther
Ezekiel	Eve
Isaiah	Joanna
Jacob	Judith
Jesus	Julia
Job	Leah
John	Magdalene
Jonah	Martha
Joseph	Mary
Joshua	Miriam
Lazarus	Naamah
Luke	Naomi
Mark	Phoebe
Matthew	Rachel
Moses	Rebekah
Noah	Ruth
Paul	Salome
Peter	Sarah
Samuel	Tamar
Solomon	Zipporah

Scandinavian Names

Boys	Girls
Aksel	Astrid
Anders	Birgit
Anton	Bonnevie
Bjorn	Dufvenius
Christian	Elsa
Claus	Erika
Dirk	Fia
Erik	Frida
Gustav	Gudrun
Hendrik	Gunilla
Ingmar	Inge
Isak	Ingrid
Johannes	Janna
Karl	Johanna
Knut	Kristina
Krister	Liv
Lars	Lotta
Matts	Mini
Mikael	Sabina
Niels	Sanna
Niklas	Sigrid
Oskar	Sofia
Per	Sonya
Rudolf	Ursula
Stellan	Wilhelmina

Italian Names

Boys	Girls
Aldo	Annamaria
Alessandro	Bella
Angelo	Cara
Arturo	Caramia
Carlo	Carissa
Carmine	Carlotta
Ciro	Chiara
Cosmo	Donna
Dante	Elda
Emilio	Elena
Enrico	Eliana
Franco	Elisa
Gianni	Elletra
Gino	Faustina
Giorgio	Fidelia
Guido	Gina
Leonardo	Isabella
Lorenzo	Maria
Luciano	Melania
Marco	Nicola
Mario	Paulina
Salvatore	Pia
Tomasso	Rosa
Vincenzo	Rosamaria
Vito	Sophia

French Names

Boys

Alain
Charles
Claude
Francois
Frederic
Gaston
Gerard
Germain
Gregoire
Guy
Henri
Isidore
Jacques
Jean
Jean-Claude
Jean-Michel
Jean-Paul
Laurent
Louis
Luc
Marcel
Maxime
Phillipe
Robert
Yves

Girls

Aimee
Amelie
Anais
Angelique
Antoinette
Arianne
Chantal
Claire
Colette
Daniele
Desiree
Dominique
Eliane
Elisabeth
Emmanuelle
Esmee
Gabrielle
Genevieve
Giselle
Maria
Michele
Monique
Simone
Yvette
Yvonne

German Names

Boys

Claus, Klaus
Erik
Folker
Freiderich
Garrick
Gerhard
Gunther
Gustaf
Heinrich
Helmut
Hendrik
Karl
Konrad
Kurt
Leopold
Max
Norbert
Oswald
Otto
Ralph
Roger
Rudy
Stefan
Wilhelm
Wolfgang

Girls

Ada
Anke
Anneliese
Annemarie
Beata
Clotilda
Constanze
Cordula
Ebba
Elisabeth
Elsa
Emma
Felicie
Gudrun
Heidi
Hilda
Juliana
Karoline
Katharina
Kristina
Margarite
Maria
Martina
Rosa
Ursula

Polish Names

Russian Names

Boys	Girls	Boys	Girls
Aleksander	Anna	Adya	Anastasiya
Andrzej	Barbara	Alek	Anninka
Aniol	Cecilia	Aleksei	Dariya
Anzelm	Celestyna	Denis	Dasha
Bogdan	Gabriela	Dmitri	Duscha
Boleslaw	Gizela	Grigori	Elena
Czeslaw	Grazyna	Igor	Evelina
Dobromir	Hanna	Ivan	Inessa
Helmut	Honorata	Karl	Irene/Irina
Jacek	Iwona	Maksimilian	Ivanna
Jozef	Jadwiga	Mikhail	Kira
Karol	Kamilia	Misha	Lara
Kazimierz	Karolina	Nikita	Lia
Krzysztof	Krysta	Nikolai	Masha
Marek	Krystyna	Oleg	Nadya
Pawel	Lucja	Pavel	Natalia
Ryszard	Maria	Sasha	Natasha
Slawomir	Marusya	Sergei	Oksana
Waclaw	Matylda	Sidor	Olga
Walenty	Mirka	Stanislav	Polina
Witold	Monika	Valentin	Sasha
Wladymir	Otylia	Valeri	Sofya
Wladyslaw	Roksana	Vlad	Sonya
Wojtek	Waleria	Vladimir	Svetlana
Zbigniew	Wiktoria	Vladja	Tatiana

Irish Names		Scottish Names	
Boys	*Girls*	*Boys*	*Girls*
Aidan	Aileen	Ainsley	Alexandra
Art	Amanda	Alan	Alison
Bran	Annie	Angus	Annella
Brendan	Brenda	Bean	Christy
Brian	Briana	Bennett	Dina
Colin	Catherine	Cally	Fiona
Curran	Cathleen	Cameron	Heather
Devin	Ciara	Charles	Jeanie
Farris	Deirdre	Clement	Jenny
Fergus	Dorren	Conall	Lexine
Finn	Eavan	Donald	Lexy
Ian	Eliza	Fergus	Lindsay
James	Emma	Gregor	Lucy
Jamie	Ethnea	Harry	Maidie
John	Karen	Iagan	Maisie
Kevin	Kate	Ian	Margaret
Kieran, Keiran	Kathy	James	Nan
Killian	Maggie	Jock	Netta
Liam	Molly	Jon	Nora
Lochlain	Nancy	Kenneth	Peigi
Owen	Nessa	Peader	Robina
Patrick	Polly	Roddy	Rona
Rowan	Riona	Scott	Rowena
Sean	Sally	Stewart	Sandy
Shay	Sinead	Walter	Tory

English Names

African Names

Boys	Girls	Boys	Girls
Arthur	Agnes	Addae	Aamori
Charles	Alexandra	Adio	Abayomi
Clinton	Althea	Ayo	Adia
Clive	Amanda	Bakari	Aisha
Colin	Andie	Bomani	Asabi
Earl	Angie	Dalila	Bayo
Edward	Anna/Anne	Dumisani	Eshe
George	Becky	Hamidi	Fatima
Harry	Betty	Harun	Femi
Henry	Carla	Hasani	Habiba
Jay	Connie	Hondo	Hasina
Jeff	Cynthia	Jaja	Jumoke
Max	Elizabeth	Kamal	Kibibi
Michael	Esther	Kamau	Kissa
Nicholas	Georgina	Muhhamad	Lateefa
Nigel	Hayley	Rudo	Maudisa
Norman	Ida	Runako	Nailah
Peter	Jennifer	Saeed	Nomble
Philip	Jill	Salehe	Omorose
Roger	Katherine	Salim	Oni
Roland	Margaret	Sekani	Rufaro
Ronald	Moira	Themba	Salama
Toby	Pippa	Umi	Taliba
William	Rhonda	Zikomo	Tisa
Winston	Wendy	Zuberi	Zahra

Spanish Names

Boys	Girls
Adonis	Angela
Alejandro	Beila
Alfonso	Beilarosa
Angel	Bonita
Benito	Caliopa
Carlos	Carlotta
Damaso	Carmen
Diego	Clementina
Emilio	Consuelo
Enrique	Delfina
Esteban	Delicia
Fiero	Destina
Francisco	Elena
Hector	Flora
Isidoro	Graciela
Javier	Guadalupe
Jorge	Honoria
Jose	Juanita
Juan	Maria
Julio	Mariposa
Miguel	Odelita
Mundo	Paloma
Raoul	Primalia
Roberto	Soledad
Tomas	

Greek Names

Boys	Girls
Alexandros	Aggie
Andreas	Andrianna
Ari	Ariadne
Basil	Athena
Cletus	Calista
Demetri	Calla
Demetrios	Chloe
Demos	Damalla
Flavian	Delos
Hilarion	Diona
Jason	Filia
Lucas	Gillian
Markos	Helena
Nikos	Iona
Paul	Isadora
Sander	Kali
Seth	Kalidas
Socrates	Kori
Stephanos	Kynthia
Theo	Leandra
Theodoros	Nia
Theophilos	Phyllis
Tito	Pia
Verniamin	Theodora
Zeno	Zoe

Asian Names

Future Racecar Drivers

Boys

An (Chinese)
Chang (Chinese)
Dong (Chinese)
Hiro (Japanese)
Huang (Chinese)
Ibu (Japanese)
Ji (Chinese)
Jin (Chinese)
Jing (Chinese)
Ju-Long (Chinese)
Kang (Korean)
Li (Chinese)
Liang (Chinese)
Pin (Vietnamese)
Quon (Chinese)
Shen (Chinese)
Sheng (Chinese)
Shuu (Japanese)
So (Vietnamese)
Tan (Japanese)
Tung (Chinese,
Vietnamese)
Yen (Chinese)
Yu (Chinese)
Yuan (Chinese)
Zhong (Chinese)

Girls

Bao (Chinese)
Bay (Vietnamese)
Cai (Chinese)
Connie-Kim
(Vietnamese)
De (Chinese)
Fang (Chinese)
Ha (Vietnamese)
Lei (Chinese)
Li (Chinese)
Lian (Chinese)
Ling (Chinese)
Mai (Japanese)
Min (Chinese)
Ming (Chinese)
Niu (Chinese)
Nu (Vietnamese)
Pang (Chinese)
Tam (Japanese)
Thim (Thai)
Veata (Cambodian)
Yu (Chinese)
Zan (Chinese)
Zhi (Chinese)
Zhong (Chinese)
Zi (Chinese)

A.J.
Alex
Arie
Bruno
Buddy
Dale
Dan
Dario
Denny
Eddie
Helio
Jacques
Jeff
Jimmy
Johnny
Juan
Jules
Kenny
Leo
Mario
Mauri
Oriol
Sam
Scott
Tony

Names That Will Make Jaws Drop

Boys
Charrod
Decorri
Demorrio
Drisan
Flozell
Fontel
Gibril
Jerametrius
Jerious
Kawika
Kicky
Plaxico
Quadtrine
Reche
Tanyon
Travonti
Zaza

Girls
Carousel
Chamique
Charl
DeLisha
DeMya
Edwige
Epiphanny
Essence
Jeffrey
Holiday
Hollis
Plenette
Quanitra
Sequoia
Shavonte
Swin
Tobin

Most Popular Names of the 1880s

Boys
1. John
2. William
3. James
4. George
5. Charles
6. Joseph
7. Frank
8. Robert
9. Edward
10. Henry
11. Harry
12. Thomas
13. Walter
14. Arthur
15. Fred
16. Albert
17. Clarence
18. Willie
19. Roy
20. Louis
21. Earl
22. Paul
23. Carl
24. Ernest
25. Samuel

Girls
1. Mary
2. Anna
3. Margaret
4. Helen
5. Elizabeth
6. Ruth
7. Florence
8. Ethel
9. Emma
10. Marie
11. Clara
12. Bertha
13. Minnie
14. Bessie
15. Alice
16. Lillian
17. Edna
18. Grace
19. Annie
20. Mabel
21. Ida
22. Rose
23. Hazel
24. Gertrude
25. Martha

Most Popular Names of the 1890s

Boys
1. John
2. William
3. James
4. George
5. Charles
6. Joseph
7. Frank
8. Robert
9. Edward
10. Henry
11. Harry
12. Thomas
13. Walter
14. Arthur
15. Fred
16. Albert
17. Clarence
18. Willie
19. Roy
20. Louis
21. Earl
22. Paul
23. Carl
24. Ernest
25. Samuel

Girls
1. Mary
2. Anna
3. Margaret
4. Helen
5. Elizabeth
6. Ruth
7. Florence
8. Ethel
9. Emma
10. Marie
11. Clara
12. Bertha
13. Minnie
14. Bessie
15. Alice
16. Lillian
17. Edna
18. Grace
19. Annie
20. Mabel
21. Ida
22. Rose
23. Hazel
24. Gertrude
25. Martha

Most Popular Names of the 1900s

Boys
1. John
2. William
3. James
4. George
5. Charles
6. Robert
7. Joseph
8. Frank
9. Edward
10. Thomas
11. Henry
12. Walter
13. Harry
14. Willie
15. Arthur
16. Albert
17. Clarence
18. Fred
19. Harold
20. Paul
21. Raymond
22. Richard
23. Roy
24. Joe
25. Louis

Girls
1. Mary
2. Helen
3. Margaret
4. Anna
5. Ruth
6. Elizabeth
7. Dorothy
8. Marie
9. Florence
10. Mildred
11. Alice
12. Ethel
13. Lillian
14. Gladys
15. Edna
16. Frances
17. Rose
18. Annie
19. Grace
20. Bertha
21. Emma
22. Bessie
23. Clara
24. Hazel
25. Irene

Most Popular Names of the 1910s

Boys

1. John
2. William
3. James
4. Robert
5. Joseph
6. George
7. Charles
8. Edward
9. Frank
10. Thomas
11. Walter
12. Harold
13. Henry
14. Paul
15. Richard
16. Raymond
17. Albert
18. Arthur
19. Harry
20. Donald
21. Ralph
22. Louis
23. Jack
24. Clarence
25. Carl

Girls

1. Mary
2. Helen
3. Dorothy
4. Margaret
5. Ruth
6. Mildred
7. Anna
8. Elizabeth
9. Frances
10. Virginia
11. Marie
12. Evelyn
13. Alice
14. Florence
15. Lillian
16. Rose
17. Irene
18. Louise
19. Edna
20. Catherine
21. Gladys
22. Ethel
23. Josephine
24. Ruby
25. Martha

Most Popular Names of the 1920s

Boys

1. Robert
2. John
3. James
4. William
5. Charles
6. George
7. Joseph
8. Richard
9. Edward
10. Donald
11. Thomas
12. Frank
13. Harold
14. Paul
15. Raymond
16. Walter
17. Jack
18. Henry
19. Kenneth
20. Arthur
21. Albert
22. David
23. Harry
24. Eugene
25. Ralph

Girls

1. Mary
2. Dorothy
3. Helen
4. Betty
5. Margaret
6. Ruth
7. Virginia
8. Doris
9. Mildred
10. Frances
11. Elizabeth
12. Evelyn
13. Anna
14. Marie
15. Alice
16. Jean
17. Shirley
18. Barbara
19. Irene
20. Marjorie
21. Florence
22. Lois
23. Martha
24. Rose
25. Lillian

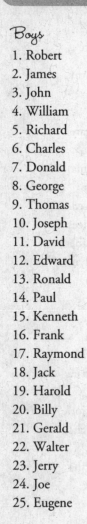

Most Popular Names of the 1930s		Most Popular Names of the 1940s	
Boys	**Girls**	**Boys**	**Girls**
1. Robert	1. Mary	1. James	1. Mary
2. James	2. Betty	2. Robert	2. Linda
3. John	3. Barbara	3. John	3. Barbara
4. William	4. Shirley	4. William	4. Patricia
5. Richard	5. Patricia	5. Richard	5. Carol
6. Charles	6. Dorothy	6. David	6. Sandra
7. Donald	7. Joan	7. Charles	7. Nancy
8. George	8. Margaret	8. Thomas	8. Sharon
9. Thomas	9. Nancy	9. Michael	9. Judith
10. Joseph	10. Helen	10. Ronald	10. Susan
11. David	11. Carol	11. Larry	11. Betty
12. Edward	12. Joyce	12. Donald	12. Carolyn
13. Ronald	13. Doris	13. Joseph	13. Margaret
14. Paul	14. Ruth	14. Gary	14. Shirley
15. Kenneth	15. Virginia	15. George	15. Judy
16. Frank	16. Marilyn	16. Kenneth	16. Karen
17. Raymond	17. Elizabeth	17. Paul	17. Donna
18. Jack	18. Jean	18. Edward	18. Kathleen
19. Harold	19. Frances	19. Jerry	19. Joyce
20. Billy	20. Beverly	20. Dennis	20. Dorothy
21. Gerald	21. Lois	21. Frank	21. Janet
22. Walter	22. Alice	22. Daniel	22. Diane
23. Jerry	23. Donna	23. Raymond	23. Janice
24. Joe	24. Martha	24. Roger	24. Joan
25. Eugene	25. Dolores	25. Steven	25. Elizabeth

Most Popular Names of the 1950s

Boys
1. Michael
2. James
3. Robert
4. John
5. David
6. William
7. Richard
8. Thomas
9. Mark
10. Charles
11. Steven
12. Gary
13. Joseph
14. Donald
15. Ronald
16. Kenneth
17. Paul
18. Larry
19. Daniel
20. Stephen
21. Dennis
22. Timothy
23. Edward
24. Jeffrey
25. George

Girls
1. Mary
2. Linda
3. Patricia
4. Susan
5. Deborah
6. Barbara
7. Debra
8. Karen
9. Nancy
10. Donna
11. Cynthia
12. Sandra
13. Pamela
14. Sharon
15. Kathleen
16. Carol
17. Diane
18. Brenda
19. Cheryl
20. Elizabeth
21. Janet
22. Kathy
23. Margaret
24. Janice
25. Carolyn

Most Popular Names of the 1960s

Boys
1. Michael
2. David
3. John
4. James
5. Robert
6. Mark
7. William
8. Richard
9. Thomas
10. Jeffrey
11. Steven
12. Joseph
13. Timothy
14. Kevin
15. Scott
16. Brian
17. Charles
18. Daniel
19. Paul
20. Christopher
21. Kenneth
22. Anthony
23. Gregory
24. Ronald
25. Donald

Girls
1. Lisa
2. Mary
3. Karen
4. Susan
5. Kimberly
6. Patricia
7. Linda
8. Donna
9. Michelle
10. Cynthia
11. Sandra
12. Deborah
13. Pamela
14. Tammy
15. Laura
16. Lori
17. Elizabeth
18. Julie
19. Jennifer
20. Brenda
21. Angela
22. Barbara
23. Debra
24. Sharon
25. Teresa

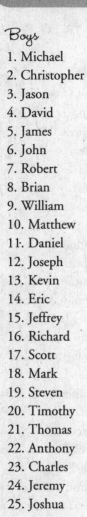

Most Popular Names of the 1970s

Boys

1. Michael
2. Christopher
3. Jason
4. David
5. James
6. John
7. Robert
8. Brian
9. William
10. Matthew
11. Daniel
12. Joseph
13. Kevin
14. Eric
15. Jeffrey
16. Richard
17. Scott
18. Mark
19. Steven
20. Timothy
21. Thomas
22. Anthony
23. Charles
24. Jeremy
25. Joshua

Girls

1. Jennifer
2. Amy
3. Melissa
4. Michelle
5. Kimberly
6. Lisa
7. Angela
8. Heather
9. Stephanie
10. Jessica
11. Elizabeth
12. Nicole
13. Rebecca
14. Kelly
15. Mary
16. Christina
17. Amanda
18. Sarah
19. Laura
20. Julie
21. Shannon
22. Christine
23. Tammy
24. Karen
25. Tracy

Most Popular Names of the 1980s

Boys

1. Michael
2. Christopher
3. Matthew
4. Joshua
5. David
6. Daniel
7. James
8. Robert
9. John
10. Joseph
11. Jason
12. Justin
13. Andrew
14. Ryan
15. William
16. Brian
17. Jonathan
18. Brandon
19. Nicholas
20. Anthony
21. Eric
22. Adam
23. Kevin
24. Steven
25. Thomas

Girls

1. Jessica
2. Jennifer
3. Amanda
4. Ashley
5. Sarah
6. Stephanie
7. Melissa
8. Nicole
9. Elizabeth
10. Heather
11. Tiffany
12. Michelle
13. Amber
14. Megan
15. Rachel
16. Amy
17. Lauren
18. Kimberly
19. Christina
20. Brittany
21. Crystal
22. Rebecca
23. Laura
24. Emily
25. Danielle

Most Popular Names of the 1990s

Boys

1. Michael
2. Christopher
3. Matthew
4. Joshua
5. Jacob
6. Andrew
7. Daniel
8. Nicholas
9. Tyler
10. Joseph
11. David
12. Brandon
13. James
14. John
15. Ryan
16. Zachary
17. Justin
18. Anthony
19. William
20. Robert
21. Jonathan
22. Kyle
23. Austin
24. Alexander
25. Kevin

Girls

1. Ashley
2. Jessica
3. Emily
4. Sarah
5. Samantha
6. Brittany
7. Amanda
8. Elizabeth
9. Taylor
10. Megan
11. Stephanie
12. Kayla
13. Lauren
14. Jennifer
15. Rachel
16. Hannah
17. Nicole
18. Amber
19. Alexis
20. Courtney
21. Victoria
22. Danielle
23. Alyssa
24. Rebecca
25. Jasmine

Most Popular Names of 2007

Boys

1. Jacob
2. Michael
3. Ethan
4. Joshua
5. Daniel
6. Christopher
7. Anthony
8. William
9. Matthew
10. Andrew
11. Alexander
12. David
13. Joseph
14. Noah
15. James
16. Ryan
17. Logan
18. Jayden
19. John
20. Nicholas
21. Tyler
22. Christian
23. Jonathan
24. Nathan
25. Samuel

Girls

1. Emily
2. Isabella
3. Emma
4. Ava
5. Madison
6. Sophia
7. Olivia
8. Abigail
9. Hannah
10. Elizabeth
11. Addison
12. Samantha
13. Ashley
14. Alyssa
15. Mia
16. Chloe
17. Natalie
18. Sarah
19. Alexis
20. Grace
21. Ella
22. Brianna
23. Hailey
24. Taylor
25. Anna

Most Popular Names of 2008

Most Popular Names of 2009

Boys	Girls	Boys	Girls
1. Jacob	1. Emma	1. Jacob	1. Isabella
2. Michael	2. Isabella	2. Ethan	2. Emma
3. Ethan	3. Emily	3. Michael	3. Olivia
4. Joshua	4. Madison	4. Alexander	4. Sophia
5. Daniel	5. Ava	5. William	5. Ava
6. Alexander	6. Olivia	6. Joshua	6. Emily
7. Anthony	7. Sophia	7. Daniel	7. Madison
8. William	8. Abigail	8. Jayden	8. Abigail
9. Christopher	9. Elizabeth	9. Noah	9. Chloe
10. Matthew	10. Chloe	10. Anthony	10. Mia
11. Jayden	11. Samantha	11. Christopher	11. Elizabeth
12. Andrew	12. Addison	12. Aiden	12. Addison
13. Joseph	13. Natalie	13. Matthew	13. Alexis
14. David	14. Mia	14. David	14. Ella
15. Noah	15. Alexis	15. Andrew	15. Samantha
16. Aidan	16. Alyssa	16. Joseph	16. Natalie
17. James	17. Hannah	17. Logan	17. Grace
18. Ryan	18. Ashley	18. James	18. Lily
19. Logan	19. Ella	19. Ryan	19. Alyssa
20. John	20. Sarah	20. Benjamin	20. Ashley
21. Nathan	21. Grace	21. Elijah	21. Sarah
22. Elijah	22. Taylor	22. Gabriel	22. Taylor
23. Christian	23. Brianna	23. Christian	23. Hannah
24. Gabriel	24. Lily	24. Nathan	24. Brianna
25. Benjamin	25. Hailey	25. Jackson	25. Hailey

Most Popular Names of 2010

Boys

1. Jacob	26. John	51. Jose	76. Cooper
2. Ethan	27. Nathan	52. Jeremiah	77. Josiah
3. Michael	28. Jonathan	53. Julian	78. Luis
4. Jayden	29. Christian	54. Robert	79. Ayden
5. William	30. Liam	55. Aaron	80. Carson
6. Alexander	31. Dylan	56. Adrian	81. Adam
7. Noah	32. Landon	57. Wyatt	82. Nathaniel
8. Daniel	33. Caleb	58. Kevin	83. Brody
9. Aiden	34. Tyler	59. Hunter	84. Tristan
10. Anthony	35. Lucas	60. Cameron	85. Diego
11. Joshua	36. Evan	61. Zachary	86. Parker
12. Mason	37. Gavin	62. Thomas	87. Blake
13. Christopher	38. Nicholas	63. Charles	88. Oliver
14. Andrew	39. Isaac	64. Austin	89. Cole
15. David	40. Brayden	65. Eli	90. Carlos
16. Matthew	41. Luke	66. Chase	91. Jaden
17. Logan	42. Angel	67. Henry	92. Jesus
18. Elijah	43. Brandon	68. Sebastian	93. Alex
19. James	44. Jack	69. Jason	94. Aidan
20. Joseph	45. Isaiah	70. Levi	95. Eric
21. Gabriel	46. Jordan	71. Xavier	96. Hayden
22. Benjamin	47. Owen	72. Ian	97. Bryan
23. Ryan	48. Carter	73. Colton	98. Max
24. Samuel	49. Connor	74. Dominic	99. Jaxon
25. Jackson	50. Justin	75. Juan	100. Brian

Most Popular Names of 2010

Girls

1. Isabella	26. Sofia	51. Peyton	76. Madelyn
2. Sophia	27. Ashley	52. Audrey	77. Madeline
3. Emma	28. Anna	53. Claire	78. Bailey
4. Olivia	29. Brianna	54. Arianna	79. Payton
5. Ava	30. Sarah	55. Julia	80. Andrea
6. Emily	31. Zoe	56. Aaliyah	81. Autumn
7. Abigail	32. Victoria	57. Kylie	82. Melanie
8. Madison	33. Gabriella	58. Lauren	83. Ariana
9. Chloe	34. Brooklyn	59. Sophie	84. Serenity
10. Mia	35. Kaylee	60. Sydney	85. Stella
11. Addison	36. Taylor	61. Camila	86. Maria
12. Elizabeth	37. Layla	62. Jasmine	87. Molly
13. Ella	38. Allison	63. Morgan	88. Caroline
14. Natalie	39. Evelyn	64. Alexandra	89. Genesis
15. Samantha	40. Riley	65. Jocelyn	90. Kaitlyn
16. Alexis	41. Amelia	66. Gianna	91. Eva
17. Lily	42. Khloe	67. Maya	92. Jessica
18. Grace	43. Makayla	68. Kimberly	93. Angelina
19. Hailey	44. Aubrey	69. Mackenzie	94. Valeria
20. Alyssa	45. Charlotte	70. Katherine	95. Gabrielle
21. Lillian	46. Savannah	71. Destiny	96. Naomi
22. Hannah	47. Zoey	72. Brooke	97. Mariah
23. Avery	48. Bella	73. Trinity	98. Natalia
24. Leah	49. Kayla	74. Faith	99. Paige
25. Nevaeh	50. Alexa	75. Lucy	100. Rachel

Top Twin Names of 2010

Female Twins

1. Ella, Emma
2. Olivia, Sophia
3. Gabriella, Isabella
4. Faith, Hope
5. Ava, Emma
6. Isabella, Sophia
7. Madison, Morgan
8. Ava, Ella
9. Ava, Olivia
10. Mackenzie, Madison
11. Abigail, Isabella
12. Abigail, Emma
13. Hailey, Hannah
14. Makayla, Makenzie
15. Addison, Avery
16. Elizabeth, Emily
17. Ava, Mia
18. Heaven, Nevaeh
19. Abigail, Emily
20. Emma, Olivia
21. London, Paris
22. Chloe, Claire
23. Mia, Mya
24. Anna, Emma
25. Arianna, Brianna
26. Isabella, Olivia
27. Abigail, Lillian
28. Addison, Ava
29. Emma, Isabella
30. Samantha, Sophia
31. Ella, Olivia
32. Emma, Hannah
33. Emma, Mia
34. Faith, Grace
35. Madison, Makenzie
36. Madison, Olivia
37. Abigail, Olivia
38. Anabella, Isabella
39. Chloe, Zoe
40. Elizabeth, Isabella
41. Elizabeth, Victoria
42. Jada, Jade
43. Julia, Sophia
44. Kayla, Kylie
45. Madison, Megan
46. Mia, Sophia
47. Natalie, Olivia
48. Paige, Payton
49. Serenity, Trinity
50. Valentina, Valeria

Female and Male Twins

1. Madison, Mason
2. Emma, Ethan
3. Taylor, Tyler
4. Madison, Michael
5. Jayda, Jayden
6. Madison, Matthew
7. Samuel, Sophia
8. Addison, Aiden
9. Olivia, Owen
10. Zachary, Zoe
11. Addison, Jackson
12. Aiden, Ava
13. Emily, Ethan
14. Emma, Ryan
15. Isaac, Isabella
16. Natalie, Nathan
17. Abigail, Benjamin
18. Andrew, Emma
19. Isabella, Isaiah
20. Jada, Jaden
21. Brian, Brianna
22. Emma, Jack
23. Aiden, Emma
24. Eli, Ella
25. Jacob, Olivia
26. Lily, Logan
27. Michael, Michelle
28. Naomi, Noah
29. Abigail, Alexander
30. Abigail, Andrew
31. Brandon, Brianna
32. Chloe, Christian
33. Elizabeth, William
34. Emily, Matthew
35. Emma, Jacob
36. Emma, William
37. Jacob, Sarah
38. Lilly, Logan
39. Nicholas, Sophia
40. Noah, Sophia
41. Oliver, Olivia
42. Sophia, William
43. Abigail, Jacob
44. Addison, Austin
45. Alexander, Sophia
46. Ella, Jackson
47. Emma, Evan
48. Emma, James
49. Jayla, Jaylen
50. Zachary, Zoey

Male Twins

1. Jacob, Joshua
2. Ethan, Evan
3. Jayden, Jordan
4. Daniel, David
5. Matthew, Michael
6. Landon, Logan
7. Elijah, Isaiah
8. Jacob, Joseph
9. Jayden, Jaylen
10. Isaac, Isaiah
11. Caleb, Joshua
12. Andrew, Matthew
13. James, John
14. Alexander, Nicholas
15. Jeremiah, Josiah
16. Joseph, Joshua
17. Nathan, Nicholas
18. Jonathan, Joshua
19. Logan, Lucas
20. Ethan, Nathan
21. Aiden, Ethan
22. Jeremiah, Joshua
23. Alexander, Andrew
24. Alexander, Benjamin
25. Logan, Luke
26. Jacob, Lucas
27. Jonathan, Joseph
28. Nathan, Noah
29. Andrew, Anthony
30. Brandon, Bryan
31. Daniel, Michael
32. Daniel, Samuel
33. Isaiah, Jeremiah
34. Jaden, Jordan
35. Jayden, Kayden
36. John, Joseph
37. Matthew, Ryan
38. Aiden, Austin
39. Benjamin, Samuel
40. Christopher, Nicholas
41. Taylor, Tyler
42. Benjamin, William
43. Hayden, Hunter
44. Santiago, Sebastian
45. Alexander, Anthony
46. Alexander, William
47. Brandon, Brian
48. Carter, Cooper
49. Evan, Owen
50. Evan, Ryan

Boys

Aabid (Arabic) loyal

Aalam (Arabic) universal spirit

Aarcuus (Greek) rambunctious

Aaron ✪ (Hebrew) revered; sharer
Aahron, Aaran, Aaren, Aareon, Aarin, Aarone, Aaronn, Aarron, Aaryn, Aeron, Aharon, Ahran, Ahren, Ahron, Aranne, Aren, Arin, Aron, Arron

Aashiq (Arabic) fights evil

Aasif (Hindi) brash

Aasim (Hindi) in God's grace

Aatiq (Arabic) caring

Abacus (Greek) device for doing calculations; clever
Abacas, Abakus, Abba

Abaddon (Hebrew) knows God

Abahu (Hindi) hopeful

Abana (Biblical) place name

Abanobi (Mythology) water lover

Abasi (African) strict

Abbas (Arabic) harsh
Ab, Abba

Abbey (Hebrew) spiritual
Abbie, Abie, Abby

Abbott (Hebrew) father; leader
Abbitt, Abott, Abotte

Abdi (African) serves well

Abdiel (Arabic) serving Allah

Abdon (Greek) God's worker

Abdul (Arabic) servant of Allah
Ab, Abdal, Abdeel, Abdel, Abdoul, Abdu, Abdual, Abul

Abdulaziz (Hindi) servant of a friend
Abdelazim, Abdelaziz, Abdulazaz, Abdulazeez

Abdul-Jabbar (Arabic) comforting

Abdullah (Arabic) Allah's servant
Abdalah, Abdalla, Abdallah, Abdualla, Abdulah, Abdulahi, Abdulla

Abe (Hebrew) form of Abraham: father of a multitude
Abey, Abie

Abednego (Aramaic) faithful

Abeeku (African) Wednesday-born

Abel (Hebrew) vital
Abe, Abele, Abell, Abey, Abie, Able, Adal, Avel

Abelard (German) firm
Ab, Abalard, Abbey, Abby, Abe, Abel, Abelerd, Abelhard, Abilard, Adalard, Adelard

Abelardo (Spanish) decisive

Abelino (Spanish) from biblical Abel
Abel, Able

Aben (Spanish) diligent

Abercius (Latin) open mind

Aberdeen (Place name) serene
Aber, Dean, Deen

Aberlin (German) ambitious

Abhay (Indian) unafraid

Abhijit (Indian) winner

Abi (Turkish) family's oldest brother

Abiah (Hebrew) child of Jehovah
Abia, Abiel, Abija, Abijah, Abisha, Abishai, Aviya, Aviyah

Abiasaph (Biblical) loyal to God

Abidan (Biblical) God judges him

Abidla (Arabic) worshipping

Abiezer (Hebrew) father's light

Abihu (Biblical) believer

Abijah (Hebrew) God's gift
Abish

Abilene (Place name) town in Texas; good old boy
Abalene, Abileen

Abimael (Biblical) loves God

Abimbola (African) destined for riches

Abimelech (Hebrew) believer

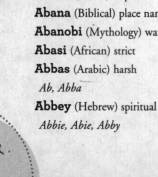

Abinadab (African) tuesday-born

Abioye (African) he loves God

Abir (Hebrew) strong

Abeer

Abisia (Hebrew) God's gift;
gifted child

Abixah, Absa

Abisoye (African) believer

Able (French) strong

Abner (Hebrew) cheerful leader

Ab, Abnir, Abnor, Avner, Ebner

Aboo (African) father; wise

Abosi (African) remembered

Abraar (Hebrew) fathers many

Abraham (Hebrew) father of a
multitude

Abarran, Abe, Aberham, Abey,
Abhiram, Abie, Abrahim, Abrahm,
Abram, Bram, Ibrahim

Abram (Hebrew) form of
Abraham: father of a multitude

Abe, Abrams, Avram, Bram

Abrasha (Hebrew) father

Abraxas (Spanish) bright

Aba

Abs (Hebrew) form of Absalom:
my father is peace

Abe

Absalom (Hebrew) my father is
peace

Abe, Abs, Absalon, Avshalom

Absolon (French) form of
Absalom: my father is peace

Abundiantus (Latin) plentiful

Abbondanzio, Abbondazio,
Abbondio

Abundio (Spanish) living in
abundance

Abun, Abund

Acacius (Latin) blameless

Ace (Latin) one; unity

Acer, Acey, Acie

Acencion (Spanish) ascends

Ace-Shane (American) gracious
God is first

Achaea (Biblical) good ancestry

Achard (French) dark mind

Achilles (Greek) heroic

Achill, Achille, Achillea, Achillios,
Ackill, Akil, Akili, Akilles

Acho (Greek) loud

Acisclo (Spanish) frantic

Acisclus (Greek) from the river
god Achelous

Ack (Scandinavian) peaceful

Acker (American) oak tree

Aker

Ackerley (English) born of the
meadow; nature-loving

Accerley, Ackerlea, Ackerleigh,
Ackersley, Acklea, Ackleigh, Ackley,
Acklie

Actium (Biblical) place name

Acton (English) sturdy; oaks

Acten, Actin, Actohn, Actone

Adad (Mythology) stormy

Adael (Hebrew) decorated by
God

Adair (Scottish) negotiator

Adaire, Adare, Ade

Adal (German) noble man

Adall, Adel

Adalai (Hebrew) my witness

Adalard (German) brave

Adalberto (Spanish) bright;
dignified

Adal, Berto

Adam ✿ (Hebrew) first man;
original

Ad, Adahm, Adama, Adamo, Adas,
Addam, Addams, Addie, Addy,
Adem, Adham

Adamson (Hebrew) Adam's son

Adams, Adamsen, Adamsson,
Addamson

Adan (Irish) bold spirit

Aden, Adin, Adyn, Aidan, Aiden

Adar (Hebrew) fire; spirited

Addar

Adarsh (Spanish) first man (Adam)

Adbeel (Biblical) crowned

Add (Greek) steadfast

Addae (African) the sun

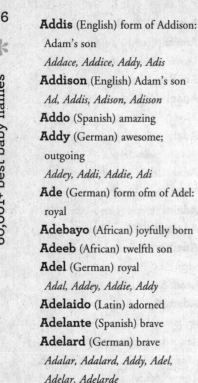

Addis (English) form of Addison:
Adam's son
Addace, Addice, Addy, Adis

Addison (English) Adam's son
Ad, Addis, Adison, Adisson

Addo (Spanish) amazing

Addy (German) awesome;
outgoing
Addey, Addi, Addie, Adi

Ade (German) form ofm of Adel:
royal

Adebayo (African) joyfully born

Adeeb (African) twelfth son

Adel (German) royal
Adal, Addey, Addie, Addy

Adelaido (Latin) adorned

Adelante (Spanish) brave

Adelard (German) brave
*Adalar, Adalard, Addy, Adel,
Adelar, Adelarde*

Adelmo (German) protects others

Adelpho (Greek) breathes
Adelfo

Aden (Irish) fiery

Adeniyi (Biblical) believer

Adeone (Welsh) royal
Addy, Adeon

Adeoye (Latin) God-given

Adewale (Welsh) in flight; soars

Adhinav (Indian) newest

A'Dhron (American) warm

Adi (Arabic) fair

Adigun (American) distinctive

Adilson (Jewish) son of justice

Adin (Hebrew) good-looking
Adan

Adina (Biblical) slight

Adio (African) devout

Adir (Hindi) lightning

Adit (Sanskrit) bright

Aditya (Sanskrit) sun

Adlai (Hebrew) ornamented
Ad, Addy, Adlay, Adley, Adlie

Adlay (Hebrew) God's haven
Adlei, Adley

Adler (German) eagle-eyed
Ad, Addler, Adlar

Admer (English) noble

Adna (Hebrew) physical

Adnee (English) loner
Adni, Adny

Ado (American) respected
Ad, Addy

Adofo (German) sly

Adolf (German) sly wolf
Ad, Adolfe, Adolph

Adolphus (German) noble wolf
Adolfus, Adulphus

Adom (African) blessed

Adomas (African) blessed

Adonai (Biblical) my Lord

Adonaldo (Spanish) baby of hope

Adonijah (Hebrew) believer

Adonis (Greek) gorgeous;
Aphrodite's love in mythology
*Addonis, Adon, Adones, Adonnis,
Adonys, Andonice*

Adoren (Hebrew) my Lord

Adorjan (Welsh) birdlike

Adrastos (Mythology) tenacious

Adrian ✪ (Latin) wealthy; dark-
skinned
*Adarian, Ade, Addie, Adorjan,
Adrain, Adreeyan, Adreian,
Adreyan, Adriaan, Adriane,
Adriann, Adrien, Adrion, Adron,
Adryan, Adryon, Aydrien, Aydrienne*

Adriano (Italian) wealthy
Adriannho, Adrianno

Adrie (Hungarian) leader of men

Adriel (Hebrew) God's follower
Adrial, Adryel

Adrien (French) form of Adrian:
wealthy; dark-skinned
Ade, Adriene, Adrienn

Adya (Russian) man from Adria

Adyn (Irish) manly
Adann, Ade, Aden, Aidan, Ayden

Adzel (Native American) fruitful

Aedan (Welsh) fire; fiery
temperament

Aedron (Welsh) fiery

Aegle (Mythology) light

Aemilios (German) nobility

Aeneas (Greek) worthy of praise
Aineas, Aineias, Eneas, Eneis

Aeolus (Greek) ruler of the winds

Aerin (Welsh) berry

Aeron (Mythology) masculine
god

Aesoh (Biblical name spelled
backward) revered

Aeson (Mythology) steady

Afan (Russian) form of Afanasy:
forever

Afanasy (Russian) forever
Afanasi

Afdhaal (Arabic) quiet

Affie (Arabic) pure

Afililio (Hispanic) commentator

Afra (Arabic) pale red hair

Afton (English) dignified
Affton, Aftawn, Aften

Afzal (Arabic) best

Agaf (Greek) martyr

Agamemnon (Greek) slow but
sure
Agamem

Agapito (Spanish) loving

Agapius (Greek) love

Agaue (Greek) worker

Aggie (English) works the soil

Aggis (Asian) good

Aglay (Russian) splendid

Agnar (Irish) purity

Agricola (Irish) farms

Agripino (Hispanic) grieves

Agron (Spanish) farmer

Agrona (Celtic) combative

Aguayo (Spanish) smart

Agueda (Spanish) gives

Agueleo (Greek) wise one

Agurs (Spanish) good; often a
girl's name

Agus (Spanish) form of Agustin:
dignified

Agustin (Latin) dignified
Aguste, Auggie, Augustin

Agustive (Spanish) thoughtful

Ahab (Hebrew) father's brother;
sea captain in *Moby Dick*

Ahaziah (Hebrew) beloved

Ahearn (Irish) horse tender
*Ahearne, Aherin, Ahern, Aherne,
Hearn*

Aherin (Hebrew) held on high
Aharon, Ahern, Aherne

Ahimelech (Biblical) religious
support

Ahmad (Arabic) praised man
*Achmad, Achmed, Ahamad,
Ahamada, Ahamed, Ahmaad,
Ahmaud, Amad, Amahd, Amed*

Ahmed (Arabic) praised man

Ahmoz (African) praised

Ahsan (Hindi) gracious; (Arabic)
grateful

Ahti (Mythology) water god

Ahura (Mythology) wise

Aiah (Biblical) shepherd

Aidan ○ ❶ (Irish) fiery spirit
Adan, Aden, Adin, **Aiden,** *Aydan,
Ayden, Aydin*

Aided (Irish) spirited

Aigars (Russian) content

Aignan (Greek) pure

Aijalon (Biblical) place name

Aiken (English) hardy; oak-hewn
Aicken, Aikin, Ayken, Aykin

Ailbhe (Irish) saint

Ailill (Irish) small; elfin

Ailred (English) spiritual

Aimery (German) leader
*Aime, Aimerey, Aimeric, Amerey,
Aymeric, Aymery*

Aimo (Scandinavian) plenty

Aino (Scandinavian) the best one

Ainsley (Scottish) in a meadow
*Ainslee, Ainslie, Ainsleigh, Ainsli,
Ansley, Aynslee, Aynsley, Aynslie*

Ainsworth (English) joyful

Aiolos (Greek) fleet

Aisha (Arabic) living; typically a
female name

Aiwar (Arabic) form of Anwar:
shining

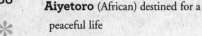

Aiyetoro (African) destined for a peaceful life

Ajani (African) victorious

Ajax (Greek) daring
Ajacks

Ajay (American) spontaneous
A.J., Aj, Ajah, Ajai

Ajmal (African) depressed

Akan (Biblical) blessed

Akando (Asian) smart boy

Akar (Hindi) lightning
Akara

Akash (Indian) of the sky

Akbar (Hindi) Muslim king; giving

Ake (Scandinavian) inherits

Akeem (Arab) form of Hakim: brilliant
Ackeem, Ackim, Akieme, Akim, Hakeem

Akevy (Hebrew) form of Akiva: cunning

Aki (Scandinavian) blameless

Akil (Arabic) intelligent
Ahkeel, Akeel, Akeyla, Akhil, Akiel, Akili

Akilles (Greek) form of Achilles: heroic

Akim (Russian) loved by God
Achim, Ackeem, Ackim, Ahkieme, Akeam, Akee, Akeem, Akiem, Akima, Arkeem

Akinori (Japanese) spring flower

Akins (African) brave

Akira (Japanese) intellectual

Akiva (Hebrew) cunning
Akiba, Kiva

Akram (Arabic) kind

Akren (American) in jeopardy

Aksel (Scandinavian) calm

Akwasi (African) hopes

Akwete (African) second-born twin

Al (Irish) form of Alexander: great leader; helpful; form of Alan: handsome boy

Aladdin (Arabic) believer
Al, Ala, Alaa, Alaaddin, Aladdein, Aladean, Aladen

Alain (French) form of Alan: handsome boy
Alaen, Alainn, Alayn, Allain, Alun

Alair (Gaelic) happy
Alaire

Alan (Irish) handsome boy
Ailin, Al, Aland, Alen, Allan, Allen, Alley, Allie, Allin, Allyn, Alon, Alun

Alander (American) argumentative; cogitative

Alando (Spanish) form of Alan: handsome boy
Al, Alaindo, Alan, Aland, Alano, Allen, Allie, Alun, Alundo, Alyn

Alanson (Celtic) son of Alan; handsome
Alansen, Alenson, Allanson

Alarcon (French) dominant; (German) rules

Alaric (German) ruler
Alarick, Alarik, Aleric, Allaric, Allarick, Alric, Alrick

Alasdair (Scottish) form of Alastair: strong leader
Al, Alaisdair, Alasdaire, Alasdare, Alisdair, Allysdair

Alastair (Scottish) strong leader
Alaistair, Alastaire, Alasteir, Alastere, Alastor, Aleistere, Alester, Alistair, Allaistar, Allastair, Allastir, Alystair

Alaster (American) form of Alastair: strong leader
Alaste, Alester, Allaster

Albair (Welsh) rules

Alban (Latin) white man; from Alba's white hill
Abion, Albain, Albany, Albean, Albee, Albein, Alben, Albi, Albie, Albin, Alby, Auban

Albanse (American) form of
Albany: town in New York;
restless
*Alban, Albance, Albanee, Albany,
Albie, Alby*

Albany (American) town in New
York; restless
Albanee, Albanie

Albe (Latin) from Alba's white
hill

Alberic (German) ruler; tough
Albric

Albert (German) distinguished
*Al, Alberto, Alberts, Albie,
Albrecht, Alby, Ally, Aubert*

Alberto (Italian) distinguished
Al, Albert, Bertie, Berto

Albie (German) form of Albert:
distinguished
Albee, Albi, Alby

Albion (Greek) old-fashioned
Albionne, Albyon

Albis (Spanish) unaware

Alby (Irish) white

Alcario (Spanish) delight

Alcide (Spanish) spirited

Alcippe (Greek) strong horse

Alcordia (American) in accord
with others
Alcord, Alkie, Alky

Alcott (English) cottage-dweller
*Alcot, Alkokt, Alkott, Allcot,
Allcott, Allkot, Allkott*

Aldee (American) friend

Aldegundo (Spanish) old soul

Alden (English) wise
Al, Aldan, Aldin, Aldon, Elden

Alder (English) revered; kind

Aldest (Last name used as first
name) great

Aldo (Italian) older one; jovial
Aldoh

Aldor (Spanish) elder

Aldorse (American) form of
Aldo: older one; jovial
Al, Aldorce, Aldors

Aldous (German) wealthy
Aldas, Aldis, Aldus

Aldred (English) advisor;
judgmental
Al, Aldrid, Aldy, Alldred, Eldred

Aldren (English) old friend
*Al, Aldie, Aldran, Aldrun, Aldryn,
Aldy*

Aldrich (English) wise advisor
*Aldie, Aldric, Aldrick, Aldridge,
Aldrige, Aldrish, Aldritch, Alldric,
Alldrich, Alldrick, Alldridge,
Eldridge*

Aldrin (English) old ruler

Aldwin (English) old friend

Aldyn (Irish) veteran

Alec (Greek) high-minded
Al, Aleck, Alek, Alic

Alecs (Scandinavian) defends man

Aleden (English) old friend

Alejandro (Spanish) defender;
bold and brave
Alejandra, Alejo, Alex, Alexjandro

Alek (Russian) form of Aleksei:
defender; brilliant
Aleks

Aleka (Slavic) form of Alex: great
leader; helpful

Aleksander (Greek and Polish)
defender
Alek, Sander

Aleksei (Russian) defender;
brilliant
Alek, Alexi, Alik

Aleksey (Russian) smart

Aleman (Spanish) protects

Alemet (African) world leader

Aleph (Hebrew) first letter of the
Hebrew alphabet

Aleppo (Place name) easygoing
Alepo

Aleric (Scandinavian) rules all
Alarik, Alerick, Alleric, Allerick

Aleron (French) the knight's
armor; protected

Alessandro (Italian) helpful;
defender
Alessand, Allessandro

Alessio (Italian) defensive

Alex ✪ (Greek) form of
Alexander: great leader; helpful
Alax, Alecs, Alix, Allax, Allex

Alexander ✪ ❶ (Greek) great
leader; helpful
*Al, Alec, Alecsander, Aleksandar,
Aleksander, Aleksandur, Alex,
Alexandar, Alexandor, Alexandr,
Alexis, Alexsander, Alexxander,
Alexzander, Alisander, Alixander,
Alixandre*

Alexandros (Greek) form of
Alexander: great leader; helpful
Alesandros, Alexandras

Alexdann (Hawaiian) helpful

Alexis ✪ (Greek) form of
Alexander: great leader; helpful
*Alexace, Alexei, Alexes, Alexey,
Alexi, Alexie, Alexius, Alexiz,
Alexy, Lex*

Alf (Italian) form of Alfonso:
bright; prepared

Alfa (Spanish) first

Alfalfa (Botanical) sprite

Alfeo (Italian) different

Alfeus (Hebrew) follower
Alpheus

Alfie (English) form of Alfred:
counselor
Alf, Alfi, Alfy

Alfon (Spanish) bright

Alfonso (Spanish) bright;
prepared
*Alf, Alfie, Alfons, Alfonsin, Alfonso,
Alfonsus, Alfonz, Alfonza, Alfonzo,
Alfonzus, Alphonsus, Fons, Fonzie,
Fonzy*

Alford (English) wise

Alfred (English) counselor
Al, Alf, Alfeo, Alfie, Alfrede, Alfryd

Alfredo (Italian) alf
Alfie, Alfreedo, Alfrido

Algas (English) has spears

Alger (German) hardworking
Algar, Allgar

Algernon (English) man with
facial hair
*Al, Algenon, Alger, Algie, Algin,
Algon, Algy*

Algia (German) prepared; kind
Alge, Algie

Algirdas (Scandinavian) chariot
rider; believer

Algo (American) lovable

Ali (Arabic) greatest
Alee, Aly

Ali-Baba (Literature) from *A
Thousand and One Nights*; cunning

Alicio (Spanish) noble; dignified

Alick (English) defends

Alim (Arabic) musical

Alipi (Spanish) calm

Alipio (Spanish) place name

Alireza (Hebrew) joyful

Alirio (Spanish) alert

Alisander (Greek) form of
Alexander: great leader; helpful
*Alisander, Alissander, Allisandre,
Alsandair, Alsandare, Alsander*

Alisen (Irish) honest

Allan (Irish) form of Alan:
handsome boy
Allane, Allayne

Allard (English) brave man
Alard, Ellard

Alleem (American) bold

Allegheny (Place name)
mountains of the Appalachian
system; grand
Al, Alleg, Alleganie, Alleghenie

Allen (Irish) handsome boy
*Al, Alen, Alley, Alleyn, Alleyne,
Allie, Allin, Allon, Allyn, Alon*

Allett (Biblical) hides

Allie (Arabic) divine

Allington (English) calm

Allward (Polish) brave

Almagor (Hebrew) courageous

Almar (German) strong
Al, Almarr, Almer
Almedia (Spanish) place name
Almee (German) ruler
Almere (American) director
Almer
Almez (Spanish) dependable
Almo (American) form of Elmo:
gregarious
Almodad (Biblical) sturdy
Almon (Biblical) place name
Almund (Botanical) from
almond; wise
Alois (Czech) famous warrior
Aloisio, Aloysius
Alonzo (Spanish) enthusiastic
*Alano, Alanzo, Alon, Alonso,
Alonza, Alonze, Elonzo, Lon, Lonnie*
Alouis (French) sun king
Aloys (French) king
Aloysius (German) famed
Alaois, Alois, Aloisio, Aloisius
Alpar (Hindi) champions
downtrodden
Alpheus (Hebrew) form of
Alfeus: follower
Alphaeus
Alphin (German) leads first

Alphonse (German)
distinguished
*Alf, Alfonse, Alphons, Alphonsa,
Alphonso, Alphonzus, Fonsi, Fonsie,
Fonz, Fonzie*
Alpin (Scottish) man from alpine
area
Alps (Place name) climber
Alp
Alquince (American) old; fifth
*Al, Alquense, Alquin, Alquins,
Alquinse, Alqwence*
Alrick (German) leader
Alrec, Alric
Alston (English) serious;
nobleman
Allston, Alsten, Alstin
Alsworth (English) from a
manor; rich
Alta (Latin) high; elevated
Al
Altair (Scottish) defender
Altan (Turkish) dawn
Altarius (African American)
form of Altair: defender
*Al, Altare, Altareus, Alterius,
Alltair*
Altemease (Turkish) dawn light
Alter (Hebrew) old; will live to
be old
Altilio (Spanish) bright

Altman (German) wise
Altmann, Atman
Alton (English) excellent; kind
Allton, Altawn, Alten, Altyn
Altonio (Spanish) form of
Antonio: superb
Altus (Latin) form of Alta: high;
elevated
Al
Alula (Latin) winged
Alun (Welsh) adored
Alva (Hebrew) intelligent;
beloved friend
Alvah
Alvado (Spanish) fair
Alvah (Biblical) high God
Alvan (Biblical) friend
Alvar (Spanish) careful
Alvaro, Alver
Alvarado (Spanish) peacemaker
Alvaradoh, Alvaro, Alvie, Alvy
Alvaro (Spanish) just
*Alvaroh, Alvarro, Alvey, Alvie,
Alvy*
Alvern (English) old friend
Al, Alverne, Alvurn
Alvim (Slavic) pale friend
Alvin (Latin) light-haired; loved
*Alv, Alvan, Alven, Alvie, Alvy,
Alvyn*

Alvin-Don (American) combo of
Alvin and Don

Alvis (American) form of Elvis:
all-wise
Al, Alviss, Alvy

Alvord (Greek) cautious

Alwin (German) form of Alvin:
light-haired; loved
Allwyn, Alwyn, Alwynn, Aylwin

Alzado (Arabic) forlorn

Amaan (African) loyal
Aman, Amman

Amable (French) amiable

Amac (Mythology) wise

Amadayus (Invented) form of
Amadeus: God-loving
Amadayes

Amadeo (Italian) blessed by God;
artistic

Amadeus (Latin) God-loving
Amad, Amadayus, Amadeaus,
Amadei, Amadio, Amadis, Amado,
Amador, Amadou, Amedeo,
Amodaos

Amado (Spanish) loved
Amadee, Amadeo, Amadi, Amadis,
Amadus, Amando

Amadour (French) loved
Amador, Amadore

Amadus (Latin) adores God
Amandus

Amal (Hebrew) hardworking;
optimistic
Amahl, Amhall

Amalek (Biblical) place name;
works hard

Amancio (Spanish) faithful

Amandeep (Hindi) light of peace
Amandip, Amanjit, Amanjot,
Amanpreet

Amando (Spanish) God-loving

Amandor (Spanish) affectionate

Amanus (Biblical) place name

Amar (Arabic) making a home
Amari, Amario, Amaris, Ammar,
Ammer

Amaramto (Latin) beauty does
not fade

Amarbir (Spanish) forevermore

Amardeep (Indian) loved

Amarillo (Place name) town in
Texas; in Spanish
Amarille, Amarilo

Amarion (Hebrew) believes in
God

Amasa (Hebrew) carries a heavy
load

Amathus (Biblical) place name

Amato (Italian) loving
Amahto, Amatoh

Amaury (Spanish) slanted; power

Amazu (Hebrew) burdened

Ambert (Arabic) golden boy

Amblin (English) of nobility

Ambrel (Spanish) amber

Ambrogia (Italian) everlasting

Ambrose (German) everlasting
Amba, Ambie, Ambroce, Ambrus,
Amby

Ambrosio (Spanish) everlasting

Ambrus (Slavic) immortal

Ameer (Arabic) rules

Amer (Spanish) leader

America (Place name) patriotic

Americo (Spanish) patriotic
Ame, America, Americus, Ameriko

Amerigo (Italian) ruler; name of
Italian explorer
Amer, Americo, Ameriko

Amery (Arabic) regal birth
Amory

Ames (French) friendly
Aims

Amias (Latin) devoted to God
Amyas

Amichai (Hebrew) my nation lives

Amiel (Hebrew) my people's God
Ameal, Amheel, Ammiel

Amin (Arabic) honorable;
dependable
Aman, Ameen

Amine (Arabic) honest

Amir (Arabic) royal; ruler
Ameer, Amire

Amiren (American) leader

Amit (Hindi) forever;
Amitan, Amreet, Amrit

Amiti (Japanese) endless friend

Ammen (Mythology) hides

Ammiel (Biblical) adventurer

Ammon (Irish) hidden
Amnon

Amodeo (Invented) loving

Amol (Hebrew) perseveres

Amon (Egyptian) secretive

Amor (Latin) love
Amerie, Amoree, Amori, Amorie

Amory (German) home ruler
Amery, Amor

Amos (Hebrew) strong
Amus

Ampah (African) certainty

Amparo (Spanish) winding

Ampy (American) fast
Amp, Ampee, Ampey, Amps

Amram (Biblical) uplifted

Amran (Biblical) spirited

Amund (Scandinavian) fearless

Amyas (Latin) lovable
Aimeus, Ameus, Amias, Amyes

An (Chinese) peaceful; safe
Ana

Anah (Biblical) the answer

Anaitis (Mythology) pure

Anamim (Biblical) windy

Anan (Irish) outdoorsy
An, Annan

Ananan (Biblical) hopes

Anand (Hindi) delightful
Ananda, Anant, Ananth

Ananiah (Biblical) place name

Ananias (Biblical) pious

Anant (Indian) forever

Ananta (Sanskrit) forever

Anarolio (Spanish) called forth

Anas (Czech) born again

Anast (Russian) born again

Anastasius (Greek) reborn
*Anas, Anastagio, Anastas, Anastase,
Anastasi, Anastasio, Anastastios,
Anastice, Anasticius, Anastisis,
Athanasius*

Anatole (French) exotic
*Anatol, Anatoli, Anatolijus,
Anatolio, Anatoly, Anitolle*

Anatu (Hebrew) water

Ancel (French) creative
Ance, Ancell, Anse, Ansel, Ansell

Andalf (Norse) leads with staff

Andel (Scandinavian) honored

Ander (English) form of Andrew:
manly and brave

Anders (Swedish) masculine
*Ander, Andersen, Anderson, Andirs,
Andries, Andy*

Ando (Slavic) form of Andrew:
manly and brave

Andrade (Scandinavian) manly

Andrae (Slavic) form of Andrew:
manly and brave

Andras (French) form of
Andrew: manly and brave
*Andrae, Andres, Andrus, Ondrae,
Ondras*

André (French) masculine
*Andra, Andrae, Andre, Andree,
Andrei, Anrecito, Aundré*

Andreas (Greek) masculine
Adryus, Andrieas, Andries, Andy

Andrej (Slavic) masculine; manly

Andren (English) masculine

Andrere (Greek) manly

Andres (Spanish) macho
Andras, Andrés, Andrez, Andy

Andre-Shaun (French) combo
of Andre and Shaun; kind boy

Andretti (Italian) speedy
Andrette, Andy

Andrew ✪ ● (Greek) manly and
brave
*Aindrew, Anders, Andery, Andi,
Andie, Andreas, Andres, Andrews,
Andru, Andrue, Andy, Audrew*

Andrick (Scandinavian) masculine

Andromache (Greek) manly

Andronek (Greek) wins

Andronico (Italian) victor

Andronicus (Greek) clever

Andros (Polish) masculine
Andris, Andrus

Andru (Greek) form of Andrew: manly and brave
Andrue

Andrzej (Polish) manly

Andy (Greek) form of Andrew: manly and brave
Andee, Andie

Anekin (Slavic) manly

Aner (Biblical) well-born

Aneurin (Welsh) golden child
Aneirin

Anfanio (Spanish) secretive

Anferny (American) variation of Anthony
Andee, Anfernee, Anferney, Anferni, Anfernie, Anfurny

Angel ⚬ (Greek) angelic messenger
Ange, Angele, Angell, Angie, Angy

Angelberto (Spanish) shining angel
Angel, Angelbert, Bert, Berto

Angelo (Italian) angelic
Ange, Angelito, Angeloh, Angelos, Anglo, Anjelo

Angharad (Welsh) loving

Angits (Celtic) divine

Angle (Word as name) spin doctor
Ange, Angul

Anglin (Greek) angelic
Anglen, Anglinn, Anglun

Angra (Mythology) dark spirit

Angus (Scottish) standout; important
Ange, Angos, Aonghas

Anh (Vietnamese) smart

Anibal (Spanish) brave noble

Aniceto (Spanish) invincible

Anick (Hebrew) gracious

Aniello (Italian) risk-taker

Anil (Hindi) air
Aneel, Anel, Aniel, Aniello

Aniol (Polish) angel
Ahnjol, Ahnyolle

Anju (Indian) younger

Anka (Polish) gracious; stems from Anna

Ankoma (African) last-born child

Ankur (Indian) blooms

Annan (African) second; from Annar

Annatto (Botanical) tree; tough
Annatta

Anndo (Scandinavian) protects

Annibale (Phoenician) form of Hannibal: leader

Anniel (Biblical) angel

Annis (English) God's gift

Anok (Slavic) reliable

Anolus (Greek) masculine
Ano, Anol

Anrue (American) masculine
Anrae, Anroo

Ans (Scandinavian) dramatic

Anscom (English) awesome man
Anscomb

Ansel (French) creative
Ancell, Ansa, Anse, Ansell

Anselm (German) protective
Anse, Ansehlm, Ansellm

Anselmo (Spanish) protected by God
Ancel, Ancelmo, Anse, Ansel, Anselm, Anzelmo, Selmo

Ansgar (German) spear of God

Anshel (Hindi) blessed
Anshl

Anskar (German) brusque

Ansley (English) loner
Anslea, Anslee, Ansleigh, Anslie, Ansly, Ansy

Anson (German) divine male
Anse, Ansonn, Ansun

Anssi (Scandinavian) protected

Antal (Latin) princely

Ante (Slavic) flourishes; (Spanish) special

Antero (Greek) moves with grace
Anthonisamy (Indian) form of
Anthony: priceless
Anthony ✪ ❶ (Latin) priceless
Anathony, Anothony, Anth,
Anthawn, Anthey, Anthoney,
Anthoni, Anthonie, Anthonio,
Anthyonny, Anton, Antony, Tony
Antioch (Biblical) place name
Antioco (Spanish) best
Antipas (Greek) father
Antjuan (American) form of
Anthony: priceless
Antoan (Latin) form of Anthony:
priceless
Antoine (French) worthy of
praise
Antone, Antons, Antos, Antwan,
Antwon, Antwone
Antolin (Slavic) unusual
Anton (Latin) outstanding
Antan, Antawn
Antonce (African American)
form of Anthony: priceless
Antawnce
Antonio (Spanish) superb
Antinio, Antoino, Antone,
Antonello, Antonino, Antonioh,
Antonnio, Antonyia, Antonyio,
Antonyo, Tony

Antony (Latin) good
Antawny, Antini, Antonah,
Antone, Antoney, Antoni, Antonie,
Anty, Tone, Tony
Antran (Spanish) energetic
Antrinell (African American)
valued
Antrie, Antrinel, Antry
Antroy (African American) form
of Anthony: priceless
Antroe, Antroye
Antuane (Slavic) first
Antwan (American) form of
Antoine: worthy of praise
Antawan, Antawn, Anthawn,
Antowine, Antown, Antowne,
Antwain, Antwaine, Antwaion,
Antwane, Antwann, Antwanne,
Antwaun, Antwen, Antwian,
Antwine, Antwion, Antwoan,
Antwoin, Antwoine, Antwon,
Antwonn, Antwonne, Antwuan,
Antyon, Antywon
Antwone (American) form of
Antoine: worthy of praise
Antwonn
Anubis (Egyptian) royal
Anulf (Scandinavian) royal
Anwar (Arabic) shining
Anouar, Anour, Anwhour

Anwyl (Welsh) beloved
Anwell, Anwyll
Anyon (Latin) form of Anthony:
priceless
Anzelm (Polish) protective
Ahnzselm
Apatin (Slavic) aggressive
Apearen (Native American) armed
Apen (Irish) likes horses
Aplin (American) strong
Apolinar (Spanish) manly and wise
Apollo
Apolinard (Spanish) strong
Apolla (Greek) strong
Apollo (Greek) masculine; a god
in mythology
Apolloh, Apolo, Apoloniah,
Applonian, Appollo
Apolonio (Greek) form of
Apollo: masculine; a god in
mythology
Apostle (Greek) follower; disciple
Apos
Apostolos (Greek) disciple
Apos
Apple (American) favorite;
wholesome
Apel
Aquan (Native American)
tranquil

Aquila (Spanish) eagle-eyed
Acquilla, Aquil, Aquilas, Aquile,
Aquilla, Aquillino

Aquileo (Spanish) warrior
Akweleo, Aquilo

Ara (Slavic) integrity

Arachne (Greek) spider

Aracin (Latin) ready; heaven's
gate

Araldo (German) army leader

Aralis (Hawaiian) godlike

Aralt (Irish) army leader

Aram (Syrian) noble; honorable
Ara, Aramia, Arra

Aramis (French) clever
Airamis, Arames, Aramith,
Aramys, Aramyse, Arhames

Arann (Slavic) calm

Arbel (Biblical) prayerful

Arber (American) from arbor;
adorned

Arbet (Last name as first name)
high
Arb, Arby

Arbogast (German) covered

Arcana (Latin) esoteric wisdom

Arcen (English) virile

Arceneaux (French) friendly;
heavenly
Arce, Arcen, Arceno

Arch (English) form of Archibald:
bold leader
Arche

Archard (English) bold

Archer (English) athletic; bowman
Arch, Archie

Archibald (German) bold leader
Arch, Archibold, Archie

Archie (English) form of
Archibald: bold leader
Arch, Archi, Archy

Arcis (Spanish) from war god
Arecio

Ard (Thai) woodsy

Ardan (Latin) passion; eagle

Ardee (American) ardent
Ard, Ardie, Ardy

Ardell (Latin) go-getter
Ardel

Arden (Latin) ball of fire
Ard, Arda, Ardie, Ardin, Ardon,
Arrden

Ardley (English) with dedication

Ardmohr (Latin) more ardent
than others
Ard, Ardmoor, Ardmore

Ardolph (German) ardent

Ardor (French) loving

Ardouin (French) ardent

Arecin (French) smooth

Areeb (Arabic) passionate

Areeg (Welsh) gold

Arellano (Scandinavian) unique

Arelus (Latin) form of Aurelius:
golden son

Aren (Dutch) form of Aaron:
revered; sharer

Arenas (Spanish) eager

Arenda (Spanish) eager

Ares (Mythology) combats

Arethuse (Greek) excels

Arfel (Welsh) struggles

Argan (American) leader
Argee, Argen, Argey, Argi, Argie,
Argun

Argento (Spanish) silver
Arge, Argey, Argi, Argy

Argeroula (Greek) shines

Argus (Greek) careful; bright
Agos, Arjus

Argyl (Irish) from Ireland; aware

Argyle (English) diamond
pattern; planning
Argile

Ari (Greek) best
Ahree, Aria, Arias, Arie, Arih, Arij,
Arri

Arian (Welsh) form of Arion:
enchanted man

Aribert (German) holy

Aribold (German) holy

Aric (English) leader
Aaric, Arec, Areck, Arick, Arik,
Arric, Arrick, Arrik

Arie (English) God's lion

Ariel (Hebrew) God's spirited lion
Airel, Arel, Arell, Ari, Arie, Ariele,
Arielle, Ariya, Ariyel, Arrial, Arriel

Aries (Greek) god of war;
mythology
Arees, Arie, Ariez

Arik (German) leads; (Welsh)
form of Erik: powerful leader

Arild (Hebrew) God's lion

Arimas (Literature) form of
Aramis: clever

Arines (Spanish) strong

Ario (Spanish) warring
Ari, Arrio

Arioch (Biblical) dignity

Arion (Greek) enchanted man
Ari, Arian, Ariane, Arie, Arien,
Ariohn, Arrian

Arisbe (Spanish) believer

Arisodemos (Greek) best person

Arist (Greek) God-fearing

Aristeo (Spanish) best
Aris, Aristio, Aristo, Ary

Aristeus (Greek) quintessential

Aristides (Greek) son of the
outstanding
Ari, Aris, Aristidis

Aristophanes (Greek)
playwright

Aristotle (Greek) best man
Ari, Aris, Aristie, Aristito, Aristo,
Aristokles, Aristotelis, Aristottle

Ariwin (Spanish) best friend

Arj (Welsh) white

Arjan (Hindi) archer
Arjun

Arkady (Russian) revered

Arkan (Scandinavian) king's baby

Arkell (Scandinavian) of the king

Arki (Greek) ruler

Arkos (Biblical) people's master

Arkyn (Scandinavian) royal
offspring
Aricin, Ark, Arkeen, Arken, Arkin

Arle (Irish) sworn
Arlee, Arley, Arly

Arledge (English) lives by a lake
Arleedj, Arles, Arlidge, Arlledge

Arleigh (Irish) sworn
Arly

Arlen (Irish) dedicated
Arl, Arlan, Arland, Arle, Arlend,
Arlin, Arlyn, Arlynn

Arley (English) meadow-loving;
outdoorsy
Arleigh, Arlie, Arly

Arlindo (Italian) dedicated

Arlis (Hebrew) dedicated; in charge
Arlas, Arles, Arless, Arly

Arliss (English) wise eyes

Arlo (German) strong
Arloh

Arlonn (Irish) sworn; cheerful
Arlan, Arlann, Arlen, Arlon

Arlyn (Irish) form of Arlen:
dedicated

Arlys (Hebrew) pledged
Arlis

Arm (English) arm
Arma, Arman, Arme

Arman (German) army man;
defender
Armaan

Armand (German) strong soldier
Armad, Armanda, Armando,
Armands, Armanno, Armaude,
Arme, Armenta, Armond, Ormand

Armando (Spanish) entertainer
Armand, Arme, Armondo

Armani (Italian) army;
disciplined talent
Amani, Arman, Armanie, Armon,
Armoni

Armel (French) royal; sturdy

Armen (Spanish) from Armenia
Arme, Arment, Armenta

Armetris (Greek) prepared;
armed

Armineh (Armenian) from
Armenia

Armino (Teutonic) warrior

Armitage (Last name as first
name) safe haven
Armi, Armita, Army

Armon (Hebrew) strong as a
fortress
*Arman, Arme, Armen, Armin,
Armino, Armoni, Armons*

Armstrong (English) strong-armed
Arme, Army

Arnaud (French) strong
Arnaldo, Arnauld

Arnborn (Scandinavian) eagle-
bear; animal instincts
Arn, Arnborne, Arnbourne, Arne

Arndt (German) strong
Arne, Arnee, Arney, Arni, Arnie

Arne (German) form of Arnold:
ruler; strong
Arn, Arna, Arnel, Arnell

Arnell (American) strong

Arnette (Dutch) little eagle
Arnat, Arnet, Arnot, Arnott

Arnic (Scandinavian) eagle-eyed

Arnie (German) form of Arnold:
ruler; strong
Arne, Arney, Arni, Arnny, Arny

Arno (German) farsighted
Arn, Arne, Arnoh, Arnou, Arnoux

Arnold (German) ruler; strong
*Arnald, Arndt, Arne, Arnie,
Arnoll, Arny*

Arnome (Invented) powerful
Arnom

Arnon (German) eagle

Arnot (French) form of Arnold:
ruler; strong
Arnart, Arnett, Arnott

Arnov (Slavic) resolved

Arnst (Scandinavian) eagle-eyed
Arn

Arnulfo (Spanish) strong
Arne, Arnie, Arny

Arocles (Greek) masterful

Aroldo (German) eagle; strong

Aron (Hebrew) generous
Aaron, Arron, Erinn

Aronon (Welsh) blond

Arpad (Hungarian) prince; sunny

Arper (Slavic) fruitful

Arquimides (Spanish)
philosopher

Arran (Scandinavian) form of
Aaron: revered; sharer

Arrigo (Italian) ruler

Arsenio (Greek) macho; virile
*Arne, Arsen, Arsenius, Arseny,
Arsinio, Arsonio*

Arshad (Iranian) revered

Arshaq (Arabic) supports

Arsinoe (Biblical) place name

Arslan (Spanish) form of Arsenio:
macho; virile

Arson (Greek) masculine

Art (English) bearlike; wealthy
Arte, Artie

Artax (Biblical) rules

Artemus (Greek) gifted
*Art, Artemas, Artemio, Artemis,
Artie, Artimas, Artimis, Artimus*

Arthel (Slavic) royalty

Arthi (Scandinavian) masculine

Arthisus (Origin unknown) stuffy
Arth, Arthi, Arthy

Arthur (Celtic) bear; stone
*Art, Arth, Arther, Arthor, Artie,
Artor, Artur, Arty, Aurther, Aurthur*

Artie (English) form of Arthur:
bear; stone
Art, Artee, Arty

Artin (Slavic) form of Arthur:
bear; stone

Artra (Scandinavian) bear boy

Arturo (Italian) talented
Art, Arthuro, Artur, Arture, Arturro

Arun (Hindi) the color of the sky
before dawn
Aruns

Arund (Hindi) free spirit

Arundel (English) lives with
eagles; soars

Arv (Scandinavian) worthwhile

Arvai (Hebrew) roams
Arve

Arvel (German) friendly

Arvid (Hebrew) full of
wanderlust
*Arv, Arvad, Arve, Arvie, Arvind,
Arvinder, Arvydas*

Arvin (German) friendly
*Arv, Arven, Arvie, Arvind,
Arvinder, Arvon, Arvy*

Arvo (Spanish) friend

Arwen (German) friend
Arwee, Arwene, Arwhen, Arwy

Arwey (Welsh) priceless

Arwin (American) assertive friend

Ary (Hebrew) lion; fierce
Ari, Arye

Arya (Indian) analytical

Aryan (English) white

Asa (Hebrew) healer
Ase, Aza

As·d (Arabic) happy
Asaad, Asad, Asid, Assad, Azad

Asafa (Biblical) collector

Asbury (Last name used as first
name) dignified

Ascencion (Spanish) ascends

Ascot (English) cottage-dweller

Asgar (Scandinavian) God's
home

Ash (Botanical) tree; bold
Ashbey, Ashby, Ashe

Asha (Hebrew) fire

Asharious (Mythology) from
Ashur, god of war

Ashbel (Hebrew) fiery god

Ashby (Scandinavian) brash
Ashbee, Ashbey, Ashie, Ashy

Asher (Hebrew) joyful
Ash, Ashar, Ashor, Ashur

Ashfaaq (Arabic) honorable

Ashford (English) spunky
Ash, Ashferd, Ashtin

Ashkenaz (Biblical) sincere

Ashley (English) smooth
*Ash, Asheley, Ashelie, Ashely, Ashie,
Ashlan, Ashlee, Ashleigh, Ashlen,
Ashlie, Ashlin, Ashling, Ashlinn,
Ashlone, Ashly, Ashlyn, Ashlynn,
Aslan*

Ashlin (English) form of Ashley:
smooth

Ashmon (English) of the ash trees

Ashok (Indian) content

Ashraf (Arabic) honors others

Ashrin (English) of the ash trees

Ashton (English) handsome
Asheteen, Ashtin

Ashtoreth (Biblical) staunch

Ashur (Hebrew) happy

Ashvin (English) ash tree

Asifa (Hebrew) gathers

Askew (Last name used as first
name) distinguished

Askia (American) worthy

Aslan (Literature) from CS
Lewis's Narnia series; lionlike

Asmer (Last name used as first
name) ash tree

Asmus (German) well-known

Asner (Hebrew) giving

Asriel (Hebrew) praised

Asshurim (Biblical) of the ash-
tree land

Assir (Biblical) hawk-like

Aston (English) eastern
Asten, Astin

Aswin (English) from the land of
ash trees

Atam (American) form of Adam:
first man; original
Atame, Atom, Atym

Atanacio (Spanish) everlasting
Atan, Atanasio

Atanase (Spanish) forever

Atch (American) lively

Ateeq (Arabic) affectionate

Athan (Biblical) form of Dathan:
fountain of hope

Athanasius (Greek) immortal
Atanas, Atanasio

Athar (English) lives on a farm

Atherton (English) coming from a farm

Athos (Greek) high

Atilano (Greek) strong

Atilio (Spanish) aggressor

Atinuwa (African) aware

Atkins (Last name as first name) linked; known
Atkin

Atlas (Greek) courier of greatness
Atlass

Atley (English) from the meadow
Atlea, Atlee, Atleigh, Atli, Attley

Aton (Egyptian) sun child

Ator (Scandinavian) born of thunder

Atropos (Greek) unbinding

Atsu (African) second-born twin

Atticus (Greek) ethical
Aticus, Attikus

Attila (Gothic) powerful
Atalik, Atila, Atilio, Atiya, Atlya, Att

Attillio (Italian) hero

Atul (German) good

Atwater (English) living by the water

Atwell (English) the well; full of gusto

Atwood (English) the woods; outdoorsy

Atworth (English) farmer

Atyab (Arabic) cultivated

Auberon (German) like a bear; highborn
Aube, Auberron, Aubrey

Aubert (German) leader
Auber, Aubey

Aubin (French) ruler; elfin
Auben

Aubrey (French/German) ruler
Aubary, Aube, Aubery, Aubree, Aubry, Aubury, Bree

Auburn (Latin) brown with red cast; tenacious
Aubern, Aubie, Auburne

Auday (American) strong

Audelon (French) wealthy

Auden (English) old friend
Aude, Audie

Audencio (Spanish) companion
Auden

Audie (German) strong man
Aude, Audee, Audi, Audiel, Audley

Audley (English) rich
Audlea, Audlee, Audleigh, Audly

Audon (Scandinavian) alone

Audran (American) purposeful

Audras (Scandinavian) having wealth
Audres

Audric (French) wise ruler

Audun (Scandinavian) form of Audon: alone

Audwin (English) rich

Augie (Latin) form of Augustus: highly esteemed
Aug, Auggie, Augy

August (Latin) determined
Auge, Augie

Augustine (Latin) serious and revered
Agostino, Agoston, Agustin, Aug, Augie, August, Augustene, Augustin

Augustive (Spanish) serious

Augusto (Spanish) respected; serious
Agusto, Augey, Auggie, Austeo

Augustus (Latin) highly esteemed
Aug, Auge, Augie, August

Aulderay (American) old soul

Aulie (English) form of Audley: rich
Awlie

Aurek (Latin) golden

Aurelius (Latin) golden son
Arelian, Areliano, Aurel, Aurey, Aurie, Auriel, Aury

Aureo (Spanish) gold; pleases

Ausburn (English) reddish-brown

Aust (American) form of Austin: serious and revered

Austin ○ ① (Latin) form of Augustine: serious and revered
Astin, Aust, Austen, Austine, Auston, Austyn

Austreberto (Spanish) austere

Auther (American) form of Arthur: bear; stone
Authar, Authur

Autry (Latin) golden

Avanindra (Hindi) king of the earth
Avan

Avdis (Slavic) providential

Avelino (Spanish) nature-lover

Avenall (English) from the woods; calm
Avenel, Avenell

Avent (French) up-and-coming
Aventin, Aventino

Averill (French) April-born child
Ave, Averel, Averell, Averiel, Averil, Averyl, Averyll, Avrel, Avrell, Avrill, Avryl

Avery (English) soft-spoken
Avary, Ave, Aveary, Averey, Averie, Avry

Avi (Hebrew) springlike
Avian, Avidan, Avidor, Aviel, Avion

Aviaz (Hebrew) believer

Aviden (Hebrew) God judges him

Avinoam (Biblical) pleasant brother

Avion (French) flyer
Aveonn, Avyon, Avyun

Avison (Hebrew) believes

Avitol (Hebrew) vital

Aviv (Hebrew) spring; (French) vibrant

Avner (Hebrew) father of light
Avneet, Avniel

Avniel (Hebrew) God is my rock

Avon (Hebrew) spring birth; (English) place name

Avram (Hebrew) almighty father
Arram, Avraham, Avrom, Avrum

Avren (Hebrew) uplifts God

Avrum (Yiddish) form of Abraham: father of a multitude

Avrylle (French) hunter
Avryll

Axel (German) peaceful; contemporary
Aksel, Ax, Axe, Axil, Axill, Axl

Axie (Scandinavian) peaceful child

Axton (German) town of peace; peacemaker

Ayal (English) highborn

Ayden (Turkish) knowing

Aydin (Irish) masculine

Aydinus (Slavic) knowing

Ayers (Last name as first) industrious

Aylen (Native American) joy

Aylmer (English) of noble birth

Aylward (English) guards best

Aylwin (Welsh) elf friend

Ayman (Arabic) fortunate

Ayo (African) happy

Ayson (Origin unknown) lucky
Aison

Aytekin (American) friend

Azad (Arabic) lucky

Azael (Spanish) God-loved

Azar (Biblical) form of Azariah: aided by Jehovah

Azariah (Biblical) aided by Jehovah

Azeem (Arabic) cherished
Aseem, Asim

Azeez (Arabic) strong

Azhar (Arabic) flourishes

Azi (African) a child

Azia (Biblical) powerful

Azim (Arabic) grandiose

Aziz (Arabic) powerful; (African) adorable

Azizi (African) beloved

Azmon (Biblical) place name

Azrae (Mythology) Azrael

Azriel (Hebrew) the Lord's angel

Azuriah (Hebrew) aided by God
Azaria, Azariah, Azuria
Azzie (Slavic) strong

Babak (Iranian) the father
Babar (Turkish) lion
Baber
Babe (American) athlete
Babu (Hindi) fierce
Bacchus (Greek) reveler; jaded
Baakus, Bakkus, Bakus
Bach (Last name as first name)
talented
Bok
Bachar (Hebrew) eldest
Bachir (Hebrew) oldest son;
reliable
Bachur
Bacon (English) literary; outspoken
Baco, Bake, Bakon
Badar (Hindi) full moon
Bade (Welsh) wild boar
Baden (German) bathes; cleansed
Badge (American) moon-watcher

Badger (Last name as first name)
difficult
Badge, Badgeant, Bage, Bagent
Badget (English) moon-loving
Badr (African) full moon; lucky
Badru (African) full moon; lucky
Baghai (Arabic) form of Bahij:
delighted
Bagher (American) magnificent
Bagley (English) boy from the field
Bagor (English) fun
Baha (Arabic) splendid
Bahij (Arabic) delighted
Bahir (Arabic) magnificent
Bai (Chinese) white
Bailey (French) attentive
Baile, Baily, Baley, Baylie
Bainbridge (Irish) bridge;
negotiator
Bain, Banebridge, Beebee
Baines (Last name as first name)
pale
Baine, Baynes
Bainlon (American) form of
Bailey: attentive
Baily
Baird (Irish) singer/poet; creative
Bard, Bayrde
Bairon (Spanish) creative
Baka (Biblical) place name
Bakari (African) promising

Baker (English) cook
Baiker, Baykar
Bal (Hindi) strong
Bala (Hindi) young
Balan (Indian) youthful
Balbino (Italian) mumbler
Baldemar (Spanish) form of
Balthasar: God save the king
Baldy
Balder (Scandinavian) good prince
Baldur, Baudier
Baldev (Hindi) strong God
Baldie (German) nickname for
Baldwin: brave friend
Baldric (German) leader
Baldrick, Baledric, Bauldric
Baldridge (English) persuasive
Baldwin (German) steadfast friend
Baldwinn, Baldwynn, Bally
Balendin (Place name) balen
Baley (American) form of Bailey:
attentive
Baleye
Balfour (Scottish) landowner
Balf, Balfore
Balfre (Spanish) brave
Balin (Hungarian) from Balint:
strong and healthy
Balint (Latin) strong and healthy
Ballance (American) courageous
Balance, Ballans

Ballard (German) brave
Ballerd

Balraj (Hindi) strong king

Balthasar (Greek) God save the
king
Bath, Bathazar

Balu (Hindi) young

Balun (English) bold friend

Balwin (Last name as first name)
friendly; brave
Ball, Winn

Bamboo (Malay) botanical

BaNaire (Slavic) of God's peace

Banan (Irish) white

Bancroft (English) bean field;
gardener
Banc, Bankie, Bankroft

Bandy (Origin unknown)
gregarious
Bandee, Bandi

Banjo (Word as name)

Banks (Last name as first name)
focused
Bank

Banning (Irish) fair-haired
Bannie, Banny, Bannyng

Bao (Chinese) prized boy

Baptist (Latin) one who has been
baptized

Barak (Hebrew) lightning; success
Barrak, Barack

Baram (Hebrew) son of the people

Barclay (Scottish) audacious
man; birch tree meadow
Bar, Barclaye, Bark, Barklay, Barky

Bard (Irish) singer
Bar, Barr

Barden (English) peaceful; valley-
dweller
Bardon

Bardolf (German) wily hero

Bardrick (English) sings ballads
Bardric

Barek (English) flash

Barend (Scandinavian) bearlike

Baret-Carlyle (American)
combo of Baret and Carlyle

Bargo (Last name as first name)
outspoken
Barg

Bari (Irish) fair-haired

Baris (Slavic) calm

Barison (English) son of peaceful
man

Baritta (Last name used as first
name) able

Bark (English) form of Barker:
handles bark; lumberjack
Birk

Barker (English) handles bark;
lumberjack
Bark, Barkker

Barlaam (History) hermit

Barlam (Hebrew) giving

Barlow (English) hardy
Barloe, Barlowe

Barman (Last name as first name)
bright; blessed
Barr

Barn (American) word as name;
works in barns
Barnee, Barney, Barny

Barnabas (Hebrew) seer; comforter
*Barn, Barnaby, Barnebus, Barney,
Barnie, Barny*

Barnaby (Hebrew) companionable
*Barn, Barnabee, Barnabie, Barnie,
Barny*

Barnali (Last name used as first
name) son of the gatekeeper

Barneo (Place name) barn boy

Barner (English) mercurial
Barn, Barnerr, Barney, Barny

Barnes (English) powerful; bear

Barnett (English) leader of men
Barn, Barnet, Barney

Barney (English) form of
Barnett: leader of men
Barn, Barni, Barnie, Barny

Barnum (German) safe; barn
Barnham, Barnhem, Barnie

Baron (English) noble leader
Bare, Baren, Barren, Baryne

B

Barra (Irish) fair-haired

Barragan (Irish) fenced in

Barrance (Last name used as first name)

Barrett (German) strong and bearlike
Bar, Baret, Barett, Barette, Barry

Barrington (English) dignified
Bare, Baring, Berrington

Barry (Irish) candid
Barre, Barrie, Bary

Barryrex (American) combo of Barry and Rex

Bart (Hebrew) persistent
Bartee, Bartie, Barty

Bartelt (English) form of Bartholomew: friendly; earthy

Barth (Hebrew) protective
Bart, Barthe, Barts

Bartholomew (Hebrew) friendly; earthy
Bart, Barthlolmewe, Bartie

Bartlett (Last name as first name) motivated

Bartley (Last name as first name) rural man
Bart, Bartle, Bartlee, Bartli, Bartly

Barto (Spanish) form of Bartholomew: friendly; earthy
Bartelo, Bartol, Bartoli, Bartolo, Bartolomeo

Barton (English) persistent man; Bart's town
Bart, Barty

Bartosz (Slavic) form of Bartholomew: friendly; earthy

Bartoz (Slavic) form of Bartholomew: friendly; earthy

Bartram (English) intelligent
Bart, Barty

Baruch (Hebrew) most blessed
Barry

Baruti (African) teaches

Basant (Arabic) smiling

Basford (American) charming; low-profile
Bas, Basferd, Basfor

Bash (American) party-loving
Bashey, Bashi, Bashy

Basil (Greek) regal
Basel, Basey, Basile, Bazil

Basim (Arabic) smiles
Bassam

Basir (Turkish) smart

Bass (Last name as first name) fish; charmer
Bassee, Bassey, Bassi, Bassy

Bassam (Arabic) smiles

Bassett (English) small man
Baset, Basett, Basey, Basse

Bastete (Egyptian) fiery cat

Bastian (Greek) respected
Bastien, Bastyun

Basye (American) home-based; centered
Base, Basey

Batch (French) from bachelor; unmarried man
Bat, Bats, Batsh

Bates (English) romantic
Bate

Baudelio (Spanish) bold

Baudoin (Latin) winning

Baudouin (French) bold friend

Bauer (French) small

Baul (Gypsy) slow-moving

Baurice (African American) form of Maurice: dark

Bavan (Welsh) Evan's son

Bavol (Gypsy) windblown

Baxley (English) from the meadow; outdoorsy
Bax, Baxlee, Baxli

Baxter (English) tenacious
Bax, Baxey, Baxie, Baxther

Bay (English) hair of russet; vocal
Baye, Bayie

Bayard (English) russet-haired
Bay, Baye, Bayerd

Bay-Atlas (American) combo of Bay and Atlas; seventh from heaven

Baylon (English) from the bay; outdoorsman

Bayro (Spanish) from the barn

Bazel (French) form of Basil: regal

Bazooka (American) fun-loving; unusual
Bazookah

Bazzy (American) loud
Bazzee, Bazzi, Bazzie

Beacan (Irish) small boy
Beag, Bec, Becan

Beach (English) fun-loving
Bee, Beech

Beacher (English) pale-skinned; beech tree
Beach, Beachie, Beachy, Beecher

Beagan (Irish) small
Beagen, Beagin

Beale (French) attractive
Beal, Beally

Beall (English) handsome

Beaman (English) tends bees
Beamann, Beamen, Beeman

Beamer (English) musician
Beam, Beamy, Beemer

Bean (Scottish) lively
Beann

Beanon (Irish) good boy
Beinean, Beineon, Binean

Bear (Scottish) lively

Beara (American) athletic

Bearach (Irish) spearing
Bearchan, Bercnan, Bergin

Beasley (English) nurturing; pea field
Beas, Beasie, Beesly

Beate (German) serious
Bay, Bayahtah, Baye, Beahta, Beahtae

Beattie (Irish) happy

Beau (French) handsome man
Beaubeau, Bo, Boo, Bow

Beauford (French) attractive
Beau, Beauf, Beaufort

Beaumont (French) attractive and strong
Beau, Bo, Bomont, Bowmont

Beauregard (French) a face much admired
Beau, Beauregarde, Beaurigard, Bobo

Beaver (French) tenacious
Beav, Beave, Beever, Bevoh

Bebe (Spanish) baby
Be-Be

Becher (Hebrew) firstborn
Bee

Beck (English) stream; laid-back
Bec, Becc, Becke, Becker, Bek

Becker (English) calm
Bekker

Becket (English) by the brook

Beckett (English) methodical
Beck, Beket, Bekette

Bede (English) prayerful
Bea, Bead, Beda, Bedah

Bedford (Last name as first name) laid-back

Bedrich (Czech) rules peacefully

Bedro (Spanish) form of Pedro: dependable; rock
Bed

Bedros (Spanish) prays

Beebe (English) tending bees; tenacious
B.B., Bee-be, Beebee

Beechum (English) of the trees (beech)

Beeson (Last name as first name) son of beekeeper; wary
Bees

Beggs (Last name as first name) admired
Begg, Begs

Behlin (Spanish) from Bethlehem

Behrad (Indian) form of Bharat: fire

Beig (English) mouth

Beige (American) calm
Bayge

Beinish (Latin) form of Benedict: blessed man

Beircheart (Welsh) spears

Bela (Hawaiian) beauty

Belden (English) plain-spoken
Beld, Beldene, Beldon, Bell,
Bellden, Belldon

Beldon (English) pretty valley
child

Belen (Greek) following the
arrow's straight path

Belizario (Spanish) archer

Bell (French) handsome man

Bellamy (French) beautiful friend
Belamie, Bell, Bellamie, Bellmee,
Belmy

Bellindo (German) ferocious;
attractive
Balindo, Belindo, Belyndo

Bello (African) advocates Islam

Belman (English) handsome

Belmount (French) gracious
Belmon, Belmond, Belmonde,
Belmont, Belmonta

Belosi (Slavic) humble

Belton (English) from a lovely
town of bells
Beltan, Belten

Belvin (American) form of
Melvin: friendly
Belven

Belvon (Welsh) smart

Bem (African) peaceful

Ben (Hebrew) form of Benjamin:
son of the right hand; son of the
south
Benjy, Bennie, Benno, Benny

Benaiah (Hebrew) God-built;
wars
Benaya, Benayahu

Benammi (Biblical) comes into
his own

Bence (American) form of
Benson: son of Ben; brave heart
Bens, Bense, Binse

Bend (American) word as name;
lithe

Bendell (Last name used as first
name) loving
Ben

Bender (American) tweaker;
diplomatic
Ben, Bend

Bendo (American) soothing
Ben, Bend

Benedict (Latin) blessed
Ben, Benedik, Benne, Bennie, Benny

Benes (Czech) blessed

Benesh (Yiddish) blessed

Bengt (Scandinavian) blessed

Beni (Slavic) blessing

Beniah (Hebrew) articulate
Benia, Benyah

Benicio (Spanish) adventurous
Benecio, Benito

Benigno (Latin) kind child

Benito (Italian) blessed
Benedo, Beni, Beno

Benjamin ○ ❶ (Hebrew) son of
the right hand; son of the south
Behnjamin, Ben, Benjamen,
Benjamine, Benjie, Benjy, Benni,
Bennie, Benny, Benyamin

Benjiro (Japanese) promotes
peace

Bennell (Last name used as first
name) blessed

Benner (English) blessed

Bennett (French) blessed
Ben, Benet, Benett, Bennet,
Bennette, Benny

Benno (Italian) form of Ben: son
of the right hand; son of the south
Beno

Benny (Hebrew) form of
Benjamin: son of the right hand;
son of the south
Benge, Benjy, Benni, Bennie

Benoit (French) growing and
flourishing
Ben, Benoyt

Benoni (Hebrew) sorrow

Bensey (American) easygoing; fine
Bence, Bens, Bensee

Benson (Hebrew) son of Ben; brave heart
Bensahn, Bensen

Bent (English) form of Benton: formidable
Bynt

Bentley (English) clever
Bent, Bentlee, Leye

Benton (English) formidable
Bentan, Bentawn, Bentone

Benvenuto (Italian) welcomed child
Ben

Benz (German) from carmaker Mercedes-Benz; upscale
Bens

Benzi (Hebrew) blessed

Beowulf (Literature) warrior

Ber (Hebrew) bear

Berar (French) speaks well

Berdy (German) bright

Beresford (English) place of spears
Berresford

Berfit (Origin unknown) farming; outdoorsman
Berf

Berg (German) tall; mountain
Bergh, Berj, Burg, Burgh

Bergen (Irish) little spear man
Bergin, Birgin

Berger (French) watchful; shepherd
Bergher, Bergie

Bergin (Swedish) loquacious; lives on the hill
Bergan, Berge, Bergen, Berger, Bergin, Birgin

Berj (Scandinavian) form of Birger: helpful

Berk (Turkish) rough-hewn

Berkeley (English) idolized; (place name) town in California *Berk, Berkeley, Berki, Berkie, Berklee, Berkley, Berklie, Berkly, Berky*

Berko (Hebrew) bear
Ber

Berks (American) adored
Berk, Berke, Berkelee, Berkey, Berkli, Berksie, Berkslee, Berky, Birklee, Birksey, Burks, Burksey

Berlon (German) loyal

Berman (German) steady
Bermahn, Bermen, Bermin

Bermudez (Spanish) place name; battles

Bernabe (German) bold
Bernabee, Bernabey, Bernaby, Bernby, Bernebe, Berns, Bernus, Burnby

Bernal (German) bearlike
Bern

Bernar (Last name used as first name) hardy

Bernard (German) brave and dependable
Bern, Bernarde, Bernee, Bernerd, Bernie, Berny, Burnard

Bernardo (Spanish) brave; bear
Berna, Bernardo, Barnardoh, Berny

Bernave (American) form of Bernard: brave and dependable
Bernav, Bernee, Berneve, Berni

Bernd (German) bearlike
Bern, Berne, Bernee, Berney, Berny

Berndt (German) hardy

Berne (German) courageous
Bern, Berni, Bernie, Bernne, Berny

Berner (English) bearlike

Bernhard (German) brave

Bernie (German) brave boy
Bern, Berni, Berny, Birnie, Burney

Bernstein (Last name used as first name) brave

Berrios (Spanish) the berries

Berry (English) botanical; flourishing

Bert (English) shining example
Berti, Bertie, Berty, Birt, Burt

Berthold (German) bold ruler
Bert, Berthol, Berthuld, Bertolt, Berty

Berthrand (German) form of
Bertram: outstanding
Bert, Berthran, Bertie, Bertrand, Berty

Bertil (Scandinavian) bright
Bertel

Bertin (English) form of Burton:
protective; town that is well-fortified
Berton, Burtun

Bertoldo (Spanish) ruler
Bert

Berton (American) form of
Burton: protective; town that is
well-fortified
Bert, Bertan, Berty

Bertram (German) outstanding
*Bert, Bertie, Bertrem, Bertrom,
Berty*

Bertrand (German) bright
*Bert, Bertie, Bertran, Bertrund,
Birtryn*

Bertren (German) smart

Berts (English) bright

Bertus (Last name used as first
name) child of Bert

Berty (English) form of Bert:
shining example
Bert, Bertie, Burty

Bervick (American) upwardly
mobile; brave
Bervey

Berwyn (English) loyal friend
*Berrie, Berwin, Berwynd,
Berwynne*

Besley (Last name as first name)
calm
Bes, Bez

Best (American) word as name;
quintessential man
Beste

Betel (Biblical) man of God

Bethel (Hebrew) loves the house
of God
Bethell

Bethuel (Biblical) religious

Bettis (American) vocal
Bettes, Bettus, Betus

Beuford (Last name as first
name) form of Buford: diligent
Beuf, Bu, Bueford

Beval (Welsh) vivacious

Bevan (Welsh) beguiling
Bev, Bevahn, Beven, Bevin

Bevell (Last name used as first
name) craftsman

Bever (English) form of Bevis:
strong-willed

Beverly (English) from a stream
of beavers; natural

Bevil (English) form of Bevis:
strong-willed

Bevis (French) strong-willed
Bev, Bevas, Beves, Bevvis, Bevys, Bevyss

Bexal (American) studious
Bex, Bexlee, Bexly, Bexy

Bexley (Place name)
distinguished

Bezalel (Biblical) loyal

Bhakati (Hindi) devoted man

Bhanu (Hindi) sun-loving

Bharat (Hindi) fire

Bhaskar (Hindi) shining

Bhupen (Indian) forest

Biaggio (Italian) stutters; unsure
Biage, Biagio

Bialas (Polish) white-haired
Bialy

Bicken (Last name used as first
name) boy with ax

Bickford (English) wields an ax;
chops

Bickley (Last name used as first
name) boy with ax

Biffy (American) popular
Bibbee, Biff

Bigram (Origin unknown)
handsome
Bigraham, Bygram

Bijou (French) jewel

Bijoy (Indian) winning

Biju (French) joy

Bilal (Arabic) selected one

Bill (German) form of William:
staunch protector
Billi, Billie, Billy

Billings (Place name)
sophisticated

Billy (German) form of William:
staunch protector
Bilie, Bill, Billee, Billi, Billie, Bily

Binden (Last name used as first
name) binds closely

Bindo (Italian) blessed

Bing (German) outgoing
Beng

Bingo (American) spunky
Bengo, Bingoh

Binh (Vietnamese) a part of the
whole

Binkie (English) energetic
Bink, Binki, Binky

Binnie (American) devoted son

Bion (Greek) life

Birch (English) white and
shining; birch tree
Berch, Bir, Burch

Bird (American) soaring
Byrd

Biren (American) form of Byron:
reclusive; small cottage
Biran

Birger (Scandinavian) helpful

Birinder (Indian) devout

Birkett (English) living in
birches; calming
*Birk, Birket, Birkie, Birkitt,
Burkett, Burkette, Burkitt*

Birkey (English) from the birch
tree isle
Birkee, Birkie, Birky

Birley (English) outdoorsy;
meadow
Berl, Birl, Birlee, Birly

Birney (English) single-minded;
island
Birne, Birni, Birny, Burney

Birtle (English) from the hill of
birds; natural

Bish (Hindi) universal

Bishamon (Mythology) Japanese
god of war and luck

Bishop (Greek) supervisor;
serving the bishop
Bish, Bishie, Bishoppe

Bix (American) hip
Bicks, Bixe

Bizzo (American) lively

Bjorn (Swedish) athletic
*Bjarn, Bjarne, Bjonie, Bjorne,
Bjorny*

Black (Scottish) dark
Blacke, Blackee, Blackie

Blackburn (Scottish) lives by a
brook; dark

Blade (Spanish) prepared; knife
Bladie, Blayd

Blades (American) sporty

Blagden (English) likes the dark
valley

Blaine (Irish) svelte
Blain, Blane, Blayne

Blainen (American) pious

Blair (Irish) open
Blaire, Blare, Blayree

Blaise (French) audacious
Blasé, Blayse, Blaze

Blake ○ (English) dark and
handsome
Blaike, Blakey, Blakie

Blakeley (English) outdoorsy;
meadow
Blake, Blakelee, Blakely, Blakie

Blame (American) sad
Blaim, Blaime

Blanchard (Last name as first
name) white
Blan

Blanco (Spanish) light
Blancoh, Blonco, Blonko

Blandon (American) form of
Brandon: hill; high-spirited

B

Blanford (English) from the gray ford
Blandford

Blank (American) word as name; blank slate; open
Blanc

Blanket (Invented) security
Blank, Blankee, Blankett, Blankey, Blankie, Blanky

Blanton (English) mild-mannered
Blanten, Blantun

Blasio (Spanish) stutterer
Blaseo, Blasios, Blaze

Blaynn (Last name used as first name) form of Blaine: svelte

Blaze (English and American) daring
Blaase, Blaise, Blazey, Blazie

Blazej (Czech) stutters; insecure

Blazer (American) fiery

Bleddyn (Welsh) heroic

Blendan (Last name used as first name) edge

Bliss (English) happy
Blice, Blyss

Blithe (English) merry
Bly, Blye, Blythe

Blitzer (German) adventurous
Blitz, Blitze

Block (English) on the block; engaged

Blocker (Last name as first name) block
Bloc, Block, Blok

Bloo (American) zany

Blue (Color name) hip
Bleu, Blu

Blunt (Last name used as first name) candid

Blye (American) joyful
Blie

Bo (Scandinavian) lively
Beau

Boat (American) word as name; sea-loving
Bo

Boaz (Hebrew) strong; swift
Bo, Boase, Boaze, Boz

Bob (English) form of Robert: brilliant; renowned
Bobbi, Bobbie, Bobby

Bobby (English) form of Robert: brilliant; renowned
Bob, Bobbie, Bobi

Bobo (African) Tuesday-born

Bocko (English) fair-haired

Bodaway (Native American) fire maker

Boden (French) communicator
Bodin, Bodun, Bowden

Bodhi (Chinese) founder of Ch'an Buddhism in China
Bodhee

Bodhi (American) form of Bodie: laid-back

Bodie (American) laid-back

Bodil (Scandinavian) living

Bodua (African) last one

Bodun (Scandinavian) shelter

Bodynam (Scandinavian) flourishes

Boele (Scandinavian) helpful

Bogan (Slavic) godlike

Bogart (German) bold
Bo, Bobo, Bogardte, Boge, Bogert, Bogey, Bogie

Bogdan (Polish) God's gift

Bogdari (Polish) gift from God
Bogdi

Boggle (American) confusing
Bogg

Boghos (Slavic) strong

Bogumil (Polish) loves God

Bohumil (Polish) favored by God

Bohus (Slavic) favored

Bojan (Czech) fighter

Bojesse (American) comical
Boje, Bojee, Bojeesie, Bojess

Bola (American) careful; bold
Bolah, Boli

Bolden (American) bold man
Boldun

Boleslaw (Polish) in glory
Boleslav

Bolin (Last name as first name)
bold
Bolen

Bolivar (Spanish) aggressive
Bolley, Bollivar, Bolly

Bolley (American) strong
Bolly

Bolton (English) town of the bold

Bomani (African) fighter
Boman

Bon (French) good
Bonne

Bonam (English) decent

Bonar (French) gentle
Bonarr, Bonnar, Bonner

Bonaventura (Spanish) good
fortune: (Italian) good luck
*Bona, Bonavento, Buenaventura,
Buenaventure, Ventura*

Bonaventure (Latin) humble
*Bonaventura, Bonnaventura,
Buenaventure*

Bond (English) farmer; renegade
Bondee, Bondie, Bondy

Bondee (English) close

Bongani (African) thankful

Bongo (American) type of drum;
musical
Bong, Bongy

Boni (Latin) fortunate
Bonne

Bonif (American) giving

Bonifacio (Spanish) benefactor
Bona, Boni, Boniface

Bonner (American) good

Bono (Spanish) good
Bonno

Bonocorso (Italian) good path

Bonsi (Italian) good

Bonyer (American) hopeful

Boo (Literature) recluse in *To Kill
a Mockingbird*

Booker (English) lover of books
Book, Booki, Bookie, Booky

Boone (French) blessed; good
Boon, Boonie, Boony

Boonen (English) asset

Bootaan (Unknown) deserted

Booth (German) protective *Boot,
Boothe, Boothie, Bootsie*

Boots (American) cowboy
Bootsey, Bootsie, Bootz

Booveeay (Invented) form of
Bouvier: elegant; sturdy; ox
Boo

Bordan (English) secretive; of
the boar
*Borde, Bordee, Borden, Bordi,
Bordie, Bordy*

Border (American) word as
name; fair-minded; aggressive
Bord

Borg (Scandinavian) fortified;
castle
Borge, Borgh

Borges (Last name as first name)
labyrinthine

Borgey (Scandinavian) castle

Borim (Biblical) place name

Boris (Russian) combative
Boras, Bore, Bores

Borka (Slavic) battles

Bornami (Asian) conflicted

Borr (Russian) contentious

Bos (English) woodsman
Boz

Boscoe (English) woodsman

Boseda (African) Sunday-born

Bosley (English) thriving; grove
Bos, Boslee, Boslie, Bosly

Bosor (Biblical) place name

Bosque (Russian) fighter

Bosser (Scandinavian) lively

Bost (Place name) from Boston
Bostt

Boston (Place name) distinctive
Boss, Bost

Bosvely (English) child from the grove

Boswell (English) well near woods; dignified
Bos, Bosswell, Boz, Bozwell

Botan (Japanese) long-living

Botolf (English) wolf; standoffish
Botof

Bouck (Last name used as first name) worldview

Bour (English) loves the stream

Bourbon (Place name) jazzy
Borbon, Bourbonn, Bourbonne

Bourey (Vietnamese) countryman

Bourne (French) planner; boundary
Bourn, Bourney, Bournie, Byrn, Byrne, Byrnie

Bouvier (French) elegant; sturdy; ox
Bouveah, Bouveay, Bouviay

Bovo (Last name as first name) macho
Bovoh

Bowen (Welsh) shy
Bowie, Bowin

Bowie (Irish) brash; western
Booie, Bowen

Bowing (Last name as first name) blond and young
Beau, Bo, Bow, Bowen

Bowlin (Irish) blond

Bowman (Last name as first name) young; archer
Bow

Bowry (Irish) form of Bowie: brash; western
Bowy

Boy (American) boy child of the family

Boyce (French) defender
Boice, Boy, Boyce

Boyd (Scottish) fair-haired
Boide, Boydie

Boydine (French) from the woods
Boyse

Boydine (American) God's gift

Boydon (Last name used as first name) fair-haired

Boyer (French) woodsman

Boyette (Last name used as first name) joyful

Boyko (Slavic) fearful

Boylingston (Last name used as first name) sedate

Boyne (Irish) cow; grows

Boysey (Last name used as first name) treasured

Bozarth (Last name used as first name) gifted

Bozidar (Polish) God's precious
Bovza, Bovzek

Brack (English) from the plant bracken; fine
Bracke

Bracken (English) plant name; debonair
Brack, Brackan, Brackin, Brackun

Brackson (English) son of Brack

Bracy (Last name used as first name) holding

Brad (English) form of Bradley: prosperous; expansive
Braddie, Braddy

Brada (American) steadfast

Bradan (English) open-minded
Braden, Bradin, Brady, Bradyn, Braedyn, Braid

Bradford (English) mediator
Brad, Brady

Bradley (English) prosperous; expansive
Brad, Bradie, Bradlee, Bradlie, Bradly

Bradshaw (English) broad-minded
Brad, Brad-Shaw, Bradshie

Brady (Irish) high-spirited
Brade, Bradee, Bradey

Brahma (Hindi) worshipful

Braid (English) form of Bradan: open-minded
Brane

Brain (Word as name) brilliant
Brane

Brainard (English) princely
Brainerd

Brait (American) in demand

Braith (Welsh) spotted

Brak (American) support

Bram (Hebrew) form of Abraham: father of a multitude
Brahm, Bramm

Bramb (Dutch) form of Abraham: father of a multitude

Bramly (English) brambles

Bran (Irish) raven; blessed
Brann

Brance (Welsh) dark

Branch (Latin) growing
Bran, Branche

Branco (Last name as first name) authentic
Brank, Branko

Brand (English) fiery
Brandd, Brande, Brandy, Brann

Brandeis (Czech) has a charitable nature

Brandell (Last name used as first name) beacon of light

Brando (American) talented
Brand

Brandon ⚥ ❶ (English) hill; high-spirited
Bradonn, Bran, Brandan, Brandin, Branny

Brandt (English) dignified
Bran, Brandtt, Brant

Brandy (English) firebrand; bold; brandy drink
Brand, Brandee, Brandey, Brandi, Brandie

Brannon (Irish) bright-minded
Bran, Brann, Brannen, Branon

Bransby (Last name used as first name) beacon of light

Branson (English) persistent
Bran, Brans, Bransan, Bransen

Brant (English) hothead
Brandt

Brantley (English) proud child

Brants (English) proud child

Brashier (French) brash
Brashear, Brasheer

Brasil (Irish) disagrees
Brazil, Breasal, Bresal

Bratcher (Last name as first name) aggressive
Bratch

Bratumil (Polish) brother's love

Braulio (Italian) from a meadow

Braunsen (Last name used as first name) son of brown-haired man

Bravillo (Spanish) brave
Braville

Bravo (Italian) top-notch
Bravoh, Bravvo

Brawley (English) meadow man

Brax (Spanish) scrappy

Braxton (English) worldly
Brack, Brackston, Brax, Braxsten, Braxt

Bray (English) vocal
Brae

Brayan (Origin unknown) to yell out
Brayen

Brayd (English) loyal

Brayden ⚥ (English) effective
Braedan, Braedon, Braydon, Braydun

Braylon (English) steadfast

Brayton (English) town of Bray

Braz (American) mysterious

Brazan (American) mystery

Brazil (Portuguese) reddish brown tree

Brecht (Last name as first) playwright

Breck (Irish) fair and freckled
Breckie, Breckle, Brek

Brecken (Irish) freckled

Brede (Scandinavian) glacier; cold heart

Breeahno (Invented) form of Briano: strong man of honor

Breeon (American) strong

Breer (English) fine

Breeson (American) strong
Breece, Breese, Bresen

Breeze (American) happy
Breese, Breez, Breezy

Bref (American) brave

Brekett (Irish) freckled

Brencis (Russian) sad

Brendan (Irish) armed
Brend, Brenden, Brendie, Brendin, Brendon

Brennan (English) pensive
Bren, Brenn, Brennen, Brennon, Brenny

Brennan (Irish) raven

Brenson (Last name as first name) disturbed; masculine
Brens, Brenz

Brent (English) prepared; on the mountain
Bren, Brint

Brenton (English) forward-thinking; hill town boy
Brent, Brenten, Brintin

Breslin (English) land of Bres

Brett (Scottish) man from Britain; innovative
Bret, Breton, Brette, Bretton, Britt

Brettson (American) manly man; Briton
Brett

Brewer (English) brews

Brewster (English) creative; brewer
Brew, Brewer

Breyen (Irish) strong; aggressive
Brey, Breyan

Brian ♥ ❶ (Irish) strong man of honor
Bri, Briann, Brien, Brienn, Bry, Bryan

Briand (English) jolly

Briander (American) inquisitive; rider of waves

Briano (Celtic) form of Brian: strong man of honor

Briant (American) form of Bryant: honest; strong

Briareus (Mythology) giant with one hundred arms; strong

Brice (Welsh) go-getter
Bryce

Brick (English) alert; bridge
Bricke, Brik

Brickle (American) surprising
Brick, Brickel, Brickell, Bricken, Brickton, Brickun, Brik

Brider (English) of the bride

Bridgely (English) coming from the bridge
Bridgeley

Bridger (English) makes bridges
Bridge

Bridges (English) bridge boy

Bridon (English) bright-eyed

Brielton (English) Briel town

Brig (English) punished

Brigdo (American) leader
Brigg, Briggy

Brigham (English) place name; mediator
Brigg, Briggie, Briggs, Brighum

Brighton (English) from the shining town

Brike (American) creative

Briley (English) calm
Bri, Brilee, Brilie, Brily

Brill (English) climbs

Brimmer (English) hill

Brinden (English) tawny

Brinell (English) tawny

Brink (English) on the precipice

Brinkley (English) meadow on edge

Brinley (English) of the joyful meadow; sweet
Brindley, Brinly, Brynley, Brynly

Briscoe (Last name as first name) forceful
Brisco, Brisko, Briskoe

Brishen (English) craftsman

Bristol (English) place name

Britt (English) humorous; from Britain
Brit, Britts

Brittin (American) boy from Britain

Britton (English) loyal; from Britain

Brock (English) forceful
Broc, Brocke, Brockie, Brocky, Brok

Brockly (English) aggressive
Brocklee, Brockli, Broklee, Broklie, Brokly

Brockton (English) badger; stuffy
Brock

Brod (English) form of Broderick: broad-minded; brother
Broddie, Broddy

Brodall (Irish) rules

Brode (Irish) broad wall

Broder (Scandinavian) true brother
Brolle, Bror

Broderick (English) broad-minded; brother
Brod, Broddee, Broddie, Broddy, Broderic, Broderik, Brodric, Brodrick

Brodie ♥ (Irish) builder
*Brode, Brodee, **Brody***

Brodny (Irish) falling aside; brash

Brodrick (Last name used as first name) ruler's son

Brogan (Irish) sturdy shoe; dependable
Brogann

Bromley (English) meadow of shrubs; unpredictable
Brom, Bromlee, Bromlie, Bromly

Bron (Irish) sadness

Bronc (Spanish) wild; horse
Bronco, Bronk, Bronko

Bronco (Spanish) wild; spirited
Broncoh, Bronko, Bronnco

Brondo (Last name as first name) macho
Bron, Brond

Brone (Irish) sorrow

Bronick (English) brown

Bronnie (American) brown

Bronson (English) Brown's son
Bron, Brondson, Bronni, Bronnie, Bronny, Bronsan, Bronsen

Bronto (American) from brontosaurus; thunderous
Bront, Brontee, Brontey, Bronti, Bronty

Bronze (Metal) alloy of tin and copper; brown
Bronz

Brook (English) easygoing
Brooke, Brookee, Brookie

Brooker (English) stream boy

Brooks (English) easygoing
Brookes, Brooky

Brosio (Spanish) son of the stream

Brost (Spanish) able

Broughton (English) from a protected place

Brow (American) snob
Browy

Brown (English) tan
Browne, Brownie, Browny

Brownie (American) brown-haired
Brown

Brownlee (English) brown-haired

Brownson (Last name used as first name) son of Brown

Broylon (English) noble

Broze (American) soulful

Brubaker (English) brown-haired

Bruce (French) complicated; from a thicket of brushwood
Bru, Brucie, Brucy, Brue

Bruck (English) brown-haired

Bruder (Last name used as first name)

Bruiser (American) tough guy
Bruezer, Bruser, Bruzer

Brumley (French) smart; scattered
Brum

Brundage (Last name used as first name)

Brundo (Spanish) brown-haired

Brune (German) brown-haired

Bruni (German) brown-haired

Bruno (German) brown-skinned
Brune, Brunne, Brunoh

Brunon (Polish) brown-haired

Brush (American) confident

Bruton (Latin) brutal

Brutus (Latin) aggressive; a bully

Bry (American) form of Bryan:
ethical; strong

Bryan ✿ ❶ (Irish) ethical; strong
Brye, Bryen

Bryand (English) form of Bryan:
ethical; strong

Bryant (Irish) honest; strong
Bryan, Bryent

Bryce (Welsh) spunky
Brice, Bry, Brye

Brycen (English) fast

Brychan (Welsh) speckled

Brycy (Welsh) lively

Brydon (American)
magnanimous
Bridon, Brydan, Bryden, Brydun

Brydson (American) well-liked

Brylee (American)

Bryn (Welsh) hill-dweller

Brynmor (Welsh) big hill

Bryon (American) form of Byron:
reclusive; small cottage

Brys (Welsh) spotted

Brysen (English) son of Brice

Bryson (Welsh) Bryce's son; smart
Briceson, Bry, Bryse

Bryton (Welsh) hill town

Bu (Irish) winner; form of Buagh

Bual (English) son of speed

Bubba (German) a regular guy
Bub, Buba, Bubb, Bubbah

Bub-Joo (Asian)

Buck (English) studly; buck deer
Buckey, Buckie, Bucko, Bucky

Buckingham (Last name used as
first name) male deer

Buckley (English) outdoorsy; a
meadow for deer
*Buckey, Buckie, Bucklee, Bucklie,
Bucks, Bucky*

Bucko (American) macho
Bukko

Bucky (American) warmhearted
Buck, Buckey, Buckie

Bud (English) courier
*Budd, Buddie, Buddy, Budi,
Budster*

Buddy (American) courier
Bud, Buddi, Buddie, Budi

Budington (English) awakened

Budrys (Spanish)

Buell (German) upward; hill
Bue

Buf (English) castle

Buffalo (American) tough-minded
Buff, Buffer, Buffy

Buffington (Last name used as
first name) town of Buffing

Buford (English) diligent
Bueford, Bufe, Buforde

Bulgara (Slavic) hardworking
Bulgar, Bulgarah, Bulgaruh

Bulldog (American) rough-and-
tough
Bull, Dawg, Dog

Bullock (Last name as first name)
practical

Bulmarck (Spanish)

Bulmaro (Spanish) fair

Bumpus (Last name as first
name) humorous
Bump, Bumpey, Bumpy

Bunard (English) good
Bunerd, Bunn

Bune (American) free

Bunyan (English) good and burly
Bunyan, Bunyen

Buran (American) complex
Burann, Burun

Burch (English) strong

Burchard (English) tree trunks;
sturdy
*Burckhardt, Burgard, Burgaud,
Burkhart*

Burdell (English) in the dell

Burdette (English) shielded

Burditt (Last name as first name) shy
Burdett, Burdette, Burdey

Burford (Last name as first name) from the water

Burge (English) form of Burgess: businessman
Burges, Burgis, Burr

Burgess (English) businessman
Berge, Burge, Burges, Burgiss

Burhan (Last name as first name) complex

Burke (German) fortified
Berk, Berke, Burk, Burkie

Burl (German) homespun

Burley (English) nature-lover; wooded meadow
Burl, Burlea, Burlee, Burli, Burly, Burr

Burnaby (English) brook man

Burne (English) lives by the brook
Bourn, Bourne, Burn, Byrn, Byrne, Byrnes

Burnell (English) of the brook
Burnel

Burnell (French) brown-haired

Burnett (English) by the small brook
Burnet, Burnitt

Burney (English) loner; island
Burn, Burne, Burnie, Burny

Burnie (American) form of Bernie: brave boy

Burnis (English) by the brook; brown-haired
Burn, Burnes, Burney, Burr

Burr (English) prickly; brusque
Burry

Burrell (American) safe

Burrick (English) townsman
Bur, Burr, Burry

Burrin (English) safe haven

Burris (English) sophisticated; living in the town
Berris, Buris, Burr, Burres

Burston (English) safe haven

Burt (English) shining man
Bert, Bertee, Burtie, Burty

Burtard (English) from the stronghold town

Burton (English) protective; town that is well-fortified
Burt, Burty, Brutie

Busby (Scottish) artist; village
Busbee, Busbi, Buzbie, Buzz, Buzzie

Busher (Last name as first name) bold
Bush

Buster (American) fun
Bustah

Bustos (Spanish) jovial

Butcher (English) worker
Butch, Butchy

Butler (English) directing the house; handsome
Butler, Butlir, Butlyr, Buttler

Buxton (Last name as first name) kind

Buz (Biblical) hateful

Buzz (Scottish) popular
Buzy, Buzzi, Buzzie, Buzzy

Byelo (Slavic) white

Byford (English) leaving the cottage; forever young

Byorn (American) form of Bjorn: athletic

Byram (English) stealthy; yard that houses cattle
Bye, Byrem, Byrie, Byrim

Byrd (English) birdlike
Bird

Byrne (English) loner
Birn, Birne, Byrn, Byrni, Byrnie, Byrny

Byrnett (Last name as first name) stable
Burn, Burnett, Burney, Burns, Byrne, Byrney

Byron (English) reclusive; small cottage
Biron, Biryn, Bye, Byren, Byrom, Byrone, Byryn

Cab (American) word as name
Cabby, Kab

Cabbon (Biblical) place name

Cabell (Last name as first name) spontaneous

Cable (French) rope-making boy; crafty
Cabel

Cabot (French) loves the water
Cabbott

Cabral (African) Tuesday's child

Cabree (Irish) rides

Cabrera (Spanish) able
Cabrere

Cacal (Last name used as first name) noisy

Cack (American) laughing
Cackey, Cackie, Cacky, Cassy, Caz, Kass, Kassy, Khaki

Cactus (Botanical) prickly
Cack, Kactus

Cadas (Biblical) place name

Cadby (Norse) spirited heritage

Caddock (Last name as first name) high spirits

Cade (English) stylish; bold; round
Cadye, Kade

Cadel (Welsh) fierce

Caden (English) spirited
Cadan, Cade, Cadun, Caiden, Kaden, Kayden

Cadman (Irish) fighter
Cadmann

Cadmar (Greek) fiery
Cadmarr

Cadmus (Greek) one who excels; prince
Cad, Cadmuss, Kadmus

Cadon (American) friendly

Cadou (Welsh) fights

Cady (American) forthright
Cadee, Cadey, Cadie

Cael (Irish) slim

Caesar (Latin) focused leader
Caeser, Caez, Caezer, Cesaro, Cezar, Seezer

Caetan (Irish) slim

Cage (American) dramatic
Cadge

Caglar (American) able

Cagle (Spanish) winner

Cailen (American) gentle
Kail, Kailen, Kale

Cain (Hebrew) aggressive
Caine, Cainen, Cane, Kain, Kane

Cairn (Welsh) stone; sturdy
Cairne

Caj (Scandinavian) from Gaius (Caesar's first name); masculine

Caja (American) close proximity

Cal (Latin) form of Calvin: bald
Callie, Kal

Calah (Scandinavian) outdoors

Calam (Scottish) peaceful

Calbert (American) cowboy
Cal, Calbart, Calberte, Calburt, Callie, Colbert

Calcher (American) peaceful

Calden (English) singer

Calder (English) stream; flowing
Cald, Kalder

Calderon (Spanish) stream; flowing
Cald, Kald, Kalder, Kalderon

Caldwell (English) refreshing; cold well

Cale (Hebrew) slim; good heart
Kale

Caleb ○ ⊤ (Hebrew) faithful; brave
Cal, Calab, Cale, Caley, Calie, Calub, Kaleb

Calek (American) fighter; loyal
Calec, Kalec, Kalek

Calen (Irish) slim
Cailun

Calendt (American) slim

Caler (English) promising

Caley (Irish) slender

Calf (American) cowboy
Kalf

Calfray (American) singer

Calhoun (Irish) limited; from the narrow woods
Cal, Calhoon, Calhoune, Callie

Calixto (Spanish) handsome
Calex, Calexto, Cali, Calisto, Calix, Callie, Cally, Kalixto

Call (Native American) flourish

Callahan (Irish) spiritual
Cal, Calahan, Calihan, Callie

Callard (Last name used as first name) thrives

Callie (American) form of Calvin: bald
Cal, Calley, Calli, Cally

Callistua (Greek) most beautiful man

Callo (American) attractive
Cal, Cally, Kallo

Cally (Scottish) peacemaker

Calman (Last name as first name) caring
Cal

Calno (Biblical) place name

Calum (Irish) cal
Callum, Calym, Calyme

Calv (American) form of Calvert: respected; herding

Calvary (American) word as name; herding all
Cal, Kal, Kalvary

Calvert (English) respected; herding
Cal, Calber, Calbert, Calver, Kal, Kalvert

Calvin (Latin) bald
Cal, Calvie, Kal

Cam (Scottish) form of Cameron: mischievous; crooked nose
Camm, Cammey, Cammie, Cammy, Kam

Camara (African) instructs

Cambell (American) form of Campbell: bountiful; crooked mouth
Cam, Cambel, Cammy, Kambell

Camberg (Last name as first name) valley man
Cam

Cambio (Italian) short

Cambridge (Place name) city in England; twisting; mover
Cambrydge

Camden (Scottish) conflicted
Cam, Camdan, Camdon

Camerero (Last name as first name) charismatic

Cameron ♥ (Scottish) mischievous; crooked nose
Cam, Camaron, Camerohn, Cami, Cammy, Camren, Camron

Camiel (Spanish) helps

Camilo (Latin) helpful; (Italian) free *Cam, Camillo*

Cammer (Spanish) hall worker

Campbell (Scottish) bountiful; crooked mouth
Cambell, Cammie, Camp, Campie, Campy

Campillo (Spanish) form of Camilo: helpful

Campion (English) champion

Camrin (American) form of Cameron: mischievous; crooked nose

Camron (Scottish) form of Cameron: mischievous; crooked nose
Camren

Can (Turkish) vibrant

Canaan (Biblical) spiritual leanings
Cane, Kanaan, Kanan

Canada (Place name) from Canada

Canal (Word as name) waterway
Kanal

Candelario (Spanish) bright and glowing
Cadelario

Cander (American) candid
Can, Candor, Candy, Kan, Kander, Kandy

Candido (Spanish) pure; candid
Can, Candi, Candide, Candy

Candle (American) bright; hip
Candell

Cangelo (Spanish) vibrant

Canice (Spanish) seamless

Cannon (French) courageous
Canney, Canni, Cannie, Canny, Canon, Canyn, Kannon, Kanon

Cano (Scottish) attractive

Canow (American) like a canon

Canten (American Indian) hunter

Canute (Scandinavian) great
Knut, Knute

Canyon (Nature) hip

Capan (American) bird; jaunty

Capi (American) high energy

Capon (American) bird; captain

Capone (Last name used as first name) risk-taker

Capote (Italian) bright

Cappy (French) breezy; lucky
Cappey, Cappi

Capua (Biblical) place name

Caractacus (Latin) bold

Carad (American) wily
Karad

Caradine (Spanish) birdlike

Caravaggio (Italian) painter

Caravale (Last name used as first name) dear valley girl

Carballo (Spanish) explosive

Card (English) form of Cardan: crafty; carder
Kard

Cardan (English) crafty; carder
Card, Carden, Cardon

Cardente (Spanish) clarity; craftsman

Carder (Last name used as first name) confident

Cardew (Welsh) dark

Cardin (Irish) dark home

Cardoc (Welsh) loved

Cardozo (Spanish) supportive

Cardwell (English) craftsman
Kardwell

Carel (Dutch) free

Carew (Latin) runner
Carrew

Carey (Welsh) masculine; by the castle
Care, Cari, Cary, Karey

Cari (English) masculine
Care, Carie, Cary

Carino (Last name as first name) strong

Carl (Swedish) kingly
Karl

Carland (Last name as first name) land of free men

Carlin (Irish) winning
Carlan, Carle, Carlen, Carlie, Carly

Carlisle (English) strengthens
Carl, Carly, Carlyle

Carlo (Italian) sensual; manly
Carl, Carloh

Carlon (Irish) form of Carl: kingly
Karlon, Carlonn

Carlos ✪ (Spanish) manly; sensual
Carl, Carlo

Carlson (English) son of a manly man
Carls, Carlsan, Carlsen

Carlton (English) leader; town of Carl
Carleton, Carltan, Carlten, Carltown, Carltynne

Carmel (Hebrew) growing; garden
Carmell, Karmel

Carmello (Italian) flourishing
Carm, Carmel, Carmelo, Karmello

Carmi (Biblical) beloved son;
(Italian) garden

Carmichael (Scottish) bold;
Michael's follower
Car, Kar, Karmichael

Carmine (Italian) carmane
Carmin, Carmyne, Karmen, Karmine

Carmo (Italian) songs

Carmody (French) manly; adult
Carmodee

Carn (English) winner

Carneg (Slavic) horner

Carnell (Irish) victor
Car, Carny, Kar, Karnell, Karney

Carney (Irish) winner
Carn, Carnay, Carnee, Carnie,
Carny

Caro (Hungarian) horn boy

Carol (Irish) champion
Caroll, Carrol, Carroll

Carpus (Greek) bountiful

Carr (Scandinavian) outdoorsy
Car, Kar

Carrew (Latin) runner

Carrick (Irish) lives on rocky place

Carrier (Last name used as first
name) growth

Carroll (German) masculine;
winner
Carall, Care, Carell, Caroll,
Carrol, Carrolle, Carry, Caryl

Carson ❂ (English) confident
Carr, Cars, Carsan, Carsen

Carsten (German) a Christian

Carswell (English) diligent

Cart (American) word as name;
practical
Cartee, Cartey, Kart

Carter ❂ ❶ (English) insightful
Cart, Cartah, Cartie

Cartrell (English) practical
Car, Cartrelle, Cartrey, Cartrie,
Cartrill, Kar, Kartrel, Kartrell

Cartwright (English) creative
Cart, Cartright, Kart, Kartwright

Carungay (Spanish) crass

Caruso (Italian) musically
inclined
Karuso

Carvell (English) innovative
Carvel, Carvelle, Carver, Karvel

Carver (English) carver
Carve, Carvey, Karver, Karvey

Cary (English) pretty brook;
charming
Carey

Casady (English) curly-haired

Casdeen (American) assertive;
ingenious
Kassdeen

Case (Irish) highly esteemed
Casey

Caseen (Dutch) together

Casel (English) boisterous

Casen (Last name used as first
name) bound

Casey (Irish) courageous
Case, Casi, Casie, Kacie, Kacy,
Kase, Kaysie

Cash (Latin) conceited
Casha, Cashe, Cazh

Cashmere (American) smooth;
soft-spoken
Cash, Cashmeer, Cashmyre, Kashmere

Cashone (American) cash-loving
Casho

Casiano (Latin) empty

Casimir (Polish) peace-loving
Casmer, Casmir

Casimiro (Spanish) famous;
aggressor
Casmiro, Kasimiro

Caslu (Biblical) turmoil

Casper (German) secretive
Caspar, Caspey, Caspi, Caspie, Cass

Caspian (Place name) sea near
Iran; daring

Caspin (Biblical) place name

Cass (Irish) form of Cassidy: humorous
Cash, Caz, Kass

Cassell (English) saintly

Cassian (Last name used as first name) thinker

Cassidy (Irish) humorous
Casidy, Cass, Cassadie, Cassidee, Cassidie, Kasidy, Kass, Kassidy

Cassie (Irish) form of Cassidy: humorous
Casi, Cass, Cassy

Cassius (Latin) protective
Cass, Casseus, Casshus

Cast (Greek) form of Castor: eager protector
Casta, Caste, Kast

Castellan (Spanish) adventurer

Caster (English) saint

Castern (Last name used as first name) reliable

Castle (Last name used as first name) sturdy

Casto (Mythology) form of Castor: eager protector; (Spanish) star; (Greek) truthful
Cass, Kasto

Castor (Greek) eager protector
Cass, Caster, Castie

Castulo (Spanish) aggressor
Castu, Kastulo

Cata (American) form of Catarino: unflawed; perfect

Catarino (Spanish) unflawed; perfect
Catrino

Cathal (Irish) leader

Cather (Last name used as first name) virile

Cathmor (Irish) brave warrior

Cato (Latin) zany and bright
Catoe, Kato

Catou (French) wise

Cauda (Biblical) place name

Caudell (Last name used as first name) pure

Caughtry (Welsh) fighter

Cavan (Irish) attractive man
Cavahn, Caven, Cavin

Cavance (Irish) handsome
Caeven, Cavanse, Kaeven, Kavance

Cavell (Last name as first name) opinionated
Cavil, Cavill

Cavin (Irish) safe; stylish

Cavinal (Irish) not of substance; hollow

Cawley (Last name as first name) brash

Cayce (American) form of Casey: courageous
Cace, Case, Kayce

Caycen (American) of the case

Cayern (Last name used as first name) makes cases

Cayetano (Spanish) feisty; destiny

Cayeto (Spanish) survivor

Caynce (Invented) form of Cayce: courageous
Caincy, Cainse, Kaynse

Cayo (American) smart

Cazare (Last name as first name) daring
Cazares

Ceabron (Last name used as first name) giving

Cease (American) rowdy

Cebriane (Spanish) form of Cyprus: island south of Turkey; outgoing

Cebron (Spanish) generous

Cecil (Latin) unseeing; hard-headed; blind
Cece, Cecel, Cecile, Cecilio, Cicile

Cedar (Botanical) tree name; sturdy
Ced, Sed, Sedar

Cedric (English) leader
Ced, Ceda, Cedrick

Ceferino (Spanish) careful

Celedonio (Spanish) heavenly

Celius (Spanish) celestial

Celso (Italian) heavenly
Celesteno, Celestino, Celesto, Celestyno, Celsus, Selso

Celsorio (Last name used as first name) soars

Celum (Spanish) holly berries

Celumiel (Spanish) of the heavens
Celu

Celvan (Slavic) winning

Cemal (Arabic) handsome

Cender (Spanish) articulate; peace

Cened (Slavic) wins

Cengiz (Inventive) weapon

Cenobio (Spanish) shy

Centola (Spanish) tenth child
Cento

Century (Invented) remarkable
Cen, Cent

Cerb (Greek) dark mind

Cerber (Mythology) three-headed

Cerbulo (Spanish) serene

Cerce (Greek) form of Circe; thinker

Ceres (Greek) loving

Cerf (French) buck

Cerlito (Spanish)

Ceron (Greek) thunders

Cerone (French) serene; creative
Serone

Cervacio (Spanish) serves

Cervando (Spanish) fawning

Cervant (Spanish) original

Cervantes (Literature) for the Spanish author; original
Cervantez

Cesaire (French) form of Caesar

Cesar (Spanish) leader
Cesare, Cezar, Zarr

Cesar-Vega (Spanish) combo of Cesar and Vega; famed star

Cetrell (Spanish) centered

Chaban (American) form of Chabe: from Shabe in Bible

Chabe (Biblical) from Shabe in the Bible

Chacko (Spanish) form of Chico: boy

Chad (English) firebrand
Chadd, Chaddy

Chadburn (English) spirited

Chaden (English) battles

Chadley (English) cautions

Chads (English) aggressive

Chadson (English) son of Chad; comforts

Chadwick (English) warrior
Chad, Chadwyck

Chaffee (Last name as first name) bold adventurer

Chaggy (American) cocky
Chagg, Shagg, Shaggy

Chaicus (Biblical) strong

Chaika (Hebrew) life
Chai, Chaikeh, Chaikel, Chaiki

Chaim (Hebrew) life
Chai, Chayim, Haim, Hy, Hyman, Hymie, Khaim, Manny

Chaise (French) chases
Chayse

Chaker (Arabic) best

Chalen (American) strong

Chalfie (American)

Chalfin (Last name used as first name)

Challen (American) form of Allen: handsome boy

Chalmer (Scottish) the Lord's son
Chall, Chally, Chalmers

Chalmers (French) chambers; surrounded; (Scottish) Lord's child
Chalm

Chamara (Asian) diligent

Chamb (American) messenger

Chambers (English) regal boy

Chamblin (American) easygoing
Cham

Chan (Chinese) bright; Vietnamese *truthful*

Chanan (Hebrew) filled with God's compassion

Chance (English) good fortune; happy
Chancey, Chanci, Chancy, Chanse, Chanz, Chauncey

Chancela (American) dedicated

Chancellor (English) book keeper
Chance, Chancey

Chand (Indian) sun

Chanda (Indian) brightness

Chandell (African American) innovator
Chandelle, Chandey, Chandie, Shandel, Shandell

Chanderkala (Hindi) luminous

Chandler (English) ingenious; (French) maker of candles
Chand, Chandey, Chandlor

Chandru (Indian) moon

Chaney (French) strong
Chane, Chanie, Chayne, Chaynee

Chang (Chinese) free; flowing

Chanina (Hebrew) compassionate by virtue of God

Channing (English) brilliant
Chann, Channy

Chanoch (Hebrew) dedicated; loyal

Chantan (Indian) sparkle

Chante (French) singer
Chant, Chanta, Chantay, Chantie

Chapa (Last name as first name) merchant; spirited
Chap, Chappy

Chaparro (Spanish) from chaparral southern landscape; cowboy
Chap, Chaps

Chapel (Last name used as first name) singer

Chapell (Hindi) spiritual

Chapen (French) clergyman
Chapin, Chapland, Chaplin

Chaplin (Last name used as first name) pious

Chapman (English) businessman
Chap, Chappy

Chappelle (French) of the chapel

Char (French) truthful; spiritual

Charilaos (Greek) giving

Charlem (English) of Charles

Charlemagne (French) historic; King of the Franks "Charles the great"

Charles ○ (German) manly; well-loved
Charl, Charley, Charli, Charlie, Charly, Chas, Chaz, Chazz, Chuck

Charleston (English) Charles's town; confident
Charlesten

Charlie (German) manly
Charl, Charley, Charli, Charly

Charlie-John (American) combo of Charlie and John

Charlton (English) leader
Charles, Charley, Charlie, Charlt

Charome (American) masculine
Char, Charoam, Charom, Charrone, Charry

Charon (Greek) mythological ferryman of the underworld

Charro (Spanish) wild-spirited cowboy
Charo, Charroh

Charudata (Hindi) beautiful

Charvaka (Hindi) form of Charudata: beautiful

Chas (American) form of Charles: manly; well-loved

Chase ○ ❶ (French) hunter
Chace, Chass

Chaskel (Hebrew) strong

Chason (French) hunts
Chansen

Chat (American) happy
Chatt

Chatham (Last name as first name) serious

Chatsworth (English) warrior's place

Chatwin (Last name as first name) thoughtful

Chaucer (Literature) for Geoffrey Chaucer; distinguished
Chauce, Chauser

Chaudray (French) hopeful

Chauncey (English) fair-minded
Chance, Chancey, Chanse, Chaunce

Chausse (English) form of Chauncey: fair-minded

Chavers (English) stern

Chavivi (Hebrew) beloved

Chavlier (French) elegant

Chayne (Scottish) swagger
Chane, Channe, Chay

Chaz (German) form of Charles: manly; well-loved
Chas, Chazz, Chazzie, Chazzy

Ché (Spanish) form of José: asset; favored
Chay, Shae, Shay

Ched (French) form of Shad: joyful

Chee (American) high-energy
Che

Chekhov (Russian) playwright; genius

Chen (Chinese) great

Cheney (French) outdoorsman
Chenay, Cheney

Cheramy (American) form of Jeremy: talkative
Charamie, Cheramee, Chermy

Cheran (Biblical) dearest

Chermon (French) my dear

Cherno (Slavic) black

Chesed (Biblical) difficult

Chesley (American) patient
Ches, Cheslee, Chez, Chezlee

Chesman (Last name used as first name) hard

Chester (English) comfy-cozy
Ches, Chessie, Chessy

Chesterfield (English) field of Rochester; comforting

Chet (English) creative
Chett

Chetan (Indian) vibrant

Chetny (Native American) determined

Chetwin (English) winding road

Chevalier (French) gallant
Chev, Chevy

Chevalle (French) dignified
Chev, Chevi, Chevy

Cheven (Invented) playful
Chevy

Chever (Place name)

Chevery (French) form of Chevy: clever
Chev, Shevery

Chevy (French) clever
Chev, Chevi, Chevie, Chevv

Chew (Chinese) mountain

Chiamaka (African) God is good

Chibale (Hebrew) loving

Chick (English) form of Charles: manly; well-loved
Chic, Chickie, Chicky

Chico (Spanish) boy
Chicoh, Chiko

Chief (Word as name) leader

Chieko (Spanish) boy

Chiel (Hebrew) God lives

Chijoke (African) talented

Chikosi (African) the ruins

Chili (American) appetite for hot food

Chillen (American) form of Chilton: serene; farm

Chilton (English) serene; farm
Chill, Chillton, Chilly, Chilt

Chimanga (African) grain

Chimento (Italian) of the chimes

Chin (Korean) precious boy

Chip (English) chip off the old block; like father
Chipp, Chipper

Chiram (Hebrew) held in high esteem

Chiriga (Indian) lights the way

Chisholm (Place name) from Chisholm Trail: pioneer spirit
Chis, Chishom, Chiz

Chita (Spanish) fiery

Chito (American) fast-food eater; hungry
Cheetoh, Chitoh

Chiura (Italian) light; textured

Chiztam (Hebrew) imbued with God's strength

Chobi (Spanish) buddy

Chogie (Spanish) friendly

Choicey (American) word name; picky
Choicie, Choisie

Chombel (American) birdlike

Chonito (Spanish) friend
Chonit, Chono

Chopo (American) cowhand
Chop, Choppy

Choto (Spanish) kid
Shoto

Chotto (Last name as first name) child

Chovev (Hebrew) companion

Chow (Chinese) everywhere

Chris (Greek) form of Christopher: the bearer of Christ
Cris, Chrissy, Chrys

Christer (Norwegian) religious
Krister

Christian ✪ ⓣ (Latin) follower of Christ
Chris, Christen, Christiaan, Christiane, Christyan, Cristian, Kris, Krist, Kristian

Christo (Spanish) christian

Christodoulous (Greek) filled with sweet love for Christ

Christop (Greek) christian

Christophe (French) beloved of Christ
Cristoph, Kristophe

Christopher ✪ ⓣ (Greek) the bearer of Christ
Chris, Christofer, Crista, Cristopher, Cristos, Kit, Kristopher

Christopherson (English) son of Christopher; religious
Christophersen, Cristophersen, Cristopherson

Christos (Greek) form of Christopher: the bearer of Christ
Chris, Kristos

Chubby (American) oversized
Chubbee, Chubbey, Chubbi, Chubbie

Chuck (German) rash
Chuckee, Chuckey, Chuckie, Chucky

Chuckles (American) clown

Chucky (German) impulsive
Chuckey, Chucki, Chuckie

Chuey (Spanish) form of Charles: manly; well-loved

Chuhei (Japanese) shy

Chuna (Hebrew) warm

Chuneh (Hebrew) with the Lord's grace

Chunky (American) word name; large
Chunk, Chunkey, Chunki

Chur (American) form of Churchian: spirited

Churchian (American) spirited

Churchill (English) bright
Church

Chutar (Spanish) aiming for goals
Chuter

Chux (American) clear

Chuxin (American) clear

Chuyen (Native American) clear

Cian (Irish) old soul

Ciano (Irish) old

Cibab (German) giving

Cicero (Latin) strong speaker
Cice

Ciceron (Latin) chickpea

Cicil (English) shy
Cecil, Cice

Cid (Spanish) leader; lord
Ciddie, Ciddy, Cyd, Sid

Cielo (Spanish) light

Cieran (Spanish) clarity

Cigler (Last name used as first name)

Cimarron (Place name) city in New Mexico; cowboy
Cimaronn

Cinco (Spanish) fifth child
Cinko, Sinko

Cione (Italian) Last name used as first name

Ciprian (Latin) from the island of Cyprus
Cipriano

Ciriaco (Italian) lordly

Ciriak (Spanish) believer

Ciriako (Italian) lord's child

Cirill (English) form of Cyril: regal

Cirillo (Spanish) lordly
Cirilo

Ciro (Italian) lordly
Ciroh, Cirro, Cyro

Cirrus (Latin) thoughtful; cloud formation
Cerrus, Cirrey, Cirri, Cirrie, Cirry, Cirus, Serrus, Serus

Cisco (American) clever
Sisco, Sysco

Cisto (Spanish) form of Francisco: free spirit; from France

Citlalis (Spanish) star

Citronella (American) oil from fragrant grass; pungent
Cit, Citro, Cytronella, Sitronella

Cival (English) form of Percival: mysterious

Civille (American) form of Saville: willow town

Clady (French) form of Claude: slow-moving; lame

Claiborn (English) born of earth
Claiborne

Clair (English) renowned
Claire, Clare

Clairon (French) clear

Clamente (Spanish) form of Clemente: pleasant

Clance (Irish) form of Clancy: lively; feisty redhead
Clancy, Clanse, Klance, Klancy

Clancy (Irish) lively; feisty redhead
Clancey, Clancie

Claney (American) form of Clancy: lively; feisty redhead

Clant (American) form of Clancy: lively; feisty redhead

Clanton (Last name used as first name)

Claran (Latin) bright
Clarance, Claranse, Claransi, Clare, Claren, Clarence, Clary, Klarense

Clarence (Latin) intelligent
Clarance, Clare, Clarens, Clarense, Clarons, Claronz, Clarrence, Klarence, Klarens

Clarinett (Invented) plays the clarinet
Clare, Clarinet, Clary, Klare, Klari

Clark (French) personable; scholar
Clarke

Clarkey (Last name used as first name) scholar

Clarson (American) clarity

Clary (English) clear

Clater (English) premier

Claude (Latin) slow-moving; lame
Claud, Claudey, Claudie, Claudy, Klaud, Klaude

Claudemir (Slavic) lame

Claudene (Italian) lame

Claudimir (Slavic) lame

Claudio-Clyde (Slavic) combo of Claudio and Claude

Claus (Greek) victorious
Klaas, Klaus

Clausen (English) form of Nicholas: the people's victory

Claven (English) endorsed
Klaven

Clavero (Spanish) lame

Clavey (Last name used as first name)

Clawdell (American) form of Claude: slow-moving; lame
Clawd

Claxton (English) townie
Clax, Klax

Clay (English) reliable
Claye, Klae, Klay

Claybey (American) southern; earthly
Claybie, Klaybee

Clayborne (English) earthly
Clabi, Claybie, Clayborn, Claybourne, Klay

Claybrook (English) sparkling smile
Claibrook, Clay, Claybrooke, Clayie

Clayeo (Spanish) form of Clay: reliable

Clayton (English) stodgy
Clay, Claytan, Clayten

Claywell (English) by the clay well

Cleadis (American) form of Cletus: creative; selected
Famed

Cleary (Irish) smart
Clear, Clearey, Clearie

Cleavon (English) daring
Cheavaughn, Cleavaughn, Cleave, Cleevaughan, Cleevon

Clegg (Last name used as first name)

Clem (Latin) casual
Cleme, Clemmey, Clemmie, Clemmy, Clim

Clemen (American) forgives

Clement (Scottish) gentle
Clem, Clemmyl

Clemente (Spanish) pleasant
Clemen, Clementay

Clements (Latin) forgiving man
Clem, Clement, Clemmants, Clemment

Clemer (Latin) mild
Clemmie, Clemmy, Klemer, Klemmie, Klemmye

Clemmie (Latin) mild
Clem, Klem, Klemmee, Klemmy

Clenzy (Spanish) forgiving; cleansed
Clense, Clensy, Klenzy

Cleofas (African American) brave lion

Cleofe (Greek) famed

Cleon (Greek) famed man
Clee, Cleone, Kleon

Cleophas (Greek) seeing glory; known
Cle, Cleofus, Cleoph, Klee, Kleofus, Kleophus

Clete (Greek) form of Cletus: creative; selected
Cleet, Cleete

Cletus (Greek) creative; selected
Clede, Cledus, Cletis

Cleve (English) precarious
Clive

Cleveland (English) daring
Cleavelan, Cleve, Clevon, Clevy, Cliveland

Clevis (Greek) prolific
Cleviss, Clevys, Clevyss

Cliff (English) form of Clifford: dashing
Clif, Cliffey, Cliffie, Cliffy

Cliffen (American)

Clifford (English) dashing
Cleford, Cliff, Cliffy, Clyford

Clift (American) cliff-dweller
Clifte

Clifton (English) risk-taker
Cliff, Cliffian, Clifften, Cliffy

Clim (American) form of Clem: casual

Cline (Last name as first name) musical

Clint (English) form of Clinton: town on a hill
Clent, Clynt, Klint

Clinton (English) town on a hill
Clenton, Clint, Clinten, Clynton, Klinten, Klinton

Clipper (American) boatsman

Clive (English) daring; living near a cliff
Cleve, Clyve

Clive-John (English) combo of Clive and John

Cliven (English) cliff boy

Clodagh (Scottish) winning

Clooney (American) dramatic
Cloone, Cloonie, Cloony, Clune, Cluney, Clunie, Cluny

Clotaire (French) famous
Clotie, Klotair, Klotie

Clovis (German) famed warrior
Clove, Cloves, Clovus, Klove, Kloves, Klovis

Clowry (Last name used as first name)

Cloyd (American) form of Floyd: practical; hair of gray
Cloy, Cloye, Kloy, Kloyd

Cloyd (American) form of Clyde: adventurer

Clske (Dutch) dark

Clue (Word as name)

Cluny (American) dramatic

Clwe (Dutch) face of a mountain

Clyde (Welsh) adventurer
Clide, Clydey, Clydie, Clydy, Clye, Klyde, Klye

Clydell (American) countrified
Clidell, Clydel

Clydenestra (Spanish) form of Clyde: adventurer

Coad (English) form of Coady: comforted

Coady (English) comforted

Coal (American) word as a name
Coale, Koal

Coat (Native American) snake

Cobalt (Word as name) from the cottage

Cobb (English) cozy
Cob, Cobbe

Cobbie (American) form of Jacob: he who supplants

Coben (Last name as first name) creative
Cob, Cobb, Cobe, Cobee, Cobey, Cobi, Coby, Kob, Kobee, Koben, Kobi, Koby

Cobern (English) stream spot

Cobian (American) form of Jacob: he who supplants

Coble (English) cobler

Cobo (American) friendly

Cobus (Dutch) friend

Coby (American) friendly
Cob, Cobe, Cobey, Cobie

Coca (American) excitable
Coka, Cokey, Cokie, Koca, Koka

Cochise (Native American) warrior
Cocheece, Cochize

Cochran (Last name used as first name)

Cocinero (Italian) slippery

Coco (French) brash
Coko, Koko

Coder (Last name used as first name) form of Cody: comforting

Codrington (Last name used as first name) form of Cody: comforting

Codryll (Last name used as first name) form of Cody: comforting

Cody (English) comforting
Coday, Code, Codee, Codey, Codi, Codie

Coe (American) form of Cody: comforting

Coenraad (Dutch) form of Conrad: optimist

Coffey (English) Friday's child

Coffie (English) Friday's child

Coffman (Last name used as first name)

Cog (American) form of Cogdell: needed
Kog

Cogan (English) form of Kegan: ball-of-fire

Cogdell (Last name as first name) needed
Cogdale

Coggin (Last name used as first name)

Cohn (American) winner
Kohn

Coil (Hebrew) giving

Coitlee (American) silver

Coitoine (French) silver

Cokie (American) bright
Cokey, Coki, Cokki, Kokie

Col (American) the colonel

Colak (Irish) bright

Colbert (English) cool and calm
Colbey, Colbi, Colbie, Colburt, Colby, Cole

Colborn (English) intimidating; cold brook
Colbey, Colborne, Colburn, Colby, Cole

Colby (English) bright; secretive; dark farm
Colbey, Colbi, Colbie, Cole, Colie

Colden (English) haunting
Coldan, Coldun, Cole

Cole ✪ (Greek) lively; winner
Coal, Coley, Colie, Kohl, Kole

Colee (American) victor

Coleman (English) lively; peacemaker
Cole, Colemann, Colman, Kohlman

Coley (American) victor

Colgate (English) passway
Colgait, Colgaite, Kolgate

Colier (Last name as first name) sophisticated

Colin (Irish) young and quiet; peaceful; the people's victor
Colan, Cole, Colen, Collin, Collyn

Colis (English) he who delights others

Collan (Irish) farms

Coller (Irish) farms

Collett (English) black hair

Colley (English) dark-haired
Col, Colli, Collie

Collier (English) hardworking; miner
Colier, Collie, Colly, Colyer

Collies (English) delights

Collin (Scottish) shy
Collen, Collie, Collon, Colly

Collins (Irish) shy; holly
Collens, Collie, Collons, Colly, Kolly

Colm (Irish) dove; peaceful

Colorado (Place name) U.S. state; multicolored

Coloss (Biblical) colossal

Colson (English) precocious; son of Nicholas
Cole, Colsan, Colsen

Colster (English) colts

Colston (English) young horse town

Colt (English) frisky; horse trainer
Colty, Kolt, Koltt

Colten ✪ (English) dark town; mysterious
Cole, Collton, Colt, Coltan, Coltawn, Colton, Kol

Colter (English) keeping the colts
Colt, Coltor, Colty

Colum (Latin) peaceful; dove
Colm, Kolm, Kolum

Columba (Latin) dove; calm

Columbus (Latin) peaceful; discovered America
Colom, Colombo, Columbe

Colvint (Spanish) river

Colwen (Irish) peaceful
Colvin, Colwin

Comanche (Native American) tribe; wild-spirited; industrious
Comanch, Komanche

Combs (English) Last name used as first name

Commander (Word as name) leader

Commodore (French) commander

Como (Spanish) similar
Comoh

Comus (Greek) humorous
Comas, Comes, Commus, Komus

Con (Irish) form of Conan:
worthy of praise

Conal (Irish) strong; wolflike;
Conall

Conall (Scottish) highly regarded
Conal

Conan (Irish) worthy of praise
Conen, Connie, Conny, Conon

Conant (Irish) top-notch
Conent, Connant

Concini (Italian) Last name used
as first name

Concord (English) agreeable
*Con, Concor, Conny, Koncord,
Konny*

Conde (Last name as first name)
driven

Cong (Chinese) bright

Conger (Irish) tall

Coniah (Irish) pure
Conias, Conah

Conk (Invented) from conch
mollusk of the ocean; jazzy
*Conch, Conkee, Conkee, Conky,
Kanch, Konk, Konkey*

Conkel (Last name used as first
name)

Conkey (Last name used as first
name)

Conklin (English) Last name
used as first name

Conlach (Irish) in accord

Conlan (Irish) winner
*Con, Conland, Conlen, Conleth,
Conlin, Connie, Conny*

Conleth (Welsh) hero

Conley (Celtic) hero

Connable (Last name used as
first name)

Connaughton (American) sapient

Connell (Irish) strong
*Con, Conal, Connall, Connel,
Connelle, Connie, Conny*

Connelly (Celtic/Gaelic)
Last name used as first name;
friendship

Connery (Scottish) daring
*Con, Conery, Connarie, Connary,
Connie, Conny*

Connie (Irish) form of Connor:
brilliant; form of Conrad: optimist
*Con, Conn, Connee, Connery,
Conney, Connie, Conny*

Connor ✪ (Scottish) brilliant
*Con, Conn, Conner, Conor, Kon,
Konnor*

Conra (Irish) wise

Conrad (German) optimist
*Con, Connie, Conny, Conrade,
Konrad*

Conrado (Spanish) bright advisor
Conrad, Conrod, Conrodo

Conradt (Welsh) Last name used
as first name; bold in counsel

Conreed (Welsh) brave

Conridge (Last name as first
name) advisor
Con, Conni, Connie, Conny, Ridge

Conroy (Irish) wise writer
Conrie, Conroye, Conry, Roy, Roye

Conrye (American) form of
Conrad: optimist

Considine (Last name used as
first name) considerate

Consis (Mythology) flourishing

Constant (French) devotee; loyal

Constantine (Latin) constant;
steadfast
*Con, Conn, Consta, Constance,
Constant, Constantin, Constantyne,
Konstantin*

Consydin (American) form of
Considine: considerate

Conte (Italian) accountable

Conway (Irish) vigilant
Con, Connie, Kon, Konway

Cooke (Latin) cook
Cook, Cookie, Cooky

Cooker (English) cooks

Coolidge (Last name as first name) wary
Cooledge

Cooney (Last name as first name) giving

Cooper ○ ❶ (English) handsome; maker of barrels
Coup, Couper, Koop, Kooper, Kouper

Coos (Dutch) friend

Cope (English) able
Cape

Coptos (Biblical) place name

Coral (Nature) from Hebrew goral; pebble

Corbell (Latin) raven; dark
Corbel

Corbet (Latin) dark
Corb, Corbett, Corbit, Corbitt, Korb, Korbet

Corbie (Latin) raven

Corbin (Latin) dark and brooding
Corban, Corben, Corby

Corbitt (Last name as first name) brooding
Corbet, Corbett, Corbie, Corbit, Corby

Corblee (American) dark

Corby (Latin) dark
Corbey, Korbee, Korby, Korry

Corcoran (Irish) ruddy-skinned
Corkie, Corky

Cord (Origin unknown) soap opera hunk
Corde, Kord

Cordaro (Italian) roped

Cordel (French) practical
Cordell, Cordelle, Cordie, Cordill, Cordy

Cordell (Latin) bound; rope

Cordero (Spanish) gentle
Cordara, Cordaro, Cordarro, Kordarro, Kordero

Cordi (Spanish) makes ropes

Cordry (American) makes ropes

Corentin (French) stormy

Coret (French) stormy

Corey (Irish) laughing
Core, Corie, Corry, Cory, Korey, Korrie, Kory

Coril (American) coral

Corin (Latin) combative
Coren, Dorrin, Koren, Korrin

Corinth (Biblical) from Corinthians

Cork (Place name) county in Ireland
Corkee, Corkey, Corki, Corky, Kork

Corkeen (American) form of Corky: casual

Corkel (American) form of Corky: casual

Corkson (American) son of Corky

Corky (American) casual
Corkee, Corkey, Korky

Corl (English) cheery

Corlan (English) of good cheer

Corlon (American) tasteful

Cormac (Irish) the raven's offspring; watchful
Cormack, Cormak

Cormic (Irish) raven

Cormick (Last name as first name) old-fashioned
Cormac, Cormack

Corn (Latin) form of Cornelius: horn; loquacious
Korn

Cornall (Irish) form of Cornelius: horn; loquacious

Cornelio (Spanish) horn blower

Cornelius (Greek) horn; loquacious
Coarn, Conny, Corn, Corni, Cornie, Corny, Kornelius, Neel, Neely, Neil, Neiley

Cornell (French) fair
Corne, Cornelle, Corny, Kornell

Cornellian (Greek) horn color

Coro (Spanish) form of Coronnel: colonel

Corodon (Greek) lark

Coronnel (Spanish) colonel

Corrado (Italian) worthy advisor

Corrigan (Irish) aggressive
Coregan, Corie, Correghan, Corrie,
Corry, Koregan, Korrigan

Cors (Spanish) from Corsica

Corso (Spanish) form of Kyros:
masterful
Sun

Cort (German) eloquent
Corte, Court, Kort

Cortal (Last name used as first
name) intellectual

Cortant (Spanish) bitter

Cortazar (Last name as first)
creative

Cortell (Spanish) cuts

Cortez (Spanish) victorious;
explorer
Cortes

Corum (English) form of
Corwin: heart's delight

Corvey (Greek) crest

Corvin (English) friend
Corwin, Corwynn, Korry, Korvin

Corwen (English) delights the
heart

Corwin (English) heart's delight
Corrie, Corry, Corwan, Corwann,
Corwyn, Corwynne

Cory (Latin) humorous
Coarie, Core, Corey, Corrie, Kohry,
Kori

Coryell (Greek) lark; devious

Cos (Biblical) place name; orderly

Cosell (French) outgoing

Cosgrove (Irish) winner
Cosgrave, Cossy, Kosgrove, Kossy

Cosimo (Greek) orderly

Cosma (Greek) universal
Cos, Kosma

Cosmas (Greek) universal
Cos, Kosmas, Koz

Cosmedin (Spanish) harmony

Cosmo (Greek) in harmony with
life
Cos, Cosimo, Cosimon, Cosme,
Cosmos, Kosmo

Cosner (English) organized;
handsome
Cosnar, Kosner

Costas (Greek) constant
Costa, Costah

Coste (Greek) form of
Constantine: constant; steadfast

Costel (Slavic) constant

Costello (Italian) form of
Constantine: constant; steadfast

Cotledge (Last name used as first
name) by the cottage ledge

Cotrer (Last name used as first
name) contrary

Cotter (American) gregarious

Cottingham (Last name used as
first name) day by day

Cottlings (English) in the cottage

Cotton (Botanical name) casual
Cottan

Cottrell (English) in the cottage

Coty (French) comforter
Cotey, Coti, Cotie, Koty

Coug (American) from cougar;
fierce
Cougar, Koug, Kougar

Couland (French) from court
land

Coulter (English) dealing in
colts; horseman
Colter, Coult, Kolter, Koulter

Council (French) advisor

Counsel (Latin) advisor
Consel, Council, Kounse, Kounsell

Country (Word as name) cowboy

Court (English) royal

Courtland (English) born in the
land of the court; dignitary

Courtnay (English) sophisticated
Cort, Corteney, Court, Courtney,
Courtny

Covell (English) warm
Covele, Covelle

Covet (American) word as name;
desires
Covett, Covette, Kovet

Covington (English) distinctive
Covey, Coving, Kovey, Kovington

Cowan (Irish) cozy
Cowen, Cowie, Cowy

Cowboy (American) western

Cowden (Irish) cave in the hill

Cowell (English) brash; frank
Kowell

Cowey (Irish) reclusive
Cowee, Cowie, Kowey

Coye (English) outdoorsman
Coy, Coyey, Coyie

Coyle (English) in the woods

Coylie (American) coy
Coyl, Koyl, Koylie

Coyne (French) demure

Coystal (American) bashful
Coy, Koy, Koystal

Crad (American) practical
Cradd, Krad, Kradd

Craddock (Last name as first name) practical

Crager (Scottish) from the crags

Crago (Last name as first name) macho
Crag, Craggy, Krago

Craig (Irish) brave climber
Crai, Craigie, Cray, Craye, Crayg, Creg, Cregge, Kraig

Crain (English) cranes

Crandal (English) open
Cran, Crandall, Crandell, Crane

Crandale (English) from the land of cranes
Crandall, Crandell

Crandan (English) from the cranes

Cranley (English) lives in a field of cranes

Cranston (English) from the town of cranes

Cranyon (English) from the cranes

Craon (Greek) leader

Crawford (English) flowing
Crafe, Craford, Craw, Fordy

Cray (English) place name

Crayton (English) substantial
Craeton, Cray, Creighton

Creach (Scottish) home-loving

Creasy (English) Last name used as first name

Creed (American) believer
Crede, Creede, Creyd, Kreed

Creek (English) word as name

Creigh (English) lives near rocks

Creighton (English) sophisticated
Criton

Crenshaw (Last name as first name) good intentions

Crescin (Latin) expansive

Cresencio (Spanish) integrity

Creshaun (African American) inspired
Creshawn, Kreshaun

Cresp (Latin) man with curls
Crisp, Crispen, Crispun, Crispy, Cryspin, Kresp, Krisp, Krispin, Krispyn

Crever (Irish) sly fox

Crevin (Irish) sly fox

Crew (American) word as name; sailor
Krew

Crey (English) form of Creighton: sophisticated
Craedie, Cray, Creigh, Creydie

Crider (English) creek

Cris (Welsh) form of Crisiant: crystallike

Crisanto (Spanish) anoint

Crisiant (Welsh) crystallike

Crisman (Greek) golden

Crisoforo (Spanish) gold clothing; form of Christopher; bearer of Christ

Crispin (Latin) man with curls
Chrispy, Crespen, Crispo, Crispy, Krispin, Krispo

Crispo (Latin) curly-haired
Crisp, Krispo

Crist (Spanish) Christian

Cristhian (Greek) Christian

Cristian (Greek) form of
Christian: follower of Christ
Kristian

Cristino (Greek) christian

Cristo (Spanish) mountain of
Christ
Kristo

Cristobal (Spanish) bearing Christ

Cristovo (Greek) serves Christ

Criten (American) form of of
Critendon: critical
Critan, Kriten

Critendon (Last name as first
name) critical
Crit, Criten, Krit, Kritendon

Crofton (Irish) comforter
Croft, Croften

Crolley (English) Last name used
as first name

Cromaci (Greek) decorated

Cromer (English) adorned

Crompton (Last name as first
name) giving

Cromwell (Irish) giving
Chromwell, Crom, Crommie

Cronin (German) timely

Cronus (Greek) reigning

Croom (American) giving

Crosby (Irish) easygoing
*Crosbee, Crosbie, Cross, Krosbie,
Krosby*

Crosson (English) of the cross

Croston (English) by the cross
Cro, Croton, Kroston

Croswell (English) cross on the
well

Crosy (American) of the cross

Crosz (American) of the cross

Crothers (Scottish) Last name
used as first name

Crow (English) crow

Crowson (English) son of Crow

Crue (American) form of Crew:
word as name; sailor

Cruo (Spanish) cross

Crutcher (English) fighter

Cruz (Spanish) cross

Cruze (Spanish) cross
Cruise, Cruse, Kruise, Kruze

Cruzon (Spanish) cross

Csaba (Hungarian) shepherd

Ctirad (Czech) long-suffering

Cuauhtemoc (Spanish) eagle

Cuba (Place name) distinctive;
spicy
Cubah, Cueba, Kueba, Kuba

Cubbenah (African) Wednesday

Cubby (American) child

Cucuta (Place name) city in
North Colombia; sharp
Cucu

Cudjo (Jamaican) Monday

Cuelly (American) wild spirit

Cuernavaca (Place name) city
in Mexico; cow horn
Vaca

Cuffy (Jamaican) Friday
Cuffee, Cuffey

Cuke (American) zany
Kook, Kooky, Kuke

Culber (American) woods child

Culbert (Last name as first name)
practical

Culkin (American) child actor
Culki, Kulkin

Cull (American) selective
Cullee, Cullie, Cully, Kulley

Cullen (Irish) attractive
*Culen, Cull, Cullan, Cullen,
Cullie, Cully, Kullen, Kully*

Culley (Irish) secretive
Cull, Cullie, Cully, Kull, Kully

Cullom (American) wood

Culver (English) peaceful
Colver, Cull, Culley, Culli, Cully

Culverado (American) peaceful
Cull, Cullan, Culver, Culvey, Kull

Cumal (Native American) thunders

Cummings (Literature) for the
poet E.E. Cummings; innovative
Cumming, Kummings

Cuney (Last name as first name) serious
Cune, Kune, Kuney

Cuneyt (Scandinavian) warmth

Cunning (Irish) from surname Cunningham; wholesome
Cuning

Cunningham (Irish) milk-pail town; practical
Cuningham

Cupid (Latin) heart's desire

Curb (American) dynamic
Kurb

Curbey (American) form of Kirby: brilliant
Curby

Curbow (Last name used as first name) stone

Curer (French) helps

Curgus (Greek) cunning

Curie (French) innovator

Curley (American) cowboy
Curly, Kurly

Curo (Spanish) sheltered

Curran (Irish) smiling hero
Curan, Curr, Curren, Currey, Currie, Curt

Currere (French) sheltered

Currey (English) messenger; calm

Currie (English) messenger; courteous
Kurrie

Curro (Spanish) form of Curtis: gracious; kindhearted

Curt (French) form of Curtis: gracious; kindhearted
Kurt

Curtis (French) gracious; kindhearted
Curdi, Curdis, Curt, Curtey, Curtice, Curtie, Curtiss, Curty, Kurt

Cush (American) thrives

Custer (Last name as first name) watchful; stubborn
Cust, Kust, Kuster

Cuthah (Biblical) place name

Cuthbert (English) intelligent

Cutle (English) makes knives

Cutler (English) wily
Cutlar, Cutlur, Cuttie, Cutty

Cutlon (English) knife maker

Cutrer (French) knife dealer

Cutsy (English) form of Cutler: wily
Cutlar, Cuttie, Cutty, Kutsee, Kutsi, Kutsy

Cutter (English) man who cuts gemstones

Cuttino (African American) athletic
Kuttino

Cuyler (American) form of Schuyler: protective
Kuyler

Cy (Greek) shining example
Cye, Si

Cybor (American) leader

Cygan (Last name used as first name) shines

Cyler (Irish) protective chapel
Cuyler, Cyle

Cyll (American) bright
Cyl, Syll

Cynric (Greek) thorn

Cyone (Greek) whirlwind

Cyprien (French) religious
Cyp, Cyprian

Cyprus (Place name) island south of Turkey; outgoing

Cyrano (Greek) shy heart
Cyranoh, Cyre, Cyrie, Cyrno, Cyry

Cyree (Greek) Lord

Cyril (Greek) regal
Ciril, Cyral, Cyrell, Cyrille

Cyrilon (Spanish) lofty

Cyrus (Persian) sunny
Cye, Syrus

Cyrx (American) conniving
Cyrxie

Czech (Slavic) Czech

Czeslaw (Polish) honorable
Slav, Slavek

Dablo (Spanish) form of Diablo:
devil

Dabney (English) careful; funny
Dab, Dabnee, Dabnie, Dabny

Dabriel (American) teaches

Dacey (Irish) southerner
Dace, Dacian, Dacius, Dacy,
Daicey, Daicy

Dacga (Slavic) emotional

Dachary (English) form of
Dachry: stream

Dache (Latin) audacious

Dachry (English) stream

Dacias (Latin) brash
Dace, Daceas, Dacey, Dacy, Dayce,
Daycie

Dacko (American) zany

Dacosta (Italian) from the coast

Dacus (Last name used as first
name)

Dada (African) curly-haired

Dade (Place name) county in
Florida; renegade
Daide, Dayde

Dadean (English) curly

Dadley (English) curly

Daedalus (Greek) father of
Icarus; inventor
Daidalos, Dedalus

Dag (Scandinavian) sunny
Dagg, Dagget, Daggett, Dagny

Dagan (Hebrew) earthy
Dagon

Dagfinn (Scandinavian) sunshine

Daggan (Scandinavian) day

Daggs (Scandinavian) day

Dagny (Scandinavian) day
Dag

Dagoberto (Spanish) day
Dagbert, Dagobert

Dagwood (English) comic
Dag, Dawood, Woody

Dahryan (Indian) compassionate

Dahy (Irish) lithe
Dahey

Dai (Japanese) great man

Daigle (Last name used as first
name) dark

Daiki (Japanese) shining

Dailey (English) form of Dale:
valley
Daily, Daley, Daly

Dain (Scandinavian) from Denmark

Dainard (Irish) loved
Dainehard, Dainhard, Daneard,
Daneardt, Danehard, Danehardt,
Daynard

Dairus (Invented) daring
Daras, Dares, Darus

Daithi (Irish) speedy

Daivat (Hindi) powerful man

Dakarai (African) happy
Dakarrai, Dakk

Dako (American) form of Dakota:
friendly

Dakota (Native American) friendly
Daccota, Dack, Dak, Dakoda,
Dakodah, Dakoetah, Dakotah,
Dekota, Dekohta, Dekowta, Kota

Dakote (Place name) from the
Dakotas
Dako

Dalai (Indian) peaceful
Dalee

Dalanee (Invented) form of
Delaney: challenging
Dalaney, Dalani

Dalbert (English) man who lives
in the valley
Del, Delbert

Dalcher (Last name used as first
name) gathers

Dale (English) valley
Dail, Daile, Daley, Dallan, Dalle,
Dallin, Day, Dayl, Dayle

Dalen (English) up-and-coming
Dalan, Dalin, Dallen, Dallin,
Dalyn

Daley (Irish) organized
Dailey, Daily, Dale

Dalgienuz (Slavic) valor

Dalgus (American) loving the
outdoors

Dalhart (Place name) city in Texas
Dal

Dalin (Spanish) proud

Dallard (English) proud

Dallas (Place name) good old
boy; city in Texas
Dal, Dall, Dalles, Dallice, Dallis,
Dallus, Delles

Dallin (English) valley-born; fine
Dal, Dallan, Dallen, Dallon

Dallin (American) form of Dylan:
sea god; creative

Dalphy (French) dolphin

Dalsten (English) smart
Dal, Dalston

Dalt (English) abundant
Dall, Daltey, Daltt

Dalton (English) farmer
Daleton, Dall, Dallton, Daltan,
Dalten

Daltrey (English) high river

Dalvis (Invented) form of Elvis:
all-wise
Dal, Dalves, Dalvus, Dalvy

Daly (Irish) together
Daley, Dawley

Dalziel (Scottish) from the field

Damacio (Spanish) calm; tamed
Damas, Damasio, Damaso, Damazio

Damarcus (African American)
confident
D'Marcus, Damarkes, Damarkus,
Demarcus

Damare (Greek) form of
Damario: tamer of wild things

Damari (Greek) gentle

Damario (Spanish) tamer of wild
things
Damarios, Damarius, Damaro,
Damero

Damarion (Greek) form of
Damario: tamer of wild things

Damary (Greek) tame
Damaree, Damarie

Damascus (Place name) capital
of Syria; dramatic
Damas, Damask

Damaskenos (Greek) form of
Damascus: dramatic
Damaskinos

Damaso (Spanish) taming
Damas

Damean (American) form of
Damian: fate
Dama, Daman, Damas, Damea

Dameetre (Invented) form of
Dimitri: fertile; flourishing

Damek (Czech) earth
Adamec, Adamek, Adamik,
Adamok, Adha, Damick, Damicke

Dameone (Greek) form of
Damian: fate

Dameron (American) form of
Cameron: mischievous; crooked
nose

Damian (Greek) fate
Daemon, Daimen, Daimon,
Daman, Dame, Damean, Damen,
Dameon, Damey, Damiano,
Damianos, Damianus, Damien,
Damion, Damon, Damyan,
Damyean, Damyen, Damyon,
Damyun, Dayman, Daymian,
Daymon, Demyan

Damiko (Slavic) gentle

Damin (Greek) comforts

Damon (Greek) dramatic; spirited
Damonn, Damyn

Damron (Greek) comforts

Damyi (American) comforts

Dan (Hebrew) form of Daniel:
judged by God; spiritual
Dahn, Dannie, Danny

Dana (Scandinavian) light-haired
Danah, Dane, Danie, Dayna

Danar (English) from Denmark;
dry

Danaus (Mythology) king of Argos
Denaus, Dinaus

Dand (Scottish) form of Andrew: manly and brave

Dandin (Hindi) holy man

Dandre (American) light
Aiondrae, Dan, Dandrae, Dandray, DeAndrae, DeAndray

Dandrer (French) form of Dandre: light

Dandridge (English) Last name used as first name

Dandy (Hindi) form of Dandin: holy man

Dane (English) man from Denmark; light
Dain, Daine, Daney, Danie, Danyn, Dayne, Dhane

Daneck (American) well-liked
Danek, Danick, Danik, Danike, Dannick

Danel (Hebrew) God judges

Danely (Scandinavian) Danish
Dainely, Daynelee

Danerin (Slavic) giving

Danez (English) helpful

Danfer (Slavic) faithful

Danford (English) place name; the way or ford of the Danes

Dang (Vietnamese) worthy

Dangelle (Italian) angelic

Dangelo (Italian) angelic
Danjelo

Danger (American) dangerous
Dang, Dange, Dangery

Danial (Hebrew) form of Daniel: judged by God; spiritual

Daniel ✡ ❶ (Hebrew) judged by God; spiritual
Da, Danal, Dane, Daneal, Danek, Dani, Danial, Daniele, Danil, Danilo, Danko, Dann, Dannel, Danney, Danni, Dannie, Danniel, Danny, Danyal, Danyel, Danyell, Danyyell, Deiniol

Danilo (Slavic) form of Daniel: judged by God; spiritual

Danilon (Slavic) form of Daniel: judged by God; spiritual

Danne (Biblical) form of Daniel: judged by God; spiritual
Dann

Danner (Last name as first name) rescued by God
Dan, Dann, Danny

Danno (Hebrew) kind
Dannoh, Dano

Danny (Hebrew) form of Daniel: judged by God; spiritual
Dan, Dann, Dannee, Danney, Danni, Dannie

Danon (French) remembered
Danen, Danhann, Dannon, Danton

Danron (American) combo of Dan and Ron

Dante (Latin) enduring
Dan, Danne, Dantae, Dantay, Dantey, Dauntay, Dayntay, Dontae, Dontay, Donté

Danter (Latin) form of Dante: enduring

Dantin (American) form of Daniel: judged by God; spiritual

Danton (Last name as first name) Dan's town

Dantre (African American) faithful
Dantrae, Dantray, Dantrey, Dantri, Dantry, Don, Dont, Dontre, Dontrey, Dontri

Dantrell (African American) spunky
Dantrele, Dantrill, Dantrille

Dantzler (American) form of Daniel: judged by God; spiritual

Danube (Place name) flowing; river
Dannube, Danuube, Donau

Danut (Slavic) form of Dan: judged by God; spiritual

Danyo (Hebrew) form of Daniel: judged by God; spiritual

Danza (English) form of Denzel: sensual

Daphnis (Greek) attractive

Daquan (African American) rambunctious
Dakwan, Daquanne, Dekwan, Dekwohn, Dekwohnne, Dequan, Dequanne

Dar (English) deerlike

Darb (Irish) form of Darby: free spirit

Darbrie (Irish) free man; lighthearted
Dar, Darb, Darbree, Darbry

Darby (Irish) free spirit
Dar, Darb, Darbee, Darbey, Darbie, Darre, Derby

Darce (Irish) dark
D'Arcy, Darcy, Dars, Darsy

Darcel (French) dark
Dar, Darce, Darcelle, Darcey, Darcy, Darsy

Darcell (Irish) dark hair

Darcus (Irish) dark hair

Darcy (French) slow-moving
Darce, Darse, Darsey, Darsy

Dard (Greek) clever

Dardanos (Greek) adored
Dar, Dardanio, Dardanios, Dardanus

Darhen (American) form of Darwin: dearest friend

Darian (American) inventive
Dari, Darien, Darion, Darrian, Darrien, Darrion, Derreynn

Darin (Irish) great
Daren, Darren, Darrie, Daryn

Dario (Spanish) rich
Darioh, Darrey

Darion (Irish) great potential
Dare, Darien, Darrion, Daryun

Daris (Greek) form of Darius: affluent

Darius (Greek) affluent
Dare, Dareas, Dareus, Darias, Dariess, Dario, Darious, Darrius, Derrius, Derry

Darji (American) rich

Dark (Slavic) form of Darko: macho
Dar, Darc

Darkell (English) brunette

Darko (Slavic) macho
Dark

Darko (English) brunette

Darlen (American) darling
Darlan, Darlun

Darman (English) hidden

Darnell (English) secretive
Dar, Darn, Darnall, Darnel, Darnie, Darny

Darnley (English) sly

Darold (American) clever
Dare, Darrold, Darroll, Derold

Daron (Irish) great
Darren, Dayron

Daros (Greek) loved

Darr (English) loved

Darrah (Irish) dark
Darach, Darragh

Darrel (Aboriginal) blue sky
Darral, Darrell, Darrill, Darrol, Darroll, Darry, Darryl, Darryll, Daryl, Derrel, Derrell, Derril, Derrill, Deryl, Deryll

Darrell (French) loved man
Darel, Darol, Darrel, Darrey, Daryl, Derrel, Derrell

Darren (Irish) great
Daren, Darin, Daron, Darran, Darrin, Darring, Darron, Darryn, Derrin, Derron, Derry

Darrett (American) form of Garrett: brave; watchful
Dare, Darry

Darrick (American) form of Derrick: bold heart

Darrien (Greek) with riches
Darian, Darion, Darrian, Darrion, Darryan, Darryen

Darrien (Irish) greatness

Darris (Greek) rich

Darrti (American) fast; deer
Dart, Darrt

Darryl (French) darling man
Darrie, Daryl, Derrie, Deryl, Deryll

Darshak (Sanskrit) insight

Darshan (African American) pious

Dart (English) decisive
Darte, Dartt

D'Artagnan (French) leader; ostentatious

Darton (English) swift; deer

Darty (American) Last name as first name

Darvin (English) friendship

Darwin (English) dearest friend
Dar, Darwen, Darwinne, Darwon, Darwyn, Derwin, Derwynn

Daryn (American) form of Darin: great
Darynn, Deryn

Darynth (English) form of Darren: great

Dash (American) speedy; dashing
Dashy

Dashawn (African American) unusual
Dashaun, Deshaun, Deshawn, D'Sean, D'Shawn

Dashell (African American) dashing
Dashiell

Dasher (American) dashing; fast
Dash

Dashiell (English) from author Dashiell Hammett

Dasno (Latin) royal

Dassinger (Last name as first name)

Dathan (Biblical) fountain of hope

Dauer (Last name as first name)

Daufen (French) dolphin

Dault (English) valley boy

Davao (Place name) city in the Philippines; exotic
Davo

Dave (Hebrew) form of David: beloved
Davey, Davi, Davie, Davy

Daven (American) dashing
Davan

Davender (Hebrew) form of David: beloved

Davenport (Last name as first name) of the old school; sea-loving

Davey (Hebrew) form of David: beloved
Dave, Davee, Davi, Davie, Davy

Davian (Hebrew) dear one
Daivian, Daivyan, Daveon, Davien, Davion, Davyan, Davyen, Davyon

David ☼ ❶ (Hebrew) beloved
Daffy, Daffyd, Dafydd, Dai, Davad, Dave, Daved, Davee, Daven, Davey, Davi, Davide, Davie, Davies, Davin, Davis, Davon, Davy, Davyd, Davydd

Davidpaul (American) beloved
David-Paul

Davidson (English) son of David
Davidsen, Davison

Davik (Slavic) form of David: beloved

Davin (Scandinavian) smart
Dave, Daven, Dayven

Davinal (American) form of David: beloved

Davinno (English) bright

Davins (American) form of David: beloved
Davens

Davion (American) form of David: beloved

Davis (Welsh) David's son; heart's child
Dave, Daves, Davidson, Davies, Davison, Daviss, Davy

Davon (American) sweet
Davaughan, Davaughn, Dave, Davone, Devon

Davonnae (African American) form of David: beloved
Davawnae, Davonae

Davonne (American) form of Davin: smart

Davonte (African American) energetic
Davontay, Devonta, D'Vontay

Daw (English) quiet
Dawe, Dawes

Dawber (Last name as first name) funny
Daw, Dawb, Dawbee, Dawbey, Dawby, Daws

Dawes (Last name used as first name) form of David: beloved

Dawk (American) spirited
Dawkins

Dawkins (Last name used as first name) form of David: beloved

Daws (English) dedicated
Daw, Dawsen, Dawz

Dawson (English) David's son; loved
Daw, Dawe, Dawes, Dawsan, Dawse, Dawsen, Dawsey, Dawsin

Dax (French) unique; water-loving
Dacks, Daxie

Day (English) calm
Daye

Dayanand (Hindi) a loving man

Dayman (Greek) form of Damon: dramatic; spirited

Daymond (Invented) compassionate

Dayt (Last name used as first name) day

Dayton (English) the town of David; planner
Daeton, Day, Daye, Daytan, Daytawn, Dayten, Deytawn, Deyton

Dazh (Slavic) giver

Dazo (American) form of David: beloved

Dazon (American) form of David: beloved

Deacon (Greek) giving
Deakin, Decon, Deecon, Deekon, Dekawn, Deke, Dekie, Dekon, Diakonos

Deadon (French) form of Dieudonne: loves a gracious God

Deagan (Last name as first name) capable
Degan

Deak (American) form of Richard: wealthy leader

Dean (English) leader
Deane, Deanie, Deany, Deen, Dene, Deyn, Dino

DeAndré (African American) very masculine
DeAndrae, D'André, DeAndray, Diandray, Diondrae, Diondray

Deangelo (Italian) sweet; personable; angelic
Dang, Dange, DeAngelo, D'Angelo, Deanjelo, Deeanjelo, DiAngelo, Di-Angelo

Deans (English) sylvan; valley
Dean, Deaney, Deanie

Deanthony (African American) rambunctious
Deanthe, Deanthoney, Deanthonie, Deeanthie, Dianth

Deanza (Spanish) smooth
Denza

Dearborn (Last name as first name) endearing; kind from birth
Dearbourn, Dearburne, Deerborn

Dearing (Last name as first name) endearing
Dear

Dearmon (Last name used as first name) man of deer

Dearon (American) dear one
Dear

Deason (Invented) cocky
Deace, Deas, Dease, Deasen, Deasun

Debdan (Indian) God's gift

Debonair (French) with a beautiful air; elegant and cultured
Debonaire, Debonnair, Debonnaire

Debrum (Czech) kindness

Debythis (African American) strange
Debiathes

Decatur (Place name) city in Illinois; special
Dec, Decatar, Decater, Deck

Deccan (Place name) region in India; scholar
Dec, Dek

Decimus (Latin) tenth child
Decio

Deck (Irish) form of Declan: strong; prayerful
Decky

Declan (Irish) strong; prayerful
Dec, Deck, Dek, Deklan, Deklon

Dedal (Greek) artistic

Dedan (Indian) form of Deodan: serving God

Deddrick (American) form of Dedric: leader
Dead, Dedric, Dedrick, Dedrik, Dietrich

Dedeaux (French) sweet
Dede, Dee

Dederic (American) substance

Dedlus (Greek) industrious

Dedric (German) leader
Dedrick, Deidrich

Dee (American) form of names that start with D
D, De

Deek (American) form of Deacon: giving
Deke

Deeley (Irish) assembly

Deems (English) merits

Deepak (Sanskrit) light of knowledge
Depak, Depakk, Dipak

Dees (Slavic) desires

Deeter (American) friendly
Deter

DeForest (French) of the forest
Defforest

DeFoy (French) child of Foy
Defoy, Defoye

Degner (Slavic) of the day

Degraf (French) child of Graf
DeGraf

Dehlin (American) form of Dylan: sea god; creative

Deicy (Latin) God-loving

Deidric (German) rules

Deidrich (German) leader
Dedric, Dedrick, Deed, Deide, Deidrick, Diedrich

Deinol (Greek) form of Daniel: judged by God; spiritual

Deinorus (African American) vigorous
Denorius, Denorus

Deion (Greek) form of Dion: joyous celebrant; god of wine
Dee

Dejanee (Slavic) action-oriented

Dejuan (African American) talkative
Dajuan, Dajuwan, Dejuane, Dejuwan, Dewaan, Dewan, Dewaughan, Dewon, Dewonn, Dewuan, Dwon, Dwonn, Dwonne

Dejuon (American) form of Dejuan: talkative

Deke (Hebrew) form of Dekel: palm tree
Deek

Dekel (Hebrew) palm tree

Del (English) valley; laid-back and helpful
Dail, Dell, Delle

DeLane (Irish) form of Delaney: challenging

Delaney (Irish) challenging
Del, Delaine, Delainey, Delainie, Delane, Delanie, Delany, Dell

Delano (Irish) dark
Del, Delaynoh, Dell

Delanoy (Irish) darkness

Delayme (American) form of Delaney: challenging

Delber (English) daylight

Delbert (English) sunny
Bert, Bertie, Berty, Dalbert, Del, Delburt, Dell, Dilbert

Deleon (Spanish) Last name used as first name

Delete (Origin unknown) ordinary
Delette

Delfino (Spanish) dolphin; sea-loving
Define, Fino

Delgado (Spanish) slim

Delin (English) of the sea

Delius (Greek) from the island Delos
Deli, Delia, Delios, Delos

Delk (American) celebrant

Dell (English) from the country; sparkles

Delley (Scandinavian) fascinates

Dellin (Scandinavian) fascinates

Delling (Norse) shines

Delm (Scandinavian) charismatic

Delman (French) from the mountain

Delmar (Last name as first name) friendly
Delm

Delmer (American) country
Del, Delmar, Delmir

Delmis (Spanish) friend
Del, Delms

Delmore (French) seagoing
Del, Delmar, Delmer, Delmor, Delmoor, Delmoore

Delmy (American) form of Delmore: seagoing
Delmi

Delp (Indian) form of Dilip: protests; royal

Delphin (French) dolphin
Delfin, Delfino, Delfinos, Delfinus, Delphino, Delphinos, Delphinus, Delvin

Delrin (English) of the dell

Delroy (French) royal; special
Del, Dell, Dellroy, Delroi, Roi, Roy

Delsen (Native American) of a just God

Delsi (American) easygoing
Delci, Delcie, Dels, Delsee, Delsey, Delsy

Delt (American) fraternity boy
Delta

Delton (English) friend
Delt, Deltan, Delten

DeLuca (Italian) lucky

Delvan (English) form of Delwin: companion
Del, Dell, Delly, Delven, Delvin, Delvun, Delvyn

Delvern (English) proud

Delvie (English) proud

Delwin (English) companion
Dalwin, Dalwyn, Delavan, Delevan, Dellwin, Delwen, Delwins, Delwince, Delwinse, Delwy, Delwyn

Deman (Dutch) man

Demarco (Italian) daring
Deemarko, Demarkoe, Demie, Demmy, Dimarco, D'Marco

Demarcus (American) zany; royal
Damarcus, DaMarkiss, DeMarco, DeMarcus, Demarkes, Demarkess, DeMarko, DeMarkus, Demarkus, DeMarquess, DeMarquez, Demarquiss, DeMarquiss

Demario (Italian) bold
Demarioh, Demarrio, Demie, Demmy, Dimario, D'Mareo, D'Mario

Demarion (American) combo of De and Marion

Demarques (African American) son of Marques; noble
Demark, Demarkes, Demarquis, Demmy

Demarris (American) combo of De and Marris; loud

Demas (Greek) well-liked
Dimas

Dement (French) mountain

Demesio (Italian) treacherous

Demete (American) form of Demetrius: follower of Demeter
Deme, Demetay

Demetrice (Greek) form of Demetrius: follower of Demeter

Demetrick (African American) earthy
Demetrik, Demi, Demitrick

Demetrios (Greek) earth-loving
Demeetrius, Demetreus, Demetri, Demetrious, Demetris, Demi, Demie

Demetrius (Greek) follower of Demeter
Dametrius, Dem, Demetri, Demetrice, Demetris, Demitrios, Demmy, Demos, Dhimitrios, Dimetre, Dimitri, Dimitrios, Dimitrious, Dimitry, Dmitri, Dmitrios, Dmitry

Demian (Slavic) form of Damian: fate

Demin (Spanish) form of Demos: of the people

Deming (English) form of Demos: of the people

Demitree (American) form of Dimitri: fertile; flourishing

Demitri (Greek) fertile; earthy
Demetrie, Demetry, Demi, Demie, Demitry, Dmitri

Democri (Greek) judges

Demond (African American) worldly
Demonde

Demondre (American) of the world

Demos (Greek) of the people
Demas, Demmos

Demosthenes (Greek) orator; eloquent
Demos

Demps (Irish) form of Dempsey: respected; judge
Demps, Dempse, Dempz

Dempsey (Irish) respected; judge
Dem, Demi, Demps, Dempsie, Dempsy

Den (Greek) form of Dennis: reveler

Denali (Hindi) great

Denard (Last name as first name) envied
Den, Denar, Denarde, Denny

Denby (Scandinavian) adventurous
Danby, Denbee, Denbey, Denbie, Denney, Dennie, Denny

Dene (Hungarian) reveler

Deneki (Slavic) star of the day

Denham (Scandinavian) hamlet of Danes

Denholm (Scandinavian) house of Danes

Deni (English) form of Dionysius: joyous celebrant; god of wine
Denni

Denim (French) cotton fabric

Denk (American) sporty
Denky, Dink

Denley (English) dark
Denlie, Denly

Denman (English) dark; valley-dweller
Den, Deni, Denmin, Denney, Denni, Dennie, Dennman, Denny, Dinman

Denmark (Place name) from Denmark

Dennar (English) valley boy

Dennard (English) valley boy

Dennell (English) valley boy

Dennis (Greek) reveler
Den, Denes, Deni, Denies, Denis, Deniss, Dennes, Dennet, Denney, Denni, Dennie, Dennies, Dennison, Denniz, Denny, Dennys, Deno, Denys, Deon, Dino, Dion, Dionisio, Dionysius, Dionysus, Diot

Dennisen (English) Dennis's son; partier
Den, Denison, Dennison, Dennizon, Dennyson, Tennyson

Denno (Greek) form of Dennis: reveler

Denny (Greek) form of Dennis: reveler

Den, Denee, Deni, Denney, Denni

Denoy (Greek) form of Dennis: reveler

Densey (English) place name

Dent (American) form of Denzel: sensual

Denton (English) valley settlement; happy

Denny, Dent, Dentan, Denten, Dentie, Dentin

Denver (Place name) capital of Colorado; climber

Den, Denny

Denzel (English) sensual

Den, Denny, Densie, Denz, Denze, Denzell, Denzelle, Denziel, Denzil, Denzill, Denzille, Denzyl, Denzylle, Dinzie

Denzie (English) place name

Deo (Sanskrit) God

Deodan (Latin) serving God

Deodar (Sanskrit) cedar

Deondray (African American) romantic

Deandre, Deeon, Deondrae, Deondrey, Deone

Deone (Greek) form of Dionysius: joyous celebrant; god of wine

Deion, Deonah, Deonne, Dion

Deonnetaye (American) extrovert

Deonté (French) outgoing

De'On, Deontae, Deontay, Deontie, Diontay, Diontayye

Deordre (African American) outgoing

Deordray

Depp (American) dashing

Dep

Derby (Irish) guileless

Derbey, Derbie

Derek (German) ruler; bold heart

Darrick, Darriq, Derak, Dere, Dereck, Deric, Derick, Derik, Deriq, Deriqk, Derk, Derreck, Derrek, Derrick, Derrik, Derryck, Derryk, Deryk, Deryke, Dirk, Dirke, Dyrk

Derenzo (Italian) form of Darren: great

Derett (American) form of Derrick: bold heart

Derlam (American) form of Derlin; form of Derland: from the land of deer

Derland (English) from the land of deer

Durland

Derlin (English) from the land of deer

Derl, Derlan, Derlen, Derlyn, Durland, Durlin

Dermod (Irish) form of Dermot: unabashed; giving

Dermud

Dermond (Irish) unassuming

Dermon, Dermun, Dermund, Derr

Dermot (Irish) unabashed; giving

Der, Dermod, Dermott, Derree, Derrey, Derri, Diarmid, Diarmuid

Dern (Hebrew) form of Deron: smart

Deron (African American) form of Darren: smart

Dare, Daron, DaRon, Darone, Darron, Dayron, Dere, DeRronn

Deronce (American) form of Direnc: resistance

Derrell (French) form of Darrell: loved

Dere, Derrel, Derrill

Derrence (American) form of Direnc: resistance

Derrett (French) form of Darren: great

Derri (American) breezy

Derree, Derry

Derrick (German) bold heart

Derak, Derick

Derry (Irish) red-haired
Dare, Darry, Derrey, Derri, Derrie

Dervando (Italian) friend

Derward (Last name as first
name) clunky
Der, Derr, Derwy, Dur, Durr, Ward

Derwent (Last name as first
name) of deer

Derwin (English) bookish
*Darwin, Darwyn, Derwyn,
Derwynn, Durwen, Durwin*

Derya (Slavic) from the ocean

Des (Irish) form of Desmond:
from Munster

Desaro (Spanish) desired

Deseo (Spanish) desire
Des, Desi, Dezi

Deshan (Hindi) patriot
Deshad, Deshal

Deshawn (African American)
brassy
*Dashaun, Dashawn, Desean,
Deshaun, Deshaune, Deshawnn,
Deshon, D'Sean, D'Shawn*

Deshea (American) confident
Desh, DeShay, Deshay, Deshie

Deshon (African American) bold;
open
Desh, Deshan, Deshann

Desi (Latin) form of Desmond:
from Munster; form of Desiderio:
yearning; sorrow; desired

Desiderio (Latin) yearning;
sorrow; desired
*Deri, Derito, Des, Desi,
Desideratus, Desiderios, Desiderius,
Desie, Diderot, Didier, Dizier*

Desidoro (Spanish) desirable

Desire (American) desirable
Des, Desi, Desidero

Desley (American) form of
Lesley: strong-willed

Desmee (Irish) form of
Desmond: from Munster
*Desi, Desmey, Dessy, Dezme,
Dezmee, Dezmie, Dezmo, Dezzy*

Desmond (Irish) from Munster
*Des, Desi, Desmon, Desmund,
Dezmond, Dizmond*

Desmondae (Irish) loyal
Irishman

Desmun (Irish) form of
Desmond: from Munster
Dez, Dezmund

Desoto (Spanish) explores

Desperado (Spanish) renegade
Des, Desesperado, Dessy, Dezzy

Dessles (African) happy

Destin (Place name) city in
Florida; destiny; fate
Desten, Destie, Deston, Destrie

Detleff (Germanic) decisive
Detlef, Detlev

Detler (German) decides

Detrick (German) rules

Detries (German) form of
Dedric: leader

Detroy (African American)
outgoing
Detroe

Detry (German) rules

Detton (Last name as first name)
determined
Deet, Dett

Deuce (American) two in cards;
second child
Doos, Duz

DeUndre (African American)
child of Undre
Deundrae, DeUndray, Deundry

Deuter (German) warrior

Dev (Irish) form of Devlin:
fearless
Deb, Deo

Deval (Hindi) godlike
Deven

Devann (American) divine child
DeVanne, Deven

Devaughan (American) bravado
Devan, Devaughn, Devonne

Devdan (Hindi) God's gift
Debdan, Deodan

Devend (Indian) from Hindu
god Indra Devendra

Devender (American) poetic
Devander, Deven, Devendar

Dever (American) generous

Deverell (American) special
*Dev, Devee, Deverel, Deverelle,
Devie, Devy*

Devereux (French surname)
divine
Deveraux

Deverges (French) diverges

Devin ✪ (Irish) poetic; writer
*Dev, Devan, Deven, Devinn,
Devon, Devvy, Devyn, Devynn*

Devine (Latin) divine
Dev, Devinne

Devinson (Irish) poetic
*Davin, Dev, Devan, Devee, Deven,
Devy*

Devland (Irish) courageous
Dev, Devlend, Devlind, Devvy

Devlin (Irish) fearless
*Devlan, Devlen, Devlon, Devlyn,
Devy*

Devo (American) quirky; fun
Divo

Devoe (French) Last name used as
first name; lives near beautiful valley

Devon (Irish) writer
*Deavon, Dev, Deven, Devin,
Devohne, Devond, Devonn, Devy,
Devyn*

Devonte (African American)
form of writer
Devontae, Devontay

Devroy (French) God as royalty

Dew (English) word as name

Dewalt (Last name as first name)

Dewan (American) form of
Dejuan: talkative
Dewey

Deward (Spanish) holy

Deway (American) invented

Dewayne (American) spirited
*Dewain, Dewaine, Duwain,
Dwain*

Dewell (Last name as first name)

Dewey (Welsh) valued
Dew, Dewi, Dewie, Dewy, Duey

DeWhayne (American) form of
Dewayne: spirited

Dewitt (English) fair-haired
*Dewie, DeWitt, Dwight, Witt,
Wittie, Witty*

DeWittay (African American)
witty
Dewitt, DeWitt, Witt, Witty

Dewon (African American) clever
Dejuan, Dewan

Dex (Latin) form of Dexter:
skillful; right-handed
Dexe

Dexee (American) form of
Dexter: skillful; right-handed
Dex, Dexey, Dexi, Dexie

Dexter (Latin) skillful; right-handed
*Decster, Dex, Dext, Dextah,
Dextar, Dextor*

Dezi (Irish) form of Desi: from
Munster; yearning; sorrow; desired

Dhan (Indian) rich

Dhananjay (Indian) rich

Dhaval (Indian) purity

Dhiaa (African) winning

Dhillon (American) form of
Dillon: devoted

Dhrga (Indian) unreachable

Dhruv (Indian) star

Diablo (Spanish) devil

Dial (Word as name)

Diamon (American) luminous
Diamund, Dimon, Dimun

Diamond (English) bright; gem
Dimah, Dime, Dimond, Dimont

Diante (English) form of Deonte:
outgoing

Diarmid (Irish) happy for others' successes
Diarmaid, Diarmait, Diarmi

Diaz (Spanish) rowdy
Dias, Diazz

Dice (English) risk-taking
Dicey, Dies, Dize, Dyce, Dyse

Dick (German) form of Richard: wealthy leader
Dickey, Dicki, Dickie, Dicky, Dik

Dickens (Literature) for Charles Dickens; articulate

Dickinson (Last name as first name) poetic

Dickon (Last name as first name) strong king

Didier (French) desirable

Didionne (French) form of Didier: desirable

Diedrich (German) form of Dedric: leader
Dedrick, Deed, Died, Dietrich

Diego ✪ (Spanish) form of James: he who supplants
Dago, Deago, Deagoh, Dee, Diago

Dierkes (Scandinavian) rules

Dierks (Scandinavian) rules

Diesel (American) rugged
Dees, Deez, Desel, Dezsel, Diezel

Diet (German) form of Dedric: leader

Dieter (German) prepared
Dedrick, Deke, Derek, Detah, Deter, Diederick, Dirk

Dietmar (German) famous

Dieudonne (French) loves a gracious God

Digby (Irish) man of simplicity

Diggory (French) lost
Diggery, Diggorey, Digory

Diggs (Last name as first name)

Digna (Scandinavian) worthwhile

Digneo (Latin) worthwhile

Dijon (Place name) city in France; refined
Dejawn

Dilean (Irish) loyal

Dilip (Hindi) protests; royal
Duleep

Dill (Irish) faithful
Dillard, Dilly

Dilley (Irish) loyal

Dillion (Irish) form of Dillon: devoted

Dillon (Irish) devoted
Dill, Dillan, Dillen, Dilly, Dilon, Dylan, Dylanne, Dyllon, Dylon

Dimas (Spanish) frank

Dimitri (Russian) fertile; flourishing
Demetry, Demi, Demitri, Demitry, Dmitri

Dimitrios (Greek) earth-loving

Dimter (Last name used as first name) form of Dimitri: fertile; flourishing

Dinesh (Hindi) day Lord

Dingo (Animal) wild spirit

Dink (American) from *Dink, the Little Dinosaur* television series

Dino (Italian) form of Dean: leader
Dean, Deanie, Deano, Deinoh, Dinoh

Dinos (Greek) form of Constantine: proud
Dean, Dinohs, Dynos

Dinose (American) form of Dino: leader
Denoze, Dino, Dinoce, Dinoz, Dinoze

Dins (American) climber
Dinse, Dinz

Dinsdale (English) hill protector; innovator

Dinsmore (Irish) guarded
Dinnie, Dinnsmore, Dinny, Dins

Diogenes (Greek) honest man
Dee, Dioge, Dioh

Diogo (Spanish) form of Diego: he who supplants

Diohne (Greek) form of Dion: joyous celebrant; god of wine

Dion (Greek) form of Dionysius: joyous celebrant; god of wine
Deion, Deon, Deonn, Deonys, Deyon, Dio, Dionn

Dionel (Welsh) form of Daniel: judged by God; spiritual
Deinel

Dionisio (Spanish) form of Dionysius: joyous celebrant; god of wine
Dionis, Dioniso, Dionysio

Dionysus (Greek) joyous celebrant; god of wine
Dee, Deonysios, Dion, Dionio, Dioniso, Dionysios, Dionysius, Dionysos,

Diosdado (Spanish) wise; loves God

Direnc (Turkish) resistance

Direnzo (Italian) rules

Dirk (Scandinavian) leader
Derk, Dierck, Dieric, Dierick, Dirck, Dirke, Dirky, Durk,

Diron (American) form of Darin: great
Diran, Dirun, Dyronn

Dishan (Biblical) a threshing

Distan (American) invented

Diven (Last name as first name)

Divina (Spanish) divine

Dix (American) energetic
Dex

Dixen (English) jovial

Dixie (American) southerner
Dix, Dixee, Dixey, Dixi

Dixon (English) Dick's son; happy
Dickson, Dix, Dixie, Dixo

Dizon (Spanish) form of Dixon: Dick's son; happy

D'Marques (American) form of Demarco: daring

Doak (Scottish) St. Cadoc's servant

Doan (English) hills; quiet
Doane, Doe

Dobbs (English) fire

Dobes (American) unassuming
Dobe, Doe

Dobie (American) reliable; southern
Dobe, Dobee, Dobey, Dobi

Dobine (Slavic) goodness

Dobrin (Slavic) goodness

Dobro (Slavic) goodness

Dobromir (Polish) good
Dobe, Dobry, Doby

Dobry (Polish) good
Dobe, Dobree, Dobrey

Dobson (Slavic) goodness

Dodd (English) swaggering; has a small-town sheriff feel
Dod

Dodge (English) swaggering
Dod, Dodds, Dodgson

Dodgen (English) Last name as first name; son of Dodd or Dodda

Dodsworth (English) Last name as first name

Dody (Greek) God's gift
Doe

Dogan (English) Last name as first name

Doherty (Irish) rash
Docherty, Doh, Doughertey, Douherty

Dolan (Irish) dark
Dolen

Dolbin (American) dark

Dolce (Italian) sweet

Dolek (American) doleful

Dolen (Irish) dark

Dolgen (American) tenacious
Dole, Dolg, Dolgan, Dolgin

Dollester (Last name as first name) dark

Dollus (American) dark

Dolon (Irish) brunette
Dole, Dolen, Dolton

Dolph (German) form of Rudolph: wolf
Dolf, Dolfie, Dollfus, Dollfuss, Dollphus, Dolphus

Dolson (Last name as first name) son of Dolan; dark

Dom (Latin) form of Dominic:
child of the Lord; saint
Dome, Dommie, Dommy

Domaneke (Latin) loves the
Lord; dynamic

Domasz (Slavic) form of
Thomas: twin; look-a-like

Domenico (Italian) confident
Dom, Domeniko

Domero (Spanish) courageous

Dominador (Latin) seeks love

Domingo (Spanish) Sunday-born
boy
Demingo, Dom, Domin, Dominko

Dominic ☺ (Latin) child of the
Lord; saint
*Demenico, Demingo, Dom,
Domenic, Domenico, Domenique,
Domingo, Domini, Dominick,
Dominie, Dominik, Dominique,
Domino, Dominy, Nick*

Dominiel (American) form of
Dominic: child of the Lord; saint

Dominique (French) spiritual
*Dom, Dominick, Dominike,
Domminique*

Domino (Latin) winner
Domeno, Dominoh, Domuno

Domizio (Italian) form of
Dominic: child of the Lord; saint

Dommond (Latin) form of
Dominic: child of the Lord; saint

Domon (Latin) form of Dominic:
child of the Lord; saint

Domy (Italian) of the Lord

Don (Scottish) form of Donald:
world leader; powerful
*Dahn, Doni, Donn, Donney,
Donni, Donnie, Donny*

Donaciano (Spanish) dark
Dona, Donace, Donae, Donase

Donahue (Irish) fighter
Don, Donahoe, Donohue

Donald (Scottish) world leader;
powerful
*Don, Donal, Donaldo, Donall,
Donalt, Donaugh, Donel, Doneld,
Donelson, Donild, Donn, Donnel,
Donnell, Donney, Donni, Donnie,
Donny*

Donat (French) gives

Donatello (Italian) giving
*Don, Donatelo, Donetello, Donny,
Tello*

Donatien (French) generous
Don, Donatyen, Donn, Donnatyen

Donato (Italian) donates; giving

Donatus (Greek) giving

Donav (Irish) form of Donovan:
combative

Donaway (Last name as first name)

Donder (Dutch) thunder

Donegan (Last name as first name)

Dong (Chinese) from the east

Donker (African) modest

Donley (American) generous

Donnan (Irish) brown-haired;
popular

Donne (Irish) brave

Donnel (Irish) brave

Donnell (Irish) courageous
*Dahn, Don, Donel, Donell,
Donhelle, Donnie, Donny*

Donnelly (Irish) righteous
*Donalee, Donally, Donelli, Donely,
Donn, Donnell, Donnellie, Donnie*

Donnis (American) form of
Donald: world leader; powerful
Don, Donnes, Donnus

Donny (Irish) fond leader
Donney, Donni, Donnie

Donovan (Irish) combative
*Don, Donavan, Donavon,
Donavaughn, Donavyn, Donevin,
Donevon, Donivin, Donny,
Donoven, Donovon*

Dont (American) dark; giving
Don, Dontay

Dontae (African American)
capricious
Dontay, Donté

Dontave (African American) wild
spirit
Dontav, Donteve

Dontavious (African American)
giving
*Dantavius, Dawntavius,
Dewontavius*

Donté (Italian) lasting forever
*Dantae, Dantay, Dohntae, Dontae,
Dontay, Dontey*

Donton (American) confident
Don, Donnee, Dont, Dontie

Dontrell (African American)
jaded
*Dontray, Dontree, Dontrel,
Dontrelle, Dontrey, Dontrie,
Dontrill*

Donyale (African American)
regal; dark
Donyel, Donyelle

Donyell (African American) loyal
Danyel, Donny, Donyal

Donzell (African American) form
of Denzel: sensual
Dons, Donsell, Donz, Donzelle

Doocey (American) clever
Dooce, Doocee, Doocie, Doos

Dool (American) form of Dooley:
shy hero

Dooley (Irish) shy hero
Doolee, Dooli, Dooly

Dop (American) form of Dophy:
wise one

Dophy (French) wise one

Dor (Aboriginal) energetic
Doram, Doriel, Dorli

Doran (Irish) adventurer
*Dore, Dorian, Doron, Dorran,
Dorren*

Dorcel (French) fleet

Dore (Greek) form of Isidore:
special gift

Dorell (Scottish) brave

Dorgan (American) form of
Dragan: dragon

Dorian (Greek) the sea's child;
mysterious; youthful forever
*Dora, Dore, Dorean, Dorey,
Dorie, Dorien, Dorrian, Dorrien,
Dorryen, Dory*

Doriano (Spanish) thriving

Dorin (Romanian) form
of Dorian: the sea's child;
mysterious; youthful forever

Dorman (Last name as first
name) practical
Dor, Dorm

Dorn (Slavic) form of Dorin: the
sea's child; mysterious; youthful
forever

Doro (Greek) God's gift

Doron (Greek) unlimited passion
Doran, Doroni

Dorral (Last name as first name)
vain
Dorale, Dorry

Dorset (Place name) county in
England
Dorsett, Dorzet

Dorsey (French) sturdy as a
fortress
Dorsee, Dorsie

Dorum (American) form
of Dorian: the sea's child;
mysterious; youthful forever

Dorval (Irish) poet

Doss (Latin) wealthy

Dotan (African) hardworking
Dotann

Dothan (Biblical) obeys

Dotson (Last name as first name)
loquacious; son of Dot
Dotsen, Dottson

Doug (Scottish) form of Douglas:
powerful; dark river
Dougie, Dougy, Dug, Dugy

Dougal (Irish) dark
*Dougall, Doyle, Dugal, Dugald,
Dugall*

Douglas (Scottish) powerful;
dark river
Doug, Douggie, Dougie, Douglace,
Douglass, Douglis, Dugaid

Dougray (Irish) dwells by the
dark stream

Dov (Hebrew) bear

Dovan (Asian) village in
Himalayas (Nepal)

Dovie (American) peaceable
Dove, Dovee, Dovey, Dovi, Dovy

Dow (Irish) brunette
Dowan, Dowe, Dowson

Dowd (American) serious
Doud, Dowdy, Dowed

Dowden (Irish) dark

Dowding (American) dark

Dowell (Welsh) Last name as first
name; dark

Dowen (Irish) dark

Downie (American) form of
surname Downey

Dowrick (Last name as first name)

Dox (American) form of Dax:
unique; waterloving

Doxey (American) form of Dox:
unique; water-loving

Doy (American) form of Douglas:
powerful; dark river

Doyal (American) form of Doyle:
deep; dark
Doile, Doyl

Doyle (Irish) deep; dark
Doil, Doy, Doyal, Doye, Doyl

Doylton (Last name as first
name) pretentious
Doyl, Doyle

Dozier (German) Last name as
first name

Draco (Italian) dragon

Dracy (American) form of Stacey:
hopeful
Dra, Drace, Dracee, Dracey,
Draci, Drase, Drasee, Drasi

Dradell (American) serious
Drade, Dray

Dragan (Slavic) dragon

Drake (English) dragonlike; fire-
breathing
Drago, Drakie, Drako

Draper (English) precise; maker
of drapes
Draiper, Drape

Draphus (English) draper

Draven (American) capable; cool

Dravey (American) groovy
Dravee, Dravie, Dravy

Dravis (American) form of
Travis: conflicted

Dray (Hindi) ambient light

Dren (Scandinavian) courage

Drew (Welsh) wise; well-liked
Dru, Druw

Drexel (American) thoughtful
Drex

Drexie (American) thinker

Dries (Dutch) brave
Dre

Drigger (English) Last name as
first name

Driscoll (Irish) pensive
Driscol, Drisk, Driskell

Driver (English) driver

Dru (English) wise; popular
Drew, Drue

Drulon (English) adoring

Drummar (English) drums

Drummon (English) drums

Drummond (Scottish) practical
Drum, Drumon, Drumond

Drurius (American) form of
Darius: affluent

Drury (French) loving man
Drew, Drewry, Dru, Drure,
Drurey, Drurie

Dryden (English) writer; calm
Driden, Drydan, Drydin

Drystan (Welsh) form of Tristan:
sad; wistful
Drestan, Dristan, Drystyn

Dua (Arabic) prays

Dual (American) two

Duan (English) form of Dwayne: swarthy

Duane (Irish) dark man
Dewain, Dewayne, Duain, Duwain, Duwaine, Duwayne, Dwain, Dwaine, Dwayne

Duarte (Spanish) rich

Dub (Irish) form of Dublin: city in Ireland; trendy
Dubby

Dubai (Arabic) place name

Dubak (African) eleventh child

Dubi (Slavic) dark

Duble (Slavic) dark

Dublin (Place name) city in Ireland; trendy

Dubray (English) dark

Duc (Vietnamese) honest

Ducio (Italian) docile

Ducy (Spanish) leads

Dude (American) cool guy

Dudley (English) compromiser; rich; stuffy
Dud, Dudd, Dudlee, Dudlie, Dudly

Dueart (American) kind
Art, Duart, Due, Duey

Duff (Scottish) dark
Duf, Duffey, Duffie, Duffy

Duffin (Last name as first name) dark

DuFrane (French) of the frame

Dugal (Irish) dark

Dugan (Irish) dark man
Doogan, Dougan, Douggan, Duggan, Duggie, Duggy, Dugin

Dugar (French) dark

Dugas (French) dark

Duke (Latin) leader of the pack
Dook, Dukey, Dukie

Dulay (African) works cloth

Duleep (Indian) protects

Dulio (Italian) combative

Dulley (American) popular

Dumah (Biblical) in the mist

Dumas (French) Last name as first name

Dumisani (African) leader

Dumont (French) monumental
Dummont, Dumon, Dumonde, Dumonte, Dumontt

Dunbar (Irish) castle-dweller
Dunbarr

Dunbaron (American) dark
Baron, Dunbar

Duncall (American) form of Dunkle: handsome

Duncan (Scottish) spirited fighter
Dunc, Dunk, Dunkan, Dunn, Dunne

Dunce (English) hill

Dundee (Australian) spunky

Dune (English) word as name

Dunham (Last name as first name) dark

Dunia (American) dark
Dunya

Dunk (Scottish) form of Duncan: spirited fighter
Dunc, Dunk

Dunlap (Scottish) hill

Dunlavy (English) sylvan
Dunlave

Dunley (English) meadow-loving
Dunlea, Dunlee, Dunleigh, Dunli, Dunlie, Dunly, Dunnlea, Dunnleigh, Dunnley

Dunlop (English) sylvan

Dunmore (Scottish) guarded
Dun, Dunmohr, Dunmoore

Dunn (Irish) neutral
Dun, Dunne

Dunney (Scottish) hill

Dunnigan (Scottish) hill

Dunning (Scottish) hill

Dunnson (Scottish) son of Donald

Dunphy (American) dark; serious
Dun, Dunphe, Dunphee, Dunphey

Dunstan (English) well-girded
Dun, Duns, Dunse, Dunsten, Dunstin, Dunston

Dunstand (English) form of Dunstan: well-girded
Dunsce, Dunse, Dunst, Dunsten, Dunstun

Dupree (French) smooth

Durand (Latin) form of Durant: lasting; alluring
Duran, Durayn

Durango (Spanish) place name; Basque durango; fertile lowland surrounded by elevations

Durant (Latin) lasting; alluring
Dante, Duran, Durand, Durante, Durr, Durrie, Durry

Duray (American) endures

Durban (Place name) city in South Africa
Durb, Durben

Durbon (Last name as first name)

Duren (Latin) lasts

Durg (Hindi) out of reach

Durham (Last name as first name) supportive
Duram

Durke (American) form of Dirk: leader

Durmot (French) has no malice

Durnford (English) Last name as first name

Duro (Place name) palo Duro Canyon; enduring
Dure

Duron (American) form of Doran: adventurer

Durrell (English) protective
Durel, Durell, Durr, Durrel, Durry

Durward (English) gatekeeper

Durwin (English) dear friend
Derwin, Derwyn, Durwen, Durwinn, Durwyn

Durwood (English) vigilant; home-loving
Derrwood, Derwood, Durr, Durrwood, Durward, Durwould

Duryea (Hindi) invincible

Duskin (German) form of Dustin: bold and brave

Dusky (English) born at dusk

Dussen (Dutch) energetic

Duster (American) form of Dusty: bold and brave
Dust, Dustee, Dustey, Dusti, Dusty

Dustin (German) bold and brave
Dust, Dustan, Dusten, Duston, Dustie, Dusty, Dustyn

Dusty (German) form of Dustin: bold and brave
Dust, Dustee, Dustey, Dusti, Dustie

Dusty-Joe (American) cowboy
Dustee, Dusti, Dusty, Dustyjoe

Dutch (Dutch) from Holland; optimistic
Dutchie, Dutchy

Duth (Dutch) boy from the Netherlands

Duthrie (American) form of Guthrie: windy; heroic

Duval (French) valley; peaceful
Dovahl, Duv, Duvall, Duvalle

Duvin (French) of the wine

Dwain (American) form of Dwayne: swarthy
Dwaine

Dwan (African American) fresh
Dewan, D'wan, D'Wan, Dwawn, Dwon

Dwanae (African American) dark; small
Dwannay

Dwayne (Gaelic) swarthy
Duane, Duwain, Duwane, Duwayne, Dwain, Dwaine

Dweezel (American) creative
Dweez, Dweezil

Dwight (English) intelligent; white
Dwi, Dwite

Dwighton (English) Dwight's town

Dwyer (Irish) wise
Dwire, Dwyyer

Dwyke (American) form of
Dwight: intelligent; white

Dyam (Native American) eagle

Dybry (Slavic) good

Dyer (English) creative
Di, Dier, Dyar, Dye

Dykins (English) near the dike

Dylan ⚬ (Welsh) sea god;
creative
*Dill, Dillan, Dillon, Dilloyn,
Dilon, Dyl, Dylahn, Dylen, Dylin,
Dyllan, Dylon, Dylonn*

Dyle (Welsh) form of Dylan: sea
god; creative

Dylion (Welsh) form of Dylan:
sea god; creative

Dym (Russian) form of Dimitri:
fertile; flourishing

Dynell (African American)
seaman; gambler
Dinell, Dyne

Dyre (Scandinavian) dearest

Dyron (African American)
mercurial; sea-loving
Diron, Dyronn, Dyronne

Dyron (Scandinavian) dearest

Dyson (English) sea-loving
*Dieson, Dison, Dysan, Dysen,
Dysun, Dyzon*

Dyvet (English) worker; dyes
Dye

Eagan (Irish) form of Egan: spirited
Egon

Eagle (Native American) sharp-eyed
Eagal, Egle

Eagul (American) eagle

Eamon (Irish) form of Edmond:
protective
Amon, Eamen, Emon

Ean (English) form of Ian:
believer; handsome

Earl (English) promising; noble
Earle, Earley, Earlie, Early, Eril, Erl

Earldon (English) noble

Earlen (Irish) form of Earl:
promising; noble

Early (English) punctual
Earl, Earlee, Earley

Earnest (English) genuine
Earn, Earnie, Ern, Ernie

Earon (American) form of Aaron:
revered; sharer
Earonn

Earvin (English) sea-loving
Dervin, Ervin

Easau (Biblical) equivocates

Easey (American) easygoing
Easy, Ezey

East (English) from the East
Easte

Easter (English) born on Easter day

Eastland (English) boy from the
East

Easton (English) outdoorsy; east
town
Easten

Eaton (English) wealthy
Eaten, Etawn, Eton

Eaves (English) edges by

Eb (Hebrew) form of Ebenezer:
base of life; rock

Ebal (Biblical) merciful

Ebbe (Scandinavian) brave

Ebby (Hebrew) form of Ebenezer:
base of life; rock
Ebbey, Ebbi

Eben (Hebrew) helpful; loud
Eban

Ebenezer (Hebrew) base of life;
rock
*Eb, Ebbie, Ebby, Eben, Ebeneezer,
Ebeneser*

Eberhardt (German) brave
Eb, Eber, Eberhard

Ebert (French) bright

Ebo (African) Tuesday-born

Ebun (Hebrew) rock solid

Eckhardt (German) iron-willed
Eck, Eckhard, Eckhart, Ekhard

Ecklee (Last name as first name) strong

Ector (Slavic) dedicated

Ed (English) form of Edward: prospering; defender
Edd, Eddie, Eddy, Edy

Eda (Scottish) fiery

Edan (Scottish) fiery
Edon

Eday (Irish) fiery

Edbert (German) courageous
Ediberto

Edcell (English) focused; wealthy
Ed, Edcelle, Eds, Edsel

Eddie (English) form of Edward: prospering; defender
Eddee, Eddey, Eddy

Edel (German) of noble birth
Adel, Edelmar, Edelweiss

Edeltraud (German) young

Eden (Hebrew) delight
Eadon, Edin, Edon, Edye, Edyn

Edenir (Hebrew) delights

Edenson (Hebrew) son of Eden; delight
Edence, Edens, Edensen

Edgar (English) success
Ed, Eddie, Edghur, Edgur

Edgard (English) spear thrower
Ed, Eddie, Edgarde

Edgardo (English) successful
Edgar, Edgard, Edgardoh

Edge (American) cutting edge; trendsetter
Eddge, Edgy

Edgin (Last name as first name)

Edilberto (Spanish) noble
Edilbert

Edison (English) Edward's son; smart
Ed, Eddie, Edisen, Edyson

Ediwon (Slavic) form of Edward: prospering; defender

Edmond (English) protective
Ed, Edmon, Edmund

Edmun (Polish) rich

Edmundo (Spanish) wealthy protector
Ed, Eddie, Edmond

Edor (Spanish) snowy

Edrick (English) rich leader
Ed, Edri, Edrik, Edry

Edsel (English) rich
Ed, Eddie, Edsil, Edsyl

Edson (English) form of Edison: Edward's son; smart

Eduar (Spanish) form of Edward: prospering; defender

Eduardo (Spanish) flirtatious
Ed, Eddie, Edwardo

Eduviges (Italian) contentious

Edward (English) prospering; defender
Ed, Eddey, Eddi, Eddie, Eddy, Edwar, Edwerd

Edwards (English) Last name as first name; prospers

Edwiges (Spanish) contentious

Edwin (English) prosperous friend
Ed, Edwinn, Edwynn

Edzel (English) affluent

Efemy (Greek) eloquent

Efrain (Hebrew) form of Ephraim: fertile
Efren

Efrat (Spanish) brave

Efremel (Russian) cheerful

Efrim (Hebrew) form of Ephraim: fertile
Ef, Efrem, Efrum

Efton (American) form of Ephraim: fertile
Ef, Eft, Eften, Eftun

Egan (Irish) spirited
Eggie, Egin, Egon

Egbert (English) bright sword
Egber, Egburt, Eggie, Eggy

Egborn (English) ready; born of Edgar
Eg, Egbornem, Egburn, Eggie

Eger (English) form of Edgar: success

Egerton (English) town of a spearman
Edgarton, Edgartown, Edgerton, Egeton

Egeus (American) protective
Aegis, Egis

Eggleston (Last name as first name) town of Edgar

Eghert (German) smart
Eghertt, Eghurt

Egil (Scandinavian) the sword's edge
Eigil

Egmon (German) protective
Egmond, Egmont, Egmun, Egmund, Egmunt

Egon (Irish) passionate

Egypt (Place name) mysterious; majestic

Ehab (Irish) vibrant

Ehren (Hebrew) form of Aaron: revered; sharer

Ehrlich (Last name as first name) aware

Eikki (African) strong

Eilam (Hebrew) form of Elam: eternal

Einar (Scandinavian) lone fighter

Eirene (American) peaceful

Eiton (Hebrew) strong

Ejuan (Spanish) form of Ewan: youthful spirit

Ekels (Last name as first name) Echols variant

Eklund (Last name as first name) honored

Ekon (African) muscular

Ekul (Last name as first name) honored

El (English) old friend

El Fego (Spanish) bird; articulate

El Mahdi (Spanish) loved

Elam (Hebrew) eternal

Elan (French) finesse
Elann, Elen, Elon, Elyn

Elbis (American) exalted
Elb, Elbace, Elbase, Elbus

Elbridge (American) presidential
Elb, Elby

Elcim (Spanish) dignified

Eldaah (Biblical) battles

Eldan (Biblical) God loves

Eldemar (Slavic) old soul

Elder (English) older sibling
El, Eldor

Eldon (English) charitable
Edwin, El, Elden, Eldin

Eldorado (Place name) city in Arkansas
El, Eld, Eldor

Eldread (English) wise advisor
El, Eldred, Eldrid

Eldridge (English) supportive
Eldredge

Eleazar (Hebrew) helped by God
Elazar, Eleasar, Eliasar, Eliazar, Elieser, Elizar

Elegy (Spanish) memorable
Elegee, Elegie, Elgy

Elendor (Invented) special
Elen, Elend

Eleuter (Greek) freedom of integrity

Eleuterio (Greek) freedom of integrity

Elex (American) form of Alex: great leader; helpful

Elger (German) of noble birth
Ellgar, Ellger

Elgin (English) elegant
Elgen

Elham (English) Last name as first name; place name

Eli ♂ ⚤ (Hebrew) faithful man; high priest
El, Elie, Eloy, Ely

Elian (Spanish) spirited
Eliann, Elyan

Elias (Greek) spiritual
El, Eli, Eliace, Elyas

Eliason (Greek) form of Elias:
spiritual

Eliazar (Hebrew) God assists him

Elic (American) form of Alec:
high-minded

Eliel (Hebrew) religious

Eliett (Spanish) form of Elliott:
God-loving

Eliezer (Origin unknown) of God
Elieser, Elyeser

Elige (Latin) God has chosen him

Elighie (American) form of
Elijah: religious; Old Testament
prophet

Elihu (Hebrew) true believer
Elih, Eliu, Ellihu

Elijah ✪ ❶ (Hebrew) religious;
Old Testament prophet
El, Elie, Elija

Elik (Hawaiian) form of Eric:
powerful leader

Eliniod (American) God helps him

Eliphaz (Biblical) the endeavor
of God

Elis (Hebrew) form of Eliseo:
darling

Eliseo (Spanish) darling
Elizeo

Elisha (Hebrew) of God's
salvation
Elishah, Elysha, Elyshah

Elkanah (Biblical) obedient to God

Elkin (Hebrew) obedient to God

Ellard (German) brave man
Ell, Ellarde, Ellee, Ellerd

Ellery (English) dominant
El, Ell, Ellary, Ellerie, Ellie

Ellezer (English) believer

Ellion (American) form of Elliott:
God-loving

Elliott (English) God-loving
Elie, Elio, Ell, Elliot

Ellis (English) form of Elias:
spiritual
Ellice, Ells

Ellison (English) circumspect
Ell, Ellason, Ellisen, Ells, Ellyson

Ellkan (Hawaiian) saved by God
Elkan, Elkin

Ellory (Cornish) graceful swan
Elory, Elorey, Ellorey

Ellsha (Hebrew) saved by the Lord
*Elljsha, Elisee, Elish, Elishia,
Elishua*

Elman (American) protective
El, Elle, Elmen, Elmon

Elmer (English) famed
*Ell, Elm, Elmar, Elmir, Elmo,
Elmoh*

Elmerre (English) form of Elmer:
famed

Elmito (Spanish) form of Elmer:
famed

Elmo (Greek) gregarious
Ellmo, Elmoh

Elmore (English) radiant; sassy;
royal
Elm, Elmie, Elmoor, Elmor

Elmot (American) lovable
Elm

Elof (Swedish) the one heir
Loff

Elohim (Hebrew) chosen

Eloi (French) chosen one
Eloie, Eloy

Elois (Spanish) chosen

Elonzo (Spanish) sturdy; happy
El, Elon, Elonso

Elrad (Hebrew) God rules his life

Elran (Spanish) God directs him

Elreno (Spanish) God directs him

Elrette (Spanish) God directs him

Elrid (Hebrew) God directs him

Elrin (American) God helps him

Elroy (French) giving
Elroi, Elroye

Elsden (English) spiritual
Els, Elsdon

Elson (English) form of Elston: sophisticated
Elsen

Elster (Scottish) form of Alastair: strong leader

Elston (English) sophisticated
Els, Elstan, Elsten

Elsworth (Last name as first name) pretentious
Ells, Ellsworth

Elton (English) settlement; famous
Ell, Ellton, Elt, Eltan, Elten

Elusha (Slavic) treasured

Eluteria (Russian) believer

Eluye (Spanish) integrity

Elvie (Spanish) fair

Elvin (English) friend of elves
El, Elv, Elven

Elvind (American) form of Elvin: friend of elves
Elv

Elvis (Scandinavian) all-wise
El, Elvyse, The King

Elvy (English) elfin; small

Elwell (English) born in the old-well area

Elwen (English) friend of elves
Elwee, Elwin, Elwy, Elwyn, Elwynn, Elwynt

Elwond (Last name as first name) steady
Ellwand, Elwon, Eldwund

Elwood (English) old wood; everlasting
Ell, Elwoode, Elwould, Woodie, Woody, Woodye

Elwyne (English) elf-friend

Ely (Hebrew) lifted up
Eli

Elyden (English) from the hill

Elyus (Hebrew) form of Elias: spiritual

Elzaphan (Biblical) God assists him

Emanuel (Hebrew) with God
Em, Eman, Emanuele

Embers (Spanish) fiery

Emberto (Italian) pushy
Berty, Embert, Emberte

Embree (American) fiery

Emerick (German) form of Emery: hardworking leader

Emerit (German) form of Emery: hardworking leader

Emeritus (Latin) having fully earned

Emerson (German) Emery's son; able
Emers, Emersen

Emery (German) hardworking leader
Em, Emeri, Emerie, Emmerie, Emory, Emrie

Emig (Greek) brown

Emigdio (Greek) brown

Emil (Latin) ingratiating
Em, Emel, Emele

Emiliano (Italian) charms

Emilio (Italian) competitive; (Spanish) excelling
Emil, Emile, Emilioh, Emlo

Emjay (American) reliable
Em-J, Em-Jay, M.J., MJ

Emmanuel (Hebrew) with God
Em, Eman, Emmannuel, Emmanuele, Manny

Emmaus (Biblical) place name; safe in God

Emmett (Hebrew) truthful; sincere
Emit, Emmet, Emmit, Emmitt, Emmyt, Emmytt

Emory (German) industrious leader
Emery, Emmory, Emorey, Emori, Emorie

Emre (Turkish) bond of brothers
Emra, Emrah, Emreson

Emress (Spanish) proud

Emric (Slavic) form of Emery; hardworking leader

Emrick (Welsh) immortal
Emryk

Emser (American) hard worker

Emuel (Hebrew) form of Emmanuel: with God
Emanuel, Imuel

Enam (Biblical) place name

Enan (Welsh) hard

Encarnacion (Spanish) embodiment of life

Enda (Slavic) masculine

Ender (Slavic) form of Andrew: manly and brave

Eneas (Hebrew) much-praised
Ennes, Ennis

Engel (German) angel

Engelbert (German) angel-bright
Bert, Bertie, Berty, Engelber, Inglebert

Engen (American) smart

Enger (Scandinavian) angel

England (English) from England

Englun (American) from England

Engram (English) angelic

Engus (Irish) form of Angus: standout; important

Enlai (Chinese) thankful

Enlow (Last name as first name)

Ennis (Irish) reliable

Enno (Hebrew) form of Enos: mortal

Enny (American) form of Enos: mortal

Enoch (Hebrew) dedicated instructor
En, Enoc, Enok

Enos (Hebrew) mortal
Enoes

Enosh (Biblical) man

Enrick (Spanish) cunning
Enric, Enrik

Enrico (Italian) ruler
Enrike, Enriko, Enryco

Enrique (Spanish) charismatic ruler
Enrika, Enrikae, Enriqué, Enryque, Quiqui

Enrsto (Spanish) form of Ernesto: sincere

Ensor (Slavic) form of Ernest: sincere

Enver (Turkish) brightest child

Enzi (African) strong boy

Enzo (Italian) fun-loving

Eodis (Biblical) good

Epher (Biblical) plenty

Ephesian (Biblical) gifted

Ephraim (Hebrew) fertile
Eff, Efraim, Efram, Efrem, Ephraime, Ephrame, Ephrayme

Epifanio (Spanish) showing intelligence

Eppey (Spanish) smart

Eran (Hebrew) watchful

Erasmus (Greek) beloved
Eras, Erasmas, Erasmis

Erastus (Greek) loved baby

Erazmo (Spanish) loved
Erasmo, Eraz, Ras, Raz

Erbert (German) form of Herbert: famed warrior
Ebert, Erberto

Erby (German) aggressive

Ercell (Italian) the gift

Ercole (Italian) glorious God's child

Ereb (Greek) dark

Erebus (Greek) nether darkness

Ergo (Latin) word as name; therefore; consequently

Erhardt (German) strong-willed
Erhar, Erhard, Erhart, Erheart

Eric ⚬ (Scandinavian) powerful leader
Ehrick, Erek, Erick, Erik, Eryke

Erie (Place name) one of the Great Lakes; vast

Erikson (Scandinavian) Erik's son; bold man
Ericksen, Eriksen, Erycksen, Eryksen, Erykson

Erin (Irish) peace-loving
Aaron, Arin, Aron, Eryn

Eris (Greek) hard life

Erlan (English) aristocratic
Earlan, Earland, Erland, Erlen, Erlin

Erling (English) highborn

Ermitt (English) form of Kermit: droll

Ermot (French) form of Ernest: sincere

Ernest (English) sincere
Earnest, Ern, Ernie, Erno, Ernst, Erny, Ernye

Ernesto (Spanish) sincere
Ernie, Nesto, Nestoh

Ernie (English) form of Ernest: sincere
Ernee, Erney, Erny

Erno (Slavic) form of Ernest: sincere

Ernold (English) sincere

Ernst (Dutch) form of Ernest: sincere

Ernulfo (Spanish) sincere

Erol (American) noble
Eral, Eril, Errol

Erold (Welsh) form of Errol: noble

Erolden (English) wanders

Eronlon (American) form of Aaron: revered; sharer

Eros (Greek) sensual
Ero

Erose (Greek) form of Eros: sensual
Eroce

Errett (American) form of Aaron: revered; sharer

Errick (American) form of Eric: powerful leader

Errin (American) form of Aaron: revered; sharer

Errington (Last name as first name) Aaron's town

Errol (German) noble
Erol, Erold, Erroll, Erryl

Ershcel (American) form of Herschel: deer; swift

Erskine (Scottish) high-minded
Ers, Ersk, Erskin

Erst (Scottish) cliff

Erv (English) good-looking

Ervin (English) sea-loving
Earvin, Erv, Ervan, Erven, Ervind, Ervyn

Ervine (English) sea-lover
Ervene, Ervin

Erving (Scottish) good-looking

Erwey (American) form of Irving: attractive

Erwin (English) friendly
Erwyn

Esau (Hebrew) rough-hewn; raw
Es, Esa, Esauw, Esaw

Escobar (Spanish) swept up

Escobedo (Spanish) Last name as first name

Escoto (Spanish) shy

Esdras (Biblical) form of Ezra: helpful; strong

Eshban (Biblical) fire of discernment

Eshcol (Hebrew) the grapes

Eshter (Indian) form of Eshwar: Hindu god

Eskew (English) Last name as first name

Eskil (Scandinavian) divine

Esmaeil (Spanish) loved

Esmaiel (Spanish) outcast son

Esmail (Indian) God listens

Esmé (French) beloved
Es, Esmae, Esmay

Esmer (Slavic) affluent

Esmond (French) handsome
Esmand, Esmon, Esmund

Esmun (American) kind
Es, Esman, Esmon

Esos (Irish) godlike

Espen (German) bear of God; (Danish) the bear

Esperanza (Spanish) hopeful
Esper, Esperance, Esperence

Espie (Scandinavian) big

Espy (Scandinavian) of God

Esraa (Hebrew) form of Ezra: helpful; strong

Esser (Spanish) reassuring

Essex (English) dignified
Ess, Ez

Estanisiao (Spanish) glorified

Este (Spanish) form of Esteban: royal; friendly

Esteban (Spanish) royal; friendly
Estabon, Estebann, Estevan, Estiban, Estyban

Estel (American) from the East

Esterlin (Last name as first name) Easterner

Estes (English) Eastern; open
Estas, Este, Estis

Estevan (Spanish) crowned
Estivan, Estyvan

Estridge (Last name as first name) fortified
Es, Estri, Estry

Esvin (English) friend of Esser

Etam (Biblical) place name

Etan (Irish) watchful

Etano (Italian) form of Ethan: firm will

Etereo (Spanish) heavenly; spiritual
Etero

Ethan ✪ ❶ (Hebrew) firm will
Eth, Ethen, Ethin, Ethon

Ethaniel (Italian) form of Gaetano: from the city of Gaeta; Italian man

Etheal (English) of good birth
Ethal

Ethelbert (German) principled
Ethelburt, Ethylbert

Etren (American) form of Ethan: firm will

Ettore (Italian) loyal; steadfast
Etor, Etore

Etwin (American) friend of Ethan; resolved

Eual (Jewish) form of Eyal: deer-like

Euclid (Greek) brilliant
Euclide, Uclid

Eudin (Greek) leads

Eufronio (Greek) bright

Eugene (Greek) blue-blood
Eugean, Eugenie, Ugene

Eural (American) from Ural Mountains; upward
Eure, Ural, Ury

Eurby (Last name as first name) sea
Erby, Eurb

Eurskie (Invented) dorky
Ersky

Eurus (Greek) form of Eros: sensual

Eusebio (Spanish) devoted to God
Eucebio, Eusabio, Eusevio, Sebio, Usibo

Eustace (Latin) calming
Eustice, Eustis, Stace, Stacey, Ustace

Eustacio (Spanish) calm; visionary
Eustacio, Eustase, Eustasio, Eustazio, Eustes, Eustis

Eustorgio (Greek) beloved

Euxinus (Greek) highborn

Evagelos (Greek) form of Andrew: manly and brave
Evaggelos, Evangelo, Evangelos

Evan ✪ ❶ (Irish) warrior
Ev, Evann, Evanne, Even, Evin

Evander (Greek) manly; champion
Evand, Evandar, Evandir

Evans (Welsh) believer in a gracious God
Evens, Evyns

Evanus (American) form of Evan: warrior
Evin, Evinas, Evinus

Evar (Scandinavian) courageous

Evaristo (Spanish) form of Evan: warrior
Evariso, Evaro

Eve (Invented) form of Yves: honest; handsome
Eeve

Evelle (American) vibrant

Evelyn (American) writer
Ev, Evlinn, Evlyn

Even (Latin) does well

Ever (German) strong wild boar

Everard (German) tough
Ev, Evrard

Everest (Place name) highest mountain peak in the world

Everestin (American) everlasting

Everett (English) strong
Ev, Everet, Everitt, Evret, Evrit

Everette (English) brave

Everhart (Scandinavian) vibrant
Evhart, Evert

Everly (American) singing
Everlee, Everley, Everlie, Evers

Evert (Dutch) of the wild boars

Everton (English) from the town of boars; fearless

Every (English) word as name

Evetier (French) good

Evett (American) bright
Ev, Evatt, Eve, Evidt, Evitt

Evince (American) invincible

Evitt (American) invincible

Evodio (Spanish) righteous

Evon (Welsh) form of Evan: warrior
Even, Evin, Evonn, Evonne, Evyn

Evre (American) form of Everett: strong

Evres (American) form of Everettt: strong

Evret (American) form of Everettt: strong

Evzek (Slavic) brave

Ewald (Polish) fair ruler

Ewan (Scottish) youthful spirit
Ewahn, Ewon

Ewand (Welsh) form of Evan: warrior
Ewen, Ewon

Ewanell (American) form of Ewan: youthful spirit
Ewanel, Ewenall

Ewart (English) shepherd; caring
Ewar, Eward, Ewert

Ewen (Scottish) form of Eugene: blue-blood

Ewing (English) law-abiding
Ewin, Ewyng

Excell (American) competitive
Excel, Exsel, Exsell

Exek (American) God gives strength

Exia (Spanish) demanding
Ex, Exy

Exios (Spanish) finds a way

Exiquio (Spanish) exacting

Exod (Spanish) his exodus

Exzel (American) form of Edsel: rich

Eyal (American) form of Eagle: sharp-eyed

Eydis (Scandinavian) island god

Eytin (American) form of Ethan: firm will

Eza (Hebrew) form of Ezra: helpful; strong
Esri

Ezekiel (Hebrew) God's strength
Eze, Ezek, Ezekhal, Ezekial, Ezikiel, Ezikyel, Ezkeil, Ezykiel, Zeke

Ezequiel (Spanish) devout

Ezer (Hebrew) helpful boy

Ezion (Biblical) place name

Ezira (Hebrew) helpful
Ezirah, Ezyra, Ezyrah

Ezno (Spanish) humble

Ezra (Hebrew) helpful; strong
Esra, Ezrah

Ezri (Hebrew) my help
Ezrey, Ezry

Ezron (American) created

Ezzie (Hebrew) form of Ezra: helpful; strong
Ez

F

Faakhir (Arabic) proud

Faber (German) grower
Fabar, Fabir, Fabyre

Faberto (Latin) form of Fabian:
grower
Fabe, Fabey, Fabien, Fabre

Fabian (Latin) grower
*Fab, Fabe, Fabean, Fabeone,
Fabiano, Fabie, Fabien,*

Fabio (Italian) seductive;
handsome
Fab, Fabioh

Fabish (American) form of
Fabrice: skilled worker

Fable (American) storyteller
Fabal, Fabe, Fabel, Fabil

Fablo (American) form of Fabio:
seductive; handsome

Fabrice (French) skilled worker
*Fabriano, Fabricius, Fabritius,
Fabrizio, Fabrizius*

Fabrizio (Italian) fabulous

Fabron (French) blacksmith

Fabryce (Latin) crafty
*Fab, Fabby, Fabreese, Fabrese,
Fabrice*

Fabulous (American) vain
Fab, Fabby, Fabu

Fachan (Last name as first name)
precocious

Factor (English) entrepreneur

Facundo (Last name as first
name) profound

Faddis (American) loner; deals
in beans
Faddes, Fadice, Fadis

Faddy (American) faddish
Fad, Faddey, Faddi

Fadi (Arabic) saved by grace

Fadil (Arabic) giving

Faeus (Biblical) form of Alfeus:
follower

Fagan (Irish) fiery
Fagane, Fagen, Fagin, Fegan

Fahd (Arabic) fierce; panther; brave
Fahad

Faheem (Arabic) brilliant

Fahim (Arabic) intelligent

Fahren (American) form of
Faran: sincere

Fahrer (French) leader

Faino (American) the start

Fair (English) blond

Fairbairn (Scottish) fair-haired
child

Fairbanks (English) bank along
the pathway
Fairbanx, Farebanks

Fairchild (English) fair-haired
child

Fairfax (English) full of warmth
Fairfacks, Farefax, Fax, Faxy

Faisal (Arabic) authoritative
Faisel, Faizal, Fasel, Fayzelle

Faizon (Arabic) understanding

Fakhr (Arabic) proud

Faladrick (Origin unknown)
form of Frederick: plainspoken
leader; peaceful
Faldrick, Faldrik

Falcon (American) bird as name;
dark; watchful
Falk, Falkon

Falcone (Latin) of the falcons

Faldo (Last name as first) brassy

Falguni (Indian) Hindi for month
Falgun

Faline (Hindi) fertile

Falk (Hebrew) falcon
Falke

Falkner (French) handles falcons
Faulkner, Fowler

Fallows (English) inactive
Fallow

Falvey (English) of the falcons

Fam (American) family-oriented
Fammy

Famous (American) ambitious
Fame

Fane (English) exuberant
Fain, Faine

Fanlie (American) free

Fannin (English) happy
Fane

Fant (Latin) guileless

Fantroy (French) naive, royal

Fany (Spanish) freedom

Faolan (Irish) wolf; sly
Felan, Phelan

Far (English) traveler
Farr

Faraji (African) he who comforts
others

Faralito (Spanish) comforts

Faramond (English) protected
*Faramund, Farrimond,
Farrimund, Pharamond,
Pharamund*

Faran (American) sincere
*Fahran, Faren, Faron, Feren,
Ferren*

Fardan (Arabic) unique

Fareed (Arabic) special

Fargo (American) jaunty
Fargouh

Farhad (Arabic) unusual

Faris (Arabic) knighted

Farkas (Last name as first name)
strong man

Farley (English) open
*Farl, Farlee, Farleigh, Farlie,
Farly, Farlye*

Farmer (English) he farms

Farnall (Last name as first name)
strong man
Farnell, Fernald

Farnham (English) windblown;
field
Farnhum, Farnie, Farnum, Farny

Farnley (English) from a place
of ferns

Farno (Italian) in ferns

Farold (Invented) lively

Farolito (Spanish) little ferns

Farouk (Arabic) knowing what's
true
Faruq, Faruqh

Farquar (French) masculine

Farr (English) adventurer
Far

Farrar (French) distinguished
Farr

Farre (English) wanders

Farrell (Irish) brave
Farel, Farell, Faryl

Farren (English) mover
Faran, Faron, Farrin, Farron

Farris (Arabic) rider; (Irish) rock;
reliable
Fare, Farice, Faris

Farro (Italian) grain
Farron, Faro

Farrow (English) tends the pigs

Fasta (Spanish) offering

Fattah (Arabic) conqueror

Faughn (Italian) raven

Faulkner (English) disciplinarian
*Falcon, Falconner, Falkner,
Falkoner*

Faunus (Latin) god of nature
Fawnus

Fausatino (Spanish) lucky

Faust (Latin) lucky
Fauston

Faustino (Italian) lucky

Favero (French) insightful

Favian (Latin) knowing
Fav, Favion

Favor (French) gives

Fawad (Arabic) victorious

Fawcett (American) audacious
*Fawce, Fawcet, Fawcette, Fawcie,
Fawsie, Fowcett*

Faxan (Anglo-Saxon) outgoing
Faxen, Faxon

Faxon (German) lush hair

Fay (Irish) raven-haired
Faye, Fayette

Fayne (English) happy

Faysal (Arabic) judgmental

Fazio (Italian) diligent

Fe (Latin) shining

Fearon (American) keen

Febronio (Spanish) bright

Fedde (Dutch) ruler

Federico (Spanish) peaceful and
affluent
Federik

Fedil (French) excellence

Fedor (German) form of
Theodore: God's gift; a blessing
Faydor, Feodor, Fyodor

Fedrick (American) form of
Cedric: leader
Fed, Fedric, Fedrik

Feeney (Irish) Last name as first
name; soldier

Feibush (Last name as first name)
particular

Feivel (Hebrew) bright

Feixon (Hebrew) helped by God

Feldronio (Spanish) from the field

Felimy (Irish) good

Felipe (Spanish) horse-lover
Felepe, Filipe, Flippo

Felix (Latin) joyful
Felixce, Filix, Phelix, Philix

Felker (English) Last name as
first name

Fellini (Last name as first)
carnivalesque

Felman (Last name as first name)
smart
Fel, Fell

Felton (English) farming the field

Fenimore (Last name as first
name) creative

Fenner (English) capable
Fen, Fenn, Fynner

Fennessey (English) form of
Phineas: farsighted

Fenris (Scandinavian) fierce

Fenton (English) nature-loving
Fen, Fenn, Fennie, Fenny

Fentress (English) natural
Fentres, Fyntres

Fenwick (English) from the
marsh village; able

Feo (Native American) confident
Feeo, Feoh

Ferdinand (German) adventurer
Ferdie, Ferdnand, Ferdy, Fernand

Ferenc (Hungarian) free

Ferg (Irish) strong

Fergall (Irish) bravest man
Fearghall, Forgael

Fergonn (French) strong

Fergus (Irish) man of strength
Feargus, Ferges, Fergie, Fergis, Fergy

Ferguson (Irish) bold; excellent
*Fergie, Fergs, Fergus, Fergusahn,
Fergusen, Fergy, Furgs, Furgus*

Ferlin (American) countrified
Ferlan

Ferll (Irish) strong

Fermin (Spanish) strong-willed
Fer, Fermen, Fermun

Fernan (Spanish) risk-taker

Fernando (Spanish) bold leader
*Ferd, Ferdie, Ferdinando, Ferdy,
Fernand*

Fernao (Spanish) form of
Fernando: bold leader

Fernley (English) from the fern
meadow; natural
*Farnlea, Farnlee, Farnleigh,
Farnley, Fernlea, Fernlee, Fernleigh*

Feroza (Persian) lucky

Feroze (Persian) lucky

Ferrand (French) gray-haired
Farrand, Farrant, Ferrant

Ferraro (Italian) fiery

Ferrell (Irish) hero
Fere, Ferrel, Feryl

Ferret (English)

Ferris (Irish)
Farris, F

Fery

Fest

Festive (American) word as name; joyful
Fest, Festas, Festes

Festus (Latin) happy
Festes

Feven (Russian) sees God

Fhoki (Japanese) discriminating

Fiachra (Irish) raven; watchful

Fico (Italian) form of Frederick: plainspoken leader; peaceful

Fidel (Latin) faithful
Fidele, Fidell, Fydel

Fideles (Latin) loyal

Fidencio (Spanish) confidence
Fidens, Fido

Fides (Greek) calms

Field (English) outdoorsman
Fields

Fielding (English) outdoorsman; working the fields

Fien (American) elegant
Fiene, Fine

Fiero (Spanish) fiery

Fierro (Spanish) fiery

Fife (Scottish) bright-eyed
Fyfe, Phyfe

Fi__l (Scottish) form of Fife: __-eyed

__e name) Fiji Islands;

__jie

Fikry (American) industrious
Fike, Fikree, Fikrey

Filbert (English) genius
Fil, Filb, Bert, Phil

Filemon (Greek) loves horses

Filetus (Biblical) beloved

Filinto (Spanish) friendly

Filip (Greek) horse-lover; (Belgium) form of Philip: outdoorsman *Fil, Fill*

Filmer (English) form of Filmore: famed
Fill, Filmar

Filmore (English) famed
Fill, Fillie, Fillmore, Filly, Fylmore

Filomelo (Spanish) friend

Filson (Last name as first name) son of Phil; meanders

Fimy (African) loved by God

Finbar (Irish) blond

Finbarr (Irish) blond

Finch (Last name as first name) birdlike

Fineas (Egyptian) dark

Finell (Irish) blond

Finesse (English) word as name; extreme delicacy or subtlety in action

Finian (Irish) fair
Fin, Finean, Finn, Fynian

Finis (Latin) finished

Finlan (Irish) blond

Finlay (Irish) blond soldier
Finley, Findlay, Findley

Finley (Irish) magical
Fin, Finny, Fynn, Fynnie

Finn (Scandinavian) fair-haired; from Finland
Fin, Finnie, Finny

Finna (Scandinavian) blond

Finnegan (Irish) fair
Finegan, Finigan, Finn, Finny

Finnian (German) from Finland

Finoch (Scottish) blond

Fintan (Irish) small blond man

Finton (Irish) magical
Finn, Finny, Fynton

Fiorello (Italian) flowering

Firdaus (Arabic) from the garden of paradise

Firman (French) loyal
Farman, Farmann, Fermin, Firmin

Firoozeh (Arabic) succeeds

Fishel (Hebrew) fish
Fish, Fysh

Fisher (English) he fishes
Fish, Fischer, Fisscher, Visscher

Fisk (Scandinavian) fisherman
Fiske

Fitch (French) throws spears

Fito (Spanish) little

Fitz (French) bright young man; son
Fitzy

Fitzgerald (English) bright
young man; Gerald's son

Fitzhugh (French) Hugh's son;
big-hearted

Fitzmorris (Last name as first
name) son of Morris
Fitz, Morrey, Morris

Fitzpatrick (French) Patrick's
son; noble

Fitzroy (French) son of Roy; lively

Fitzsimmons (English) bright
young man; Simmons's son

Five (Word as name)

Fiven (American) five

Flabia (Spanish) light-haired
Flavia

Flag (American) patriotic
Flagg

Flame (Last name as first name)
confident

Flaminio (Spanish) priest;
thoughtful
Flamino

Flann (Irish) red-haired
Flainn, Flannan, Flannery

Flannan (Irish) red-haired

Flannigan (Last name as first
name) red-haired

Flappan (Last name as first name)

Flass (Last name as first name)

Flaubert (French) fame, bright

Flavean (Greek) form of Flavian:
blond

Flavian (Greek) blond
Flovian

Flavio (Italian) shining
Flav, Flavioh

Fleada (American) introvert
Flayda

Fleetwood (English) from the
woods

Flemmer (English) a native of
Flanders

Flemming (English) a native of
Flanders; confident
Fleming, Flyming

Fletcher (English) kindhearted;
maker of arrows
Fletch, Fletchi, Fletchie, Fletchy

Flimmel (Last name as first
name)

Flint (English) stream; nature-lover
Flinn, Flintt, Flynt, Flynnt

Flintlee (English) of the stream

Flip (English) loves horses; wild
movements

Flippin (Spanish) form of Felipe:
horse-lover

Floan (American) form of Flynn:
brash

Floran (Spanish) flourishing like
a flower garden

Florante (Spanish) flowers

Florecio (Spanish) flowering

Florencione (Italian) flowering

Florentin (Italian) blooming
Florencio

Florian (Latin) flourishing
Florean, Florie

Floyd (English) practical; hair of
gray
Floid

Flux (Middle English) flowing

Flynn (Irish) brash
Flin, Flinn, Flinnie, Flinny, Flyne

Flynt (English) flowing; stream
Flint, Flinte, Flinty, Flynte

Fobbs (Last name as first name)
flourishing

Fobo (Greek) fearful

Fogle (Last name as first name)

Folan (Last name as first name) of
the folks

Foley (Last name as first name)
creative
Folee, Folie

Folke (German) of the people

Folker (German) watchful
Folke, Folko

Follis (Last name as first name) of
the folks

Fonseca (Italian) form of Alphonse: distinguished

Fontayne (French) giving; fountain
Font, Fontaine, Fontane, Fountaine

Fontenot (French) fountain

Fonzie (German) form of Alphonse: distinguished
Fons, Fonsi, Fonz, Fonzi

For (American) representative
Fore

Foran (American) derivative of foreign; exotic
Foren, Forun

Forbes (Irish) wealthy
Forb

Ford (English) strong
Feord, Forde, Fyord

Fordan (English) river crossing; inventive
Ford, Forday, Forden

Foreign (American) word as name; foreigner
Foran

Foreman (Last name as first name) leader

Forend (American) forward
Fore, Foryn, Forynd

Forest (French) nature-loving
Forrest, Fory, Fourast

Forester (English) protective; of the forest
Forrester, Forry

Forge (English) crosses stream

Foros (Greek) carries forward

Forsey (Scottish) Last name as first name; man of peace

Fortino (Spanish) fortune

Fortney (Latin) strength of character
Fortenay, Forteney, Forteny, Fortny, Fourtney

Fortune (French) fortunate man
Fortounay, Fortunae

Fortuno (Spanish) lucky man
Fortunio

Fost (Latin) form of Foster: worthy
Foste, Fostee, Fosty

Foster (Latin) worthy
Fauster, Fostay

Fotis (Greek) light

Fouad (Arabic) good heart
Fuad

Fowler (English) hunter; traps fowl
Fowller

Foy (American) foible

Frace (American) fragile

Fraime (Anglo-Saxon) newcomer

Fraine (English) ash tree; tall
Frayne, Freyne

Fralin (Last name as first name) frail

Francesco (Italian) flirtatious
Fran, Francey, Frankie, Franky

Franchot (French) free

Francis (Latin) free spirit; from France
Fran, Frances, Franciss, Frank, Franky, Frannkie, Franny, Frans

Francisco (Spanish) form of Francis: free spirit; from France
Chuco, Cisco, Francisk, Franco, Frisco, Paco, Pancho

Francista (Spanish) Frenchman; free
Cisco, Cisto, Francisco, Franciscus, Fransico

Franckie (German) dynamic

Franco (Spanish) defender; spear
Francoh, Franko

Francois (French) smooth; patriot; Frenchman
Frans, Franswaw, French, Frenchie, Frenchy

Frank (English) form of Franklin: outspoken; landowner
Franc, Franco, Frankee, Frankie, Frankey, Franko, Franky

Frankel (German) free

Franklin (English) outspoken; landowner
Francklin, Franclin, Frank, Frankie, Franklinn, Franklyn, Franklynn, Franky

Franqueli (Italian) free

Frantisek (Czech) free man

Franz (German) man from France; free
Frans

Frasher (English) curls

Frasier (English) attractive; man with curls
Frase, Fraser, Fraze, Frazer

Frayley (English) of the ash meadow

Frayne (English) foreigner
Fraine, Frayn, Frean, Freen, Freyne

Fraze (English) curls

Fred (German) form of Frederick: plainspoken leader; peaceful
Fredde, Freddo, Freddy, Fredo

Fredder (German) form of Fred: plainspoken leader; peaceful

Freddie (German) form of Frederick: plainspoken leader; peaceful
Freddee, Freddey, Freddi, Freddy

Freddis (German) form of Frederick: plainspoken leader; peaceful
Freddus, Fredes, Fredis

Fredell (German) form of Frederick: plainspoken leader; peaceful

Frederic (French) peaceful king
Fred, Freddy

Frederick (German) plainspoken leader; peaceful
Fred, Freddy, Frederic, Fredrich, Fredrik, Fryderyk

Freeborn (English) born free

Freed (English) free boy
Fried

Freedom (American) loves freedom

Freedy (English) free

Freeman (English) free man
Free, Freedman, Freman

Fremont (German) protective; noble

Fren (Spanish) form of Francisco: free

French (English) boy from France

Francisco (Spanish) free

Fres (Spanish) fresh air

Fresco (Spanish) open

Freslev (American) freshness

Frewen (Anglo-Saxon) free
Frewin

Frey (Scandinavian) fertility god

Frick (English) brave man

Frid (German) peaceful

Fridmann (Last name as first name) free man

Fridolf (Scandinavian) relishes peace
Freydolf, Freydulf, Friedolf, Fridulf

Fridolin (German) free

Frieder (German) peaceful leader
Frie, Fried, Friedrich

Friederich (German) form of Frederick: plainspoken leader; peaceful
Fridrich, Friedrich

Friedhelm (German) peaceful helmet
Friedelm

Frisco (American) form of Francisco: free spirit; from France
Cisco, Frisko

Friso (Anglo-Saxon) best self

Fritz (German) form of Frederick: plainspoken leader
Firzie, Firzy, Frits, Fritts, Fritzi, Fritzie, Fritzy

Fritzie (German) peaceful

Fritzon (Norse) peacemaker

Frode (Scandinavian) intellectual

Froilan (German) popular leader

Fromel (Hebrew) outgoing

Frosino (Italian) merry

Frost (English) cold; freeze

Frosten (American) of the winter

Froyim (Hebrew) kind

Fructuoso (Spanish) fruitful
Fru, Fructo

Fry (English) new sprout; growing
Frye, Fryer

Fu (Japanese) form of Fudo: the god of fire and wisdom

Fuddy (Origin unknown) bright-eyed
Fuddie, Fudee, Fudi

Fudo (Japanese) the god of fire and wisdom

Fukuda (Japanese) field

Fulbright (German) brilliant; full of brightness
Fulbrite

Fulgentius (Latin) full of kindness; shines
Fulgencio

Fulke (English) folksy
Fawke, Fowke, Fulk

Fuller (English) tough-willed
Fuler

Fullerton (English) strong
Fuller, Fullerten

Fulton (English) fresh mind; field by the town

Funge (Last name as first name) stodgy
Funje, Funny

Furlo (American) macho
Furl

Furman (German) form of Firman: loyal
Fuhrman, Fuhrmann, Furmann

Fursey (Irish) spiritual

Fyfe (Scottish) craftsman
Fife, Fyffe, Phyfe

Fyodor (Russian) divine
Feodor, Fyodr

Gabae (Biblical) loves God

Gabaldon (English) Last name as first name

Gabata (Biblical) place name

Gabbana (Italian) creative
Gabi

Gabe (Hebrew) form of Gabriel: God's hero; devout
Gabbee, Gabbi, Gabbie, Gabby, Gabi, Gabie, Gaby

Gabino (Spanish) strong believer
Gabby, Gabi

Gable (French) dashing

Gablen (American) form of Gabriel: God's hero; devout

Gabor (Last name as first name) believer; colorful

Gabriel ○ (Hebrew) God's hero; devout
Gabby, Gabe, Gabi, Gabreal, Gabrel, Gabriele, Gabrielle, Gabryel

Gad (Hebrew) lucky; audacious
Gadd

Gaddi (Arabic)

Gaddiel (Hebrew) fortunate; loves God
Gadiel

Gaddis (American) hard to please; picky
Gad, Gaddes, Gadis

Gadi (Hebrew) form of Gaddiel: fortunate; loves god
Gadish

Gael (English) speaks Gaelic; independent

Gaetano (Italian) from the city of Gaeta; Italian man
Gaetan, Geitano, Guytano

Gaffar (Arabic) from the stream

Gagan (French) form of Gage: dedicated

Gage (French) dedicated

Gager (French) dedicated

Gaghe (American) jaunty

Gaham (Biblical) searches

Gahuj (African) hunts

Gailen (French) healer; physician
Galan, Galen, Galun

Gain (Word as name) gainful

Gaines (English) increase in wealth
Ganes, Gaynes

Gair (Irish) little boy
Gaer, Geir

Gaither (French) victor

Gaius (Latin) joyful
Gal

Galatian (Biblical) bible book
Galatians

Galavis (Greek) white

Galax (Spanish) of the galaxy

Galbraith (Irish) sensible
Gal

Galbreath (Irish) practical man
Galbraith, Gall

Galdin (American) calm

Galdino (Spanish) calm

Gale (English) cheerful
Gael, Gail, Gaile, Gaille, Gayle

Galegina (Native American) lithe; deer

Galen (Greek) calming; intelligent
Gaelin, Gailen, Gale, Galean, Galey, Gaylen

Galene (Spanish) shining

Galfrid (Last name as first name) uplifted
Galfryd

Gali (Spanish) shining

Galileo (Italian) from Galilee
Galilayo

Gallagher (Irish) helpful
Galagher, Gallager, Gallie, Gally

Gallant (American) savoir-faire
Gael, Gail, Gaila, Gaile, Gayle

Gallman (Last name as first name) lively
Gallway, Galman, Galway

Galloway (Irish) outgoing
Gallie, Gally, Galoway, Galway

Galo (Spanish) enthusiastic
Gallo

Galt (German) empowered

Galton (English) landowner; reclusive

Galvin (Irish) sparrow; flighty
Gallven, Gallvin, Galvan, Galven, Galway

Gamal (Arabic) camel; travels long distances

Gamaliel (Hebrew) rewarded by God
Gamaleel, Gamalyel

Gamba (African) warring

Gamberro (Spanish) hooligan
Gami

Gamble (Scandinavian) mature wisdom
Gam, Gamb, Gambel, Gambie, Gamby

Gamel (Hebrew) God rewards him

Gamliel (Arabic) camel; wanders
Gamaliel

Gammon (Last name as first name) game
Gamen, Gamon, Gamun

Gan (Chinese) wanders wide

Gandy (American) adventurer

Ganesh (Hindi) Lord of all

Ganit (American) leader

Ganon (Irish) fair-skinned
Gannon, Ganny

Ganso (Spanish) goose; goofy
Gans, Ganz

Ganya (Russian) strong

Gar (English) form of Garbin: pure

Garai (African) settled

Garbhan (Irish) rough boy

Garbin (Spanish) pure

Garbini (Spanish) pure

Garcia (Spanish) strong
Garce, Garcey, Garsey

Gard (English) guard
Garde, Gardey, Gardi, Gardie, Gardy, Guard

Gardner (English) keeper of the garden
Gar, Gard, Gardener, Gardie, Gardiner, Gardnyr, Gardy

Garee (English) form of Gary: strong man

Garek (Polish) brave boy
Garreck, Garrik, Gerek

Gareth (Irish) kind
Gare

Garfiel (English) form of Garfield: armed

Garfield (English) armed
Gar, Garfeld

Gariana (Hindi) shout

Garin (American) form of Darin: great
Gare, Gary

Garis (Biblical) place name

Garl (French) form of Garland: adorned

Garland (French) adorned
Gar, Garlan, Garlend, Garlind, Garlynd

Garlando (Spanish) wreath

Garlon (French) wreath

Garmon (German) man who throws spears
Garmen

Garn (American) prepared
Gar, Garnie, Garny, Garr

Garner (French) guard
Gar, Garn, Garnar, Garnir

Garnett (English) armed; spear
Gar, Garn, Garnet, Garny

Garnock (Welsh) from the alder-tree place; outdoor spirit

Garoa (Spanish) morning dew

Garold (American) form of Harold: leader of an army

Garon (American) gentle
Garonn, Garonne

Garonzick (Last name as first name) secure
Gare, Garon, Garons, Garonz

Garr (English) form of Garrett: brave; watchful; form of Garth: sunny; gardener
Gar

Garrad (English) form of Gerard: brave

Garren (American) kind

Garreth (German) brave
Gareth, Garryth, Garyth

Garrett (Irish) brave; watchful
Gare, Garet, Garitt, Garret, Garritt, Gary, Gerrot

Garrick (English) ruler with a spear; brave
Garey, Garic, Garick, Garik, Garreck, Gary, Gerrick, Gerrieck

Garridan (English) form of Gary: strong man

Garrison (French) prepared
Garris, Garrish, Garry, Gary

Garrist (English) form of Garrison: prepared

Garroway (English) throws spears; physical presence
Garraway

Garson (English) son of Gar; fort home; industrious

Garth (Scandinavian) sunny; gardener
Gar, Gare, Garry, Gart, Garthe, Gary

Garthay (Irish) form of Gareth: gentle
Garthae

Garton (English) place of spear man; rowdy

Garv (English) peaceful
Garvey, Garvy

Garvan (English) throws spears; athletic

Garver (English) friend

Garvy (Irish) peacemaker
Garvey

Garwin (English) friend who struggles

Garwood (English) natural
Garr, Garwode, Garwoode, Woody

Gary (English) strong man
Gare, Garrey, Garri

Garyle (German) form of Gary: strong man

Gask (American) form of Gaskill

Gaskill (Last name as first name)

Gasos (Greek) form of Pegasus: horse; rider

Gaspard (French) holds treasure
Gaspar, Gasper

Gaspare (Italian) treasure-holder
Casper, Gasp, Gasparo

Gassia (Slavic) treasure

Gaston (French) native of Gascony; stranger
Gastawn, Gastowyn

Gat (American) form of Gatam: their lowing; their touch

Gatam (Biblical) their lowing; their touch

Gataz (Spanish) open-minded

Gatch (American) jaunty

Gate (English) open
Gait, Gates

Gath (Biblical) place name

Gathen (American) form of Gath: place name

Gathrir (American) form of Gath: place name

Gatlin (Last name as first name)

Gatsby (Literature) from Fitzgerald's *The Great Gatsby*; ambitious; tragic

Gaudencio (Spanish) content

Gaudy (American) word as name; colorful
Gaudin

Gauge (French) form of Gage: dedicated

Gauran (French) form of George: land-loving; farmer

Gaurav (Hindi) proud

Gauri (Indian) white

Gautier (French) form of Walter: army leader
Gauther, Gauthier

Gavard (Last name as first name) creative
Gav, Gaverd

Gavin ✪ (English) alert; hawk
Gav, Gaven, Gavinn, Gavon, Gavvin, Gavyn

Gavine (French) hawk

Gavino (Italian) hawk

Gavra (Hebrew) dedicated to God

Gavri (Hebrew) form of Gavriel: filled by God's strength

Gavriel (Herbew) filled by God's strength
Gavryel

Gavril (Hebrew) strong
Gavrill, Gavryl, Gavryll

Gawain (Hebrew) archangel
Gawaine, Gawayne, Gwayne

Gawath (Welsh) form of Gawain: archangel

Gawin (Scottish) watchful; wise
Gawyn

Gayathri (Russian) God-fearing

Gaylin (Greek) calm
Gaelin, Gayle, Gaylen, Gaylon

Gaylord (French) high-energy
Gallerd, Galurd, Gaylar, Gayllaird, Gaylor

Gaynor (Irish) spunky
Gainer, Gaye, Gayner

Gayton (Irish) fair
Gayten, Gaytun

Gaza (Arabic) place name; strong

Gazara (Biblical) place name

Gean (American) form of Gene: noble

Gearld (English) changes

Gearn (English) changes

Geary (English) flexible
Gearey

Gebby (German) gifted

Gedaliah (Hebrew) great in
Jehovah's love
*Gedalia, Gedaliahu, Gedalya,
Gedalyahu*

Gedion (French) form of Gideon:
power-wielding

Gedor (Biblical) place name

Geer (German) spearman
Geere

Gefaniah (Hebrew) vineyard of
the Lord; grows
*Gefania, Gefanya, Gephania,
Gephaniah*

Geibe (American) bright

Geir (Biblical) shining

Geka (Scandinavian) armed

Gelo (Russian) nobility

Gemini (Astrology) zodiac twins;
intelligent

Gen (Slavic) family man

Genaro (Latin) dedicated
Genaroe, Genaroh

Gene (Greek) noble
Geno, Jene, Jeno

General (American) military rank
as name; leader

Genio (Spanish) blue blood

Gennaro (Latin) devout

Geno (Italian) spontaneous

Genoah (Place name) city in Italy
Genoa, Jenoa, Jenoah

Genoris (Italian) giving

Genovese (Italian) spontaneous;
from Genoa
Genno, Geno, Genovise, Genovize

Gent (American) from gentleman;
mannerly
Gynt, Jent, Jynt

Gentil (Spanish) charming
Gentilo

Gentry (American) high breeding
Genntrie, Gent, Gentree, Gentrie

Genty (Irish) man of snow; changes

Geo (Greek) form of George:
land-loving; farmer
Gee

Geoff (English) form of Geoffrey:
peaceful
Jeff

Geoffrey (English) peaceful
*Geffry, Geoff, Geoffie, Geoffry,
Geoffy, Geofry, Jeff*

Geordan (Scottish) from the hill

Georg (German) works with the
earth

George (Greek) land-loving; farmer
*Georg, Georgi, Georgie, Georgy,
Jorg, Jorge*

George-Hamilton (American)
star quality

Georgio (Italian) earth-worker
Giorgio, Jorgio, Jorjeo, Jorjio

Georgios (Greek) land-loving

Georgy (Greek) form of George:
land-loving; farmer
Georgee, Georgi, Georgie

Geraint (English) old

Gerald (German) strong; ruling
with a spear
Geralde, Gerrald, Gerre, Gerry

Gerant (Welsh) eldest

Gerar (French) brave

Gerard (French) brave
Gerord, Gerr, Gerrard

Gerardus (American) brave

Gerben (Dutch) spear-wielder

Gerber (Last name as first name)
particular
Gerb

Gerbold (German) bold with a
spear
Gerbolde

Gerdano (Italian) descends

Gere (English) spear-wielding;
dramatic
Gear

Gereon (German) old soul

Gerhard (German) forceful;
(French) finds
Ger, Gerd

Gerico (American) form of
Jericho: nocturnal

Gerlach (German) athlete with
spears; musical

Gerlie (Spanish) wins

Germain (French) growing; from
Germany
Germa, Germaine, Germane,
Germay, Germayne, Jermaine

German (German) from the
country of Germany

Gerod (English) form of Gerard:
brave
Garard, Geraldo, Gerarde, Gere,
Gererde, Gerry, Gerus, Giraud,
Jerade, Jerard, Jere, Jerod, Jerott, Jerry

Gerodi (Italian) form of Gerod:
brave

Gerold (Danish) rules with spears
Gerrold, Gerry

Geronimo (Italian) sacred name
Geronimoh

Gerrist (Slavic) strong

Gerrit (Dutch) protective

Gerry (English) form of Gerald:
strong; ruling with a spear
Gerr, Gerre, Gerree, Gerrey, Gerri,
Gerrie

Gersh (Biblical) form of Gershon:
his banishment; the change of
pilgrimage
Gershe, Gursh, Gurshe

Gershom (Hebrew) exile

Gershon (Biblical) his
banishment; the change of
pilgrimage

Gerson (English) Gary's son

Gerton (English) town of Gary

Gervaise (French) man of honor
Gerv, Gervase, Gervay

Gervasio (Spanish) aggressive
Gervase, Gervaso, Jervasio

Gervis (German) honored
Gerv, Gervace, Gervaise, Gervey,
Jervaise, Jervis

Gerwyn (Welsh) fair and lovely

Geshem (Hebrew) raining

Geter (Origin unknown) hopeful
Getterr, Getur

Gether (Biblical) in the dark

Gethin (Welsh) dark skin

Gevariah (Hebrew) strength
Gevaria, Gevarya, Gevaryah,
Gevaryahu

Ghalby (Origin unknown)
winning
Galby

Ghalib (Arabic) wins

Ghassan (Arabic) in the prime
of life

Ghayth (Arabic) victor
Ghaith

Gheorgh (Welsh) form of
George: land-loving; farmer

Ghorm (American) form of
Gorm: blue-eyed

Ghoshal (Hindi) the speaker
Ghoshil

Ghulam (Arabic) slave; servant

Gi (Italian) form of Giann:
believer in a gracious God

Giacomo (Italian) replacement;
musical
Como, Gia

Giann (Italian) believer in a
gracious God
Ghiann, Giahanni, Gian, Gianni,
Giannie, Gianny

Gianni (Italian) calm; believer in
God's grace
Giannie, Gianny

Gibbon (Scottish) strong
Gibben, Gibbons

Gibbs (English) form of Gibson:
smiling
Gib, Gibb, Gibbes

Gibeah (Biblical) a hill

Gibeon (Biblical) place name

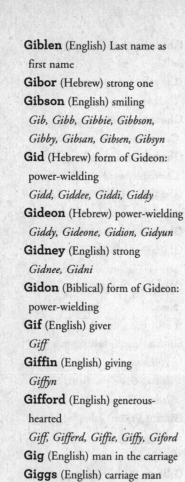

Giblen (English) Last name as first name

Gibor (Hebrew) strong one

Gibson (English) smiling
Gib, Gibb, Gibbie, Gibbson, Gibby, Gibsan, Gibsen, Gibsyn

Gid (Hebrew) form of Gideon: power-wielding
Gidd, Giddee, Giddi, Giddy

Gideon (Hebrew) power-wielding
Giddy, Gideone, Gidion, Gidyun

Gidney (English) strong
Gidnee, Gidni

Gidon (Biblical) form of Gideon: power-wielding

Gif (English) giver
Giff

Giffin (English) giving
Giffyn

Gifford (English) generous-hearted
Giff, Gifferd, Giffie, Giffy, Giford

Gig (English) man in the carriage

Giggs (English) carriage man

Gil (Hebrew) form of Gilam: joyful people
Gill

Gilad (Hebrew) testimonial hill; outspoken
Giladi, Gilead

Gilam (Hebrew) joyful people

Gilbert (English) intelligent
Gil, Gilber, Gilburt, Gill, Gilly

Gilberto (Spanish) bright
Bertie, Berty, Gil, Gilb, Gilburto, Gillberto, Gilly

Gilboa (Biblical) place name

Gilbran (Spanish) thinker

Gilby (Irish) blond
Gilbie, Gill, Gillbi

Gilchrist (Irish) open
Gill

Gildardo (German) excellent

Gildea (Irish) God's servant

Gildo (Italian) macho
Gil, Gill, Gilly

Giles (French) protective
Gile, Gyles

Gilesp (Irish) form of Gillespie: humble

Gilford (English) kindhearted
Gill, Gillford, Guilford

Gilgal (Biblical) place name

Gill (Hebrew) happy man
Gil, Gilli, Gillie, Gilly

Gillanders (Scottish) serves

Gillean (Scottish) able server
Gillan, Gillen, Gillian

Gillent (French) form of Gilbert: intelligent

Gilles (French) miraculous
Geal, Zheal, Zheel

Gillespie (Irish) humble
Gilespie, Gill, Gilley, Gilli, Gilly

Gillett (French) hospitable
Gelett, Gelette, Gillette

Gilley (American) countrified
Gill, Gilleye, Gilli, Gilly

Gillian (Irish) devout
Gill, Gilley, Gilly, Gillyun

Gillor (American) serves well

Gilman (Irish) serving well
Gilley, Gilli, Gillman, Gillmand, Gilly, Gilmand, Gilmon

Gilmer (English) riveting
Gelmer, Gill, Gillmer, Gilly

Gilmi (Irish) devout

Gilmore (Irish) riveting
Gill, Gillmore, Gilmohr

Gilo (Hebrew) joyful

Gilon (Hebrew) joyful
Gill

Gilroy (Irish) king's devotee
Gilderoy, Gildray, Gildrey, Gildroy, Gillroy

Gilson (Irish) devoted son

Gilus (Scottish) Jesus's servant

Gimarrai (Biblical) place name

Gimzo (Biblical) place name

Ginnesar (Biblical) place name

Gino (Italian) of good breeding; outgoing
Geeno, Geino, Ginoh

Gins (Greek) life-giving

Ginton (Hebrew) garden

Giona (Italian) form of Giovanni: jovial; happy believer

Giordano (Italian) delivered
Giorgie, Jiordano

Giorgio (Italian) earthy; creative
George, Georgeeo, Georgo, Jorge, Jorgio

Giovanni (Italian) jovial; happy believer
Geovanni, Gio, Giovani, Giovannie, Giovanny, Vannie, Vanny, Vonny

Gipsy (English) travels widely

Girioel (Welsh) Lord

Girolamo (Italian) form of Jerome: holy name; blessed

Giron (American) form of Garon: gentle

Girvin (Irish) tough-minded
Girvan, Girven, Girvon

Gisbert (French) aggressor

Gisli (French) loyal

Gitel (Hebrew) good

Gittaim (Biblical) place name

Gitte (Scandinavian) celebrated

Gittel (Hebrew) good

Giulio (Italian) youth

Giuseppe (Italian) capable
Beppo, Giusepe, Gusepe

Given (Last name as first name) gift
Givens, Gyvan, Gyven, Gyvin

Givon (Hebrew) boy of heights

Gizmo (American) playful
Gis, Gismo, Giz

Gizon (Spanish) morning

Glad (American) happy
Gladd, Gladde, Gladdi, Gladdie, Gladdy

Gladspell (Last name as first name) happy

Gladston (Last name as first name) happy

Gladstone (English) cheering

Gladus (Welsh) lame; rueful

Gladwyn (English) friend who has a light heart
Glad, Gladdy, Gladwin, Gladwynn

Glaisne (Irish) serene
Glasny

Glancy (American) form of Clancy: lively; feisty redhead
Glance, Glancee, Glancey, Glanci

Glanville (French) serene

Glasgow (Place name) city in Scotland

Glasson (Scottish) from Glasgow, Scotland

Glause (Spanish) blue eyes

Glen (Irish) natural wonder
Glenn

Glenard (Irish) from a glen; nature-loving
Glen, Glenerd, Glenn, Glennard, Glenni, Glennie

Glendon (Scottish) fortified in nature
Glen, Glend, Glenden, Glenn, Glynden

Glendower (Welsh) water valley boy

Glenmore (English) valley boy

Glenn (Irish) natural wonder
Glen, Glenni, Glennie, Glenny, Glynn, Glynny

Glennon (Last name as first name) living in a valley
Glenen, Glennen, Glenon

Glenward (Last name as first name)

Gloster (Place name) from Gloucester

Glyndwr (Welsh) water valley life
Glyn, Glynn, Glynne

Glynn (Welsh) lives in a restful glen
Glin, Glinn, Glyn

Gobi (Place name) desert in Central Asia; audacious
Gobee, Gobie

Gobind (Sanskrit) the name of a Hindu deity
Govind

Gockley (Last name as first name) peaceful
Gocklee

Goddard (German) staunch in spirituality
Godard, Godderd, Goddird

Godfred (German) peaceful; God's child

Godfrey (Irish) peaceful
Godfree, Godfrie, Godfry

Godfried (German) imbued with God's peace
Godfreed

Godinez (Spanish) loves God

Godofredo (Spanish) form of Godfrey: peaceful

Godric (English) man of God
Godrick, Godrik, Godryc, Godryck, Godryk

Godridge (Last name as first name) place of God

Godwin (English) close to God
Godwinn, Godwyn, Godwynn

Goel (Hebrew) redeemed

Goethe (Last name as first name) poet

Goforth (English) peace wish

Gofraidh (Irish) God's peace child
Gothfraidh, Gothraidh

Goger (Last name as first name) paternal

Gohn (African American) spirited
Gon

Golan (Biblical) place name

Golding (English) golden boy

Goldo (English) golden
Golo

Goliath (Hebrew) large
Goliathe

Gombos (Last name as first name) thorough

Gomda (Native American) wind's moods

Gomer (English) famed fighter
Gomar, Gomher, Gomor

Gomorr (Place name) the battle

Gong (American) forceful

Gonz (Spanish) form of Gonzalo: feisty wolf
Gons, Gonz, Gonza, Gonzales, Gonzalez

Gonzales (Spanish) feisty
Gonzalez

Gonzalo (Spanish) feisty wolf
Gonz, Gonzoloh

Goode (English) good
Good, Goodey, Goody

Goodman (Last name as first name) a good man
Goodeman

Goodreau (French) good

Goodrich (Last name as first name) giving; good
Goodriche

Gopin (Indian) cow song

Gor (Last name as first name) hill

Goran (Croatian) good

Gordion (Biblical) place name

Gordo (American) jovial guy

Gordon (English) nature-lover; hill
Gord, Gordan, Gorden, Gordi, Gordie, Gordy

Gordy (English) form of Gordon: nature-lover; hill
Gordee, Gordi, Gordie

Gore (English) practical; pie-shaped land

Gorgey (Latin) gorge

Gorgonio (Greek) trouble

Gorham (English) sophisticated; name of a silver company
Goram

Gorky (Place name) Russian amusement park in the novel *Gorky Park*; mysterious
Gork, Gorkee, Gorkey, Gorki

Gorm (Irish) blue-eyed

Gorman (Irish) small man
Gormann, Gormen

Gormlee (Irish) blue-eyed

Goro (Japanese) fifth son

Goron (Welsh) handsome

Gosheven (Native American) leaps well; athletic

Goss (English/German) Last name as first name

Gotam (Hindi) best cow; cherished
Gautam, Gautoma

Gottfried (German) form of Godfried: imbued with God's peace

Gotzon (German) angel

Goulet (French) Last name as first name

Gouriet (French) charming

Govannon (Welsh) craftsman

Gower (Welsh) unblemished

Gowon (African) rainmaking

Gozal (Hebrew) baby bird; trying his wings

Gozan (Biblical) place name

Gradin (Irish) diligent

Grady (Irish) hardworking
Grade, Gradee, Gradey

Grae (Scottish) grand

Graem (Scottish) homebody
Graeme

Graffen (Last name as first name) distinguished

Graffin (American) form of Griffin: unconventional

Graham (English) wealthy; grand house
Graeham, Graeme, Grame

Graig (American) form of Craig: brave climber

Grail (Word as name) desired; sought after
Grale, Grayle

Grajeda (Spanish) crow

Gram (American) form of Graham: wealthy; grand house

Granace (American) gray

Granados (Spanish) grand

Granbel (Last name as first name) grand and attractive
Granbell

Granberry (English) farms berries

Granderson (Last name as first name) grand
Grand, Grander

Grange (French) lonely; on the farm
Grainge, Granger, Grangher

Granicus (Biblical) place name

Granison (Last name as first name) son of Gran; grandiose
Gran, Grann

Granit (English) great

Granite (American) rock; hard
Granet

Grant (English) expansive
Grandt, Grann, Grannt

Grantland (French) tall

Grantly (French) tall; lithe
Grantlea, Grantleigh, Grantley

Granvar (English) grand

Granville (French) grandiose
Grann, Granvel, Granvelle, Gravil

Grarol (English) gray

Grasshopper (American) lively

Gratton (Last name as first name) God loved

Graven (English) gray

Gravette (Origin unknown) grave
Gravet

Gravitt (English) gray

Gray (English) hair of gray
Graye, Grey

Grayce (English) gray hair

Graydon (Last name as first name) graceful

Grayer (English) gray

Graylon (English) gray-haired
Gray, Grayan, Graylan, Graylin

Grayson (English) son of man with gray hair
Gray, Grey, Greyson

Graz (Place name) city in Austria

Grazi (Italian) gracious

Graziano (Italian) dearest
Graciano, Graz

Greco (Italian) kind

Gredy (Last name as first name)

Greek (American) Greek

Greeley (English) careful
Grealey, Greel, Greely

Greenlee (English) outdoorsy
Green, Greenlea, Greenly

Greenwood (English) untamed;
forest
*Greene, Greenwoode, Greenwude,
Grenwood*

Greer (Last name as first name) sly
Greere, Grier

Greerzen (American) son of
Greer

Greg (Latin) form of Gregory:
careful
Gregg, Greggie, Greggy

Greger (Scandinavian) form of
Gregory: careful

Gregoire (French) watchful
Gregorie

Gregor (Greek) cautious
Greger, Gregors, Greig

Gregorio (Greek) careful

Gregory (Greek) careful
*Greg, Greggory, Greggy, Gregori,
Gregorie, Gregry*

Gregson (Last name as first
name) son of Greg; careful
Greggsen, Greggson, Gregsen

Grekel (American) vigilant

Grenville (New Zealand)
outdoorsy
Granville, Gren

Gresham (English) of pasture
village; sylvan
Grisham

Greville (English) thoughtful

Grey (Last name as first name)
quiet; grey-haired
Greyson

Griden (Norse) peacemaker

Griffaw (Latin) ruddy

Griffin (Latin) unconventional
*Greffen, Griff, Griffee, Griffen,
Griffey, Griffie, Griffon, Griffy*

Griffith (Welsh) able leader
*Griff, Griffee, Griffey, Griffie,
Griffy*

Grigg (Welsh) vigilant

Grigori (Russian) watchful
Grig, Grigor

Grimbald (Last name as first
name) dark
Grimbold

Grimes (English) spunky

Grimm (English) grim; dark
Grim, Grym

Grimshaw (English) from a dark
forest; quiet

Grindon (Last name as first
name)

Gris (German) gray
Griz

Grischa (German) form of
Gregory: careful

Griswald (German) bland
Greswold, Gris, Griswold

Grogan (Last name as first name)

Grosvenor (French) hunts well

Grover (English) thriving
Grove

Gruver (Origin unknown)
ambitious
Gruever

Gualberto (Spanish) believer

Gualter (Spanish) form of
Walter: army leader

Guanjone (Spanish) strong

Guapo (Spanish) looker

Guard (American) protects

Guasparre (Italian) values

Gudy (German) good

Guenter (German) warrior

Guerdon (English) combative

Guerino (Italian) protects

Guerry (English) aggressive

Guido (Italian) form of Guy: wood
Guidoh, Gwedo, Gweedo

Guilford (English) from a ford with yellow flowers; nature-lover
Gilford, Guildford

Guillerm (German) form of William: staunch protector

Guillermo (Spanish) attentive
Guilermo, Gulermo

Gull (Scandinavian) godlike

Gullen (Scandinavian) godlike

Gullet (Latin) throat

Gulshan (Hindi) gardener; flourishes

Gultekin (Turkish) Last name as first name

Gulzar (Arabic) thrives

Gumecindo (Spanish) excellent

Gunder (Scandinavian) form of Gunnar: bold

Gundy (American) friendly
Gundee

Gunion (Last name as first name)

Gunn (Scandinavian) macho; gunman
Gun, Gunner

Gunnar (Scandinavian) bold
Gunn, Gunner, Gunnir

Guntersen (Scandinavian) macho; gunman
Gun, Gunth

Gunther (Scandinavian) able fighter
Gunn, Gunnar, Gunner, Guntar, Gunthar, Gunthur

Gunvor (Scandinavian) watchful

Gunyon (American) tough; gunman
Gunn, Gunyun

Gur (Hindi) from guru; teacher

Gurd (Scandinavian) guards

Gurjeet (Indian) at the feet of the guru

Gurley (Last name as first name) leads

Gurmot (German) speared

Gurpreet (Hindi) devoted follower

Guryon (Hebrew) lionlike
Garon, Gorion, Gurion

Gus (Scandinavian) form of Augustus: highly esteemed; form of Gustaf: armed; vital
Guss, Gussi, Gussy, Gussye

Gustachian (American) pretentious
Gus, Gussy, Gust

Gustaf (German) armed; vital
Gus, Gusstof, Gustav, Gustovo

Gustavo (Spanish) vital; gusto
Gus, Gustaffo, Gustav

Gustin (Spanish) serious

Gusto (Spanish) pleasure
Gusty

Gustus (Scandinavian) royal
Gus, Gustaf, Gustave, Gustavo

Guth (Irish) form of Guthrie: windy; heroic
Guthe, Guthry

Guthrie (Irish) windy; heroic
Guthree, Guthry

Gutierre (Spanish) form of Walter: army leader

Guto (Welsh) royal; tired

Guy (French) wood
Guye

Guyon (French) leads

Guzet (American) bravado
Guzz, Guzzett, Guzzie

Gwandoya (African) miserable fate

Gweedo (Invented) form of Guido: wood

Gwent (Place name) city in Wales

Gwill (American) dark-eyed
Gewill, Guwill

Gwynedd (Welsh) fair-haired
Gwyn, Gwynfor, Gwynn, Gwynne

Gwynn (Welsh) fair
Gwen, Gwyn

Gyan (Hindi) knowledgeable
Gyani

Gyanee (Italian) form of Gianni: calm; believer in God's grace

Gyasi (African) terrific man

Gye (American) knowing

Gylfi (Scandinavian) king; stealthy

Gyllen (Last name as first name) young

Gylmar (German) loyal

Gyorgy (Italian) form of George: land-loving; farmer

Gyronne (Hindi) wise

Gysen (Hindi) wise

Gysley (English) excellent

Gyth (American) capable
Gith, Gythe

Gyuri (Slavic) form of George: land-loving; farmer

Haadee (Arabic) leader

Haafiz (Arabic) protector

Haakon (Scandinavian) chosen son

Haaris (Arabic) good man

Haas (Last name as first name) good

Habakkuk (Hebrew) embrace

Habby (Hebrew) loved

Habib (Arabic) well-loved
Habeeb

Habie (Origin unknown) jovial
Hab

Habimama (African) believer in God

Habor (Biblical) place name

Hachiro (Japanese) eighth son

Hachman (Last name as first name) chops
Hachmann, Hachmin

Hackett (Last name as first name) chops

Hackman (German) fervent; hacks wood
Hackmann

Hadad (Arabic) calm; blacksmith

Hadar (Hebrew) respected
Hadaram, Hadur, Heder

Hadaway (English) from the heather hill

Hadden (American) bright; natural
Haddan, Haddin, Haddon, Haden, Hadon

Haddy (English) form of Hadley: lover of nature; meadow with heather
Had, Haddee, Haddey, Haddi

Hade (Arabic) leads in the right way

Hades (Mythology) Greek god of the dead

Hadi (Arabic) guide

Hadle (English) from the meadow of heather

Hadley (English) lover of nature; meadow with heather
Haddleye, Hadlee, Hadlie, Hadly

Hadran (Latin) dark

Hadrian (Roman) from Hadria

Hadriel (Hebrew) blessed

Hadwin (Last name as first name) natural man
Hadwyn

Haffey (Indian) protects

Haffi (Indian) protects

Hafiz (Arabic) guards others
Hafeez, Hapheez, Haphiz

Hagan (German) defender
Hagen, Haggan, Haggin

Hagar (Hebrew) wanders

Hagen (German) chosen one
Hagan, Haggen

Haggai (Biblical) festive

Haggerty (Irish) Last name as first name; unjust

Hagins (German) strong

Hagit (Last name as first name) defends

Hagley (Last name as first name) defensive

Hahn (Last name as first name) asks

Haidar (Hindi) lionlike
Haider, Haydar, Hyder

Haig (Armenian) strong ancestry

Haike (Asian) of the water

Hailen (Irish) clever

Haim (Hebrew) alive
Hayim, Hayyim

Haines (Last name as first name) confident
Hanus, Haynes

Hajile (Arabic) wanders

Hajir (Arabic) powerful

Hakan (Arabic) fair

Hakim (Arabic) brilliant
Hakeam, Hakeem, Hakym

Hako (Japanese) honorable

Hakon (Scandinavian) chosen son
Haaken, Haakin, Haakon, Hacon, Hagan, Hagen, Hakan, Hako

Hal (English) home ruler

Haland (Last name as first name) island
Halland

Halbert (Last name as first name) island
Bert, Hal

Haldane (German) fierce; person who is half Danish
Haldayn, Haldayne

Haldas (Last name as first name) dependable

Halden (German) man who is half Dane
Haldan, Haldane, Haldin, Halfdan

Haldin (Scandinavian) half-Danish

Haldor (Scandinavian) thunderous rock

Hale (English) heroic
Hal, Halee, Haley, Hali

Halen (Swedish) portal to life
Hailen, Hale, Haley, Hallen, Haylen, Haylin

Haley (Irish) innovative
Hail, Hailee, Hailey, Hale, Halee, Hayley

Halford (Last name as first name) kind

Hali (Greek) loves the sea

Hall (English) solemn

Hallahan (Last name as first name)

Hallam (African) gentle

Hallberg (English) comes from a town of valleys
Halberg, Halburg, Hallburg

Halle (Scandinavian) rocklike dependability

Hallen (Scandinavian) from the hall

Halley (English) holy man

Halliwell (Last name as first name) sea-loving

Hallman (English) his hall

Hallmark (English) stalwart

Hallward (English) guards the hall; wily
Halward, Halwerd, Hawarden

Halmer (English) robust

Halos (Greek) halo

Halse (English) on the island
Halce, Halsi, Halsy, Halzee, Halzie

Halsey (English) isolated; island

Halstead (Last name as first name) home on the rock
Halsted

Halston (Origin unknown) fashionable

Halton (English) town on a hill; country boy
Hallton, Halten

Halvard (Scandinavian) staunch
Halvor, Hallvard

Halver (Scandinavian) protects

Halwell (English) special
Hallwell, Halwel, Halwelle

Halyna (Slavic) calm

Ham (Last name as first name) praising

Hamaker (Last name as first name) industrious
Ham

Hamal (Arabic) lamb

Hamar (Scandinavian) hammer

Hamath (Biblical) place name

Hamby (Last name as first name)

Hamid (Arabic) grateful
Hameed

Hamidi (Arabic) ham
Hamedi, Hameedi, Hamm, Hammad

Hamil (English) rough-hewn
Hamel, Hamell, Hamill, Hamm

Hamilton (English) benefiting
Hamelton, Hamil, Hammilton

Hamish (Irish) form of James: he who supplants

Hamlet (German) ham
Hamlette, Hamlit, Hamm

Hamlin (German) homebody
Hamaline, Hamelin, Hamlen, Hamlyn

Hamm (English) Last name as first name; low-lying land by a stream

Hammer (German) works with a hammer; able
Hammar, Hammur

Hammond (English) ingenious
Ham, Hamm, Hammon, Hamond

Hamon (Scandinavian) leader
Hamo

Hamor (Hebrew) organized

Hamp (American) fun-loving
Ham, Hampton

Hampden (English) distinctive; valley home

Hampton (English) distinctive
Ham, Hamm, Hamp, Hampt

Hamza (Arabic) endures

Han (Arabic) form of Hani: happy

Hanan (Arabic) forgiving

Hanani (Arabic) merciful

Hancock (English) has a farm; practical

Handel (German) form of John: God is gracious

Haneef (Arabic) believer

Hanford (Last name as first name) forgiving
Hamford

Hani (Arabic) happy

Hanif (Arabic) Islam believer

Hanisi (African) Thursday-born

Hank (English) form of Henry: leader
Hankey, Hanks, Hanky

Hanley (English) natural; meadow high
Han, Hanlee, Hanleigh, Hanly

Hannelore (Scandinavian) combo of Hanne and Lore

Hannes (Scandinavian) form of Johannes: God is gracious
Hahnes

Hannibal (Slavic) leader
Hanibal, Hanibel, Hann

Hannon (Hebrew) boy of gracefulness

Hanoch (Hebrew) loyal

Hanry (American) form of Henry: leader

Hans (Scandinavian) believer; warm
Hahns, Hanz, Hons

Hansa (Scandinavian) traditional; believer in a gracious Lord
Hans

Hansel (Scandinavian) gullible; open
Hans, Hansie, Hanzel

Hansen (Scandinavian) warm; Hans's son
Han, Handsen, Hans, Hansan, Hanson, Hanssen, Hansson, Hanz

Hans-Joachim (Scandinavian) combo of Hans and Joachim

Hansonn (Scandinavian) son of Hans

Hansraj (Hindi) king of swans; smooth

Hany (Arabic) happy

Haon (Hawaiian) relaxed

Hap (American) form of Hapney: happenstance

Hapney (English) happenstance

Haqq (Arabic) truth

Haran (Biblical) place name; Abraham's brother

Harbin (English) optimist

Harcourt (English) loves nature

Hardeep (Indian) God-loving

Hardell (German) bold

Hardeman (German) bold

Hardesty (German) brave

Hardin (English) lively; valley of hares
Hardee, Harden

Harding (English) fiery
Harden, Hardeng

Hardwick (English) castle boy
Harwyck

Hardwin (English) keeps hares

Hardy (American) fun-loving; substantial
Harday, Hardey, Hardie, Harding

Harean (African) aware

Harel (Scandinavian) ruler

Harence (English) swift

Harford (English) jolly
Harferd

Hargis (English) Last name as first name; baptismal name of son of Agace

Hargrave (Saxon) Last name as first name; provider or commissary of an army

Hargrove (English) fruitful

Hari (Hindi) brownish-orange

Harim (Arabic) above all

Harish (Indian) generous

Harjit (Indian) lights the way

Hark (American) word as name; behold
Harko

Harkin (Irish) red-faced
Harkan, Harken

Harlan (English) army land; athletic
Hal, Harl, Harlen, Harlon, Harlynn

Harland (English) strong fighter's land

Harld (Scandinavian) form of Harold: leader of an army

Harlemm (African American) dancer
Harl, Harlam, Harlem, Harlems, Harlum, Harly

Harley (English) wild-spirited
Harl, Harlee, Harly

Harlow (English) bold
Harlo, Harloh

Harmon (German) dependable
Harm, Harman, Harmen

Harmony (Mythology) from Harmonia; in harmony with life
Harmonio

Harness (English) word as name

Harod (Biblical) king
Harrod

Harold (Scandinavian) leader of an army
Hal, Harald, Hareld, Harry

Haron (Arabic) praiseworthy

Harper (English) artistic and musical; harpist
Harp

Harpo (American) jovial
Harpoh, Harrpo

Harpreet (Indian) God-loving

Harreal (Indian) happy

Harrell (Hebrew) likes the mountain of God; religious

Harrington (English) comes from the town of Harry; old-fashioned

Harris (English) dignified
Haris, Harriss

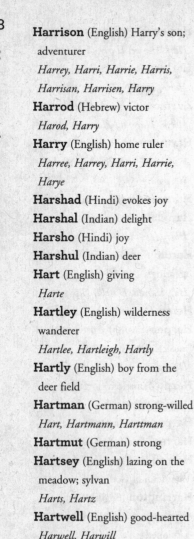

Harrison (English) Harry's son; adventurer

Harrey, Harri, Harrie, Harris, Harrisan, Harrisen, Harry

Harrod (Hebrew) victor

Harod, Harry

Harry (English) home ruler

Harree, Harrey, Harri, Harrie, Harye

Harshad (Hindi) evokes joy

Harshal (Indian) delight

Harsho (Hindi) joy

Harshul (Indian) deer

Hart (English) giving

Harte

Hartley (English) wilderness wanderer

Hartlee, Hartleigh, Hartly

Hartly (English) boy from the deer field

Hartman (German) strong-willed

Hart, Hartmann, Harttman

Hartmut (German) strong

Hartsey (English) lazing on the meadow; sylvan

Harts, Hartz

Hartwell (English) good-hearted

Harwell, Harwill

Hartwig (German) strong

Haruki (Japanese) child of the spring

Harun (Arabic) highly regarded

Harv (German) able combatant

Har

Harve (French) strong fighter

Harvey (German) fighter

Harv, Harvi, Harvie, Harvy

Harwin (American) safe

Harwen, Harwon

Harwood (English) from the deer wood; artistic

Harewood

Hasan (Arabic) attractive

Hasani (African) good

Hasees (Arabic) good

Hashim (Arabic) force for good

Hasheem

Hashum (African) crushes

Heshum

Hasin (Arabic) handsome

Hasen, Hassin

Hask (Hebrew) form of Haskell: ingratiating

Haske

Haskell (Hebrew) ingratiating

Hask, Haskel, Haskie, Hasky

Haslett (English) land of hazel trees; worthy

Haslit, Haslitt, Hazel, Hazlett, Hazlitt

Hassan (Arabic) good-looking

Hasan

Hasso (German) sun

Hasson

Hastings (English) leader

Haste

Haswell (English) dignified

Has, Haz

Hattan (Place name) from Manhattan; sophisticate

Hatt

Hauran (Biblical) place name

Haval (Biblical) waste

Havard (Scandinavian) guardian of the home

Hav

Havelock (Czech) form of Paul: small; wise

Haven (English) sanctuary

Haiv, Hav

Haward (English) guards the hedge; border man

Hawarden

Hawes (English) stays by the hedges

Haws

Hawke (English) watchful; falcon

Hauk, Hawk

Hawley (English) boy from the hedge

Hawthorne (English) observer

Hay (English) hedge

Hayde (English) hedge

Hayden ○ ❶ (English) respectful
Haden, Hadon, Hay, Haydon,
Haydyn, Hayton

Haye (English) open

Hayes (English) open
Haies, Hay, Haye

Hayman (English) hedging
Hay

Haymo (Last name as first name)
good-natured

Hayne (English) working
outdoors
Haine, Haines, Haynes

Hayres (English) aware

Hayward (English) creative; good
work ethic
Hay, Heyward

Hayword (English) open-minded
Haword, Hayward, Haywerd

Haz (Hebrew) sees God

Hazael (Old English) hazel tree

Hazaiah (Hebrew) believes God's
decisions

Hazard (Origin Unknown)
hazzard

Hazen (English) form of Hayes:
open
Hazin

Hazleton (English) from woods
of hazel trees

Hazlewood (English) from
woods of hazel trees

Hearn (English) optimistic
Hearne, Hern

Heath (English) open space;
natural
Heathe, Heith, Heth

Heathcliff (English) mysterious

Heaton (English) high-principled
Heat, Heatan, Heaten

Heber (Hebrew) partner;
togetherness
Hebor

Hebron (Biblical) friend

Hector (Greek) loyal
Hec, Heck, Heco, Hect, Hectar,
Hecter, Hekter, Tito

Heddwyn (Welsh) peaceful; fair-
haired
Hedwin, Hedwyn, Hedwynn

Hedeon (Russian) woodsman

Hedgardo (Spanish) vigilant

Hedley (English) natural

Hedwig (German) combative

Hedwin (German) peaceful ally

Hefastus (Greek) clear

Heffington (Last name as first
name)

Heike (Welsh) peaceful

Heiko (Dutch) rowdy

Heimdall (Scandinavian) white god
Heiman, Heimann

Hein (German) advising
Heiiri, Heiner, Heini, Heinlich

Heinrich (German) form of
Henry: leader
Hein, Heine, Heinrick, Heinrik

Heinz (German) advisor
Heinze

Heladio (Spanish) boy born in
Greece; ingenious
Eladio, Elado, Helado

Heleph (Biblical) place name

Helger (Slavic) holy

Helgi (Scandinavian) happy
Helge

Helio (Hispanic) bright

Heliodor (Greek) sun's adoration

Heliodoro (Greek) sun's
adoration

Helios (Greek) sun

Heller (German) brilliant

Hellerson (German) brilliant
one's son; smart
Helley

Helm (German) bravery

Helmand (German) helmet;
protected

Helmar (German) protected;
smart
Helm, Helmer, Helmet, Helmut

Helmut (German) courageous

Helon (Biblical) window; grief

Heman (Last name as first name) direct

Hemant (Indian) season

Hemin (Hebrew) loyal
Heman

Hender (German) ruler; illustrious
Hend

Henderson (English) reliable
Hender, Hendersen, Hendersyn

Hendrik (German) home ruler
Heinrich, Hendrick, Henrick, Hindrick

Hendtrax (Hebrew) gifted

Henech (Last name as first name) leading the pack
Henach

Henley (English) surprising
Henlee, Henly, Henlye, Hinley

Henning (Scandinavian) ruler

Henrik (Norwegian) leader
Henric, Henrick

Henry ✪ (German) leader
Hal, Hank, Harry, Henny, Henree, Henri

Hensarling (Last name as first name)

Henshaw (Last name as first name)

Henson (Last name as first name) son of Hen; quiet

Heraldo (Spanish) divine

Herb (German) energetic
Herbi, Herbie, Herby, Hurb

Herber (French) valiant

Herbert (German) famed warrior
Bert, Herb, Herbart, Herberto, Herbie, Herbirt, Herby, Hurb, Hurbert

Herbertson (German) famed soldier's son

Hercule (French) strong
Harekuel, Hercuel, Herkuel

Hercules (Greek) grand gift
Herc, Herk, Herkules

Heriberto (Spanish) form of Herbert: famed warrior
Heribert

Herkamer (Last name as first name)

Herman (Latin) fair fighter
Heremon, Herm, Hermahn, Hermann, Hermie, Hermon, Hermy

Hermangildo (Spanish) combative

Hermes (Greek) courier of messages
Hermez

Hermod (Scandinavian) greets and welcomes

Hermosillo (Spanish) fighter

Hernand (Spanish) form of Hernando: bold

Hernando (Spanish) bold
Hernan

Herndon (English) nature-loving
Hern, Hernd

Herne (English) from the bird heron; inventive
Hearne, Hern

Hernley (English) from the heron meadow; easygoing
Hernlea, Hernlee, Hernlie, Hernly

Herodotus (Greek) the father of history

Heroico (Spanish) hero

Herol (American) form of Harold: leader of an army

Herrick (Last name as first name) never alone

Herris (German) rules

Herrod (Biblical) king
Herod

Herron (Latin) heroic

Herschel (Hebrew) deer; swift
Hersch, Hersh, Hershel, Hershell, Hershelle, Herzl, Hirchel, Hirsch, Hirshel

Hershall (Hebrew) deer; swift
Hersch, Herschel, Hersh, Herzl, Heshel, Hirschel, Hirsh, Hirshel

Hertzel (Hebrew) form of
Herschel; deer; swift
Hert, Hertsel, Hyrt

Herve (French) ready for battle

Hervey (American) form of
Harvey: fighter
Herv, Herve, Hervy

Herzon (American) fast
Herz, Herzan, Herzun

Hesed (Hebrew) sweet

Hesperos (Greek) evening star
Hesperios, Hespers

Hess (Last name as first name)
bold
Hes, Hys

Hessel (Dutch) bold man

Heston (Last name as first name)
star quality

Hetrick (Last name as first name)

Hevel (Hebrew) alive

Hewis (German) smart

Hewitt (German) smart
*Hew, Hewet, Hewett, Hewie,
Hewit, Hewy, Hugh*

Hewney (Irish) smart
Owney

Hewson (Irish) son of Hugh;
smart; giving

Heywood (Last name as first
name) thoughtful
Haywood

Hezekiah (Biblical) strong man
Hezeklah, Zeke

Hezron (Biblical) strength

Hiawatha (Native American)
Iroquois chief
Hia

Hibah (Arabic) the gift

Hickam (English) Last name as
first name; enclosed dwelling

Hickok (American) from Wild
Bill Hickok

Hidalgo (American) westerner

Hidde (Japanese) excellent

Hideaki (Japanese) cautious

Hideo (Japanese) excellent
Hideyo

Hieremias (Greek) God lifts
him up

Hieronymos (Greek) alternate
of Jerome
Heronymous

Hifz (Arabic) memorable

Higinio (Hispanic) forceful

Hilaire (French) happy child

Hilarion (Greek) cheery;
hilarious
Hilary, Hill

Hilary (Latin) joyful
*Hilaire, Hill, Hillarie, Hillary,
Hillery, Hilly, Hilorie*

Hildebrand (German)
combative; sword
Hill, Hilly

Hill (English) lives on a hill;
dreamy

Hillard (German) wars; diligent
Hilliard, Hillier, Hillyer

Hillel (Hebrew) praised; devout
Hilel, Hill

Hillery (Latin) happy; cheerful
Hill

Hilliard (German) brave;
settlement on the hill
*Hill, Hillard, Hillierd, Hilly,
Hillyerd, Hylliard*

Hills (Last name as first name)
brave; from the hills

Hilton (English) sophisticated
*Hillten, Hillton, Hiltan, Hiltawn,
Hiltyn, Hylton*

Himesh (Hindi) snow king

Hines (Last name as first name)
strong
Hine, Hynes

Hipolito (Spanish) man who
rides horses

Hippocrates (Greek)
philosopher
Hipp

Hippolyte (Greek) frees horses
Hippolit, Hippolitos, Hippolytus,
Ippolito

Hiram (Hebrew) most admired;
highly praised
Hi, Hirom, Hirym

Hiramatsu (Japanese) exalted

Hiranya (Indian) rich

Hiresh (Indian) treasured

Hiro (Japanese) giving

Hirsh (Hebrew) deer; swift
Hersh, Hershel, Hirschel, Hirshel

Hirza (Hebrew) lithe; deer

Hisham (Arabic) generous nature

Hitchcock (English) creative;
spooky
Hitch

Hixon (Last name as first name)
high-energy

Hjalmar (Scandinavian)
protective warrior
Hjalamar, Hjallmar, Hjalmer

Ho (Chinese) good

Hoan (Asian) complete child

Hoashis (Japanese) God

Hobart (German) haughty
Hobb, Hobert, Hoebard

Hobbes (English) form of
Robert: brilliant; renowned
Hob, Hobbs

Hobe (German) hill child

Hobert (German) studious

Hobson (English) helpful backer
Hobb, Hobbie, Hobbson, Hobby,
Hobsen

Hock (Asian) smart

Hockley (English) high meadow
boy
Hocklea, Hocklee, Hocklie, Hockly

Hockney (English) from a high
island
Hockny

Hodge (English) form of Roger:
famed warrior
Hodges

Hodgie (English) short for
Hodge: famed warrior
Hodgy

Hodgson (English) boy born to
Roger; up-and-coming
Hodge, Hodges

Hoffman (Last name as first
name) sophisticated

Hogan (Irish) high-energy;
vibrant
Hogahn, Hoge, Hoghan

Hogue (Last name as first name)
youth
Hoge

Hojar (American) wild spirit
Hobar, Hogar

Hoke (Origin unknown) popular

Hoken (American) liked

Holbert (German) capable
Hilbert

Holbrook (English) educated
Brooke, Brookie, Brooky, Holb,
Holbrooke

Holcomb (Last name as first
name) bright

Holday (American) form of
Holiday: born on a holy day

Holden (English) quiet; gracious
Holdan, Holdin, Holldun

Holder (English) musical
Hold, Holdher, Holdyer

Holdern (Last name as first
name)

Holegario (Spanish) superfluous
Holegard

Holger (Last name as first name)
devoted

Holiday (English) born on a holy
day
Holliday

Holling (English) holly

Hollis (English) flourishing
Holl, Hollace, Hollice, Hollie, Holly

Holloway (Last name as first
name) jovial
Hollo, Hollway, Holoway

Hollywood (Place name) city in California; showoff
Holly, Wood

Holm (English) natural; woodsy
Holms

Holmes (English) safe haven; from the river; natural home
Holmm, Holmmes

Holmfrid (Last name as first name) prefers home-and-hearth

Holon (Biblical) place name

Holt (English) shaded view
Holte, Holyte

Homain (Last name as first name) homebody
Holman, Holmen

Homarl (Greek) form of Homer: secure

Homaros (Greek) form of Homer: secure

Homer (Greek) secure
Hohmer, Home, Homere, Homero

Honda (African) form of Hondo: warrior

Hondo (African) warrior

Honesto (Spanish) truthful
Honesta, Honestoh

Hong (Vietnamese) pink; tasteful

Honorato (Spanish) full of honor
Honor, Honoratoh

Honoré (Latin) man who is honored
Honor, Honoray

Hood (Last name as first name) easygoing; player
Hoode, Hoodey

Hooker (English) shepherd

Hoolihan (American) hooligan
Hool, Hoole, Hooli

Hoop (American) ball player
Hooper, Hoopy

Hoover (Last name as first name)

Hopkins (Welsh) Robert's son; famous
Hopkin, Hopkinson, Hopkyns, Hopper, Hoppner

Hopper (Last name as first name) creative

Hoppy (American) lively

Horace (Latin) poetic
Horaace, Horase, Horice

Horatio (Latin) poetic; dashing
Horate, Horaysho

Horeb (Biblical) place name

Horgan (Last name as first name)

Hori (Biblical) prince; freeborn

Hornal (German) gardens

Horsley (English) calm field of horses; keeper
Horslea, Horsleigh, Horslie, Horsly

Horst (German) deep; thicket
Hurst

Horstman (German) profound
Horst, Horstmen, Horstmun

Horstmar (German) from the thicket; emphatic

Horston (German) thicket; sturdy
Horst

Horton (English) brash
Horten, Hortun

Horus (Egyptian) kind

Hosa (Native American) crow

Hosaam (Arabic) handsome

Hosea (Hebrew) prophet

Hoshea (Hebrew) saved

Hosie (Hebrew) form of Hosea: prophet
Hosaya, Hose

Hosni (Arabic) excellent

Houchan (English) spirited

Houghton (English) boy from the town on high

Houston (English) Texas city; rogue; hill town
Houst, Hust, Huston

Hovannes (Hebrew) form of Johannes: God is gracious

How (American) word as a name
Howe, Howey, Howie

Howard (English) well-liked
*How, Howerd, Howie, Howurd,
Howy*

Howart (Origin unknown) admired
Howar

Howden (English) careful

Howe (German) high-minded
How, Howey, Howie

Howell (Welsh) outstanding
Howel, Howey, Howie, Howill

Howent (English) distinctive

Howerd (English) form of
Howard: well-liked

Howlan (English) living on a hill;
high

Howland (American) well-known
Howlend, Howlond, Howlyn

Howze (American) form of
Howard: well-liked

Hoyt (Irish) spirited
Hoit, Hoye

Hrothgar (Literature) king

Huang (Chinese) rich

Hubbard (German) fine
Hubberd, Hubert, Hubie

Huber (German) intelligent

Hubert (German) intellectual
*Bert, Bertie, Burt, Hubart,
Huberd, Hue, Huebert, Hugh*

Hubie (English) form of Hubert:
intellectual
Hube, Hubee, Hubey, Hubi

Huck (Literature) from
Huckleberry Finn

Huckleberry (American) glossy
black berry; from *Huckleberry
Finn*; mischevious

Hud (English) charismatic cowboy
Hudd

Hudson (English) Hugh's son;
charismatic adventurer
Hud, Hudsan, Hudsen

Hudspeth (English) form of
Hud: charismatic cowboy

Hudya (Arabic) going the right
way

Huelett (American) bright;
southern
Hu, Hue, Huel, Hugh, Hulette

Huey (French) hearty

Hugh (English) intelligent
*Hue, Huey, Hughey, Hughi,
Hughie, Hughy*

Hughes (English) smart

Hughie (English) intelligent;
lucky in parentage
Hughee, Hughi, Hughy

Hugo (Latin) spirited heart

Huitt (English) smart

Hul (Biblical) pain; infirmity

Huland (English) bright
Hue, Huel, Huey, Hugh

Hulbard (Last name as first
name) singing; bright
Hulbert, Hulburt

Hull (English) spirited; confident

Hulsey (English) wise eye

Humbert (German) famous
giant; renowned warrior

Humberto (Spanish) brilliant
Hum, Humb, Humbie

Hume (Last name as first name)
daunting

Humphrey (German) strong
peacemaker
*Hum, Humfry, Hump, Humphry,
Humprey*

Hundy (Last name as first name)

Hunghui (Asian)

Hunn (German) combative
Hun

Hunt (English) active

Hunter ○ ❶ (English) hunter;
adventurer
Hunt

Hunting (English) hunter
Huntyng

Huntington (Last name as first
name) town of hunters

Huntler (English) hunter
Huntt

Huntley (English) hunter
Hunt, Hunter, Huntlea, Huntlee, Huntlie, Huntly

Huon (Hebrew) form of John: God is gracious

Hur (Biblical) liberty; whiteness; hole

Hurd (Last name as first name) tends the herd

Hurlbert (English) shining army man
Hulbert, Hurlburt, Hurlbutt

Hurley (Irish) the tide; flowing
Hurlea, Hurlee, Hurli, Hurly

Hurst (Last name as first name) entrepreneurial

Hurston (English) boy from town of thickets

Husham (Biblical) good-looking

Husky (American) big
Husk, Huskee, Huskey, Huski

Huss (American) small

Hussein (Arabic) attractive man; handsome
Husain, Husane, Husein, Hussain

Hust (American) form of Houston: Texas city; rogue; hill town

Huston (English) form of Houston: Texas city; rogue; hill town

Hutch (American) safe haven; unique
Hut, Hutchey, Hutchie, Hutchy

Hutner (Last name as first name) child of the house

Hutter (Last name as first name) tough
Hut, Hutt, Huttey, Huttie, Hutty

Hutton (English) sophisticated
Hutt, Huttan, Hutten, Hutts

Huxford (Last name as first name) outdoorsman

Huxley (English) outdoorsman
Hux, Huxel, Huxle, Huxlee, Huxlie

Hwang (Japanese) yellow

Hyacinthe (French) flowering
Hyacinthos, Hyacinthus, Hyakinthos

Hyatt (English) secure
Hy, Hye, Hyett, Hyut

Hyde (English) special; a hyde is 120 acres
Hide, Hy

Hyden (English) tans hides

Hyghner (Last name as first name) lofty goals
High, Highner, Hygh

Hylan (Asian) hopeful

Hyll (Origin unknown) open-minded
Hy, Hye, Hyell

Hyman (Hebrew) life
Hy, Hymen, Hymie

Hyo (Vietnamese) optimist

Iagan (Scottish) fire

Iago (Spanish) feisty villain
Iagoh, Jago

Iah (Egyptian) moonlike

Iain (Scottish) believer

Ian ✪ (Scottish) believer; handsome
Iain, Ean, Eon, Eyon

Iathan (Spanish) form of Nathan: God's gift to mankind

Ib (Arabic) joy

Ibrahim (Arabic) fathering many
Ibraham, Ibrahem

Ibu (Japanese) creative

Icarus (Mythology) ill-fated
Ikarus

Ich (Hebrew) form of Ichabod: glory in the past; slim
Ick, Ickee, Ickie, Icky

Ichabod (Hebrew) glory in the past; slim
Ich, Icha, Ickabod, Ika, Ikabod, Ikie

Idelfonso (Spanish) ready

Idi (Swahili) born during the Idd festival

Idris (Welsh) impulse-driven
Idriss, Idriys

Idwal (Welsh) known

Iefan (Welsh) form of John: God is gracious

Ieuan (Welsh) form of Ivan: believer in a gracious God; reliable one

Ifan (Welsh) form of John: God is gracious

Ifor (Welsh) archer

Igal (Biblical) redeemed; defiled

Iggy (Latin) form of Ignatius: firebrand
Iggee, Iggey, Iggi, Iggie

Ignace (French) fiery
Iggy, Ignase

Ignash (Latin) form of Ignatius: firebrand

Ignasha (Latin) form of Ignatius: firebrand

Ignatius (Latin) firebrand
Ig, Iggie, Iggy, Ignacius, Ignashus, Ignatious, Ignnatius

Igor (Russian) warrior

Igoran (Russian) army boy

Ihsan (Arabic) charitable

Ijon (Biblical) place name

Ike (Hebrew) form of Isaac: laughter
Ika, Ikee, Ikey, Ikie

Ilan (Hebrew) tree
Illan

Ilesh (Indian) earth king

Illtyd (Welsh) from the well-populated homeland
Illtud

Ilmar (Scandinavian) airy

Ilom (Welsh) happy

Immanuel (Hebrew) with God
Emmanuel, Imanuel

Imran (Arabic) host

Imre (Slavic) form of Emery: hardworking leader

Inder (Hindi) the Lord of sky gods is Indra; ethereal
Inderjeet, Inderjit, Inderpal, Indervir, Indra, Indrajit

Indiana (Place name) U.S. state; rowdy; dashing
Indio, Indy

Indore (Place name) city in India
Indor

Indra (Hindi) Lord of sky gods

Ing (Scandinavian) he who is foremost
Inge

Ingan (Scandinavian) prolific

Ingeborg (Scandinavian) fertile

Ingelbert (German) combative
Ing, Inge, Ingelbart, Ingelburt, Inglebert

Inger (Scandinavian) fertile
Ingemar, Ingmar

Ingmar (Scandinavian) famous son
Ing, Ingamar, Ingamur, Inge, Ingemar, Ingmer

Ingra (English) form of Ingram: angelic; kind
Ingie, Ingrah, Ingrie

Ingram (English) angelic; kind
Ing, Ingraham, Ingre, Ingrie, Ingry

Ingvar (Scandinavian) fertility god
Ingevar

Inigo (Spanish) form of Ignatius: firebrand

Iniko (Japanese) serves

Innis (Irish) isolated
Ines, Inis, Innes, Inness, Inniss

Innocencio (Spanish) innocent

Inteus (Native American) proud

Into (Scandinavian) excitable

Ioan (Slavic) believer

Ionel (Slavic) believer

Ior (Welsh) form of Iorwerth: worthy Lord

Iorgos (Greek) outgoing
Iorwerth (Welsh) worthy Lord
Ira (Hebrew) cautious
Irae, Irah
Irakli (Slavic) athletic
Iram (English) smart
Irem, Irham, Irum
Iranga (Sri Lankan) special
Irfan (Arabic) grateful child
Irind (American) peaceful
Irineo (Spanish) peaceful
Irish (English) boy from Ireland
Irmtraud (German) strong
soldier
Irv (English) form of Irving:
attractive
Irvin (English) attractive
Irv, Irvine
Irving (English) attractive
Irv, Irve, Irveng, Irvy
Irwin (English) practical
*Irwen, Irwhen, Irwie, Irwinn,
Irwy, Irwynn*
Isa (African) saved
Isaac ⚪ ⓣ (Hebrew) laughter
Isaak, Isack, Izak, Ize, Izek, Izzy
Isadore (Greek) special gift
*Isador, Isedore, Isidore, Issy, Izzie,
Izzy*
Isai (Hebrew) believer

Isaiah ⚪ ⓣ (Hebrew) saved by God
Isa, Isay, Isayah, Isey, Izaiah, Izey
Isak (Scandinavian) laughter
Isac
Isam (Arabic) protector
Isamu (Japanese) bravery
Isas (Japanese) worthwhile
Isham (Last name as first name)
athletic
Ishan (Hindi) sun
Ishbak (Biblical) protector
Ishmael (Hebrew) God hears
Hish, Ish, Ishmel, Ismael
Ishtar (Mythology) goddess of
fertility and love
Isidore (Greek) gift of Isis
Izzie
Isidoro (Spanish) gift
*Cedro, Cidro, Doro, Izidro, Sidro,
Ysidor*
Isidro (Greek) gift
Isydro
Israel (Hebrew) God's prince;
conflicted
Israyel, Issy, Izzy
Israj (Hindi) king of gods
Issa (Hebrew) laughing
Issachar (Biblical) reward
Isser (Slavic) creative
Ithamar (Biblical) island of the
palm tree

Ithiel (Biblical) with God beside
him
Itil (Welsh) has a giving nature
Itlus (Roman) from Italy
Itsik (Hebrew) form of Isaac:
laughter
Itzak (Hebrew) form of Isaac:
laughter
Itzik
Iuri (Slavic) form of Yuri: dashing
Ivan (Russian) believer in a
gracious God; reliable one
Ivahn, Ive, Ivey, Ivie
Ivanore (Scandinavian) child of
God
Ivar (Scandinavian) Norse god
Ive (English) able
Ivee, Ives, Ivey, Ivie
Ives (American) musical
Ive
Ivo (Polish) yew tree; sturdy
Ivar, Ives, Ivon, Ivonnie, Yvo
Ivon (Slavic) believer
Ivor (Scandinavian) outgoing; ready
Ifot, Ivar, Ive, Iver, Ivy
Izaak (Polish) full of mirth
Izacz (Slavic) spicy; happy
Isaac, Izak, Izie, Izze, Izzee
Izador (Spanish) gift
*Dorrie, Dory, Isa, Isador, Isadoro,
Isidoros, Isodore, Iza, Izadoro*

Izaiah (Czech) form of Isaiah: saved by God

Izaith (Spanish) form of Isaiah: saved by God

Izan (Slavic) asks

Izedin (Spanish) gives

Izhar (Indian) serves well

Izrail (American) form of Isaiah: saved by God

Izzy (Hebrew) friendly
Issie, Issy, Izi, Izzee, Izzie

Ja (Korean) gorgeous

Jaak (Scandinavian) form of Jack: God is gracious

Jaan (Scandinavian) form of John: God is gracious

Jabal (Place name) form of Japalpur; a city in India: attractive

Jabari (African American) brave

Jabbar (Arabic) comforting

Jaber (American) form of Jabir: supportive
Jabar, Jabe

Jabez (Hebrew) sorrow

Jabin (Hebrew) God's own

Jabir (Arabic) supportive
Jabbar

Jabon (American) wild
Jabonne

Jabot (French) shirt ruffle

Jace (American) audacious
Jase, Jhace

Jacek (Polish) hyacinth; growing
Jack, Yahcik

Jacen (Greek) form of Jason: healer; the Lord is salvation

Jacett (Invented) jaunty
Jaycett

Jachin (Biblical) ready

Jachym (Hebrew) form of Jacob: he who supplants
Jach

Jacinto (Spanish) hyacinth; fragrant
Jacint

Jack ✪ ❶ (Hebrew) form of John: God is gracious
Jackee, Jackie, Jacko, Jacky, Jax

Jackal (Sanskrit) wild dog; betrays
Jackel, Jackell, Jackyl, Jackyll

Jackie (English) personable
Jackee, Jackey, Jacki, Jacky, Jaki

Jackie-Lee (American) combo of Jackie and Lee

Jackson ✪ (English) Jack's son; full of personality
Jackee, Jackie, Jacks, Jacsen, Jakson, Jax, Jaxon

Jacksonville (Last name as first name) town of Jack's son; sturdy
Jacsonville, Jaksonville

Jaclo (Spanish) combo of Jack and Lo

Jacob ✪ ❶ (Hebrew) he who supplants
Jaccob, Jacobe, Jacobee, Jake, Jakes, Jakey, Jakob

Jacoben (American) replaces; friend

Jacobo (Spanish) warm
Jake, Jakey

Jacobs (Biblical) replacing
Jakey, Jakobs

Jacobus (Latin) form of Jacob: he who supplants
Jakobus

Jacoby (Hebrew) form of Jacob: he who supplants
Jacobey, Jakobey, Jakoby

Jacquard (French) class act
Jackard, Jackarde, Jacquarde, Jaqard, Jaquard, Jaquarde

Jacques (French) romantic; ingenious
Jacquie, Jacue, Jaques, Jock, Jok

Jacy (American) form of Jacob: he who supplants

Jadaan (Last name as first name) content

Jadall (Invented) punctual
Jada, Jade

Jade (Spanish) valued jade stone
Jadee, Jadie, Jayde

Jaden ❶ (Hebrew) Jehovah has heard
Jade, Jadin, Jadon, Jadun, Jadyn, Jaiden, Jaydie, Jaydon

Jadney (Last name as first name) pleased
Jad

Jadran (Slavic) form of Adrian: wealthy; dark-skinned

Jae (French) form of Jay: colorful

Jaegel (English) salesman
Jaeg, Jaeger, Jael

Jaeger (German) outdoorsman
Jaegir, Jagher, Jagur

Jael (Hebrew) climber

Jaewon (African American) form of Juwon: devout; lively
Jaewan, Jaywan, Jaywon

Jaeyel (Hebrew) form of Jael: salesman

Jafar (Arabic) from the stream
Gafar, Jafari

Jafeth (Hebrew) handsome

Jaffar (Arabic) directs

Jaffe (Hebrew) beautiful

Jaffey (English) form of Jaffe: beautiful
Jaff

Jaffiel (Spanish) loves the water

Jafon (Dutch) growth

Jagan (English) confident
Jagen, Jago, Jagun

Jagannath (Indian) Hindi god Vishnu; world leader

Jagger (English) brash
Jagar, Jager, Jaggar, Jagir

Jaggerton (English) brash
Jag, Jagg

Jagit (Invented) brisk
Jaggett, Jaggit, Jagitt

Jago (English) self-assured

Jaguar (Spanish) fast
Jag, Jagg, Jaggy, Jagwar, Jagwhar

Jahan (Sanskrit) worldly

Jaheim (Hindi) worldly

Jahi (African) runs well; dignity

Jahlel (Biblical) God helps

Jahmal (Arabic) beautiful
Jahmaal, Jahmall

Jahmil (Arabic) beautiful
Jahmeel, Jahmyl

Jai (American) adventurer
Jay

Jaidev (Hindi) God's victory

Jaidov (Indian) winning

Jailo (Hindi) worldwise

Jaime (Spanish) follower
Jaimey, Jaimie, Jamee, Jaymie

Jaimini (Hindi) winner

Jaimo (Asian) form of James: he who supplants

Jair (Hebrew) teacher
Jairo

Jairaj (Hindi) Lord's victor

Jairam (Slavic) God informs him

Jaircineo (Spanish) enlightened

Jairemaine (French) form of Germain: growing; from Germany

Jairo (Spanish) God enlightens
Jaero, Jairoh

Jairus (Biblical) faithful

Jaison (American) form of Jason: healer; the Lord is salvation
Jaizon

Jaja (African) praise-worthy

Jakar (Place name) from Jakarta
Jakart, Jakarta, Jakarte

Jake (Hebrew) form of Jacob: he who supplants
Jaik, Jakee, Jakey, Jakie, Jayke

Jakeem (Arabic) has been lifted

Jakey (American) nickname for Jake; friendly
Jaky

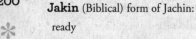

Jakin (Biblical) form of Jachin: ready

Jakiren (American) playful

Jakob (Hebrew) form of Jacob: he who supplants
Jakab, Jake, Jakeb, Jakey, Jakie, Jakobe, Jakub

Jal (English) wanderer

Jalal (Hindi) glory

Jalam (Biblical) victor

Jaleel (Arabic) handsome
Jalil

Jalen (American) vivacious
Jalon, Jaylen, Jaylin, Jaylon

Jalenal (American) wins

Jaliseo (Spanish) modest

Jallen (American) winner

Jalmar (Scandinavian) soldier

Jamail (Arabic) good-looking
Jahmil, Jam, Jamaal, Jamahal, Jamal, Jamil, Jamile, Jamy

Jamaine (Arabic) good-looking

Jaman (American) wonder

Jamar (American) form of Jamail: good-looking
Jamarr, Jemar, Jimar

Jamari (African American) attractive

Jamarr (African American) attractive; formidable
Jam, Jamaar, Jamar, Jamel, Jammy

Jamerson (English) son of James

James ○ ⊤ (English) form of Jacob: he who supplants
Jaimes, Jamsey, Jamze, Jaymes, Jim, Jimmy

James-Bolton (American) musical

Jameson (English) able; James's son
Jamesan, Jamesen, Jamesey, Jamison, Jamsie

Jamie (English) form of James: he who supplants
Jaimey, Jaimie, Jamee, Jamey, Jay, Jaymey, Jaymsey

Jamil (Arabic) beautiful
Jameel, Jamyl

Jamile (Arabic) handsome

Jamin (Hebrew) favored son
Jamen, James, Jamie, Jamon, Jaymon

Jamisen (American) form of James: he who supplants
Jami, Jamie, Jamis, Jamison

Jan (Dutch) form of John: God is gracious
Jaan, Jann, Janne

Janardan (Indian) helper

Jance (Scandinavian) form of John: God is gracious

Janesh (Hindi) thankful

Janier (French) form of John: God is gracious

Janis (Slavic) devout

Janko (Slavic) happy

Janon (Hebrew) chosen

Janson (Scandinavian) Jan's son; hardworking
Jan, Janne, Janny, Jansahn, Jansen, Jansey

Jantz (Scandinavian) form of Jantzen: God is gracious
Janson, Janssen, Jantzon, Janz, Janzon

Jantzen (Scandinavian) form of John: God is gracious

Janus (Latin) Roman god of beginnings and endings; optimistic; born in January
Jan, Janis

Januson (Scandinavian) son of Janus; year's gateway

Japheth (Hebrew) grows
Japhet

Jaquanace (American) growth

Jaquawn (African American) rock
Jacquon, Jakka, Jaquan, Jaquie, Jaqwen, Jequon, Jock

Jaquier (French) form of Jacques: romantic; ingenious

Jarah (Hebrew) sweet

Jarat (American) form of Jared: descendant; giving

Jaraus (American) form of Jaran: sings

Jard (American) form of Jared: descendant; giving
Jarra, Jarrd, Jarri, Jerd, Jord

Jareb (Hebrew) contender
Jarib, Yarev, Yariv

Jared (Hebrew) descendant; giving
Jarad, Jarod, Jarode, Jarret, Jarrett, Jerod, Jerrad, Jerrod

Jarek (Slavic) fresh
Jarec

Jarell (Scandinavian) giving
Jare, Jarelle, Jarey, Jarrell, Jerrell

Jaren (Hebrew) vocal
Jaron, Jayrone, J'ron

Jarenal (American) form of Jaren: vocal
Jaranall, Jaret, Jarn, Jaronal, Jarry, Jerry

Jarenn (American) form of Jaran: sings

Jarent (French) sings

Jares (Biblical) form of Jairus: faithful

Jareth (American) open to adventure
Jarey, Jarith, Jarth, Jary

Jariath (American) sings

Jarib (Hebrew) competes

Jaribon (American) laughs

Jario (Hebrew) believer

Jarius (Spanish) generous

Jarkko (Finnish) form of George: land-loving; farmer

Jarl (Scandinavian) noble

Jarles (Scandinavian) noble

Jarman (German) stoic
Jerman

Jarmuth (Biblical) place name

Jarnigan (German) German boy

Jaro (Polish) spring child

Jaroe (American) form of Gerald: strong; ruling with a spear

Jarol (English) form of Gerald: strong; ruling with a spear

Jarold (Polish) form of Gerald: strong; ruling with a spear

Jaromil (Czech) spring love
Jarmil

Jaron (Hebrew) spirited singer

Jarons (Hebrew) spirited singer

Jarred (Hebrew) form of Jared: descendant; giving
Jere, Jerod, Jerred, Jerud

Jarrell (English) jaunty
Jare, Jarell, Jarrel, Jarry, Jerele, Jerrell

Jarrett (English) confident
Jare, Jaret, Jaritt, Jarret, Jarrit, Jarritt, Jarry, Jarryt, Jarrytt, Jerot, Jerret, Jerrett, Jurett, Jurette

Jarrod (Hebrew) form of Jared: descendant; giving
Jare, Jarod, Jarry, Jerod

Jarvett (American) form of Jarrett: confident

Jarvey (German) celebrated
Garvey, Garvy, Jarvee, Jarvi, Jarvy

Jarvis (German) athletic
Jarv, Jarvee, Jarves, Jarvey, Jarvhus, Jarvie, Jarvus, Jarvy

Jary (Spanish) form of Jerry: strong; ruling with a spear
Jaree

Jaryn (Hebrew) sings

Jasdeep (Indian) bright light

Jase (American) hip

Jaskarn (Indian) praises

Jason ⚬ (Greek) healer; the Lord is salvation

Jaspal (Pakistani) pure

Jasper (English) guard
Jasp, Jaspur, Jaspy, Jaspyr

Jasraj (Indian) famous

Jassel (Spanish) form of Jason: healer; the Lord is salvation

Jasson (American) form of Jason: healer; the Lord is salvation

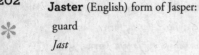

Jaster (English) form of Jasper:
guard
Jast

Jasvir (Indian) famous

Jatauan (American) joker

Jatin (American) form of
Gaetano: from the city of Gaeta;
Italian man

Jattir (Biblical) place name

Jaumet (French) foremost

Jaun (American) form of John:
God is gracious

Javan (Biblical) righteous
Javin, Javon

Javaris (African American)
prepared
Javares, Javarez

Javas (Sanskrit) bright eyes

Jave (American) form of Jove:
Roman sky god

Javed (American) form of
Jove: Roman sky god

Javen (Hebrew) form of Javan:
righteous

Javier (Spanish) affluent;
homeowner
Havyaire, Javey, Javiar

Javion (American) form of Javan:
righteous

Javon (Hebrew) hopeful
*Javan, Javaughn, Javen, Javonn,
Javonte*

Javonte (African American)
jaunty
*Javaughantay, Javawnte,
Ja-Vonnetay, Ja-Vontae*

Javor (Slavic) sturdy tree

Javy (American) form of Javaris;
prepared
Javey, Javie

Jawahir (Arabic) gems

Jawdat (Arabic) excellent
Gawdat

Jawhar (Arabic) gem

Jawon (African American) shy
*Jawan, Jawaughn, Jawaun,
Jawuane, Jewan, Jewon, Jowon*

Jax (American) form of Jackson:
Jack's son; full of personality
Jacks, Jaxx

Jaxon (English) form of
Jackson: Jack's son; full of
personality

Jaxson (English) form of
Jackson: Jack's son; full of
personality

Jay (English) form of a name
starting with J; colorful
Jai, Jaye

Jaya (American) jazzy
Jay, Jayah

Jayan (Indian) wins

Jayant (Hindi) winner

Jayashree (Indian) victor

JayC (American) combo of Jay
and C

Jayden ○ ❶ (American) bright-
eyed
*Jayde, Jaydey, Jaydi, Jaydie,
Jaydon, Jaydun, Jaydy*

Jayes (English) form of Jay: form
of a name starting with J; colorful

Jayesh (Indian) victor

Jaylon ❶ (American) combo of
Jay and Lon*Jaylen*

Jayme (English) form of Jamie:
he who supplants

Jaymee (English) form of Jamie:
he who supplants

Jaymes (American) form of
James: he who supplants
Jaimes

Jaymz (American) form of James:
he who supplants

Jayson (Greek) form of Jason:
healer; the Lord is salvation

Jaz (American) form of Jazz: jazzy

Jazeps (Latvian) God will increase

Jazer (American) form of Jazz: jazzy

Jazon (Polish) heals

Jazz (American) jazzy
Jazze, Jazzee, Jazzy

Jean (French) form of John: God is gracious
Jeanne, Jeannie, Jene

Jeanis (French) form of John: God is gracious

Jean-Marc (French) combo of Jean and Marc

Jean-Pierre (French) combo of Jean and Pierre

Jean-Sebastien (French) combo of Jean and Sebastian

Jeardo (Polish) form of Jerard: confident

Jearoslav (Polish) glory

Jeb (Hebrew) jolly
Jebb, Jebby

Jebben (Hebrew) form of Jebediah: close to God

Jebediah (Hebrew) close to God
Jeb, Jebadiah, Jebby, Jebedyah

Jebus (Biblical) place name

Jecori (American) exuberant
Jekori

Jed (Hebrew) helpful
Jedd, Jeddy, Jede

Jediah (Hebrew) God's help
Jedi, Jedyah

Jedidiah (Hebrew) close to God
Jed, Jeddy, Jeddyah, Jedidyah

Jedrek (Polish) virile
Jedrick, Jedrus

Jedwog (Polish) manly

Jeeps (French) jaunty

Jeevan (African American) form of Jevan: spirited (Hebrew) religious
Jevaughn, Jevaun

Jeevik (Indian) water

Jeff (English) form of Jeffrey: peaceful; form of Jefferson: dignified
Geoff, Jeffie, Jeffy

Jeffers (English) form of Jeffrey: peaceful

Jefferson (English) dignified
Jeff, Jeffarson, Jeffersen, Jeffursen, Jeffy

Jeffery (English) form of Jeffrey: peaceful
Jeffrie, Jeffry, Jefry

Jeffrey (English) peaceful
Geoffrey, Jeff, Jeffree, Jeffrie, Jeffry, Jeffy, Jefree

Jehan (French) form of John: God is gracious

Jehu (Hebrew) true believer

Jela (African) honors

Jelani (African American) trendy
Jelanee, Jelaney, Jelanne

Jem (English) form of James: he who supplants
Jemmi, Jemmy, Jemmye, Jemy

Jemarr (African American) worldly
Jemahr

Jemonde (French) man of the world
Jemond

Jenda (Czech) form of John: God is gracious

Jenkins (Last name as first name) God is gracious
Jenkin, Jenks, Jenky, Jenkyns, Jenx, Jinx

Jennett (Hindi) heavenly
Jennet, Jennit, Jennitt, Jennyt, Jennytt, Jinnat

Jennings (Last name as first name) attractive
Jennyngs

Jensi (Hungarian) noble
Jenci, Jens

Jenson (English) son of Jen; blessed
Jensen, Jenssen, Jensson

Jep (American) easygoing
Jepp

Jephtha (Biblical) judges others; outgoing

Jerald (English) form of Gerald: strong; ruling with a spear
Jere, Jereld, Jerold, Jerrie, Jerry

Jeramy (Hebrew) exciting
Jeramah, Jeramie, Jere, Jeremy

Jerard (French) confident
Jerrard

Jere (Hebrew) form of Jeremy: talkative
Jeree, Jerey

Jeremiah ✿ ✝ (Hebrew) prophet uplifted by God; farsighted
Jeramiah, Jere, Jeremyah, Jerome, Jerry

Jeremie (Hebrew) loquacious
Jeremee, Jeremy

Jeremy ✝ (English) talkative
Jaramie, Jere, Jeremah, Jereme, Jeremey, Jerrey, Jerry

Jeriah (Hebrew) form of Jeremiah: prophet uplifted by God; farsighted

Jericho (Arabic) nocturnal
Jerako, Jere, Jerico, Jeriko, Jerycho, Jerycko, Jeryco, Jeryko

Jerick (American) form of Jericho: nocturnal
Gericho, Jereck, Jerik, Jero, Jerok, Jerrico

Jeril (American) form of Jarrell: leader
Jerill, Jerl, Jerry

Jerma (American) form of Germaine: growing; from Germany
Jermah, Jermane, Jermayne

Jermain (French) from Germany
German, Germane, Germanes, Germano, Germanus, Jermaine, Jerman, Jermane, Jermayn, Jermayne

Jermaine (German) form of Germaine: growing; from Germany
Germain, Germaine, Jere, Jermain, Jermane, Jermene, Jerry

Jermey (American) form of Jermaine: growing; from Germany
Jermy

Jermon (African American) dependable
Jermonn

Jerney (Hebrew) exalted of the Lord

Jernigan (Last name as first name) spontaneous
Jerni, Jerny

Jero (American) jaunty
Jeroh, Jerree, Jerri, Jerro, Jerry

Jerod (Hebrew) form of Jared: descendant; giving

Jerold (English) merry
Jerrold, Jerry

Jerome (Latin) holy name; blessed
Jarome, Jere, Jerohm, Jeromy, Jerree, Jerrome, Jerry, Jirome

Jerone (English) hopeful
Jere, Jerohn, Jeron, Jerrone

Jeronimo (Italian) form of Geronimo: sacred name
Gerry, Jero, Jerry

Jerral (American) form of Jerald: strong; ruling with a spear
Jeral, Jere, Jerry

Jerram (Hebrew) God has uplifted
Jeram, Jerem, Jerrem, Jerrym, Jerym

Jerrell (American) exciting
Jarell, Jerre, Jerrel, Jerrie, Jerry

Jerrett (Hebrew) form of Jarrett: confident
Jeret, Jerete, Jerod, Jerot, Jerret

Jerry (German) form of Gerald: strong; ruling with a spear
Gerry, Gery, Jerre, Jerri, Jerrie, Jerrye

Jerse (Place name) calm; rural
Jerce, Jercey, Jersey, Jersy, Jerzy

Jervis (Greek) honorable
Gervase

Jesmar (American) form of Jesse: wealthy
Jess, Jessie, Jezz, Jezzie

Jesper (American) easygoing
Jesp, Jess

Jess (Hebrew) wealthy
Jes

Jesse (Hebrew) wealthy
Jess, Jessee, Jessey, Jessi, Jessye

Jessup (Last name as first name)
rich
Jesop, Jesopp, Jess, Jessa, Jessie,
Jessopp, Jessupp, Jessy, Jesup, Jesupp

Jesuan (Spanish) devout

Jesus ✪ (Hebrew) saved by God
Hesus, Jesu, Jesuso, Jezus

Jet (English) black gem

Jetal (American) zany
Jetahl, Jetil, Jett, Jettale, Jetty

Jethro (Hebrew) fertile
Jeto, Jett, Jetty

Jeton (French) a chip for
gamblers; wild spirit
Jet, Jetawn, Jets, Jett, Jetty

Jett (American) free
Jet, Jets, Jetty, The Jet

Jettie (American) form of Jett:
free
Jette, Jettee, Jetti

Jetty (American) form of Jett:
free
Jettey

Jevan (African American) spirited
Jevaughn, Jevaun, Jevin, Jevon

Jex (American) form of Jack: God
is gracious

Jhonatan (African) spiritual
Jhon, Jon

Ji (Chinese) organized; orderly

Jibben (American) form of Jivon:
living; vibrant

Jibri (Arabic) angel

Jie (Chinese) wonderful

Jiggins (English) lost

Jiles (American) form of Giles:
protective

Jilve (American) form of Jiles:
protective

Jim (Hebrew) form of James: he
who supplants
Jem, Jihm, Jimi, Jimmee, Jimmy

Jimbo (American) cowhand;
endearment for Jim
Jim, Jimb, Jimbee, Jimbey, Jimby

Jimbob (American) countrified
Gembob, Jim Bob, Jim-Bob, Jymbob

Jimere (Biblical) from Gemar

Jimmy (English) form of James:
he who supplants
Jim, Jimi, Jimmey, Jimmi, Jimmye,
Jimy

Jimmy-John (American)
country boy
Jimmiejon, Jimmyjohn, Jimmy-Jon,
Jymmejon

Jimoh (African) Friday's child

Jin (Chinese) golden

Jinan (Place name) city in China
Jin

Jindrich (Czech) ruling
Jindra, Jindrik, Jindrisek,
Jindrousek

Jing (Chinese) unblemished;
capital

Jinghua (Asian) ruler

Jinkon (American) vibrant

Jiri (Czech) working the earth
Jira, Jiricek

Jiro (Japanese) second boy born

Jiten (Indian) conquers

Jivon (Hindi) living; vibrant
Jivan

Joab (Hebrew) praising God;
hovering
Joabb

Joachim (Hebrew) a king of
Judah; powerful; believer
Akim, Jakim, Yachim, Yakim

Joah (Greek) form of Jonah:
peacemaker

Joanus (German) form of
Johann: God is gracious

Joao (Spanish) form of John: God
is gracious

Joaquin (Spanish) bold; hip
Joakeen, Joaquim, Juakeen,
Jwaqueen

Joar (Biblical) form of Jair: teacher

Job (Hebrew) patient
Jobb, Jobe, Jobi, Joby

Jobab (Biblical) sorrowful

Jobin (Biblical) perceives

Jobo (Hebrew) patient

Jobse (American) patient

Jobson (English) son of Job;
patient

Joby (Hebrew) patient; tested
Job, Jobee, Jobi

Jochen (German) established

Jock (Hebrew) grace in God;
athlete
Jockie, Jocky

Joda (Hebrew) devout

Jodbin (Hebrew) combo of Jod
and Bin

Jody (Hebrew) believer in
Jehovah; (American) combination
of Joe and Dee
Jodee, Jodey, Jodie, Jodye, Joe

Joe (Hebrew) form of Joel:
prophet in the Bible; form of
Joseph: He will add
Jo, Joey, Joeye, Joie

JoeGee (American) combo of Joe
and Gee

Joel (Hebrew) Jehovah is the Lord
Joelie, Joell, Jole, Joly

Joerd (Dutch) guards

Joergen (Scandinavian) earth
worker

Joest (Scandinavian) just

Joey (Hebrew) form of Joel:
prophet in the Bible; form of
Joseph: He will add
Joee, Joie

Joffre (German) form of Jeffrey:
peaceful

Johann (German) form of John:
God is gracious
Johan, Johane, Yohann, Yohanne,
Yohon

Johannes (Hebrew) form of
John: God is gracious
Johan, Jon

Johar (Hindi) gem

John ✪ ❶ (Hebrew) God is
gracious
Jahn, Jhan, Johne, Johnne, Johnni,
Johnnie, Johnny, Johnnye, Jon

Johnny (Hebrew) form of John:
God is gracious
Gianni, Johnie, Johnnie, Jonni,
Jonny

Johnny-Dodd (American)
country sheriff
Johnniedodd, Johnny Dodd

Johnny-Ramon (Spanish)
renegade
Johnnyramon, Johnny Ramon

Johnson (English) John's son;
credible
Johnsen, Johnsonne, Jonsen, Jonson

Joji (Japanese) form of John: God
is gracious

JoJo (American) friendly; popular
Jo-Jo

Jokel (American) form of Joachim:
king of Judah; powerful; believer

Jokshan (American) form
of Jackson: Jack's son; full of
personality

Joktan (Biblical) small

Jole (American) jolly

Jolly (American) jolly

Jolon (Native American) oak
valley dweller

Joloyd (American) combo of Jo
and Lloyd

Jomar (African American) helpful
Joemar, Jomarr

Jomei (Japanese) lightens

Jomo (American) grows crops

Jon (Hebrew) alternative for John
Jonni, Jonnie, Jonny, Jony

Jonah (Hebrew) peacemaker
Joneh

Jonald (Hebrew) combo of Jon and Ronald

Jonas (Hebrew) capable; active
Jon

Jonathan ✪ ❶ (Hebrew) gift of God
Johnathan, Johnathon, Jonathon

Jonavon (Hebrew) calm

Jonaz (Hebrew) form of Jonas: capable; active

Jones (American) saucy

Jonnie (Hebrew) form of John: God is gracious

Jonnley (American) form of John: God is gracious
Jonn, Jonnie

Jonte (American) form of John: God is gracious
Johatay, Johate, Jontae

Jools (English) form of Julius: attractive

Joplin (Place name) city in Montana; sings
Joplyn

Joppa (Biblical) place name

Joram (Biblical) giving

Joran (Scandinavian) dependable

Jord (Scandinavian) strong

Jordahno (Invented) form of Giordano: delivered

Jordan ✪ ❶ (Hebrew) downflowing river
Jorden, Jordon, Jordun, Jordy, Jordyn

Jordane (Hebrew) form of Jordan: downflowing river

Jordan-Michael (American) athletic

Jordison (American) son of Jordy; glowing
Jordisen, Jordysen, Jordyson

Jordy (Hebrew) form of Jordan: downflowing river
Jordey, Jordi, Jordie

Jorge (Spanish) form of George: land-loving; farmer
Jorje, Quiqui

Jorgen (Scandinavian) farmer
Jorgan

Jorger (Scandinavian) form of George: land-loving; farmer

Jorget (French) mutinous

Jorine (French) form of George: land-loving; farmer

Joris (Dutch) form of George: land-loving; farmer

Jory (Hebrew) descendant
Jorey

Jos (Place name) city in Nigeria

Josa (Hebrew) God judges him

José ✪ (Spanish) asset; favored
Joesay, Jose, Pepe, Pepito

Joseph ✪ ❶ (Hebrew) He will add
Jodie, Joe, Joey, Josef, Josep, Josephe, Jozef, Yusif

Josh (Hebrew) form of Joshua: devout
Joshuam, Joshyam, Josue, Jozua

Josha (Hebrew) form of Joshua: devout

Joshua ✪ ❶ (Hebrew) devout

Josia (Hebrew) form of Josiah: supported by the Lord
Josea

Josiah ✪ (Hebrew) supported by the Lord
Josyah

Joson (English) form of Jason: healer; the Lord is salvation

Joss (English) form of Joseph: He will add
Josslin, Jossly

Josue (Spanish) devout

Jotham (Biblical) a king of Judah; believer in perfect Jehovah
Jothem, Jothym

Jour (French) form of Jourdain: flowing

Jourdain (French) flowing
Jordane, Jorden

Jourdyun (Slavic) form of
Jourdain: flowing

Jovan (Slavic) gifted
Jovahn, Jovohn

Jovani (Italian) form of Jove:
Roman sky god
Jovanni, Jovanny, Jovany

Jove (Mythology) Roman sky god

Jovi (American) sky

Jovito (Spanish) jubilant

Joza (Czech) form of Joseph: He
will add

Jozef (Polish) supported by
Jehovah; asset
Joe, Joze

Jozo (Slavic) little Joe

Juan ✿ (Spanish) devout; lively
Juann, Juwon

Juanie (Spanish) form of John:
God is gracious

Jubal (Hebrew) celebrant

Jubilo (Spanish) rejoicing; jubilant
Jube

Judah (Biblical) praised
Juda

Judas (Latin) praised

Judd (Latin) secretive
Jud

Jude (Latin) form of Judas: praised
Judah

Judge (English) judgmental
Judg

Judges (Biblical) judgmental

Judson (Last name as first name)
mercurial
Juddsen, Juddson, Judsen, Judssen

Judule (American) form of
Judah: praised
Jud, Judsen, Judsun

Juhi (Indian) flowers

Julan (American) attractive

Jules (Greek) young Adonis
Jewels, Jule

Julian ✿ (Greek) gorgeous
Juliane, Julien, Julyon, Julyun

Julias (Biblical) place name

Julio (Spanish) handsome; youthful
Huleeo, Hulie, Julie

Julius (Greek) attractive
Juleus, Jul-yus, Jul-yuz

Ju-Long (Chinese) powerful

Jumaane (African) Tuesday-born

Jumah (African) born on Friday
Juma

Jumahl (African) form of Jumah:
born on Friday

Jumbe (African) strong
Jumbey, Jumby

Jumble (American) awry

Jumoke (African) beloved

Jun (Japanese) follows the rules

Jund (Arabic) soldier

Juneau (Place name) capital of
Alaska
Juno, Junoe

Junior (Latin) young son of the
father
Junnie, Junny, Junyer

Junius (Latin) youngster
Junie, Junnie, Junny

Junny (Asian) honest

Juper (German) form of Joseph:
He will add

Jupiter (Roman) god of thunder
and lightning; guardian
Jupe

Jur (Czech) form of George: land-
loving; farmer

Jura (Place name) mountain
range between France and
Switzerland
Jurah

Juraj (Slavic) form of George:
land-loving; farmer

Jurass (American) from Jurassic
period of dinosaurs; daunting
Jurases, Jurassic

Jurate (Slavic) forgives

Jurg (Dutch) form of Jurgen:
working the earth

Jurgen (Scandinavian) working
the earth

Jurgin (Dutch) form of Jurgen: working the earth

Jurgs (Dutch) form of Jurgen: working the earth

Juri (Slavic) farms

Juric (Slavic) form of George: land-loving; farmer

Jus (French) just
Just, Justice, Justis

Juste (French) law-abiding
Just, Zhuste

Juster (American) fair and honest

Justice (Latin) just
Jusees, Just, Justiz, Justus, Juztice

Justie (Latin) honest; fair
Jus, Justee, Justey, Justi

Justin ✪ (Latin) fair
Just, Justan, Justen, Justun, Justyn, Justyne

Justinian (Latin) ruler; Roman emperor
Justinyan

Justino (Spanish) fair
Justyno

Justiz (American) judging; fair
Justice, Justis

Justo (Scandinavian) handsome

Justus (German) fair

Jute (Botanical) practical

Juven (Latin) youthful

Juvenal (Latin) young
Juve

Juventino (Spanish) young
Juve, Juven, Juvey, Tino, Tito

Juver (Spanish) form of Javor: sturdy tree

Juwon (African American) form of Juan: devout; lively
Jujuane, Juwan, Juwonne

Jvon (American) form of Juan: devout; lively

Jyles (American) form of Giles: protective

Jyree (Scandinavian) form of George: land-loving; farmer

Kaar (American) form of Kar: bold; Michael's follower

Kaarlo (American) form of Carlo: sensual; manly

Kabir (Hindi) spiritual leader
Kabar

Kabonero (African) symbol

Kabonesa (African) born in hard times

Kacancu (Rukonjo) firstborn

Kacy (American) happy
K.C., Kace, Kacee, Kase, Kasee, Kasy, Kaycee

Kadar (Arabic) empowered
Kader

Kade (American) exciting
Cade, Caden, K.D., Kadey, Kaid, Kayde, Kydee

Kadeem (Arabic) servant
Kadim

Kaden ✪ (American) exciting
*Cade, Caden, Caiden, Caidin, Caidon, Caydan, Cayden, Caydin, Caydon, Kadan, Kadon, Kadyn, Kaiden, **Kayden***

Kading (Last name as first name) powerful

Kadir (Hindi) talented
Kadeer, Qadeer, Qadir

Kadjaly (African) born from God

Kadmiel (Hebrew) God-loving

Kado (Japanese) through life's gate

Kaelan (Irish) strong
Kael, Kaelen, Kaelin, Kaelyn

Kaemon (Japanese) happy

Kaeto (American) form of Cato: zany and bright
Cayto, Caytoe, Kato

Kafele (African) supreme

Kafus (American) laughing boy

Kaha (Hawaiian) domesticated

Kahale (Hawaiian) homebody

Kahane (Egyptian) brave

Kahil (Turkish) ingenue; (Arabic) friend; (Greek) handsome *Cahill, Kaleel, Kalil, Kayhil, Khalil*

Kaholo (Hawaiian) boy who runs

Kai (Hawaiian) kay
Keh

Kaid (English) round; happy *Caiden, Cayde, Caydin, Kaden, Kadin, Kayd*

Kaihe (Hawaiian) spear

Kailey (Hawaiian) religious

Kailin (Irish) sporty
Kailyn, Kale, Kalen, Kaley, Kalin, Kallen, Kaylen

Kaine (Irish) handsome

Kainen (Irish) handsome

Kaipo (Hawaiian) embraces

Kairo (Arabic) from Cairo; exotic

Kaiser (German) title that means emperor

Kaiyan (Indian) place name

Kaj (Scandinavian) earthy

Kajah (Biblical) form of Caja: close proximity

Kal (Hawaiian) born of the sun

Kala (Hawaiian) sun boy

Kalama (Hawaiian) source of light
Kalam

Kalani (Hawaiian) of one sky
Kalan

Kalb (Hawaiian) studies

Kale (American) healthy; vegetable
Kail, Kayle, Kaylee, Kayley, Kaylie

Kaleb (American) form of Caleb: faithful; brave

Kalebbe (Hebrew) form of Kaleb: faithful; brave

Kalen (Hawaiian) young

Kalgan (Place name) city in China
Kal

Kali (Polynesian) comforts

Kalidas (Indian) creative

Kalil (Arabic) best friend
Kahil, Kahleel, Kahlil, Kaleel, Khaleel, Khalil

Kalin (Arabic) young

Kalkin (Hindi) tenth child

Kallahan (American) form of Callahan: spiritual

Kallen (Greek) handsome
Kallan, Kallin, Kallon, Kallun, Kalon, Kalun, Kalyn

Kalman (Irish) slim

Kalogeros (Greek) beautiful in aging

Kalonn (Irish) strong

Kalunga (African) watchful; the personal god of the Mbunda of Angola

Kalvim (Latin) form of Calvin: bald

Kalvin (Latin) form of Calvin: bald
Kal

Kalyan (Indian) handsome

Kama (Sanskrit) perfection

Kamaka (Hawaiian) pretty face

Kamal (Arabic) perfect; (African) lotus child
Kameel, Kamil

Kamari (African) moonlight child

Kamau (African) quiet soldier
Kamall

Kamden (Scottish) form of Camden: conflicted

Kameron (Scottish) form of Cameron: mischievous; crooked nose
Kameren, Kammeron, Kammi, Kammie, Kammy, Kamran, Kamrin, Kamron

Kammer (African) moon; pained

Kamon (American) alligator; (Biblical) place name
Cayman, Caymun, Kame, Kammy, Kayman, Kaymon

Kamran (American) form of Cameron: mischievous; crooked nose

Kamrino (Italian) form of Cameron: mischievous; crooked nose

Kamyar (Indian) handsome

Kan (American) good-looking

Kana (Japanese) strength of character

Kanah (Biblical) form of Elkanah: obedient to God

Kanak (Indian) golden child

Kanan (Hindi) forest

Kandall (American) form of Kendall: shy

Kane (Gaelic) warlike; honor; tribute
Cahan, Cahane, Cain, Kaince, Kaine, Kaney, Kanie, Kayne

Kang (Korean) healthy

Kaniel (Hebrew) confident; supported by the Lord; hopeful
Kane, Kan-El, Kanel, Kanelle, Kaney

Kano (Place name) city in Nigeria
Kan, Kanoh

Kant (German) philosopher
Cant

Kantu (Hindi) joyous

Kany (Australian) stone

Kanye (American) unbreakable

Kanzler (German) Last name as first name

Kaori (Japanese) scented

Kaper (American) capricious
Cape, Caper, Kahper, Kape

Kapila (Hindi) foresees
Kapil

Kapono (Hawaiian) anointed one

Kapp (Greek) form of the surname Kaparos
Kap, Kappy

Kapple (English) Last name as first name; from Cable; son of Cabel

Kar (American) form of Carr: outdoorsy

Karan (Hindi) listens

Karau (English) loyal

Karcher (German) beautiful blond boy

Kare (Scandinavian) large
Karee

Kareem (Arabic) generous
Karam, Karehm, Karem, Karim, Karreem, Krehm

Karekin (Scandinavian) large

Karel (Slavic) form of Carl: kingly

Karey (Greek) form of Cary: pretty brook; charming; form of Carey: masculine; by the castle
Karee, Kari, Karrey, Karry

Kari (Scandinavian) hair curls

Kariah (Biblical) form of Zechariah: Lord remembers

Karif (Arabic) fall-born
Kareef

Karime (Arabic) distinctive

Karimen (Scandinavian) big

Karkor (Biblical) place name

Karl (German) manly; forceful
Carl, Kale, Karel, Karlie, Karll, Karol, Karoly

Karlen (Slavic) form of Carl: kingly

Karmel (Hebrew) red-haired
Carmel, Carmelo, Karmeli, Karmelli, Karmelo, Karmello, Karmi

Karmmer (Hebrew) form of Carmel: growing; garden

Karnaim (Biblical) place name

Karney (Irish) wins
Carney

Karolek (Polish) form of Charles: manly; well-loved
Karol

Karp (Russian) abundant; (Greek) fruitful

Karr (Scandinavian) curly hair
Carr

Karst (Greek) anointed

Karstell (Last name as first name)

Karsten (Greek) chosen one

Kartik (Indian) hopes

Karu (Hindi) cousin
Karun

Karyim (Arabic) divisive

Kaseem (Arabic) divides
Kasceem, Kaseym, Kasim, Kazeem

Kaseko (African) ridiculed

Kasem (Asian) joyful

Kasen (Spanish) helmet; protected

Kasey (Irish) form of Casey:
courageous
Kasi, Kasie

Kasi (Egyptian) form of Kasiya:
leaving
Kasee, Kasey, Kasie

Kasim (Hindi) shining

Kasimir (Arabic) serene
Kasim, Kazimir, Kazmer

Kasin (Slavic) wolf; safety

Kasiya (Egyptian) leaving

Kason (Spanish) safe

Kasper (German) reliable
Caspar, Casper, Kasp, Kaspar, Kaspy

Kass (German) standout among
men
Cass, Kasse

Kassidy (Irish) form of Cassidy:
humorous
Kass, Kassidi, Kassidie, Kassie

Kastor (Greek) wins

Katell (Scandinavian) pure

Kato (African) second of twins

Katzir (Hebrew) reaping
Katzeer

Kauai (Place name) Hawaiian
island; breezy spirit
Kawai

Kaufman (Last name as first
name) serious
Kauffmann, Kaufmann

Kauri (Scandinavian) blessed

Kaushal (Indian) smart

Kavan (Irish) good-looking
Cavan, Kaven, Kavin

Kavi (Hindi) poetic

Kavin (Irish) form of Kevin:
handsome; gentle

Kawai (Hawaiian) form of Kauai:
Hawaiian island; breezy spirit

Kay (Greek) joyful
Kai, Kaye, Kaysie, Kaysy, Keh

Kayin (African) desired baby

Kayle (Hebrew) faithful
Kail, Kayl

Kaylen (Irish) form of Kellen:
strong-willed
Kaylan, Kaylin, Kaylon, Kaylyn

Kayo (Sanskrit) wordsmith

Kayode (African) joy-giver

Kayven (Irish) handsome
Cavan, Kavan, Kave

Kaz (Greek) creative

Kazan (Greek) creative
Kazann

Kazar (Slavic) kind

Kazimierz (Polish) practical
Kaz

Kazuo (Japanese) peace-loving;
good son

Kealoha (Hawaiian) bright path

Keane (German) attractive
Kean, Keen, Keene, Kiene

Keanu (Hawaiian) cool breeze
over mountains
Keahnu

Kearn (Irish) outspoken
Kearny, Kern, Kerne, Kerney

Kearney (Irish) sparkling
*Karney, Karny, Kearns, Kerney,
Kirney*

Kearon (Irish) form of Kieran:
handsome brunette

Keary (Irish) form of Kerry: dark

Keat (English) hawk

Keatal (English) hawk

Keaton (English) nature-lover
Keaten, Keatt, Keatun, Keton

Keats (Literature) for poet John Keats; melancholy
Keatz

Keawe (Hawaiian) lovable

Keb (Egyptian) loves the earth

Kecalf (American) inventive
Keecalf

Kechel (African American) kach
Kachelle

Keda (Hindi) form of Kedar: powerful

Kedar (Hindi) powerful
Kadar, Keder

Kedding (English) Last name as first name

Kedem (Hebrew) old soul

Kedemah (Biblical) old

Kedrick (American) form of Kendrick: heroic
Ked, Keddy, Kedric, Kedrik

Kedron (Biblical) place name; King

Kee (Irish) from Keefe: handsome

Kee-Bun (Taiwanese) good news
Keebun

Keefa (Irish) loved and lovely

Keefe (Irish) handsome
Keaf, Keafe, Keef, Keeffe, Kief

Keegan (Irish) ball-of-fire
Keagan, Keagin, Kegan, Kege, Keghun

Keelan (Irish) slim
Kealan, Keallan, Keallin, Keilan, Keillan, Kelan

Keeley (Irish) handsome
Kealey, Kealy, Keelee, Keelie, Keely, Keilie

Keen (German) smart
Kean, Keane, Keene, Keeney, Kene

Keenan (Irish) bright-eyed
Kenan

Keeney (American) incisive
Kean, Keane, Keaney, Keene, Kene

Keesen (Dutch) adored

Keever (Irish) form of Kevin: handsome; gentle

Keevin (Irish) form of Kevin: handsome; gentle

Keffry (American) form of Jeffrey: peaceful

Kefil (African) given by God

Kefir (Hebrew) young lion; high spirits

Kefiwy (African) loyal

Kehlor (American) friend

Keir (Irish) brunette

Keirer (Irish) dark
Kerer

Keiron (Irish) dark
Keiren, Keronn

Keitaro (Japanese) blessed baby
Keita

Keith (English) witty
Keath, Keeth, Keithe

Keithen (Scottish) gentle
Keith

Keizo (American) spice

Keko (Hawaiian) bold

Kekoa (Hawaiian) one warrior; (Asian) brave

Kel (Irish) fighter; energetic
Kell

Kelby (English) snappy; charming
Kel, Kelbey, Kelbi, Kelbie, Kelbye, Kell, Kellby, Kelly

Kelcy (English) helpful
Kelci, Kelcie, Kelcye, Kelsie

Kele (Hawaiian) watches like a hawk

Kelemen (Hungarian) soft-spoken

Kell (English) fresh-faced
Kel, Kelly

Kellagh (Irish) hardworking
Kellach

Kellam (Scottish) calm

Kelle (Scandinavian) springlike

Kellen (Irish) strong-willed
Kel, Kelen, Kelin, Kell, Kellan, Kellin, Kelly, Kelyn

Keller (Last name as first name) bountiful
Kel, Keler, Kelher, Kell, Kylher

Kellins (Irish) strong

Kelly (Irish) able combatant
Keli, Kellee, Kelley, Kelli, Kellie

Kelmen (Hungarian) form of
Kelemen: soft-spoken

Kelsen (English) port town child

Kelsey (Scandinavian) unique
among men
Kel, Kells, Kelly, Kels, Kelsi, Kelsie,
Kelsy, Kelsye, Kelzie, Kelzy

Kelto (Greek) unrequited love

Kelton (Irish) energetic
Keldon, Kelltin, Kellton, Kelten,
Keltin, Keltonn

Kelts (Origin unknown) energetic
Kel, Kelly, Kelse, Kelsey, Keltz

Kelvin (English) goal-oriented
Kellven, Kelvan, Kelven, Kelvon,
Kelvun, Kelvynn, Kilvin

Kemal (Turkish) honored infant;
generous

Kemmer (American) ethical

Kemp (English) champion

Kemper (American) high-minded
Kemp, Kempar

Kempton (American) takes the
high road

Kemuel (Hebrew) God's advocate

Ken (Scottish) form of Kenneth:
good-looking
Kenn, Kenny, Kinn

Kenan (Irish) strong

Kenaz (Hebrew) bright

Kendall (English) shy
Ken, Kend, Kendahl, Kendal,
Kendoll, Kendy, Kenney, Kennie,
Kenny, Kindal

Kendan (English) strong; serious
Ken, Kend, Kenden

Kendrick (English) heroic
Kendricks, Kendrik, Kendryck,
Kenric, Kenrick, Kenricks, Kenrik

Kenel (Invented) form of
Kendall: shy
Kenele

Kenelm (English) handsome boy
Kenhelm, Kennelm

Kenitsu (Asian) many summers

Kenix (American) form of
Kenneth: good-looking

Kenji (Asian) careful

Kenley (English) distinguished
Kenlea, Kenlee, Kenleigh, Kenlie,
Kenly

Kenn (English) river; flowing

Kennard (English) courageous;
selfless; (Irish) bold leader
Ken, Kenard, Kennaird, Kennar,
Kenny

Kennavy (Irish) brave

Kennean (Scottish) little Ken

Kennedy (Irish) leader
Canaday, Canady, Kennedey,
Kennedie, Kennidy

Kenner (English) capable
Kennard

Kennern (American) able

Kennet (Scandinavian) form of
Kenneth: good-looking
Kenet, Kennete

Kenneth (Scottish) good-looking
Ken, Keneth, Kenith, Kennath,
Kennie, Kenny

Kenny (Scottish) form of
Kenneth: good-looking
Kennee, Kenney, Kenni, Kennie

Kenric (English) bold

Kenrick (English) heroic boy

Kensil (English) form of
Kenneth: good-looking

Kent (English) fair-skinned
Kennt, Kentt

Kentaro (Japanese) large baby boy

Kentlee (Last name as first name)
dignified
Ken, Kenny, Kent, Kentlea,
Kentleigh, Kently

Kentley (English) meadow boy

Kenton (English) form of Kent:
fair-skinned
Kentan, Kentin

Kentos (American) form of Quintus: fifth child

Kentrell (English) white

Kenward (Last name as first name) bold

Kenway (Last name as first name) bold

Kenyatta (African) from Kenya; patriotic

Kenyon (Irish) dear blond boy
Ken, Kenjon, Kenny, Kenyawn, Kenyun

Kenzel (Scottish) wise

Kenzie (Scottish) form of Kinsey: affectionate; winning
Kensie

Kenzo (American) form of Ken: good-looking

Keola (Hawaiian) vibrant

Keon (American) unbridled enthusiasm
Keion, Keonne, Keyon, Kion, Kionn

Keontay (African American) outrageous
Keon, Keontae, Keontee

Kepler (German) loves astrology; starry-eyed
Kappler, Keppel, Keppeler, Keppler

Kepner (German) Last name as first name

Kerbie (American) form of Kirby: brilliant

Kerel (African) forever young

Kerem (Hebrew) works in vineyard

Keren (Hebrew) of the horns

Kerey (Irish) dark

Kerm (Irish) form of Kermit: droll
Kurm

Kermit (German) droll
Kerm, Kermee, Kermet, Kermey, Kermi, Kermie, Kermy

Kern (Irish) dark; musically inclined
Curran, Kearn, Kearne, Kearns

Kernaghan (Last name as first name) dark
Carnahan, Kernohan

Kernis (Invented) dark; different
Kernes

Kerr (Scandinavian) serious; (Scottish) surname
Karr, Kerre, Kurr

Kerrick (English) rules

Kerrins (English) of the horns

Kerry (Irish) dark
Keary, Kere, Keri, Kerrey, Kerrie

Kers (Indian) an Indian plant

Kersen (Indonesian) cherry bright

Kerstie (American) spunky
Kerstee, Kersty

Kert (American) form of Curt/Curtis: gracious; kindhearted

Kerwyn (Irish) energetic
Kerwen, Kerwin, Kerwun, Kir, Kirs, Kirwin

Keshawn (African American) friendly
Kesh, Keshaun, Keyshawn, Shawn

Keshet (Hebrew) rainbow; bright hopes

Keshon (African American) sociable
Kesh

Kesin (Hindi) needy

Kesley (American) derivative of Lesley: active
Keslee, Kesli, Kezley

Kesse (American) attractive
Kessee, Kessey, Kessi, Kessie

Kester (Scottish) form of Christopher: the bearer of Christ

Kestrel (English) soars

Ketchum (Place name) city in Idaho
Catch, Ketch, Ketcham, Ketchim

Keth (Irish) form of Keith: witty

Kettil (Scandinavian) self-sacrificing
Keld, Ketil, Ketti, Kjeld

Keung (Chinese) universal spirit

Kevann (Irish) good-looking

Kevin ✿ (Irish) handsome; gentle
Kev, Kevahngn, Kevan, Keven,
Kevvie, Kevvy

Kevis (Irish) form of Kevin:
handsome; gentle
Handsome

Kevontay (American) combo of
Kevon and Tay

Kevork (English) noble

Key (English) key
Keye, Keyes

Keylor (Irish) friend

Keyon (Irish) form of Ewan:
youthful spirit

Keyshawn (African American)
clever; believer

Keyth (Welsh) form of Keith: witty

Keyvan (American) form of
Kevin: handsome; gentle

Khaalis (Greek) beauty

Khadijah (Arabic) premature
baby

Khadim (Hindi) forever
Kadeem, Kadeen, Kahdeem,
Khadeem

Khak (American) form of Khaki:
laughing

Khaldoun (Arabic) everlasting

Khaldun (Arabic) everlasting

Khalid (Arabic) everlasting
Khalead, Khaled, Khaleed

Khalil (Arabic) good friend

Khaliq (Arabic) ingenious
Kaliq, Khalique

Khambrel (American) articulate
Kambrel, Kham, Khambrell,
Khambrelle, Khambryll, Khamme,
Khammie, Khammy

Khan (Turkish) shares; prince

Khayrat (Arabic) good

Khayru (Arabic) giving
Khiri, Khiry, Kiry

Khevin (American) form of
Kevin: handsome; gentle
Khev

Khiam (American) old

Khosrow (Slavic) denies

Khouri (Arabic) spiritual
Couri, Khory, Khourae, Kori

Khyber (Place name) pass
on border of Pakistan and
Afghanistan
Kibe, Kiber, Kyber

Kibbe (Nayas) nocturnal bird

Kibo (Place name) mountain
peak; highest peak of Kilimanjaro;
spectacular
Kib

Kibwy (African) God blesses

Kidd (Last name as first name)
adventurous

Kidder (Last name as first name)
brash; confident

Kidron (English) youthful

Kiefer (Irish) loving
Keefer, Kiefert, Kieffer, Kieffner,
Kiefner, Kuefer, Kueffner

Kiel (Place name) city in North
Germany; (Irish) form of Kyle:
serene

Kien (Irish) form of Keenan:
bright-eyed

Kier (Icelandic) large vat or tub

Kieran (Scottish) dark-haired;
(Irish) handsome brunette
Keiran, Keiren, Keiron, Kern,
Kernan, Kier, Kieren, Kierin,
Kiernan, Kieron, Kiers, Kyran

Kiet (Asian) respected

Kiev (Place name) capital city of
Ukraine

Kiho (Hawaiian) moves carefully

Kilbane (English) Last name as
first name

Kilgore (Scottish) Last name as
first name

Killam (Irish) slim

Killi (Irish) form of Killian:
effervescent
Killean, Killee, Killey, Killyun

Killian (Irish) effervescent
Kilean, Kilian, Killean, Killee, Killi, Killie, Killyun, Kylian

Killion (Irish) slim

Kilroy (Irish) royal

Kilyun (American) form of Killion: slim

Kim (Vietnamese) gold
Kimmie, Kimmy, Kimy, Kym

Kimball (Greek) inviting
Kim, Kimb, Kimbal, Kimbie, Kimble, Kymball

Kimberly (English) bold
Kim, Kimbo, Kimberleigh, Kimberley

Kin (Japanese) golden

Kincaid (Scottish) vigorous
Kincaide, Kinkaid

Kincannon (Scottish) Last name as first name; I'll defend

Kinch (Last name as first name) knife blade

King (English) royal leader

Kingman (Last name as first name) gracious man

Kingsley (English) royal nature
King, Kings, Kingslea, Kingslee, Kingsleigh, Kingsly, Kins

Kingston (English) gracious
King, Kingstan, Kingsten

Kingswell (English) royal; king

Kinnard (Last name as first name) leaning
Kinnaird

Kinnel (Gaelic) dweller at the head of the cliff

Kinney (English) simplifies

Kinsey (English) affectionate; winning
Kensey, Kinsie

Kinton (Hindi) adorned

Kioshi (Japanese) thoughtful silence

Kip (English) focused
Kipp, Kippi, Kippie, Kippy

Kipling (Literature) for writer Rudyard; adventurous
Kiplen, Kippling

Kipp (American) hill; upward bound
Kip, Kyp

Kipster (English) boy from the hill

Kirabo (African) treasured

Kiral (Greek) Lord

Kiran (Hindi) light

Kirann (American) purehearted

Kirby (English) brilliant
Kerb, Kirb, Kirbee, Kirbey, Kirbie, Kyrbee, Kyrby

Kiri (Vietnamese) like mountains

Kiril (Russian) Lord
Cyril, Cyrill, Kirill, Kirillos, Kyril, Kyrill

Kirk (Scandinavian) believer
Kerk, Kirke, Kurk

Kirkan (Scandinavian) of the church

Kirkland (Last name as first name) church land

Kirkley (Last name as first name) church wood
Kirklea, Kirklee, Kirklie, Kirkly

Kirkor (English) of the church

Kirkson (English) church son

Kirkwell (Last name as first name) wood; giving of faith

Kirkwood (English) heavenly
Kirkwoode, Kurkwood

Kirton (English) from the town of churches

Kirvin (American) form of Kevin: handsome; gentle
Kerven, Kervin, Kirv, Kirvan, Kirven

Kishore (Indian) little colt

Kit (Greek) mischievous
Kitt

Kitchell (American) form of Mitchell: optimistic

Kito (African) precious

Kiva (Hebrew) form of Akiva: cunning

Kizza (African) child born after twins' birth

Kjeld (Scandinavian) form of Carl: kingly

Kjell-Ake (Scandinavian) form of Carl: kingly

Kjetil (Scandinavian) form of Carl: kingly

Klaus (German) wealthy
Klaas, Klaes, Klas, Klass

Klausen (German) victor

Klay (English) form of Clay: reliable
Klaie, Klaye

Kleber (Last name as first name) serious
Klebe

Kleef (Dutch) boy from the cliff; daring

Kleigh (American) form of Clay: reliable

Klein (Last name as first name) bright
Kleiner, Kleinert, Kline

Klemens (Latin) gentle
Klemenis, Klement, Kliment

Kleng (Scandinavian) claw; struggles

Klev (Invented) form of Cleve: precarious
Kleve

Knight (English) protector
Knighte, Nighte

Knightley (English) protects
Knight, Knightlea, Knightlee, Knightlie, Knightly, Knights

Knoll (American) flamboyant
Noll

Knollie (English) form of Knowles: outdoorsman

Knossos (Biblical) place name

Knoten (Native American) windy

Knowah (American) form of Noah: peacemaker

Knowles (English) outdoorsman
Knowlie, Knowls, Nowles

Knowlton (English) from the grassy knoll

Knox (English) bold

Knud (Scandinavian) ruler

Knut (Scandinavian) aggressive
Canute, Cnut, Knute

Kobi (Hebrew) cunning; smart
Cobe, Cobey, Cobi, Cobie, Coby, Kobe, Kobee, Kobey, Kobi, Kobie, Koby

Kobin (African) Tuesday's child

Kobus (Dutch) form of Jacob: he who supplants

Kodiak (American) bear; daunting

Kody (English) brash
Kodee, Kodey, Kodi, Kodie, Kodye

Kofi (African) Friday-born

Kohana (Hawaiian) best

Kohath (Biblical) congregation

Kohl (English) form of Cole: lively; winner

Kohler (German) coal

Koji (African) Monday's baby

Kojo (African) Monday-born

Koka (Hawaiian) man from Scotland; strategist

Kolby (American) form of Colby: bright; secretive; dark farm
Kelby, Kole, Kollby

Kole (English) form of Cole: lively; winner

Kolen (Irish) beautiful; light

Kolibar (American) form of Colbert: cool and calm

Kolton (English) coal town

Kombs (American) from catacombs

Komic (Invented) funny
Com, Comic, Kom

Konane (Hawaiian) spot of moonlight

Kondo (African) fights

Kone (Word as name) cone

Kong (Chinese) heavenly

Konnor (Irish) another spelling of Connor; brilliant
Konnar, Konner

Kono (African) industrious

Konrad (German) bold advisor
Khonred, Kon, Konn, Konny, Konraad, Konradd, Konrade, Kord, Kort

Konsa (American) form of Constantine: constant; steadfast

Konstandin (Slavic) steadfast

Konstantin (Greek) loyal
Kon, Konny, Kons, Konstance, Konstantine, Konstantyne

Konstantinos (Greek) loyal
Constance, Konstance, Konstant, Tino, Tinos

Koralion (Greek) coral

Korb (German) form of Korbel: black raven

Korbel (German) black raven

Kore (Greek) pure

Koren (Greek) strong-willed

Korent (English) form of Corentin: stormy

Koresh (Hebrew) farms
Choresh

Korey (Irish) lovable
Kori, Korrey, Korrie

Korling (American) bold

Kornel (Czech) horn; communicator
Kornelisz, Kornelius, Kornell

Kornelius (Latin) form of Cornelius
Korne, Kornellius, Kornelyus, Korney, Kornnelyus

Korrigan (Irish) form of Corrigan
Koregan, Korigan, Korre, Korreghan, Korri, Korrigon

Kort (German) talkative

Korten (German) of the court

Kory (Irish) hollow
Kori, Korre, Korrey, Korrye

Kosana (African) prince

Kosey (African) temperamental; lionlike

Koshua (American) form of Joshua: devout

Koshy (American) jolly
Koshee, Koshey, Koshi

Kosmo (Greek) likes order
Cosmos, Kosmy

Kostas (Russian) form of Konstantin: loyal

Koster (American) spiritual
Kost, Kostar, Koste, Koster

Kosumi (Native American) fishes with a spear; smart

Kosyantyn (Slavic) leader

Kovit (Asian) talented

Krael (Slavic) form of Kyryl: Lord's child

Kraig (Irish) form of Craig: brave climber
Krag, Kragg, Kraggy

Kramer (German) shopkeeper; humorous

Krater (American) form of the word crater

Krause (German) outdoorsy

Krayton (Russian) kind

Kreig (Irish) form of Craig: brave climber

Kres (Slavic) peaceful

Kreso (Slavic) peaceful

Kricker (Last name as first name) reliable
Krick

Krikor (Armenian) form of Gregory: careful

Kris (Greek) form of Kristian: follower of Christ; form of Kristopher: the bearer of Christ
Krissy, Krys

Krishna (Hindu) pleasant
Krishnah

Krispin (Irish) form of Crispin: man with curls

Krissel (German) curly-haired

Krister (Scandinavian) religious

Kristian (Greek) form of Christian: follower of Christ
Kris, Krist, Kristyan

Kristiyan (Slavic) Christian

Kristo (Greek) form of Kristopher: the bearer of Christ

Kristoffer (Scandinavian) form of Christopher: the bearer of Christ

Kristopher (Greek) form of Christopher: the bearer of Christ
Kris, Krist, Kristo, Kristofer

Kroenen (Polish) form of Cronin: timely

Kronos (Greek) black

Kruz (Spanish) delight

Krystyn (Polish) Christian
Krys, Krystian

Krzysztof (Polish) bearing Christ
Kreestof

Kubrick (Last name as first name) creative
Kubrik

Kueng (Chinese) of the universe; fine

Kugonza (African) in love

Kumar (Hindi) boy

Kundayo (African) joy

Kunig (Dutch) clever

Kuno (German) courageous

Kunyo (African) brave

Kuper (Hebrew) copper

Kurt (Latin) wise advisor
Curt, Kurty

Kurtis (Latin) form of Curtis: gracious; kindhearted
Kurt, Kurtes, Kurtey, Kurtie, Kurts, Kurtus, Kurty

Kuster (American) form of Custer: watchful; stubborn

Kutrer (Last name as first name) form of Cutrer: knife dealer

Kutter (American) form of Cutter: man who cuts gemstones

Kutty (English) knife-wielding
Cutty

Kwadjo (African) Monday-born

Kwako (African) Wednesday-born

Kwame (African) Saturday's child
Kwamee, Kwami

Kwan (Korean) bold character

Kwasi (African) born on Sunday
Kweisi, Kwesi

Kwintyn (Polish) fifth child
Kwint, Kwintin, Kwynt

Ky (Irish) form of Kyle: serene

Kyan (Place name) village in Japan
Kyann

Kylan (Irish) form of Kyle: serene

Kyland (Irish) calm

Kyle ✪ (Irish) serene
Kiel, Kiyle, Kye, Kyl, Kyley, Kylie, Kyly

Kyler (English) peaceful
Cuyler, Kieler, Kiler, Kye, Kylor

Kylerly (English) unusual

Kylerton (American) form of Kyle: serene
Kylten

Kymond (American) brave

Kynan (Welsh) leads

Kynaston (English) serene

Kyne (English) blue-blooded

Kyran (Irish) form of Kieran: handsome brunette

Kyriacos (Greek) masterful

Kyriak (Greek) loves God

Kyros (Greek) masterful

Kyryl (Slavic) Lord's child

Kyston (American) form of Constantine: constant; steadfast

Kyzer (American) wild spirit
Kaizer, Kizer, Kyze

La Var (American) combo of La and Var

Laasch (Scandinavian) forward-thinking

Laban (Hebrew) white
Lavan

Labarne (American) form of Laban: white
Labarn

Labaron (French) the baron
LaBaron, LaBaronne

Labhras (Irish) form of Lawrence: honored
Lubhras

LaBryant (African American) son of Bryant; brash
Bryant, La Brian, La Bryan, Labryan, Labryant

Lachean (Scottish) from place of lakes

Lachlan (Scottish) feisty
Lachlann, Lacklan, Lackland, Laughlin, Lock, Locklan

Lachman (Scottish) prospers

Lachtna (Irish) gray; aging with grace

Lacido (Spanish) bright

Lacy (Scottish) warlike
Lacey

Ladan (Hebrew) having seen; aware

Ladd (English) helper; smart
Lad, Laddee, Laddey, Laddie, Laddy

Ladden (American) athletic

Laddie (English) youthful
Lad, Ladd, Laddee, Laddey, Laddy

Laden (English) from Layton: musical

Ladisiao (Spanish) helpful
Laddy

Ladislav (Czech) form of Walter: army leader

Lado (Spanish) artistic

Lael (Hebrew) belonging to Jehovah
Lale

Laertes (Literature) from Shakespeare's Hamlet; action-oriented

Lafaye (American) cheerful
Lafay, Lafayye, Laphay, Laphe

Lafayetta (Spanish) form of Lafayette: ambitious
Lafay

Lafayette (French) ambitious
Lafayet, Lafayett

Lafe (American) punctual
Laafe, Laife, Laiffe

Lafen (English) dearest friend

Lafett (French) form of Lafayette: ambitious

Lafi (Polynesian) shy

Lagos (Place name) city in Nigeria
Lago

Lagrand (African American) the grand
Grand, Grandy, Lagrande

Lahahana (Hawaiian) warm as sunshine

Laionela (Hawaiian) lion boldness

Laird (Scottish) rich
Layrd, Layrde

Lais (Indian) leonine

Laish (Biblical) place name

Laizer (French) form of Lazarus: helped by God

Lajos (Hungarian) famed

Lake (English) tranquil water

Lakista (African American) bold man

Laksen (Scandinavian) lucky son

Lakshman (Hindi) promising; (Indian) rich

Lal (Hindi) beloved

Lalit (Indian) handsome

Lalo (Latin) singer of a lullaby
Laloh

Lam (African) picks lemons

Lamalcom (African American) son of Malcolm; kingly
LaMalcolm, LaMalcom, Mal, Malcolm, Malcom

Lamar (Latin) renowned
Lamahr, Lamarr, Lemar, Lemarr

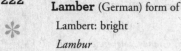

Lamber (German) form of
Lambert: bright
Lambur

Lambert (German) bright
Lamb, Lamer, Lambie, Lamburt,
Lammie, Lammy

Lamberto (Spanish) bright

Lamech (Biblical) to lower

Lamek (Biblical) form of Lamech:
to lower

Lament (Biblical) from
Lamentations

Lamis (Arabic) speaks softly

Lamond (French) worldly
Lammond, Lamon, Lamonde,
Lemond

Lamont (Scandinavian) lawman
Lamon

Lamonte (French) mountain

Lan (Chinese) orchid

Lance (German) confident
Lanse, Lantz, Lanz

Lancelot (French) romantic
Lance, Lancelott, Launcelot,
Launcey

Land (English) form of Landon:
plain; old-fashioned

Landan (English) from the plains;
quiet

Lander (English) landed
Land, Landor

Landers (English) wealthy
Land, Landar, Lander, Landor

Landis (English) owning land;
earthy
Land, Landes, Landice, Landise,
Landly, Landus

Lando (American) masculine
Land

Landon ♂ ❶ (English) plain;
old-fashioned
Land, Landan, Landen

Landry (French) entrepreneur
Landré, Landree

Lane (English) secure
Laine, Laney, Lanie, Lanni, Layne

Lang (English) top
Lange

Langdon (English) long-winded
Lang, Langden, Langdun

Langen (English) tall

Langerson (Scandinavian) long

Langford (English) healthy
Lanford, Langferd

Langham (Last name as first
name) long
Lang

Langilea (Polynesian) loud as
thunder

Langiloa (Polynesian) stormy;
moody

Langley (English) natural
Lang, Langlee, Langli, Langly

Langston (English) long-
suffering
Lang, Langstan, Langsten

Langton (English) long
Lange

Langundo (Polynesian) graceful

Langward (Last name as first
name) long

Langworth (Last name as first
name) of long worth

Lani (Hawaiian) lithe

Lanie (Scandinavian) son of tall
man

Laning (Last name as first name)

Lanndson (English) Last name as
first name

Lanny (American) popular
Lann, Lanney, Lanni, Lannie

Lansing (Place name) city in
Michigan
Lance, Lans

Lanty (Irish) lively
Laughun, Leachlainn, Lochlainn,
Lochlann

Lantz (American) form of Lance:
confident

Lanu (Native American) circular

Lanzo (Italian) lance

Laoghaire (Irish) caretaker of cows

Laoiseach (Place name) from the county Leix in Ireland

Lap (Vietnamese) independent

Laphonso (African American) prepared; centered

Lapidos (Greek) cologne
Lapidus

Laramie (French) pensive
Laramee

Lare (American) wealthy
Larre, Layr

Laredo (Spanish) place name

Larence (English) form of Lorenzo: honored

Largel (American) intrepid
Large

Lari (American) form of Larry: extrovert

Lariat (American) roper
Lare, Lari

Larios (Spanish) form of Lawrence: honored

Larkin (Irish) brash
Lark, Larkan, Larken, Larkie, Larky

Larndell (American) generous
Larn, Larndelle, Larndey, Larne

Larne (Place name) district in Northern Ireland
Larn, Larney, Larny

Larnell (American) giving
Larne

Laron (American) outgoing
Larron, Larrone

Laroyce (French) royal

Larrimore (Last name as first name) loud
Larimore, Larmer, Larmor

Larrmyne (American) boisterous
Larmie, Larmine, Larmy, Larmyne

Larry (Latin) extrovert
Lare, Larrey, Larri, Larrie, Lary

Lars (Scandinavian) form of Lawrence: honored
Larrs, Larse, Larsy

Larsa (Biblical) ancient Babylonian city

Larson (Scandinavian) son of Lars

Lasha (Biblical) place name (east of the Dead Sea); fissure

Lashaun (African American) enthusiastic
Lashawn, La-Shawn, Lashon, Lashond

Lashe (Scandinavian) form of Lasse: winner; the people's victory

Laskey (Last name as first name) jovial
Lask, Laski

Lasse (Scandinavian) form of Nicholas: winner; the people's victory

Lassen (Place name) a peak in California in the Cascade Range
Lase, Lasen, Lassan, Lassun

Lassit (American) broad-minded
Lasset, Lassitte

Lassiter (American) witty
Lassater, Lasseter, Lassie, Lassy

Laszlo (Hungarian) famous leader
Laslo, Lazuli

Lateef (Arabic) a gentle man

Lath (Scandinavian) boy from the barn

Latham (Scandinavian) farmer; knowing
Lathe, Lay

Lathrop (English) home-loving
Lathe, Lathrap, Latrope, Lay, Laye, Laythrep

Latif (Arabic) nice

Latimer (English) interprets; philanthropic
Latymer

Latorris (African American) notorious
LaTorris

Latoure (French) torn

Latravious (African American) healthy
Latrave

Latty (English) giving
Lat, Latti, Lattie

Laughlin (Irish) servant

Laurence (Latin) form of Lawrence: honored
Larence, Laurance, Laurans, Laure, Lorence

Laurens (German) brilliant
Larrie, Larry, Laure, Laurins, Lorens, Lors

Laurent (French) martyred
Laurynt

Laurie (Latin) form of Lawrence: honored

Lavan (Latin) pure

Lavaughn (African American) perky
Lavan, Lavon, Lavonn, Levan, Levaughn

Lavaughor (African American) laughing
Lavaugher, Lavawnar

Lavay (Italian) form of Livia: place name

Lavega (French) eagle star

Laven (Hebrew) white

Lavesh (Hindi) little piece; calm

Lavi (Hebrew) uniter

Lavunn (American) form of Levon: forward-thinking

Law (American) feisty

Lawerence (Latin) form of Lawrence: honored

Lawford (English) dignified
Laford, Lauford, Lawferd

Lawler (Last name as first name) honoring; teacher
Lawlor, Lollar, Loller

Lawrence (Latin) honored
Larrie, Larry, Laurence, Lawrance, Lawrunce

Lawrie (Latin) form of Lawrence: honored
Lowrie

Lawson (English) Lawrence's son; special
Law, Laws, Lawsan, Lawsen

Lawton (Last name as first name) honored town

Laylan (English) from land of Leigh

Layneln (English) form of Lane: secure

Layshaun (African American) merry
Laysh, Layshawn

Laysy (Last name as first name) sophisticated
Lay, Laycie, Laysee

Layt (American) fascinating
Lait, Laite, Late, Layte

Layte (English) meadow boy

Layton (English) musical
Laytan, Laytawn, Layten

Laz (Spanish) form of Lazarus: helped by God

Lazar (Hebrew) form of Lazarus: helped by God
Lazare, Lazaro, Lazear, Lazer

Lazaro (Italian) form of Lazarus: helped by God

Lazarus (Greek) helped by God
Eleazer, Lasarus, Lazerus, Lazoros

Lazo (Spanish) form of Lazarus: helped by God

Leal (Spanish) form of Lael: belonging to Jehovah; (Greek) self-assured

Leamon (American) powerful
Leamm, Leamond, Leemon

Leand (Greek) form of Leander: ferocious; lionlike

Leander (Greek) ferocious; lionlike
Anders, Leann, Leannder

Leandro (Spanish) of Leander

Lear (Greek) royal
Leare, Leere

Learly (Last name as first name) terrific
Learley

Leary (Irish) herds; high goals

Leather (American) word as name; tough
Leath

Leavery (American) giving
Leautree, Leautri, Leautry, Levry, Lo, Lotree, Lotrey, Lotri, Lotry

Leben (Last name as first name) small; hopeful

Lebna (African) soulful

Lebrun (French) brown-haired
Lebron, Labron

Lechoslaw (Polish) glorious Pole; envied
Lech, Leslaw, Leszek

Lecil (American) form of Cecil: unseeing; hard-headed; blind

Leckto (Greek) everlasting

Lectoy (American) form of Leroy: king; loyal
Lec, Lecto, Lek

Lee (English) loving
Lea, Leigh

Leeander (Invented) form of Leander: ferocious; lionlike

Legario (Spanish) cheerful

Leger (French) sent to earth

Leggett (Last name as first name) able
Legate, Leggitt, Liggett

Lei (Hawaiian) wreath; decorative

Leibel (Hebrew) lion

Leif (Scandinavian) loved one
Laif, Leaf, Leife

Leigh (English) smooth

Leighton (Last name as first name) hearty
Laytan, Layton, Leighten, Leightun

Leith (Scottish) broad

Lel (Gypsy) taker

Leland (English) protective
Leeland, Leighlon, Leiland, Lelan, Lelond

Leldon (American) form of Eldon: charitable
Leldun

Lem (Hebrew) form of Lemuel: loves God

Lemar (American) form of Lamar: renowned
Lemarr

Lemmy (Hebrew) loves God

Lemon (American) fruit; tart
Lemonn, Lemun, Limon

Lemuel (Hebrew) loves God
Lem, Lemmie, Lemmy, Lemy

Lemus (Spanish) loves God

Len (German) form of Leonard: courageous
Lennie, Lynn

Lenard (American) form of Leonard: courageous
Lenerd

Lencio (Spanish) valiant; gentle

Leni (Polynesian) lives for today

Lenjun (Dutch) helps

Lennan (Irish) gentle

Lennart (Scandinavian) brave
Lenn, Lenne

Lenno (Italian) brave

Lennon (Irish) renowned; caped
Lenin, Lenn, Lennan, Lennen

Lennor (Last name as first name) brave

Lennox (Scottish) authoritative
Lennix, Lenocks, Lenox, Linnox

Lenny (German) form of Leonard: courageous
Lenn, Lenney, Lenni, Lennie, Leny, Linn

Lensar (English) stays with parents

Lentin (English) summery

Lenton (American) religious
Lent, Lenten, Lentun

Lenvil (Invented) typical
Lenval, Level

Leny (German) form of Leonard:
courageous

Leo (Latin) lionlike; fierce

Leobardo (Italian) lionlike

Leocadio (Spanish) lionhearted
Leo

Leolin (Polynesian) watchful
Leoline, Llewelyn

Leon (Greek) tenacious
Lee, Leo, Leone, Leonn

Leonard (German) courageous
Lee, Leo, Leonar, Leonerd,
Leonord, Lynar, Lynard, Lynerd

LeOnarda (Spanish) form of
Leonardo: lionhearted

Leonardo (Italian) lionhearted
Leo

Leoncio (Spanish) lionhearted
Leon, Leonce, Leonse

Leondras (African American)
leonine
Leon, Leondre, Leondrus, Leonid

Leondus (Spanish) lion

Leone (Spanish) lion

Leonel (American) form of
Lionel: fierce

Leonidus (Latin) strong
Leon, Leone, Leonidas, Leonydus

Leontes (German) lion's courage

Leonzo (Spanish) lion's courage

Leopold (German) brave
Lee, Leo

Leor (Latin) listens

Leoti (American) outdoorsy
Lee, Leo

Leovardo (Spanish) form of
Leonardo: lionhearted
Leo, Leovard

Leovigildo (Spanish) lion heart

Lepern (Italian) leonine

Lepoldo (Spanish) form of
Leopold: brave
Lee, Lepold, Poldo

Lepolo (Polynesian) handsome

Lerby (French) circular life

Lerett (Last name as first name)
gentle

Lerey (American) form of Larry:
extrovert
Lerrie, Lery

Leroy (French) king; royal
Leeroy, Leroi, Le-Roy, Roy, Roye

Leroye (French) royal

Les (English) form of Leslie: fortified
Lez, Lezli

Leshawn (African American)
cheery
Lashawn, Leshaun, Le-Shawn

Leslie (Scottish) fortified
Lee, Les, Lesley, Lesli, Lezlie, Lezly

Lesner (Last name as first name)
serious
Les, Lez, Lezner

Lester (American) large persona
Les, Lestor

Letian (Spanish) happy

Leto (Latin) happy

Letrae (French) joyful

Letushim (Biblical) hammermen;
filemen

Leuk (Irish) form of Lake:
tranquil water

Leumas (Biblical) name spelled
backward

Leummim (Biblical) countries,
without water.

Lev (Russian) lionine

Levar (American) soft-spoken
Levarr

Levega (French) star

Leven (Hebrew) heart's child

Leveratto (Italian) organized

Leverett (Last name as first
name) planner
Lev, Leveret, Leverit, Leveritt

Leverton (Last name as first
name) town of Lever; organized

Levesque (French) gatekeeper

Levi ◐ (Hebrew) harmonious
Lev, Levey, Levie, Levy

Levonne (African American) forward-thinking
Lavonne, Leevon, Levon

Lew (Polish) form of Louis: famous warrior
Leu

Leward (French) contentious
Lewar, Lewerd

Lewie (French) form of Louis: famous warrior
Lew, Lewee, Lewey, Lewy

Lewin (Last name as first name) lionlike

Lewis (German) form of Louis: famous warrior
Lewey, Lewie, Lewus, Lewy

Lewy (Irish) giving

Lex (English) form of Alexander: great leader; helpful
Lexa, Lexe, Lexi, Lexie, Lexy

Lexonne (American) form of Alexander: great leader; helpful

Leyland (Last name as first name) protective

Leyth (Scottish) river

Li (Chinese) strong man

Liam ☉ (Irish) protective; handsome
Leam, Leeam, Leeum

Liang (Chinese) good man

Libardo (Spanish) free

Liber (Roman) freedom

Liberio (Spanish) liberated
Libere, Lyberio

Liberty (American) freedom-loving
Lib

Libni (Slavic) love

Libor (Czech) free

Licien (French) form of Lucian: soothing

Lidio (Greek) pleasant man

Lidon (Hebrew) judge

Liem (Vietnamese) truthful

Lienad (Biblical) name spelled backward

Lif (Scandinavian) full of life

Lifen (Dutch) beloved

Lige (Spanish) form of Ligia: clear

Ligi (Spanish) form of Ligia: clear

Ligia (Spanish) clear

Lihau (Hawaiian) cool; fresh

Like (Asian) soft-spoken

Liko (Hawaiian) budding; flourishing

Lillo (American) triple-threat talent
Lilo

Limo (Invented) from limousine; sporty
Lim

Limu (Polynesian) seaweed; natural

Linc (English) form of Lincoln: leader; lake colony
Link, Links

Lincoln (English) leader; lake colony
Link

Lindberg (German) linden-tree mountain
Lin, Lind, Lindburg, Lindie, Lindy, Lyndberg, Lyndburg

Lindell (Last name as first name) in harmony with nature
Lindall, Lindel, Lyndall, Lyndell

Linden (Botanical) tree
Lindun

Lindoh (American) sturdy
Lindo, Lindy

Lindsay (English) natural
Lind, Lindsee, Lindsey, Linz, Linzee, Lyndsey, Lyndzie, Lynz, Lynzie

Lindy (German) form of Lindberg: linden-tree mountain
Lind

Linford (Last name as first name) bold man
Lynford

Linfred (Last name as first name) proactive

Linley (English) open-minded
Lin, Linlee, Linleigh, Lynlie

Linnard (German) form of Leonard: courageous
Linard, Lynard

Lino (American) form of Linus: blond

Linos (Spanish) praised

Linton (English) lives near lime trees
Lintonn, Lynton, Lyntonn

Linus (Greek) blond
Linas, Line, Lines

Linvel (English) from flax town

Linwood (American) open

Lionel (French) fierce
Li, Lion, Lionell, Lye, Lyon, Lyonel, Lyonell

Liron (Hebrew) my song
Lyron

Lisiate (Polynesian) courageous

Lisimba (African) attacked by lion; victim

Lister (Origin unknown) intelligent

Littlejoe (Spanish) small

Litton (English) centered
Lyten, Lyton, Lytton

Liu (Asian) quiet

Liuz (Polish) light

Livias (Biblical) place name

Livingston (English) comforting
Liv, Livey, Livingstone

Liwanu (Asian) released

Llano (Place name) river in Texas; flowing
Lano

Llewellyn (English) fiery; fast
Lew, Lewellen, Lewellyn

Lleyton (Slavic) of the garden

Lloy (Welsh) holy

Lloyd (English) spiritual; joyful
Loy, Loyd, Loydde, Loye

Lobo (Spanish) wolf
Loboe, Lobow

Loc (English) of the forest

Lochan (Irish) lively

Lochlain (Irish) assertive
Lochlaine, Lochlane, Locklain

Lock (English) natural
Locke

Lod (Biblical) place name

Lodewuk (Scandinavian) warrior
Ladewijk, Ludovic

Lodge (English) safe haven

Lodi (American) place name

Lodovico (Italian) famous

Lodur (Scandinavian) vivid

Loey (American) daring
Loie, Lowee, Lowi

Lofton (Last name as first name) lofty
Loften

Logan ✪ ❶ (Irish) eloquent
Logen, Loggy, Logun

Lohan (Last name as first name) capable

Lokela (Hawaiian) famed spear-thrower

Lokene (Hawaiian) form of Rodney: open-minded

Lokesh (Indian) hindu god Brahma

Lokie (Mythology) chaotic

Loknath (Indian) world leader

Lokni (Hawaiian) red rose

Loman (Irish) bare

Lomas (Spanish) good man

Lomax (English) Last name as first name

Lombain (French) peaceful (from the name Colombain)

Lombard (Teutonic) long-beard

Lombardi (Italian) winner
Bardi, Bardy, Lom, Lombard, Lombardy

Lon (Irish) intense

Lonata (Spanish) bravery

Lonato (Native American) flint stone; calm

Loncel (French) gentle

Lond (English) form of London: ethereal; capital of great Britain

London (English) ethereal; capital of great Britain
Londen

Long (Last name as first name) Chinese dragon; methodical

Lonnie (Spanish) form of Alonzo: enthusiastic
Lonney, Lonni, Lonny

Lono (Hawaiian) god of peace and agriculture

Loocho (Invented) form of Lucho: lucky; light

Loomis (American) young

Loramie (American) form of Laramie: pensive

Loran (American) form of Lauren: laurel-crowned

Lorance (Latin) form of Lawrence: honored
Lorans, Lorence

Lorca (Last name as first) poet

Lorcan (Irish) fiery

Lord (English) regal
Lorde

Lordlee (English) regal
Lordly, Lords

Lordson (English) Lord's son

Loredo (Spanish) smart; cowboy
Lorado, Loredoh, Lorre, Lorrey

Loren (Latin) hopeful; winning
Lorin, Lorrin

Lorens (Scandinavian) form of Lawrence: honored

Lorenzo (Spanish) form of Lawrence: honored
Larenzo, Loranzo, Lore, Lorence, Lorenso, Lorentz, Lorenz, Lorrie, Lorry

Loreto (Italian) form of Lawrence: honored

Loriano (Italian) form of Lorenzo; form of Lawrence: honored

Lorimer (Last name as first name) brash
Lorrimer

Loring (German) brash; (Greek) son of soldier
Looring, Lorrie, Louring

Lorl (English) laurel plant

Lorne (Latin) grounded
Lorn, Lorny

Lorry (English) form of Laurie: honored
Lore, Lorri, Lorrie, Lorry, Lory

Loryn (Latin) praised

Lot (Hebrew) furtive
Lott

Lotan (Biblical) secret

Lothario (German) lover
Lotario, Lothaire, Lotherio, Lothurio

Lou (German) form of Louis: famous warrior
Lew

Loudin (German) from low valley; blessed child

Loudon (American) enthusiastic
Louden, Lowden, Lowdon

Louie (German) form of Louis: famous warrior
Louey

Louis (German) famous warrior
Lewis, Lou, Louie, Lue, Luie, Luis

Louks (Dutch) mysterious

Loundis (American) visionary
Lound, Loundas, Loundes, Lowndis

Louvain (English) city in Belgium; wanderer

Love (Swedish) form of Louis: famous warrior

Lovell (English) brilliant
Lovall, Love, Lovelle, Lovie

Lovett (Last name as first name) loving
Lovat, Lovet

Low (American) word as a name; low-key
Lowey

Lowell (English) loved
Lowall, Lowel

Lowry (Last name as first name) leader
Lowree, Lowrey

Loy (English) loyal

Loyal (English) true to the word
Loy

Loys (American) loyal
Loyce, Loyse

Loza (Spanish) form of Louis: famous warrior

Lozano (Spanish) Last name as first name

Luas (Slavic) combative

Lubin (Slavic) loving

Lubomil (Polish) loves grace

Lubomir (Slavic) loves peace

Lubos (Slavic) loving

Luboslaw (Polish) loves glory

Luc (French) light; laidback
Lucca, Luke

Luca (Italian) lighthearted
Louca, Louka, Luka

Lucan (Irish) light

Lucas ✪ ❶ (Greek) patron saint of doctors/artists; creative
Lucca, Luces, Luka, Lukas, Luke, Lukes, Lukus

Lucason (German) son of Lucas; light

Lucho (Spanish) lucky; light

Lucian (Latin) soothing
Lew, Luciyan, Lushun

Luciano (Italian) lighthearted
Luca, Lucas, Luke

Lucious (African American) light; delicious
Luceous, Lushus

Lucius (Latin) sunny
Lucca, Luchious, Lushus

Lucky (American) lucky
Luckee, Luckey, Luckie

Lud (Biblical) warring

Luddey (Scandinavian) warring

Ludger (Scandinavian) wielding spears

Ludie (English) glorious
Ludd

Ludim (Biblical) warring

Luding (English) warrior

Ludington (English) warrior

Ludlow (German) respected
Ludlo, Ludloe

Ludolf (English) form of Rudolf: wolf

Ludomir (Polish) of well-known ancestry

Ludoslav (Polish) of glorified people

Ludovic (Slavic) smart; spiritual
Luddovik, Lude, Ludovik, Ludvic, Vick

Ludrie (Last name as first name) respected

Ludwig (German) talented
Ludvig, Ludweg, Ludwige

Ludwin (English) friend of Ludwig

Lugus (Irish) shining

Luigi (Italian) famed warrior
Lui, Louie

Luis ✪ (Spanish) outspoken
Luez, Luise, Luiz

Luisito (Spanish) form of Louis: famous warrior

Luister (Irish) form of Louis: famous warrior

Lujo (Spanish) luxurious
Luj

Luka (Italian) form of Luca: lighthearted
Luke

Lukae (Slavic) form of Luke: worshipful

Lukah (Invented) form of Luca: lighthearted

Lukas (Greek) lighthearted; creative
Lucus

Luke ✪ ❶ (Latin) worshipful
Luc, Lucc, Luk, Lukus

Lukman (Last name as first name) vivacious

Lulani (Hawaiian) light sky

Lullo (American) form of Luke: worshipful

Lumer (American) light
Lumar, Lume, Lumur

Luna (Spanish) moon

Lund (Scottish) island grove child

Lundy (Scandinavian) island-lover

Lunell (Irish) light

Lunn (Irish) smart and brave
Lun, Lunne

Lunt (Scandinavian) grove-dweller

Luo (Hawaiian) light

Luong (Vietnamese) from the land of bamboo

Lusk (Last name as first name) hearty
Lus, Luske, Luskee, Luskey, Luski, Lusky

Lussier (French) Last name as first name

Lutalo (African) bold fighter

Lute (Polynesian) pigeon; inconspicuous

Luther (German) reformer
Luthar, Luth, Luthur

Luthus (American) form of Luther: reformer
Luth, Luthas

Luto (Greek) from Pluto

Lux (English) light

Lyal (English) form of Lyle: unique
Lye

Lyall (Scottish) faithful

Lycur (Greek) sly

Lydan (Irish) gray

Lyfe (American) life

Lyle (French) unique
Lile, Ly

Lyleon (Scottish) of the isles

Lyles (English) of the isles

Lyman (English) meadow-man; sportsman
Leaman, Leyman

Lyndall (English) nature-lover
Lynd, Lyndal, Lyndell

Lyndles (English) of nature

Lyndon (English) verbose
Lindon, Lyn, Lynd, Lyndonn

Lynge (Scandinavian) sylvan nature

Lynn (English) water-loving
Lin, Linn, Lyn, Lynne

Lynton (English) town of nature lovers
Linton

Lynus (Greek) flax

Lynusse (American) form of Lynus: flax

Lynwood (English) forest

Lyon (Place name) city in France
Lyone

Lyr (Welsh) sea god

Lyron (Hebrew) my song

Lysande (Greek) freewheeling
Lyse

Lysander (Greek) lover
Lysand

Lyulf (German) haughty; combative
Lyulfe, Lyulff

Maarten (Welsh) form of Martin: warlike; god of war

Mablevi (African) do not deceive

Mac (Irish) mack
Mackee, Macki, Mackie, Macky

Macabee (Biblical/Hebrew) hammer

MacAdam (Scottish) son of Adam; first

Macadee (Scandinavian) headstrong

Macaffie (Scottish) charming
Mac, Mack, Mackey, McAfee, McAffee, McAffie

Macario (Spanish) blessed
Macareo, Makario

Macarlos (Spanish) manly
Carlos

Macarthur (Irish) arthur's son

Macaru (Spanish)

Macaul (Scottish) form of
Macaulley: devout son

Macauley (Scottish) righteous;
dramatic
Mac, Macaulay, McCauley

Macauliffe (Last name as first
name) bookish
Macaulif, Macauliff

Macaulley (Scottish) devout son

Macbey (American) form of
Mackie: friendly
Mackbey, Makbee, Makbi

Macdowell (Last name as first
name) giving
Macdowl

Mace (French) club

Macedonio (Spanish) from
Macedonia; travels

MacEgan (Last name as first
name) son of Egan; capable

Maceo (Spanish) form of
Macedonio: from Macedonia;
travels

Maceson (French) son of Mace

Macgowan (Irish) able; gallant
Macgowen, Macgowyn

Machen (Slavic) winner

Mackay (Scottish) form of
Mackie: friendly

Mackeane (Last name as first
name) attractive
Mackeene

Macken (Scottish) from Mackay

Mackenna (Irish) giving; leader
Mackena

Mackenzie (Irish) giving
*Mack, Mackenzy, Mackinsey,
Makinzie, McKenzie*

Mackeon (Last name as first
name) smiling

Mackie (Irish) friendly
Mackey

MacKinley (Irish) son of Kinley;
educated

Mackinney (Last name as first
name) good-looking
Mackinny

Macklin (Irish) good-humored

Maclain (Irish) natural wonder
McLain, McLaine, McLean

Maclean (Irish) dependable
Macleen

MacMurray (Irish) loves the sea

Macnair (Scottish) practical

Macon (Place name) city in
Georgia; creative
Makon

Macy (French) lasting; wealthy
Mace, Macee, Macey, Macye

Madai (Biblical) of the Medes
(ancient Persians)

Madan (Hindi) god of love; loving

Madden (Pakistani) planner
*Maddin, Maddyn, Maden, Madin,
Madyn*

Maddock (Welsh) generous
*Maddoc, Maddox, Madocock,
Madox*

Maddok (Welsh) form of
Maddock: generous

Maddox (English) giving
Maddocks, Maddy, Madox

Madeo (Italian) form of
Mateo: God's gift

Madhav (Hindi) sweet
Madhu

Madhavi (Indian) sweet as honey

Madison (English) good
*Maddison, Maddy, Madisan,
Madisen, Son*

Madock (American) giving
Maddock, Maddy, Madoc

Madon (Irish) giving

Madras (Place name) city in India

Madu (African) manly

Madzimoyo (African) nourished
by water; simple

Magaidi (African) last

Magalirio (Spanish) charming

Magee (Irish) practical; lively

Mackie, Maggy, McGee

Magellan (Spanish) explorer

Magene (Latin) creative

Magglio (Hispanic) athletic

Magic (American) magical

Majic

Magick (American) magical

Magli (Icelandic) magnanimous

Magne (Latin) great

Magni (Latin) greatness

Magno (Latin) greatness

Magnus (Latin) outstanding

Maggy, Magnes

Magog (Biblical) son of Gog;

place name

Maguire (Irish) subtle

Macky, Maggy, McGuire

Mahadev (Indian) omnipotent

Mahali (Biblical) unhealthy

Mahan (American) cowboy

Mahahn, Mahand, Mahen, Mayhan

Maharba (Biblical) name spelled backward

Mahatma (Sanskrit) spiritually elevated

Maheshkumar (Indian) son of Lord Shiva

Mahir (Arabic) skilled

Mahler (Last name as first) famous composer; sweeping

Mahli (Hebrew) brilliant

Mahlon (English) astute

Mahluli (African) conqueror

Mahmud (Arabic) remarkable

Maikan (Welsh) calm

Maimon (Arabic) of good fortune

Main (Place name) river in Germany; leader

Mainess, Mane, Maness

Maisel (Persian) warrior

Meisel

Maitland (English) of the meadow; fresh ideas

Maj (Arabic) form of Majid: glorious

Majeed (Arabic) majestic

Majid

Majid (Arabic) glorious

Major (Latin) leading

Mage, Magy, Majar, Maje, Majer

Makale (Invented) form of Mikhail: godlike

Makaz (Biblical) place name

Makhi (American) form of Mikhail: godlike

Makio (Hawaiian) great

Makoto (Japanese) sincere; honest

Maks (Russian) form of Maksimilian: competitor

Maksimilian (Russian) competitor

Maksim

Makya (Native American) hunter

Mal (Hindi) gardens; flourishes

Mala (Indian) necklace

Malachi (Hebrew) angelic; magnanimous

Malachy, Malakai, Malaki, Maleki

Malachil (Hawaiian) angel

Malack (American) form of Malakai: God's angel

Malakai (Hebrew) God's angel

Malaki (Hebrew) God's angel

Malakinn (African) lordly

Malawa (African) flowering

Malcolm (Scottish) peaceful

Mal, Malkalm, Malkelm, Malkolm

Maldon (French) strong and combative

Maldan, Malden

Malfred (German) feisty

Malfrid, Mann

Malidan (English) meets

Malik (Arabic) angelic; masterful

Malic

Malikah (Hindi) royalty

Malise (French) masterful

Malk (Hindi) royal

Malla-Ki (Invented) form of Malachi: angelic; magnanimous

Malley (German) form of Mallory: wild spirit

Mallin (English) rowdy; warrior
Malen, Malin, Mallan, Mallen, Mallie, Mally

Mallory (French) wild spirit
Mal, Mallie, Malloree, Mallorie, Mally, Malory

Mallun (English) soldier's strength

Maloney (Irish) religious
Mal, Malone, Malonie, Malony

Malta (Biblical) place name

Malvin (English) open-minded
Mal, Malv, Malven, Malvyne

Mamre (Biblical) rebellious; bitter; set with trees

Mamun (Arabic) trustworthy

Manahath (Biblical) among men

Manasseh (Hebrew) cannot remember
Manases

Manchester (English) dignity; (Place name) city in England

Manchu (Chinese) unflawed

Mandar (Indian) flower

Mandell (German) tough; almond
Mandee, Mandel, Mandela, Mandie, Mandy

Mandla (African) powerful

Mandy (Latin) lovable
Mandey

Manfred (English) peaceful
Manferd, Manford, Mannfred, Mannie, Manny, Mannye

Manfredo (Italian) strong peacefulness

Mani (Spanish) God's gift

Manila (Place name) capital of Philippines
Manilla

Maninder (Hindi) masculine; potent

Manish (Indian) mind god

Manjuk (Arabic) lightness

Manley (English) virile; haven
Man, Manlee, Manlie, Manly

Mann (German) masculine
Mannes, Manning

Manning (English) heroic
Man, Maning, Mann

Mannis (Irish) great
Manish, Manus

Mannix (Irish) spiritual
Manix, Mann, Mannicks

Mannon (French) exciting

Manny (Spanish) form of Manuel: with God
Manney, Manni, Mannie

Manoj (Sanskrit) cupid

Manolito (Spanish) God loves

Manolo (Spanish) from Spanish shoe designer Manolo Blahnik; cutting-edge

Manpreet (Indian) beloved; calm

Manriquez (German) brave

Manse (English) winning

Mansfield (English) outdoorsman
Manesfeld, Mans, Mansfeld, Mansfielde

Manshel (English) of the house; domestic
Mansel

Mantel (English) formidable
Mantell, Mantle

Manton (English) man's town; special

Manu (Hindi) father of people; masculine

Manuel (Hebrew) form of Emmanuel: with God
Mannuel, Manny, Manual, Manuelle

Manus (American) strong-willed; (Slavic) daybreak
Manes, Mann, Mannas, Mannes, Mannis, Mannus

Manvel (French) great town; hardworking
Mann, Manny, Manvil, Manville

Manzo (Japanese) third-born

Mao (Chinese) hair

Maquinn (Native American) generous

Marat (Russian) desirable

Marathon (Biblical) place name

Marathus (Biblical) place name

Marble (English) word as name

Marc (French) combative
Markee, Markey, Markeye, Markie
Mark, Marko, Marky

Marcel (French) singing God's praises
Marcell, Mars, Marsel

Marceli (French) form of Marcellus: romantic; persevering

Marcellin (French) combative

Marc-Elliott (French) combination of Marc and Elliott

Marcellus (Latin) romantic; persevering
Marcel, Marcelis, Marcey,
Marsellus, Marsey

Marcelno (Slavic) combative

Marcelo (Italian) combative

March (English) fruitful month
Marche

Marchand (French) merchant

Marchell (English) has limits

Marcial (Spanish) martial; combative
Mars

Marciano (Italian) manly; macho
Marcyano

Marciel (French) warring

Marcin (Polish) form of Martin: warlike; god of war

Marcio (Italian) warring

Marcion (Italian) warring

Marcionne (Italian) form of Martin: warlike; god of war

Marco (Italian) tender
Marc, Mark, Markie, Marko, Marky

Marconi (Italian) inventive; tough

Marcos (Spanish) outgoing
Marco, Marko, Markos, Marky

Marco-Tulio (Spanish) fighter; substantial
Marco Tulio, Marcotulio

Marcoux (French) aggressive; manly
Marce, Mars

Marcus (Latin) combative
Marc, Mark, Markus, Marky

Marcus-Anthony (Spanish) valuable; aggressive
Marc Anthony, Marc-Antonito,
Marcus-Antoneo, Marcusantonio,
Markanthony, Taco, Tonio, Tono

Marduk (Hindi) bothered

Mardy (Jewish) competitive

Marek (Polish) masculine

Marekel (Slavic) form of Marcus: combative

Marett (Greek) pearl

Margarito (Italian) pearl

Marguez (Spanish) noble
Marguiz

Mariano (Italian) combative; manly
Mario

Marico (Italian) reasonable

Marin (French) ocean-loving
Maren, Marino, Maryn

Mariner (Greek) form of Myron: aromatic oil

Mario (Italian) masculine
Marioh, Marius, Marrio, Morio

Marion (Latin) suspicious
Mareon, Marionn

Marios (Italian) combative

Marius (German) masculine; virile
Marrius

Marjuan (Spanish) contentious
Marhwon, Marwon, Marwond

Mark (Latin) form of Marcus: combative

Markan (Latin) form of Marcus: combative

Markay (American) manly

Markee (Polish) warring

Markel (Latin) form of Mark: combative

Markell (African American) personable
Markelle

Marker (American) form of Mark: combative

Markham (English) homebody
Marcum, Markhum, Markum

Markos (Greek) warring; masculine

Markys (French) form of Marcus: combative

Marl (English) rebel
Marley, Marli

Marley (English) secretive; boy of the woods
Marlee, Marleigh, Marly

Marlin (English) opportunistic; fish
Marllin

Marlo (English) hill by a lake; optimistic
Mar, Marl, Marlow, Marlowe

Marlon (French) wizard; strange
Marlan, Marlen, Marlin, Marly

Marlones (French) form of Marlon: wizard; strange

Marlous (English) boy from lake

Marlowes (English) boy from lake

Marmaduke (English) haughty
Duke, Marmadook, Marmahduke

Marmion (French) famed
Marmeonne, Marmyon

Marnin (Hebrew) ebullient

Maroulis (Greek) dark

Marq (French) noble
Mark, Marque, Marquie

Marque (French) noble; smart
Marcqe, Marcque, Marqe

Marquel (French) nobleman

Marques (African American) noble
Marqes, Marqis, Marquez, Marquis

Marquise (French) noble
Mark, Markese, Marky, Marq, Marquese, Marquie, Marquis

Marquison (Last name as first name) capable

Mars (Latin) warlike; god of war
Marrs, Marz

Marsdon (English) comforting
Marr, Mars, Marsden, Marsdyn

Marsh (English) handsome
Marr, Mars, Marsch, Marsey, Marsy

Marshall (French) giving care
Marsh, Marshal, Marshel, Marshell, Marsy

Marson (English) Mark's son

Marston (English) personable
Mars, Marst, Marstan, Marsten

Martand (Indian) sunny

Marte (English) warring

Martial (French) form of Mark: combative

Martim (Latin) form of Martin: warlike; god of war

Martin (Latin) form of Mars: warlike; god of war
Mart, Marten, Marti, Martie, Marton, Marty

Martone (French) form of Martin: warlike; god of war

Marty (Latin) form of Martin: warlike; god of war
Mart, Martee, Martey, Marti, Martie, Martye

Martyn (French) form of Martin: warlike; god of war

Marv (English) form of Marvin: steadfast friend
Marve, Marvy

Marvell (French) marvelous man
Marvel, Marvil, Marvill, Marvyl, Marvyll

Marvie (English) form of Marvin: steadfast friend

Marvin (English) steadfast friend
Marv, Marven, Marvy

Marvous (American) marvelous

Marwood (English) forest man

Masa (African) centered

Masaaki (Japanese) correct brightness

Masada (Hebrew) stronghold

Masajiro (Japanese) integrity
Masahiro, Masaji

Masamba (African) departs

Masamitsu (Japanese) feeling

Masanao (Japanese) good

Masayuki (Japanese) problematic

Mash (African) delights

Mashael (Invented) form of
Michael: like the Lord

Mashane (English) form of
Maxime: greatest

Mashawn (African American)
vivacious
Masean, Mashaun, Mayshawn

Maslen (American) promising
Mas, Masline, Maslyn

Mason ♂ ♀ (French) ingenious;
reliable; stone mason
Mace, Mase

Masood (Iranian) helpful

Massa (Biblical) a burden;
prophecy

Massey (English) doubly excellent
Maccey, Masey, Massi

Massiel (Slavic) best; from
Massimo

Massim (Italian) best; from
Massimo

Massimo (Italian) great
Masimo, Massey, Massimmo

Masson (French) stone mason

Master (English) masterful

Masura (Japanese) fated for good
life

Mate (Spanish) form of
Mateo: God's gift

Matej (Polish) form of Matthew:
God's gift

Mateo (Italian) God's gift

Mateus (Italian) God's gift

Mathan (Hebrew) fine gift

Mathau (American) spunky
Mathou, Mathow, Mathoy

Mather (English) leader; army;
strong
Mathar

Matheson (English) son of God's
gift
*Mathesen, Mathisen, Mathison,
Mathysen, Mathyson*

Matheu (French) form of
Matthew: God's gift
Matt, Matty

Mathias (German) form of
Matthew: God's gift
*Mathies, Mathyes, Matt, Matthias,
Matty*

Mathieson (German) son of
Mathias

Mathieu (French) form of
Matthew: God's gift

Matias (Spanish) form of
Matthew: God's gift
Mathias, Matios, Mattias

Matin (Hebrew) gift

Matine (French) kind

Matisse (French) gifted

Matland (English) mat's land;
homesteader

Matlock (American) rancher
Lock, Mat, Matt

Mato (Native American) bear;
brawler

Matson (Hebrew) son of
Matthew
Matsan, Matsen, Matt, Matty

Matt (Hebrew) form of Matthew:
God's gift
Mat, Matte

Matteo (Spanish) God's gift

Matteson (English) son of Matt;
God's gift

Matthew ♂ ♀ (Hebrew) God's
gift
*Math, Matheu, Mathieu, Matt,
Mattie, Mattsy, Matty*

Matthewson (Last name as first
name) son of Matthew; devout
*Mathewsen, Mathewson,
Matthewsen*

Matthias (Scandinavian) form of
Matthew: God's gift

Matti (Scandinavian) form of
Mathias: God's gift
Mat, Mats

Mattison (Last name as first
name) son of Matti; worldly
*Matisen, Matison, Mattysen,
Mattyson, Matysen, Matyson*

Matts (Swedish) form of
Matthew: God's gift

Matty (Hebrew) form of
Matthew: God's gift
Mattey, Matti

Matun (Biblical) treasure

Matunde (African) form of
Matthew: God's gift

Matus (Czech) form of Matthew:
God's gift

Mauli (Hawaiian) spirited

Maurice (Latin) dark
*Maur, Maurie, Maurise, Maury,
Moorice, Morice, Morrie, Morry*

Mauricio (Italian) dark
Mari, Mauri, Maurizio

Mauricion (Latin) dark

Maurizio (Italian) dark
*Marits, Miritza, Moritz, Moritza,
Moritzio*

Mauro (Latin) form of Maurice:
dark

Maury (Latin) form of Maurice:
dark
Mauree, Maurey, Mauri

Maven (American) dramatic

Maverick (American)
unconventional
*Mav, Mavarick, Mavereck,
Mavreck, Mavvy*

Mavis (French) bird; thrush; free
Mavas, Mavus

Mawali (African) vibrant

Mawulol (African) thanks God

Max (Latin) best
*Mac, Mack, Macks, Maxey, Maxie,
Maxx, Maxy*

Maxcy (Slavic) form of
Maximilian: most wonderful

Maxence (French) excellent

Maxfield (English) of the great
field; lives large

Maxime (French) greatest
Max, Maxeem, Maxim

Maximeen (French) best

Maximilian (Latin) most
wonderful
*Max, Maxemillion, Maxie,
Maxima, Maximillion,
Maxmyllyun, Maxy*

Maximino (Spanish) maximum;
tops
*Max, Maxem, Maxey, Maxi,
Maxim, Maxy*

Maximinole (Italian) best

Maximus (Greek) best

Maxinen (Spanish) maximum
Max, Maxanen, Maxi

Maxwell ❶ (English) full of
excellence
*Maxe, Maxie, Maxwel, Maxwill,
Maxy*

Mayer (Hebrew) smart
Mayar, Maye, Mayor, Mayur

Mayfield (English) grace

Maynard (English) reliable
Mayne, Maynerd

Mayne (English) power figure

Mayner (English) form of
Maynard: reliable

Mayo (Irish) nature-loving
*Maio, Maioh, May, Mayes,
Mayoh, Mays*

Mayon (Place name) volcano in
the Philippines
May, Mayan, Mays, Mayun

Mays (English) of the field;
athlete

Mayz (Arabic) form of Mazin:
mannered

Maz (Hebrew) aid
Maise, Maiz, Mazey, Mazi,
Mazie, Mazy

Mazaca (Biblical) place name

Mazal (Arabic) sedate

Mazin (Arabic) mannered

McCoy (Irish) jaunty; coy
Coye, MacCoy

McDonald (Scottish) open-minded
Mac-D, Macdonald

McFarlin (Last name as first name) son of Farlin; confident
Far, Farr

McGill (Irish) tricky

McGowan (Irish) feisty
Mac-G, Mcgowan

McGregor (Irish) philanthropic
Macgregor

McKay (Scottish) connives

McKinley (Last name as first name) son of Kinley; holding his own
Kin, Kinley, McKinlee

McLean (Scottish) stays lithe

McLin (Irish) careful
Mac, Mack

Mead (English) outdoorsman
Meade, Meede

Meadey (English) child of the meadow

Meallan (Irish) sweet
Maylan, Meall

Meant (American) closed

Mearl (French) form of Merlin: clever

Mechell (French) strong ancestry

Medad (Hebrew) loves

Medan (Biblical) judgment; process

Medardo (Spanish) power figure

Medford (French) natural; comical
Med, Medfor

Medgar (German) strong

Medina (Spanish) place name

Medwin (German) friendly

Megiddo (Biblical) place name

Mehmet (Sanskrit) royal

Mehrdad (Persian) sun

Mehul (Indian) rainy

Meindert (German) hearty boy
Meinhard, Meinrad

Meir (Hebrew) teacher
Mayer, Myer

Mek (Scandinavian) spiritual

Mekhi (Asian) vision

Mel (Irish) form of Melvin: friendly
Mell

Melanio (Spanish) royal

Melar (English) mill man; pleases

Melbourne (Place name) city in Australia; serene; (English) from the mill stream
Mel, Melborn, Melbourn,
Melburn, Melburne

Melburn (English) sylvan; outdoorsy
Mel, Melbourn, Melburne,
Milbourn, Milburn

Melch (Hebrew) royalty

Melchor (Polish) city's king

Meldon (English) destined for fame
Melden, Meldin, Meldyn

Meldric (English) leader
Mel, Meldrik

Melech (Jewish) king

Melecio (Spanish) cautious
Melesio, Melezio, Mesio

Meletius (Greek) ultra-cautious
Meletios, Meletus

Melford (English) boy from mill ford

Melito (Spanish) small and calm

Meliton (Greek) malta child

Melle (English) masculine form of Mary: star of the sea; sea of bitterness

Melos (Greek) favorite
Milos

Melquiades (Spanish) gypsy

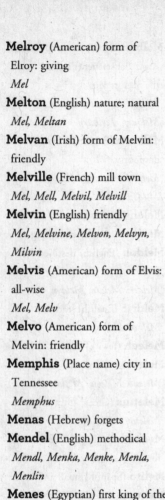

Melroy (American) form of Elroy: giving
Mel

Melton (English) nature; natural
Mel, Meltan

Melvan (Irish) form of Melvin: friendly

Melville (French) mill town
Mel, Mell, Melvil, Melvill

Melvin (English) friendly
Mel, Melvine, Melvon, Melvyn, Milvin

Melvis (American) form of Elvis: all-wise
Mel, Melv

Melvo (American) form of Melvin: friendly

Memphis (Place name) city in Tennessee
Memphus

Menas (Hebrew) forgets

Mendel (English) methodical
Mendl, Menka, Menke, Menla, Menlin

Menes (Egyptian) first king of the 1st Egyptian Dynasty

Menlus (Greek) endures

Menno (Dutch) strong

Mensa (African) third son; genius
Mensah

Ment (Greek) teaches

Menter (Greek) helper; mentor

Merari (Biblical/Hebrew) bitter

Merce (English) merchant

Mercer (English) affluent
Merce, Mercur, Murcer

Merch (English) merchant

Merchant (English) merchant

Mercury (Latin) mercurial

Mercutio (Literature) from Shakespeare's Romeo and Juliet; mercurial

Merdyth (Welsh) form of Meredith: protector

Meredith (Welsh) protector
Merdith, Mere, Meredyth, Meridith, Merrey

Mereld (Irish) form of Merrill: renowned

Merika (Slavic) sea child

Merlin (English) clever
Merl, Merlan, Merle, Merlinn, Merlun, Murlin

Merlot (Word as name) wine

Merrical (American) miracle

Merrick (English) bountiful seaman
Mere, Meric, Merik, Merrack, Merrik

Merrie (English) giving
Merey, Meri, Merri

Merrill (French) renowned
Mere, Merell, Merill, Merrell, Merril, Meryll

Merritt (Latin) worthy
Merid, Merit, Merret, Merrid

Merson (Irish) son of the sea

Merv (Irish) form of Mervin: bold
Murv

Mervin (Irish) bold
Merv, Merven, Mervun, Mervy, Mervyn, Murv, Murvin

Merwin (Irish) friend of the sea

Merzian (American) sea child

Meshach (Hebrew) fortunate
Meeshak, Meshack, Meshak

Meson (Spanish) of the house

Mesquite (American) rancher; spiny shrub
Meskeet

Messiah (Biblical) delivered the Jews

Metheus (Greek) form of Prometheus: friend of man; bringer of fire

Methuse (Biblical) from Methuselah

Metin (Turkish) dominant

Metzger (Last name as first name)

Meyer (Hebrew) brilliant
Maye, Meier, Mye, Myer

Meyshaun (African American) searching
Maysh, Mayshaun, Mayshawn, Meyshawn

Mibsam (Biblical) smelling sweet

Micah (Hebrew) prophet; sees all
Mica, Micha, Michah

Mican (Hebrew) form of Michael: like the Lord

Michael ☉ ✪ (Hebrew) like the Lord
Mical, Michaelle, Mickey, Mikael, Mike, Mikey, Mikiee, Miko

Michel (French) fond
Mich, Michelle, Mike, Mikey

Michelangelo (Italian) God's angel/messenger; artistic
Michel, Michelanjelo, Mikalangelo, Mike, Mikel, Mikelangelo

Michitt (American) form of Michael: like the Lord

Michon (French) form of Michel: fond
Mich, Michonn, Mish, Mishon

Mick (Hebrew) closest to God
Mic, Mik

Mickel (American) form of Michael: like the Lord
Mick, Mikel

Mickey (American) enthusiastic
Mick, Micki, Mickie, Micky, Miki, Myck

Mickey-Lee (American) friendly
Mickey Lee, Mickeylee, Mickie-Lee

Miga (Spanish) persona; essence

Migdol (Biblical) place name

Migio (Spanish) form of Remigio: from Rheims

Migron (Biblical) place name

Miguel ☉ (Spanish) form of Michael: like the Lord
Megel, Migel, Migelle

Miguelangel (Spanish) angelic
Miguelanjel

Mihir (Hindi) sunny

Mika (Hebrew) form of Micah: prophet; sees all
Mikah, Mikie, Myka, Mykie, Myky

Mikael (Scandinavian) warrior
Michael, Mikel, Mikkel

Mikahael (Slavic) form of Michael: like the Lord

Mikaile (Scandinavian) form of Michael: like the Lord

Mikas (Russian) form of Mikhail: godlike

Mike (Hebrew) form of Michael: like the Lord
Meik, Miik, Myke

Mikel (Slavic) form of Mikhail: godlike

Mikelis (Slavic) form of Michael: like the Lord

Mikhail (Russian) godlike
Mika, Mikey, Mikkail, Mykhey

Mikolaj (Polish) form of Michael: like the Lord

Mikolas (Greek) form of Nicholas: winner; the people's victory
Mick, Mickey, Mickolas, Mik, Miko, Mikolus, Miky

Mil (Slavic) loved

Milagros (Spanish) miracle
Milagro

Milam (Last name as first name) uncomplicated
Mylam

Milan (Place name) city in Italy; smooth
Milano

Milburn (Scottish) volatile
Milbyrn, Milbyrne, Millburn

Miles (German) forgiving
Mile, Miley, Myles, Myyles

Miletus (Biblical) loved

Miley (American) reliable; forgiving
Mile, Miles, Mili, Mily, Myles, Myley

Milford (English) from a calm mill setting; country setting; country, *Milferd, Milfor*

Milid (Biblical) place name

Milko (Czech) form of Michael: like the Lord

Millard (Latin) old-fashioned *Milard, Mill, Millerd, Millurd, Milly*

Miller (English) practical *Mille, Myller*

Milli (English) miller

Millian (English) miller

Millo (German) form of Miles: forgiving

Mills (English) safe *Mill, Milly, Mylls*

Milo (German) soft-hearted *Miles, Milos, Mye, Mylo*

Milos (Slavic) kind *Mile, Miles, Myle, Mylos*

Milou (French) mill man

Milton (English) innovative *Melton, Milt, Miltey, Milti, Miltie, Milty, Mylt, Mylton*

Mimi (Greek) outspoken *Mims*

Miner (Last name as first name) hardworking; miner *Mine, Miney*

Mingo (American) flirtatious *Ming-O, Myngo*

Minnow (American) beachcomber

Minter (Last name as first name) dull

Mirko (Slavic) glory in peace

Mirlam (American) great *Mir, Mirsam, Mirtam*

Mirsab (Arabic) judicious

Misa (Slavic) form of Michael: like the Lord

Misael (Hebrew) godlike

Misha (Russian) form of Mikhail: godlike; graceful

Mishael (Hebrew) form of Michael: like the Lord

Mishma (Biblical) hearing; obeying

Mitch (English) form of Mitchell: optimistic

Mitchell (English) optimistic *Mitch, Mitchel, Mitchelle, Mitchie, Mitchill, Mitchy, Mitshell, Mytchil*

Mitchum (Last name as first name) dramatic; known *Mitchem*

Mithun (Indian) Gemini; couple; soft

Mitul (Indian) basic

Mizzah (Biblical/Hebrew) despair

Moab (Biblical) of his father; son of Lot; place name (east of Dead Sea)

Modein (Biblical) place name

Modesto (Spanish) modest *Modysto*

Modi (Norse) son of Thor

Modred (Greek) unafraid *Modrede, Modrid*

Moe (American) form of names beginning with Mo or Moe; easygoing *Mo*

Moey (Hebrew) easygoing *Moe, Moeye*

Moges (Dutch) power

Mohammad (Arabic) praiseworthy *Mohamad, Mohamid, Mohammed, Mohamud, Muhammad*

Mohan (Hindi) compelling; riveting

Mohana (Sanskrit) handsome *Mohann*

Mohawk (Place name) river in New York

Mohit (Indian) seeks beauty

Mohsen (Persian) one who does good deeds *Mosen*

Mois (Hebrew) humble

Moises (Hebrew) drawn from the water
Moe

Mojave (Place name) desert in California; towering man
Mohave, Mohavey

Mokei (Hawaiian) Moses child

Molim (African) softspoken

Moline (American) narrow
Moleen, Molene

Momo (American) rascal

Monaco (Place name) unique, alone

Monahan (Irish) believer
Mon, Monaghan, Monehan, Monnahan

Mondo (Spanish) world

Money (American) word as name; popular
Muney

Monico (Spanish) player
Mon

Monroe (Irish) delightful; presidential
Mon, Monro, Munro, Munroe

Montague (French) forward-thinking
Mont, Montagew, Montagu, Montegue, Monty

Montana (Spanish) mountain; (Place name) U.S. state; (American) sports icon *Mont, Montane, Montayna, Monty*

Monte (Spanish) form of Montgomery: wealthy; form of Montague: forward-thinking
Mont, Montee, Monti, Monts, Monty

Montero (Spanish) mountain

Montes (French) discriminating

Montford (English) of the mount

Montgomery (English) wealthy
Mongomerey, Monte, Montgomry, Monty

Montoi (French) mountain

Montrae (French) ostentatious

Montraie (African American) fussy
Mont, Montray, Montraye, Monty

Montrel (African American) popular
Montrell, Montrelle, Monty

Montrese (American) form of Montgomery: wealthy

Montrose (French) high and mighty
Mont, Montroce, Montros, Monty

Monty (English) form of Montgomery: wealthy; form of Montague: forward-thinking
Monte, Montee, Montey, Monti

Moody (American) expansive
Moodee, Moodey, Moodie

Moon (African) dreamer

Mooney (American) dreamer
Moon, Moonee, Moonie

Moore (French) dark-haired
Mohr, Moores, More

Mooring (Last name as first name) centered
Moring

Moose (American) large guy
Moos, Mooz, Mooze

Moray (Scottish) place name

Mordchai (Hebrew) combative

Mordecai (Hebrew) combative
Mord, Morde, Mordekai, Morducai, Mordy

Mordechay (American) form of Mordecai: combative

Moreland (Last name as first name) of wealth
Mooreland, Moorland, Moorlande, Morland, Morlande

Morell (French) secretive
More, Morelle, Morey, Morrell, Mourell, Murell

Moretti (Italian) desired child

Morey (Latin) dark
Morrie, Morry

Morgan (Celtic) confident; seaman
Morg, Morgen, Morghan

Moriah (Hebrew) Jehovah is my teacher

Moric (Slavic) form of Maurice: dark

Morland (English) from the land of moors

Morlen (English) outdoorsy
Morlan, Morlie, Morly

Morones (Spanish) joyful

Moroni (Place name) city in Comoros; joyful
Maroney, Maroni, Marony, Moroney, Morony

Morph (Greek) changing

Morpheus (Greek) god of dreams; shapes

Morrell (French) dark

Morris (Latin) dark
Maurice, Moris, Morse, Mouris

Morrison (Last name as first name) son of Morris; dark
Morrisen, Morrysen, Morryson

Morrley (English) outdoors-loving
More, Morlee, Morley, Morly, Morrs

Morrow (Last name as first name) follower
Morrowe

Morry (Hebrew) taught by God; old friend
Morey, Morrey, Mory

Morse (English) bright; code-maker
Morce, Morcey, Morry, Morsey

Mortimer (French) deep
Mort, Mortemer, Mortie, Morty, Mortymer

Morton (English) town of moors; dark
Mort, Mortan, Mortun, Morty

Mos (American) special

Moschi (Jewish) form of Moses: appointed for special things

Moses (Hebrew) appointed for special things
Mosa, Mose, Mosesh, Mosie, Mozes, Mozie

Moshe (Hebrew) special
Mosh, Moshie

Mosi (African) firstborn

Moss (Irish) giving
Mossy

Mostin (Welsh) settler

Mostyn (Welsh) mossy

Motaz (Slavic) form of Matthew: God's gift

Motor (American) word as name; speedy; active
Mote

Mottel (Hebrew) form of Max: best

Moushegh (Welsh) form of Moses: appointed for special things

Moylan (American) lights in the sky

Mozam (Place name) from Mozambique
Moze

Mudge (Last name as first name) friendly
Mud, Mudj

Muhammad (Arabic) form of Mohammad: praiseworthy
Muhamed, Muhammed

Mukul (Hindi) bird; beginnings

Mulder (American) of the dark

Muldoon (Last name as first name) different
Muldoone, Muldune

Muna (Arabic) wished for

Munday (English) Monday's child

Mundo (Spanish) form of Edmundo: wealthy protector
Mun, Mund

Mungo (Scottish) loved; congenial
Mongo, Mongoh, Munge, Mungoh

Munir (Arabic) shines strongly

Munnin (Scandinavian) memorable

Murcia (Place name) region in Spain
Mursea

Murdoch (Scottish) rich
Merdock, Merdok, Murd, Murdock, Murdok, Murdy

Murfain (American) bold spirit
Merfaine, Murf, Murfee, Murfy, Murphy

Murff (Irish) form of Murphy: fighter
Merf, Murf

Murk (Slavic) content

Murl (English) nature-lover; sea

Murli (Hindi) flute

Murlie (Hindi) form of Murli: flute

Murphy (Irish) fighter
Merph, Merphy, Murfie, Murph

Murray (Scottish) sea-loving; sailor
Mur, Muray, Murrey, Murry

Murrell (English) nature-lover; sea

Murrill (English) nature-loving

Murt (American) happy

Murthy (American) form of Murphy: fighter

Murtough (Irish) of the sea
Murtagh, Murrough

Murugan (Last name as first name)

Musa (African) forgiving

Mushi (Biblical) giving

Mushki (Biblical) place name

Muslim (Arabic) religious

Musri (Biblical) place name

Mustafa (Arabic) chosen one; Turkish
ingenious

Mustapha (Arabic) the right one

Mutka (African) New Year's baby

Mycheal (African American) devoted
Mysheal

Myle (Latin) soldier

Myles (German) form of Miles: forgiving

Mylie (German) form of Miles: forgiving

Mylik (Slavic) form of Miles: forgiving

Mylos (Slavic) kind
Milos

Mynor (Latin) form of Miner: hardworking; miner

Mynton (English) town of miners

Myrden (Irish) fragrant

Myren (Greek) form of Myron: aromatic oil

Myreon (Greek) aromatic oil
Myron

Myrle (American) able
Merl, Merle, Myrie, Myryee

Myron (Greek) aromatic oil
Mi, Miron, My, Myrayn

Myrzon (American) humorous
Merzon, Myrs, Myrz

Mystikal (American) musician; mystical

Mystry (American) mysterious

Nabil (Arabic) of noble birth; honored
Nabeel, Nobila

Nabor (Hebrew) light of the future

Nachman (Last name as first name) unique
Menachem, Menahem, Nacham, Nachmann, Nahum

Nachson (Last name as first name) son of Nach; up-and-coming

Nachum (Hebrew) comforts others.

Nad (Biblical) name spelled backward

Nada (Arabic) morning dew; giver
Nadah

Nadab (Biblical) free and voluntary gift; prince

Nader (Arabic) dearest

Nadim (Arabic) fellow celebrant
Nadeem

Nadir (Arabic) rare man
Nadeer, Nadeir

Naeem (Arabic) happy

Nafis (Hebrew) struggles

Naftali (African) runs in woods
Naphtali, Neftali, Nefthali,
Nephtali, Nephthali

Nag (Indian) form of Nagesh:
Hindi serpent god

Nagel (English) smooth
Naegel, Nageler, Nagelle, Nagle,
Nagler

Nagesh (Indian) Hindi serpent god

Nagid (Arabic) regal

Nahath (Biblical) rest; a leader

Nahbi (Biblical) very secret

Nahir (Hebrew) light
Naheer, Nahor

Nahshon (Biblical) that foretells; that conjectures

Nahum (Arabic) content;
(Biblical) comforter; penitent
Nemo

Naim (Arabic) content
Naeem

Naima (arabic) comforting

Nain (Biblical) place name

Nairi (Biblical) place name

Nairn (Last name as first name) born again
Nairne

Nairobi (Place name) city in Kenya; starting out

Naissus (Biblical) place name

Najib (Arabic) noble
Nageeb, Nagib, Najeeb

Naldo (Italian) form of Reynaldo: knowledgeable tutor

Nalin (Hindi) lotus; pretty boy
Naleen

Namir (Hebrew) leopard; fast
Nameer

Nana (African) king

Nanda (Indian) achiever

Nando (Spanish) form of Fernando: bold leader

Nandor (Hungarian) form of Ferdinand: adventurer

Nandy (Hindi) from the god Nandin; destructs

Nano (Hawaiian) springtime

Nanson (American) spunky
Nance, Nanse, Nansen, Nansson

Nansor (Indian) defiant

Napier (French) mover
Neper

Napoleon (German) lion of Naples; domineering
Nap, Napo, Napoleone, Napolion,
Napolleon, Nappy

Narayana (Indian) secure

Narciso (Latin) lily; daffodil
Narcis

Narcissus (Greek) self-loving; vain
Narciss, Narcissah, Narcisse, Nars

Nardino (Spanish) kind

Naren (Hindi) best

Narendar (Indian) king

Narendra (Indian) king

Narithier (Indian) king

Narjis (Indian) lord

Narmad (Indian) delights

Nartan (Indian) dancing

Nasario (Spanish) dedicated to God
Nasar, Nasareo, Nassario, Nazareo,
Nazarlo, Nazaro, Nazor

Nash (Last name as first name) exciting
Nashe, Nashey

Nashe (Arabic) soothing advisor

Nashua (Native American) thunderous

Nasir (Arabic) wins

Nason (Biblical) perseveres

Nasser (Arabic) winning
Naser, Nasir, Nasr, Nassar, Nasse, Nassee, Nassor

Nat (Hebrew) form of Nathaniel: God's gift to mankind
Natt, Natte, Nattie, Natty

Natal (Hebrew) gift of God
Natale, Natalino, Natalio, Nataly

Natan (Hebrew) magnanimous

Natchio (Spanish) form of Nathan: God's gift to mankind

Nate (Hebrew) form of Nathan and Nathaniel: God's gift to mankind
Natey

Nath (Hebrew) form of Nathan: God's gift to mankind

Nathan ○ ❶ (Hebrew) form of Nathaniel: God's gift to mankind
Nat, Nate, Nathen, Nathin, Natthaen, Natthan, Natthen, Natty

Nathaniel ○ (Hebrew) God's gift to mankind
Nat, Nate, Nathan, Nathaneal, Nathanial, Nathe, Nathenial

Nation (American) patriotic

Natividad (Spanish) a child born at Christmastime

Nato (American) gentle
Nate, Natoe, Natoh

Navarro (Spanish) wild spirit
Navaro, Navarroh, Naverro

Naveed (Hindi) wishing you well
Navid

Naveen (Hindi) new

Navnit (Indian) smooth

Nayan (Hebrew) form of Nathan: God's gift to mankind

Naylor (English) likes order
Nailer, Nailor

Nazaire (Biblical) from Nazareth; religious boy
Nasareo, Nasarrio, Nazario, Nazarius, Nazaro, Nazor

Neal (Irish) winner
Neale, Nealey, Neall, Nealy, Neel, Neelee, Neely, Nele

Nebaioth (Biblical) firstborn

Nebo (Mythology) Babylonian god of wisdom

Nebraska (Place name) U.S. state
Neb

Nebulous (Word as name)

Nectarios (Greek) sweet nectar; immortal man
Nectaire, Nectarius, Nektario, Nektarios, Nektarius

Ned (English) form of Edward: prospering; defender
Neddee, Neddie, Neddy

Nedrun (American) difficult
Ned, Nedd, Neddy, Nedran, Nedro

Neely (Scottish) winning
Neel, Neels

Negasi (African) destined for royalty

Negeb (Arabic) well-known

Nehemiah (Hebrew) compassionate
Nechemia, Nechemiah, Nechemya, Nehemyah, Nemo

Neiel (Biblical) place name

Neil (Scottish) victor
Neal, Neale, Neall, Nealle, Nealon, Neel, Neile, Neill, Neille, Neils, Nels, Nial, Niall, Niel, Niles

Neirin (Irish) light

Nekane (Spanish) saddened

Nellie (English) form of Nelson: broad-minded
Nell, Nellee, Nelli, Nells, Nelly

Nelo (Spanish) form of Daniel: judged by God; spiritual

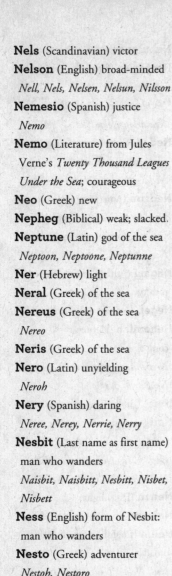

Nels (Scandinavian) victor

Nelson (English) broad-minded
Nell, Nels, Nelsen, Nelsun, Nilsson

Nemesio (Spanish) justice
Nemo

Nemo (Literature) from Jules
Verne's *Twenty Thousand Leagues
Under the Sea*; courageous

Neo (Greek) new

Nepheg (Biblical) weak; slacked

Neptune (Latin) god of the sea
Neptoon, Neptoone, Neptunne

Ner (Hebrew) light

Neral (Greek) of the sea

Nereus (Greek) of the sea
Nereo

Neris (Greek) of the sea

Nero (Latin) unyielding
Neroh

Nery (Spanish) daring
Neree, Nerey, Nerrie, Nerry

Nesbit (Last name as first name)
man who wanders
*Naisbit, Naisbitt, Nesbitt, Nisbet,
Nisbett*

Ness (English) form of Nesbit:
man who wanders

Nesto (Greek) adventurer
Nestoh, Nestoro

Nestor (Greek) wanderer
Nest, Nester, Nestir, Nesto, Nesty

Netar (African American) bright
Netardas

Nethanel (Hebrew) form of
Nathaniel: God's gift to mankind

Nets (American) athletic

Netuno (Spanish) form of
Neptune: god of the sea

Netzer (American) form of
Nestor: wanderer
Net

Nevada (Place name) U.S. state
Nev, Nevadah

Nevardo (Spanish) masculine

Never (English) word as name

Neville (French) innovator
*Nev, Nevil, Nevile, Nevvy, Nevyle,
Niville*

Nevin (Irish) small holy man
*Nev, Nevan, Neven, Nevins,
Nevon, Niven*

Nevins (Irish) devout

Newbie (American) novice
New, Newb

Newbury (Last name as first
name) renewal
Newbery, Newberry

Newcomb (Last name as first
name) renewal
Newcombe

Newell (English) new hall
New, Newall, Newel, Newy, Nywell

Newland (Last name as first
name) of a new land

Newlin (Welsh) able; new pond
Newl, Newlynn, Nule

Newman (English) attractive
young man
*Neuman, Neumann, New,
Newmann*

Newport (Last name as first
name) from a new seaport

Newt (English) new

Newton (English) bright; new
mind
New, Newt

Neyman (American) son of Ney;
bookish
Ney, Neymann, Neysa

Nezer (Arabic) winning boy

Nezib (Biblical) place name

Nga (Asian) herb

Niall (Irish) winner
Nial

Niambi (African (Swahili)) melody

Niaz (Hindi) gift

Nibshan (Biblical) place name

Nicah (Greek) victorious
Nik, Nike

Nicandro (Spanish) a man who
excels
*Nicandreo, Nicandrios, Nicandros,
Nikander, Nikandreo, Nikandrios*

Nicasio (Spanish) winning

Nicholas ○ ❶ (Greek) winner; the people's victory
Nichelas, Nicholus, Nick, Nickee, Nickie, Nicklus, Nickolas, Nicky, Nikolas, Nyck, Nykolas

Nichols (English) kindhearted
Nicholes, Nick, Nicky, Nikols

Nick (English) form of Nicholas: victorious; winner; the people's victory
Nic, Nik

Nickel (English) word as name

Nicklaus (Greek) form of Nicholas: winner; the people's victory
Nicklaws, Niklus

Nickleby (Last name as first name) betting on the odds

Nickler (American) fleet-footed; perspicacious

Nicko (Greek) form of Nico: victors

Nicky (Greek) form of Nicholas: winner; the people's victory
Nick, Nickee, Nickey, Nicki, Nik, Nikee, Nikki

Nico (Italian) victor
Nicos, Niko, Nikos

Nicodemus (Greek) people's victory
Nicodemo, Nicodema

Nicol (Scottish) form of Nicholas: winner; the people's victory

Nicolas (Italian) form of Nicholas: winner; the people's victory
Nic, Nico, Nicolus

Nicomedes (Greek) thinking of victory
Nicomedo, Nikomedes

Nieblas (Spanish) winner

Niels (Scandinavian) victorious
Neels

Nigel (English) champion
Nigie, Nigil, Nygelle

Night (American) nocturnal

Nike (Greek) winning
Nykee, Nykie, Nyke

Nikhil (Russian) form of Nicholas: winner; the people's victory

Nikita (Russian) not yet won
Nika

Niklas (Scandinavian) winner
Niklaas, Nils, Klaas

Nikolai (Russian) winning
Nika

Nikolas (Greek) form of Nicholas: winner; the people's victory
Nik, Nike, Niko, Nikos, Nyloas

Nikolaus (Greek) form of Nicholas: winner, the people's victory

Nikom (Greek) winning

Nikon (Greek) victorious

Nikos (Greek) victor
Nicos, Niko, Nikolos

Nikostratos (Greek) the army's victory
Nicostrato, Nicostratos, Nicostratus

Niles (English) smooth
Ni, Nile, Niley, Nyles, Nyley

Nimro (American) form of Nimrod: renegade

Nimrod (Hebrew) renegade
Nimrodd, Nymrod

Ninad (Indian) gentle noise

Ninian (Gaelic) name given in honor of a fifth-century Irish saint

Nino (Spanish) child; young boy

Ninus (Biblical) place name

Ninyun (American) spirited
Ninian, Ninion, Ninyan, Nynyun

Niran (Indian) everlasting

Nissan (Hebrew) omen
Nisan, Nissyn

Nissim (Hebrew) Nisan is seventh Jewish month; believer

Nitin (Indian) attractive

Nito (Italian) form of Benito: blessed

Nivea (Spanish) reborn

Niven (Last name as first name) smooth

Nix (American) negative
Nicks, Nixy

Nixon (English) audacious
Nickson, Nixen, Nixun

Nizam (Arabic) leader

Njord (Scandinavian) man of the north
Njorth

Noah ○ ❶ (Hebrew) peacemaker
Noa, Noe, Nouh

Noam (Hebrew) sweet man; pleases others
Noahm, Noe

Nob (Biblical) place name

Noble (Latin) regal
Nobe, Nobee, Nobel, Nobie, Noby

Noblen (American) protected

Nocona (Native American) leads man

Nod (Biblical) vagabond; fugitive

Noden (Native American) windy day

Noe (Spanish) quiet;
Noeh, Noey

Noean (Spanish) calm

Noel (French) born on Christmas
Noelle, Noelly, Nole, Nollie

Noey (Spanish) form of Noah: peacemaker
Noe, Noie

Nofri (Italian) ancestor

Nolan (Irish) outstanding; noble
Nole, Nolen, Nolline, Nolun, Nolyn

Nolden (American) noble
Nold

Noll (Scandinavian) form of Oliver; loving nature

Nolly (Scandinavian) hopeful
Nole, Noli, Noll, Nolley, Nolleye, Nolli, Nollie

Nonan (Latin) superb

Noon (English) word as name, from Latin nona: ninth hour

Noor (Hindi) light
Nour, Nur

Noph (Biblical) place name

Norb (Scandinavian) innovative
Noberto, Norbie, Norbs, Norby

Norberito (Spanish) form of Norbert: bright north

Norbert (German) bright north
Norb, Norbie, Norby

Norberto (Spanish) form of Norbert: bright north

Nordin (Nordic) handsome
Nord, Nordan, Norde, Nordee, Nordeen, Nordi, Nordun, Nordy

Noriel (Spanish) hero

Norin (French) from the north

Norka (Scandinavian) charming

Norman (English) sincere; man of the north
Norm, Normen, Normey, Normi, Normie, Normon, Normun, Normy

Norrell (French) from the north

Norris (English) from the north

Norrison (French) northerner

Norriston (French) northern town

Norse (English) scandinavian boy

Norshell (African American) brash
Norshel, Norshelle

North (American) directional
Norf, Northe

Northcliff (English) from the north cliff
Northcliffe, Northclyff, Northclyffe

Northrop (English) northerner
Northrup

Norton (English) dignified man of the north
Nort, Nortan, Norten

Norval (English) from the north
Norvan

Norvell (French) northern town

Norville (French) resident of a northern village; warmhearted
Norval, Norvel, Norvil, Norvill, Norvyl

Norward (English) going north
Norwerd

Norwell (English) northward bound

Norwin (English) friendly
Norvin, Norwen, Norwind, Norwinn

Norwood (English) of the north woods

Novae (Biblical) place name

Novak (Slavic) Last name as first name

Novio (Spanish) boyfriend

Nowell (Last name as first name) dependable
Nowe

Nowey (American) knowing
Nowee, Nowie

Nuad (Welsh) tolerant

Nueces (Place name) river in Texas

Nuell (American) form of Newell: new hall
Nuel

Numa (Arabic) nice

Nun (Biblical) from the ocean

Nuncio (Spanish) messenger; informant
Nunzio

Nunry (Last name as first name) giving
Nunri

Nuri (Arabic) light
Noori, Nur, Nuriel, Nuris

Nuriel (Hebrew) light of God
Nooriel, Nuriya, Nuriyah, Nurya

Nuys (Place name) from Van Nuys
Nies, Nyes, Nys

Nye (Welsh) focused
Ni, Nie, Nyee

Nyle (American) form of Niles: smooth
Nyl, Nyles

Nyron (English) form of Neil: victor

Nyx (American) humorous

Oak (English) sturdy
Oake, Oakes, Oakie

Oakes (English) sturdy oak

Oakley (English) sturdy; strong
Oak, Oakie, Oaklee, Oakleigh, Oakly, Oklie

Oat (English) word as name

Oba (Hebrew) form of Obadiah: serving God

Obadiah (Hebrew) serving God
Obadyah, Obediah, Obee, Obie, Oby

Obal (Biblical) leader

Obasi (African) God-loving

Obataiye (African) world leader

Obayana (African) king by the fire

Obba (African) form of Obi: big heart

Obbie (Biblical) form of Obadiah: serving God
Obey, Obi, Obie

Obed (Hebrew) serves

Obedience (American) strict
Obie

Ober (Scandinavian) famed

Oberon (German) strong-bearing
Auberon, Auberron, Obaron, Oberahn, Oberone, Oburon

Obert (German) rich man

Obey (American) form of Obadiah: serving God
Obe, Obee, Obie, Oby

Obi (African) big heart

Obie (Hebrew) form of Obadiah: serving God
Obbie, Obe, Oby

Obike (African) loved by his family

Oboth (Biblical) place name

Ocean (Greek) ocean; child born under a water sign
Oceane, Oceanus

Ocie (Greek) form of Ocean: ocean; child born under a water sign
Osie

O'Connor (Irish) son of Connor

Octavio (Latin) eight; able
Octave, Octavian, Octavien, Octavioh, Octavo, Ottavio

Oda (Scandinavian) precise

Odakota (Native American) has many friends

Ode (Greek) poetry as a name; poetic
Odee, Odie

Oded (Hebrew) supportive

Odegard (Scandinavian) powerful guard

Odell (American) musical
Dell, Odall, Ode, Odey, Odyll

Oder (Place name) river in Europe
Ode

Odessus (Biblical) place name

Odhran (Irish) green; creative
Odran, Oran

Odie (English) form of Odell: musical

Odilon (German) rich

Odin (Scandinavian) Norse god of magic; soulful
Odan, Oden

Odinan (Hungarian) rich; powerful

Odion (African) the first twin

Odisoose (Invented) form of Odysseus: wanderer
Ode

Odissan (African) wanderer

Odolf (Japanese) from the field of deer; lithe

Odom (African) the oak; strong

Odysseus (Greek) wanderer
Ode, Odey, Odie

Oelen (Spanish) giving

Oescus (Biblical) place name

Ofer (Hebrew) deer

Og (Aramaic) king

Ogano (Japanese) wise

Ogdon (English) literate
Og, Ogdan, Ogden

Ogen (German) invincible

Oghe (Irish) horse rider
Oghie, Oho

Ogle (American) word as name; leer; stare
Ogal, Ogel, Ogll, Ogul

Ogun (Japanese) undaunted

Ohad (Biblical) praising; confessing

Ohanko (Japanese) invincible

Ohanzee (Native American) shadowy figure

Ohin (Japanese) wanted child

Oisin (Irish) fawn; gentle

Oistin (Latin) much revered

Ojas (Indian) shiny

Ojay (American) brash
O.J., Oojai

Ojo (African) he came of a hard birth

Okan (Turkish) horse
Oke

Okapi (African) graceful

Okechuku (African) God's blessing

Okello (African) child after twins were born

Okemos (African) advises

Okie (American) man from Oklahoma
Okey, Okeydokey

Oko (Japanese) evoker; charming

Okon (Japanese) from the darkness

Okoth (African) sad child; born during rainfall

Okpara (African) first son

Oktawian (African) eighth child

Ola (African) child much honored

Olabisi (African) rich

Oladele (African) honored at home

Olaf (Scandinavian) watchful
Olay, Ole, Olef, Olev, Oluf

Olafemi (African) lucky child

Olafur (Scandinavian) forunate

Olajuwon (Arabic) honorable
Olajuwan, Olujuwon

Olakeakua (Hawaiian) living
for God

Olamina (African) rich of spirit

Olan (Scandinavian) royal
ancestor
Olin, Ollee

Olaniyan (African) honored all
around

Olav (Scandinavian) traditional
Ola, Olov, Oluf

Oldrich (Czech) leader; strong
*Olda, Oldra, Oldrisek, Olecek,
Olik, Olin, Olouvsek*

Ole (Scandinavian) watchful
Olay

Oleg (Russian) holy; religious
Olag, Ole, Olig

Olegario (Spanish) aggressor

Olek (Scandinavian) holy

Olin (English) holly; jubilant
Olen, Olney, Olyn

Olindo (Latin) sweet fragrance

Oliver ✚ (Latin) loving nature
*Olaver, Olive, Ollie, Olliver, Olly,
Oluvor*

Olivier (French) eloquent
Oliveay

Oliwa (Hawaiian) from an army
of elves

Ollie (English) form of Oliver:
loving nature
Olie, Ollee, Olley, Olly

Olliem (Scandinavian) form of
William: staunch protector

Olmos (Spanish) altruistic

Olney (English) lonely field

Olo (Spanish) form of Orlando:
famed; distinctive

Olorun (African) blessed;
counsels others

Olsen (Scandinavian) Last name
as first name

Olubayo (African) full of happiness

Olufemi (African) God's loved
child
Olviemi

Olugbala (African) the people's
God

Olujimi (African) hand in hand
with God

Olumide (African) God has come

Olumoi (African) blessed by God

Olushegun (African) marches
with God

Olushola (African) blessed

Oluwa (African) believer

Oluyemi (African) man full of God

Olvera (Spanish) form of Oliver:
loving nature

Olvery (English) draws others
near

Omaha (Place name) city in
Nebraska

Omanand (Hindi) joyful thinker

Omar (Arabic) spiritual
Omahr, Omarr

Omari (African) in high esteem

Ombre (Spanish) man

Omedes (Greek) ponders

Omer (Arabic) form of Omar:
spiritual

Omie (Italian) homebody
Omey, Omi, Omye

Omri (Hebrew) Jehovah's servant;
giving

On (African) desirable

Onacona (Native American)
white owl; watchful

Onam (Biblical) success

Onan (Turkish) rich

Onaney (African) sees all

Onani (Asian) sweet

Onaona (Hawaiian) fragrant

Onder (Scandinavian) form of
Andrew: manly and brave

Ondraze (Scandinavian) form of
Andrew: manly and brave

Ondrej (Czech) masculine
Ondra, Ondravsek, Ondrejek,
Ondrousek

Onesimo (Spanish) number one;
important
Onie

Onkar (Hindi) purest one

Ono (Biblical) place name

Onofrio (German) smart
Ono, Onofreeo, Onofrioh

Onorato (Spanish) honored

Onslow (Arabic) climbing
passion's hill
Ounslow

Onur (Turkish) promising boy

Onwoachi (African) God's world

Ophel (Biblical) place name

Ophir (Hebrew) loyal

Ophlas (Biblical) place name

Oqwapi (Native American) red
cloud

Oracio (Spanish) oracle

Oral (Latin) eloquent

Oran (Irish) pale
Orin, Orran, Orren, Orrin

Orangel (Greek) angel of truth

Oranos (Greek) universal

Orban (Hungarian) city man;
sophisticated

Orbie (Slavic) sophisticated

Orchard (English) botanical
name

Ordell (Latin) the start

Oregon (Place name) state

Oren (Hebrew) form of Owen:
wellborn; high-principled

Orenthiel (American) sturdy as
a pine
Ore, Oren

Orenthiem (American) sturdy
as a pine
Orenth, Orenthe

Orest (Greek) form of Orestes:
leader

Orestes (Greek) leader
Oresta, Oreste, Restie, Resty

Orestis (Greek) form of Orestes:
leader

Orev (Hebrew) raven; observing

Orford (Last name as first name)
noble

Ori (Hebrew) flame of truth

Orie (English) form of Orrin:
river boy

Oriol (Spanish) best
Orioll

Orion (Greek) fiery hunter
Oreon, Ori, Orie, Ory

Orji (African) sturdy tree

Orlando (Spanish) famed;
distinctive
Orl, Orland, Orlie, Orlondo, Orly

Orlay (Spanish) famed

Orlean (Latin) gold

Orleans (Latin) the golden boy
Orlins

Orlis (English) bearlike

Orman (Latin) noble
Ormand, Ormond, Ormonde

Orme (English) kind
Orm

Ormond (English) kindhearted
Ormand, Ormande, Orme,
Ormon, Ormonde, Ormund,
Ormunde

Orn (Latin) form of Oren: well
born; high-principled

Oro (Spanish) golden child

Oron (Hebrew) light spirit

Orontes (Biblical) place name

Orpheus (Greek) darkness of
night; mythological musician

Orr (English) form of Orrick:
sturdy as an oak

Orran (Irish) green-eyed
Ore, Oren, Orin

Orrent (Greek) excites

Orrial (Latin) form of Uriel: light; God-inspired

Orrick (English) sturdy as an oak
Oric, Orick, Orreck, Orrik

Orrie (American) form of Orson: strong as a bear
Orry

Orrin (English) river boy

Orris (Latin) form of Horatio: poetic; dashing
Oris, Orriss

Orry (Latin) oriental; exotic
Oarrie, Orrey, Orrie

Orso (Latin) form of Orson: strong as a bear

Orson (Latin) strong as a bear
Orsan, Orsen, Orsey, Orsun

Orth (English) honest
Orthe

Orton (English) town on the shore; reaching

Orturo (Spanish) form of Arturo: talented

Ortwin (English) shore friend

Orunjan (African) god of the noon-time sun

Orval (American) form of Orville: brave; (Scandinavian) eagle-eyed
Orvale

Orven (English) spears

Orville (French) brave
Orv, Orvelle, Orvie, Orvil

Orvin (Last name as first name) fated for success
Orwin, Orwynn

Orway (American) kind
Orwaye

Osai (Afghanistan) deerlike

Osakwe (Japanese) good destiny

Osanmwesr (Japanese) leaving

Osayaba (Japanese) wonders

Osbert (English) smart

Osborne (English) strong-spirited
Osborn, Osbourne, Osburn, Osburne, Ossie, Oz, Ozzie, Ozzy

Osburt (English) smart
Osbart, Osbert, Ozbert, Ozburt

Oscar (Scandinavian) divine
Ozkar

Oscard (Greek) fighter
Oscar, Oskard

Osceola (Native American) black drink

Osciel (Spanish) gracious

Osei (African) gracious

Osgood (English) good man
Osgude, Ozgood

Oshea (Hebrew) kind spirit

Osileani (Polynesian) talking forever

Osin (Irish) small deer

Osk (Scandinavian) spears

Oslo (Place name) capital of Norway
Os, Oz

Osman (Spanish) verbose
Os, Osmen, Osmin, Ossie, Oz, Ozzie

Osmar (English) amazing; divine

Osménio (Spanish) talkative

Osmond (English) singing to the world
Os, Osmonde, Osmund, Ossie, Oz, Ozzy

Ospe (Russian) form of Joseph: He will add

Osrec (Scandinavian) leader
Os, Ossie

Osred (Scandinavian) leads mankind

Osric (Scandinavian) leader
Osrick

Ossie (Hebrew) powerful
Os, Oz, Ozzy

Osten (Last name as first name) religious leader
Ostin, Ostyn

Osval (Slavic) form of Oswald: divine power

Osvaldo (German) divine power
Osvald, Oswaldo

Oswald (English) divine power
Oswalde, Oswold, Oswuld, Oszie,
Oz

Oswin (English) God's ally
Osvin, Oswinn, Oswyn, Oswynn

Ota (Czech) affluent

Otadan (Native American)
abundance

Otey (Slavic) wealthy

Othar (Slavic) leader

Othell (African American)
thriving
Oth, Othey, Otho

Othello (Spanish) bold
Otello, Othell

Othman (Last name as first
name) man of bravery

Othnel (Biblical) God's lion

Othniel (Hebrew) rendered brave
by God's love

Othon (German) rich

Otik (German) lucky

Otis (Greek) intuitive
Oates, Odis, Otes, Ottes, Ottis

Otokar (Czech) prudent in wealth

Otoniel (Spanish) fashionable
Otonel

Otskai (Native American) leaving

Ottah (African) thin boy

Ottar (Scandinavian) warring
Otomars, Ottomar

Otto (German) wealthy
Oto, Ott, Ottoh

Ottokar (German) can-do spirit;
fighter
Otokars, Ottocar

Ottway (German) fortunate
Otwae, Otway

Otu (Native American) industrious

Oukounaka (Asian) from the surf

Ouray (Native American) arrow
man

Oved (Hebrew) serving
Obed

Overton (Last name as first
name) leader
Ove, Overten

Ovidio (Spanish) from Roman
poet Ovid; creative
Ovido

Ovido (Spanish) tends sheep

Owen ♂ ♥ (Welsh) wellborn;
high-principled
Owan, Owin, Owwen

Owney (Irish) old one
Oney

Ox (American) animal; strong
Oxy

Oxford (English) scholar; ox
crossing
Fordy, Oxferd, Oxfor

Oya (African) vocal

Oz (Hebrew) courageous; unusual

Ozais (Hebrew) strong in God

Ozden (Hebrew) good in God

Ozeas (Italian) strong

Ozell (English) strong
Ozel

Oziel (Spanish) strong

Ozni (Hebrew) knows God

Ozuru (Japanese) stork; lively
hope

Ozzie (English) form of Oswald:
divine power
Oz, Ozzee, Ozzey, Ozzy

Paal (Scandinavian) form of Paul:
small; wise

Pablo (Spanish) strong; creative
Pabel, Pabo, Paublo

Pace (English) peace

Pacian (Spanish) peaceful
Pacien, Pace

Packer (Last name as first name)
orderly
Pack

Paco (Spanish) energetic
Pak, Pakkoh, Pako, Paquito

Padden (English) form of Patton:
warrior's town
Paddin, Paddyn

Paddy (Irish) form of Patrick:
noble
Paddey, Paddi, Paddie, Padee

Paden (English) form of Patrick:
noble

Padget (French) learning;
growing
Padgett, Pagas

Padraic (Irish) form of Patrick:
noble
*Padraick, Padraik, Padrayc,
Padrayck, Padrayk*

Padre (Spanish) father; cajoles
Padrae, Padray

Paeter (Scandinavian) form of
Peter: dependable; rock

Page (French) helpful
Pagey, Paige, Payg

Pageman (Last name as first
name) sharp

Pagiel (Hebrew) worships

Pago (Place name) for Pago Pago
Pay

Pagolo (Italian) placid

Pahan (Native American)
summons

Paine (Latin) countryman
Payne

Paki (African) has seen the truth

Palani (Slavic) long-suffering

Pall (Scandinavian) form of Paul:
small; wise

Palladin (Greek) confrontational;
wise
*Palidin, Palladyn, Palleden, Pallie,
Pally*

Pallaton (Native American)
tough; fighter
Palladin

Pallav (Indian) new growth

Pallu (Biblical) distinct

Palma (Latin) successful

Palmer (English) open; grows
palms
Pallmar, Pallmer, Palmar, Palmur

Palti (Hebrew) getaway

Pampa (Place name) city in Texas

Pan (Greek mythology) god of
forest and shepherds
Pann

Panama (Place name) canal
connecting North and South
America; rounder
Pan

Pancho (Spanish) form of
Francisco: free spirit; from France
Panchoh, Ponchito

Pancrazio (Italian) all-powerful
Pankraz

Pandy (English) from Panda

Panfilo (Spanish) loving all
nature

Pankaj (Hindi) lotus flower

Panos (Greek) rock; sturdy

Pantaleon (Spanish) pants;
trousers; manly
Pant, Pantalon

Pantias (Greek) philosophical

Pao (Italian) form of Paul: small;
wise

Paolo (Italian) form of Paul:
small; wise
Paoloh, Paulo

Paphos (Biblical) place name

Papillion (French) butterfly

Paquito (Spanish) dear Paco

Parah (Biblical) place name

Paran (Biblical) place name

Parindra (Indian) lion

Paris (English) lover; France's
capital
Pare, Paree, Parris

Parish (French) priest's place;
lovely boy
Parrish, Parrysh, Parysh

Park (English) calming
Parke, Parkey, Parks

Parker ⚬ (English) manager
Park, Parks

Parley (Scottish) reluctant
Parly

Parnell (French) ribald
Parle, Parne, Parnel, Parnelle,
Perne

Parnelli (Italian) frisky
Parnell

Parnes (French) form of Peter:
dependable; rock

Paros (Place name) Greek island;
charming
Par, Paro

Parr (English) protective
Par, Parre

Parris (French) priest's place;
lovely boy
Paris, Pariss, Parriss, Parrys,
Parryss

Parrish (French) separate and
unique; district

Parry (Welsh) young son
Parrie, Pary

Parryth (American) up-and-
coming
Pareth, Parre, Parry, Parythe

Parson (English) clergyman
Parsen

Parthik (Greek) virginal

Partholon (Irish) form of
Bartholomew: friendly; earthy
Parlan

Parvati (Indian) best

Pascal (French) boy born on
Easter or Passover; spiritual
Pascalle, Paschal, Pasco, Pascual,
Paskalle, Pasky

Pascasio (Spanish) Easter baby

Pasko (English) form of Pascal:
boy born on Easter or Passover;
spiritual

Pasquale (Italian) spiritual
Pask, Paskwoll, Pasq, Pasquell,
Posquel

Pass (Russian) form of Paul:
small; wise

Pastor (English) clergyman
Pastar, Paster

Pat (English) form of Patrick:
noble
Pattee, Pattey, Patti, Patty, Pattye

Patcher (American) unusual

Pate (Latin) form of Patrick:
noble
Pait, Payte

Patek (Latin) form of Patrick:
noble
Patec, Pateck

Pater (Greek) father

Paterno (Spanish) fatherly

Paterson (Last name as first
name) intelligent father

Patricio (Spanish) form of
Patrick: noble
Patricyo

Patricius (Latin) noble

Patrick (Irish) noble
Paddy, Partric, Patric, Patrik,
Patriquek, Patryk, Pats, Patsy

Patriot (American) patriotic

Patterson (English) intellectual
Paterson, Pattersen, Pattersun,
Pattersund

Pattison (English) son of Pat;
noble
Pattisen, Pattysen, Pattyson,
Patysen, Patyson

Patton (English) warrior's town
Patten, Pattun, Patun, Peyton

Paul (Latin) small; wise
Pauley, Paulie, Pauly

Paul-Erik (Scandinavian)
combination of Paul and Erik

Pauli (Italian) dear Paul
Paulee, Pauley, Paulie, Pauly

Paulin (German) form of Paul:
small; wise
Paulyn

Paulis (Latin) form of Paul:
small; wise
Pauliss, Paulys, Paulyss

Paulo (Spanish) form of Paul: small; wise

Paulos (Greek) form of Paul: small; wise

Paulus (Latin) small
Paul, Paulie, Paulis, Pauly

Paun (American) form of Paul: small; wise

Pavan (Indian) wind

Pavel (Russian) inspired
Pasha

Paviter (Indian) pure

Pavlof (Last name as first name) reactive; small
Pavel

Pavol (Slavic) form of Paul: small; wise

Pavun (Indian) belonging to the middle

Pawel (Polish) believer
Pawl

Pax (Latin) peace-loving
Paks, Paxy

Paxon (German) peaceful
Packston, Packton

Paxton (English) from a town of peace; gentle boy
Paxten

Payam (Slavic) message

Payan (Indian) ornamented

Payne (Latin) countryman
Paine, Payn

Payton ❶ (English) soldier's town
Pate, Paton, Payten, Paytun, Peyton

Peabo (Irish) rock

Peader (Scottish) rock or stone; reliable
Peder, Peter

Peak (English) word as name

Peale (English) bell-ringer in a church; religious
Peal, Peel, Peele

Pearson (English) dark-eyed
Pearse, Pearsen, Pearsun, Peerson

Peat (English) form of Pete: dependable; rock

Peck (American) peaceful

Pecos (Place name) Texas river; cowboy
Peck, Pekos

Pedaias (Biblical) God loves
Pedaiah

Peder (Scandinavian) form of Peter: dependable; rock

Pederson (Scandinavian) form of Peterson: son of Peter
Pedersen

Pedram (Indian)

Pedro (Spanish) form of Peter: dependable; rock
Pedra, Pedrin, Pedroh

Peer (Scandinavian) rock

Peerson (English) son of Peter; smart
Peersen

Pegasus (Mythology) horse; rider

Peili (Spanish) joyful

Peirano (Italian) form of Peter: dependable; rock

Peleg (Greek) the sea

Pelle (Swedish) for Peter; rock
Pele, Pelee

Pelly (English) happy
Peli, Pelley, Pelli

Pelon (Spanish) joyful

Pelton (Last name as first name) town of Pel; respectful

Pembroke (French) sophisticated
Brookie, Pemb, Pembrooke, Pimbroke

Pender (Last name as first name) loves music

Penley (Last name as first name) strong

Penn (German) strong-willed
Pen, Pennee, Penney, Pennie, Penny

Penrod (German) respected leader

Penrose (Last name as first name) liked

Pentecost (Religion) pious person
Penticost, Pentycost

Pentige (Last name as first name) worthy

Pentz (Last name as first name) visionary

Penuel (Hebrew) face of God

Pepic (German) perseveres

Pepin (German) ardent
Pepen, Pepi, Pepp, Peppi, Peppy, Pepun

Pepper (Botanical) live wire
Pep, Pepp, Peppy

Peppino (Spanish) energetic

Per (Scandinavian) secretive

Peralta (Italian) pearl

Percival (French) mysterious
Parsival, Perc, Perce, Perceval, Percey, Percy, Perseval, Purcival, Purcy

Percy (French) form of Percival: mysterious
Percee, Percey, Perci, Percie

Peregrino (Italian) bird; ordinary

Perfecto (Spanish) perfect
Perfek

Peri (English) form of Perry: tough-minded

Perick (French) form of Peter: dependable; rock

Pericles (Greek) fair leader
Periklees, Perikles, Perry

Perine (Latin) adventurer
Perrin, Perrine, Perry, Peryne

Perk (American) perky
Perkey, Perki, Perky

Perkin (English) opinionated
Parkin

Perkins (English) political
Perk, Perkens, Perkey

Pernell (French) form of Parnell: ribald; form of Peter: dependable; rock
Pernel

Peron (Last name as first name) leader

Perre (English) form of Peter: dependable; rock

Perrin (Latin) traveler
Perrine, Pero, Per

Perrince (American) form of Terrence: calm

Perris (Greek) legendary kidnapper of Helen of Troy; daring
Paris, Peris, Periss, Perrys, Perys

Perry (English) tough-minded
Parry, Perr, Perrey, Perri, Perrie

Perryman (Last name as first name) nature-lover
Perry

Perseus (Greek) destroyer; mythological hero

Persis (Biblical) place name

Perth (Place name) capital of Western Australia
Purth

Perun (Slavic) thunder; god of lightning

Pete (English) form of Peter: dependable; rock
Petey, Petie

Peter (Greek) dependable; rock
Per, Petar, Pete, Petee, Petey, Petie, Petur, Pyotr

Peterson (Scandinavian) son of Peter
Petersen

Pethuel (Aramaic) God's vision

Petra (Place name) city in Arabia; dashing

Petre (Slavic) form of Peter: dependable; rock

Petru (Slavic) form of Peter: dependable; rock

Petrus (Scandinavian) dependable

Petter (Scandinavian) form of
Peter: dependable; rock
Petya

Peverel (Latin) peverell
Peveril

Peyman (English) form of
Peyten: soldier's town

Peyton (English) form of Payton:
soldier's town
Pey, Peyt

Pharaton (Biblical) place name

Pharis (Irish) heroic
Farres, Farrus, Pharris

Pharo (Latin) ruler

Pharpar (Biblical) place name

Pharrington (Last name as first
name)

Phasael (Biblical) place name

Phelan (Irish) the small wolf;
fierce

Phelgen (Last name as first
name) stylish
Phelgon

Phelim (Irish) wolfish; fierce
Phelym

Phelps (English) droll
Felps, Filps

Phex (American) kind
Fex

Phil (Greek) form of Philip:
outdoorsman; horse-lover
Fill, Phill

Philander (Greek) lover of
many; infidel
*Filander, Phil, Philandyr,
Philender*

Philemon (Greek) showing
affection; (Biblical) loves others
Filemon, Philamon, Philo

Philetus (Greek) collector

Philip (Greek) outdoorsman;
horse-lover
*Felipe, Filipp, Flippo, Phil, Phillie,
Phillip, Phillippe, Philly*

Philippe (French) form of Philip:
outdoorsman; horse-lover
Felipe, Filippe, Philipe

Philo (Greek) lover
Filo

Phineas (English) farsighted
*Fineas, Finny, Pheneas, Phineus,
Phinny*

Phoenix (Greek) bird of
immortality; everlasting
Fee, Feenix, Fenix, Nix

Photius (Greek) scholarly

Picardus (Hispanic) adventurous

Pickford (Last name as first
name) old-fashioned

Pico (Spanish) the epitome; peak

Pier (Dutch) for Peter

Pierce (English) insightful;
piercing
*Pearce, Peerce, Peers, Peersey,
Percy, Piercy, Piers*

Piero (Italian) form of Peter:
dependable; rock
Pierro

Pierre (French) socially adroit
Piere

Pierrepont (French) social
Pierpont

Pierre-Yves (French)
combination of Pierre and Yves

Pierrick (English) form of Pier:
for Peter

Piers (English) form of Philip:
outdoorsman; horse-lover

Pierson (English) son of Pier;
rock
Pearson, Peirsen

Pietro (Italian) reliable
Pete

Pike (English) word as name

Pilar (Spanish) basic
Pilarr

Pildash (Biblical) biblical relative
of Abraham

Pilgrim (English) a traveler
Pilgrym

Pillion (French) excellence
Pilion, Pillyon, Pilyon

Pilot (French) excellence

Pim (Dutch) precise

Pin (Vietnamese) joyful

Pincus (American) dark
Pincas, Pinchas, Pinchus, Pinkus

Pinechas (Hebrew) form of Paul: small; wise

Pineda (Spanish) Last name as first name

Pinero (Spanish) springtime

Piney (American) living among pines; comfortable
Pine, Pyney

Pinkston (Last name as first name) different
Pink, Pinky

Pinky (American) familiar form of Pinchas

Pinya (Hebrew) loyal

Pio (Italian) pious

Piotr (Slavic) form of Peter: dependable; rock

Pip (German) ingenious
Pipp, Pippin, Pippo, Pippy

Pippin (English) shy

Pippo (Italian) gift

Pirney (Scottish) from the island

Pirro (Greek) red hair

Pitch (American) musical

Pithom (Biblical) place name

Piton (Spanish) form of Felix: joyful

Pitt (English) swerving dramatically

Pittman (English) blue-collar worker

Pius (Polish) pious

Placid (Latin) calm
Plasid

Placido (Italian) serene songster
Placeedo, Placidoh, Placydo

Placidon (Spanish) serene

Plan (American) word as name; organized

Plash (American) splashy; zany

Plat (French) from the flatlands; landowner
Platt

Platinum (English) worthwhile

Plato (Greek) broad-minded
Plata, Platoh

Playtoh (Invented) form of Plato: broad-minded

Plicerio (Spanish) capable

Plinio (Spanish) talented

Pluck (American) audacious; plucky

Plutarco (Greek) nefarious

Po (Biblical) place name

Poe (Last name as first name) dark spirit

Poet (American) writer
Poe

Pola (Biblical) place name

Polemos (Greek) warlike

Policarpo (Greek) with much fruit

Polja (Russian) creative

Polk (Last name as first name) political

Pollard (German) closed-minded
Polard, Pollar, Pollerd, Polley

Pollock (Last name as first name) creative

Pollux (Last name as first name) underdog

Polo (Greek) adventurer
Poloe, Poloh

Polonice (Polish) respects

Polygnotos (Greek) lover of many

Pomeroy (Last name as first name) polite

Pomposo (Spanish) pompous

Ponce (Spanish) fifth; wanderer
Poncey, Ponciano, Ponse

Ponciano (Spanish) of the sea

Poncio (Spanish) of the sea

Ponipake (Hawaiian) good luck

Pons (Spanish) fifth; explores
Ponse

Pontius (Latin) the fifth
Pontias, Pontus

Pontos (Greek) sea

Pony (Scottish) dashing
Poney, Ponie

Poogie (American) snuggly
Poog, Poogee, Poogi, Poogs, Pookie

Poole (Place name) area in
England
Pool

Pope (Greek) father
Po

Porfirio (Spanish) audacious

Port (Latin) gatekeeper
Porte

Porter (Latin) decisive
Poart, Port, Portur, Porty

Portnoy (Latin) gate

Potiphar (Biblical) bull of Africa;
a fat bull

Poul (Scandinavian) small

Powder (American) cowboy
Powd, Powe

Powell (English) ready

Powers (English) wields power

Pragedis (Spanish) prays

Prairie (American) rural man or
rancher
Prair, Prairey, Prairi, Prairy

Prakash (Indian) light

Pramad (Indian) happy

Pranav (Indian) om (syllable)

Prasanna (Indian) happy

Prashant (Indian) calm

Pratt (Last name as first name)
talkative

Pravat (Indian) leads

Pravin (Indian) talented

Praxedes (Last name as first
name) prayerful

Preemoh (Invented) form of
Primo: top-notch

Prentice (English) learning
Prenticce, Prentis, Prentiss, Printiss

Prescott (Last name as first
name) sophisticated

Presley (English) songbird;
meadow of the priest
Preslee, Preslie, Presly

Prest (English) priest

Preston (English) spiritual
Prestyn

Preston (Last name as first name)
village of a priest; religious home

Pretio (Spanish) prays

Pretivo (Spanish) prays

Preto (Latin) important

Priamos (Greek) saved

Price (Welsh) vigorous
Pricey, Pryce

Priestley (English) cottage of
the priest
Priestlea, Priestlee, Priestly

Primerica (American) from
America; patriotic
Prime

Primitivo (Spanish) primitive
Primi, Tito, Tivo

Primitivus (Spanish) first

Primo (Italian) top-notch
Preemo, Primoh, Prymo

Prince (Latin) regal leader
Preenz, Prins, Prinz, Prinze

Prine (English) prime

Priore (Italian) first

Prisciliano (Spanish) wise old
man

Procopio (Greek) progressive

Procter (Last name as first name)
leads
Proctor

Prometheus (Mythology) friend
of man; bringer of fire

Promiz (Slavic) first

Prop (American) word as name;
fun-loving
Propp

Prospen (French) prospers

Prosper (Italian) having good
fortune
Pros

Proteus (Greek) first

Prudencio (Spanish) wise

Prusa (Biblical) place name

Pry (Latin) before

Pryor (Latin) spiritual director
  Pry, Prye

Publias (Greek) thinker
  Publius

Puck (Literature) vibrant

Pullman (English) train man;
  motivator
  Pulman, Pulmann, Pullmann

Pullum (Greek) song

Puneet (Indian) purest

Punon (Biblical) place name

Pura (Spanish) pure of heart

Pureza (Spanish) pure

Purley (Welsh) caring

Pursey (American) form of
  Percy: mysterious

Purvin (English) helpful
  Pervin

Purvis (French) provider
  Pervis, Purviss

Pushkin (Last name as first) poet;
  playful

Puskar (Indian) fountain

Putiel (English) inquiring mind

Putnam (English) fond of water
  Puddy, Putnum, Puttie, Putty

Pyke (English) a spear

Pynchon (Last name as first)
  brilliant; inventive

Pyre (Latin) fire; excitable

Qabil (Arabic) capable

Qadim (Arabic) able

Qadir (Arabic) talented
  Qadar, Qadeer, Quadeer, Quadir

Qamar (Arabic) moon; dreamy

Qasim (Arabic) generous

Qidri (Biblical) place name

Qimat (Hindi) valued

Quaashie (African American)
  ambitious

Quaddus (African American)
  bright

Quadrees (Latin) fourth
  Kwadrees, Quadrhys

Quais (American) form of Qusay:
  rough hewn

Quan (Vietnamese) dignified

Quanah (Native American) good-
  smelling
  Quan

Quannell (African American)
  strong-willed
  *Kwan, Kwanell, Kwanelle, Quan,
  Quanelle, Quannel*

Quant (Latin) knowing his worth
  *Quanta, Quantae, Quantal,
  Quantay, Quantea, Quantey,
  Quantez*

Quanza (Spanish) giving

Quaronne (African American)
  haughty
  Kwarohn, Kwaronne, Quaronn

Quashawn (African American)
  tenacious
  *Kwashan, Kwashaun, Kwashawn,
  Quasha, Quashie, Quashy*

Qudamah (Arabic) courage

Quebrado (Spanish) broken

Qued (Native American)
  decorated robe

Quelatikan (Native American)
  blue horn

Quenby (English) giving
  Quenbee, Quenbie, Quenbey

Quennell (French) strength of
  an oak
  Quenell, Quennel

Quentel (Latin) fifth

Quentin (Latin) fifth
  *Kwent, Qeuntin, Quantin, Quent,
  Quenten, Quenton, Quientin,
  Quienton, Quint, Quintin, Quinton,
  Qwent, Qwentin, Qwenton*

Quention (Latin) fifth

Querubin (Hebrew) fast bull

Radimir (Polish) joyful

Radko (Slavic) happy child

Radley (English) sways with the
wind
Radlea, Radlee, Radleigh

Radnor (English) boy of the
bright shore; natural

Radolf (Anglo-Saxon) warrior

Radomir (Slavic) delightful

Radonir (Polish) form of
Radomir: delightful

Radovan (Czech) delighted

Rady (Filipino) happy

Raekwon (African American)
proud
Raykwonn

Raenn (American) form of Rain:
helpful; smart

Raeshawn (American) brainy

Raeshon (American) form of
Raeshawn; brainy
Rayshawn, Rashone, Reshawn

Raf (Spanish) healed by God

Rafael (Hebrew) rafaelle
*Rafayel, Rafayelle, Rafe, Raphael,
Raphaele*

Rafe (Irish) tough
Raff, Raffe, Raif

Rafeeq (Arabic) gregarious

Rafferty (Irish) wealthy
*Rafarty, Rafe, Raferty, Raff,
Raffarty, Raffertie, Raffety*

Raffin (Hebrew) form of Raphael:
God has healed

Rafi (Arabic) musical; friend
Rafee, Raffy

Rafik (Arabic) friendly

Rage (American) trendsetter

Raghib (Arabic) rapturous

Ragin (Biblical) in God's circle

Ragnar (Scandinavian) power
fighter

Ragu (Indian) fast

Ragul (Scandinavian) advises

Raheem (Arabic) having empathy
Rahim

Rahime (Arabic) sweet

Rahman (Arabic) full of
compassion
Raman, Rahmahn

Rahn (American) form of Ron:
kind
Rahnney, Rahnnie, Rahnny

Rahn (American) form of Ron:
kind

Rahsaan (Arabic) organized

Rai (Japanese) next child

Raibeart (Gaelic) form of
Robert: brilliant; renowned

Raiden god

Ra

Rain *Raine, Rain
Raney, Rayne*

Rainer (German) a
Rainor, Rayner, Raynor

Rainey (German) generous
Rain, Raine, Raney, Raynie

Rainier (Place name)
distinguished

Rainy (German) advises

Raj (Sanskrit) with stripes
Rajiv

Raja (Sanskrit) king
Raj

Rajab (Arabic) glorified

Rajan (Pakistani) kingly

Rajendra (Hindi) strong king

Rajendran (Indian) Indra is the
king

Rajesh (Hindi) king rules

Rajnish (Indian) night rules

Rake (American) mischief

Rakesh (Hindi) king

Raleigh (English) jovial
*Ralea, Ralee, Raleighe, Rawlee,
Rawley, Rawlie*

Quick (A...
Quico
friend...
Pac...

...merican) fast; remarkable

... (Spanish) stands by his
...

...idem (American) believer

...uiessencia (Spanish) essential;
essence
Quiess, Quiessence

Quigley (Irish) loving nature
Quiglee, Quigly, Quiggly, Quiggy

Quilaq (Native American) seal

Quillan (Irish) club; joined
Quill, Quillen, Quillon

Quimby (Norse) woman's house

Quincy (French) fifth; patient
Quensie, Quincee, Quincey,
Quinci, Quincie, Quinnsy, Quinsey

Quinlan (Irish) fit physique
Quindlen, Quinlen, Quinlin,
Quinn, Quinnlan

Quinlin (Irish) strong

Quinn (Irish) form of Quintin:
planner
Kwen, Kwene, Quenn, Quin

Quinnton (Latin) fifth

Quinntone (Latin) fifth

Quintavius (African American)
fifth child
Quint

Quintin (Latin) planner
Quenten, Quint, Quinton

Quinto (Spanish) fifth
Quiqui

Quintus (Spanish) fifth child
Quin, Quinn, Quint

Quiqui (Spanish) friend; form of
Enrique
Kaka, Keke, Quinto, Quiquin

Quirin (English) a magic spell

Quirinus (Latin) spear; Roman
god of war

Quito (Spanish) lively
Kito

Qumran (Biblical) place name

Qunnoune (Native American)
tall

Quoitrel (African American)
equalizer
Kwotrel, Quoitrelle

Quon (Chinese) bright; light

Qusay (Arabic) rough hewn
Qussay

R

Raamah (Hebrew) thunders

Raashid (Arabic) form of Rashad:
wise

Rab (Scottish) form of Raibeart:
brilliant; renowned
Rabbie

Rabbaanee (African) easygoing

Rabbi (Hebrew) master

Rabbit (Literature) for John
Updike's novels; fast
Rab

Rabul (Hispanic) rich

Race (English) one who races

Racelis (Spanish) of the sky

Racey (English) form of Race:
one who races

Rachins (Hebrew) merciful

Racine (French) Last name as
first name; root

Racqueab (Arabic) homebody

Rad (Scandinavian) helpful;
confident
Radd

Radbert (English) intelligent
Rad

Radborne (English) born happy
Radbourne, Radburn

Radcliff (English) from the
bright cliff; able

Raddy (Slavic) cheerful
Rad, Radde, Raddie, Radey

Radford (English) helpful
Rad, Raddey, Raddie, Raddy,
Radferd

Ralf (American) form of Ralph:
advisor to all
Raulf

Ralik (Hindi) purified

Ralis (Latin) thin
Rallus

Ralph (English) advisor to all
Ralf, Ralphie, Ralphy, Raulf, Rolf

Ralpheal (American) form of
Raphael: God has healed

Ralphie (English) form of Ralph:
advisor to all
Ralphee, Ralphi

Ralston (English) Ralph's town;
quirky boy
Ralfston, Rolfston

Ralton (Last name as first name)
from the rail town

Ram (Sanskrit) compelling;
pleasant
Rama, Ramm

Ramah (Indian) pleases

Rambert (German) pleasant kid
Ramburt

Rambo (American) daring;
action-oriented
Ram

Ramel (Hindi) godlike
Raymel

Rameshwar (Indian) Rama Lord

Rami (Spanish) form of Ramiro:
judicious
Ramiah

Raminz (Indian) charms

Ramiro (Spanish) judicious
Rameero, Ramero, Ramey, Rami

Ramjee (Indian) pleasing

Ramman (Biblical) form of Ram:
compelling; pleasant

Rammy (Spanish) charming

Ramone (Spanish) wise advocate;
romantic
Ramond, Raymond, Romon

Ramono (Spanish) form of
Raymond: strong

Ramp (American) word as name;
hyper
Ram, Rams

Rams (English) form of Ramsey:
savvy
Ramm, Ramz

Ramsden (English) born in ram
valley; loves the outdoors

Ramsey (English) savvy
*Rams, Ramsay, Ramsy, Ramz,
Ramzee, Ramzy*

Ramsis (Egyptian) born

Ramzan (Indian) pleases

Ramzey (American) form of
Ramsey: savvy

Ran (Scottish) form of Ronald:
kind
Ranald

Rance (American) renegade
Rans, Ranse

Ranceford (English) from the
ford of Laurence; rooted in reality

Rancye (American) form of
Rance: renegade
Rancel, Rancy

Rand (Place name) ridge of gold-
bearing rock in South Africa

Randall (English) secretive
*Randahl, Randal, Randel, Randey,
Randull, Randy*

Randic (American) form of
Randall: secretive

Randolph (English) protective
Rand, Randolf, Randolphe, Randy

Randy (English) form of Randall:
secretive; form of Randolph:
protective
Randee, Randey, Randi, Randie

Ranean (Biblical) from
Mediterranean

Ranen (Hebrew) joyful

Rangarajan (Hindi) charming

Ranger (French) vigilant
Rainge, Range, Rangur

Rangini (Polynesian) celestial

Rani (Hebrew) joyful
Ran, Ranie, Rannie

Ranien (American) counsels

Ranjan (Hindi) delightful

Rank (American) top
Ran

Rankin (English) shielded

Rannon (Jewish) renewed

Ransell (English) form of
Lawrence: honored; form of
Ransom: wealthy
Rancell

Ransford (English) the raven's
ford; watchful

Ransley (English) the raven's
field; watchful

Ransom (Latin) wealthy
*Rance, Ranse, Ransome, Ransum,
Ransym*

Ranson (English) form of
Ransom: wealthy

Rant (English) word as name;
from Dutch ranten: to talk
foolishly

Rante (American) form of Randy:
secretive; protective

Ranteen (Italian) prudent

Ranuel (Hebrew) God's own

Ranulf (English) a Lord
chancellor; regal

Rao (French) form of Raoul:
advisor to all

Raoul (Spanish) form of Raul:
advisor to all
Raulio

Raous (French) form of Raoul:
advisor to all

Raphael (Hebrew) God has
healed
Rafael, Rafe, Rapfaele

Raphon (Biblical) place name

Raqib (Arabic) glorified

Rascheed (Arabic) giving

Rashad (Arabic) wise
*Rachad, Rashaud, Rashid, Rashod,
Roshad*

Rashard (American) good

Rasheed (Arabic) intelligent

Rashid (Arabic) focused

Rasmus (Greek) form of
Erasmus: beloved

Rasool (Arabic) herald

Rasputin (Russian) a Russian
mystic
Rasp

Rastus (Greek) form of Erastus:
loved baby
Rastas

Rasul (Arabic) brings message

Rathik (Slavic) vengeful

Raudel (African American) rowdy
Raudell, Rowdel

Rauf (Arabic) compassionate

Raul (Spanish) form of Ralph:
advisor to all
Rauly, Rawl

Raven (American) bird; dark and
mysterious
Rave, Ravey, Ravy, Rayven

Ravenel (English) darkness of
ravens

Ravi (Hindi) sun god
Ravee

Ravid (Hebrew) searching

Ravin (Indian) sun

Ravindra (Hindi) a strong sun

Ravis (Sanskrit) sunny

Rawdan (English) hilly;
adventurous
Rawden, Rawdin, Rawdon

Rawle (American) form of Raul:
advisor to all

Rawleigh (American) jovial;
(English) from the dear meadow
Rawlee, Rawli

Rawlins (French) form of
Roland: renowned

Ray (French) royal; king
Rae, Raye, Rayray

Rayal (Irish) form of Ray: royal;
king

Radimir (Polish) joyful

Radko (Slavic) happy child

Radley (English) sways with the wind
Radlea, Radlee, Radleigh

Radnor (English) boy of the bright shore; natural

Radolf (Anglo-Saxon) warrior

Radomir (Slavic) delightful

Radonir (Polish) form of Radomir: delightful

Radovan (Czech) delighted

Rady (Filipino) happy

Raekwon (African American) proud
Raykwonn

Raenn (American) form of Rain: helpful; smart

Raeshawn (American) brainy

Raeshon (American) form of Raeshawn; brainy
Rayshawn, Rashone, Reshawn

Raf (Spanish) healed by God

Rafael (Hebrew) rafaelle
Rafayel, Rafayelle, Rafe, Raphael, Raphaele

Rafe (Irish) tough
Raff, Raffe, Raif

Rafeeq (Arabic) gregarious

Rafferty (Irish) wealthy
Rafarty, Rafe, Raferty, Raff, Raffarty, Raffertie, Raffety

Raffin (Hebrew) form of Raphael: God has healed

Rafi (Arabic) musical; friend
Rafee, Raffy

Rafik (Arabic) friendly

Rage (American) trendsetter

Raghib (Arabic) rapturous

Ragin (Biblical) in God's circle

Ragnar (Scandinavian) power fighter

Ragu (Indian) fast

Ragul (Scandinavian) advises

Raheem (Arabic) having empathy
Rahim

Rahime (Arabic) sweet

Rahman (Arabic) full of compassion
Raman, Rahmahn

Rahn (American) form of Ron: kind
Rahnney, Rahnnie, Rahnny

Rahn (American) form of Ron: kind

Rahsaan (Arabic) organized

Rai (Japanese) next child

Raibeart (Gaelic) form of Robert: brilliant; renowned

Raiden (Japanese) storm; thunder god

Railee (American) gregarious

Raimund (German) wise

Rain (English) helpful; smart
Raine, Rainey, Raini, Rains, Raney, Rayne

Rainer (German) advisor
Rainor, Rayner, Raynor

Rainey (German) generous
Rain, Raine, Raney, Raynie

Rainier (Place name) distinguished

Rainy (German) advises

Raj (Sanskrit) with stripes
Rajiv

Raja (Sanskrit) king
Raj

Rajab (Arabic) glorified

Rajan (Pakistani) kingly

Rajendra (Hindi) strong king

Rajendran (Indian) Indra is the king

Rajesh (Hindi) king rules

Rajnish (Indian) night rules

Rake (American) mischief

Rakesh (Hindi) king

Raleigh (English) jovial
Ralea, Ralee, Raleighe, Rawlee, Rawley, Rawlie

Quick (American) fast; remarkable

Quico (Spanish) stands by his friends
Paco

Quidem (American) believer

Quiessencia (Spanish) essential; essence
Quiess, Quiessence

Quigley (Irish) loving nature
Quiglee, Quigly, Quiggly, Quiggy

Quilaq (Native American) seal

Quillan (Irish) club; joined
Quill, Quillen, Quillon

Quimby (Norse) woman's house

Quincy (French) fifth; patient
Quensie, Quincee, Quincey, Quinci, Quincie, Quinnsy, Quinsey

Quinlan (Irish) fit physique
Quindlen, Quinlen, Quinlin, Quinn, Quinnlan

Quinlin (Irish) strong

Quinn (Irish) form of Quintin: planner
Kwen, Kwene, Quenn, Quin

Quinnton (Latin) fifth

Quinntone (Latin) fifth

Quintavius (African American) fifth child
Quint

Quintin (Latin) planner
Quenten, Quint, Quinton

Quinto (Spanish) fifth
Quiqui

Quintus (Spanish) fifth child
Quin, Quinn, Quint

Quiqui (Spanish) friend; form of Enrique
Kaka, Keke, Quinto, Quiquin

Quirin (English) a magic spell

Quirinus (Latin) spear; Roman god of war

Quito (Spanish) lively
Kito

Qumran (Biblical) place name

Qunnoune (Native American) tall

Quoitrel (African American) equalizer
Kwotrel, Quoitrelle

Quon (Chinese) bright; light

Qusay (Arabic) rough hewn
Qussay

R

Raamah (Hebrew) thunders

Raashid (Arabic) form of Rashad: wise

Rab (Scottish) form of Raibeart: brilliant; renowned
Rabbie

Rabbaanee (African) easygoing

Rabbi (Hebrew) master

Rabbit (Literature) for John Updike's novels; fast
Rab

Rabul (Hispanic) rich

Race (English) one who races

Racelis (Spanish) of the sky

Racey (English) form of Race: one who races

Rachins (Hebrew) merciful

Racine (French) Last name as first name; root

Racqueab (Arabic) homebody

Rad (Scandinavian) helpful; confident
Radd

Radbert (English) intelligent
Rad

Radborne (English) born happy
Radbourne, Radburn

Radcliff (English) from the bright cliff; able

Raddy (Slavic) cheerful
Rad, Radde, Raddie, Radey

Radford (English) helpful
Rad, Raddey, Raddie, Raddy, Radferd

Rayan (Irish) form of Ryan: royal; good-looking

Raybourne (English) from the deer brook; sylvan
Rayburn, Raybin

Rayce (American) form of Raymond: strong
Rays, Rayse

Rayfield (English) woodsy; capable
Rafe, Ray, Rayfe

Rayk (American) form of Rake: mischief

Rayland (English) streamland boy

Rayman (English) form of Raymond: strong

Raymond (English) strong
Rai, Ramand, Ramond, Ray, Raymie, Raymonde, Raymun, Raymund, Raymy

Raynard (French) judge; sly
Ray, Raynaud, Renard, Renaud, Rey, Reynard, Reynaud

Rayner (French) form of Raymond: strong
Ray, Rayne

Rayon (English) word as name; fabric; from "ray" as in "ray of light"

Raypheon (American) form of Raphael: God has healed

Raysh (American) form of Rayshan: inventive

Rayshan (African American) inventive
Ray, Raysh, Raysha, Rayshun

Rayson (American) son of Ray

Razi (Aramaic) secretive

Razus (American) happy

Reace (Welsh) passionate
Reece, Rees, Reese

Read (English) red-haired
Reade, Reed, Reid

Reagan (Irish) kingly
Ragan, Raghan, Reagen, Reegan, Regan

Reaman (Irish) prolific

Reaner (Last name as first name) even-tempered
Rean, Rener

Rearden (Irish) creative

Reaser (Welsh) excitable

Reavis (American) enthusiastic

Rebal (American) variant on Rebel: outlaw

Rebel (American) outlaw
Reb, Rebbe, Rebele

Red (English) man with red hair
Redd, Reddy

Redford (English) handsome man with ruddy skin
Readford, Red, Reddy, Redferd, Redfor

Redin (Last name as first name) red-haired

Redmon (German) protective
Redd, Reddy, Redmond, Redmun, Redmund

Redney (American) form of Rodney: open minded

Reece (Welsh) vivacious
Rees, Reese, Reez

Reed (English) red-haired
Read, Reede, Reid

Reed-Kanan (Scandinavian)

Reef (Nature) water-loving boy

Reem (Hebrew) horned animal or unicorn

Rees (Welsh) form of Rhys: loving
Reece, Reese, Reez, Rez

Reese (Welsh) vivacious
Reis, Rhys

Reesey (Welsh) form of Reese: vivacious

Reeves (English) giving
Reave, Reaves, Reeve

Reez (American) form of Reese: vivacious

Reg (Scandinavian) form of
Reginald: wise advisor

Regal (American) debonair
Regall

Regane (Scandinavian) decides

Regen (English) leader

Regent (Latin) royal; grand

Reggie (English) form of
Reginald: wise advisor
Reg, Reggey, Reggi, Reggye

Reginald (English) wise advisor
Reg, Reggie, Reginal, Regineld

Reginaldo (Spanish) leader

Regine (French) artistic
Regeen

Regis (Latin) kingly
Reggis

Regney (Slavic) leader

Regulo (Italian) form of
Reginald: wise advisor

Rehob (Biblical) place name

Rehoboam (Biblical) son of
Solomon

Reid (English) red-haired
Reide

Reidar (Scandinavian) soldier

Reider (Scottish) red-skinned

Reillon (Spanish) realm

Reilly (Irish) daring
Rilee, Riley, Rilie

Rein (German) advises

Reinald (French) judges

Reinder (German) wins

Reine (Scandinavian) victor

Reinhart (German) brave-hearted
Reinhar, Reinhardt, Rhinehard,
Rhinehart

Reith (American) shy

Relio (Spanish) gold

Rema (English) form of Remus:
fast

Remberto (Spanish) pious

Remeth (Biblical) place name

Remi (French) fun-loving
Remee, Remey, Remmy, Remy

Remiel (Hebrew) saved by God

Remigio (Italian) from Rheims;
religious

Reming (English) raven

Remington (Last name as first
name) intellectual
Rem, Remmy

Remko (Last name as first name)
believes

Remo (Italian) confident

Remuda (Spanish) herd of horses
Rem, Remmie, Remmy

Remus (Latin) fast
Reemus, Remes, Remous

Renaloza (Spanish) reborn

Renard (French) smart; brave; fox
Renardt

Renato (Italian) born again
Renata, Renate

Renaud (English) powerful
Renny

Renba (Biblical) name spelled
backward

Render (Dutch) draws

René (French) born again
Renee, Rennie, Renny, Re-Re

Renferd (English) peace-loving
Renfred

Renfro (Welsh) calm
Renfroe, Renfrow, Renphro, Rinfro

Renji (Japanese) truthful

Rennell (Irish) advises

Renny (French) able
Renney, Renni, Rennye

Rennye (Irish) advises

Reno (Place name) city in Nevada
Reen, Reenie, Renoh

Renshaw (English) born in the
raven wood

Renson (Last name as first name)
son of Ren

Renton (English) born in the
town of deer

Renwick (English) born in the
village of deer

Renze (Italian) excellence

Renzo (Italian) form of Lorenzo:
honored

ReShard (African American) rough
Reshar, Reshard

Reshma (Indian) sun

Resk (American) variant on Rex: kingly

Reslie (American) form of Leslie: fiesty; beautiful and smart

Restes (Greek) form of Orestes: leader

Reston (English) form of Royston: town of Royce

Reth (American) form of Seth: chosen

Reto (German) resides

Rett (Literature) form of Rhett: romantic

Reuben (Hebrew) behold, a son
Rube, Rubey, Rubie, Rubin, Ruby, Rubyn

Rev (Invented) ramped up
Revv

Revera (Spanish) values God

Revin (American) distinctive
Revan, Revinn, Revun

Rex (Latin) kingly
Rexe

Rexel (Latin) king

Rexford (American) form of Rex: kingly
Rexferd, Rexfor, Rexy

Rey (Spanish) form of Reynaldo: knowledgable tutor
Ray, Reye, Reyes

Reymund (French) honored

Reymundo (Spanish) form of Raymond: strong

Reynaldo (Spanish) knowledgeable tutor

Reynard (French) brilliant
Raynard, Rayne, Renardo

Reynaud (French) advisor; judge

Reynold (English) knowledgeable tutor
Ranald, Ranold, Reinold, Renald, Renalde, Rey, Reye, Reynolds

Reza (Iranian) content

Rezeile (Biblical) name spelled backward

Rezeph (Biblical) place name

Rhagae (Biblical) place name

Rhegium (Biblical) place name

Rhene (American) smiley
Reen, Rheen

Rhett (American) romantic
Rhet, Rhette

Rho (Welsh) rose

Rhoden (Greek) rose

Rhodes (Greek) lovely
Rhoades, Rodes

Rhodree (Welsh) ruler
Rodree, Rodrey, Rodry

Rhondel (English) form of Rondel: poetic

Rhoris (Irish) red hair

Rhymen (American) form of Ryan: royal; good-looking

Rhyon (Irish) form of Ryan: royal; good-looking
Rhyan, Rhyen

Rhyph (Welsh) jovial

Rhys (Welsh) loving
Reece, Reese

Rian (Irish) little king

Riano (Italian) king

Riao (Spanish) form of Rio: water-loving

Ribal (American) from ribald; revels

Ribog (Slavic) of God

Ricardo (Spanish) snappy
Recardo, Ric, Riccardo, Ricky

Ricardoph (Spanish) energetic

Riccardio (Italian) brave

Rice (English) rich
Ryes

Rich (English) affluent
Richie, Ritchie

Richard (English) wealthy leader
Rich, Richerd, Richey, Richi, Richie, Rickie, Ricky, Ritchie

R

Richey (German) ruler
Rich, Richee, Richie, Ritch, Ritchee, Ritchee, Ritchey

Richie (English) form of Richard: wealthy leader
Richey, Richi, Ritchey, Ritchie

Richman (German) has power

Richmond (German) rich and protective
Rich, Richie, Richmon, Richmun, Ricky, Ritchmun

Richshae (English) form of Richard: wealthy leader

Richter (Last name as first name) hopeful
Rick, Ricky, Rik, Rikter

Rick (German) form of Richard: wealthy leader
Ric, Rickey, Ricki, Rickie, Ricky, Rik

Rickard (Scandinavian) form of Richard: wealthy leader
Rick, Rickert, Rickward, Rikkert

Rico (Italian) spirited; ruler
Reco, Reko, Ricko, Rikko, Riko

Ricod (American) form of Rico: spirited; ruler

Ricsi (American) form of Richie: wealthy leader

Riddle (Word as name) perplexes

Riddock (Irish) man of the field

Rider (American) horse rider
Ryder

Ridge (English) on the ridge; risk-taker

Ridglee (English) man of the ridge
Ridgley, Ridglea

Ridhaa (Arabic) delight

Ridley (English) ingenious
Redley, Rid, Ridlie, Ridly, Rydley

Riemer (English) from Rheims

Rien (Dutch) mariner

Rigby (English) high-energy
Rigbie, Rigbye, Rygby

Rigel (Arabic) foot; star in constellation Orion

Rigney (Greek) power

Rigo (Spanish) ridge boy

Rigoberto (Spanish) strong; ridge boy
Bert, Berto, Rigo

Rike (American) form of Nike: winning
Rikee, Rykee, Rykie, Ryky

Rikken (Slavic) form of Rik: hopeful

Rilan (English) land of rye

Rilee (American) form of Riley: brave
Rilea, Rileigh

Rileigh (American) form of Riley: brave
Ryleigh

Riley (Irish) brave
Reilly, Rylee, Ryley, Rylie, Ryly

Rimme (French) form of Remi: fun-loving

Rimmon (Biblical) place name

Rimon (Hebrew) pomegranate

Ringo (English) funny
Ring, Ringgoh, Ryngo

Rinus (American) form of Ryan: royal; good-looking

Rinzel (American) thinker

Rio (Spanish) water-loving
Reeo

Rio Grande (Spanish) a river in Texas
Rio, Riogrande

Rion (American) form of Ryan/ Rian: royal; good-looking; little king

Rione (Spanish) flowing
Reo, Reone, Rio

Rionn (Greek) form of Orion: fiery hunter

Riordan (Irish) lordly
Rearden

Riordene (Irish) poetic

Rip (English) serene
Ripp, Rippe

Ripley (English) serene
Riplee

Ris (English) outdoorsman; smart
Rislea, Rislee, Risleigh, Riz, Rizlee

Rise (Welsh) form of Rhys: loving

Rishab (American) form of
Rashad: wise

Rishi (Arabic) first; (Indian) wise
man

Rishon (Hebrew) first

Risley (English) smart and quiet
Rislee, Risleye, Rizlee, Rizley

Risto (Scandinavian) bears Christ

Ristoffer (American) form of
Christopher: the bearer of Christ

Ristoph (German) form of
Christopher: the bearer of Christ

Ritch (American) leader
*Rich, Richee, Richey, Ritch,
Ritchal, Ritchee, Ritchi*

Ritchell (English) controller

Ritchie (English) form of Richie:
wealthy leader
Ritchee, Ritchey, Ritchy

Rito (American) spunky
Reit

Ritt (German) debonair
Rit, Rittie, Rittly

Ritter (German) debonair
Riter, Rittyr

Rivan (Literature) from Eddings's
The Rivan Codex; esoteric

River (English) flowing water; hip
Riv, Ryver

Rivers (English) flowing river

Riverson (English) son of River

Rixus (Greek) excites

Rizal (Spanish) athletic

Rizalino (Spanish) pleased

Rizo (Italian) lively

Roald (Scandinavian) famous
ruler

Roam (American) wanderer
Roamey, Roamy, Roma, Rome

Roan (English) form of Rogan:
spirited redhead

Roar (Irish) form of Roarke: ruler

Roarke (Irish) ruler
Roark, Rork, Rourke

Rob (English) form of Robert:
brilliant; renowned
Robb

Robbie (English) form of Robert:
brilliant; renowned
Robbee, Robbey, Robbi, Robby

Robert ○ (English) brilliant;
renowned
*Bob, Bobbie, Bobby, Rob, Robart,
Robbie, Robby, Roberto, Robs,
Roburt*

Robert-Lee (American) patriotic
*Bobbylee, Robby Lee, Robert-E-Lee,
Robert Lee, Robertlee*

Roberto (Spanish) form of
Robert: brilliant; renowned
Berto, Rob, Robert, Tito

Roberts (Last name as first
name) luminous
Rob, Robards, Robarts, Roburts

Robeson (English) Rob's son;
bright
Roberson, Robison

Robhert (Welsh) form of Robert:
brilliant; renowned

Robin (English) gregarious
Robb, Robbin, Robby, Robyn

Roble (Last name as first name)
divine
Robel, Robl, Robley

Roblee (American) patriot

Robles (English) royal

Robson (English) sterling
character
Robb, Robbson, Robsen

Roc (Italian) form of Rocco:
tough

Rocal (American) form of Rocco:
tough

Rocco (Italian) tough
*Roc, Rock, Rockie, Rocko, Rocky,
Rok, Rokee, Rokko, Roko*

Roch (English) form of Rock: hardy

Rochester (English) guarded
Roche

Rocio (Spanish) form of Rocco: tough

Rock (American) hardy
Roc, Rocky, Rok

Rocket (American) word as a name; snappy
Rokket

Rockleigh (English) dependable; outdoorsy
Rocco, Rock, Rocklee, Rockley, Rocky, Roklee

Rockmun (English) man who rests

Rockne (English) form of Rocco/ Rock: tough; hardy

Rockney (American) brash

Rockwell (American) spring of strength
Rock, Rockwelle, Rocky

Rocky (English) hardy; tough
Rocco, Rock, Rockee, Rockey, Rocki, Rockie

Rocquin (Spanish) form of Joaquin: bold; hip

Rod (English) brash
Rodd, Roddy

Rodalfo (Spanish) form of Rudolph: wolf

Rodas (Spanish) Spanish name for the Rhone River in France; of Rhodes
Rod, Roda

Rodden (English) powerful

Roddick (Last name as first name) goes far

Roddy (German) form of Roderick: effective leader
Roddee, Roddi, Roddie

Rodel (American) generous
Rodell, Rodey, Rodie

Rodeo (Spanish) roundup; cowboy
Rodayo, Roddy, Rodyo

Roderick (German) effective leader
Roddy, Roddyrke, Roderic, Roderik, Rodreck, Rodrick, Rodrik

Rodger (German) form of Roger: famed warrior
Rodge, Roge

Rodion (Biblical) form of Herodion: heroic

Rodman (German) hero
Rodmin, Rodmun

Rodney (English) open-minded
Rod, Roddy, Rodnee, Rodni, Rodnie

Rodo (French) wolflike

Rodolfo (Spanish) spark
Rod, Rudolfo, Rudolpho

Rodree (American) leader
Rodrey, Rodri, Rodry

Rodrigo (Spanish) feisty leader
Rod, Roddy, Rodrego, Rodriko

Rodriguez (Spanish) hot-blooded
Rod, Roddy, Rodreguez, Rodrigues

Rodwell (German) renowned

Roe (English) deer

Roel (Dutch) famed hero

Roemello (Italian) form of Romulus: presumptuous

Rogan (Irish) spirited redhead

Rogasiano (Spanish) red hair

Rogelio (Spanish) aggressive
Rojel, Rojelio

Rogell (Dutch) strong

Roger (German) famed warrior
Rodge, Rodger, Roge, Rogie, Rogyer, Rogers

Rognan (Slavic) upward

Rohan (Hindi) going higher

Rohanee (Indian) comes down to earth

Rohit (Hindi) he fishes

Roi (French) form of Roy: king

Roisin (Irish) the rose

Rokee (Slavic) peaceful boy

Rokel (Scandinavian) a ewe

Roland (German) renowned
Rolend, Rollan, Rolland, Rollie,
Rollo, Rolund

Rolando (Spanish) famous
Rolan

Roldan (Spanish) leader

Role (American) brash
Roel, Roll

Rolf (German) kind advisor
Rolfee, Rolfie, Rolfy, Rolph

Rolfon (Norwegian) overbearing

Rollan (Russian) from Roland:
renowned

Rollie (English) form of Roland:
renowned
Rollee, Rolley, Rolli, Rolly

Rollins (German) form of
Roland: renowned
Rolin, Rolins, Rollin, Rolyn

Rollo (German) famous

Rolly (English) famous

Rolt (Latin) wolfish

Roly (English) form of Roland:
renowned

Roman (Latin) fun-loving
Romain, Romen, Romey, Romi,
Romun, Romy

Romano (Italian) from Rome

Romar (English) from Rome

Rombert (Latin) from Rome

Rome (Place name) city in Italy
Romeo

Romedios (Spanish) Roman

Romeo (Italian) romantic lover
Romah, Rome, Romeoh, Romero,
Romey, Romi, Romy

Romer (American) form of
Rome: city in Italy
Roamar, Roamer

Rommel (Latin) from Rome

Romney (Welsh) roamer
Rom, Romnie

Romo (French) boy from Rome

Romulo (Spanish) man from
Rome; of Rome
Romo

Romulon (Mythology) of Rome

Romulus (Latin) presumptuous
Rom, Romules, Romulo

Romy (German) form of
Romulus: presumptuous

Ron (English) form of Ronald:
kind
Ronn

Ronak (Scandinavian) powerful

Ronald (English) kind
Ron, Ronal, Ronel, Ronney, Ronni,
Ronnie, Ronuld

Ronalk (Slavic) form of Ronald:
kind

Ronan (Irish) seal; playful

Rond (American) from the word
round

Rondel (French) poetic
Ron, Rondal, Rondell, Rondie,
Rondy

Ronen (Jewish) joyful

Ronford (English) distinguished
Ronferd, Ronnforde

Rong (Chinese) warring

Roni (Hebrew) joyful
Rone, Ronee

Ronicle (American) form of Ron:
kind

Ronit (Jewish) sings

Ronneal (American) leaving

Ronnie (English) form of Ronald:
kind
Ronnee, Ronney, Ronni, Ronny

Ronomy (Biblical) from
Deuteronomy

Ronson (Scottish) Ron's son;
likable

Rook (Spanish) form of Roque:
rock

Roon (Scandinavian) form of
Rune: secretive

Roone (Irish) distinctive; bright
face
Rooney, Roune

Rooney (Irish) man with red hair
Rooni, Roony

Roose (Last name as first name) high-energy
Rooce, Roos, Rooz, Ruz

Roosevelt (Dutch) strong leader
Rooseveldt, Rosevelt, Rosy, Velte

Rooster (American) loud
Roos, Rooz

Roper (American) roper
Rope

Roque (Portuguese) rock

Rorden (Irish) creative

Rorelle (English) red-haired

Rorick (French) red-haired

Rorin (American) form of Rory: strong

Rory (German) strong
Roree, Rorey, Roreye, Rorie

Rosalio (Spanish) rose; charmer

Rosano (Italian) rosy prospects; romantic

Roscoe (English) woods; nature-loving
Rosco, Roskie, Rosko, Rosky

Rosembelt (Spanish) beauty of roses

Rosendo (Italian) rose

Roser (American) redhead; outgoing
Rozer

Roshanek (Slavic) bright flower

Roshaun (African American) loyal
Roshawn

Roshni (Indian) brightness

Rosk (American) swift
Roske

Rosley (English) of the rosary

Rosling (Scottish) redhead; explosive
Roslin, Rosy, Rozling

Ross (Latin) attractive
Rossey, Rossie, Rossy

Rossa (American) exuberant
Ross, Rosz

Rossain (American) hopeful
Rossane

Rossan (French) rose

Rossano (Italian) handsome

Rossell (French) rose

Rossi (Italian) rose red

Roston (English) rusting

Roswell (English) fascinating
Roswel, Roswelle, Rosy, Rozwell, Well

Roteus (Greek) form of Proteus: first

Roth (German) man with red hair
Rauth, Rothe

Rouel (French) form of Rule: emphatic

Roumen (Slavic) Roman

Roupen (American) quiet
Ropan, Ropen, Ropun

Roven (English) wanders

Rover (English) wanderer
Rovar, Rovey, Rovur, Rovy

Roverb (Invented) from Proverb

Rovere (French) travels

Rovonte (French) roving

Rowan (English) red-haired; adorned
Rowe, Rowen

Rowand (Last name as first name) reliable

Rowdy (English) athletic; loud
Roudy, Rowdee, Rowdi, Rowdie

Rowe (English) outgoing
Roe, Row, Rowie

Rowel (English) famed

Rowell (English) rocker
Roll, Rowl

Rowenam (English) red-haired

Rowland (Scandinavian) form of Roland: renowned

Rowley (English) from the rough meadow; spirited

Rown (English) form of Rowan: red-haired; adorned

Roxen (English) precise

Roy (French) king
Roi

Royal (French) king
Roy, Royall, Royalle, Roye

Royalton (French) king
Royal, Royallton

Royce (German) famous
Roy, Royse

Roycell (French) form of Royce:
famous

Roycie (American) form of
Royce: famous
Rory, Roy, Royse, Roysie

Royd (English) good humor

Roydean (American) combo of
Roy and Dean

Roydee (English) natural

Royden (English) outdoors; regal
Roy, Roydin

Royderrick (English) form of
Roderick: effective leader

Royelio (Spanish) royal

Royle (English) kingly

Roysell (American) form of
Royce: famous

Royst (American) form of Royce:
famous

Royston (English) town of Royce

Ruadhan (Hindi) brash

Ruari (Irish) red-haired
Ruairi, Ruaridh

Rube (Spanish) form of Ruben:
behold, a son
Rubino

Ruben (Spanish) form of Reuben:
behold, a son
Rube, Ruby

Rubens (Dutch) son

Rubi (Hebrew) form of Rubin:
behold, a son

Ruchirat (French) rich

Rudder (English) ruddy skin

Ruddy (English) ruddy skin

Rudeger (German) friendly
*Rudger, Rudgyr, Rudigar, Rudiger,
Rudy*

Rudo (African) loving

Rudolf (German) wolf
Rodolf, Rudy

Rudolph (German) wolf
*Rodolf, Rodolph, Rud, Rudee,
Rudey, Rudi, Rudolpho, Rudy*

Rudow (German) lovable

Rudy (German) form of Rudolph:
wolf
Rude, Rudee, Rudey, Rudi

Rudyard (English) closed off
Rud, Rudd, Ruddy

Rueban (American) form of
Reuben: behold, a son
Ruban

Rued (Spanish) dishonest

Ruel (French) variant on Rule:
emphatic

Ruelas (Spanish) ambitious

Rufaro (African) gives happiness

Ruffo (Spanish) form of Rufus:
redhead

Rufine (French) red hair

Rufino (Spanish) redhead

Rufus (Latin) redhead
*Fue, Rufas, Rufes, Ruffie, Ruffis,
Ruffy, Rufous*

Rugby (English) braced for
contact
Rug, Rugbee, Rugbie, Ruggy

Rugerd (Slavic) famed

Ruggier (French) form of Roger:
famed warrior

Rugo (Italian) famed

Rui (Spanish) powerful fighter

Ruiden (Irish) red-haired

Ruiz (Spanish) chummy

Rujul (Indian) truthful

Rule (English) emphatic

Rulei (French) unit

Rulon (Native American) spirited
Rulonn

Rumford (English) lives at river
crossing; grounded

Rummel (American) form of
Rommel: from Rome

Rumont (French) red mountain

Runa (German) keeps score

Runako (African) attractive

Rune (German) secretive
Roone, Runes

Rupad (Hindi) secretive
Rupesh

Rupchand (Sanskrit) as beautiful as the moon

Rupert (English) prince
Rupe

Rupin (Indian) handsome

Rurik (Russian) famous

Rush (English) loquacious
Rusch

Rushford (English) from the ford of rushes; found

Rushon (French) red hair

Rusi (English) red-haired

Rusim (Biblical) traditional

Rusk (Spanish) innovator
Rusck, Ruske, Ruskk

Ruskin (French) red-haired

Ruslan (English) rusty hair

Russ (French) form of Russell: man with red hair; charmer

Russell (French) man with red hair; charmer
Russ, Russel, Russy, Rusty

Russo (Italian) russet

Russon (French) red hair

Rustice (French) rusty hair

Rustin (English) redhead
Rustan, Ruston, Rusty

Rusty (French) form of Russell: man with red hair; charmer
Rustee, Rustey, Rusti

Rutherford (English) dignified
Ruthe, Rutherfurd, Rutherfyrd

Rutil (Spanish) faithful

Rutilio (Spanish) faithful

Rutland (Norse) red land

Rutledge (English) substantial
Rutlidge

Rutley (English) from red country; fertile

Ruud (Dutch) like a wolf; well-known

Ruvim (Hebrew) meaningful

Ryall (American) capable

Ryan ○ ❶ (Irish) royal; good-looking
Rhine, Rhyan, Rhyne, Ry, Ryane, Ryann, Ryanne, Ryen, Ryun

Ryander (American) competitive; obstinate

Ryden (English) form of Ryder: outdoorsy; man who rides horses

Ryder (English) outdoorsy; man who rides horses
Rider, Rye

Ryderin (Welsh) caring

Rye (Botanical) grain; basic

Ryerson (English) fit outdoorsman
Rye

Rygel (Spanish) regal

Ryk (American) form of Rick: wealthy leader

Ryke (Slavic) form of Richard: wealthy leader

Ryken (Slavic) form of Richard: wealthy leader

Ryker (English) of the rye land; farms

Rykey (American) easygoing

Ryland (English) excellent
Rilan, Riland, Rye, Rylan

Rylandar (English) farmer
Rye, Rylan, Ryland

Rylant (American) form of Ryland: excellent

Ryle (American) form of Kyle: serene

Ryman (English) man of rye; fundamental

Rymmy (Spanish) form of Romy: presumptuous

Ryne (Irish) form of Ryan: royal; good-looking
Rine, Ryn, Rynn

Ryoun (American) form of Ryan: royal; good-looking

Ryston (English) form of Royston: town of Royce

Ryszard (Polish) courageous leader
Reshard

Ryton (English) from the town of rye; fundamental

Ryvers (American) form of Rivers: flowing river

Saad (Aramaic) helping others

Saahdia (Aramaic) helped by the Lord
Saadya, Seadya

Saarik (Hindi) sings like a bird
Saariq, Sareek, Sareeq, Sariq

Sabene (Latin) optimist
Sabe, Sabeen, Sabin, Sabyn, Sabyne

Saber (French) armed; sword
Sabar, Sabe, Sabre

Sabin (Latin) sabine
Sabeeno, Sabino, Savin, Savino

Sable (French) animal; brown-haired child

Sacha (Russian) defends; charms
Sascha, Sasha

Sachar (Hebrew) well-rewarded
Sacar

Sachetan (Indian) logical

Saddam (Arabic) powerful ruler
Saddum

Sadiki (African) loyal
Sadeeki

Sadler (English) practical
Sadd, Saddle, Sadlar, Sadlur

Sae (American) talkative
Saye

Saeed (African) lucky

Safford (English) boy from the river of willows

Saffron (Botanical) spice/plant; orange-haired
Saffran, Saffren, Saphron

Sagar (Indian) ocean

Sagaz (Spanish) clever
Saga, Sago

Sage (Botanical) wise
Saje

Sageal (Spanish) smart

Sagel (Indian) ocean

Sager (American) rewarded; short
Sayger

Sagi (Hebrew) best

Saginaw (Place name) city in Michigan; (Native American) bold
Sag, Saggy

Sagiv (Hebrew) the best
Segev

Saguaro (Botanical) cactus; prickly
Seguaro

Sahak (Slavic) jovial

Sahil (Hindi) leader
Sahel

Sahn (Hindi) held high

Sai (Arabic) sword

Saied (Arabic) fortunate

Sail (American) water; natural

Sailan (American) of the sea

Sainsbury (English) from the home of saints; religious
Sainsberry

Saint (Latin) holy man

Saith (English) to speak
Saithe, Saythe

Sajan (Hindi) beloved

Sakar (Biblical) form of Issachar: reward

Sal (Italian) form of Salvador: savior; spirited; form of Salvatore: rescuer; spirited
Sall, Sallie, Sally

Saladin (Arabic) devout
Saladdin

Salado (Spanish) funny
Sal

Salath (Biblical) generous

Salehe (African) good

Salem (Hebrew) peaceful

Salford (Place name) city in
England

Salim (Arabic) safe; peaceful
Saleem

Salisbury (English) born in the
willows
Salisbery, Salisberry, Saulisbury,
Saulsberry, Saulsbery, Saulsbury

Salm (Biblical) from Psalms

Salman (Arabic) protected

Salom (Biblical) form of
Absalom: my father is peace

Salomaa (Spanish) ideal

Salt (American) salt-of-the-earth
Salty

Salustia (Spanish) healthy

Salute (American) patriotic

Salvacion (Spanish) salvation

Salvador (Spanish) savior;
spirited
Sal, Sally, Salvadore

Salvatore (Italian) rescuer;
spirited
Sal, Sallie, Sally, Salvatori,
Salvatorre

Salvio (Latin) saved
Salvian, Salviano, Salviatus

Salvoterre (Spanish) salvation

Sam (Hebrew) form of Samuel:
man who heard God; prophet
Samm, Sammey, Sammi, Sammy

Samaga (Biblical) place name

Samal (Biblical) place name

Saman (Hebrew) hears all

Samce (Biblical) form of Samson:
strong man

Samed (Arabic) everlasting

Sami (Lebanese) high

Samilo (Italian) upward

Samir (Arabic) special
Sameer, Samere, Samyr

Sammon (Arabic) grocer
Sammen

Sammy (Hebrew) wise
Samie, Sammee, Sammey, Sammi,
Sammie, Samy

Samos (Place name) casual

Samrat (Indian) of the emperor

Samson (Hebrew) strong man
Sam, Sampson

Samuel ✪ ❶ (Hebrew) man who
heard God; prophet
Sam, Samael, Sammeul, Sammie,
Sammo, Sammuel, Sammy, Samual

Samvel (Hebrew) know the name
of God
Samvell, Samvelle

Sanborn (English) one with
nature
Sanborne, Sanbourn, Sandy

Sancho (Latin) genuine
Sanch, Sanchoh

Sandage (English) form of
Sander: savior of mankind; nice

Sandalio (Spanish) wolflike

Sandberg (Last name as first
name) writer
Sandburg

Sander (Greek) savior of
mankind; nice
Sandor

Sanders (English) kind
Sandars, Sandors, Saunders

Sanderson (Last name as first
name) defender
Sandersen

Sandhurst (English) from the
sandy thicket; undaunted
Sandhirst

Sandiego (Spanish) place name

Sanditon (English) from the
sandy town; perseveres

Sandro (Italian) form of
Alexander: great leader; helpful

Sandy (English) personable
Sandee, Sandey, Sandi
Sanford (English) negotiator
Sandford, Sandy, Sanferd, Sanfor
Sangarius (Biblical) place name
Sango (Asian) coral
Sanjay (Sanskrit) wins every time
Sanjiv (Hindi) longlasting
Sanjog (Indian) lucky chance
Sanogo (Spanish) brave
Sanorelle (African American)
honest
Sanny, Sano, Sanorel, Sanorell
Sansone (Italian) strong
Santana (Spanish) saintly
Santa, Santanah, Santanna, Santee
Santiago ❶ (Spanish) sainted;
valuable
*Sandiago, Santego, Santiagoh,
Santy, Tago*
Santino (Italian) sacred
Santeeno, Santyno
Santon (English) sandy home
Santos (Italian) holy; blessed
Sant, Santo
Santosh (Hindi) happy
Sapir (Hebrew) sapphire; jewel
Safir, Saphir, Saphiros
Saral (Indian) straightforward
Sarang (Indian) deer

Sarday (American) extrovert
Sardae, Sardaye
Sardica (Biblical) place name
Sardis (Biblical) place name
Sargent (French) officer/leader
Sarge, Sergeant
Sargis (Slavic) serves
Sargon (Persian) sun king
Sarid (Biblical) place name
Sarkis (Greek) the Lord
Sasan (Hebrew) happy
Sasha (Russian) helpful
Sacha, Sash
Sassacus (Native American) wild
soul
Sasso (Hebrew) happy
Sasson (Hebrew) happy
Sastry (Indian) safe
Satchel (American) unique
Satch, Satchell
Saturnin (Spanish) from planet
Saturn; melancholy
Saturnino
Satya (Indian) honesty
Saul (Hebrew) gift
Saulie, Sawl, Sol, Solly
Saunder (English) defensive;
focused
Saunders
Sava (Slavic) aware

Savage (Last name as first name)
wild
Sav
Saverio (Spanish) bright
Saviero (Spanish) form of Xavier:
home; shining
Saville (French) willow town
Savelle, Savile, Savill, Seville
Savini (Italian) bright
Savio (Italian) smart
Savone (Italian) form of Savino:
sabine
Savoy (Place name) region in
France
Savoe
Savyon (Spanish) great attitude
Sawyer (English) hardworking
Saw, Sawyrr
Saxe (English) form of Saxon:
sword-fighter; feisty
Sax, Saxee, Saxey, Saxie
Saxon (English) sword-fighter;
feisty
Sackson, Sax, Saxan, Saxe, Saxen
Saxton (Place name) stern
Saxten
Sayan (Asian) standing
Sayre (Welsh) skilled
Saye, Sayer, Sayers
Scafell (Place name) mountain in
England

Scanlon (Irish) devious
Scan, Scanlin, Scanlun, Scanne

Scant (American) word as name; too little
Scanty

Schae (American) safe; careful
Schay

Schaffer (German) watchful
Schaffur, Shaffer

Schawn (American) form of Shawn/Sean: God is gracious

Schelde (Place name) river in Europe; calm
Shelde

Schelte (German) sheltie

Schmidt (German) hardworking; blacksmith
Schmit

Schneider (German) stylish; tailor
Sneider, Snider

Schubert (German) cobbler
Shubert

Schumann (Last name as first) famous composer; romantic

Schuyler (Dutch) protective
Skylar, Skyler

Scipio (Greek) leader

Scirocco (Italian) warmth of the wind
Cirocco, Sirocco

Scopus (Biblical) place name

Scorpio (Latin) lethal
Scorp, Scorpioh

Scotland (Place name) from Scotland

Scott (English) from Scotland; happy
Scot, Scotty

Scotty (English) happy
Scottee, Scottey, Scotti

Scout (French) hears all; scouts for information

Scribner (English) the one who writes

Scully (Irish) vocal
Scullee, Sculley, Scullie

Scupi (Biblical) place name

Seabert (English) shines like the sea
Seabright, Sebert, Seibert

Seabrook (English) outdoorsy
Seabrooke

Seabury (English) lives by the sea
Seaberry, Seabry

Seaby (American) form of Sebastian: dramatic; honorable

Seaman (English) seafarer

Seamus (Gaelic) replacement; bonus
Seemus, Semus

Sean ⚬ (Irish) God is gracious
Seann, Shaun, Shaune, Shawn

Searcy (English) fortified
Searcee, Searcey

Searles (English) fortified
Searl, Searle, Serles, Serls

Seaton (Place name) seaton
Seaten, Seeten, Seeton

Seaver (Last name as first name) safe
Seever

Sebastian ⚬ (Latin) dramatic; honorable
Bastian, Seb, Sebashun, Sebastien, Sebastion, Sebastuan, Sebo

Sebbie (American) form of Sebastian: dramatic; honorable

Sebe (Latin) form of Sebastian: dramatic; honorable
Seb, Sebo, Seborn, Sebron, Sebrun

Secondo (Italian) second-born boy
Segundo

Sedgley (American) classy
Sedg, Sedge, Sedgeley, Sedgely

Sedgwick (English) from the place of swords; defensive
Sedgewick, Sedgewyck, Sedgwyck

Seely (Last name as first name) fun-loving
Sealy, Sealey, Seeley

Seerath (Indian) great

Sef (Egyptian) yesterday

Seferino (Spanish) flying in the
wind
Cefirino, Sebarino, Sephirio,
Zefarin, Zefirino, Zephir, Zephyr

Sefre (Welsh) peace

Sefton (English) from the town
in the rushes; safe

Seger (Last name as first name)
singer
Seager, Seeger, Sega, Segur

Segundo (Spanish) second child

Seidon (Greek) from Greek
mythology Poseidon

Sekani (African) laughing

Sela (Hebrew) from the cliff; dares
Selah

Selby (English) from a village of
mansions; rich
Selbey, Shelbey, Shelbie, Shelby

Seldon (English) from the willow
valley; swaying
Selden, Sellden, Shelden

Selestino (Spanish) heavenly
Celeste, Celestino, Celey, Sele,
Selestyno

Selig (German) blessed boy
Seligman, Seligmann, Zelig

Selim (Turkish) safe haven

Selkirk (Scottish) church home
boy; conflicted

Sellers (English) dweller of
marshland; sturdy
Sellars

Selmo (Spanish) form of
Anselmo: protected by God

Selmy (French) form of Anselme:
protective

Selo (Biblical) place name

Selvin (English) from the woods

Selvon (American) gregarious
Sel, Selman, Selv, Selvaughn,
Selvawn

Selwyn (English) friend from the
mansion; wealthy
Selwin, Selwinn, Selwynn,
Selwynne

Semaj (Turkish) named

Semath (American) unites

Semeon (Biblical) form of
Simon: good listener; thoughtful

Seminole (Native American)
tribe name; unyielding

Semion (Slavic) form of Simon:
good listener; thoughtful

Senath (Biblical) belongs

Sender (Hebrew) form of
Alexander: great leader; helpful

Seneca (Native American) tribe
name; revered

Senen (Irish) wise boy

Senior (French) older
Sennyur, Senyur, Sinior

Sennen (English) aged

Sennett (French) old spirit
Sennet

Sentino (Italian) form of
Santino: sacred

Seppel (German) loved

Sepph (Biblical) place name

Septimus (Latin) seventh child;
neglected

Sequoia (Native American) tree;
sturdy

Serafin (Spanish) form of
Seraphim: full of fire

Seraphim (Hebrew) full of fire
Sarafim, Saraphim, Serafim,
Serephim

Sereno (Latin) serene
Cereno

Serf (Spanish) serves

Serge (French) gentle man
Serg

Sergeant (French) officer; leader
Sarge, Sargent

Sergei (Russian) good looking
Serg, Serge, Sergie, Sergy, Surge

Sergio (Italian) handsome
Serge, Sergeeo, Sergeoh, Sergyo

Serguej (Slavic) serves well

Sero (Italian) sun

Servacio (Spanish) saved

Servando (Spanish) services

Servas (Latin) saved
Servaas, Servacio, Servatus

Sesame (Botanical) seed; flavors
Sesamey, Sessame, Sessamee

Seth ⚪ (Hebrew) chosen
Sethe

Seton (English) from the sea
town; loves the water

Sevastian (American) form of
Sebastian: dramatic; honorable

Seven (American) dramatic;
seventh child
Sevene, Sevin

Several (American) multiplies
Sevral, Sevrull

Severence (French) strict
Severince, Severynce

Severin (Latin) severe
Saverino, Severinus, Seweryn

Severn (English) having
boundaries

Severo (Italian) unbending; harsh

Sevester (American) form of
Sylvester: forest-dweller; heavy-duty
Seveste, Sevy

Sevrin (Scandinavian) severe

Seward (English) guarding the sea
Sew, Sewerd, Sward

Sewell (Last name as first name)
seaward
Seawel, Seawell, Sewel

Sexton (English) church-loving
Sextan, Sextin, Sextown

Sextus (Latin) sixth child;
mischievous
Sesto, Sixto, Sixtus

Seymour (French) prayerful
Seamore, See, Seye, Seymore

Shaamar (Biblical) name spelled
backward

Shabat (Hebrew) the end
Shabbat

Shachar (Hebrew) the dawn

Shad (African) joyful

Shade (English) secretive
Shadee, Shadey, Shady

Shadman (Hebrew) farm

Shadow (English) mystique
Shade, Shadoe

Shadrach (Biblical) godlike;
brave
*Shad, Shadd, Shadrack, Shadreck,
Shadryack*

Shadrie (Biblical) form of
Shadrach: godlike; brave

Shaff (American) companion

Shafiq (Arabic) forgiving
Shafeek, Shafik

Shafir (Hebrew) handsome
Shafeer, Shafer, Shefer

Shago (American) casual

Shahzad (Persian) royalty; king

Shai (Hebrew) the gift

Shaikh (French) severe

Shak (Arabic) attracts

Shakil (Arabic) attractive
*Shakeel, Shakill, Shakille,
Shaqueel, Shaquil, Shaquille*

Shakir (Arabic) appreciative
Shakee, Shakeer

Shakunt (Indian) bluebird

Shakur (Arabic) thankful
Shakurr

Shale (Hebrew) form of Shalev:
calm
Shaile, Shayle

Shalev (Hebrew) calm

Shalom (Hebrew) peaceful
Sholem, Sholom

Shalu (American) peace

Sham (Biblical) armed

Shaman (Russian) mystical
Shamain, Shamon, Shayman

Shamar (Indian) proud

Shamir (Hebrew) thorn
Shameer

Shammah (Biblical) devout

Shamus (Irish) seizing
Schaemus, Schamus, Shamuss

Shan (Hindi) bright sun

Shanahan (Irish) giving
Shanihan, Shanyhan

Shance (American) form of
Chance: good fortune; happy
Shan, Shanse

Shand (English) loud
Shandy

Shandee (English) noisy
Shandi, Shandy

Shane (Irish) easygoing
Shain, Shay, Shayne

Shani (African) a wonder;
(Hebrew) red

Shanley (Irish) old soul
Shannley

Shannon (Irish) wise
Shana, Shanan, Shane, Shanen,
Shann, Shannen, Shanon

Shantam (Hindi) bright sun

Shantan (Sanskrit) peaceful

Shante (American) poised
Shantae, Shantay

Shap (English) form of Shep:
watchful

Shapleigh (English) form of
Shepley: from the sheep meadow;
tender

Shaq (Arabic) form of Shaquille:
handsome
Shack, Shak

Shaquille (Arabic) handsome
Shak, Shakeel, Shaq, Shaquil,
Shaquill

Sharad (Indian) fall season

Sharif (Arabic) truthful
Shareef, Sheref

Sharkie (American) crafty

Sharman (American) magic man

Sharp (Word as name) bright

Shashee (Indian) moon

Shashhi (Hindi) moon

Shasta (Place name) Oregon
mountain; high hopes

Shaun (Irish) form of Sean: God
is gracious
Seanne, Shaune, Shaunn

Shaw (English) safe; in a tree
grove
Shawe

Shawn (Irish) form of Sean: God
is gracious
Shawnay, Shawne, Shawnee,
Shawney

Shawnell (African American)
talkative
Shaunell

Shawner (American) form of
Shawn: God is gracious

Shawon (African American)
optimistic
Shawan, Shawaughn, Shawaun

Shay (Irish) form of Shamus:
seizing
Shai

Shayan (Native American) from
Cheyenne; tribe; erratic

Shayde (Irish) confident
Shaedy, Sheade

Shaykeen (African American)
successful
Shay, Shaykine

Shea (Irish) vital
Shay

Sheamus (Irish) form of James:
he who supplants

Sheban (Biblical) sworn

Shechem (Biblical)

Sheehan (Irish) clever
Shehan, Shihan

Sheen (English) bright and
shining; talented
Shean, Sheene

Shehzad (Arabic) prince

Shel (Hebrew) mine

Shelah (Biblical) vivacious

Shelby (English) established
Shel, Shelbee, Shelbey, Shelbie,
Shell, Shelly

Sheldon (English) quiet
Shel, Sheld, Shelden, Sheldin,
Shell, Shelly

Shell (English) form of Sheldon: quiet

Shelley (English) form of Shelby: established
Shelly

Shelton (English) from the village of ledges

Shem (Hebrew) famous

Shen (Chinese) introspective

Shenandoah (Place name) valley; nostalgic

Sheng (Chinese) winning

Shep (English) watchful
Shepp, Sheppy

Shepal (English) herds sheep

Shepher (English) sheep herder

Shepherd (Last name as first name) vigilant; (English) herds sheep
Shepard, Sheperd, Shephard

Shepho (Biblical) herds sheep

Shepley (English) from the sheep meadow; tender
Sheplea, Shepleigh, Shepply, Shipley

Sherag (Jewish) bright

Sherborn (English) from the bright shiny stream; careful
Sherborne, Sherbourn, Sherburn, Sherburne

Sheridan (Irish) wild-spirited
Sharidan, Sheridon, Sherr, Sherrey, Shuridun

Sheridun (Irish) confident

Sherill (English) from the shining hill; special
Sherrill

Sherlock (English) fair-haired; smart
Sherlocke, Shurlock

Sherm (English) worker; shears
Shermy

Sherman (English) tough-willed
Cherman, Shermann, Shermy, Shurman

Sherrerd (English) from open land; rancher
Sherard, Sherrard, Sherrod

Sherrick (Last name as first name) already gone
Sherric, Sherrik, Sherryc, Sherryck, Sherryk

Sherris (English) herds sheep

Sherwin (English) fleet of foot
Sherwind, Sherwinn, Sherwyn, Sherwynne

Sherwood (English) bright options
Sherwoode, Shurwood, Woodie, Woody

Shevon (African American) zany
Shavonne, Shevaughan, Shevaughn

Shiloh (Hebrew) gift from God; charmer
Shile, Shilo, Shy, Shye

Shimron (Biblical) place name

Shin (Korean) faithful

Shine (American) shines

Shiney (American) luminescent

Shing (Chinese) wins

Shingo (Japanese) clutch

Shipley (English) meadow of sheep
Ship

Shipton (English) from the ship village; sailor

Shire (Place name) English county; humorous
Shyre

Shirely (English) of the shire

Shishir (Indian) season

Shiva (Hindi) of great depth and range; life/death
Shiv

Shlomo (Hebrew) form of Solomon: peaceful and wise
Shelomi, Shelomo, Shlomi

Shmuel (Hebrew) form of Samuel: man who heard God; prophet

Shomer (Hebrew) watches

Shon (American) form of Shawn:
God is gracious
Sean, Shaun, Shonn

Shontae (African American)
hopeful
Shauntae, Shauntay, Shawntae,
Shontay, Shontee, Shonti, Shontie,
Shonty

Shorty (American) small in
stature
Shortey, Shorti

Shoshone (Native American)
tribe; wanderer
Shoshoni

Shoval (Hebrew) on the right path

Shreya (Indian) best

Shuan (Mythology) dark place

Shunem (Biblical) place name

Shur (Biblical) place name

Shura (Russian) protective
Schura, Shoura

Shuu (Japanese) responsible

Shyam (Hindi) dark

Si (Hebrew) form of Simon: good
listener; thoughtful
Sy

Sichuan (Place name) Chinese

Sicily (Place name) traveler
Sicilly

Sid (French) form of Sidney:
attractive
Cyd, Sidd, Siddie, Siddy, Syd, Sydd

Side (Biblical) place name

Sidel (English) valley child

Sidney (French) attractive
Ciddie, Cidnie, Cyd, Cydnee,
Sidnee, Sidnie, Syd, Sydney

Sidon (Biblical) place name

Sidonio (Spanish) form of
Sidney: attractive

Sidor (Russian) gifted
Isidor, Sydor

Sidromio (Spanish) form of
Sydney: attractive

Sidus (Latin) star
Sydus

Siegbert (German) wins

Siegfried (German) victor
Siegfred, Sig, Sigfred, Sigfrid,
Siggee, Siggie, Siggy

Siello (Indian) superb

Sierra (Spanish) dangerous
See-see, Serra, Siera, Sierrah

Sig (German) form of Sigmund
and Siegfried: victor
Siggey, Siggi, Sigi, Syg

Sigga (Scandinavian) form of
Siegfried: victor
Sig

Sigge (German) form of
Sigmund: victor

Sigmund (German) victor
Siegmund, Sig, Siggi, Siggy, Sigi,
Sigmon, Sigmond

Signe (Scandinavian) victor
Signy

Sigoph (Biblical) place name

Sigurd (Scandinavian) winning
personality

Sigus (German) winner

Sigwald (German) leader
Siegwald

Sil (Spanish) light

Silar (American Indian) leader

Silas (Latin) saver
Si, Siles, Silus

Sill (English) beam of light
Sills

Silo (Scandinavian) legendary

Siloam (Biblical) place name

Silous (American) form of Silas:
saver
Si, Silouz

Silvano (Latin) of the woods;
unique
Silvan, Silvani, Silvio, Sylvan

Silvanus (Mythology) woodland

Silver (Latin) silver
Sylver

Silverman (German) works with silver; craftsman

Silverton (English) from the town of silversmiths
Silvertown

Silvester (Latin) from the woods
Silvestre, Silvestro, Sylvester

Silvio (Italian) sylvan

Sim (African) form of Simba: lionlike

Simba (African) lionlike

Simcha (Hebrew) joyful

Siment (Scandinavian) form of Simon: good listener; thoughtful

Simeon (French) listener
Si, Simion, Simone, Simyon, Sy

Simington (English) devout

Simmon (Hebrew) devout

Simms (Hebrew) good listener
Sims

Simon (Hebrew) good listener; thoughtful
Si, Siman, Simen, Simeon, Simmy, Sye, Symon, Syms

Simpson (Hebrew) simplistic
Simpsen, Simpsun, Simson

Simran (Indian) God loves

Simus (Biblical) form of Onesimus: profits

Sinc (Native American) leader

Sinclair (French) prayerful
Clair, Sinc, Sinclare, Synclaire

Sinclar (French) prays

Sindbad (Literature) from *The Arabian Nights*; daring
Sinbad

Sindry (Mythology) shines

Singer (Last name as first name) vocalist
Synger

Singh (Hindi) lion's courage

Singo (American) genuine

Sinjin (English) form of St. John

Sion (Hebrew) heavenly peak
Zion

Sione (African) believer

Sipher (American) treasure

Siraj (Arabic) shines

Sirion (Biblical) place name

Siris (Egyptian) starlike

Sirius (Greek) shining

Sissel (Greek) difficult

Sisto (American) cowboy

Sisyphus (Greek) in mythology

Sivney (Irish) satisfied
Sivneigh, Sivnie

Six (American) number as name
Syx

Sixto (Greek) well-mannered

Sixtus (Latin) sixth child

Skay (Native American) white

Skeeter (English) fast
Skeater, Skeet, Skeets

Skeetz (American) zany
Skeet, Skeeter, Skeets

Skelly (Irish) bard
Scully

Skerry (Scandinavian) from the island of stone; pragmatist

Ski (Scandinavian) sends out

Skilling (English) masterful
Skillings

Skinner (English) skins for a living

Skip (American) form of Skipper: shipmaster
Skipp, Skyp, Skyppe

Skipper (American) shipmaster

Skippy (American) fast
Skippee, Skippie, Skyppey

Skye (Dutch) goal-oriented
Sky

Skylar (Dutch) protective
Skilar, Skye, Skyeler, Skylir

Slade (English) quiet child
Slaid, Slaide, Slayd, Slayde

Sladen (English) valley child

Sladkey (Slavic) glorious
Sladkie

Slam (American) friendly
Slams, Slamz

Slane (Irish) good health

Slap (American) casual

Slater (Last name as first name) precocious

Slaiter, Slayter

Slatter (English) works on roofs

Slav (Russian) glorified

Slava (Russian) form of Stanislav: glory in leading

Slavek (Polish) smart; glorious

Slavec, Slavik

Slavin (Irish) mountain man; hermit

Slaven, Slawin

Slawomir (Slavic) great glory; famed

Slavek, Slavomir

Slim (English) nickname for slim guy

Sloan (Irish) sleek

Sloane, Slonne

Slocum (Last name as first name) happy

Slo, Slocom, Slocumb

Slover (Last name as first name) slove

Sly (Latin) form of Sylvester: forest-dweller; heavy-duty

Smedley (English) of the flat meadow

Smedleigh, Smedly

Smerdyakov (Russian) sinister

Smith (English) crafty; blacksmith

Smid, Smidt, Smit, Smitt, Smitti, Smitty

Smithson (Last name as first name) son of Smith; craftsman

Smitty (English) craftsman

Smittey

Smokey (American) smokin'

Smoke, Smokee, Smoky

Snake (Place name) U.S. river

Snead (English) Last name as first name

Snowden (English) from a snowy hill; fresh

Snowdon

Snyder (German) tailor's clothing; stylish

Schneiger, Snider

So (Vietnamese) smart

Socorro (Spanish) helpful

Sokorro

Socrates (Greek) philosophical; brilliant

Socratez, Socratis, Sokrates

Soeren (Scandinavian) sun ray

Sofian (Arabic) devoted

Sofus (Greek) wise

Sophus

Sogane (Biblical) place name

Sohan (Hindi) charmer; handsome

Sohil (Hindi) beautiful

Sol (Hebrew) form of Solomon: peaceful and wise

Solly

Solano (Latin) from the east

Solly (Hebrew) form of Solomon: peaceful and wise

Sollee, Solley, Solli, Sollie

Solomon (Hebrew) peaceful and wise

Salamon, Sol, Sollie, Solly, Soloman

Somerby (English) from the summer village; lighthearted

Somerbie, Somersby, Sommersby

Somerley (Irish) summer sailor

Somerled, Sorley

Somers (English) loving summer

Sommers

Somerset (English) talented

Somer, Somers, Sommerset, Summerset

Somerton (English) from the summer town

Somervile, Somerville

Sommar (English) summer

Somer, Somers, Somm, Sommars, Sommer

Son (English) boy
Sonni, Sonnie, Sonny

Sonny (English) boy
Son, Sonney, Sonni, Sonnie

Sonteeahgo (Invented) form of Santiago: sainted; valuable

Sophocles (Greek) playwright

Sorel (Botanical) form of Sorrel: reddish-brown horse; horse lover

Soren (Scandinavian) good communicator
Soryn

Sorrel (French) reddish-brown horse; horse lover
Sorre, Sorrell, Sorrey

Sorren (Scandinavian) sun ray

Sosimo (Spanish) promise

Sothern (English) from the south; warmhearted
Southern

Sound (American) word as a name; dynamic

Sousan (French) underdog

Southwell (English) living by the southern well

Sovann (Asian) golden

Spanky (American) outspoken; stubborn
Spank, Spankee, Spankie

Sparks (English) happy

Sparky (Latin) ball of fire; joyful
Spark, Sparkee, Sparkey, Sparki, Sparkie

Sparta (Biblical) place name

Spas (Slavic) saved by God

Spaulding (Last name as first name) comic
Spalding, Spaldying, Spauldyng

Specie (American) special child

Speed (English) plucky

Speedy (English) fast

Speers (English) good with spears; swift-moving
Speares, Spears, Spiers

Spence (English) form of Spencer: giver; provides well
Spens, Spense

Spencer (English) giver; provides well
Spence, Spencey, Spenser, Spensor, Spensy

Sperry (Last name as first name) inventive
Sperrey

Spider (American) scary
Spyder

Spidey (American) zany

Spike (American) word as name
Spiker

Spiker (English) go-getter
Spike, Spikey, Spyk

Spillane (American) funloving

Spiridon (Greek) like a breath of fresh air
Speero, Spero, Spiridon, Spiro, Spiros, Spyridon, Spyros

Spiro (Greek) coil; spiral
Spi, Spiroh, Spiros, Spy, Spyro

Sprague (French) high-energy

Springer (English) fresh
Spring

Sprinter (American) runner

Spud (English) energetic

Spunk (American) spunky; lively
Spunki, Spunky

Spurgeon (Botanical) from the shrub spurge; natural
Spurge

Spurs (American) boot devices used to spur horses; cowboy
Spur

Spyros (Greek) round

Squire (English) land-loving
Squirre, Skwyre

Sravanthi (Indian) old soul

Stace (English) optimist
Stayce

Stacey (English) hopeful
Stace, Stacee, Stacy, Stase, Stasi

Stackler (Last name as first name) aligned

Stadler (Last name as first name)
staid
Stadtler

Staffan (Slavic) crowned

Stafford (English) dignified
*Staff, Staffard, Stafferd, Staffi,
Staffie, Staffor, Staffy*

Stagio (Italian) of the stage

Stajonne (Slavic) form of Stoyan:
loyal

Stamos (Greek) reasonable
Stammos, Stamohs

Stan (Latin) form of Stanley:
traveler

Stanbury (English) fortified
*Stanberry, Stanbery, Stanburghe,
Stansberry, Stansburghe, Stansbury*

Stancliff (English) from the
stone cliff; prepared
*Stancliffe, Stanclyffe, Stanscliff,
Stanscliffe*

Standa (Slavic) glory

Standish (English) farsighted
Standysh

Standley (English) travels

Stanfield (English) from the
stone field; able
Stansfield

Stanford (English) dignified
Stan, Stanferd, Stann

Stanislaus (Latin) glorious
*Staneslaus, Stanis, Stanislus, Stann,
Stanus*

Stanislav (Russian) glory in
leading
Slava, Stasi

Stanley (English) traveler
*Stan, Stanlea, Stanlee, Stanli,
Stanly*

Stanmore (English) lake of
stones; ill-fated

Stanton (English) stone-hard
Stan

Stanway (English) came from the
stone road
Stanaway, Stannaway, Stannway

Stanwick (English) born in
village of stone; hard
Stanwicke, Stanwyck

Stanwood (English) stone woods
man; tough

Stark (German) high-energy
Starke, Starkey

Starling (English) singer; bird
Starlling

Starr (English) bright star
Star, Starri, Starrie, Starry

Stash (Russian) form of Stanislav:
glory in leading

Stavros (Greek) winner
Stavrohs, Stavrows

Stavrus (Greek) cross

Steadman (English) landowner;
wealthy
Steadmann, Sted, Stedmann

Steaven (Scottish) form of
Steven: victorious

Steed (English) horse of high
spirits

Steele (English) hardworking
Steel, Stille

Stefan (Scandinavian) crowned;
(German) chosen one
*Stefawn, Steff, Steffan, Steffie,
Steffon, Steffy, Stefin, Stephan*

Stefano (Italian) supreme ruler
*Stef, Steffie, Steffy, Stephano,
Stephanos*

Stehlin (Last name as first name)
genius
Staylin, Stealan, Stehlan

Stein (German) stonelike
Steen, Sten, Steno

Steinar (Scandinavian) muse;
rock
Steinard, Steinart, Steinhardt

Steinbeck (Last name as first)
writer John

Stelios (Greek) community hero

Stellan (Swedish) star

Sten (Scandinavian) star stone
Stene, Stine

Stennis (Scottish) prehistoric standing stones; eternal

Stepan (English) form of Stephen: victorious
Stepen, Stepyn

Steph (English) form of Stephen: victorious
Stef, Steff, Steffy

Stephan (Greek) form of Stephen: victorious

Stephanos (Greek) crowned; martyr
Stef, Stefanos, Steph, Stephanas

Stephen (Greek) victorious
Stephan, Stephon, Stevee, Steven, Stevey, Stevi, Stevie, Stevy

Stephene (French) form of Stephen: victorious
Stef, Steff, Steph

Stephine (French) wins

Sterl (English) valuable

Sterling (English) worthwhile

Stern (German) bright; serious
Stearn, Sterns

Stetson (American) cowboy
Stetsen, Stetsun, Stettson

Steubing (Last name as first name) stepping
Steuben, Stu, Stuben, Stubing

Steve (Greek) form of Steven or Stephen: victorious
Stevie

Steven (Greek) victorious
Stevan, Steve, Stevey, Stevie

Steveo (American) form of Steve: victorious

Stevie (English) form of Steven: victorious
Stevee, Stevey, Stevi, Stevy

Stevland (English) steve's place

Stewart (English) form of Stuart: careful; watchful
Stewert, Stu, Stuie

Stian (Scandinavian) traveler

Stieran (Scandinavian) wandering
Steeran, Steeren, Steeryn, Stieren, Stieryn

Stig (Scandinavian) upwardly mobile
Stigg, Styg, Stygg

Stiles (English) practical
Stile, Stiley, Styles

Stillman (English) quiet boy

Sting (English) spike of grain

Stoat (English) small mammal also called ermine; white
Stoate, Stote

Stobart (German) harsh
Stobe, Stobey, Stoby

Stock (American) macho
Stok

Stockard (English) dramatic
Stock, Stockerd, Stockord

Stockdale (English) from meadow with trees

Stocker (English) foundation
Stock

Stockett (English) from meadow with trees

Stockley (English) in a field of tree stumps stock; rooted in reality

Stockton (English) strong foundation
Stockten

Stockwell (English) from the well by tree stumps; grounded

Stoddard (English) caretaker of horses
Stoddart

Stokley (English) stokes the fire

Stoli (Russian) celebrant

Stone (English) athletic
Stonee, Stoney, Stonie, Stony

Stonewall (English) fortified
Stone, Stoney, Wall

Stoney (American) form of Stone: athletic
Stonee, Stoni, Stonie

Stonne (English) stone

Storey (English) one story of a house; storyteller
Story

Storm (English) impetuous; volatile
Storme, Stormy

Stowe (English) secretive
Stow, Stowey

Stoy (Slavic) steadfast

Stoyan (Slavic) loyal

Strahan (Irish) sings stories
Strachan

Stratan (Greek) from the army

Stratford (English) river-crossing boy; happy
Strafford

Strato (Invented) strategic
Strat, Stratt

Stratton (Scottish) home-loving
Straton, Strattawn

Straus (German) ostrich; in disbelief
Strauss

Strausser (Last name as first name)

Stretch (American) easygoing
Stretcher

Strickland (English) field of flax; outdoorsy

Strider (Literature) from Tolkien's *Lord of the Rings*; great warrior

Strike (American) word as name; aggressive
Striker

Stroheim (Last name as first name) great director

Strom (German) water-lover
Strome, Stromm

Strong (English) strength of character

Strother (Irish) strict
Strothers, Struther, Struthers

Struther (Last name as first name) flowing
Strother, Strothers, Struthers

Stu (English) form of Stuart: careful; watchful
Stew, Stue, Stuey

Stuart (English) careful; watchful
Stewart, Stu, Stuey

Studs (American) cocky; (English) wears studs; masculine
Studd, Studds

Sture (Scandinavian) difficult
Sturah

Styles (English) practical
Stile, Stiles, Style

Stylianos (Greek) stylish
Styli

Sudal (Indian) good

Sudarshan (Indian) handsome

Sudbury (English) southern town boy; lackadaisical
Sudbery, Sudberry, Sudborough

Sudhakar (Indian) good; sweet nectar

Suede (Arabic) leader

Suffield (English) man from the south field

Suffolk (English) from southern folks

Sugar-Ray (American) strong; singer
Sugar Ray

Sujay (Hindi) good
Sujit

Sujit (Indian) wins

Sulaiman (Arabic) loves peace
Suleiman, Suleyman

Sullivan (Irish) dark-eyed; quiet
Sullavan, Sullie, Sullivahn, Sully

Sully (Irish) melancholy; hushed
Sull, Sullee, Sulley, Sullie

Sultan (American) bold
Sultane, Sulten, Sultin

Suman (Hindi) ingenious

Sumano (Spanish) smart

Sumarto (Indian) good

Sumit (Indian) measured

Sumner (Last name as first name) honorable; fortified

Sumney (American) ethereal
Summ, Summy, Sumnee, Sumnie
Sunder (Indian) handsome
Sunil (Hindi) blue; sad
Sunny (American) happy baby boy
Sunney, Sunnie
Suresh (Indian) sun
Surian (Sanskrit) sun
Surinder (Indian) believes in
Indra
Surya (Indian) sun
Sutcliff (English) from the south
cliff; edgy
Sutcliffe
Sutherland (Scandinavian)
sunny; southerner
Southerland
Sutter (English) southern
Sutt, Suttee, Sutty
Sutterly (English) southerner
Sutton (English) sunny;
southerner
Suvomoy (Indian) religious
Suvrat (Indian) devout
Svatomir (Slavic) known for
being spiritual
Svatoslav (Slavic) having the
glory of being devout
Sven (Scandinavian) young boy
Svein, Svend, Swen
Svendin (Scandinavian) young

Svere (Scandinavian) untamed
Swahili (Arabic) language of East
Africa; verbal
Swain (English) rigid; leading the
herd
Swaine, Swayne
Swanton (English) where swans
live; sylvan boy
Swapnil (Indian) fantasy
Sween (Irish) ambitious
Sweeney (Irish) hero
Schwennie, Sweeny
Swen (Scandinavian) form of
Sven: young boy
Swift (English) fast
Swifty
Swinburne (English) seeing pigs
in the stream
*Swinborn, Swinbourne, Swinburn,
Swinbyrn, Swynborne*
Swindell (English) polished
Schwindell, Swin, Swindel
Swinford (English) seeing pigs in
the ford
Swynford
Swinton (English) from the town
of swine
Swithin (English) swift
Swithinn, Swithun
Sy (Latin) form of Silas: saver
Si, Sylas

Sychar (Biblical) place name
Sydney (French) form of Sidney:
attractive
Cyd, Syd, Sydie
Sye (Latin) form of Silas: saver
Syfron (American) form of
Saffron: spice/plant; orange-haired
Sylvain (Latin) reclusive
Syl
Sylvan (Spanish) nature-loving
Silvan, Syl, Sylvany, Sylvin
Sylvester (Latin) forest dweller;
heavy-duty
Sil, Silvester, Sly, Syl
Symms (Last name as first name)
landowner
Symotris (African American)
fortunate
Sym, Symetris, Symotrice, Syms
Synklair (American) form of
Sinclair: prayerful
Syon (Sanskrit) lucky boy
Syrtis (Biblical) place name

Taanach (Biblical) place name

Tab (German) intelligent
Tabbey, Tabby

Tabbai (Hebrew) good boy

Tabbebo (Native American) boy
of the sun

Tabib (Turkish) physician
Tabeeb

Tabor (Aramaic) unfortunate
Taber, Taibor, Tayber, Taybor

Tack (American) popular

Taco (Spanish) thoughtful

Tad (Greek) form of Thaddeus:
courageous
*Tadd, Taddee, Taddey, Taddie,
Taddy*

Tadashi (Japanese) loyal

Taddeo (Italian) form of
Thaddeus: courageous

Taden (Native American)
bountiful

Tadeu (Slavic) praised

Tadeusz (Polish) praise-worthy;
(Slavic) worthy
Tad, Taduce

Tadhg (Irish) poetic
Taidghin, Teague, Teige

Tadi (Native American) wind
child

Tadmor (Biblical) place name

Tadros (Slavic) brave

Tadzi (Polish) praised

Tae (Irish) poetic

Tafar (African) impressive

Taff (American) sweet
Taf, Taffee, Taffey, Taffi, Taffy

Taft (English) flowing
Tafte, Taftie, Taffy

Taggart (Last name as first
name) keeps track; singer

Taghee (Native American) chief
Taighe, Taihee, Tyee, Tyhee

Tague (Scandinavian) star of the
day

Taha (Polynesian) first
Tahatan

Taher (Arabic) cleansed

Taheton (Native American) like
a hawk

Tahi (Polynesian) by the sea

Tahir (African) pure

Tahj (African) crowned

Tahl (Hebrew) rainy

Tahoe (Place name) Lake Tahoe
Taho

Tahoma (Native American)
mountain peak; high hopes
Tohoma

Tahti (Scandinavian) shining star

Tai (Vietnamese) talented

Taillam (French) works iron

Taima (Native American) storm
baby

Taimah (Native American)
thunder

Tair (Arabic) form of Tahir: pure

Taisto (Scandinavian) fighter

Tait (Scandinavian) form of Tate:
happy

Taiwo (African) first of twins

Taizo (Japanese) third son

Taj (Sanskrit) royal; crowned

Takao (Asian) strong

Takeshi (Japanese) unbending

Taklishim (Native American)
gray-haired

Takoda (Native American) friend

Tal (Hebrew) worrier
Tallee, Talley, Talli, Tally

Talal (Indian) prayerful

Talan (American) opportunistic

Talat (Arabic) prays

Talbot (French) skillful
*Tal, Talbert, Talbott, Tallbot,
Tallbott, Tally*

Talcot (English) lake-cottage
dweller; laidback

Tale (African) green; open

Talfryn (Welsh) on the high hill

Talib (African) looking for
enlightenment

Taliesin (Welsh) head that shines
Taltesin

Talli (Hebrew) dew; fresh

Talm (Aramaic) hurt

Talmadge (English) natural; living by lakes
Tal, Tally, Tamidge

Talmai (Aramaic) born on a hill

Talman (Hebrew) from my hill
Tallie, Tally, Talmon

Talon (French) wily
Tallie, Tallon, Tally, Tawlon

Talor (French) cutter; tailor

Tam (Hebrew) truthful
Tammy

Taman (Hindi) needed

Tamar (Hebrew) grows dates

Tamarius (African American) stubborn
Tam, Tamerius, Tammy, T'Marius

Tamer (Arabic) tall

Tamir (Arabic) owner

Tammany (Native American) friendly boy
Tamanend

Tammy (English) form of Thomas: twin; look-alike; form of Tamarius: stubborn
Tammee, Tammey, Tammie

Tan (Japanese) high achiever

Tanafa (Polynesian) drumbeat

Tanaki (Polynesian) boy who counts

Tanay (Hindi) son

Tandie (African American) virile

Tandy (English) together

Tane (Polynesian) sky god; fertile
Tain

Tangaloa (Polynesian) gutsy

Tangie (French) battles

Tanh (Vietnamese) having his way

Tani (African American) form of Tanier: tanner of skins

Tank (American) big; bullish

Tankie (American) large
Tank, Tankee, Tanky

Tanmay (Indian) mesmerizing

Tanner ❶ (English) tanner of skins
Tan, Tanier, Tann, Tannar, Tanne, Tanney, Tannie, Tannor, Tanny

Tano (Ghanese) named for the river

Tanom (American) creative

Tanton (English) town of tanners

Tanveer (Indian) informed

Taos (Place name) town in New Mexico
Tao, Tayo

Tap (American) light touch
Tapp, Tappi, Tappy

Tapan (Indian) sun

Tarek (Indian) star

Tarem (American) the son

Taren (French) God's gift

Tarentum (Biblical) place name

Tarhe (Native American) strength of a tree

Tarick (American) form of Tarek: star

Tarik (Arabic) knocks
Taril, Tarin, Tariq

Tariq (African American) conqueror
Tarik

Tarking (Arabic) summons

Tarlach (Hebrew) wild

Tarleton (English) stormy
Tally, Tarlton

Tarm (Scandinavian) energy

Tarmo (Scandinavian) energy

Taro (Japanese) firstborn son

Tarquin (Roman clan) impulsive

Tarrance (Latin) smooth
Terance, Terrance, Terry

Tarrant (Place name) county in Texas; lawful

Tarri (American) form of Terry: tender
Tari, Tarree, Tarrey, Tarry

Tarso (Italian) dashing

Tarsus (Biblical) place name

Tarum (Indian) young

Tarun (Arabic) knocks

Tarvin (English) on the hill

Tary (American) form of Terry: tender

Taryll (American) form of
Terrell: puller
Tarell

Tas (Place name) from Tasmania
Taz

Tashunka (Native American)
horse lover
Tasunke

Tasi (Greek) on the mark

Taso (Greek) on the mark

Tassilo (Scandinavian) fearless
protector

Tasso (Greek) on the mark

Tassos (Italian) dark

Tatankamimi (Native
American) the buffalo walks

Tate (English) happy
Tait, Taitt, Tatey, Tayt, Tayte

Taten (Scandinavian) happy

Tatlock (English) happy

Tatonga (Native American) deer;
swift

Tatry (Place name) mountains in
Poland
Tate, Tatree, Tatri

Tau (African) leonine

Taufiq (Arabic) wins

Tauney (English) form of Tawny:
tan-skinned

Taurean (African American)
reclusive; quiet
Taureen

Taurino (Italian) reserved

Taurus (Astrological sign) macho
Tar, Taur, Tauras, Taures

Tava (Polynesian) fruit; fertile

Tavares (African American)
hopeful
Tavarus

Tavarius (African American)
fun-loving
Tav, Taverius, Tavurius, Tavvy

Tavas (Hebrew) peacock;
handsome

Taven (Scandinavian) form of
Tavi: good

Tavi (Scandinavian) form of
David: beloved; (Aramaic) good

Tavish (Scottish) upbeat
Tav, Taven, Tavis, Tevis

Tavium (Biblical) place name

Tavor (Aramaic) unfortunate
Tabor

Taw (African) form of Tau:
leonine

Tawa (Native American) sun boy

Tawagahe (Native American)
builder

Tawanima (Native American)
measures the sun
Tewanima

Tawfiq (Arabic) fortunate
Tawfi

Tawl (Arabic) tall
Taweel

Tawno (American) small

Tay (Scottish) river in Scotland;
jaunty
Tae, Taye

Tayhan (Last name as first name)

Tayib (Arabic) city in Israel;
spiritual

Taylor ❶ (English) tailor
Tailor, Talor, Tayler, Tayley

Tayton (American) form of
Payton: soldier's town
Tate, Taye, Tayte, Tayten, Taytin

Tayve (Scandinavian) form of
David: beloved

Taz (Arabic) cup; vibrant

Teagu (Irish) poetic

Teague (Celtic) poet
Teaguey, Tege

Teal (English) duck

Tearlach (Scottish) adult man;
bold

Techomir (Czech) famed comfort

Techoslav (Slavic) glorious
comfort

Tecumseh (Native American) shooting star; bright

Ted (English) form of Theodore: God's gift; a blessing
Teddee, Teddey, Teddi, Teddy

Teddy-Blue (American) smiley
Blu, Blue, Teddie-Blue, Teddy, Teddyblu, Teddy-Blu, Teddyblue

Tedmund (American) shy
Tedmond

Tedrick (African American) form of Cedric: leader
Ted, Tedrik

Tegan (Celtic) doe
Tege, Tegen, Tegun, Teige

Tego (Irish) form of Teague: poetic

Tehaney (English) reddish-brown

Tejomay (Hindi) glorious
Tej

Tejraj (Indian) sharp

Teklad (Slavic) wonder

Tekoa (Biblical) place name

Tekonsha (Native American) caribou

Telamon (Greek) mythological hero

Telek (Polish) ironworker

Telem (Hebrew) their dew; their shadow

Telemachus (Mythological) son of Ulysses

Telesforo (Spanish) country boy

Telesphoros (Greek) leading to an end; centered

Telford (English) cutting iron; targeted
Telfer, Telfor, Telfour

Teller (English) relates stories; storytelling
Tellie, Telly

Tello (German) reformed

Telmo (English) works earth

Telvis (American) form of Elvis: all-wise
Telly

Tem (African) form of Teman: spiritual

Tema (Biblical) southerner

Teman (Hebrew) spiritual (Temani are Jews from Yemen)

Tempest (French) stormy; volatile
Tempie, Tempy, Tempyst

Templar (Latin) form of Temple: spiritual

Temple (Latin) spiritual; temple
Tempie, Templle, Tempy

Templeton (English) from a religious place
Temp, Tempie, Temple, Temps

Temre (American) spices

Ten (American) tenth

Tendoy (Native American) he who climbs higher
Tendoi

Teneangopte (Native American) bird; flies high

Tennant (American) capable
Tenn

Tennessee (Native American) able fighter; U.S. state
Tenns, Tenny

Tennison (English) creates

Tenny (English) creative

Tennyson (English) storyteller
Tenie, Tenn, Tenney, Tenneyson, Tennie, Tenny, Tennysen

Tensk (Native American) open

Teo (Greek) gift of God

Teodo (Greek) form of Theodore: God's gift; a blessing

Teodoro (Spanish) God's gift
Tedoro, Teo, Teodore, Theo

Teofanes (Spanish) God-loving

Teofilo (Greek) God-loving

Tephon (Biblical) place name

Teppo (Scandinavian) from Stephen: victorious

TeQuarius (African American) secretive
Teq, Tequarius, Tequie

Terach (Hebrew) wild goat; contentious
Tera, Terah

Terak (Biblical) established

Terard (Invented) form of Gerard: brave
Terar, Tererd, Terry

Tercer (Spanish) third baby

Tercero (Spanish) third baby

Terence (Irish) tender
Tarrance, Terencio, Terrance, Terrence, Terrey, Terri, Terry

TeRez (African American) creative

Terhea (American) from the oak tree

Terl (German) ruler

Term (Latin) terminates

Termell (Invented) form of Terrell: puller
Termel

Teron (Greek) hunter; calms

Terrance (Latin) calm
Terance, Terence, Terre, Terree, Terrence, Terrie, Terry

Terrell (French) puller

Terrelle (German) thunderous; outspoken
Terel, Terele, Terell, Teril, Terille, Terral, Terrale, Terre, Terrel, Terril, Terrill, Terrille, Terry, Tirill, Tirrill, Tyrel, Tyril

Terrien (Greek) hunts; calms

Terron (Greek) hunts

Terry (English) form of Terence: tender
Terree, Terrey, Terri, Terrie

Tesher (Hebrew) gift

Teshombe (African American) able

Tet (Vietnamese) Vietnamese New Year

Teunis (Dutch) form of Antonio: superb

Teva (Hebrew) natural
Tevah

Tevaughn (African American) tiger
Tev, Tevan, Tevaughan, Tivan, Tivaughan

Tevey (Hebrew) good
Tev, Tevi, Tevie

Tevin (African American) outgoing
Tev, Tevan, Tivan

Tevis (American) flamboyant
Tev, Tevas, Teves, Teviss, Tevy

Tex (American) from Texas; cowboy
Texas, Texx

Texas (Place name) U.S. state; cowboy
Tex

Thabiti (African) real man

Thabo (African) joyful

Thad (Greek) form of Thaddeus: courageous
Thadd, Thaddy

Thaddeous (Greek) form of Thaddeus: courageous

Thaddeus (Greek) courageous
Taddeo, Tadeo, Tadio, Thad, Thaddaus, Thaddius, Thaddy, Thadeus, Thadius

Thaddus (African) brave

Thady (Irish) thankful
Thad, Thaddee, Thaddie, Thaddy, Thads

Thai (Vietnamese) winner

Thais (Asian) flourishes

Thalan (Irish) charming

Thamar (Biblical) form of Ithamar: island of the palm trees

Thamer (American) helpful

Thanatos (Greek) dies

Thandiwe (African) loved

Thane (English) protective
Thain, Thaine, Thayn, Thayne

Thang (Vietnamese) victorious

Thanh (Vietnamese) tops

Thanos (Greek) praiseworthy
Thanasis

Thanus (American) landowner; wealthy
Thainas, Thaines

Thao (American) variant on Theo: godlike

Thatcher (English) practical
Thacher, Thatch, Thatchar, Thaxter

Thavin (Greek) shows love for God

Thaw (Word as name) cool

Thayer (English) protected; sheltered
Thay, Thayar

Thayle (Jewish) form of Tal: worrier

Thebez (Biblical) place name

Thel (Hebrew) upper story

Themba (African) hopeful

Themis (Greek) lawful

Thena (Greek) honoree

Thenan (Greek) honored

Thenard (American) form of Leonard: courageous

Theo (Greek) godlike

Theobald (German) brave man
Thebaud, Thebault, Thibault, Thibaut, Tibold, Tiebold

Theodis (English) spirited

Theodore (Greek) God's gift; a blessing
Teador, Ted, Tedd, Teddey, Teddie, Teddy, Tedor, Teodor, Teodoro, Theeo, Theo, Theodor, Theos

Theodoric (African American) God's gift
Thierry

Theodoros (Greek) God's gift
Theo, Theodor

Theodorus (Greek) form of Theodore: God's gift; a blessing

Theophilos (Greek) loved by God
Teofil, Theo, Theophile

Theopoline (Greek) open

Therman (Scandinavian) thunderous
Thur, Thurman, Thurmen

Theron (Greek) industrious
Therron, Theryon

Theseus (Mythology) brave

Thessal (Biblical) martyr

Thiago (Spanish) saint

Thiassi (Scandinavian) wily
Thiazi, Thjazi

Thibaud (French) form of Theobald: brave man

Thibaut (French) form of Theobald: brave man

Thierno (American) humble
Therno, Their

Tho (Vietnamese) long-living

Thom (American) form of Thomas: twin; look-alike

Thomas ○ (Greek) twin; look-alike
Thom, Thomes, Thommy, Thomus, Tom, Tomas, Tommi, Tomus

Thompson (English) prepared
Thom, Thompsen, Thompsun, Thomson, Tom, Tommy

Thor (Scandinavian) protective; god of thunder
Thorr, Tor, Torr

Thorald (Scandinavian) thundering
Thorold, Torald

Thoralf (Scandinavian) thunder

Thorbert (Last name as first name) warring

Thorburn (Last name as first name) warlike

Thord (Scandinavian) thunder

Thorer (Scandinavian) warrior
Thorvald

Thorin (Scandinavian) form of Thor: protective; god of thunder
Thorrin, Thors

Thorley (Last name as first name) warrior
Thorlea, Thorlee, Thorleigh, Thorly, Torley

Thormond (Last name as first name) world of thunder
Thurmond, Thurmund

Thorn (English) thorny; bothersome

Thorndike (Last name as first name) powerful
Thorndyck, Thorndyke

Thorne (English) complex
Thorn, Thornee, Thorney, Thornie, Thorny

Thornley (Last name as first name) empowered
Thornlea, Thornleigh, Thornly

Thornston (Scandinavian) protected
Thornse, Thors

Thornton (English) difficult
Thorn, Thornten

Thorpe (English) homebody
Thor, Thorp

Thrace (Place name) region in southeast Europe
Thrase

Thu (Vietnamese) born in the fall

Thuan (Asian) aware

Thuc (Vietnamese) alert

Thuel (Biblical) form of Bethuel: religious

Thunor (Mythology) thunder

Thuong (Vietnamese) in pursuit

Thurlow (Last name as first name) helping

Thurm (Greek) form of Theron: industrious

Thurman (Last name as first name) popular
Thurmahn, Thurmen, Thurmie, Thurmy

Thurmond (Norse) sheltered
Thurman, Thurmon

Thurso (Scandinavian) thunders

Thurston (Scandinavian) thundering
Thor, Thors, Thorst, Thorstan, Thorstein, Thorsteinn, Thorsten, Thur, Thurs, Thurstain, Thurstan, Thursten, Torstein, Torsten, Torston

Thurstron (Scandinavian) volatile
Thorst, Thorsten, Thorstin, Thurs, Thurstran

Thuy (Vietnamese) kind

Tiago (Hispanic) brave
Ti, Tia

Tiaone (Spanish) form of Tiago: brave

Tiarnach (Irish) lordlike
Tighearnach

Tiber (Biblical) place name

Tiberius (Biblical) place name

Tibor (Czech) artist
Tybald, Tybalt, Tybault

Ticio (Spanish) heroic

Tien (Vietnamese) first and foremost

Tiernan (Irish) regal
Tierney

Tifton (English) Last name as first name

Tige (American) easygoing
Tig, Tigg

Tiger (American) ambitious; strong
Tig, Tige, Tigur, Tyg, Tyge, Tyger, Tygur

Tigny (Irish) poetic

Tigran (Latin) tiger

Tigrano (Biblical) place name

Tiki (Mythology) first man

Tilak (Hindi) leader; troubled; spot on forehead

Tildan (English) man who tills

Tilden (Place name) tilden

Tilene (Slavic) religious

Tilford (Last name as first name) tilling the soil

Till (German) form of Tillman: tiller of soil

Tillery (German) ruler
Till, Tiller

Tillman (German) tiller of soil
Tilman

Tillo (German) devout

Tilon (Hebrew) mound; giver

Tilton (English) prospering
Till, Tillie, Tylton

Tim (Greek) form of Timothy: reveres God
Timmy, Tym

Timber (American) word as name
Timb, Timby, Timmey, Timmi, Timmy

Timenn (Indian) child from the sea

Timin (Irish) honors God

Timmy (Greek) truthful
Timi, Timmee, Timmey, Timmie

Timna (Biblical) place name

Timnah (Biblical) place name

Timo (Finnish) form of Timothy: reveres God; form of Timon: from Shakespeare's *Timon of Athens*; wealthy man

Timon (Literature) from Shakespeare's *Timon of Athens*; wealthy man
Tim

Timothy (Greek) reveres God
Tim, Timathy, Timmie, Timmothy, Timmy, Timo, Timon, Timoteo, Timothe, Timothey, Timothie, Timuthy, Tymmothy, Tymothy

Timur (African) timid; ; (Slavic) conquerer

Timus (Scandinavian) powerful

Tin (Vietnamese) proud; pondering

Tingo (Italian) grateful

Tinks (American) coy
Tink, Tinkee, Tinki, Tinky, Tynks, Tynky

Tino (Spanish) respected
Tyno

Tinsley (English) personable
Tensley, Tins, Tinslee, Tinslie, Tinsly

Tinus (Slavic) leader

Tiombe (African) faith

Tione (American) form of Tyrone: self-starter; autonomous

Tip (American) small boy
Tipp, Tippee, Tippey, Tippi, Tippy, Typp

Tippen (American) Last name as first name

Tippie (Scandinavian) from Stephen: victorious

Tipu (Hindi) tiger

Tiras (Biblical) thoughtful

Tirso (Greek) religious

Tiru (Hindi) pious

Tisa (African) ninth child

Titan (Greek) powerful giant
Titun, Tityn

Tito (Latin) honored
Teto, Titoh

Titon (American) concerned

Titus (Latin) heroic
Titas, Tite, Tites

Tivon (African American) popular

Tizian (Italian) creative

Tjaru (Biblical) place name

Toa (Polynesian) brave-hearted

Toafo (Polynesian) in the wild; spontaneous

Toal (Irish) from strong roots; leader; willful

Tob (Biblical) place name

Tobbar (African American) physical

Tobby (African) excellent

Tobert (French) believer

Tobes (Hebrew) form of Tobias: believing the Lord is good
Tobee, Tobi, Tobs

Tobian (Hebrew) form of Tobias: believing the Lord is good

Tobias (Hebrew) believing the Lord is good
Tobe, Tobey, Tobi, Tobiah, Tobie, Tobin, Toby, Tobyas, Tovi

Tobikuma (Japanese) cloud; misty

Tobin (Hebrew) form of Tobias: believing the Lord is good
Toban, Toben, Tobun, Tobyn

Tobit (Biblical) form of Tobias: believing the Lord is good

Toblin (American) form of Tobias: believing the Lord is good

Toby (Hebrew) form of Tobias: believing the Lord is good
Tobe, Tobee, Tobey, Tobie, Toto

Todd (English) sly; fox
Tod, Toddy

Todor (Slavic) dignity

Todros (Hebrew) gifted; treasure
Todos

Togar (Biblical) place name

Togo (Place name) country in West Africa; jaunty

Tohon (Native American) loves the water

Tokala (Native American) fox; sly

Tokar (German) lucky

Toks (American) carefree

Tokutaro (Japanese) virtuous son

Tolan (American) studious
Tolen, Toll

Tolbert (English) bright prospects
Talbart, Talbert, Tolbart, Tolburt, Tollee, Tolley, Tollie, Tolly

Toledo (Place name) city in Ohio; casual
Tol, Tolly

Tolerence (American) unbiased

Tolero (Spanish) tolerant

Tolfe (American) outgoing

Tolin (American) form of Colin: young; quiet; peaceful; the people's victor

Toliver (American) combo of T and Oliver

Tolome (Spanish) strong

Tolomey (French) planner

Tom (English) form of Thomas: twin; look-alike
Thom, Tommy

Tomaro (Spanish) form of Thomas: twin; look-alike

Tomas (Spanish) form of Thomas: twin; look-alike

Tomasso (Italian) doubter
Maso, Tom

Tomer (Hebrew) tall

Tomi (Spanish) form of Tomas: twin; look-alike

Tomiko (Japanese) born to riches

Tomio (Italian) twin

Tomioson (Italian) son of twin

Tomlin (Last name as first name) ambitious

Tommie (Hebrew)
Tommee, Tommey, Tommi, Tomy

Tomochichi (Hawaiian) seeking truth and beauty
Tomocheechee

Tomok (Slavic) twin

Tond (Slavic) form of Tony: priceless

Tondeloro (Spanish) loud thunder

Tondy (Slavic) form of Tony: priceless

Tong (Chinese) name of a secret society; keeps a secret

Tongo (Asian) sweet aroma

Toni (Greek) *Tonee, Toney, Tonie, Tony*

Tonin (Italian) form of Antonio: superb

Tonion (American) form of Tony or Anthony: priceless

Tonny (Spanish) form of Antonio: superb

Tony (Greek) priceless

Tooling (American) vibrant

Toopweets (Native American) strong man

Toph (Greek) valued

Topher (Greek) form of Christopher: the bearer of Christ

Toppin (English) from the hill

Tops (American) best

Topwe (American) jovial

Tor (Scandinavian) thunder; brash
Thor, Torr, Torri, Torrie, Torry

Torao (Japanese) tiger male; wild

Torb (Scandinavian) form of Tor: thunder; brash

Torben (Scandinavian) form of Tor: thunder; brash

Torbie (Scandinavian) form of Tor: thunder; brash

Torcall (Scandinavian) summoned by thunder

Tord (Dutch) peaceful

Tordin (Scandinavian) form of Tor: thunder; brash

Torell (English) form of Tor: thunder; brash

Toreth (Biblical) from Ashtoreth

Torey (English) form of Tor: thunder; brash

Torger (Scandinavian) Thor's spear
Terje, Torgeir

Torgne (American) form of Tor: thunder; brash

Torial (Irish) form of Tor: thunder; brash

Torian (Irish) form of Torin: like thunder

Toribio (Spanish) strong; bullish

Toril (Hindi) having attitude

Torin (African American) like thunder

Torio (Spanish) fierce

Torkel (Scandinavian) protective
Thorkel, Torkil, Torkild, Torkjell, Torquil

Torless (Literature) from *The Confusions of Young Torless* by Musil

Torm (Scandinavian) armed

Tormod (Scottish) man of the north

Torn (Last name as first name) whirlwind
Torne, Tornn

Toro (Spanish) bull

Toroh (Spanish) bull

Torolf (Scandinavian) wolf of Thor
Thorolf, Tolv, Torolv, Torulf

Toronto (Place name) jaded
Torontoe

Torq (Scandinavian) form of Thor: protective; god of thunder
Tork

Torquil (Scandinavian) a kettle of thunder; trouble

Torr (English) tower; tall
Torre

Torrence (Latin) smooth
Torrance, Torence, Torey, Tori, Torr, Torrance, Torrie, Tory

Torrent (Irish) form of Torrence: smooth

Torri (English) calming
Toree, Tori, Torre, Torree, Torrey, Torry

Torst (Scandinavian) thunders

Toru (Scandinavian) thundering

Torun (Scottish) manly

Tosan (Spanish) bull

Tosh (American) form of Josh: devout

Toshiro (Japanese) smart

Totan (Scandinavian) beloved

Toth (Egyptian) life in balance

Toussaint (French) saints; valued

Tov (Hebrew) good
Tovi, Toviel, Tovya, Tuvia, Tuviah, Tuviya

Tova (Hebrew) good
Tov

Tovar (Hebrew) form of Tova: good

Tovaris (Spanish) good

Tove (Scandinavian) ruling; leads
Tuve

Townie (American) jovial
Townee, Towney, Towny

Townley (Last name as first name) citified
Townlea, Townlee, Townleigh, Townlie, Townly

Townsend (Last name as first name) went to town

Toyah (Place name) town in Texas; saucy
Toy, Toya, Toye

Trace (French) careful
Trayse

Tracy (French) spunky
Trace, Tracee, Tracey, Traci

Traddesus (Greek) form of Thaddeus: brave

Trae (American) form of Trey: third-born; creatively brilliant

Trahaearn (Welsh) strong man
Trahern, Traherne

Trahan (English) handsome
Trace, Trahahn, Trahain, Trahane, Trahen

Trai (Vietnamese) pearl in the oyster

Trajan (American) form of Trahan: handsome

Trakis (American) vibrant

Tram (Scottish) form of Tramaine: protector

Tramar (Scottish) form of Tramaine: protector

Trampus (American) talkative
Amp, Tramp, Trampy

Tranis (Irish) thunders

Tranquilino (Spanish) calm

Trap (American) word as name; masculine
Trapp, Trappy

Trapezus (Biblical) place name

Trau (German) loyal

Trauti (French) believer

Travers (English) helpful

Traverse (French) form of Travers: helpful

Traves (American) traversing different roads
Trav, Travus, Travys

Travis (English) conflicted
Tavers, Traver, Travers, Traves, Travess, Travey, Travus, Travuss, Travys

Travo (American) form of Travis: conflicted

Travon (African American) brash; (Slavic) happy
Travaughn

Travor (English) form of Trevor: wise

Trawin (English) friend of Trevor

Trayton (English) third
Tray, Trey

Treat (English) pleasing

Treavon (American) form of Trevon/Trevaughan: studious

Treb (Irish) wise

Treebeard (Literature) from Tolkien's *The Lord of the Rings*; noble; strong

Trefor (Welsh) form of Trevor: wise

Treiber (Irish) form of Trevor: wise

Treil (American) form of Terrell: puller

Treit (American) form of Treat: pleasing

Tremayne (French) protector
Tramaine, Treemayne, Trem, Tremain, Tremaine, Tremane, Tremen

Tremetrice (American) loved

Trent (Latin) quick-minded
Trente, Trenten, Trentin, Trenton, Trenty, Trint, Trynt

Trento (Spanish) form of Trent: quick-minded

Trenton (Latin) fast-moving
Trent, Trentan, Trenten, Trentin

Trer (Irish) form of Trevor: wise

Trest (Welsh) form of Tristan: sad; wistful

Treton (Welsh) form of Tristan: sad; wistful

Trev (Irish) strong

Treva (Irish) wise
Trevan

Trevan (African American) outgoing
Trevahn, Trevann

Trevelyan (English) from Elyan's home; comforted

Trevey (Irish) strong

Trevin (American) form of Trevon: studious

Trevine (American) strong

Trevis (English) form of Travis: conflicted

Trevon (African American) studious
Trevaughan

Trevor (Irish) wise
Trefor, Trev, Trevar, Treve, Trever, Trevis, Trevur

Trevour (American) form of Trevor: wise

Trex (American) combo of T and Rex (as in the dinosaur)

Trey (English) third-born; creatively brilliant
Trae, Tray, Tre, Treye

Trigg (American) from Trigger; quick-witted
Trig, Trygg

Triman (English) form of Truman: honest man

Trinee (Spanish) musical
Triney, Trini

Trinity (Latin) triad
Trinitie

Trint (American) holy trinity

Trinton (American) town of trinity; holy

Trip (English) wanderer
Tripe, Tripp

Triplett (American) one of the triplets

Tripolis (Biblical) place name

Tripsy (English) dancing
Trippsie, Tryppsi

Tripton (English) town of travelers

Tris (Welsh) form of Tristan: sad; wistful

Tristan ✪ (French) form of Triste: sad; wistful
Trestan, Trestyn, Trist, Tristen, Tristie, Triston, Tristy, Tristyn

Tristannel (Welsh) form of Tristan: sad; wistful

Triste (French) sad; wistful
Tristan

Tristian (English) form of Tristan: sad; wistful

Tristram (Welsh) sorrowful

Trivett (Last name as first name) trinity
Trevett, Triv

Trivin (American) form of Devin: poetic; writer
Trevin

Troas (Biblical) place name

Trocky (American) manly
Trockey, Trockie

Troclus (Greek) glorified

Trond (Scandinavian) from Norway

Trotter (American) quick

Trovillion (English) home-loving

Trowbridge (Place name) Trowbridge Park

Troy (French) good-looking
Troi, Troye, Troyie

Troyal (Irish) form of Troy: good-looking

Trudell (English) remarkable for honesty
Trude, True

Truitt (English) honest
Tru, True, Truett, Truitte

Truk (Place name) islands in the West Pacific; tough
Truck

Truls (Scandinavian) truth

Truman (English) honest man
*Tru, True, Trueman, Trumaine,
Trumann*

Trumble (Last name as first
name) sincere
Trumball, Trumbell, Trumbull

Trusdale (English) truthful
Dale, Tru, True

Truslowe (English) truth

Tryg (Scandinavian) trustworthy

Trygve (Scandinavian)
trustworthy

Trym (Scandinavian) new

Trysten (Welsh) form of Tristan:
sad; wistful

Trystene (American) laughter

Trystenn (American) laughter

Tsalani (African) says good-bye;
leaving

Tsatoke (Native American)
hunter on a horse

Tsela (Native American) star

Tsin (Native American) riding a
horse

Tsoai (Native American) tree; big

Tu (Vietnamese) fourth

Tuan (Vietnamese) simple

Tuar (Native American) eagle-
eyed

Tubal (Biblical) place name

Tucker (English) stylish
Tuck, Tucky, Tuckyr

Tucks (English) form of Tucker:
stylish
Tuk

Tuder (Welsh) form of Tudor/
Theodore: leader; God's gift

Tudor (Welsh) leader; special

Tue (Danish) form of Thor:
protective; god of thunder

Tufe (American) energetic

Tukuli (African) moon child

Tulio (Spanish) energetic

Tullis (Latin) important
Tull, Tullice, Tullise, Tully

Tully (Irish) form of Tullis:
important
Tull, Tulley, Tulli, Tullie

Tulsa (Place name) city in
Oklahoma; rancher

Tulse (American) from Tulsa
(place name)

Tulsi (Hindi) holy

Tumaini (African) optimist

Tune (American) dancer; musical
Toone, Tuney

Tung (Vietnamese) medium

Tunney (Welsh) leader

Tunu (Place name) from Tununak

Tuong (Vietnamese) everything

Tupaar (Welsh) God's child

Tupi (Spanish) a language family
with Brazilian roots

Turah (Native American) thyme

Turang (Biblical) wave

Turck (Biblical) place name

Ture (Scandinavian) form of
Thor: protective; god of thunder

Turer (Scandinavian) soldier

Turgut (German) believer

Turi (Hindi) growth

Turk (English) tough
Terk, Turke

Turlough (Hebrew) form of
Tuvia: good

Turlow (Irish) thunder child

Turn (Latin) turner

Turner (Latin) skilled
Turn

Turone (African American)
form of Tyrone: self-starter;
autonomous
Ture, Turrey, Turry

Turston (Greek) form of
Thurston: thundering

Tushar (Indian) droplets

Tut (Arabic) brave
Tuttie, Tutty

Tuttle (Scottish) strong

Tutts (American) unique

Tuvia (Hebrew) good
Tuvyah, Tuvyeh

Tuwa (Native American) earth-loving

Tuyen (Vietnamese) angelic

Twain (English) dual-faceted
Twaine, Tway, Twayn

Twyford (English) debonair

Twymon (English) double

Ty (English) form of Tyler: industrious
Ti, Tie, Tye

Tybalt (Greek) always right

Tyce (American) lively
Tice

Tycho (Scandinavian) focused
Tyge, Tyko

Tydeus (Mythology) determined

Tyee (African American) goal-oriented

Tyerson (English) son of Tye

Tygie (American) energetic
Tygee, Tygey, Tygi

Tyke (Scandinavian) determined

Tyko (Greek) form of Tycho: focused

Tyler ✪ ❶ (English) industrious
Tile, Tiler, Ty, Tye, Tylar, Tyle, Tylir, Tylor

Tylus (Scandinavian) impact

Tyman (Scandinavian) high integrity

Tymon (Polish) honored by God

Tynan (Place name) a town in Northern Ireland; (Irish) dark

Tyobaldo (Slavic) form of Theobald: brave man

Tyones (American) form of Tyrone: self-starter; autonomous

Tyonne (African American) feisty
Tye, Tyon

Tyounes (American) form of Tyrone: self-starter; autonomous

Typhoon (English) volatile
Tifoon, Ty, Tyfoon, Tyfoonn

Tyr (Scandinavian) Norse god; daring warrior

Tyran (American) form of Tyrone: self-starter; autonomous

Tyre (English) thunders
Tyr

Tyree (African American) courteous
Ty, Tyrae, Tyrie, Tyry

Tyreece (African American) combative
Tyreese

Tyrell (African American) personable
Trelle, Tyrel, Tyrelle, Tyril, Tyrrel

Tyrellon (American) form of Tyrell: personable

Tyrese (American) form of Tyrone: self-starter; autonomous

Tyresen (American) form of Tyrese: self-starter; autonomous

Tyron (African American) self-reliant
Tiron, Tyronn

Tyrone (Greek) self-starter; autonomous
Terone, Tiron, Tirone, Tirus, Ty, Tyronne, Tyron, Tyroon, Tyroun

Tyroneece (African American) ball of fire
Tironeese, Tyronnee

Tys (American) fighter
Thysen, Tyes, Tyse, Tysen

Tyson (French) son of Ty
Tieson, Tison, Tyse, Tysen, Tysson, Tysy

Tzach (Hebrew) unblemished
Tzachai, Tzachar

Tzadik (Hebrew) fair
Tzadok, Zadik, Zadoc, Zadok, Zaydak

Tzadkiel (Hebrew) righteous
Zadkiel

Tzalmon (Hebrew) dark
Zalmon

Tzephaniah (Hebrew) man protected by God
Tzefanya, Zefania, Zefaniah, Zephania, Zephaniah

Tzevi (Hebrew) graceful; deer
Tzeviel, Zevi, Zeviel

Tzuriel (Hebrew) depends on God
Zuriel

Ualtar (Irish) strong
Ualtarr

Uan (Irish) form of Owen: well-born; high-principled

Uba (African) rich

Ubald (French) brave one
Ubaldo, Ube

Ubanwa (African) wealth in children

Uben (German) practice
Ubin, Ubyn

Ubiwe (African) of the heart

Ubrig (German) big
Ubrigg, Ubryg, Ubrygg

Ubrigens (German) bothered
Ubrigins, Ubrigyns

Uchtred (English) cries
Uchtrid, Uchtryd, Uctred, Uctrid,
Uctryd, Uktred, Uktrid

Udall (English) certain; valley of trees
Eudall, Udahl, Udawl, Yudall

Udeep (Indian) flood

Udeh (Hindi) praised

Udel (English) growing

Udell (English) from a tree grove
Del, Dell, Udale, Udall

Udenwa (African) thriving

Udo (German) shows promise

Udolf (German) stodgy

Ufer (German) dark mind

Ugo (Italian) bright mind

Uhr (German) disturbed

Uilleac (Irish) ready
Uilleack, Uilleak, Uilliac, Uilliack,
Uilliak, Uillyac, Uillyack, Uillyak

Uilleog (Irish) prepared
Uilliog, Uillyog

Ukel (American) player
Ukal, Uke, Ukil

Ukraine (Place name) republic

Ulan (Place name) city in Russia
Ulane

Uland (African) firstborn twin
Ulande

Ulas (German) noble

Ulbrich (German) aristocratic

Ulfat (Norse) wolf

Ulff (Scandinavian) wolf; wild
Ulf, Ulv

Ulfred (Norse) noble

Ulgar (German) highborn

Ulhas (Indian) mirth

Ulices (Latin) form of Ulysses: forceful
Uly

Ulick (Irish) for William; up-and-coming

Ulise (Latin) form of Ulysses: forceful

Ulissus (Invented) form of Ulysses: forceful

Ulland (English) noble Lord
Uland, Ullund

Ullock (Irish) nobleman

Ulman (German) the wolf's infamy
Ulmann, Ullman, Ullmann

Ulmer (German) wolf; cagy

Ulriah (German) form of Ulrich: ruling; power
Ulria, Ulrya, Ulryah

Ulrich (German) ruling; power
Ric, Rick, Rickie, Ricky, Ulrek,
Ulric, Ulriche, Ulrick, Ulrico

Ulrid (German) leader

Ulster (Scandinavian) wolf

Ultan (Irish) noble
Ultann

Ultar (Scandinavian) wolf
Ultarr

Ultman (Hindi) godlike

Ulton (German) highborn

Ulysses (Latin) forceful
Ule, Ulesses, Ulises, Ulisses

Umang (Indian) excited

Umar (Hindi) doing well

Umbard (German) form
of Humbert: famous giant;
renowned warrior
Umbarde

Umber (French) brown; plain

Umberto (Italian) earthy

Umed (Hindi) has an aim

Umek (Japanese) blossoms

Umher (Arabic) controlling

Umi (African) life

Unique (American) word as name
Uneek, Unik

Unitas (American) united

Univers (American) universal;
man for all

Unser (Last name as first name)
drives hard and fast

Unten (English) not a friend
Untenn

Unus (Latin) one
Unuss

Unwin (Last name as first name)
modest

Updike (Last name as first name)
from up above

Upjohn (English) creative
Upjon

Upton (English) highbrow writer
Uppton, Uptawn, Upten, Uptown

Upwood (Last name as first
name) upper woods is home

Uranus (Greek) the heavens

Urban (Latin) city dweller
*Urb, Urbain, Urbaine, Urbane,
Urben, Urbin, Urbun, Urby*

Urho (Scandinavian) courageous

Uri (Hebrew) form of Uriel: light;
God-inspired

Uriah (Hebrew) bright; led by God
Uri, Urie, Uryah

Urian (Irish) from heaven
Urion

Urias (Hebrew) Lord as my light;
old-fashioned
Uraeus, Uri, Uria, Urius

Uriel (Hebrew) light; God-
inspired

Urielon (American) form of
Uriel: light; God-inspired

Urien (Mythology) lights life

Urs (Scandinavian) bear; growly
Urso

Ursan (French) form of Orson:
strong as a bear
Ursen, Ursyn

Ursino (Spanish) dark

Urteil (German) judgment
Urteel, Urtiel

Uruk (Slavic) form of Urias: Lord
as my light; old-fashioned

Urv (Biblical) place name

Urvano (Spanish) city boy
Urbano

Urvine (Place name) form of
Irvin: attractive
Urveen, Urvene, Urvi

Ury (Hispanic) God-loving;
(Hebrew) shining

Usaid (Arabic) laughs

Usaku (Japanese) moonlit

Usher (Latin) decisive

Usman (Arabic) friend

Usry (Slavic) cultured

Utah (Place name) U.S. state

Uthman (Arabic) bird
Uthmann

Utz (American) befriends all

Uwe (Welsh) gentle

Uz (Hebrew) passion

Uzal (Hebrew) strong in God

Uziah (Hebrew) believes

Uziel (Hebrew) soothed by God's
strength

Uzondu (African) attracts others

Uzu (Biblical) strength in God

Uzzi (Biblical) place name

Uzziel (Hebrew) powerful in God

Vachel (French) keeps cows
Vachell

Vadim (French) creative
Vadeem

Vadin (Hindi) speaks well

Vaduz (Place name) city in
Germany

Vahan (Slavic) protected

Vail (English) serene
Bail, Bale, Vaile, Vaill, Vale, Valle

Vaino (Scandinavian)
wagonbuilder

Val (Latin) form of Valeri:
athletic; mighty; form of
Valentine: robust
Vall

Vala (Latin) form of Valentine:
robust

Valare (Latin) water-loving

Valdem (Scandinavian) rules

Valdemar (Scandinavian) famous
leader
Waldemar

Valensi (Spanish) valiant

Valente (Italian) form of
Valentin: valiant

Valenti (Italian) mighty; romantic
Val, Valence, Valentin, Valentyn

Valentin (Russian) valiant
Val, Valeri

Valentine (Latin) robust
*Val, Valentijn, Valentin,
Valentinian, Valentino,
Valentinus, Valentyn, Valentyne,
Valyntine*

Valentino (Italian) strong; healthy
Val

Valeri (Russian) athletic; mighty
Val, Valerian, Valerio, Valry

Valerian (Russian) strong leader
*Valerien, Valerio, Valerius, Valery,
Valeryan*

Vali (Scandinavian) brave man

Valin (Latin) form of Valentin:
valiant
Valen, Valyn

Vallance (Last name as first
name) tenacious

Vallie (Romanian) valor

Valmar (Slavic) peaceful

Valu (Polynesian) eight

Van (Dutch) descendant
Vann, Von, Vonn

Vance (English) brash
Vans, Vanse

Vanco (Slavic) form of Vincent:
victorious

Vanda (Russian) form of Walter:
army leader

Vandan (Hindi) saved

Vander (Greek) form of Evander:
manly; champion
Vand

Vandiver (American) quiet
Van, Vand, Vandaver, Vandever

Vandwon (African American)
covert
Vandawon, Vandjuan

Vandyke (Last name as first
name) educated

Vane (Last name as first name)
gifted

Vangle (Greek) brings good news

Vanhue (Armenian) protected

Vannevar (Scandinavian) form
of Evander: manly; champion

Vanni (Italian) form of Giovanni:
jovial; happy believer

Vanny (Slavic) form of Vanya:
right

Vanslow (Scandinavian)
sophisticated
Vansalo, Vanselow, Vanslaw

Vanya (Russian) right
Van, Yard, Yardy

Varady (Slavic) fortified

Vardon (French) green hill is home
Varden, Verdon, Verdun

Varen (Hindi) rain god Varun

Varesh (Hindu) God is superior

Varg (American) vigorous

Vargu (Scandinavian) wolf-like

Varick (German) defender
Varrick, Warick, Warrick

Varil (French) faithful

Varkey (American) boisterous

Varlan (American) tough
Varland, Varlen, Varlin

Varma (Hindi) fruitful

Varner (Last name as first name)
formidable
Varn

Varo (Last name as first name)

Vartan (Russian) gives roses

Vartkes (History) king of all

Varun (Hindi) water Lord;
excellent
Varoun

Vas (Slavic) protective
Vaston, Vastun, Vasya

Vasant (Sanskrit) brings spring

Vasch (Slavic) clarity

Vasco (Hindi) excellent

Vash (Spanish) from Velasco, Texas

Vashon (American) delightful
Vashaun, Vashonne

Vasil (Slavic) form of William:
staunch protector
*Vasile, Vasilek, Vasili, Vasilis,
Vasilos, Vasily, Vassily*

Vasile (Greek) form of Vasilis:
king

Vasilis (Russian) king
*Vasileios, Vasilij, Vasily, Vaso,
Vasos, Vassilij, Vassily, Vasya,
Wassily*

Vasin (Hindi) rules all

Vasken (Slavic) quiet

Vassil (Bulgarian) king
Vass

Vassilios (Greek) king

Vasu (Sanskrit) rich boy

Vatche (Armenian) loving

Vaughn (Welsh) compact
Vaughan, Vaunie, Von

Vea (Vietnamese) form of Veasna:
fortunate

Veasna (Vietnamese) fortunate

Vedn (Latin) sees

Vee (Hebrew) ash tree

Veejay (American) talkative
V.J., Vee-Jay, Vejay

Veer (English) form of Vere:
springlike

Vegas (Place name) from Las Vegas
Vega

Vejis (Invented) form of Regis:
kingly
Veejas, Veejaz, Vejas, Vejes

Velamo (Scandinavian) of the sea

Velle (American) tough
Vell, Velley, Velly, Veltree

Veltry (African American)
hopeful

Velvet (American) smooth
Vel, Velvat, Velvit

Venancio (Spanish) glorious

Venard (Spanish) starry

Venaventura (Spanish) hurts

Vencel (Hungarian) king

Vendon (Indian) fortified

Venedict (Greek) form of
Benedict: blessed man
Venedikt, Venka, Venya

Venezio (Italian) glorious
Venetziano, Veneziano

Venkat (Hindi) godlike

Venkata (Hindi) godlike

Ventura (Spanish) good fortune

Venturo (Italian) lucky
Venturio

Verdun (French) green knoll

Vere (Latin) springlike

Vered (Hebrew) rose-loving

Vergel (Spanish) writer
Vergele, Virgil

Verile (German) macho
Verill, Verille, Verol, Verrill

Verissimo (Spanish) truthful

Verlan (Latin) flourishes

Verle (American) truthful

Verlie (American) form of Verle:
truthful
Verley

Verlyn (African American)
growing
Verle, Verlin, Verllin, Verlon,
Verlyn, Virle, Vyrle

Vermont (Place name) U.S. state

Vern (Latin) form of Vernon:
fresh and bright
Verne, Vernie, Verny

Vernados (Greek) hearty

Verner (German) resourceful
Vern, Verne, Vernir, Virner

Verniamin (Greek) form of
Benjamin: son of the right hand;
son of the south

Vernie (Latin) form of Vernon:
fresh and bright

Vernon (Latin) fresh and bright
Lavern, Vern, Vernal, Verne,
Vernen, Verney, Vernin

Verona (Italian) man of Venice
or Verona
Verone

Verrier (French) faithful

Verrill (German) manly
Verill, Verrall, Verrell, Verroll, Veryl

Verron (Latin) form of Vernon:
fresh and bright

Vesa (Scandinavian) young

Vest (English) church child

Vester (Latin) form of Sylvester:
forest-dweller; heavy-duty

Vestin (English) church child

Vesuvio (Place name) mount
Vesuvius; spontaneous

Vetch (German) comforts

Vetis (Latin) life

Vettorio (Italian) victor

Vezeleo (Spanish) form of Basil:
regal

Vic (Latin) form of Victor:
victorious
Vick, Vickey, Vik

Vicason (English) son of Victor

Vicente (Spanish) winner
Vic, Vicentay, Visente

Vicken (Latin) victor

Vico (Italian) form of Victor:
victorious; winning

Victen (American) form of
Victor: victorious

Victor (Latin) victorious
Vic, Vick, Vickter, Victer,
Victorien, Victorin, Vidor, Vikki,
Viktor, Vitorio, Vittorio

Victoriano (Spanish) form of
Victor: victorious

Vid (Spanish) form of Vidal: full
of vitality

Vida (Hebrew) beloved; vibrant

Vidal (Spanish) full of vitality
Bidal, Videl, Videlio

Vidalo (Spanish) energetic
Vidal

Vidar (Scandinavian) soldier

Viddell (Spanish) vital

Vidkun (Scandinavian) gives

Vidor (Hungarian) delightful

Vidya (Indian) smart

Vidyalakshmi (Indian) bright

Viggo (Scandinavian) exuberant
Viggoa, Vigo

Vigile (American) vigilant
Vegil, Vigil

Vihs (Hindu) increase

Vijay (Hindi) winning
Bijay, Vijun

Vikas (Indian) growth

Vila (Czech) form of William:
staunch protector
Vili, Ville

Vili (Indian) bright

Viliam (Slavic) form of William:
staunch protector

Viliami (Slavic) form of William:
staunch protector

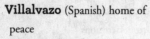

Villalvazo (Spanish) home of peace

Villantes (French) valiant

Villard (French) village man

Villen (Russian) form of Lennon: renowned; caped

Villiers (French) kindhearted

Vilmos (Italian) happy
Villmos

Vilnis (Slavic) form of Vilmos: happy

Vilok (Hindu) to see

Vimal (Hindi) unblemished

Vin (Italian) form of Vincent: victorious
Vinn, Vinney, Vinni, Vinnie

Vinay (Hindi) good manners; polite

Vince (English) form of Vincent: victorious
Vee, Vence, Vins, Vinse

Vincent (Latin) victorious
Vencent, Vicenzio, Vin, Vince, Vincens, Vincente, Vincentius, Vincents, Vincenty, Vincenz, Vincenzio, Vincenzo, Vincien, Vinciente, Vinicent, Vinn, Vinnie, Vinny, Vinzenze, Wincenty

Vincenzo (Italian) conqueror
Vincenze, Vinnie, Vinny

Vine (Latin) form of Vin: victorious

Vinicius (Indian) victor

Vinod (Hindi) effervescent; joy

Vinson (English) winning attitude
Venson, Vince, Vinny, Vins

Vinton (English) town of wine; reveler

Vinus (Slavic) ready

Vio (Indian) form of Vijay: winning

Vip (Hindi) bounty

Vir (Indian) large

Viral (Indian) mannered

Virat (Indian) big

Vireo (Latin) brave

Virgil (Latin) holding his own; writer
Verge, Vergil, Vergilio, Virge, Virgie, Virgilio, Virgy

Virginius (Latin) virginal
Virginio

Virrgilio (Spanish) form of Virgil: holding his own; writer

Virtus (Greek) virtuous

Vischer (Last name as first name) longing
Visscher

Vishal (Indian) grand

Vishnu (Indian) pervasive

Vison (Hindi) persuades

Vitale (Italian) important

Vitaliano (Italian) vital

Vitalis (Latin) bubbly; vital

Vitas (Latin) animated
Vidas, Vite

Viticus (Biblical) from Leviticus

Vito (Italian) form of Vittorio: lively; victor
Veto, Vital, Vitale, Vitalis, Vitaly, Vitas, Vite, Vitus, Witold

Vitone (Italian) form of Vitas: animated

Vitrano (Indian) great

Vittorio (Italian) lively; victor
Vite, Vito, Vitor, Vitorio, Vittore

Vittorios (Italian) victor

Vitus (Latin) winning

Vivaldo (Italian) celebrant

Vivar (Greek) alive
Viv

Vivek (Hindi) wise; knowing

Vivian (Latin) lively
Viviani, Vivien, Vivyan, Vyvian, Vyvyan

Vlad (Russian) form of Vladimir: glorious leader

Vladimir (Russian) glorious leader
Vlada, Vladameer, Vladamir, Vlademar, Vladimeer, Vlakimar, Wladimir, Wladimyr

Vladislav (Czech) glorious leader

Vladislava (Slavic) glorious ruler

Vladja (Russian) form of Vladislav: glorious leader

Vodie (Scandinavian) victor

Volf (Hebrew) form of Will: staunch protector

Volkan (Slavic) defends

Volker (German) prepared to defend
Volk

Volney (Greek) hidden

Volun (Latin) flies

Volya (Slavic) hopes

Von (German) bright
Vaughn, Vonn, Vonne

Vong (Scandinavian) tough

Vonko (Slavic) form of Vanco: victorious

Vontaire (French) noisy

Vonzie (American) form of Fonzie: distinguished
Vons, Vonze, Vonzee, Vonzey, Vonzi

Vorris (Latin) versatile

Voshon (Slavic) generous

Vui (African) saves

Vuk (Slavic) wolf-like; eloquent

Vuok (Scandinavian) flower

Vurl (American) form of Verle: truthful

Vusen (Dutch) vain

Vyacheslav (Russian) glorious child

Vyom (American) vocal

Waclaw (Polish) glorified

Wacy (Arabic) knowledgeable

Wade (English) mover; crossing a river
Wadie, Waide, Wayde

Wadell (English) southerner
Waddell, Wade

Waden (American) form of Jaden: Jehovah has heard
Wade, Wedan

Wadley (Last name as first name) by the water
Wadleigh, Wadly

Wadsworth (English) homebody
Waddsworth, Wadswurth

Wady (Slavic) water boy

Wael (English) from Wales

Wagner (German) musical; practical
Wagg, Waggner, Waggoner, Wagnar, Wagnur

Wagon (American) conveyance
Wag, Wagg, Waggoner

Wai (Asian) form of Wei: excellent

Wain (English) industrious

Wainwright (Last name as first name) works hard
Wain, Wainright, Wayne, Wayneright, Waynewright, Waynright, Wright

Waisim (Arabic) attractive

Wait (American) word as name; patient
Waite

Wake (Place name) island in the Marshall Islands

Wakefield (English) the field worker
Field, Wake

Wakely (Last name as first name) wet

Wakeman (Last name as first name) wet
Wake

Wal (Arabic) form of Waleed: newborn

Walbert (German) protective; stodgy

Walcott (Last name as first name) steadfast
Wallcot, Wallcott, Wolcott

Waldemar (German) famous leader
Valdemar, Waldermar, Waldo

Walden (English) calming
Wald, Waldan, Waldi, Waldin, Waldo, Waldon, Waldy, Welti

Waldo (German) form of Oswald: divine power
Wald, Waldoh, Waldy

Waldron (English) leader

Waleed (Arabic) newborn
Waled, Walid

Walenty (Polish) strong

Walerian (Polish) powerful

Wales (English) from Wales
Wael, Wail, Wails, Wale, Waley, Wali, Waly

Walford (English) wealthy; from Wales

Walfred (English) from Wales; loyal

Wali (Arabic) newborn

Walker (English) distinctive
Walk, Wally

Wall (English) from Wales

Wallace (English) from Wales; charming
Wallas, Walley, Walli, Wallice, Wallie, Wallis, Wally, Walsh, Welsh

Waller (English) from Wales; confident

Wallis (English) from Wales; smooth

Walls (American) walled
Walen, Wally, Waltz, Walz

Wally (English) form of Walter: army leader
Wall, Walley, Walli, Wallie

Walmir (Slavic) ruler

Walmond (Last name as first name) laidback

Walsh (English) inquisitive
Walls, Welce, Welch, Wells, Welsh

Walt (German) army leader
Waltey, Waltli, Walty

Walter (German) army leader
Walder, Wallie, Wally, Walt, Walther, Waltur, Walty, Wat

Walther (German) army leader; powerful

Walton (English) shut off; protected
Walt, Walten, Waltin

Waltrau (German) strong leader

Walu (American) form of Wally: army leader

Walworth (English) introvert

Walwyn (English) reticent
Walwin, Walwinn, Walwynn, Walwynne, Welwyn

Waman (American) form of Wymann: contentious

Wang (Chinese) hope; wish

Waqar (Arabic) talkative

Warburton (Last name as first name) still

Ward (English) vigilant; alert
Warde, Warden, Worden

Wardell (English) guarded

Warden (English) watchful
Warde, Wardie, Wardin, Wardon

Wardley (English) careful
Wardlea, Wardleigh

Ware (English) aware; cautious
Warey, Wary

Warfield (Last name as first name) cautious

Warford (Last name as first name) defensive

Waring (English) dashing
Wareng, Warin, Warring

Wark (American) watchful

Warley (Last name as first name) worthy people

Warlito (Spanish) warring

Warner (German) protective
Warne

Warren (German) safe haven
Ware, Waren, Waring, Warrenson,
Warrin, Warriner, Warron,
Warry, Worrin

Warton (English) defended town

Warvin (American) form of
Marvin: steadfast friend

Warwen (American) defensive
Warn, Warwun

Warwick (English) lavish
War, Warick, Warrick, Warweck,
Warwyc, Warwyck, Wick

Washburn (English) bountiful
Washbern, Washbie, Washby

Washington (English) leader
Wash, Washe, Washing

Wasim (Arabic) pretty baby

Wason (Arabic) form of Wasim:
pretty baby

Wat (English) form of Watkins:
able

Watford (Last name as first
name) soft-spoken

Watkins (English) able
Watkens, Wattie, Wattkins, Watty

Watson (English) helpful
Watsen, Watsie, Watsun, Watsy,
Wattsson

Waulkie (English) form of
Wilkie: willful

Wave (American) word as a name
Waive, Wayve

Waverley (Place name) city in
New South Wales
Waverlee, Waverli, Waverly

Way (English) landed; smart
Waye

Wayel (English) the road

Wayland (English) from the path
land

Wayling (English) the right way
Waylan, Wayland, Waylen, Waylin

Waylon (English) form of
Wayland: from the path land
Wallen, Walon, Way, Waylan,
Waylen, Waylie, Waylin, Waylond,
Waylun, Wayly, Weylin

Wayman (English) traveling man
Way, Waym, Waymon, Waymun

Waymon (American) knowing
the way
Waymond

Wayne (English) wheeler and
dealer
Wain, Wanye, Way, Wayn,
Waynell, Waynne

Wazir (Arabic) minister

Weather (Native American) dark

Webb (English) intricate mind
Web, Webbe, Weeb

Weber (German) intuitive
Webb, Webber, Webner

Webley (English) weaves;
intuitive
Webbley, Webbly, Webly

Webster (English) creative
Web, Webstar, Webstur

Weddel (Last name as first name)
has an angle

Wedon (Last name as first name)
inspired

Weebie (American) wily
Weebbi

Wegner (American) form of
Wagner: musical; practical

Wehrle (Last name as first name)

Wei (Chinese) excellent

Weido (Italian) bright; personable
Wedo

Welborne (Last name as first
name) where the well is
Welborn, Welbourne, Welburn,
Wellborn, Wellborne, Wellbourn,
Wellburn

Welby (German) astute; farmer
by the well
Welbey, Welbi, Welbie, Wellby

Weld (English) from the well

Weldom (American) form of
Weldon: where the well is

Weldon (Last name as first name) where the well is

Welford (English) unusual
Walferd, Wallie, Wally

Wellington (English) nobility
Welling

Wellis (American) form of Willis: youthful

Wells (English) unique
Well, Wellie, Welly

Wel-Quo (Asian) bothered
Wel

Welsh (English) form of Walsh: inquisitive
Welch, Wellsh

Welton (English) spring town

Wen (American) winter baby

Wenceslaus (Polish) glorified king
Wenceslas, Wenczeslaw, Wenzel, Wiencyslaw

Wendell (German) full of wanderlust
Wandale, Wend, Wendall, Wendel, Wendey, Wendie, Wendill, Wendle, Wendull, Wendy

Wendolid (Spanish) form of Wendell: full of wanderlust

Wenford (English) confessing
Wynford

Wenjic (Slavic) wanders

Wenli (American) form of Wendell: wanderlust

Went (American) ambitious
Wente, Wentt

Wentworth (English) Last name as first name

Wenworth (English) adventures

Werley (English) Last name as first name

Werner (German) warrior

Werther (German) worthy

Wes (English) form of Wesley: bland
Wess, Wessie, Wessy

Wesh (German) from the west

Wesley (English) bland
Wes, Weslee, Wesleyan, Weslie, Wesly, Wessley, West, Westleigh, Westley, Westly, Wezlee, Wezley

Wessell (English) westerner

Wessey (English) westerner

Wesson (American) from the west
Wess, Wessie

West (English) westerner
Weste, Westt

Westbrook (Last name as first name) from the west brook; nature-loving
Brook, West, Westbrooke

Westby (English) near the west

Westcott (English) from a western cottage
Wescot, Wescott, Westcot

Westel (English) westerner

Westie (American) capricious
West, Westee, Westey, Westt, Westy

Westleigh (English) western
Westlea, Westlie, Wezlee

Westley (English) from the west fields

Westoll (American) open
West, Westall

Weston (English) good neighbor
West, Westen, Westey, Westie, Westin, Westy

Wesze (English) westerner

Weszel (English) westerner

Wether (English) lighthearted
Weather, Weth, Wethar, Wethur

Wetherby (English) lighthearted
Weatherbey, Weatherbie, Weatherby, Wetherbey, Wetherbie

Wetherell (English) lighthearted

Wetherly (English) lighthearted

Wex (English) the fjord of the flats

Whalen (English) from the woods

Whalley (Last name as first name) predicts

Wharton (Last name as first name) provincial
Warton

Wheat (Invented) fair-haired
Wheatie, Wheats, Wheaty, Whete

Wheatley (Last name as first name) fair-haired; fields of wheat
Whatley, Wheatlea, Wheatleigh, Wheatly

Wheaton (Last name as first name) blond; wheat town

Wheel (American) important player
Wheele

Wheeler (English) likes cars; wheel maker
Weeler, Wheel, Wheelie, Wheely

Wheeless (English) off track
Whelus

Wheelie (American) big-wig
Wheeley, Wheels, Wheely

Whesk (American) self-serving

Whip (American) friendly

Whistler (English) melodic
Whis, Whistlar, Whistle, Whistlerr

Whit (English) form of Whitman: man with white hair
Whitt, Whyt, Whyte, Wit, Witt

Whitby (English) white-haired; white-walled town

Whitcomb (English) light in the valley; shining
Whitcombe, Whitcumb

White (English) white

Whitelaw (English) white
Whitlaw

Whitey (English) fair-skinned
White

Whitfield (English) from a white field

Whitford (English) the light source

Whitley (English) white area is home
Whitlea, Whitlee, Whitleigh

Whitman (English) man with white hair
Whit, Whitty, Witman

Whitmore (English) white
Whitmoor, Whittemore, Witmore, Wittemore

Whitney (English) likes white spaces
Whit, Whitnee, Whitnie, Whitt, Whittney, Widney, Widny, Witt

Whitson (English) son of Whit
Whitt, Witt

Whittaker (English) outdoorsy
Whitaker, Whitt, Witaker, Wittaker

Whitter (English) white

Whittson (English) white son

Wick (American) burning
Wic, Wik, Wyck

Wickham (Last name as first name) living in a hamlet
Wick

Wickley (Last name as first name) coming from a small home
Wicley

Wier (German) famous

Wieslaw (Polish) known

Wijnand (Slavic) form of Wymon; soldier

Wilberforce (German) wild and strong

Wilbert (German) smart
Wilberto, Wilburt

Wilbur (English) fortified
Wilbar, Wilber, Wilburt, Willbur, Wilver

Wilburn (German) brilliant
Bernie, Wil, Wilbern, Will

Wilder (English) wild man
Wildar, Wilde, Wildey

Wildon (Last name as first name) willing support
Wilden, Willdon

Wilee (English) form of Wylie: charmer

Wilen (English) form of William: staunch protector

Wiles (American) tricky
Wyles

Wiley (English) cowboy
Wile, Willey, Wylie

Wilf (English) form of Wilford:
willowy; peaceful wishes

Wilford (English) willowy;
peaceful wishes

Wilfre (German) peaceful

Wilfred (German) peacemaker
Wilferd, Wilford, Wilfrid,
Wilfride, Wilfried, Wilfryd, Will,
Willfred, Willfried, Willie, Willy

Wilfredo (Italian) peaceful
Fredo, Wifredo, Willfredo

Wilhelm (German) resolute;
determined
Wilhelmus, Wilhem, Willem

Wilke (German) form of Wilkins:
affectionate

Wilkie (English) willful

Wilkins (English) affectionate
Welkie, Welkins, Wilk, Wilkens,
Wilkes, Wilkie, Wilkin, Willkes,
Willkins

Wilkinson (English) son of
Wilkin; capable
Willkinson

Will (English) form of William:
staunch protector
Wil, Wilm, Wim, Wyll

Willard (German) courageous
Wilard, Willerd

Willeo (Spanish) form of
William: staunch protector

Willer (American) form of
Willard: courageous

Willerson (English) son of
Willard

Willialdo (Spanish) form of
William: staunch protector

William ○ ⊕ (English) staunch
protector
Bill, Will, Willeam, Willie, Wills,
Willy, Willyum, Wilyam

Williams (German) brave
Williamson

Willie (German) form of
William: staunch protector
Will, Wille, Willey, Willeye, Willi,
Willy, Wily

Willis (German) youthful
Willace, Willece, Willice, Wills,
Willus

Willits (Scandinavian) protective

Willoughby (Last name as first
name) lives with grace
Willoughbey, Willoughbie

Wills (English) willful

Wilmer (German) resolute;
ambitious
Willmar, Willmer, Wilm, Wilmar,
Wilmyr, Wylmar, Wylmer

Wilmot (German) tough-minded

Wilson (English) extraordinary
Willson, Wilsen, Wilsun

Wilt (English) talented
Wiltie

Wilton (English) practical and
open
Will, Wilt, Wiltie, Wylten, Wylton

Wiltson (English) son of Will

Wim (Slavic) go-getter

Wimmy (American) form of
William: staunch protector

Win (German) flirtatious
Winn, Winnie, Winny

Wincate (English) form of
Vincent: victorious

Winchell (English) meandering
Winchie, Winshell

Wind (American) word as name;
breezy
Windy

Windell (German) wanderer
Windelle, Windyll

Windsor (English) royal
Win, Wincer, Winnie, Winny,
Winsor, Wyndsor, Wynser

Winfield (English) peace in the country
Field, Winifield, Winnfield, Wynfield, Wynnfield

Winfried (English) peaceful

Wing (Chinese) in glory
Wing-Chiu, Wing-Kit

Wingate (Last name as first name) glorified

Wingi (American) spunky

Wings (American) soaring; free
Wing

Wink (American) vigorous

Winkel (American) bright; conniving
Wink, Winky

Winkle (American) vigorous

Winlove (Filipino) winning favor

Winn (English) form of Wyn: gregarious

Winnell (English) fair-haired

Winslone (English) form of Winslow: friendly

Winslow (English) friendly
Winslo, Wynslo, Wynslow

Winsome (English) gorgeous; charming
Wins, Winsom, Winz

Winston (English) dignified
Win, Winn, Winnie, Winny, Winstan, Winsten, Winstonn, Winton, Wynstan, Wynsten, Wynston

Winter (English) born in winter
Win, Winnie, Winny, Wintar, Winterford, Wintur, Wynter, Wyntur

Winthrop (English) winning; stuffy
Win, Winn, Winnie, Winny, Wintrop

Winton (English) winning
Wynten, Wynton

Winward (English) friendly

Wiss (American) carefree
Wissie, Wissy

Wit (Polish) life
Witt, Wittie, Witty

Witek (Polish) form of Victor: victorious

Witha (Arabic) vibrant

Witold (Polish) lively

Witt (Slavic) lively
Witte

Witter (Last name as first name) alive

Witton (Last name as first name) lively

Witty (American) humorous
Wit, Witt, Witte, Wittey, Wittie

Wize (American) smart
Wise, Wizey, Wizi, Wizie

Wladymir (Polish) famous ruler
Vladimir

Wladyslaw (Polish) good leader
Slaw

Wlodek (Polish) rules

Wohn (African American) form of John: God is gracious

Wojciech (Polish) comforts

Wojtek (Polish) comforter; warrior

Wolcott (English) home of wool

Wolf (German) form of Wolfgang: talented; a wolf walks
Wolff, Wolfie, Wolfy

Wolfe (German) wolf; ominous
Wolf, Wolff, Wulf, Wulfe

Wolfgang (German) talented; a wolf walks
Wolf, Wolff, Wolfgans, Wolfy, Wulfgang

Wolfram (Jewish) ominous

Wolley (American) form of Wally: army leader
Wolly

Wolsh (Slavic) form of Walter: army leader

Wolter (Slavic) form of Walter: army leader

Wood (English) form of Woodrow: special
Woode, Woody

Woodery (English) woodsman
Wood, Wooderree, Woodree, Woodri, Woodry, Woods, Woodsry, Woody

Woodfield (Last name as first name) enjoys the woods

Woodfin (English) attractive
Wood, Woodfen, Woodfien, Woodfyn, Woodie, Woody

Woodford (Last name as first name) forester

Woodrow (English) special
Wood, Woodrowe, Woody

Woodruff (Last name as first name) smooth; natural

Woodson (Last name as first name) son of Wood; suave

Woodville (Last name as first name) from the town of trees

Woodward (English) watchful
Wood, Woodie, Woodard, Woodwerd, Woody

Woodwer (Native American) mourning

Woody (American) jaunty
Wooddy, Woodey, Woodi, Woodie

Woolsey (English) leader
Wools, Woolsi, Woolsie, Woolsy

Worcester (English) secure

Word (American) talkative
Words, Wordy, Wurd

Worden (American) careful
Word, Wordan, Wordun

Wordsworth (English) poetic
Words, Worth

Worie (English) cautious

Worsh (American) from worship; religious
Wor

Worth (English) deserving; special
Werth, Worthey, Worthie, Worthington, Worthy, Wurth

Wortham (English) worthy

Worthington (English) fun; worthwhile
Worth, Worthey, Worthing, Worthingtun, Wurthington

Wouter (German) power figure

Wrae (English) corner

Wrangle (American) cowboy; wrangler
Wrang, Wrangler, Wrangy

Wray (American) cornered

Wren (American) leader of men
Ren, Rin, Rinn, Wrenn

Wright (English) clear-minded; correct
Right, Rite, Wrighte, Write

Wrigley (Place name) city in Tennessee

Wrisley (American) smart
Wrisee, Wrislie, Wrisly

Wriston (American) good proportions
Wryston

Wulf (Hebrew) wolf
Wolf

Wunig (Native American) believer

Wurei (Native American) windy

Wyam (American) form of Wyoming

Wyanll (Scandinavian) arises

Wyant (American) strong-willed

Wyatt ✿ (French) ready for combat
Wiatt, Wy, Wyat, Wyatte, Wye, Wyeth

Wybert (Last name as first name) good profile

Wyborn (Last name as first name) wellborn

Wyck (English) light

Wyclef (American) trendy
Wycleff

Wycliff (English) edgy
Cliffie, Cliffy, Wicliff, Wyclif, Wycliffe

Wydee (American) form of Wyatt: ready for combat
Wy, Wydey, Wydie

Wykeum (American) different

Wyland (English) charismatic

Wyler (German) creative

Wylie (English) charmer
Wiley, Wye, Wylee

Wylon (English) charismatic

Wymann (English) contentious
Wimann, Wye, Wyman

Wymel (English) famous

Wymen (English) soldier

Wymer (English) rambunctious; fighter

Wymon (English) soldier

Wyn (Welsh) gregarious

Wyndham (English) from a hamlet
Windham, Wynndham

Wynell (English) companion

Wynne (English) dear friend
Winn, Wyn, Wynn

Wynter (English) born in winter

Wynton (English) winter town child

Wyshawn (African American) friendly
Shawn, Shawny, Why, Whysean, Wieshawn, Wye, Wyshawne, Wyshie, Wyshy

Wystan (English) struggles

Wythe (English) fair

Wythel (English) of willows

Wyton (English) fair-haired; crowd-pleaser
Wye, Wytan, Wyten, Wytin

Wyze (American) sizzle; capable
Wise, Wye, Wyse

Xan (Greek) form of Alexander: great leader; helpful

Xander (Greek) form of Alexander: great leader; helpful
Xan, Xande, Xandere, Xandre

Xanthin (Greek) gold hair

Xanthos (Greek) attractive

Xanthus (Greek) golden-haired child

Xaque (American) unique

Xat (American) saved
Xatt

Xaver (Spanish) form of Xavier: home; shining

Xaverius (Spanish) form of Xavier: home; shining
Xaverious, Xaveryus

Xavier ○ (Arabic) home; shining
Saverio, Xaver, Zavey, Zavier

Xavion (Spanish) form of Xavier: home; shining

Xaxon (American) happy
Zaxon

Xayvion (African American) dwells in new house
Savion, Sayveon, Sayvion, Xavion, Xayveon, Zayvion

Xebec (French) from Quebec; cold
Xebeck, Xebek

Xen (African American) original
Zen

Xenik (Russian) sly
Xenic, Xenick, Xenyc, Xenyck, Xenyk

Xeno (Greek) gracious
Xenoes, Zene, Zenno, Zenny, Zeno, Zenos

Xenon (Greek) gracious

Xenophon (Greek) gracious

Xenos (Greek) with grace
Xeno, Zenos
Xerarch (Greek) dancing
Xerarche
Xeres (Persian) form of Xerxes:
leader
Xeries
Xerxes (Persian) leader
Xerk, Xerky, Zerk, Zerkes, Zerkez
Xhosas (African) south African
tribe
Xhoses, Xhosys
Xiaoping (Chinese) brightest star
Ximen (Spanish) obeys
Ximenes, Ximon, Ximun
Ximena (Spanish) good listener
Xing-Fu (Chinese) happy
Xi-Wang (Chinese) optimistic
Xochitl (Spanish) flowers
Xuthus (Last name as first name)
long-suffering
Xyle (American) helpful
Zye, Zyle
Xylo (Greek) form of Xylon:
forester
Xylon (Greek) forester
Xyshaun (African American)
zany
Xye, Zye, Zyshaun, Zyshawn
Xyst (English) a portico; systematic
Xist

Xystum (Greek) promenade
Xistoum, Xistum, Xysoum
Xystus (Greek) promenade
Xistus

Yaameen (Hebrew) right hand
Yachna (Hebrew) gracious
Yadid (Hebrew) friend
Yadon (Last name as first name)
different
Yado, Yadun
Yadua (Hindi) judged
Yael (Hebrew) teacher
Yail, Yaley, Yalie
Yagil (Hebrew) celebrant
Yagna (Indian) devout
Yahir (Hebrew) enlightened
Yahne (Hebrew) adored
Yahya (Arabic) vital
Yahiya
Yair (Hebrew) strong
Yakar (Hebrew) adored
Yakez (Scandinavian) celestial
Yale (German) producer
Yalen (English) old soul

Yall (English) form of Yalman:
old man
Yalman (English) old man
Yalon (English) form of Jalen:
vivacious
Yamato (Japanese) mountain;
scaling heights
Yamen (Indian) death god
Yan (Slavic) form of John: God is
gracious
Yana (Native American) bearlike
Yance (American) from England
Yancy (American) vivacious
Yanci, Yancie, Yanzie
Yanis (Hebrew) God's gift
Yannis, Yantsha
Yank (American) Yankee
Yanke
Yankel (Hebrew) supportive
Yaki, Yakov, Yekel
Yannis (Greek) believer in God;
form of John: God is gracious
Yannie
Yanny (Hebrew) learns
Yanto (French) confident
Yanton (Hebrew) form of
Jonathan: gift of God
Yao (Chinese) athletic; (African)
Thursday's child

Yaphet (Hebrew) form of
Japheth: grows
Yapheth, Yefat, Yephat

Yar (English) forest

Yarb (Gypsy) spicy

Yarbon (English) surname

Yarbrough (English) surname

Yarden (Hebrew) flowing
*Yard, Yardan, Yarde, Yardene,
Yardun*

Yardley (English) adorned;
separate
*Yard, Yarde, Yardie, Yardlea,
Yardlee, Yardly, Yardy*

Yared (Hebrew) form of Jared:
descendant; giving

Yaren (Hebrew) form of Jaren:
vocal

Yarkon (Hebrew) green

Yarom (Hebrew) sings
Yaron

Yash (Hindi) famous

Yashy (Indian) wealthy

Yasin (Arabic) seer

Yasir (Arabic) rich

Yasmuji (Asian) flowering

Yassah (Indian) famed

Yasuo (Japanese) calm

Yasutaro (Japanese) peaceful

Yates (English) smart; closed
Yate, Yattes, Yeats

Yati (Indian) beloved

Yave (Hindi) giving

Yavin (Hebrew) believes

Yaw (Akan) Thursday's child

Yawo (African) Thursday's child

Yay (African) Thursday's child

Yazeed (Arabic) growing in spirit

Yeardley (Indian) victor

Yeats (English) gates
Yates

Yeb (English) form of Jeb/Jacob:
jolly; one who supplants

Yediel (Hebrew) loved by Jehovah

Yehem (Biblical) place name

Yehoshua (Hebrew) alive by
God's salvation

Yehuda (Hebrew) praised
Yehudi

Yemin (Hebrew) guarded

Yemyo (Asian) serene

Yen (Chinese) calming; capable

Yenny (Biblical) place name

Yens (Vietnamese) yen; calm

Yeoman (English) helping
*Yeomann, Yo, Yoeman, Yoman,
Yoyo*

Yered (Jewish) form of Jared:
descendant; giving

Yerel (Indian) careful

Yero (African) studious

Yesel (Hebrew) won by God

Yeshaya (Hebrew) treasured

Yesher (Hebrew) God's salvation

Yeshurun (Hebrew) focuses on
God

Yeshya (Hebrew) gifted

Yevgeny (Russian) life-giving

Yianni (Greek) creative

Yigal (Turkish) lively

Yimer (Scandinavian) giant

Yiron (Czech) form of George:
land-loving; farmer

Yishai (Hebrew) form of Jesse:
wealthy

Yisrael (Hebrew) struggles with
God

Yitro (Hebrew) form of Jethro:
fertile

Yitzhak (Hebrew) laughing
Yitz, Yitzchak

Yngvar (Scandinavian) god of
fertility
Ingvar;

Yo (Vietnamese) truthful

Yoav (Hebrew) form of Joab:
praising God; hovering

Yobachi (African) prayerful

Yochanan (Hebrew) form of
John: God is gracious
Yohanan

Yoel (Hebrew) form of Joel:
Jehovah is the Lord

Yogesh (Hindi) another name for Hindu god Shiva

Yogi (Japanese) yoga practicer

Yoginee (Indian) yoga enthusiast

Yohance (Hebrew) form of John: God is gracious

Yohane (Hebrew) form of Johane: God is gracious

Yohann (German) form of Johann: God is gracious
Yohan, Yohn

Yohanys (German) form of Johane: God is gracious

Yoi (Hebrew) bounty

Yojiro (Japanese) hopes

Yolan (French) generous

Yolander (French) violet

Yonah (Hebrew) form of Jonah: peacemaker

Yonatan (Hebrew) form of Jonathan: gift of God
Yonathan, Yonathon

Yong (Chinese) brave

Yoosef (Hebrew) favorite
Yosef

Yoran (Hebrew) to sing

Yorick (Literature) Hamlet's jester

Yorik (English) farms

York (English) affluent
Yorke, Yorkee, Yorkey, Yorki, Yorky

Yorker (English) rich
York, Yorke, Yorkur

Yosef (Hebrew) form of Joseph: He will add
Yose, Yoseff, Yosif

Yosefu (Hebrew) form of Joseph: He will add

Yosemite (Place name) natural wonder

Yosh (Japanese) son

Yoshe (Hebrew) wise

Yoshiaki (Japanese) attractive

Yoshikatsu (Japanese) good

Yoshinobu (Japanese) goodness

Yoshio (Japanese) giving

Yossel (Hebrew) favored
Yoska, Yossi

Yosuke (Japanese) helps

Yosvani (Slavic) form of Johanne: God is gracious

Younes (Hebrew) form of Jonah: peacemaker

Young (English) fledgling
Jung, Younge

Younger (Scandinavian) young

Yoursie (American) form of Juri: farms

Yov (Russian) reliable

Yovan (Slavic) form of Jovan: gifted

Yri (Hebrew) form of Joseph: He will add

Yu (Chinese) shiny; smart

Yuan (Chinese) circle

Yudel (Hebrew) jubilant
Yudi

Yui (Chinese) moon; universal

Yuji (Japanese) snow

Yuke (American) form of Yukon: individualist

Yuki (Japanese) loves snow

Yukichi (Japanese) lucky snow

Yukien (Japanese) of the snows

Yukio (Japanese) man of snow

Yukon (Place name) individualist

Yul (Chinese) infinity

Yule (English) Christmas-born
Yuel, Yul, Yuley, Yulie

Yuli (Basque) childlike

Yuma (Place name) city in Arizona; cowboy
Yumah

Yunuen (Spanish) seer

Yunus (Turkish) young

Yurcel (Turkish) the best

Yuri (Russian) dashing
Yurah, Yure, Yurey, Yurie, Yurri, Yury

Yurik (Japanese) Yuri's child; (Slavic) form of Yorick: Hamlet's jester

Yuris (Latin) farmer
Yures, Yurus

Yuritzi (Slavic) form of Yuri:
dashing

Yursa (Japanese) lily; delicate

Yurza (Slavic) form of George:
land-loving; farmer

Yusuf (Arabic) form of Joseph:
He will add

Yuta (Native American) hunts

Yutu (African) hunter

Yuval (Hebrew) celebrant

Yuvaraj (Indian) prince

Yux (Spanish) form of Joshua:
devout

Yuz (Scandinavian) form of John:
God is gracious

Yuzhi (Slavic) form of Joseph: He
will add

Yves (French) honest; handsome
Eve, Ives

Yvonn (French) attractive
Von, Vonn, Yvon

Zaavan (Biblical) God hides him

Zab (American) slick
Zabbey, Zabbi, Zabbie, Zabby

Zabel (Biblical) place name

Zac (Hebrew) form of Zachariah:
Lord remembers
Zacary, Zach, Zachary, Zachry

Zaca (Hebrew) water movement

Zacary (Hebrew) form of
Zachary: spiritual
*Zac, Zacc, Zaccary, Zaccry,
Zaccury*

Zaccheus (Hebrew) unblemished
Zac, Zacceus, Zack

Zace (American) pleasure-seeking
Zacey, Zacie, Zase

Zach (Hebrew) form of Zachary:
spiritual
Zac, Zachy

Zachariah (Hebrew) Lord
remembers
*Zac, Zacaria, Zacarias, Zacary,
Zacaryah, Zaccaria, Zaccariah,
Zaccheus, Zach, Zachaios,
Zacharia, Zacharias, Zacharie,
Zachary, Zacheriah, Zachery,
Zacheus, Zachey, Zachi, Zachie,
Zachy, Zack, Zackariah, Zackerias,
Zackery, Zak, Zakarias, Zakarie,
Zakariyyah, Zakery, Zechariah,
Zekariah, Zeke, Zekeriah, Zhack*

Zacharias (Hebrew) devout
Zacharyas

Zachary ⊙ ❶ (Hebrew) spiritual
*Zacary, Zacchary, Zach, Zackar,
Zackarie, Zak, Zakari, Zakri,
Zakrie, Zakry*

Zack (Hebrew) form of Zachary:
spiritual
Zacky, Zak

Zade (Arabic) flourishing; trendy
Zaid

Zadok (Hebrew) unyielding
*Zadek, Zadik, Zayd, Zaydie,
Zaydok*

Zafar (Hindi) victor
Zaphar

Zafir (Arabic) wins
Zafeer, Zafyr

Zahavi (Hebrew) golden child

Zaher (American) exceeds

Zahir (Hebrew) bright
Zaheer, Zahur

Zahur (Arabic) flourishes

Zain (American) zany
Zane, Zayne

Zaire (Place name) country in
Africa; brash

Zakary (Hebrew) form of
Zachary: spiritual

Zakhar (Hebrew) pure of heart

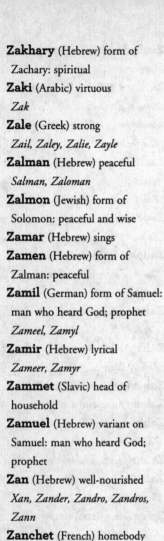

Zakhary (Hebrew) form of
Zachary: spiritual

Zaki (Arabic) virtuous
Zak

Zale (Greek) strong
Zail, Zaley, Zalie, Zayle

Zalman (Hebrew) peaceful
Salman, Zaloman

Zalmon (Jewish) form of
Solomon: peaceful and wise

Zamar (Hebrew) sings

Zamen (Hebrew) form of
Zalman: peaceful

Zamil (German) form of Samuel:
man who heard God; prophet
Zameel, Zamyl

Zamir (Hebrew) lyrical
Zameer, Zamyr

Zammet (Slavic) head of
household

Zamuel (Hebrew) variant on
Samuel: man who heard God;
prophet

Zan (Hebrew) well-nourished
*Xan, Zander, Zandro, Zandros,
Zann*

Zanchet (French) homebody

Zand (Greek) form of Zander:
great leader; helpful

Zander (Greek) form of
Alexander: great leader; helpful
*Zande, Zandee, Zandey, Zandie,
Zandy*

Zandy (American) high-energy
Zandee, Zandi

Zane (English) debonair
Zain, Zay, Zayne, Zaynne

Zano (American) unique
Zan

Zanoni (Unknown) from god
Zeus

Zaphon (Biblical) God hides him

Zappa (American) zany
Zapah, Zapp

Zappe (Persian) happy

Zappy (Persian) jovial

Zar (African) watchful

Zared (Arabic) gold

Zarek (Aramaic) light

Zarel (Slavic) watchful

Zarethan (Biblical) helped by
God

Zario (Biblical) place name

Zartavious (African American)
unusual
Zar, Zarta

Zashawn (African American)
fiery
*Zasean, Zash, Zashaun, Zashe,
Zashon, Zashone*

Zasu (Slavic) form of Jose: asset;
favored

Zauk (Slavic) form of Zac: Lord
remembers

Zaul (American) form of Saul: gift

Zavel (American) youthful

Zavier (Arabic) form of Xavier:
home; shining

Zavion (American) smiling
Zavien

Zayn (English) form of Zane:
debonair

Zazel (Arabic) handsome

Zbigniew (Polish) free of malice;
calming; relinquishes anger

Zeb (Hebrew) form of Zebediah:
gift from God
Zebe

Zebby (Hebrew) believer;
rambunctious
Zabbie, Zeb, Zebb, Zebbie

Zebediah (Hebrew) gift from
God
*Zeb, Zebadia, Zebb, Zebbie,
Zebby, Zebedee, Zebi, Zebidiah*

Zebul (Hebrew) respected

Zebulon (Hebrew) uplifted
*Zebulen, Zebulun, Zevulon,
Zevulun*

Zebulun (Hebrew) revered

Zechariah (Hebrew) form of
Zachariah: Lord remembers
Zeke

Zed (Hebrew) energetic
Zedd, Zede

Zedediah (Hebrew) form of
Zebediah: gift from God
Zededia, Zedidia, Zedidiah

Zedekiah (Hebrew) believing in
a just God
*Zed, Zeddy, Zedechia, Zedechiah,
Zedekias*

Zeeman (Dutch) seafaring
Zeaman

Zeevy (American) sly
Zeeve, Zeevi, Zeevie

Zef (Hebrew) wolf

Zeffy (American) explosive
Zeff, Zeffe, Zeffi, Zeffie

Zekarias (Dutch) impulsive

Zeke (Hebrew) friendly; outgoing
Zeek, Zekey, Zeki

Zekel (Hebrew) form of Ezekial:
God's strength

Zeker (Hebrew) form of Ezekial:
God's strength

Zekie (Turkish) bright mind

Zel (American) hearty

Zelalem (Biblical) form of Zel:
hearty

Zelbie (Hebrew) delicate

Zelig (Hebrew) holy; happy
Selig, Zel, Zeligman, Zelik

Zelmon (English) man of peace

Zemaraim (Biblical) lion-like

Zen (Japanese) spiritual

Zenas (Greek) form of Zeus:
powerful
Zenios, Zenon

Zenen (Biblical) place name

Zenib (Greek) life of Zeus

Zenith (Word as name) famous

Zeno (Greek) philosophical; stoic
Zeney, Zenie, Zenno, Zeny

Zenobios (Greek) living Zeus;
lively
Zenobius, Zinov, Zinovi

Zenon (Greek) form of Xenon:
gracious

Zenotis (Greek) form of Zeus:
powerful

Zenovial (Greek) form of Zeus:
powerful

Zent (American) zany
Zynt

Zeph (Greek) form of Zephyr:
breezy

Zephaniah (Hebrew) protected
by God
Zeph, Zephan

Zephariah (Hebrew) Jehovah's
light

Zephen (Greek) form of Zephyr:
breezy

Zepho (Greek) form of Zephyr:
breezy

Zephyr (Greek) breezy
*Zayfeer, Zayfir, Zayphir, Zefar,
Zefer, Zeffer, Zefir, Zefur, Zephir,
Zephiros, Zephirus, Zephyrus*

Zerah (Biblical) light

Zero (Arabic) nothing
Zeroh

Zerond (American) helpful
Zerre, Zerrie, Zerry, Zerund

Zes (Biblical) place name

Zeshon (African American) zany
Zeshaune, Zeshawn

Zeson (Spanish) fair

Zestler (Last name as first name)

Zete (Hebrew) shiny

Zeth (American) form of Seth:
chosen
Zethe

Zeus (Greek) powerful
Zues

Zev (Hebrew) form of Zebulon:
uplifted
Zevv

Zevediah (Hebrew) form of
Zebediah; broken dreams
Zevedia, Zevidia, Zevidiah

Zevi (Hebrew) brisk
Zevie

Zevry (Biblical) place name

Zevulon (Hebrew) form of
Zebulon: uplifted
Zevulonn

Zexi (Asian) hopeful

Zhen (Chinese) pure

Zhivago (Russian) dashing;
romantic
Vago

Zhobin (Slavic) form of George:
land-loving; farmer

Zhong (Chinese) middle brother;
loyal

Zia (Hebrew) in motion
Zeah, Ziah

Ziad (Arabic) of the light

Zibeon (Arabic) vibrant growth

Zichri (American) form of
Zachary: spiritual

Zie (American) compelling
Zye, Zyey

Ziggy (American) zany

Zigmand (American) form of
Sigmund: victor
Zig, Ziggy

Ziklag (Biblical) place name

Zikomo (African) grateful

Zilph (Biblical) place name

Zimran (Hebrew) sacred

Zimri (Hebrew) valued

Zin (Biblical) praised

Zinc (Biblical) place name

Zindel (Yiddish) form of
Alexander: great leader; helpful
Zindil

Zingo (American) zany

Zino (Greek) philosopher
Zeno

Zion (Hebrew) sign; omen
Sion, Zeione, Zi, Zione, Zye

Zional (Biblical) place name

Zior (African) sky

Ziph (Biblical) place name

Zipkiyah (Native American)
archer

Zirkle (Biblical) place name

Zito (Italian) growth

Ziv (Hebrew) energetic
Zeven, Zevy, Ziven, Zivon

Ziven (Polish) lively
Ziv, Zivan, Zyvan

Ziya (Turkish) light

Ziz (Hebrew) sign

Zlatko (Slavic) gold

Zoan (Biblical) place name

Zoar (Biblical) place name

Zobah (Biblical) place name

Zobel (Biblical) place name

Zober (African) strong

Zocco (American) form of Zach:
spiritual

Zochi (Turkish) form of Zekie:
bright mind

Zohar (Hebrew) light

Zohreh (Indian) blooms

Zoilo (Greek) life; (Spanish) lively

Zol (American) jaunty
Zoll

Zoltan (Hungarian) lively

Zolten-Penn (Hungarian) lively

Zoma (American) loquacious
Zome

Zook (American) form of Zach:
spiritual

Zoran (Slavic) dawn

Zorba (Greek) pleasure seeker
Zorbah, Zorbe

Zorby (Greek) tireless
Sorby, Zorb, Zorbie

Zorshawn (African American)
jaded
*Zahrshy, Zorsh, Zorshie, Zorshon,
Zorshy*

Zowie (Greek) life
Zowey, Zowy

Zoy (English) life-giving

Zuad (American) devout

Zuadan (American) invented
from Sudan

Zub (Russian) toothy

Zuba (Iranian) attractive

Zuberi (African) powerful
 Zooberi, Zubery

Zubren (African) strength

Zucker (English) penitent

Zuhair (Arabic) shines

Zuhayr (Arabic) flowers
 Zuhair

Zuhier (American) shines

Zulfer (American) leads

Zumrud (American) unique

Zuni (Native American) creative

Zuriel (Hebrew) believer

Zurlo (American) zany

Zury (Spanish) believer

Zuzel (Spanish) sweet

Zvon (Croatian) form of
 Zvonimir: sound of peace
 Zevon, Zevonn

Zvonimir (Croatian) sound of
 peace

Zwie (Spanish) from Jose

Zygmunt (Slavic) form of
 Sigmund: victor

Zyke (American) high-energy
 Zykee, Zyki, Zykie, Zyky

Girls

Aaliyah ○ (Hebrew) moving up
Aliya

Aamori (African) good

Aarika (Welsh) form of Erika: honorable; leading others

Aarionne (Welsh) knowing

Aaronita (American) knowing

Aaronitia (American) knowing

Abay (Native American) growing
Abai, Abbay, Abey, Abeye

Abayomi (African) giving joy

Abby (English) happy
Abbee, Abbey, Abbi, Abbie, Abbye

Abdulia (Spanish) certain

Abella (French) vulnerable; capable
Abela, Abele, Abell, Bela, Bella

Abena (African) Tuesday's child

Abery (Last name as first name) supportive
Abby, Aberee, Abrie, Abry

Abha (Hindi) lustrous

Abia (Arabic) excellent
Ab, Aba, Abiah, Abbie

Abida (Arabian) worships

Abigail ○ ○ (Hebrew, English, Irish) joyful
Abagail, Abbegayle, Abbey, Abbie, Abby, Abegail, Abey, Abigal, Abigale, Abigayle, Abygail, Abygale, Abygayle, Gail, Gayle

Abilene (Place name) Texas town; southern girl
Abalene, Abi, Abiline, Aby

Abiola (Spanish) God-loving
Abby, Abi, Biola

Abira (Hebrew) strong

Abisael (Biblical) joyful

Abra (Hebrew) example; lesson
Aba, Abbee, Abbey, Abbie, Abby

Abrianna (American) insightful
Abriana, Abryana, Abryanna, Abryannah

Abrielle (American) form of Abigail: joyful
Abby, Abree, Abrey, Abrie, Abriella, Abryelle

Acacia (Greek) everlasting; tree
Akaysha, Cacia, Cacie, Case, Casey, Casha, Casia, Caysha, Kassy, Kaykay

Acadia (Algonquian-Wakashian) place of plenty

Acalena (English) ready

Acantha (Greek) thorny; difficult

Acatia (Greek) forever tree

Accalia (Latin) stand-in
Accal, Accalya, Ace, Ackie

Achantay (African American) reliable
Achantae, Achanté

Ackalin (Greek) beloved nymph

Ackee (American) fall child

Ada (German) noble; joyful
Adah, Addah, Adeia, Aida

Adaani (French) pretty; noble
Adan, Adane, Adani, Daani, Dani

Adaeze (African) prepared
Adaese

Adah (Biblical) decorated
Ada, Adie, Adina, Dina

Adair (Scottish) innovative
Ada, Adare, Adayr, Adayre, Adda

Adalia (Spanish) spunky
Adahlia, Adailya, Adallyuh, Adaylia

Adalind (American) form of Adeline: sweet

Adalinda (French) form of Adelle: giving

Adamina (Hebrew) earth child

Adamita (Spanish) first on earth

Adanna (Spanish) beautiful baby
Adana

Adar (Hebrew) respected

Adara (Greek) lovely
Adarah, Adrah

Addison ✪ ❶ (English) awesome
Addeson, Addie, Addisen, Addison,
Addy, Addyson, Adeson, Adisen

Addy (English) nickname for
Addison: distinctive; smiling
Addee, Addie, Addye, Adie, Ady

Adea (English) decorative

Adeen (American) decorated
Addy, Adeene, Aden, Adene, Adin

Adekunle (African) crowned at sea

Adela (Polish) peacemaker

Adelaida (Spanish) noble

Adelaide (German) calming;
distinguished
Ada, Adalaid, Adalaide, Adelade,
Adelaid, Laidey

Adelbola (Spanish) brave

Adeline (English) sweet
Adaline, Adealline, Adelenne,
Adelina, Adelind, Adlin, Adline

Adelita (Spanish) form of Adela:
peacemaker
Adalina, Adalita, Adelaina, Adelaine,
Adeleta, Adey, Audilita, Lita, Lite

Adelka (German) form of
Adelaide: calming; distinguished
Addie, Addy, Adel, Adelkah, Adie

Adelle (German) giving
Adel, Adell, Addy

Adelpha (Greek) beloved sister
Adelfa, Adelphe

Adena (Hebrew) precious
Ada, Adenna, Adina, Adynna,
Deena, Dena

Adeniji (Biblical) believer

Adern (Welsh) birdlike
Adyrn

Aderyn (Hebrew) form of Adira:
strong

Adesina (African) threshold child

Adess (Hebrew) decorated

Adhelia (Spanish) of the stars

Adia (African) God's gift

Adiel (African) goat; tough-willed
Adie, Adiell, Adiella

Adil (English) noble born

Adina (Hebrew) high hopes
Addy, Adeen, Adeena, Adine,
Deena, Dena, Dina

Adira (Hebrew) strong

Adisa (Hispanic) friendly
Adesa, Adissa

Aditi (Hindi) free

Adiva (Arabic) gracious

Adjanys (Hispanic) lively
Adjanice, Adjanis

Adline (German) reliable
Addee, Addie, Addy, Adleen,
Adlene, Adlyne

Adolpha (German) noble wolf;
strong girl
Adolpham

Adonia (Greek) beauty
Adona, Adonea, Adoniah, Adonis

Adora (Latin) adored child
Adorae, Adoray, Dora, Dore,
Dorey, Dori, Dorree, Dorrie, Dorry

Adoracion (Spanish) adores

Adoraia (Spanish) adoration

Adoral (Spanish) adored baby

Adoria (Spanish) adored

Adorna (Latin) adorned

Adra (Greek) beauty

Adria (Latin) place name
Adrea

Adrian (English) rich
Adrien, Adryan, Adryen

Adriana (Latin) rich; exotic
Addy, Adree, Adrianna, Adrie,
Adrin, Anna

Adrienne (Latin) wealthy
Adreah, Adreanne, Adrenne,
Adriah, Adrian, Adrien, Adrienn,
Adrin, Adrina

Aegle (Greek) radiant

Aereale (Hebrew) form of Ariel:
God's lion
Aereal, Aeriel, Areale

Aerena (Welsh) feminine form of
Aaron: revered; sharer

Aeronwenn (Welsh) white;
aggressor
Awynn

Affrica (Irish) nice

Afiniti (American) affinity

Afiny (Hebrew) doe

Afra (Arabic) deer; lithe; reddish
Aphra, Aphrah, Ayfara

Africa (Place name) continent
Afrika

Afton (English) confident
Afi, Afian, Aften, Aftie

Afua (African) baby born on Friday
Afuah

Agafi (Greek) form of Agnes:
pure
Ag, Aga, Agafee, Agaffi, Aggie

Agapi (Greek) love
Agapay, Agape, Agappe

Agasha (Greek) form of Agatha:
kindhearted
Agashah, Agashe

Agata (Italian) good girl

Agate (English) gemstone;
precious girl
Agatte, Aget, Aggey, Aggie

Agatha (Greek) kindhearted
Agath, Agathah, Agathe, Aggey,
Aggie, Aggy

Agatta (Greek) form of Agatha:
kindhearted
Ag, Agata, Agathi, Aggie, Agi,
Agoti, Agotti

Agave (Botanical) strong-spined;
genus of plants
Ag, Agavay, Aggie, Agovay

Agentina (Spanish) form of
Argentina: confident; land of
silver
Agen, Agente, Tina

Aggie (Greek) kindhearted
Aggee, Aggy

Aggieth (English) form of Agnes:
pure

Aglae (French) splendid

Aglaia (Greek) goddess of beauty;
splendid

Agnes (Greek) pure
Ag, Aggie, Aggnes, Aggy, Agnas,
Agness, Agnie, Agnus, Nessie

Agnesa (Spanish) pure

Aharona (Hebrew) beloved
Arni, Arnina, Arona

Ahimsa (Hindu) virtuous

Ahisa (Spanish) pure

Ahtena (Hebrew) aware

Ahulani (Hawaiian) heavenly
place

Ahvanti (African) focused
Avanti

Aida (Arabic) gift
Aeeda, Ayda, Ayeeda, Ieeda

Aidan (Irish) form of the
masculine name Aidan: bold spirit
Aden, Aiden, Aidyn

Aileen (Gaelic) fair-haired beauty
Aleen, Alene, Alenee, Aline, Allee,
Alleen, Allene, Allie, Ally

Ailey (Irish) form of Aileen: fair-
haired beauty
Aila, Ailee, Ailie, Ailli, Allie

Ailsa (Irish) noble

Aimee (French) beloved
Aime, Aimey, Aimi, Aimme, Amee,
Amy

Aimer (German) leader; loved
Aimery, Ame, Amie

Ainda (American) sure

Aine (Irish) blissful
Ayne

Ainsley (Scottish) meadow;
outdoorsy
Ainslea, Ainslee, Ainsleigh, Ainslie,
Anes, Anslie, Aynslee, Aynsley

Aintre (Irish) joyous estate
Aintree, Aintrey, Antre, Antry

Aisha (Arabic) life; lively
Aaisha, Aaysha, Aeesha, Aiesha,
Aieshah, Ayeesha, Ayisha, Aysha,
Ieashia, Ieeshah, Iesha

Aisling (Irish) dreamy
Aislinn, Ashling, Isleen

Aislinn (Irish) dreamy
Aisling, Aislyn, Aislynn

Aislinning (Irish) dreamy

Aithne (Irish) fiery
Aine, Eithne, Ena, Ethne

Aja (English) leads

Ajalae (Egyptian) leader

Aka (Hawaiian) regal

Akako (Japanese) red; blushes

Akala (Hawaiian) respected

Akiva (African) morning's baby

Aky (American) lively

Ala (Arabic) excellent
Alla

Alabama (Place name) western
Bama

Alaine (Gaelic) lovely
*Alaina, Alaiyne, Alenne, Aleyna,
Aleyne, Allaine, Allayne*

Alala (Roman mythology) sister
of Mars; protected
Alalah

Alalia (German) joyful

Alama (American) lovely

Alameda (Spanish) poplar tree;
growth

Alana (Scottish) pretty girl
*Alahna, Alahnah, Alaina, Alainah,
Alanah, Alanna, Alannah, Allana,
Allie, Ally*

Alanie (Hawaiian) peace

Alanis (French) shining star
Alaniss, Alannis, Alannys, Alanys

Alaoha (American) dear child

Alason (German) form of
Allison: kindhearted
Ala, Alas

Alathea (English) heals and helps
Aleta, Letitia, Letty

Alaula (English) heals and helps

Alaygrah (Invented) form of
Allegra: snappy
Alay, Allay

Alaytheea (Invented) form of
Alethea: truthful
Alay, Thea, Theea

Alba (Italian) white

Alberta (French) bright-eyed
*Alb, Albertah, Albie, Albirta,
Alburta, Bertie, Berty*

Albertina (Portuguese) bright

Albertine (English) feminine
form of Albert: distinguished
Albertyne, Albie, Albyrtine, Teeny

Albie (American)
Albee, Albey, Alby, Albye

Albina (Italian) white
Albyna

Alcina (Greek) magical; strong-
willed
*Alcee, Alcie, Als, Alsena, Alsie.
Cina, Seena, Sina*

Alda (German) the older child

Aldine (Place name) elder

Aldona (American) sweet
Aldone

Alea (Arabic) excellent
Alaya, Aleah, Aleeah, Alia, Ally

Alechia (Greek) everlasting

Aleeza (Hebrew) joy
Aliza

Alegria (Spanish) beautiful
movement
Allegria

Alejandra (Spanish) defender
Alijandra, Alyjandra

Alejandrina (Spanish) defender
of friends

Aleksandra (Russian) form of
Alexandra: defender of mankind

Alencia (German) cleansed

Aleshia (Greek) honest
*Aleeshia, Aleeshya, Aleshya, Alyshia,
Alyshya*

Alessa (Italian) helper
Alesa

Alessandra (Italian) form of
Alexandra: defender of mankind
Aless, Alessa

Alessia (Italian) nice
Alesha, Allyshia, Alyshia

Alethea (Greek) truthful
Alathea, Aleethia, Aletha, Aletie, Altheia, Lathea, Lathey

Aletta (Greek) carefree
Aleta, Eletta, Letti, Lettie, Letty

Aleviyah (Arabic) helpful

Alex (English) protector

Alexa ○ (Greek) form of Alexandra: defender of mankind
Alecksa, Aleksah, Alex, Alexia, Alixa, Alyxa

Alexandra ○ (Greek) defender of mankind
Alejandra, Alejaundro, Alex, Alexandrah, Alexandria, Alexis, Alezandra, Allesandro, Ally, Lex, Lexi, Lexie

Alexandrine (French) helpful
Alex, Alexandrie, Ally, Lexi, Lexie

Alexcia (English) gracious

Alexi (Greek) form of Alexis: defender of mankind
Alexie, Alexy, Alixi, Alixie, Alixy, Alyxi, Alyxie

Alexia (Greek) helpful; bright
Alexea, Alexiah, Alixea, Lex, Lexey, Lexie, Lexy

Alexina (Scottish) helper

Alexis ○ ① (Greek) form of Alexandra: defender of mankind
Aleksus, Alexius, Alexus, Alexys, Lex, Lexey, Lexi, Lexie, Lexis, Lexus

Alfonsith (German) aggressive
Alf, Alfee, Alfey, Alfie, Alfonsine, Allfrie, Alphonsine, Alphonsith

Alfre (English) form of Alfreda: wise advisor
Alfree, Alfrey, Alfri, Alfrie, Alfry

Alfreda (English) wise advisor
Alfi, Alfie, Alfred, Alfredah, Alfrede, Alfredeh, Freda, Freddy

Alfreida (English) wisdom

Algorita (Spanish) eager

Ali (Greek) form of Alexandra: defender of mankind
Aley, Allee, Alley, Ally, Aly

Alia (Arabic) sky girl

Alianet (Spanish) honest; noble
Alia, Aliane

Alice (Greek) honest
Alece, Alicea, Alise, Alliss, Ally, Allys, Alyse, Alysse, Lisie, Lisy, Lysse

Alicea (Spanish) noble

Alicha (Slavic) joy

Alicia (Greek) delicate; lovely
Alisha

Alida (Greek) stylish
Aleda, Aleta, Aletta, Alidah, Alita, Lee, Lida, Lita, Lyda

Alima (Hebrew) strong

Alin (Scottish) lovely

Alina (Slavic) form of Helen: beautiful; light
Aleena, Alene, Aline, Allene, Allie, Ally, Allyne, Alyna, Lena, Lina

Alinalette (Spanish) noble

Aline (Polish) form of Alina: beautiful; light

Alisa (Hebrew) happy
Alissa, Allisa, Allissah, Alyssa

Alisha (Greek) happy; truthful
Aleesha, Alesha, Alicia, Ally, Allyshah, Alysha, Lesha, Lisha

Alison (Scottish) noble
Alisen

Alissa (Greek) pretty
Alesa, Alessa, Alise, Alissah, Allee, Allie, Ally, Allyssa, Alyssea

Alita (Native American) sparkling

Alix (Greek) form of Alexandra: defender of mankind

Aliya (Hebrew) rises; sweetheart
Aleeya, Alya

Aliza (Jewish) joy child

Alka (Polish) distinctive
Alk, Alkae

Alke (English) form of Elke: distinguished

Allaire (Scottish) open-minded

Allegra (Italian) snappy
Aligra, All, Allagrah, Allie, Alligra, Ally

Allena (Greek) outstanding
Alena, Alenah, Allana, Allie, Ally

Allene (Greek) wonderful
Alene, Alyne

Allesia (English) alyssum flower girl

Allessandra (Italian) kindhearted
Allesandra

Allicent (English) form of Alice: honest

Allie (Greek) smiling
Ali, Allee, Alli, Ally, Allye

Allison ✪ (English) kindhearted
Alisen, Alison, Allicen, Allie, Allisan, Allisen, Allisun, Ally, Allysen, Allyson, Alysen, Alyson, Sonny

Allura (Hispanic) alluring
Alura

Ally (Greek) pure heart
Allee, Alleigh, Alley, Alli, Allie

Allyson (English) another form of Allison: kindhearted
Alisaune, Allysen, Allysun, Alyson

Allysse (Greek) smooth
Allice, Allyce, Allyss

Alma (Latin) good; soulful
Almah, Almie, Almy

Almaree (Spanish) smart

Almeida (Spanish) shines; goal-oriented

Almeria (Arabic) princess
Alma, Almara, Almaria, Almer, Almurea, Als

Almira (Arabic) princess
Allmeerah, Almirah, Elmira, Mira

Alodia (Spanish) thrives; free

Alodie (Origin unknown) thriving
Alodee

Aloha (Hawaiian) love

Aloma (Jewish) form of Alona: sturdy oak

Alona (Jewish) sturdy oak
Allona

Alonda (Spanish) form of Alexandra: defender of mankind
Alona

Alondra (Spanish) bright
Alond, Alondre, Alonn

Alouette (French) birdlike
Allie, Allo, Allou, Allouetta, Alou, Alowette

Aloyse (German) renowned
Aloice, Aloise, Aloyce

Alpha (Greek) first; superior
Alf, Alfa, Alfie, Alph, Alphah, Alphia, Alphie

Alphareen (Spanish) first chosen

Alston (English) a place for a noble
Allie, Ally, Alstan, Alsten, Alstun

Alta (Latin) high place; fresh

Altagracia (Spanish) in God's grace

Altea (Polish) healer

Althaea (Greek) pure

Althea (Greek) wholesome
Althe, Althey, Althia, Althie, Althy, Thea, They

Altisha (English) other girl

Alula (Arabic) little maiden girl

Alundey (American) jaunty

Alva (Spanish) fair; bright
Alvah

Alvada (American) evasive
Alvadah, Alvayda

Alverna (English) elf friend
Alver, Alverne, Alvernette

Alvernise (English) form of Alverna: elf friend
Alvenice

Alvina (English) beloved; friendly
Alvee, Alveena, Alvie, Alvine, Alvy

Alvinetta (English) popular friend

Alvita (Latin) charismatic

Alyasha (Arabic) heaven's child

Alyda (French) soaring
Aleda, Alida, Alita, Lida, Lyda

Alynn (Dutch) intelligent

Alys (English) noble

Alysea (English) high-born

Alysia (Greek) compelling
*Aleecia, Alesha, Alicia, Alish,
Alycia*

Alyssa ✿ (Greek) flourishing
*Alissa, Allissa, Allissae, Ilyssah,
Lissa, Lyssa, Lyssy*

Alysse (English) form of Alice:
honest

Alyx (English) form of Alex:
protector

Amaba (African) amiable

Amabe (Latin) loved
Ama

Amabelle (American) loved
Amabel, Amahbel

Amada (Spanish) form of
Amanda: fit to be loved
Ama, Amadah

Amal (Arabic) optimistic
Amahl

Amalia (Hungarian/Spanish)
industrious

Amalina (German) worker
*Am, Ama, Amaleen, Amaline,
Amalyne*

Amalita (Spanish) hopeful

Amalthea (Greek) perseveres

Amanda (Latin) fit to be loved
*Amand, Amandah, Amandy,
Manda, Mandee, Mandi, Mandy*

Amandra (American) form of
Amanda: fit to be loved
*Amand, Mandee, Mandi, Mandra,
Mandree, Mandry, Mandy*

Amara (Latin) everlasting
*Am, Amarah, Amareh, Amera,
Amura, Mara*

Amarillo (Spanish) yellow
Ama, Amari, Amarilla, Amy, Rillo

Amaris (Hebrew) beloved;
dedicated
Amares

Amaryllis (Greek) fresh flower
Ama, Amarillis

Amber (French) gorgeous and
golden; semiprecious stone
Ambar, Amberre, Ambur, Amburr

Ambike (Hindi) fertile

Amboree (Last name as first
name) precocious
Ambor, Ambree

Ambre (French) kinetic energy

Ambree (French) amber color

Ambrin (Greek) long life

Ambrosette (Greek) eternal
*Amber, Ambie, Ambro, Ambrosa,
Ambrose*

Ambrosia (Greek) eternal
Ambroze, Ambrozeah, Ambrozia

Ambrosina (Greek) everlasting
Ambrosine

Amelia ✿ (German) industrious
*Amalee, Amaylyuh, Amele, Ameleah,
Ameli, Amelie, Amelya, Amilia*

Amelina (Spanish) diligent

Ameline (French) diligent

Amelita (Spanish) diligent

Amera (Arabic) of regal birth
Ameera, Amira

America (American) patriotic
*Amer, Amerca, Americah,
Amerika, Amur*

Ameth (Greek) precious gem;
amethyst

Amethyst (Greek) precious gem
Amathist, Ameth

Amia (German) loved

Amica (Latin) good friend
Ameca, Ami, Amika

Amici (Italian) friend
Amicie, Amie, Amisie

Amie (French) loved one

Amig (Slavic) loved

Amiga (Spanish) friend
Amigah

Amilla (Slavic) form of Camilla: wonderful

Amina (Arabic) trustworthy
Amena, Amine

Aminta (Latin) protects

Amira (Arabic) nurturer

Amirreza (Spanish) eloquent

Amity (Latin) a good friend
Amitee, Amitey, Amiti

Amiya (Slavic) defense

Amna (Indian) gracious

Amnette (American) haven

Amone (American) harmony

Amor (Spanish) love
Amora, Amore

Amora (Spanish) love

Amorelle (French) lover
Amoray, Amore, Amorel, Amorell

Amoretta (French) little love
Amoreta, Amorreta, Amorretta

Amorette (French) tiny love
Amorrette

Amorita (Spanish) loved

Ampar (Spanish) protected

Amrita (Indian) nectar of immortality

Amvi (Hindi) goddess

Amy ❶ (Latin) loved one
Aimee, Amee, Amey, Ameyye, Ami, Amie, Amye

Amyrka (Spanish) lively
Amerka, Amurka, Amyrk, Amyrrka

Anabelia (Slavic) well-loved

Anabril (Spanish) merciful; pretty
Anabrelle, Anna, Annabril

Anadare (Hawaiian) graceful

Anahi (Biblical) responsive

Anahita (Hindi) graceful

Anaid (Slavic) kind

Anais (French) form of Anne: loving; hospitable

Anala (Hindi) fiery

Analae (Hindi) excellent

Analeese (Scandinavian) gracious
Analece, Analeece, Annaleese

Analia (Hebrew) gracious; hopeful
Ana, Analea, Analeah, Analiah, Analya

Analisa (American) lovely

Analy (American) graceful; gracious
Analee, Anali

Anamita (Spanish) enamored

Anand (Hindi) joyful; profound
Anan, Ananda

Anandy (Indian) joy girl

Anapua (Hawaiian) flourishes

Anareli (Spanish) happy

Anastace (Spanish) form of Anastasia; resurrection
Anastayce, Anestace, Anestayce, Anystace, Anystayce

Anastasia (Greek) resurrection
Anastasiya, Anastasya

Anastay (Greek) born again; renewed
Ana, Anastae, Anastie

Anastice (Latin) form of Anastasia: resurrection
Anasteece, Anesteece, Anestice, Anysteece, Anystice

Anatola (Greek) from the east
Anatol, Anatole

Anaysis (Latin) form of Anastasia: resurrection
Anaysys

Anca (Scandinavian) alone

Ancheene (American) creative

Anchoret (Welsh) beloved girl

Ancita (Spanish) favorite

Ancret (Welsh) form of Anchoret: beloved girl

Ander (Greek) feminine

Anders (Scandinavian) stunning
Andars, Andie, Andurs, Andy

Andes (Greek) feminine
Andee

Andi (English) casual
Andee, Andey, Andie, Andy

Andraa (Greek) feminine
Andrah

Andrea ✿ (Greek) feminine
Andee, Andi, Andie, Andra,
Andrae, Andre, Andreah, Andreena

Andreana (Greek) bold heart
Andreanna, Andriana, Andrianna,
Andryana, Andryanna

Andree (Greek) strong woman
Andrey, Andrie, Andry

Andrenna (Scottish) pretty;
gracious
Andreene, Adrena

Andrianna (Greek) feminine
Andree, Andy

Andromeda (Greek) beautiful
star
Andromedah

Aneechia (Slavic) pure

Anees (Indian) grace

Aneeta (Indian) grace

Aneith (Slavic) pure

Aneka (Polish) forgiving

Anela (Hawaiian) angelic

Anelica (Spanish) pleasant

Anelka (Slavic) forgives

Anemone (Greek) breath of
fresh air

Anetra (Slavic) gracious

Anewk (Invented) form of
Anouk: loving; hospitable

Anganetta (Slavic) angelic

Ange (Greek) form of Angela:
angelic; divine

Angeele (English) lithe angel

Angel (Latin) sweet; angelic
Angelle, Angie, Anjel, Annjell

Angela (Greek) divine; angelic
Angelena, Angelica, Angelina,
Angelle, Angie, Gela, Nini

Angelia (American) angelic
messenger
Angelea, Angeliah

Angelica (Latin) angelic
messenger
Angie, Anjeleka, Anjelica, Anjelika,
Anjie

Angelika (Greek) angel
Angelyka, Angilika, Angilyka,
Angylika

Angelina ✿ (Latin) angelic
Ange, Angelyna, Angie, Anje,
Anjelina, Anjie

Angeline (American) angelic
Angelene, Angelline

Angelique (French) form of
Angelica: angelic messenger
Angel, Angeleek, Angelik, Angie,
Anjee, Anjel, Anjelique

Angelle (Latin) angelic
Ange, Angell, Anje, Anjell, Anjelle

Angerona (Mythology) angelic

Angha (Hindi) beauty

Angharad (Welsh) graceful
Angahard

Angie (Latin) angelic
Angey, Angi, Angye, Anjie

Aniani (Hawaiian) lovely
reflection

Anice (Slavic) form of Anne:
gracious

Anick (Hebrew) gracious

Aniece (Hebrew) gracious
Ana, Anesse, Ani, Anice, Annis,
Annissa

Aniela (Polish) sent by God
Ahneela

Anika (Hebrew) hospitable
Anec, Anecca, Aneek, Aneeka,
Anic, Anica, Anik, Annika

Anila (Hindi) wind girl

Anina (Aramaic) answer my
prayer

Aninda (German) form of Anina:
answer my prayer

Anisha (English) purest one
Aneesha, Anysha

Anissa (Greek) a completed spirit
Anisa, Anise, Anysa, Anyssa, Anysse

Anita (Spanish) gracious
Aneda, Aneeta, Anitta, Anyta

Anitia (Spanish) favored

Anitria (Spanish) favored

Aniyalla (Scandinavian) beloved

Anjali (Hindi) pretty; honored
Anjaly

Anjana (Hindi) merciful; pretty
Anjann

Anjelica (Latin) angelic
Anjelika

Anjeliett (Spanish) little angel
*Anjel, Anjeli, Jelette, Jeliett,
Jeliette, Jell, Jelly*

Anjul (French) jovial
Angie, Anjewel, Anji, Anjie, Anjool

Anka (Polish) favorite

Anmol (Hindi) valued

Ann (Hebrew) loving; hospitable
*Aine, An, Ana, Anna, Anne,
Annie, Ayn*

Anna ○ ❶ (Hebrew) gracious
*Ana, Anae, Anah, Annah, Anne,
Anuh*

Annabella (Italian) lovely girl
Anabela, Anabella, Annabela

Annabelle (English) lovely girl
Anabell, Anabelle, Annabell

Annal (Slavic) form of Anna:
gracious

Annalee (English) form of Anne:
gracious

Annalie (Scandinavian) form of
Annalee: gracious

Annaliea (English) form of
Annalee: gracious

Anna-Margarita (Spanish)
devout

Ann-Dee (American) courage
*Andee, Andey, Andi, Andy, Ann
Dee, Anndi*

Anne (English) gracious

Anneka (Scandinavian) form of
Anne: gracious
Anneke

Annelie (German) girl of grace

Anneliese (Scandinavian/
German) form of Anna: gracious,
and Liesa: God is bountiful
Aneliece, Aneliese

Annella (Scottish) graceful
Anell, Anella, Anelle

Annemarie (German) bitter
grace
*Anmarie, Anne-Marie, Ann Marie,
Annmarie*

Annena (Slavic) chosen

Annes (Hebrew) hospitable

Annette (American) vivacious;
giving
*Anette, Ann, Anne, Annett,
Annetta, Annie, Anny*

Anngelite (Slavic) angel

Annice (English) pure of heart

Annie (English) form of Anne:
gracious
Ann, Annee, Anney, Anni, Anny

Annika (Scandinavian) gracious
Anika

Anninka (Russian) gracious;
graceful

Annis (English) pure
Annys

Annissa (Greek) gracious;
complete
Anissa, Anni, Annie, Annisa

Annjanette (Mythology) quiet
goddess

Annletta (English) little Ann

Annunciata (Italian) noticed

Anona (Botanical) pineapple;
fresh

Anora (Latin) honored

Anouk (French) form of Ann:
loving; hospitable

Anoush (Armenian) sweetness

Anselma (German) helmet of
God

Ansley (English) happy in the meadow
Annesleigh, Ans, Anslea, Anslee, Ansleigh, Ansli, Anslie

Ansonia (Scandinavian) pure

Anstass (Greek) resurrected; eternal
Ans, Anstase, Stace, Stacey, Stass, Stassee

Anstice (Greek) everlasting
Anst, Steece, Steese, Stice

Answer (Word as name) the answer

Ansylene (English) God protects

Antenise (English) flowering

Anthea (Greek) flowering
Anthia

Antigone (Greek) impulsive; defiant

Antique (Word as name) old soul
Anteek, Antik

Antoinette (French) priceless
Antoine, Antoinet, Antwanett, Antwonette, Toinette, Tonette

Antonella (French) form of Antoinette: priceless

Antonetta (Greek) praised
Antoneta

Antonia (Latin) perfect
Antone, Antonea, Antoneah

Antonian (Latin) valuable
Antoinette, Antonetta, Toni, Tonia, Tonya

Antonine (Greek) praised
Antonyne

Antronette (English) form of Antoinette: priceless

Antwanette (African American) prized
Antwan, Antwanett

Anupama (Indian) unusual

Anusha (Armenian) sweet

Anya (Russian) grace

Aoife (Irish) beauty

Apalonia (Greek) girl with strength and light

Aphra (Hebrew) earthy; sentimental
Af, Affee, Affey, Affy, Afra, Aphree, Aphrie

Aphrodite (Greek) goddess of love and beauty
Afrodite, Aphrodytee

Api (Latin) rejoice

Apolinaria (Spanish) form of Apollonia: sun goddess
Apolinara

Apollonia (Greek) sun goddess
Apolinia, Apolyne, Appollonia

Apple (Botanical) fruit; quirky
Apel, Appell

April (Latin) month; springlike
Aprel, Aprile, Aprille, Apryl

Aptha (Biblical) growing

Aqua (Spanish) colorful
Akwa

Aquanetla (Invented) spontaneous

Aqueelah (Arabic) vigilant

Aquen (Native American) calm

Aquilline (American) eagle eye

Arabella (Latin) answer to a prayer; beauty
Arabel, Arabela, Arabelle, Arbel, Arbella, Bella, Belle, Orabele, Orabella

Arabelle (Latin) divine
Arabell

Araceli (Latin) heavenly
Ara, Aracelli, Ari

Aracelle (Spanish) flamboyant; heavenly
Ara, Aracel, Aracell, Araseli, Celi

Arachne (Greek) weaver; spider

Araiza (Spanish) innovator

Araminta (English) unique; precious dawn
Ara, Arama, Aramynta, Minta

Araxie (Spanish) creative

Arayalle (English) form of Arielle: God's lion

Araylia (Latin) golden
Araelea, Aray, Rae, Ray

Arbela (Biblical) place name

Arbra (American) form of Abra:
example; lesson
Arbrae

Arce (Spanish) gift

Arcelia (Spanish) treasured
Arcey, Arci, Arcilia, Arla, Arlia

Arcelious (African American)
treasured
Arce, Arcel, Arcelus, Arcy, Arselious

Archana (Indian) loyal
worshipper

Archon (American) capable
Arch, Archee, Archi, Arshon

Ardana (English) ardent

Ardath (Hebrew) ardent
Ardee, Ardie, Ardith, Ardon

Ardele (Latin) enthusiastic;
dedicated
Ardell, Ardella, Ardelle, Ardine

Ardelphia (Place name)
flourishes

Arden (Latin) ardent; sincere
*Ardan, Ardena, Ardin, Ardon,
Ardyn*

Ardery (English) form of Arden:
ardent; sincere

Ardiana (Spanish) ardent
Ardi, Ardie, Diana

Ardie (American) enthusiastic;
special
Ardee, Ardi

Ardienne (American) ardent

Ardina (English) ardent

Ardithan (American) sincere

Ardyss (American) ardent

Areika (Spanish) pure
Areka, Areke, Arika, Arike

Arekah (Greek) virtuous; loving

Arelie (Latin) golden girl
Arelee, Arely, Arlea

Aretha (Greek) virtuous; vocalist
Areetha

Aretta (Greek) virtuous
Arette, Arie

Argelia (Spanish) treasured

Argenta (Latin) silver

Argentina (Place name)
confident; land of silver
*Arge, Argen, Argent, Argenta,
Argie, Tina, Tinee*

Argosy (French) bright
Argosee, Argosie

Argus (Greek) bright
Arguss

Ari (Hebrew) form of Ariel: God's
lion
Aree, Arey, Arie, Ary

Aria (Hebrew) form of Ariel:
God's lion; (English) song
Arya

Ariadna (Slavic) holiest

Ariadne (Greek) holiness
Aryadne

Ariana ✪ ⊕ (Greek) righteous
Arianna

Arianda (Greek) helper
Ariand

Ariane (Greek) very gracious
Arianne, Aryahn

Arianne (French) kind
Ana, Ari, Ariann

Arianwen (Welsh) form of
Aeronwenn: white; aggressor

Arica (Scandinavian) form of
Erica: honorable; leading others

Aridatha (Hebrew) flourishing
Ar, Arid, Datha

Aridna (English) form of
Ariadne: holiness

Aridne (English) form of
Ariadne: holiness

Ariedsol (Spanish) blessed

Ariel (Hebrew) God's lion
Aeriel, Airey, Arielle

Ariella (French) lioness
Ariela, Aryela, Aryella

Aries (Latin) zodiac sign of the ram; contentious
Arees

Arin (Arabic) spreads truth
Aryn

Arina (Russian) peaceful

Aris (Greek) best

Arisca (Greek) form of Arista: wonderful
Ariska, Ariske

Arista (Greek) wonderful

Aristelle (Greek) wonder
Aristela, Aristella

Arith (Hebrew) believes

Aritha (Greek) virtuous
Arete, Aretha

Arizona (Place name) U.S. state; grand
Zona

Arketta (Invented) outspoken
Arkett, Arkette, Arky

Arlais (Welsh) magical

Arlanda (Slavic) dedicated

Arlea (Greek) heavenly
Airlea, Arlee, Arleigh, Arlie, Arly

Arleana (American) form of Arlene: dedicated
Arlena, Arlina

Arlen (Irish) devoted
Arlin, Arlyn

Arlena (Irish) dedicated
Arlana, Arlen, Arlenna, Arlie, Arlina, Arlyna, Arrlina, Lena, Lina, Linney

Arlene (Irish) dedicated
Arlee, Arleen, Arlie, Arline, Arlyne, Arlynn, Lena, Lina

Arlette (French) loyal
Arlet

Arli (English) proactive; girl from rabbit field

Arlind (American) strong; loyal

Arlitra (American) strength of character

Arlyn (Irish) dedicated

Armanda (French) disciplined

Armani (Italian) fashionable
Armanee, Armanie, Armond, Armonee, Armoni, Armonie

Armanth (English) goal-oriented

Armelle (French) armed

Armetrice (Spanish) armed

Armida (Latin) armed; prepared
Armi, Armid, Army

Arminda (Spanish) armed

Armineh (Slavic) defends

Arminell (Latin) nobility
Arminel

Arminta (Slavic) armed

Arna (Slavic) eagle watch
Arnetta

Arnette (English) little eagle; observant
Arn, Arnee, Arnet, Arnett, Ornette

Arnica (American) eagle; intense

Arnite (American) eagle; intense

Arnyx (American) eagle-eyed

Arosa (Spanish) rose

Arosell (Last name as first name) loyal
Arosel

Arpine (Romanian) dedicated
Arpyne

Array (Word as name) colorful

Arrissie (American) the sea

Artemis (Greek) moon goddess

Artemisia (Greek) belonging to Artemis
Arta, Arte, Artema

Arthel (Greek) rich

Arthlese (Irish) rich
Arth, Arthlice, Artis

Arthurena (American) feminine form of Arthur: bear; stone
Arthurene

Artranese (American) hunts

Artriece (Irish) stable
Artee, Artreese, Arty

Artulia (Spanish) high position

Aruna (Hindi) baby of dawn

Arunice (English) silver girl

Arvilla (English) climber

Arvis (American) special
Arvee, Arvess, Arvie, Arviss, Arvy

Arya (Jewish) lioness

Aryana (English) form of Ariana:
righteous

Asabi (African) outstanding

Asalia (Spanish) morning child

Asenath (Biblical) possessed of
God's spirit

Ash (Hebrew) form of Asha: lucky
Ashe

Asha (Hebrew) lucky
Aasha, Ashah, Ashra

Ashandra (African American)
dreamer
Ashan, Ashandre

Ashanti (African) graceful
Ashantay, Anshante

Ashantia (American) outgoing
Ashantea, Ashantiah

Asharaf (Hindi) wishful
Asha, Ashara

Ashby (English) farm of ash trees
Ashbee

Asher (Hebrew) blessed
Ash

Ashla (English) form of Ashley:
woodland sprite

Ashland (Irish) dreamlike
*Ashelyn, Ashlan, Ashleen, Ashlin,
Ashlind, Ashline, Ashlinn*

Ashlei (English) form of Ashley:
woodland sprite
Ashee, Ashie, Ashly, Ashy

Ashleigh (English) from the ash
tree meadow
Ashlynn, Ashton

Ashley ☺ (English) woodland
sprite
*Ash, Ashie, Ashlay, Ashlea, Ashlee,
Ashleigh, Ashli, Ashlie, Ashly*

Ashlyn (English) natural
Ashlin, Ashlinn, Ashlynn

Ashna (Indian) hopeful

Ashonika (African American)
pretty
Ashon, Ashoneka, Shon

Ashton (English) from an eastern
town; sassy
Ashe, Ashten, Ashtun, Ashtyn

Asia (Greek) sunrise
Ashah, Asiah, Asya, Aysia, Azhuh

Asli (Turkish) authentic

Asma (Arabic) exalted; loyal

Asmay (Origin unknown) special
Asmae, Asmaye

Asmillinda (Spanish) loyal

Asminda (Arabic) loyal

Asoka (Japanese) morning baby

Asp (Greek) form of Aspasia: witty

Aspasia (Greek) witty
Aspashia, Aspasya

Aspen (Place name) city in
Colorado; earth mother
Aspin, Aspyn, Azpen

Asphodel (Greek) lily beauty

Asra (Hindi) pure
Azra

Asrika (Slavic) striking

Asta (Greek) star

Astar (Greek) starry-eyed

Astera (Greek) starlike
Asteria, Astra, Astree, Astrie

Astra (Greek) starlike
Astrah, Astrey

Astraea (Greek) starlike

Astrid (Scandinavian/German)
fair; beautiful goddess
*Aster, Asti, Astred, Astri, Astridd,
Astryd, Astrydd, Atty, Estrid*

Asusena (Slavic) lovely fragrance

Asysa (Arabic) lively
Aesha, Asha, Aysah

Atalanta (Greek) athletic; fleet-
footed
Addi, Atlante, Attie

Atanasia (Spanish) form of the
name Anastasia: resurrection

Atara (Hebrew) crowned

Athalet (American) believes

Athalia (Hebrew) ambitious

Athamadia (Greek) believer

Athelean (Greek) eternal; precocious
Athey, Athi

Athena (Greek) wise woman; goddess of wisdom in mythology
Athene, Athenea, Athina, Xena, Zena

Athene (Chinese) wise

Atherine (Spanish) form of Katherine: pure

Athie (Hebrew) wise
Athee, Athey, Athy

Athinoulla (American) praiseworthy

Atianna (American) believer

Atifa (Arabic) compassionate
Ateefah

Atornett (American) off-center

Atropos (Mythology) one of the Greek Fates; cutter

Atu (American) treasured

Aube (French) form of Aubrey: ruler

Auber (French) bright

Aubrey ☉ (French/German) ruler
Aubery, Aubey, Aubrea, Aubree, Aubreye, Aubri, Aubrie, Aubry

Auburne (American) tough-minded
Aubee, Aubern, Auberne, Aubey, Aubi, Aubie, Auburn, Auby

Auden (English) oldest friend

Audia (French) noble

Audie (English) noble strength
Audee, Audey, Audi, Audy, Audye

Audra (English) exciting
Audrah, Audray

Audrea (English) highborn

Audrette (French) highborn

Audrey ☉ (Old English) strong and regal
Audi, Audie, Audra, Audree, Audreen, Audreye, Audri, Audrianna, Audrianne, Audrie, Audrina, Audry

Augusta (Latin) revered
Augustah, Auguste, Augustia, Augustyna, Austina

Augustene (English) serious

Augustina (Latin) great
Agustico, Agustin, Augusine, Augustine, Gusty, Tina, Tino

Augustine (Latin) dignified; worthwhile
Augestinn, Augusta, Augustina, Augustyna, Augustyne, Austie, Austina, Austine, Tina

Aundra (Scandinavian) highborn

Aunjanue (French) sparkling

Aunshaunte (African American) believer
Anshauntay, Aunshauntay, Aunshawntay, Aunshawnte, Shauntae, Shauntay, Shaunte

Aunzell (American) magical

Aupra (Slavic) form of Audra: exciting

Aura (Greek) breeze
Arra

Aurelia (Latin) dawn goddess
Arelia, Aura, Auralea, Aurel, Aurelie, Auria, Auriel, Aurielle

Aurelien (Slavic) golden ornament

Aurian (English) form of Arianne: kind

Auriel (Latin) gold
Auriol

Auristela (Latin) star

Aurora (Latin) morning glow
Aurorah, Aurore, Rory

Aury (American) golden dawn

Aurysia (Latin) gold
Arys, Arysia, Aurys

Austeena (American) statuesque
Austeenah, Austie, Austina

Austen (Literature) for author Jane Austen; charming
Austyn

Austine (Latin) respected
Austen, Austene, Austin

Authorea (American) dawning

Autminia (Spanish) child of autumn

Autra (Latin) gold

Autumn ✪ (Latin) joy of
changing seasons
Autum, Autumm
Ava ✪ ❶ (Latin) pretty; delicate
bird
Avah, Eva
Avalon (Celtic) paradise
Avedis (Spanish) welcomes
Avena (Latin) basic; oat field
Avengelica (Spanish) avenging
Angelica, Avenga, Avengele, Gelica
Averil (French) flighty
Ava, Averile, Averill, Averyl,
Averyll, Aviril
Avery ✪ ❶ (French) flirtatious
Avary, Averee, Averi, Averie
Aves (Greek) breath of fresh air
Aviana (Latin) fresh
Avianca (Latin) fresh
Avino (Hebrew) believes in God
Avis (Latin) little bird
Avisae (American) springlike
Ava, Avas, Aves, Avi
Aviva (Hebrew) springlike
Avivah
Avivi (Jewish) spring child
Avolonne (African American)
happy
Avalonn, Ave, Avelon, Avlon, Avo,
Avolon, Avolunne

Avon (English) graceful
Avaughn, Avaugn, Avonn, Avonne
Avonnia (English) graceful; of
Avon
Avril (French) April; springlike
Avrit (Hebrew) fresh
Avie, Avree, Avret, Avrie
Awen (Welsh) wise and gentle
Axelle (French) serene
Axel, Axell
Aya (Hebrew) bird in flight
Ayan (Hindi) pure
Ayun
Ayanna (Hindi) innocent
Ayunna
Ayda (Arabic) comes back
Ayeisha (Arabic) feminine
Aeesha, Aieshah, Asha, Ayeeshea,
Ayisa, Iasha, Yeisha, Yeishee, Yisha,
Yishie
Ayena (Native American) joyful;
pure
Ayesha (Arabic) living
Ayla (Hebrew) strong as an oak
Aylee (Hebrew) light
Ayleen (Hebrew) light-hearted
Aylene
Aylin (Spanish) strong
Aylen
Aylun (Hebrew) strong

Aylwin (Welsh) beloved
Ayle, Aylwie
Aynet (Spanish) grace
Aynona (Hebrew) form of Anne:
gracious
Ayn, Aynon, Aynonna, Aynonne
Ayo (African) joyful
Ayva (American) form on Ava:
pretty; delicate
Azadeth (Biblical) form of
Asenath: possessed of God's spirit
Azalea (Latin) earthy; flowering
Azalee, Azelea
Azalia (Spanish) flower girl
Azami (Japanese) flower
Azenet (Spanish) sun; God's gift
Aza, Azey
Azenett (Spanish) God's child
Azimah (Japanese) Azami: flower
Aziza (African) beloved; vibrant
Asisa
Azriella (Hebrew) form of
Ariella: lioness
Azriela, Azryela, Azryella
Azsure (American) form of
Azura: blue-eyed
Azucena (Spanish) lily pure
Azu, Azuce, Azucina
Azura (French) blue-eyed
Azuhre, Azur, Azure, Azurre,
Azzura

Baako (Japanese) promising; happy

Baba (American) fun-loving

Babe (Latin) little darling; baby

Babette (French) little Barbara

Babs (American) form of Barbara: traveler from a foreign land

Baca (Biblical) place name; happy

Bachi (Japanese) happy

  Bachee, Bachey, Bachie, Bochee

Bachiko (Japanese) happy

Baden (German) friendly

  Boden, Bodey

Baderinwa (African) worthy

Badger (Irish) badger

  Badge

Badri (African) moon baby

Badriyyah (Arabic) surprise

Baek (Origin unknown) mysterious

Baffin (Place name)

Bagent (Last name as first name) baggage

  Bage

Bagula (German) enthused

Bahaar (Hindi) spring

Bahama (Place name) islands; sun-loving

  Baham

Bahati (African) lucky girl

  Baha, Bahah

Bahija (Arabic) excelling

  Bahiga

Bahir (Arabic) striking

  Bah, Baheer, Bahi

Bahira (Arabic) bright mind

Bai (Chinese) outgoing

Baiben (Irish) sweet; exotic

  Babe, Bai, Baib, Baibe, Baibie, Baibin

Bailey  (English) bailiff

  Bailee, Baylee, Bayley, Baylie

Bailon (American) form of Bailey: bailiff

  Bai, Baye, Baylon

Bain (American) thorn; pale

  Baine, Bane, Bayne

Baird (Irish) ballad singer

  Bayrde

Bairn (Scottish) child

  Bairne

Baka (Hindi) crane; long-legged

  Baca

Bakara (African) noble

Bakul (Hindi) flowering

  Bakula

Bakura (Hebrew) ripe; prime

  Bikura

Balala (Hindi) hopes

Balaniki (Hawaiian) angelic

Balbina (Latin) stammers

  Balbine

Baldree (German) brave; loquacious

  Baldry

Bali (Place name) island near Indonesia; exotic

Balinda (Slavic) form of Belinda: beautiful

Ballou (American) outspoken

  Bailou, Balou

Balvino (Spanish) powerful

  Balvene, Balveno

Bambi (Italian) childlike; baby girl

  Bambee, Bambie, Bambina, Bamby

Banan (Punjabi) held close

Banht (Hindi) fire

Banita (Hindi) girl; thoughtful

Banjoko (Asian) joy

Banner (Word as name) flamboyant

Bano (Persian) bride

  Bannie, Banny, Banoah, Banoh

Bao (Chinese) adorable; creative

Bao-Jin (Chinese) precious gold

Bao-Yo (Chinese) jade; pretty

Baptista (Latin) one who
baptizes
Baptiste, Batista, Battista, Bautista

Bara (Hebrew) chosen
Bari, Barra

Barb (Latin) form of Barbara:
traveler from a foreign land

Barbara (Greek) traveler from a
foreign land
*Babb, Babbett, Babbette, Babe,
Babett, Babette, Babina, Babita,
Babs, Barb, Barbary, Barbe,
Barbette, Barbey, Barbi, Barbie,
Barbra, Barby, Basha, Basia,
Bobbie, Bobi*

Barbarette (English) form of
Barbara: traveler from a foreign
land

Barbrette (English) ill-fated

Barbro (Swedish) extraordinary
Bar, Barb, Barbar

Barcelona (Place name) city in
Spain; exotic
Barce, Lona

Barcie (American) sassy
Barsey, Barsi

Bariah (Arabic) does well

Barika (Hebrew) chosen one

Barkait (Arabic) shines
Barkat

Baronetta (English) feminine
form of Baron: noble leader

Barran (Arabic) song

Barrent (Last name as first name)
hill child

Barrett (Last name as first name)
happy girl
*Bari, Barret, Barrette, Barry,
Berrett*

Barrie (Irish) markswoman;
candid

Barron (Last name as first name)
bright
Bare, Baron, Barrie, Beren, Beron

Barrow (Last name as first name)
sharp; sly
Barow

Basey (Last name as first name)
beauty
Bacie, Basi

Bashiyra (Arabic) joyful

Basia (Greek) regal
Basha, Basya

Basilia (Greek) regal
Basila, Basilea, Basilie

Basimah (Arabic) smiling
Basima, Basma

Baskama (Biblical) place name;
fragrant

Bassen (American) queen

Bastienna (French) form of
masculine name Bastien: respected
Bastee, Bastienne

Bat (German) female warrior
Bet

Bathia (German) warrior woman
Basha, Baspa, Batia, Batya, Bitya

Bathilda (German) woman in
war
*Bathild, Bathilde, Berthilda,
Berthilde*

Bathsheba (Hebrew) beautiful;
daughter of Sheba
*Bathseva, Batsheba, Batsheva,
Batshua, Sheba*

Bathshira (Arabic) happy;
seventh

Batia (Hebrew) daughter of God
Batea, Batya

Batice (American) warrior;
attractive
Bateese, Batese, Batiece, Batty

Batini (African) ponders much

Batzra (Hebrew) daughter of
God

Bay (Vietnamese) Saturday's child;
patient; unique
Bae, Baye

Bayani (Indian) joy

Bayla (Indian) young girl
Bala

Baylor (French) of the bay;
water-loving
Bayler

Baynes (American) feminine
form of Baines: pale
Bain, Baines, Bayne

Bayo (African) bringing joy

Bayonne (Greek) joyful victor
*Bay, Baye, Bayonn, Bayonna,
Bayunn*

Bea (American) form of Beatrice:
blessed woman

Beama (English) blessed

Beata (German) blessed
Bayahta, Beate

Beatha (Latin) blessed
Betha

Beatrice (Latin) blessed woman
*Beat, Beatrisa, Beatrise, Beattie,
Bebe, Bee, Beitris, Beitriss, Bibi,
Treece, Trice*

Beatrix (Latin) happy

Beatriz (Spanish) form of
Beatrice: blessed woman

Bebe (French) baby
Babee, Baby, Bebee

Bebhinn (Irish) sweet girl

Becca (Hebrew) form of Rebecca:
loyal
Bekka

Becerra (Spanish) safe haven

Bechira (Hebrew) chosen child

Becky (English) form of Rebecca:
loyal
Becki, Beki

Bedelia (Irish) form of Bridget:
powerful

Bedriska (Irish) form of Bedelia:
powerful

Bee (American) form of Beatrice:
blessed woman

Beegee (American) laidback; calm
B.G., Begee, Be-Gee

Beeja (Hindi) the beginning;
happy
Beej

Bee-Sun (Filipino) nature-loving;
glad
Bee Sun

Bego (Hispanic) spunky
Beago

Begonia (Botanical) flower

Behira (Hebrew) shines

Behorah (Invented) friend
Be, Behi, Behie, Behora

Beige (American) tawny; calm
Bayge

Beige-Dawn (American) clear
morning
Bayge-Dawn, Beige Dawn

Beila (Spanish) beautiful

Bejoy (American) filled with joy

Bel (Latin) beauty

Bela (Czech) white
Belah

Belann (Spanish) pretty
*Bela, Belan, Belana, Belane,
Belanna*

Belay (English) white

Belem (Spanish) pretty
Bel, Beleme, Bella

Belems (American) relinquishes

Belen (Latin) beauty

Belgica (American) white
Belgika, Belgike, Belgyke, Bellgica

Belia (Spanish) beauty
*Belea, Beliano, Belica, Belicia,
Belya, Belyah*

Belicia (Spanish) believer
Belia

Belinda (Spanish) beautiful
Belynda

Belita (Spanish) little beauty

Bella ✪ (Italian) beautiful

Bellace (Invented) pretty
Bellase, Bellece, Bellice

Belle (French) beautiful
Bela, Bele, Bell, Bella

Bellina (French) beautiful

Bellona (Mythology) strong and
lovely

Belva (Latin) beautiful view

Belvia (Invented) practical
Bell, Belva, Belve, Belveah

Bemedikta (Scandinavian) form
of Benedicta: blessed
Benedikte

Bena (Native American) pheasant;
highbrow

Bendite (Latin) well-blessed
Ben, Bendee, Bendi, Bennie,
Benny, Binni

Bene (Latin) blessed

Benecia (Latin) form of
Benedicta: blessed

Benedeto (Italian) form of
Benedicta: blessed
Benedetto

Benedetta (Latin) form of
Benedicta: blessed
Benedicte, Benedikta, Benetta,
Benita, Benni, Benoite

Benedicta (Latin) feminine form
of Benedict: blessed
Benna, Benni

Benigna (Spanish) kind

Benilda (German) struggles

Bening (Filipino) blessing

Benita (Latin) feminine form of
Benedict: blessed
Bena, Benetta, Benitri, Bennie,
Binnie

Benneta (Spanish) pretty

Bennetteta (Spanish) blessing

Benni (Latin) form of Benedicta:
blessed
Bennie, Binny

Benson (Last name as first name)
Ben's child

Benta (Latin) much blessed

Bente (Latin) blessed

Bentley (English) meadow;
luxury life
Bentlea, Bentlee, Bentleigh, Bently

Beon (Biblical) place name

Beonn (American) good girl

Bera (German) bearish

Berachan (Hebrew) blessing
Beracha, Berucha, Beruchiya,
Beruchya

Berdina (German) bright; robust
Berd, Berdie, Berdine, Berdyne,
Burdine, Burdynne, Dina, Dine

Berdine (German) glows

Berecyntia (Mythology) earth
goddess

Berenjena (Spanish) eggplant

Bergen (American) pretty
Berg, Bergin

Berget (Irish) form of Bridget:
powerful
Bergette

Berit (Scandinavian) glorious
Beret, Berette

Berkley (American) smart
Berkeley, Berkie, Berklie, Berkly

Bermuda (Place name) island;
personable
Bermudoh

Bernadette (French) form of
Bernadine: brave
Berna, Bernadene, Bernadett,
Bernadina, Bernarda, Bernardina,
Bernardine, Berneta, Bernetta,
Bernette, Berni, Bernie, Bernita,
Berny

Bernadine (German) brave
Bernadene, Berni, Bernie

Bernardita (Spanish) brave little
bear

Berneen (Irish) hearty

Berney (English) brave bear

Bernice (Greek) victorious
Beranice, Berenice, Bernelle,
Berneta, Bernetta, Bernette, Berni,
Bernicia, Bernie, Bernyce

Bernie (American) winning
Bernee, Berney, Berni, Berny

Bernita (Greek) form of Bernice:
victorious

Berry (Botanical) tiny; succulent
Berree, Berri, Berrie

Bersaida (American) sensitive
Bersaid, Bersaide, Bersey, Bersy,
Sada, Saida

B

Berta (German) bright

Bertel (Slavic) smart

Bertha (German) bright
Barta, Berta, Berte, Berthe, Berti, Bertie, Bertilda, Bertilde, Bertina, Bertine, Bertita, Bertuska, Berty, Bird, Birdie, Birdy, Birtha

Bertie (German) bright
Bert, Bertee, Bertey, Berty

Bertille (German) form of Bertha: bright

Bertina (German) feminine form of Bert: shining bright

Bertrice (French) form of Beatrice: blessed woman

Berule (Greek) bright; pure
Berue, Berulle

Berura (Hebrew) chaste
Beruria

Beryl (Greek) bright and shining gem
Beril, Berlie, Berri, Berrill, Berry, Beryla, Beryle, Beryn

Bess (Hebrew) form of Elizabeth: God's promise
Bessie

Bet (Hebrew) daughter

Beta (Greek) from Greek alphabet; beginning
Betka, Betuska

Beth (Hebrew) form of Elizabeth: God's promise

Betha (Welsh) devoted to God
Bethah, Bethanne

Bethamie (English) form of Bethany: God's disciple

Bethann (English) combo of Beth and Ann; devout
B-Anne, Bethan, Beth-ann, Bethanne

Bethany (Hebrew) God's disciple
Beth, Bethanee, Bethani, Bethania, Bethanie, Bethann, Bethanne, Bethannie, Bethanny, Betheny, Bethina

Bethel (Hebrew) in God's house; holy child

Bethesda (Hebrew) child of a merry home

Bethia (Hebrew) Jehovah's daughter
Betia, Bithia

Beti (English) small woman

Betricia (American) form of Patricia: woman of nobility; unbending

Betriss (Welsh) blessed
Betrys

Bets (Jewish) God's child

Betsayra (Spanish) abundance

Betsy (Hebrew) form of Elizabeth: God's promise
Bet, Betsey, Betsi, Betsie, Betts

Betta (Italian) form of Bettina: God's promise

Bette (French) lively; God-loving

Betty (Hebrew) form of Elizabeth: God's promise
Bett, Betti, Bettye

Betuel (Hebrew) in God's house
Bethuel

Betula (Hebrew) dedicated; religious
Bee, Bet, Bethula, Bethulah, Bett, Betulah

Beulah (Hebrew) married
Bealah, Beula, Bew, Bewla

Beulahma (Biblical) marries

Bev (English) form of Beverly: beavers by the stream; friendly

Beverly (English) beavers by the stream; friendly
Bev, Beverelle, Beverle, Beverlee, Beverley, Beverlie, Beverlye, Bevvy, Verly

Bevina (Irish) vocalist
Beavena, Bev, Beve, Beven, Bevena, Bevin, Bevy, Bovana

Bevinn (Irish) royal
Bevan

Bezetha (Bibllical) place name

Bhamini (Hindi) beautiful girl

Bhanumati (Hindi) bright

Bharaati (Hindi) careful

Bhavika (Hindi) devoted girl

Bhuma (Hindi) of the earth

Bian (Vietnamese) hides from life

Bianca (Italian) white
Beanka, Beonca, Beyonca, Biancha,
Biancia, Biankah, Bionca, Bionka,
Blanca, Blancha

Bibi (Arabic) lady
Bebe, Bibiana, Bibianna,
Bibianne, Bibyana

Bibiane (Latin) vibrant

Bice (Last name as first name)
axe; sharp talent

Bidelia (Irish) form of Bridget:
powerful
Bedilia, Biddy, Bidina

Bienvenida (Spanish) welcomed
baby

Bijou (French) jewel
Bejeaux, Bejou, Bejue, Bidge, Bija,
Bijie, Bijy

Bik (Chinese) jade

Bikini (Place name) island girl;
fun-loving
Bikinee

Bilhah (Biblical) summer's child

Billie (German) feminine form of
Bill: staunch protector
Billa, Billee, Billey, Billi, Billy,
Billye

Billina (English) feminine form
of Bill: staunch protector
Belli, Bill, Billee, Billie, Billy

Billings (American) bright
Billey, Billie, Billing, Billy, Billye,
Billyngs, Byllings

Bina (Hebrew) perceptive woman;
(Indian) musical instrument
Bena, Binah, Byna

Binali (Hindi) music girl

Binase (Hebrew) bright
Beanase, Benace, Bina, Binah,
Binahse

Binti (African) dancer

Binyamina (Hebrew) right hand

Bionda (Italian) black
Beonda, Biondah

Bira (Hebrew) fortified; strong
Biria, Biriya

Bircit (Scandinavian) form of
Bridget: powerful

Bird (English) birdlike
Birdy

Birdie (English) bird
Birdee, Birdey, Birdi, Byrdie

Birdron (German) of birds

Birgit (Scandinavian) spectacular
Bergette, Berit, Birgetta, Birgite,
Britta, Byrget, Byrgitt

Birgitta (Scandinavian) form of
Bridget: powerful
Birgette, Brita, Byrgetta, Byrgitta

Birgitte (Scandinavian) strong

Birte (Scandinavian) form of
Bridget: powerful
Berty, Birt, Birtey, Byrt, Byrtee

Birthenne (American) born
lucky

Bishop (Last name as first name)
loyal
Byshop

Bita (Hebrew) form of Bithia:
Jehovah's daughter

Bitha (Biblical) blessed daughter

Bithia (Hebrew) Jehovah's
daughter

Bithron (Biblical) resounding

Bitina (Mythology) darkness
Libitina

Bitki (Spanish) form of Beatrix:
happy

Bitsie (American) small
Bitsee, Bitzee, Bitzi, Bytsey

Bitta (Scandinavian) form of
Bridget: powerful
Bit, Bitt, Bittey

Bittan (Origin unknown) gives joy

Bivona (African American) feisty
BeBe, Biv, Bivon, Bivonne

Bjork (Icelandic) unique
Byork

Blade (English) glorified
Blaide, Blayde

Blaine (Irish) thin
Blane, Blayne

Blair (Scottish) plains-dweller
Blaire, Blayre

Blaise (Latin/French) lisp; stutter
Blaize, Blasé, Blaze

Blake (English) dark

Blakely (English) dark
Blakelee, Blakeley, Blakeli

Blanca (Spanish) white
Blancah, Blonka, Blonkah

Blanche (French) white
*Blanca, Blanch, Blancha,
Blanchette, Blanka, Blanshe,
Blenda*

Blanchefleur (French) white
flower; pretty

Blanchine (French) white

Blanda (Latin) seductive
Blandina, Blandine

Blanka (Spanish) form of Blanca:
white

Blasia (Spanish) form of Blaise;
stutter

Blasie (French) blaze; stammering

Blath (Irish) flower

Blaze (Englush) fiery
Blaize, Blayze

Bleinda (American) form of
Belinda: beautiful

Blesida (Spanish) blessed

Bless (American) blessed
Blessie

Blessing (English) dedicated

Blessy (American) blessed

Bleu (French) blue
Blue

Blima (Hebrew) blossoming girl
Blimah, Blime

Bliss (English) blissful girl

Blodwen (Welsh) white flower
Blodwyn, Blodyn

Blom (Hebrew) form of Blum:
flower

Blonda (English) blonde

Blondelle (French) blonde girl
Blondell, Blondie, Blondy

Blondie (American) blonde
Blondee

Blossom (English) flower

Bluebell (Botanical) pretty
*Belle, Blu, Blubel, Blubell, Blue,
Bluebelle*

Blum (Hebrew) flower
Bluma

Blumelle (English) flowers

Blush (American) pink-cheeked
Blushe

Bly (American) soft; sensual
Blye

Blyde (English) obliging

Blydece (English) obliging

Blythe (English) carefree
Blithe, Blyth

Bo (Chinese) precious girl

Boanah (American) good
Boana, Bonaa, Bonah, Bonita

Bobbi (American) form of
Roberta: brilliant mind
*Bobbee, Bobbette, Bobbie, Bobby,
Bobbye, Bobi, Bobina*

Bobett (American) form of
Roberta: brilliant mind

Bodil (Polish) heroic
Bothild, Botilda

Bogdana (Polish) gift from God
*Boana, Bocdana, Bogda, Bogna,
Bohdana, Bohdana, Bohna*

Bogdanka (Slavic) God's gift

Bogumila (Polish) loved by God

Boguslawa (Polish) in God's
glory

Boinaiv (Native American) girl in
the grass

Bola (Origin unknown) clever
Bolo

Bolade (African) honored girl

Bolanile (African) rich in spirit

Bolda (Slavic) embolden

Boleslawa (Polish) strong

Bona (Italian) good
Bonah, Bonna

Bonbon (American) goodness

Boncela (Spanish) good

Boncie (Spanish) good

Bonda (Spanish) good
Bona

Bondeau (American) pretty

Bonett (Spanish) pretty

Bonfilia (Italian) good daughter

Bong-Cha (Korean) excellent
daughter

Bonille (Italian) goodness

Bonita (Spanish) good; pretty
*Bo, Bona, Boni, Bonie, Bonitah,
Nita*

Bonn (French) satisfied; good
Bon, Bonne

Bonnefin (Spanish) good end

Bonnevie (Scandinavian) good
life

Bonnie (Scottish) fine; attractive;
pretty
*Boni, Bonie, Bonne, Bonnebell,
Bonnee, Bonni, Bonnibel,
Bonnibell, Bonnibelle, Bonny*

Bonosse (American) generous

Booth (German) from the
dwelling; home-loving
Boothe

Bootsey (American) cowgirl
Boots, Bootsie

Bopelo (African) confident

Borghild (Scandinavian) prepared

Borgny (Scandinavian) fortified;
strong

Bors (Latin) foreign
Borse

Boske (Hungarian) strays

Boston (Place name) city in
Massachusetts; courteous
Boste, Bosten, Bostin

Boswell (Last name as first name)
intellectual
Boz, Bozwell

Boupha (Vietnamese) flower girl

Boussaina (Arabic) smiles

Bowdy (American) outgoing
Bow, Bowdee, Bowdey, Bowdie

Boxidara (Slavic) divine
Boza, Bozena, Bozka

Bozena (Polish) treasured

Bracha (Hebrew) blessed; sways
in wind
Brocha

Bradley (English) girl of the
broad meadow; carefree
Bradlee, Bradleigh, Bradlie, Bradly

Brady (Irish) spirited child
Bradee, Bradey, Bradi, Bradie

Braisly (American) cautious
Braise, Braislee, Braize, Braze

Branca (American) form of
Blanca: white

Branda (Spanish) brandy

Brandisa (English) brandy

Brandise (English) brandy

Brandy (Dutch) sweet as wine;
fun-loving
*Bran, Brandais, Brande, Brandea,
Brandee, Brandeli, Brandi,
Brandye, Brandyn, Brani,
Branndea*

Branka (Czech) glory
Bran, Branca, Bronca, Bronka

Braxton (English) from town of
Brock: safe
Braxten

Brayden (American) humorous
*Braden, Brae, Braeden, Bray,
Brayd, Braydan, Braydon*

Breana (Irish) form of Briana:
virtuous; strong
*Bre-Anna, Breanne, Breeana,
Briana, Briane, Briann, Brianna,
Brianne, Briona, Bryanna, Bryanne*

Breann (Irish) form of Briana:
virtuous; strong
Bre-Ann, Bree, Breean, Breeann

Breathine (English) breath of
fresh air

Breck (Irish) freckled

Breckina (Irish) little freckled girl

Bree (Irish) upbeat
Brea, Bria, Brie, Brielle

Breela (Irish) esteemed

Breelya (Irish) popular

Breena (Irish) glowing
Brena

Breene (English) palace child

Breeshonna (African American)
happy-go-lucky
Bree, Brie, Brieshona

Breezy (American) easygoing
Breezee, Breezie

Brehea (American) self-sufficient
Breahay, Brehae, Brehay

Breken (English) freckled

Bren (American) form of Brenda:
royal; glowing
Breyn

Brena (Irish) strong-willed
Brenna

Brenda (Irish) royal; glowing
*Bren, Brendalynn, Brenn, Brenna,
Brennda, Brenndah, Brinda,
Brindah, Brinna*

Brendelle (American) distinctive

Brendette (French) small and
royal

Brendie (American) form of
Brenda: royal; glowing
Brendee, Brendi

Brenita (Spanish) form of
Brenda: royal; glowing

Brenna (Irish) form of Brenda:
royal; glowing
Bren, Brenn, Brenie

Brenth (Welsh) hill child

Brenyatta (Welsh) hill child

Brenza (Spanish) quiet

Bresan (American) nice

Brescia (American) nice

Bretislava (Polish) glorious
Breeka, Breticka

Brett (Latin) jolly
Bret, Bretta, Brette

Breyawna (African American)
form of Brianna: virtuous; strong
Bryawn, Bryawna, Bryawne

Bria (Irish) form of Brianna:
virtuous; strong

Briandi (Irish) honorable

Brianna ○ ❶ (Irish) virtuous;
strong
*Breana, Breann, Bria, Briana,
Briannah, Brie-Ann, Bryanna*

Brianne (Irish) strong
Briane, Brienne, Bryn

Briar (French) heather
Brear, Brier

Briar-Rose (Literature) from
Sleeping Beauty: princess

Briazine (English) honored

Brice (English) quick

Briceidy (English) precocious
Brice, Bricedi, Briceidee, Briceidey

Bricene (American) aware

Bride (Scottish) form of Bridget:
powerful

Bridey (Irish) wise
Bredee, Breedee, Bride, Bryde

Bridged (Scottish) has the
strength of fire
Bridgid, Briged, Brigid

Bridget (Irish) powerful
*Birgit, Birgitt, Birgitte, Breeda,
Brid, Bride, Bridge, Bridgett,
Bridgette, Bridgey, Bridgitte,
Brigantia, Briget, Brigette, Brighid,
Brigid, Brigida, Brigit, Brigitt,
Brigitta, Brigitte, Brijette, Brygett,
Brygida, Brygitka*

Brie (French) from the French
town Rozay-en-Brie
Bree, Brielle

Brienne (French) honored

Brier (French) heather
Briar

Briesha (African American)
giving
Bri, Brieshe

Brigida (Italian) strong
Brigeeda

Brigitta (Romanian) strong
Brigeeta, Brigeetta, Brigita

Bril (American) strong
Brill

Briley (Last name as first name)
popular
BeBe, Bri, Brile

Brina (Latin) form of Sabrina:
passionate
*Breena, Brena, Brinna, Bryn,
Bryna, Brynn, Brynna, Brynne*

Brindha (Indian) sorrowful

Brindie (American) form of
Brenda: royal; glowing

Brindle (Irish) versatile
Bryndle

Brine (Irish) strong
Bryne

Brinkelle (American)
independent nature
*Binkee, Binky, Brinkee, Brinkel,
Brinkell, Brinkie*

Brinlee (American) sweetheart
Brendlie, Brenlee, Brenly

Brionna (Irish) happy
Breona, Briona

Brisa (Spanish) beloved
*Breezy, Breza, Brisha, Brisia,
Brissa, Briza, Bryssa*

Brisalle (Spanish) loved

Brisco (American) high-energy
woman
Briscoe, Briss, Brissie, Brissy

Briseis (Mythology) prized; loved

Briseyda (Spanish) happy

Brissellies (Spanish) happy
*Briselle, Briss, Brisse, Brissel,
Brissell, Brissey, Brissi, Brissies*

Brit (Latin) British

Britaney (English) girl from
Britain
*Britanee, Britani, Briteny, Britnee,
Britney, Britni, Brittaney, Brittenie*

Brites (Spanish) strong

Britt (Latin) girl from Britain
Brit

Britta (Swedish) strong woman
Brita

Brittany (English) girl from
Britain
*Brinnee, Britany, Briteney, Britney,
Britni, Brittan, Brittaney, Brittani,
Brittania, Brittanie, Brittannia,
Britteny, Brittni, Brittnie, Brittny*

Brittenne (English) girl from
Britain

Britty (Irish) form of Brittany:
girl from Britain
*Britee, Britey, Briti, Britie, Brittee,
Brittey, Britti, Brittie, Brity*

Brizalette (English) beloved

Brody (Irish) girl from the canal
Brodee, Brodey, Brodi, Brodie

Brona (Italian) brown-haired girl

Bronislava (Polish) protective
*Brana, Branislava, Branka, Brona,
Bronicka, Bronka*

Bronislawa (Polish) protective
Bronya

Bronte (Literature) for authors
Charlotte and Emily Bronte;
romantic
Brontae, Brontay

Bronty (American) form of
author surname Bronte: for
authors Emily and Charlotte
Bronte; romantic

Bronwyn (Welsh) white-breasted
*Bron, Bronwen, Bronwhen,
Bronwynn*

Brooke ✪ (English) sophisticated
Brook, Brooky

Brookette (American) girl from
the brook

Brooklyn ✪ (Place name)
neighborhood in New York
*Brookelyn, Brookelynn, Brooklynn,
Brooklynne*

Broolyn (American) form of
Brooklyn: neighborhood in New
York

Browning (Literature) for poet Elizabeth Barrett Browning; pensive

Brucie (French) feminine form of Bruce: complicated; from a thicket of brushwood
Brucina, Brucine

Bruenetta (French) brown-haired
Bru, Brunetta

Bruna (Italian) brown-haired girl

Bruneita (German) brown-haired
Broon, Brune, Bruneite, Brunny

Brunella (German) intelligent
Brun, Brunela, Brunelle, Brunetta, Brunette, Brunilla, Brunne

Brunetta (Slavic) brunette

Brunhilda (German) warrior
Brunhild, Brunhilde, Brunnhilda, Brunnhilde, Brynhild, Brynhilda, Hilda

Bruni (Spanish) brown hair

Bruno (Italian) brown

Bryanna (Gaelic) powerful female
Breanna, Brianna, Bryana

Bryanta (American) feminine form of Bryan: ethical; strong
Brianta, Bryan, Bryianta

Bryce (American) happy; (Welsh) aware
Brice

Bryleigh (English) form of Brittany: jovial
Brilee, Briley, Brily, Brilye, Brylee, Brylie

Bryn (Welsh) hopeful; climbing a hill
Brenne, Brinn, Brynn, Brynne, Brynnie

Brynn (Welsh) hopeful
Brenn, Brinn, Brynne

Brynna (Welsh) optimistic
Brinn, Brinna

Bryonie (Latin) clinging vine
Breeonee, Brioni, Bryony

Bryony (Latin) vine; clingy
Briony, Bronie, Bryonie

Bua (Vietnamese) fortunate
Boo, Bu

Bubbles (American) perky
Bubb

Buena (Spanish) goodness

Buffy (American) plains-dweller
Buffee, Buffey, Buffie

Bukola (African) wealthy
Bucola

Bule (Biblical) wed
Beul, Beulah

Bunard (American) good
Bunerd, Bunn, Bunny

Bunita (Spanish) wins

Bunmi (Hindi) earth; (Slavic) lady

Bunny (English) little rabbit; bouncy
Bunnee, Bunni, Bunnie

Burcetta (Slavic) sweet

Burgundy (French) red wine; unique
Burgandi, Burgandy

Burke (American) loud
Berk, Burk, Burkie

Burkeley (English) birches; outdoorsy
Berkeley, Burkelee, Burkeleigh, Burkeli, Burkelie, Burkely, Burklee, Burkleigh, Burkley, Burkli, Burklie, Burkly

Burma (Place name)

Burns (Last name as first name) presumptuous
Bernes, Berns, Burn, Burnee, Burnes, Burney, Burni, Burny

Buseje (African) interesting

Buthaayna (Arabic) lovely body
Busayna, Buthaynah

Butte (Place name) landscape

Butter (American) smooth

Button (American) sensitive

Buz (Biblical) angry

Buzzie (American) spirited
Buzz, Buzzi

Bwyana (African American) smart

Bwya, Bwyanne

Byhalia (Native American) strong oak

Byria (Place name)

Byronae (American) feminine form of Byron: reclusive; small cottage

Byrona, Byronay

Bythia (American) virtuous

Cabot (French) fresh-faced

Cabriole (French) adorable

Cabb, Cabby, Cabriolle, Kabriole

Cacalia (Botanical) accommodating

Cachay (African American) distinctive

Cachet (French) fetching

Cache, Cachee

Cadasa (Biblical) place name

Caddy (American) elusive; alluring

Cade (American) precocious

Kade, Kaid

Cadena (Latin) rhythmic

Cadence (American) musical

Kadence

Cadencia (Spanish) in cadence

Cadenie (American) in cadence

Cadou (French) rhythmic

Cady (English) fun-loving

Cadee, Cadey, Cadye, Caidee, Caidy, Kadee, Kady

Caesaria (Greek) feminine form of Caesar: focused leader

Cahara (American) coherent

Cai (Chinese) wealthy; girlish

Cailida (Spanish) passionate

Cailidora (Greek) gifted with a beautiful face

Cailin (American) happy

Cailyn, Cailynn, Calyn, Cayleen, Caylin, Caylyn, Caylynne

Caimile (Spanish) helps

Cainwen (Welsh) lovely treasure

Ceinwen, Kayne, Keyne

Cairo (Place name) Egypt's capital; confident

Kairo, Kayro

Caissa (American) form of Cassandra: insightful

Cait (Greek) purest

Cate, Kate

Caitlin (Irish) virginal

Cailin, Caitleen, Caitlen, Caitlinn, Caitlyn, Catlin, Catlyn, Catlynne

Caitrin (Irish) pure of heart

Caitronia (Irish) pure

Cakusola (African) lionhearted

Cala (Arabic) strong

Calla, Callah

Calandra (Greek) lark

Calendra, Calondra, Kalandra

Calanrea (Greek) form of Calantha: gorgeous flower

Calendrea

Calantha (Greek) gorgeous flower

Calanth, Calanthe, Calanthia, Callantha, Calli

Calatea (Greek) flowering

Calatee

Cale (Latin) respected

Kale

Caledonia (Latin) from Scotland

Kaledonia

Caleigh (American) beauty

Calleigh

Calenda (Irish) form of Cailin: happy

Calendun

Calent (Irish) form of Cailin: happy

Caley (American) warm

Caleigh, Kaylee

Calhoun (Last name as first name) surprising

Calia (American) beauty

Calida (Spanish) sincere; warmth

California (Place name) U.S. state; cool
Callie, Kalifornia, Kallie

Caliopa (Greek) singing beautifully
Kaliopa

Calise (Greek) gorgeous

Calista (Greek) most beautiful
Callista, Calysta, Kali, Kalista, Kalli, Kallista

Call (American) summoned

Calla (Greek) beautiful
Cala, Callie, Cally

Callen (Irish) loquacious

Callian (Irish) beauty

Callidora (Greek) gift of beauty

Callie (Greek) beautiful
Caleigh, Callee, Calley, Calli, Cally, Kali, Kallee, Kallie

Calligenia (Italian) beauty's child

Calliope (Greek) poetry muse
Kalliope, Kallyope

Callista (Greek) most beautiful
Calesta, Calista, Callista, Calysta, Kallista

Callistua (Greek) most beautiful

Callula (Latin) beautiful

Caltha (Latin) gold flower

Calumina (Scottish) calm

Calvina (Latin) has no hair
Calvine

Calypso (Greek) sea nymph

Cam (American) form of Cameron: popular; crooked nose
Cami, Camie, Cammie

Camaren (American) form of Cameron: popular; crooked nose

Cambay (American) saucy
Cambaye, Kambay

Cambee (English) of the people

Camber (American) form of Amber: gorgeous and golden; semiprecious stone
Cambie, Cambre, Cammy, Kamber

Cambree (Welsh) form of Cambria: the people
Cambre, Cambrie, Cambry, Kambree, Kambrie

Cambria (English) the people

Camden (American) glorious face
Cam, Camdon, Cammi, Cammie, Cammy

Cameka (African American) form of Tamkia: lively
Cammey, Cammi, Cammy, Kameka, Kammy

Camelina (American) form of Camilla: wonderful

Camellia (Italian) flower
Camelia, Kamelia

Camelot (English) elegant
Cam, Cami, Camie, Camy

Cameo (French) piece of jewelry; singular
Cameoh, Cammie, Kameo

Camera (Word as name) stunning
Kamera

Camerino (Spanish) unblemished
Cam, Cammy

Cameron (Scottish) popular; crooked nose
Cameran, Camren, Camryn, Kameron, Kamryn

Cameshia (American) pretty

Cametria (American) pretty

Cami (French) form of Camellia: flower
Camey, Camie, Cammie, Cammy

Camilla ✪ (Latin/Italian) wonderful
*Cam, Camelia, Camellia, **Camila**, Camile, Camille, Camillia*

Camille (French) swift runner; great innocence
Camila, Cammille, Cammy, Camylle, Kamille

Cammy (American) form of Camilla: wonderful

Camp (American) outsider
Cam, Campy

Campbell (Last name as first name) amazing
Cam, Cambell, Camey, Cami, Camie, Camy

Camrin (American) form of Cameron: popular; crooked nose
Camren, Camryn

Canace (American) form of Candace: glowing girl

Canada (Place name) country in North American; decisive
Cann, Kanada

Canain (Biblical) patient

Candace (Greek) glowing girl
Caddy, Candice, Candis, Candys, Kandace

Candelara (Spanish) spiritual
Cande, Candee, Candelaria, Candi, Candy, Lara

Candene (English) glows

Candenza (Italian) form of Candace: glowing girl

Candice-Rae (American) glows

Candida (Latin) white

Candis (American) form of Candace: glowing girl

Candlia (American) candlelight

Candra (Latin) she who glows
Candria, Kandra

Candy (American) form of Candace: glowing girl
Candee, Candi, Candie

Caneadea (Native American) the horizon; far-reaching goals

Caneeka (American) clever

Canei (Greek) pure

Canela (Spanish) pure

Cannes (Place name) town in France; selective
Can, Kan

Cannon (American) vital

Cantara (Arabic) bridge
Canta, Kanta, Kantara

Capelta (American) fanciful
Capeltah, Capp, Cappy

Caper (American) mischief

Caplice (American) spontaneous
Capleece, Capleese, Kapleese

Capote (Spanish) cloak; protected

Capri (Place name) island off coast of Italy
Caprie, Kapri

Caprice (Italian) playful; capricious
Caprece, Capreese, Capricia, Caprise

Caprik (Spanish) capricious

Capucine (French) cloak
Cappy

Car (American) driven
Carr, Kar, Karr

Cara (Latin/Gaelic) beloved friend
Carah, Kara

Caramea (Italian) dear girl

Caramenia (Spanish) dear girl

Caramia (Italian) my dear
Cara Mia, Cara-Mia

Cardea (Mythology) pivotal

Cardia (Spanish) giving
Cardi, Kardia

Careletta (Spanish) smart

Caren (American) dear
Carine, Caryn, Karen, Karyn

Caresse (Greek) well-loved

Carey (Welsh) by a castle; fond
Caree, Cari, Carrie, Cary

Cari (Latin) giving

Caria (Biblical) place name

Caribe (Place name)

Caridad (Spanish) giving; lovng
Cari

Carie (Latin) generous

Carina (French/Italian) pure; darling
Careena, Carena, Carin, Carine, Kareena, Karina

Carinthia (Place name) city in Austria; dear girl

Carissa (Greek) loving
Carisa, Caryssa, Karessa, Karissa

Carita (Latin) giving; loved
Caritta, Carrita, Carritta, Karita

Carla (German) feminine form of
Charles: well-loved
Carlah, Carlee, Carli, Carlia,
Carlie, Carly, Karla, Karlah

Carlanda (American) darling
Carlan, Carland, Carlande,
Carlee, Carlie, Carly, Karlanda

Carle (English) winner

Carleas (American) form of
Carlissa: pleasant

Carlee (German) darling
Carleigh, Carley, Carli, Carly,
Karlee, Karley

Carlen (English) winner

Carlene (American) sweet
Carleen, Carlina, Carline, Carlyn

Carlett (Spanish) affectionate
Carle, Carlet, Carletta, Carlette,
Carley, Carli

Carlice (Spanish) pleases

Carlin (Gaelic) little champion
Caline, Carlan, Carlen

Carlisle (Place name) city on the
border of England and Scotland;
sharp
Carlile, Carrie, Karlisle

Carlissa (American) pleasant
Carleeza, Carlisse

Carlita (Italian) outstanding

Carlone (Italian) winning

Carlotta (Italian) sensual
Karlotta

Carly (German) darling
Carlee, Carley, Carli, Carlie, Karlee

Carlysle (English) island of Carla

Carm (Italian) garden paradise

Carma (Hebrew) form of
Carmel: garden
Car, Carmee, Carmi, Carmie,
Karma

Carmel (Hebrew) garden
Carmela, Carmella, Karmel

Carmela (Hebrew) form of
Carmel: garden
Carmalla, Carmella, Carmie,
Carmilla

Carmen (Hebrew) crimson
Carma, Carman, Carmela,
Carmelinda, Carmita, Carmynne,
Chita, Mela, Melita

Carmensita (Spanish) dear girl
Carma, Carmens, Carmense,
Karmence

Carmi (English) garden

Carmiela (Hebrew) form of
Carmel: garden

Carmina (Italian) garden paradise

Carmine (Italian) attractive
Carmyne, Karmine

Carminia (Italian) dearest
Carma, Carmine, Carmynea,
Karm, Karminia, Karmynea

Carmiya (Hebrew) form of
Carmel: garden

Carmona (Italian) garden
paradise

Carmone (Spanish) garden

Carmyle (American) garden

Carna (Latin) horn; sound of joy

Carnation (Botanical) abundant
flower
Carn, Carna, Carnee, Carney,
Carny

Carnelian (American) gemstone

Carnelle (American) gem

Carnethia (Invented) fragrant
Carnee, Carney, Carnithia,
Karnethia

Carni (Latin) horn; vocal
Carna, Carney, Carnia, Carnie,
Carniela, Carniella, Carniya,
Carny, Karni, Karnia, Karniela,
Karniella, Karniya

Carnie (American) happy
Carni, Karni, Karnie

Carody (American) humorous
Caridee, Caridey, Carodee,
Carodey, Carrie, Karodee, Karody

Carol (English) feminine; joyful song
Carole, Carroll, Caryl, Karol, Karrole

Carole (French) joyous song
Karol, Karole

Carolena (Italian) happy

Caroli (Last name used as first name) joyous

Carolina (Italian) form of Carla: well-loved
Carrolena, Karolina

Caroline ✿ (German) little; womanly
Caraline, Carilene, Cariline, Caroleen, Carolin, Carrie, Karalyn, Karolina, Karoline, Karolyn, Karolynne

Carolleen (American) form of Carol: feminine; joyful song

Carolye (English) form of Carolina: well-loved

Carolyn (English) womanly
Carilyn, Carilynn, Carolyne, Carolynn, Karolyn

Caron (Welsh) giving heart
Carron, Karon

Caronsy (American) form of Caron: giving heart
Caronnsie, Caronsi, Karonsy

Caroun (Slavic) springtime

Carran (American) generous

Carrell (American) form of Carol: feminine; joyful song

Carrelle (American) lively
Carrele

Carrie (English) form of Caroline: little; womanly
Carey, Cari, Carri, Carry, Kari

Carron (English) form of Karen: purehearted

Carson (Nordic) dramatic
Carse, Carsen, Carsun, Karrson, Karsen, Karson

Carsyn (American) form of Carson: dramatic

Caryn (Danish) form of Karen: purehearted
Caren, Carrin, Caryne, Carynn

Carys (Welsh) love

Casey (Gaelic) alert; watchful
Casie, Cassee, Cassey, Casy, Caysee, Caysie, Caysy, Kasey

Casha (American) radiant

Cashandra (American) form of Cassandra: insightful

Cashonya (African American) monied; lively
Kashonya

Casilda (Latin) from the dwelling

Casilde (Spanish) combative
Casilda, Casill, Cass, Cassey, Cassie

Cason (Greek) seer; spirited
Case, Casey, Kason

Cassandra (Greek) insightful
Casandra, Casandria, Cass, Cassie, Cassondra, Kassandra

Cassia (Greek) spicy; cinnamon

Cassidy (Irish) clever girl
Casadee, Cass, Cassidee, Cassidi, Kassidy

Cassie (Greek) form of Cassandra: insightful
Cassey, Cassi

Cassiopeia (Greek) starry-eyed
Cass, Cassi, Kass, Kassiopia

Cassis (American) form of Carson: dramatic

Cassundra (American) form of Cassandra: insightful

Casta (Spanish) form of Castalina: pure

Castalia (Mythology) ill-fated

Castalina (Spanish) form of Catalina: chaste

Castara (Greek) form of Catherine: pure
Castera, Castora

Castille (Spanish) traditional

Cata (Spanish) pure

Catalina (Spanish) pure
Catalena, Katalena, Katalina

Catalynn (American) form of Catalina: pure

Catarina (Greek) pure
Caterina, Catrina, Katarina

Catava (Greek) uncorrupted

Catesa (American) form of Contessa: pretty

Catharina (Greek) form of Catherine: pure

Cather (Literature) for author Willa Cather; earthy
Kather

Catherine (Greek) pure
Cartharine, Cathrine, Cathryn, Katherine

Catherique (French) pure

Cathleen (Irish) pure; immaculate
Cathelin, Cathleyn, Cathlinne, Cathlyn, Cathy

Cathresha (African American) pure; outspoken
Cathrisha, Cathy, Kathresha, Resha

Cathryn (Greek) form of Catherine: pure

Cathy (Greek) pure; innocent
Cathee, Cathey, Cathie, Kathy

Catima (Greek) pure
Cattima

Catina (Italian) pure
Catin, Catine, Catinean

Catline (Irish) form of Caitlin: virginial
Cataleen, Catalena, Catleen, Catlen, Katline

Catresia (Italian) form of Catima: pure

Catrice (Greek) form of Catherine: pure
Catrece, Catreece, Catreese, Katreece, Katrice

Catrina (Greek) pure
Catreena, Catreene, Catrene, Katrina

Catriona (Greek) form of Catherine: pure
Katriona

Cauda (Biblical) place name

Cavaray (American) celestial

Cavender (American) emotional
Cav, Cavey, Kav, Kavender

Cavinessa (American) form of Kavinli: pretty; gentle

Cawleen (American) vocal

Cayen (American) form of Kay: happy; rejoicing

Cayenne (Word as name) peppery; spice

Cayla (Hebrew) unblemished
Cailie, Calee, Cayley, Caylie, Kayla

Cayley (American) joyful
Caelee, Caeley, Cailey, Cailie, Caylea, Caylee, Cayleigh, Caylie

Cayman (Place name) the islands; free spirit
Caman, Caymanne, Kayman

Cayne (American) generous
Cain, Kaine

Ceanatha (American) form of Ciana: old soul

Ceara (Irish) form of Ciara: brunette

Ceaskarshenna (African American) ostentatious
Ceaskar, Karshenna, Shenna

Cece (Latin) form of Cecilia: blind

Ceci (Latin) form of Cecilia: blind

Cecile (Latin) form of Cecilia: blind
Cecily

Cecilia (Latin) blind
Cacelia, Cece, Cecelia, Ceil, Celia, Cice, Cicilia, Cilley, Secilia, Sissy

Cedrica (English) chief; leader

Cedrice (American) feminine form of Cedric: leader
Ced, Cedrise

Ceil (Latin) blythe
Ceel, Ciel

Ceinwen (Welsh) blessed baby

Ceirra (Irish) clear-eyed
CeAirra, Cierra

Ceiteag (Scottish) purest

Celand (Latin) heavenward
Cel, Cela, Celanda, Celle

Celandine (Greek) wildflower;
natural beauty; yellow

Celaya (Spanish) serene

Celebration (American) word as
name; celebrant
Cela, Sela

Celena (Greek) form of Selena:
like the moon
Celeena, Celene

Celerina (Spanish) moves fast

Celery (Botanical) refreshing
*Cel, Celeree, Celree, Celry, Sel,
Selery, Selry*

Celes (Latin) heavens

Celeslie (Latin) celestial

Celesta (English) celestial

Celeste (Latin) gentle and
heavenly
Celest, Celestial, Celestine, Seleste

Celestia (Latin) heavenly
*Celeste, Celestea, Celestiah, Seleste,
Selestia*

Celestina (Spanish) celestial

Celestral (American) celestial

Celestyna (Polish) heavenly
*Cela, Celeste, Celesteenah,
Celestinah, Celestyne*

CeLetha (Spanish) heavenly

Celina (Greek) form of Celena:
like the moon
Selina

Celinda (American) lovely

Celine (Greek) lovely
Celeen, Celene

Celisha (Greek) flaming;
passionate

Celka (Latin) celestial
Celk, Celkee, Celkie, Selk, Selka

Celkee (Latin) form of Celeste:
gentle and heavenly
Celkea, Celkie, Cell, Selkee

Cellene (French) celestial leader

Celnie (French) heavenly

Celosia (Greek) flaming

Celta (American) form of Delta:
fourth letter of Greek alphabet

Cena (English) special
Cenna, Sena

Cene' (French) knowing

Cennetta (American) knowing

Cenobia (Spanish) power of
Zeus; strong girl
Cenobie, Zenobia, Zenobie

Censey (American) knowing

Ceola (American) clarity

Ceoline (American) clarity

Ceporah (Hebrew) form of
Zipporah: bird in flight

Cera (French) colorful; (Spanish)
growth

Cerbrenda (American) young
raven

Cerea (Greek) thriving
Serea

Cerelia (Latin) spring
Cerallua, Cerellia, Cerelly

Cerella (Latin) springlike

Ceres (Latin) joyful

Ceressa (Spanish) growth

Cerestina (Spanish) growth

Ceridwen (Welsh) poetic;
blessed
Ceri, Ceridwyn

Cerina (Latin) form of Serena:
calm

Cerise (French) cherry red
Cerese, Cerice, Cerrice, Ceryce

Cerlan (Spanish) growing

Cerrisa (French) cherry red

Cerys (Mythology) harvest
goddess
Ceri, Ceries, Cerri, Cerrie

Cesaria (Latin) feminine form of
Caesar: focused leader

Cesarina (Latin) strong spirit
Cesarea, Cesarie, Cesarin

Cesary (Polish) outspoken
Cesarie, Cezary, Ceze

Cesia (Spanish) celestial
Cesea, Sesia

Ceylon (Place name)

Chablay (American) wine

Chablis (French) white wine
Chabli

Chabulon (Biblical) place name

Chacita (Spanish) lively girl
Chaca, Chacie, Chaseeta, Chaseta

Chadawndra (African) excitable

Chadee (French) goddess
Shadee

Chadra (Indian) peacock

Chaemarique (Invented) pretty
*Chae, Chaemareek, Marique,
Shaymarique*

Chafin (Last name as first name)
sure-footed
Chaffin, Shafin

Chahna (Hindi) she lights the
world

Chai (Hebrew) life-giving
Chae, Chaeli

Chaitali (Hindi) light

Chakena (African) energy

Chakra (Sanskrit) energy
Chak, Chaka, Chakara, Chakyra

Chala (African American)
exuberant
Chalah, Chalee, Chaley, Chalie

Chalese (French) goblet; toasts
life

Chalette (American) good taste
Chalett, Challe, Challie, Shalette

Chalica (American) drinks life
fully

Chalice (French) a goblet;
toasting
*Chalace, Chalece, Chalyse,
Chalyssie*

Chalina (Spanish) rose; fragrant

Chaline (American) smiling
Chacha, Chaleen, Chalene

Chalis (African American) sunny
disposition
Chal, Chaleese, Chalise

Chalissa (African American)
optimistic
Chalisa, Chalysa, Chalyssa

Challie (American) charismatic
Challee, Challi, Chally

Chalondra (African American)
pretty
*Chacha, Chalon, Chalondrah,
Cheilonndra, Chelondra*

Chalsey (American) variation of
Chelsea: safe harbor
Chalsea, Chalsee, Chalsi, Chalsie

Chamania (Hebrew) sunflower;
bright
Chamaniya, Hamania, Hamaniya

Chamaran (Hebrew) form of
Chamania: sunflower; bright

Chamayne (American) form
of Sharmaine; form of Charles:
bountiful orchard

Chambray (French) fabric; hardy
Chambree

Chameli (Hindi) jasmine; fragrant

Chamion (American) changes

Champagne (French) sparkling;
luxurious

Chan (Vietnamese) fragrant

Chana (Hindi) moonlike

Chanah (Hebrew) graceful
Chanach, Channah

Chanal (American) moonlike

Chanchall (Hindi) energetic

Chanda (Hindi) moon goddess
Chandi, Chandie, Shanda

Chandani (Hindi) moonbeams
Chandni, Chandree, Chandrika

Chandelle (French) candle-
lighter
Chandal, Shandalle, Shandel

Chandi (Sanskrit) goddess

Chandler (English) romantic;
candle-maker
Chandlee, Shandler

Chandra (Hindi) of the moon
Chandre, Shandra, Shandre

Chandrika (Indian) moon

Chanel (French) fashionable;
designer name
Chan, Chanell, Chanelle, Channel,
Shanel, Shanell, Shanelle

Chanelle (American) stylish
Shanell, Shanelle

Chaney (English) form of
Chandler: romantic; candlemaker
Chanie, Chaynee, Chayney

Chania (Hebrew) blessed by
Lord's grace
Chaniya, Hania, Haniya

Chanicka (African American)
loved
Chaneeka, Chani, Chanika, Nicka,
Nika, Shanicka

Chanina (Hebrew) knows a
gracious Lord

Chanise (American) adored
Chanese, Shanise

Chanit (Hebrew) spear; ready for
combat
Chanita, Hanit, Hanita

Channa (Hindi) chickpea; little
thing

Channary (Vietnamese) moon
girl

Channing (Last name as first
name) clever

Chanon (American) shining
Chanen, Chann, Channon,
Chanun

Chansanique (African
American) girl singing
Chansan, Chansaneek, Chansani,
Chansanike, Shansanique

Chantal (French) singer of songs
Chandal, Chantale, Chantalle,
Chante, Chantee, Chantel,
Chantell, Chantelle, Chantile,
Chantille, Chawntelle, Shanta,
Shantel, Shawntel, Shontelle

Chantee (American) singer
Chante, Chantey, Chanti, Chantie,
Shantee, Shantey

Chanterelle (French) singer;
prized

Chanthoeun (American)
chantress

Chanti (American) melodious
Chantee, Chantie

Chantill (French) singer

Chantilly (French) beautiful lace
Chantille, Shantilly

Chantou (French) singer

Chantre (French) singer

Chantrea (Vietnamese)
moonlight

Chantrice (French) singer of
songs
Shantreece, Treece

Chanya (Hebrew) blessed by
Jehovah's love

Chanyce (American) risk-taker
Chance, Chancie, Chaneese,
Chaniece, Chanycey

Chapa (Native American) beaver

Chapawee (Native American)
active

Chapin (Last name used as first
name) factual

Chaquanne (African American)
sassy
Chaq, Chaquann, Shakwan

Chara (Greek) form of Charis:
graceful
Charo

Charbonnet (French) loving
and giving
Charbonay, Charbonet,
Charbonnay, Sharbonet,
Sharbonnet

Charde (French) wine
Charday, Chardea, Shardae

Chardonnay (French) white
wine
Char, Chardonee, Chardonnae,
Shardonnay

Charelle (French) feminine

Chari (American) cherish

Chariah (Hebrew) God's child

Charian (French) womanly

Charie (Greek) form of Charis: graceful
Chari

Charille (French) form of Charlotte: little woman
Char, Chari, Charill, Shar, Sharille

Charis (Greek) graceful
Charice, Charisse

Charish (American) cherished
Chareesh

Charisma (American) charming
Char, Karismah

Chariss (English) cherish

Charissa (Greek) giving
Char, Charesa, Charisse, Charissey

Charissma (American) magnetic

Charita (Spanish) sweet
Cherita

Charity (Latin) loving; affectionate
Carisa, Charis, Charita, Chariti, Charry, Cherry, Chirity, Sharity

Charla (French) form of Charlotte: little woman
Char

Charlaine (English) form of Charlene: petite and beautiful
Charlane

Charlana (American) form of Charlene: petite and beautiful
Chalanna

Charle (English) feminine form of Charles: well-loved

Charlene (French) petite and beautiful
Charla, Charlaine, Charleen, Charline, Sharlene

Charlesetta (German) feminine form of Charles: well-loved
Charlesette, Charlsetta

Charlesey (American) expansive; generous
Charlesee, Charlie, Charlsie, Charlsy

Charlesia (American) feminine form of Charles: well-loved
Charlese, Charlisce, Charlise, Charlsie, Charlsy, Sharlesia

Charlezet (American) feminine form of Charles: well-loved

Charli (English) feminine

Charlie (American) easygoing
Charl, Charlee, Charley, Charli

Charlize (American) pretty

Charlotee (French) small

Charlotta (French) womanly

Charlotte ○ (French) little woman
Carly, Charla, Charle, Charlett, Charletta, Charlette, Charlott, Charolot, Char

Charlottie (French) small
Charlotty

Charlsheah (American) happy

Charlsie (French) womanly

Charlton (English) feminine form of Charles: well-loved

Charluce (American) feminine form of Charles: well-loved
Charl, Charla, Charluse

Charlyn (Spanish) feminine

Charm (Greek) form of Charmian: charming; joy-baby
Charma, Charmay, Sharm

Charmaine (Latin) bountiful orchard
Charma, Charmagne, Charmain, Charmane, Charmayne, Charmian, Charmine, Charmyn, Sharmaine, Sharmane, Sharmayne, Sharmyne

Charmian (Greek) joy baby; charming

Charmine (French) charming
Charmen, Charmin

Charminique (African American) dashing
Charmineek

Charmonique (African American) charming
Charm, Charmi, Charmon, Charmoneek, Charmoni, Charmonik, Sharmonique

Charna (Slavic) darkness

Charnee (American) effervescent
Charney, Charnie, Charny

Charneeka (African American) obsessive
Charn, Charnika, Charny

Charneli (Slavic) dark

Charnelle (American) sparkling
Charn, Charnel, Charnell, Charney, Sharnell, Sharnelle

Charnesa (African American) noticed
Charnessa, Charnessah

Charnesie (American) dark hair

Charnette (American) little Charna; dark

Charney (American) dark

Charnise (American) dark

Charo (Spanish) flower
Charro

Charon (Dutch) dreamer

Charra (French) womanly

Charron (African American) form of Sharon: open heart; desert plain
Charryn, Cheiron

Charry (Spanish) rosary

Charsetta (American) form of Charlene: petite and beautiful
Charsee, Charsette, Charsey, Charsy

Chartra (American) classy
Chartrah

Chartres (French) planner
Chartrys

Charu (Hindi) gorgeous; beauty

Charudetta (Invented) combo of Charu and Detta

Charumat (Hindi) lovely and smart

Charvi (Hindi) lovely

Charvonneia (Invented) combo of Charvon and Vonneia

Charysse (Greek) graceful girl
Charece, Charese, Charisse

Chashmona (Hebrew) princess

Chasia (Hebrew) sheltered
Chasya, Hasia, Hasya

Chasida (Hebrew) religious
Chasidah, Hasida

Chasina (Aramaic) strength of character

Chasity (Latin) pure
Chassity

Chasmum (Hindi) lovely eyes

Chassie (Latin) form of Chastity: pure woman
Chass, Chassey, Chassi

Chastaine (English) chaste

Chastity (Latin) pure woman
Chasta, Chastitie

Chateria (Vietnamese) moonlight

Chatie (Spanish) lively

Chatree (Indian) daring

Chau (Aramaic) strength of character

Chaucer (English) demure
Chauser, Chawcer, Chawser

Chava (Hebrew) life-giving
Chavah, Chave, Hava

Chavi (Gypsy) girlish

Chaviva (Hebrew) beloved

Chavon (Hebrew) life
Chavonne

Chaya (Jewish) living

Chayan (Native American) form of Cheyenne: Native American tribe
Chay, Chayanne, Chi, Shayan, Shy

Chazmin (American) form of Jasmine: fragrant; sweet

Chazona (Hebrew) seer

Chea (American) witty
Cheeah

Chedra (Hebrew) happy

Cheer (American) joyful

Cheesa (American) forgiving

Cheifa (Hebrew) enjoys a safe
harbor

Chekia (Invented) cheeky
Chekie, Shekia

Chela (Spanish) exuberant
Chelan, Chelena

Cheletha (African American)
smiling
Chelethe, Cheley

Chelle (American) form of
Chelsea or Michelle: safe harbor;
like the Lord
Shell

Chelsea (Old English) safe
harbor
*Chelcy, Cheli, Chellsie, Chelse,
Chelsee, Chelsei, Chelsey, Chelsie,
Kelsey, Shelsee*

Chemarin (French) fertile; dark

Chemash (Hebrew) servant of
God
Chema, Chemesh, Chemosh

Chemda (Hebrew) charismatic

Chemdiah (Hebrew) loves God
*Chemdia, Chemdiya, Hemdia,
Hemdiah*

Chemelle (American) form of
Chanel: fashionable; designer
name

Chemikaln (American) hip

Chenchayya (American)
responsible

Chenecua (Native American)
peace

Chenia (Hebrew) lives by the
grace of God
Chen, Chenya, Hen, Henia, Henya

Chenicha (Native American) at
odds

Chenille (American) soft
Chenelle, Chenile, Chinille

Chenlei (Asian) wise

Chenoa (American) form of
Genoa: playful
Cheney, Cheno

Chenzia (American) peace

Cheops (Egyptian) pyramid
builder

Cher (French) dear
Chere, Sher

Cherelle (French) dear
Charell, Cherrelle, Sharelle

Cherian (English) darling

Cherie (French) dear
*Cherey, Cheri, Cherice, Cherree,
Cherrie, Cherry, Cherye*

Cheriel (American) darling

Cherika (French) form of
Cherry: cherry red
Chereka, Cherikah

Cherinne (American) happy
Charinn, Cherin, Cherry

Cheris (American) cherished

Cherise (French) cherry
Cherece, Cherice, Cherish, Cherrise

Cherish (French) precious girl
Charish, Cherishe, Sherishe

Cherisha (American) endearing
Cherishah, Cherishuh

Cherita (Spanish) dearest
Cheritt, Cheritta, Cherrita

Cherith (Biblical) place name;
charitable

Cheritt (American) charitable

Cheritte (American) held dear
Cher, Cherette, Cheritta

Cherly (American) form of
Shirley: bright meadow; cheerful
girl
Cherlee, Sherly

Chermelia (American) charm

Chermelle (American) charm

Chermey (American) charm

Chermona (Hebrew) goes to the
sacred mountain

Chero (American) dearest

Cherokee (Native American)
Indian tribe member

373

Cherone (Italian) dear

Cherria (American) dear

Cherrill (American) form of
Cheryl: beloved

Cherron (American) graceful
dancer
Cher, Cheron, Cherronne

Cherry (English/French) cherry
red
Cheree, Cherey, Cherrye, Chery

Cheryce (American) cherish

Cheryl (French) beloved
Charyl, Cherel, Cherelle, Cheryll

Chesley (English) pretty;
meadow
Ches, Cheslay, Cheslea, Chesleigh

Chesma (Slavic) peace-loving

Chesna (Slavic) peace
Ches, Chesnah

Chesney (English) peacemaker
Chesnee, Chesni, Chesnie, Chessnea

Chessa (Slavic) peace

Chesskwana (African American)
evoker
Chesskwan, Chessquana, Chessy

Chessteen (American) needed
Ches, Chessy, Chesteen, Chestene

Chestnut (Botanical) unique

Chet (American) vivacious
Chett

Chevona (Irish) loves a gracious
God

Chevy (American) funny
Chev, Chevee

Cheyann (Native American)
form of Cheyenne: Native
American tribe

Cheye (American) form of
Cheyenne: Native American tribe

Cheyenne (Native American)
Native American tribe
Chayanne, Cheyan, Cheyanna,
Cheyene, Chynne, Shayan,
Shayann, Sheyenne

Chezuka (Asian) quiet
Shizuka

Chhaya (Hebrew) life; vibrant;
(Indian) shadow

Chi (African) Ibo God; light

Chiante (Italian) wine
Chianti

Chiara (Italian) bright and clear
Cheara, Chiarra, Kiara, Kiarra

Chiarina (Italian) clear

Chiba (Hebrew) love

Chic (Spanish) little; strong

Chica (Spanish) girl
Chika

Chick (American) fun-loving
Chicki, Chickie

Chickadee (American) cute little
girl
Chicka, Chickady, Chickee,
Chickey, Chicky

Chidi (Spanish) cheerful

Chidori (Japanese) shorebird

Chika (Japanese) dear girl; wise

Chikira (Spanish) dancer
Shakira

Chiku (African) loquacious

Chilali (Native American)
snowbird

Childe (American) offspring
Child

Childers (Last name as first
name) dignified
Chelders, Childie, Chillders,
Chylders

Chillon (American) polished

Chimalis (Native American)
snowbird

Chimene (French) self-starter;
eager

China (Place name) unique
Chinnah, Chyna, Chynna

Chinadoll (Word as name)
delicate
China Doll, China-Doll,
Chynadoll

Chinasia (Place name) China
and Asia; different

girls

Chinenye (Place name) form of China: unique

Chinesia (Chinese) delicate

Chinnamma (Asian) wonder; summer

Chinnereth (Biblical) place name; God's child

Chinue (African) blessed by Chi

Chionne (Egyptian) kind and obedient

Chipo (African) gift

Chiquida (Spanish) form of Chiquita: small girl
Chiquide

Chiquita (Spanish) small girl
Chica, Chick, Chickie, Chikita, Chiquitia, Chiquitta, Shiquita

Chiriga (African) triumphant; capable

Chirline (American) form of Charline: petite and beautiful
Chirl, Chirlene, Shirl, Shirline

Chislaine (French) loyal

Chita (Spanish) form of Chica: girl

Chitsa (Spanish) form of Carmen: crimson

Chivonne (American) happy
Chevonne, Chivaughan, Chivaughn, Chivon, Chivonn

Chiyena (Hebrew) in the Lord's grace

Chiyoko (Japanese) forever

Chizoba (African) well-protected; strong

Chizu (Japanese) a thousand storks; bountiful

Chizuko (Japanese) abundant

Chloe ✿ ❶ (Greek) flowering
Chloee, Clo, Cloe, Cloee, Cloey, Khloe, Kloe

Chloris (Greek) pale-skinned
Chloras, Cloris, Kloris

Cho (Japanese) dawn of day
Choko, Choyo

Chofa (Polish) able

Cholena (Native American) birdlike; sings

Chonzette (English) risk-taker

Chotsani (Asian) adoring

Choye (Asian) pretty

Chris (Greek) form of Christina: follower of Christ
Chrissie, Chrissy, Kris

Chrisana (American) boisterous
Chris, Chrisanah, Crisane

Chriselda (German) form of Griselda: patient

Chrissa (Greek) form of Christina: follower of Christ
Crissa, Cryssa, Krissa

Chrissy (English) form of Christina: follower of Christ
Chrissie, Chrysie, Krissy

Christa (Latin) anointed one; Christian
Crista, Krista

Christal (Latin) form of Crystal: clear; open-minded
Christall, Christalle, Christel

Christanda (American) smart
Christandah, Christawnda

Christauna (American) spiritual
Christaun, Christawna, Christown, Christwan

Christen (Greek) form of Christiana: follower of Christ
Christan, Christin, Cristen, Kristen

Christiana (Greek) follower of Christ
Christa, Christianna, Christianne, Christie, Chrystyana, Crystianne, Crysty-Ann, Kristiana

Christie (Greek) form of Christina: follower of Christ
Christi, Kristi, Kristie

Christina (Greek) form of Christiana: follower of Christ
Chris, Chrissie, Christi, Chrystina, Crista, Kristina

Christine (French/English) form of Christina: follower of Christ
Christene, Christin, Cristine, Kristine

Christle (German) form of Christina: follower of Christ
Christian

Christmas (English) Christmas baby

Christopher (Greek) devout Christian
Kris, Krissie, Krissy, Krista, Kristofer, Kristopher

Christy (Scottish) Christian
Christee, Christi, Christie

Chrysanthemum (American) flower
Chrys, Chrysanthe, Chrysie, Mum

Chrysanthum (Invented) from flower chrysanthemum; flowering
Chrys, Chrysan, Chrysanth

Chrysolite (American) gemstone

Chuke (African) hopes

Chuki (African) born in a sour time

Chula (Native American) flower; colorful

Chulda (Hebrew) fortune-teller
Hulda, Huldah

Chulisa (Invented) clever
Chully, Ulisa

Chuma (Hebrew) warm
Chumi, Huma, Humi

Chumana (Native American) dew; morning fresh

Chumani (Native American) dewdrop

Chumba (African) darling

Chumina (Hebrew) warmth

Chun (Chinese) springlike

Chyan (American) form of Cheyenne: Native American tribe

Chylene (American) form of Cheyenne: Native American tribe

Chyler (American) feminine form of Kyler: peaceful

Chynna (Chinese) China; wise; musical
Chyna

Ciana (Irish) old soul

Ciandra (Italian) light

Ciani (Irish) old soul

Cianna (Italian) old soul

Ciannait (Irish) an old soul

Ciannata (Latin) old spirit

Ciannedra (Irish) old soul

Ciara (Irish) brunette
Cearra, Ciarah, Ciarra, Ciera, Keera, Keerah

Cicely (Latin) form of Cecilia: blind
Cicelie, Cici, Sicely

Cicylia (English) form of Cicely: blind

Cid (American) fun
Cyd, Syd

Cida (American) form of Cindy: moon goddess

Cidni (American) jovial
Cidnee, Cidney, Cidnie

Cidrah (American) unusual
Cid, Ciddie, Ciddy, Cidra

Cieara (Spanish) dark
CiCi, Ciear, Sieara

Ciemone (American) form of Simone: wise and thoughtful

Ciera (Irish) dark
Ciera, Cia, Cieera, Cierra, Cierre

Cilicia (Biblical) place name

Cilla (Greek) vivacious
Cika, Sica, Sika

Cille (American) form of Lucille: bright-eyed
Ceele

Cilvia (Spanish) form of Sylvia: girl of the forest
Sylvan

Cima (Place name) form of Cimarron: western

Cimarra (Last name used as first name) aware

Cimm (Place name) form of Cimarron: western

Cinderella (French) girl in the ashes
Cinda, Cindi, Cindie, Cindy

Cindy (Greek) form of Cynthia: moon goddess
Cindee, Cindi, Cyndee, Cyndi, Cyndie, Sindee, Syndi, Syndie, Syndy

Cinnamon (English) savory spice
Cenamon, Cinamen, Cinna, Cinnammon, Cinnamond, Cynamon

Cinta (Spanish) mountain of good

Cinthya (American) form of Cynthia: moon goddess

Cinzia (Italian) mountain; reasonable

Ciona (American) steadfast
Cinonah, Cionna, Cyona

Cipriana (Italian) form of Cyprus: island south of Turkey; outgoing
Cipri, Ciprianna, Cipriannah, Cypriana, Cyprianna, Cyprianne, Sipriana, Siprianna

Circe (Greek) sorceress deity; mysterious
Circee, Cirsey, Cirsie

Ciri (Latin) regal
Ceree, Ceri, Seree, Siri

Cirila (Latin) heavenly
Ceri, Cerila, Cerilla, Cerille, Cerine, Ciria, Cirine

Cissy (American) sweet
Ciss, Cissey, Cissi, Sissi

Cita (American) from the musical instrument sitar

Citalin (American) starlike

Citare (Greek) musical; form of the Indian lute sitar
Citara, Sitare

Citlali (Native American) starry
Citlee

Claire ○ ❶ (Latin/French) form of Clara: clear; bright
Clair, Clairee, Claireen, Claireta, Clairy, Clare, Clarette, Clarry, Klair

Clancey (American) a devil-may-care attitude
Clance, Clancee, Clancie, Clancy

Clara (Latin) clear; bright
Claire, Clare, Clareta, Clarette, Clarie, Clarine, Clary

Claresta (Greek) form of Clarissa: smart; clear-minded

Clareta (Latin) clarity; distinguished
Clarita

Clarice (Latin) form of Clara: clear; bright
Clairece, Claireece, Clairice, Clarece, Clareece, Clariece, Clarise

Clarie (French) clear

Clarieca (Latin) bright
Claire, Clare, Clari, Clarieka, Clary, Klarieca, Klarieka

Clarimond (Latin) shining defender; bright

Clarinda (Latin) form of Claire: clear; bright

Clarion (American) clear

Claris (Italian) insightful

Clarisha (Invented) clarissa

Clarissa (Latin/Greek) smart; clear-minded
Claressa, Clarice, Clarisa, Clarise, Clerissa

Clarissima (Italian) clear

Clarity (Word as name) clear-minded
Clare, Claritee, Claritie

Claronne (French) clear

Clasina (Latin) bright

Classie (American) class act

Claudette (French) persistant
Claude, Claudee, Claudet, Claudi, Claudie, Claudy

Claudia (Latin) lame
Claudelle, Claudie, Claudina,
Clodia, Klaudia

Clava (Spanish) earnest; sincere

Clavenna (American) aggressive

Clea (Invented) form of Cleanthe:
famed
Clia, Klea, Klee

Cleandrea (American) form of
Cleanthe: famed

Cleanthe (English) famed
Clea, Cleantha, Cliantha, Klea,
Kleanth

Cleatris (American) form of
Cleanthe: famed

Clelia (Latin) glorious girl

Clem (Latin) gentle; vine

Clematia (Greek) winding vine

Clematis (Greek) vine; clings

Clemence (Latin) easygoing;
merciful
Clem, Clemense, Clements,
Clemmie, Clemmy

Clementina (Spanish) kind;
forgiving
Clementas, Clementi, Clementis,
Clementyna, Clymentyna,
Klementina

Clementine (French/Latin)
merciful
Clemencie, Klementine,
Klementynne

Cleo (Greek) form of Cleopatra:
Egyptian queen

Cleodal (Latin) glory
Cleodel, Cleodell

Cleofe (Greek) glorified

Cleopatra (Greek) Egyptian
queen
Cleo, Clee, Kleeo, Kleo

Cleopatrea (American) form of
Cleopatra: Egyptian queen

Cleora (American) famed

Cleotilda (French) form of
Clotilda: famed fighter

Clerafina (Spanish) clear finish

Cleta (Greek) busy

Cletalline (Greek) busy

Cletenne (Greek) busy

Cleva (English) from the hill

Cliantha (Greek) flower of glory
Cleantha, Cleanthe, Clianthe

Clio (Greek) history muse
Kleeo, Klio

Cliodhna (Irish) dark
Clidna, Cliona

Cliona (Greek) form of Clio:
history muse

Clipper (American) topnotch

Cloe (Greek) flourishing
Cloee, Cloey

Cloi (Greek) spins life

Clois (Greek) thrives

Cloise (English) cloissone

Cloreen (American) happy
Clo, Cloreane, Cloree, Cloreene,
Corean, Klo, Klorean, Kloreen

Cloressa (American) consoling
Cloresse, Kloressa

Clorinda (Latin) happy
Cloee, Cloey, Clorinde, Clorynda,
Klorinda

Cloris (Latin) pale
Chloris

Clory (Spanish) smiling
Clori, Clorie, Kloree, Klory

Closetta (Spanish) secretive
Close, Closette, Klosetta, Klosette

Clotho (Mythology) one of the
Greek Fates; spins web of fate

Clotilda (German) famed fighter
Clotilde, Clothilde, Tilda, Tillie,
Tilly

Clotilde (French) combative

Cloud (Word as name) airy
Cloudee, Cloudie, Cloudy

Clove (Botanical) distinctive spice
Klove

Clover (Botanical) lucky
Clovah, Clove, Kloverr

Cluette (American) savvy

Clydette (American) feminine
form of Clyde: adventurer
*Clidette, Clydett, Clydie, Klyde,
Klydette*

Clymene (Greek) famous

Clytie (Greek) excellent; in love
with love
*Cly, Clytee, Clytey, Clyty, Klytee,
Klytie*

Co (American) jovial
Coco, Ko, Koko

Coahoma (Native American)
panther; stealthy

Coby (American) glad
Cobe, Cobey, Cobie

Cochava (Hebrew) star girl

Cocheta (Italian) form of
Concetta: pure female

Coco (Spanish) coconut
Koko

Cocoa (Spanish) chocolate;
spunky girl

Cody (English) softhearted; pillow
Codi, Codie, Kodie

Coffey (American) lovely
Caufey, Cofee

Cofta (Last name used as first
name) audacious

Coiya (American) coquettish
Coyuh, Koya

Cokey (American) intelligent
Cokie

Colanda (African American) form
of Yolanda: pretty as a violet flower

Colby (English) enduring
Cobie, Colbi, Kolbee

Cole (Last name as first name)
laughing
Coe, Colie, Kohl

Colemand (American) adventurer
Colmyand

Colene (American) girl

Coleteen (Invented) created;
trusted

Coletta (French) wins

Colette (French) spiritual;
victorious
Coey, Collette, Kolette

Colina (American) righteous; girl
Colena, Colin, Colinn

Coline (Greek) victory
Colinette

Colisa (English) delightful
Colissa, Collisa, Collissa

Colleen (Irish) young girl
*Coleen, Colene, Coley, Colleene,
Collen, Colli, Kolene, Kolleen*

Collena (English) girl

Colletta (English) girl

Colley (English) fearful; worrier
Col, Collie, Kolley

Collie (English) female child

Colmbyne (Latin) form of
Columbine: dove; flower

Coloma (Spanish) calm
Colo, Colom, Colome

Colossae (Biblical) place name;
colossal

Columbia (Latin) form of
Columbine: dove; flower
Colombe, Columba

Columbine (Latin) dove; flower

Colure (French) color

Colynne (American) form of
Colleen: young girl

Comfort (American) comforting;
easygoing
Komfort

Comfortyne (French) comforting
*Comfort, Comfortine, Comfurtine,
Comfy*

Comora (African) moon
Komoria

Comsa (Greek) form of Cosma:
of the universe

Concepcion (Spanish)
conceived; begins
Conception

Concetta (Italian) pure female

Conchetta (Spanish) wholesome
Concheta, Conchette

Conchie (Latin) conception
Conchee, Conchi, Konchie
Conchita (Spanish) girl of the conception
Chita, Concha, Conchi
Conchiteen (Spanish) pure
Conchita, Conchitee, Connie
Conchobarre (Irish) willful
Concordia (Latin) goddess of peace
Condoleezza (American) smart; with sweetness
Condeleesa, Condilesa, Condolissa
Coneisha (African American) giving
Conisha, Conishah, Conniesha
Conene (American) smart
Conerly (Last name used as first name) worthy
Conesa (American) free-flowing nature
Conisa, Connesa, Konesa
Conita (Dutch) consistent
Conlee (American) form of Connelly: radiant
Con, Conley, Conlie, Conly, Connie, Konlee, Konlie
Conner (American) brave
Con, Coner, Coni, Connie, Connor, Conny, Conor

Connie (English) form of Constance: loyal
Con, Conni, Conny, Konnie
Connie-Kim (Vietnamese) golden girl
Conni-Kim
Conradina (German) feminine form of Conrad: optimist
Connie, Conradine, Conradyna, Konnie, Konradina
Conroe (Place name) small town in Texas
Conn, Connie, Konroe
Conroy (Last name as first name) stately; literary
Conroi, Konroi, Konroy
Conseja (Spanish) advises
Consilletta (Italian) counsels
Consolata (Spanish) consoles others
Constance (Latin) loyal
Con, Connie, Conny, Constantia, Constantina, Constantine, Constanza
Constantina (Italian) loyal; constant
Conn, Connee, Conni, Connie, Conny, Constance, Constanteena, Constantinah
Constanza (Hebrew) constant
Constanz, Connstanzah

Constanze (German) unchanging
Con, Connie, Stanzi
Consuelo (Spanish) comfort-giver
Chelo, Consolata, Consuela
Contessa (Italian) pretty
Contesa, Contessah, Contesse
Contina (American) countess
Cookie (American) cute
Cooki
Copeland (Last name as first name) adaptable
Copelan, Copelyn, Copelynn
Copper (American) redhead
Coppyr
Coppola (Italian) theatrical
Copla, Coppi, Coppo, Coppy, Kopla, Kopola, Koppola
Coprice (American) form of Caprice: playful; capricious
Cora (Greek) maid; giving girl
Corah, Corene, Coretta, Corette, Corra, Correna, Corrie, Corinna, Kora
Coral (Latin) natural; small stone
Corall, Coralle, Coraly, Core, Corel, Koral, Koraly
Coraline (American) country girl
Coraz (Spanish) form of Corazon: heart

Corazon (Spanish) heart
Cora, Corrie, Zon, Zonn

Corazonna (Spanish) form of
Corazon: heart

Corby (Latin) raven; dark

Corday (English) prepared; heart
*Cord, Cordae, Cordie, Cordy,
Korday*

Cordelia (Latin) warmhearted
woman
*Cordalia, Cordeelia, Cordelie,
Cordi, Cordie, Cordilia, Kordelia,
Kordey, Kordi*

Cordelita (Latin/Spanish)
heartfelt
Cordelia, Cordelite, Cordella

Cordillera (Latin) form of
Cordelia: warmhearted woman

Cordula (Latin/German) heart;
jewel
*Cord, Cordie, Cordoola,
Cordoolah, Cordy*

Corenda (American) derivative of
Dorenda; adored

Corette (Greek) form of Cora:
maid; giving girl

Corey (Irish) perky
*Cori, Corree, Corrie, Korey, Korri,
Korrie*

Corgie (American) funny
Corgi, Korgee, Korgie

Cori (Greek/Irish) caring
Corey, Corri, Corrie, Cory

Coriander (Botanical) seasoning;
simplistic

Corinna (Greek) young girl
*Corina, Corrinna, Corryna,
Corynna*

Corinne (Greek/French) maiden;
protective
*Coreen, Corina, Corine, Corinna,
Corrina, Coryn, Corynn, Koreene,
Korinne*

Corintha (German) maiden

Corinthian (Place name) a town
in Greece; religious

Coris (Greek) singer
Corris, Koris, Korris

Corissa (Greek) kindhearted
Korissa

Corissah (American) mysterious

Corita (Spanish) kind

Corky (American) energetic
*Corkee, Corkey, Corki, Corkie,
Korkee, Korky*

Corliss (English) open-hearted
*Corless, Corlise, Corly, Korlis,
Korliss*

Corlisse (American) cheerful

Corlissen (American) cheerful

Corly (American) active
Corlee, Corli, Corlie, Korli, Korly

Corlyn (American) innovative
*Corlin, Corlinn, Corlynn,
Corlynne, Korlin, Korlyn*

Cormella (Italian) fiery
*Cormee, Cormela, Cormelah,
Cormellia, Cormey, Cormie*

Cornae (Origin unknown) all
seeing
Coma, Korna, Kornae

Cornecia (Latin) yellow hair;
horn

Corneitha (Latin) horn child

Cornelia (Latin) practical
Carnelia, Corney, Corni

Cornelie (Latin) horn child

Cornelius (Latin) realistic
Corneal, Corneelyus, Corney, Corny

Cornesha (African American)
talkative
Cornee, Corneshah, Cornesia

Cornish (English) Cornish

Corona (Spanish) crowned
Corone, Coronna, Korona

Correne (American) musical
*Coree, Coreen, Correen, Correna,
Korene, Korrene*

Corri (English) naive
Corry

Corrianna (American) joyful
*Coreanne, Corey, Corianna, Corri,
Corriana*

Corrie (English) form of Coral:
natural; small stone
Corrinda (French) girlish
Corri, Corrin, Korin, Korinda
Corseta (English)
unsophisticated
Cortanie (American) form of
Courtney: domain of Curtis
Cortanny, Cortany
Cortland (American) distinctive
*Cortlan, Courte, Courtland,
Courtlin*
Cortlinn (American) happy
*Cortlenn, Cortlin, Cortlyn,
Cortlynn*
Corvette (Word as name) speedy
Corv, Corva, Corve, Korvette
Corvina (Latin) raven; brunette
Cosetta (French) pretty thing
Cosette (French) warm
Cossette
Cosima (Greek) universe;
harmony
Coseema, Koseema, Kosima
Cosma (Greek) of the universe
Cosmee (Greek) organized
Cos, Cosmi, Cosmie
Cosmiss (American) harmony
with the cosmos
Cossette (French) winning
Coss, Cossie, Cossy, Kossee, Kossette

Costanza (Last name as first
name) strong-willed; funny
Costner (American) embraced
*Cosner, Cost, Costnar, Costnor,
Costnur*
Cota (Spanish) lively
Cotcha (African American)
stylish
Kasha, Katcha, Katshay, Kotsha
Cotia (Spanish) full of vitality
Cotilia (Spanish) vital
Cotrena (American) form of
Katrina: melodious
*Catreena, Catrina, Catrine,
Cotrene, Katrine, Kotrene*
Cotton (American) comforting
Cottie
Countess (English) blueblood
Contessa
Courday (French) courteous
Couria (French) courteous
Cournette (American) form of
Coronet: regal
Courney, Kournette
Courney (English) form of
Courtney: domain of Curtis
Courtney (English) domain of
Curtis
*Cortney, Courtenay, Courteney,
Courtnay, Courtnee, Courtny,
Kortnee, Kortney*

Covelina (Spanish) cave child
Covin (American) unpredictable
Covan, Cove, Coven, Covyn
Coy (American) sly
Coye, Koi, Koy
Coyah (American) singular
Coya, Coyia
Coyote (American) wild
Coyo, Kaiote, Kaiotee
Cozeth (English) rainbow
Cozetta (English) rainbow
Cozette (French) darling
Cramer (American) jolly
Cramar, Cramir, Kramer
Cramisa (Invented) nice
Cramissa, Kramisa
Creda (English) giving credence
Cree (American) wild spirit
Crea, Creeah
Creed (American) boisterous
Crede, Cree, Kreed
Creesha (English) flower
Creirwy (Welsh) lucky amulet
Cremone (French) wanted
Creola (American) desires
Cresa (English) fickle
Crescena (German) grows
Crescente (American) impressive
Crescent, Cresent, Cress, Cressie

Crescentia (Spanish) crescent-faced; smiling
Crescent, Creseantia, Cressentt

Cresenda (American) explosive

Cressa (Greek) form of Cressida: infidel
Cresa, Cressah, Cress, Cresse, Kressa

Cressell (American) growth

Cressida (Greek) infidel
Cresida, Cresiduh, Cresside

Cressie (American) growing; good
Cress, Cressy, Kress, Kressie

Creston (American) worthy
Crest, Crestan, Creste, Cresten, Crestey, Cresti, Crestie

Cresusa (English) fickle

Cricket (American) energetic
Kricket

Crimson (American) deep
Cremsen, Crims, Crimsen, Crimsonn, Crimsun

Crisanta (American) form of Chrysanthemum: flower

Crisel (English) form of Crystal: clear; open-minded

Criselda (Spanish) wild
Crisselda

Criselle (English) crystal

Crishonna (American) beautiful
Crishona, Crisshone, Crissie, Crissy, Krishona, Krishonna

Crisiant (Welsh) crystal; clear
Cris, Crissie

Crispa (Latin) curly hair

Crispina (Latin) curly-haired girl

Crispy (Invented) fun-loving; zany
Crispee, Krispy

Crista (Italian) form of Christina: follower of Christ
Krista

Cristella (English) crystal

Cristin (Irish) dedicated
Cristen, Crystyn, Kristin, Krystyn

Cristina (Greek) form of Christina: follower of Christ
Kristina

Cristos (Greek) dedicated
Christos, Criss, Crissie

Cristy (English) spiritual
Cristi, Crysti, Kristi, Krystie

Crusitee (Spanish) of the cross

Cruzita (Spanish) of the cross

Cruzitte (Spanish) of the cross

Cryange (Place name)

Crystal (Latin) clear; open-minded
Christal, Chrystal, Cristal, Cristalle, Crys, Crystelle, Krystal

Crystilis (Spanish) focused
Chrysilis, Crys, Cryssi, Cryssie, Crystylis

Csaba (Hungarian) shepherd; wanderer

Csilla (Hungarian) defensive

Cuasha (American) goodness

Cuba (Place name) island; fun-loving girl

Cullen (Irish) attractive
Cullan, Cullie, Cullun, Cully

Cumale (American) open-hearted
Cue, Cuemalie, Cue-maly, Cumahli

Cumthia (American) open-minded
Cumthea, Cumthee, Cumthi, Cumthie, Cumthy

Cupertina (Spanish) covert

Cupid (American) romantic
Cupide

Curine (American) attractive
Curina, Curinne, Curri, Currin

Curisten (Invented) form of Kirsten: follower of Christ

Curry (American) languid
Curree, Currey, Curri, Currie

Cursten (American) form of Kirsten: follower of Christ
Curst, Curstee, Curstie, Curstin

Cushaun (American) elegant
Cooshaun, Cooshawn, Cue,
Cushawn, Cushonn, Cushun

Cximara (Spanish) greatness

Cyan (American) colorful
Cyanne, Cyenna, Cyun

Cyanea (Greek) blue-eyed baby

Cyanetta (Greek) little blue
Cyan, Cyanette, Syan, Syanette

Cybele (Greek) conflicted

Cybill (Latin) prophetess
Cybell, Cybelle, Cybil, Sibyl, Sibyle

Cydell (American) country girl
Cydee, Cydel, Cydie, Cydile, Cydy

Cydney (American) perky
Cyd, Cydni, Cydnie

Cylee (American) darling
Cye, Cyle, Cylea, Cyli, Cylie, Cyly

Cylene (American) melodious
Cylena, Cyline

Cyllene (American) sweet

Cyma (Greek) does well

Cymantha (English) form of
Simone: wise and thoughtful

Cymbeline (Greek) benevolent
ruler
Beline, Cymba, Cymbe, Cymbie,
Cyme, Cymmie, Symbe

Cyn (Greek) form of Cynthia:
moon goddess
Cynnae, Cynnie, Syn

Cynara (Greek) prickly; particular
Cynarra

Cynder (English) having
wanderlust
Cindee, Cinder, Cindy, Cyn,
Cyndee, Cyndie, Cyndy

Cynista (English) leader

Cyntanah (American) singer
Cintanna, Cyntanna

Cynthia (Greek) moon goddess
Cindy, Cyn, Cyndee, Cyndy,
Cynthea, Cynthee, Cynthie

Cynthiah (American) form of
Cynthia: moon goddess

Cyntia (Greek) form of Cynthia:
moon goddess
Cyn, Cyntea, Cynthie, Cyntie,
Syntia

Cyntrille (African American)
gossipy
Cynn, Cyntrell, Cyntrelle, Cyntrie

Cypress (Botanical) swaying
Cypres, Cyprice, Cypris, Cypriss,
Cyprus

Cyra (American) willing
Cye, Cyrah, Syra

Cyreen (American) sensual
Cyree, Cyrene, Cyrie

Cyrena (American) form of
Serena: calm

Cyrene (Greek) mythological
nymph

Cyrenian (American) bewitching
Cyree, Cyren, Cyrenean, Cyrey,
Siren, Syrenian

Cyrenna (American)
straightforward
Cyrena, Cyrennah, Cyrinna,
Cyryna, Cyrynna

Cyriece (American) artistic
Cyree, Cyreece, Cyreese, Cyrie

Cyrilla (Latin) royal; little minx
Cirila

Cyrise (English) serene

Cytherea (Greek) from the
island of Cythera; celestial

Cyvie (American) clean

Czara (Slavic) leads

Czaree (American) czar-like

Czarina (Russian) royal

D

Daba (Hebrew) kindhearted

Dabaloth (Biblical) angelic

Dabaritta (Biblical) angelic

Daberath (Biblical) angelic

Dabire (Biblical) angelic

Dacey (Irish) a southerner
Dace, Dacee, Daci, Dacia, Dacie,
Dacy, Daicie, Daycee

Dacia (Latin) old soul
Dacie, Dachia, Dachi

Dae (English) day
Day, Daye

Daelan (English) aware
Dael, Daeleen, Daelena, Daelin,
Daely, Daelyn, Daelynne, Dale,
Daley, Daylan, Daylin, Daylind, Dee

Daevrissa (American) girl of
the day

Daeze (African) day

Daffodil (Botanical) flower
Daffy

Dafna (Slavic) form of Daphne:
pretty nymph

Dafnee (Greek) form of Daphne:
pretty nymph
Dafney, Dafnie

Dafo (American) form of
Daffodil: flower

Dagmar (Scandinavian/German)
glorious day
Dag, Dagmara, Dagmarr

Dagny (Scandinavian) day
Dagna, Dagnanna, Dagne, Dagney

Dahlia (Scandinavian) flower
Dahl, Dollie

Dahri (American) form of Dahlia:
flower

Dai (Welsh/Japanese) beloved one
of great importance

Dailah (American) form of
Dahlia: flower

Dainikya (Slavic) form of
Danica: star of the morning

Daira (American) outgoing
D'Aira, Daire, Dairrah, Darrah,
Derrah

Daisha (American) sparkling
D'Aisha, Daishe, Dasha, Dashah

Daisy (English) flower; day's eye
Daisee, Daisey, Daisi, Daisia,
Daisie, Daissy, Daizee, Daizi,
Daizy, Dasey, Dasi, Dasie, Dasy,
Daysee, Daysie, Daysy

Daisy-Boo (American) frivolous;
flower

Daiton (American) wondrous
Day, Dayten, Dayton

Daja (American) intuitive
Dajah

Dajanae (African American)
persuasive
Daije, Daja, Dajainay, Dayjanah

Dajon (American) gifted
Dajo, Dajohn, Dajonn, Dajonnay,
Dajonne

Dakara (American) firebrand
Dacara, Dakarah, Dakarea,
Dakarra

Daking (Asian) friendly

Dakota (Native American) tribal
name; solid friend
Dacota, Dakohta, Dakotah,
Dakotha, Dakotta, Dekoda,
Dekota, Dekotah, Dekotha

Dalacie (American) brilliant
Dalaci, Dalacy, Dalasie, Dalce,
Dalci, Dalse

Dalaina (American) spirited
Dalana, Dalayna, Delaina,
Delaine, Delayna

Dalaney (American) hopeful
Dalanee, Dalaynee, Dalayni

Dalaya (English) form of Dahlia:
flower

Dale (English) valley-life
Daile, Daleleana, Dalena, Dalina,
Dayle

Daleah (American) pretty
Dalea

Daley (Irish) leader
Dailey, Dalea, Daleigh, Dali,
Dalie, Daly

Dali (Spanish) of the day

Dalia (Spanish) flower
Daliah, Daliyah, Dayliah, Doliah,
Dolliah, Dolya

Dalian (American) joy
Dalean

Daliana (American) joyful spirit
Daliane, Dalianna, Dilial,
Dollianna

Dalice (American) able
Daleese, Dalleece

Dalila (African) gentle
Dahlila, Dahlilla, Dalia, Dalilah,
Dalilia

Dalimda (American) form
of Dalinda: beautiful; honey;
sweetheart

Dalin (American) calm
Dalen, Dalenn, Dalun

Dalinda (American) form of
Belinda: beautiful; form of
Melinda: honey; sweetheart

Dalita (American) smooth
Daleta, Daletta, Dalite, Dalitee,
Dalitta

Dallas (Place name) city in Texas;
confident
Dalis, Dalisse, Daliz, Dallice,
Dallis, Dallsyon, Dallus, Dallys,
Dalyce, Dalys

Dallen (American) outspoken
Dal, Dalen, Dalin, Dallin

Dallise (American) gentle
Dalise, Dallece, Dalleece, Dalleese

Dalmar (German) perseveres

Dalmatia (Biblical) place name

Dalondra (Invented) generous
Dalandra, Dalon, Dalondrah,
Delondra

Dalonna (Invented) generous
Dalohn, Dalona, Dalonne

Dalphine (French) form of
Delphine: calmness
Dal, Dalf, Dalfeen, Dalfene,
Dalphene

Dalton (American) smart
Dallee, Dalli, Dallie, Dallton,
Dally, Daltawyn

Daltrey (American) quiet
Daltree, Daltri, Daltrie

Dalva (American) strong

Dalyn (American) smart
Dalin, Dalinne, Dalynn, Dalynne

Dama (Hindi) temptress

Damalla (Greek) fledgling; young
Damala, Damalas, Damalis,
Damall

Damara (Greek) gentle
Damaris, Damarra

Damaris (Greek) calm
Damalis, Damar, Damara,
Damares, Damaret, Damarius,
Damary, Damarys, Dameress,
Dameris, Damiris, Dammaris,
Dammeris, Damrez, Damris,
Demaras, Demarays, Demaris

Damecia (Invented) sweet
Dameisha, Damesha, Demecia,
Demisha, Demeshe

Dami (Greek) form of Damia:
spirited
Damee, Damey, Damie, Damy

Damia (Greek) spirited
Damiah, Damya, Damyah,
Damyen, Damyenne, Damyuh

Damianne (Greek) one who
soothes
Damiana

Damica (French) open-spirited
Dameeka, Dameka, Damekah,
Damicah, Damie, Damika,
Damikah, Demeeka, Demeka,
Demekah, Demica, Demicah

Damita (Spanish) small woman
of nobility
Dama, Damah, Damee, Damesha,
Dameshia, Damesia, Dametia,
Dametra, Dametrah

Damitte (Irish) small

Damon (American) sprightly
Damoane, Damone

Damone (American) mighty
Dame

D'Amore (Invented) love

Dana (English) bright gift of God
*Daina, Dainna, Danae, Danah,
Danai, Danaia, Danalee, Danan,
Danarra, Danayla, Dane, Danean,
Danee, Daniah, Danie, Danna,
Dayna, Daynah*

Danae (Greek) bright and pure
*Danay, Danayla, Danays, Danea,
Danee, Dannae, Denae, Denee*

Danala (English) happy; golden
*Dan, Danalla, Danee, Danela,
Danney, Danny*

Danay (American) happy
Danaye, D'Nay, D·nay

Dancel (French) energetic
*Dance, Dancell, Dancelle, Dancey,
Dancie, Danse, Dansel, Danselle*

Dancie (American) from the
word dancer
Dancy

Dandelion (Botanical) flower

Daneaa (Welsh) bright day

Daneen (Greek) blessed

Daneil (Hebrew) judged by God;
spiritual
*Daneal, Daneala, Daneale,
Daneel, Daneela, Daneila*

Danelle (Hebrew) kindhearted
*Danael, Danalle, Danel, Danele,
Danell, Danella, Dani, Dannele,
Danny*

Danelly (Spanish) form of
Danielle: judged by God; spiritual
*Daneli, Danellie, Dannelley,
Dannelly*

Danena (Greek) blessed

Danessa (American) dainty
*Danesa, Danese, Danesha, Danesse,
Daniesa, Daniesha, Danisa,
Danisha, Danissa*

Danessia (American) delicate
child
*Danesia, Danieshia, Danisla,
Danissia*

Danette (American) form of
Danielle: judged by God; spiritual
Danetra, Danett, Danetta

Dangela (Latin) form of Angela:
divine; angelic
*Angee, Angelle, Angie, Dangelah,
Dangelia, Dangey, Dangi, Dangie*

Dani (Hebrew) form of Danielle:
judged by God; spiritual
*Danee, Danie, Danne, Dannee,
Danni, Dannie, Danny, Dany*

Dania (Hebrew) form of Danielle:
judged by God: spiritual
Daniah, Danya, Danyah

Daniah (Hebrew) judged
Dan, Dania, Danny, Danya

Danica (Latin/Polish) star of the
morning
*Daneeka, Danika, Danneeka,
Dannica, Dannika*

Daniella (Italian) form of
Danielle: judged by God; spiritual
Danilla

Danielle (Hebrew/French)
feminine form of Daniel: judged
by God; spiritual
*Danelle, Daniele, Daniell,
Danniella, Danyel*

Danir (American) fresh
Daner

Danit (Hebrew) judged by God
*Danett, Danis, Danisha, Daniss,
Danita, Danitra, Danitza, Daniz,
Danni*

Danita (English) form of
Danielle: judged by God; spiritual
Danni, Danny, Denita, Denny

Danla (Slavic) form of Danielle:
judged by God; spiritual

D'Anna (Hebrew) special

Danna (American) cheerful
*D'Ana, D'Anna, Dannae, Danni,
Danny*

Danner (American) morning star

Danube (Place name) river;
flowing spirit

Danuta (Polish) God's gift

Danyella (Slavic) form of Danielle: judged by God; spiritual

Danyiel (Slavic) form of Danielle: judged by God; spiritual

Danz (Last name used as first name) trendsetter

Daphiney (Greek) form of Daphne: pretty nymph
Daff, Daph

Daphne (Greek) pretty nymph
Daphane, Daphaney, Daphanie, Daphany, Daphiney, Daphnee, Daphney, Daphnie, Daphny, Daphonie, Daphy

Daphoneel (Greek) form of Daphne: pretty nymph

Daphyne (Greek) form of Daphne: pretty nymph

Daquisha (African American) talkative

Dara (Hebrew) compassionate
Dahra, Dahrah, Darah, Darra, Darrah

Daralice (Greek) beloved
Dara, Daraleese, Daraliece

Daravia (Hebrew) loving

Darby (Irish) a free woman
Darb, Darbee, Darbi, Darbie, Darbye

Darceece (Irish) form of Darci: dark

Darcelle (American) secretive
Darce, Darcel, Darcell, Darcey

Darci (Irish) dark
Darce, Darcee, Darcie, Darcy, Dars, Darsey

Darda (Hebrew) wise

Dare (Hebrew) compassion

Daretha (Slavic) loved

Dari (Czech) rich

Daria (Persian) queenly
Dare, Darea, Dareah, Dari, Darian, Darianne, Darria, Darya

Darian (Anglo-Saxon) precious
Dare, Darien, Darry, Derian

Darice (English) contemporary
Dareese, Darese, Dari, Dariece, Darri, Darrie, Darry

Darielle (French) rich
Darell, Darelle, Dariel, Darriel, Darrielle

Darienne (Greek) great

Darika (Indian) young maiden

Darilyn (American) darling
Darilin, Darilinn, Darilynn, Derilyn

Darina (Greek) rich

Darine (English) feminine form of Darren: great

Darionne (American) adventuresome
Dareon, Darion, Darionn, Darionna

Dariya (Russian) sweet
Dara, Darya

Darla (English) form of Darlene: darling girl
Darl, Darlee, Darley, Darli, Darlie, Darly

Darlee (English) darling
Darl, Darley, Darli, Darlie

Darlene (French) darling girl
Darlean, Darleen, Darlena, Darlenia, Darlin, Darling

Darlenn (French) form of Darlene: darling girl

Darless (French) form of Darlene: darling girl

Darlette (French) form of Darlene: darling girl

Darlina (French) form of Darlene: darling girl

Darling (American) precious
Darline, Darly, Darlyng

Darlonna (African American) darling
Darlona

Darlusz (Slavic) loved

Darlye (French) darling

Darmetra (American) able

Darnelle (Irish) seamstress
Darnel, Darnell, Darnella, Darnyell

Darnette (American) hides

Daroma (American) treasured

Daron (Irish) great woman
Daren, Darun, Daryn

Darquea (American) different

Darr (Slavic) form of Daria: queenly

Darras (Slavic) rules

Darrelle (English) loved

Darrien (Irish) great

Darrow (Last name as first name)
cautious
Darro, Darroh

Darryl (French/English) form of
Darlene: darling girl
Darel, Darelle, Daril, Darrell,
Darrill, Daryl, Daryll, Derel,
Derrell

Darsa (American) bright spirit

Darshelle (African American)
confident
Darshel, Darshell

Dart (English) tenacious
Darte, Dartee, Dartt

Darva (Invented) sensible
Darv, Darvah, Darvee, Darvey,
Darvi, Darvie

Daryn (Greek/Irish) gift-giver
Daryan, Darynn, Darynne

Daryna (Slavic) form of Daria:
queenly

Dash (American) fast-moving
Dashee, Dasher, Dashy

Dasha (Russian) darling
Dashah

Dashanda (African American)
loving
Dashan, Dashande

Dashawn (African American)
brash
Dashawna, Dashay

Dashawntay (African American)
careful
Dash, Dashauntay

Dashea (Hebrew) patient

Dasheena (African American)
flashy
Dashea, Dasheana

Dashelle (African American)
striking
Dachelle, Dashel, Dashell, Dashy

Dashika (African American)
runner
Dash, Dasheka

Dashiki (African) loose shirt;
casual
Dashi, Dashika, Dashka, Desheka,
Deshiki

Dashilan (American) solemn
Dashelin, Dashelin, Dashlinne,
Dashlyn, Dashlynn, Dasialyn

Dasmine (Invented) sleek
Dasmeen, Dasmin, Dazmeen,
Dazmine

Dassa (Jewish) form of Hadassah:
myrtle tree
Dassah, Dasa

Dassia (American) pretty
Dasie, Dassea, Dasseah, Dassee,
Dassi, Dassie, Deassiah

Dathema (Biblical) feminine
form of David: beloved

Dati (Hebrew) believer

Dativa (Hebrew) believer

Daufenne (French) of the
dolphin

Daulette (American) invented

Dauphinais (French) of the
dolphin

Daureen (American) darling
Dareen, Daurean, Daurie, Daury,
Dawreen

Dauria (American) form of
Daria: queenly

Daveena (Scottish) feminine
form of David: beloved
Daveen, Davena, Davey, Davina,
Davinna

Davianna (English) beloved

Davida (Hebrew) beloved one
Daveeda, Daveisha, Davesia,
Daveta, Davetta, Davette, Davika,
Davisha, Davita

Davina (Hebrew) believer; beloved
Dava, Daveena, Davene, Davida, Davita, Devina, Devinia, Devinya

Davincia (Spanish) God-loving; winner
Davince, Davinse, Vincia

Davinique (African American) believer; unique
Davin, Davineek, Vineek

Davis (American) boyish
Daves

Davisnell (Invented) vivacious
Daviesnell, DavisNell

Davonna (Scottish) well-loved
Davon, Davona, Davonda

Davonne (African American) splashy
Davaughan, Davaughn, Davion, Daviona, Davon, Davone, Davonn

Davrush (Yiddish) loves others

Daw (Asian) starlike

Dawa (Tibetan) girl born on Monday

Dawanda (African American) righteous
Dawana, Dawand, Dawanna, Dawauna, Dawonda, Dawonna, Dwanda

Dawn (English) daybreak
Daun, Dawna, Dawne

Dawna (English) eloquence of dawn
Dauna, Daunda, Dawn, Dawnah, Dawnna, Dawny, Dawnya

Dawnesha (American) dawn's child

Dawnika (African American) dawn
Dawneka, Dawneeka, Dawnica, Donika

Dawnisha (African American) breath of dawn
Daunisha, Dawnish, Dawny, Nisa, Nisha

Dawntelle (African American) morning bright
Dawntel, Dawntell, Dontelle

Dawona (African American) smart
Dawonna, Dawonne

Day (English) day; bright

Dayana (American) form of Diana: divine woman; goddess of the hunt and fertility
Dayannah, Dyana

Dayanara (Spanish) form of Deyanira: aggressor
Day, Daya, Dayan, Dianara, Diannare, Nara

Dayita (Indian) loved

Dayla (American) day's joy

Dayle (American) joyful

Daylee (American) calm; reserved
Dailee, Day, Dayley, Dayly

Dayna (English) form of Dana: bright gift of God
Daynah

Daysha (Russian) serene
Dasha, Dayeisha

Dayshanay (African American) saucy
Daysh, Dayshanae, Dayshannay, Dayshie

Dayshawna (American) laughing
Dayshauna, Dayshona, Dashonah

Dayshay (African American) lovable
Dashae, Dashay, Dashea

Dayton (Place name) town in Ohio; fast

Daytona (American) speedy
Dayto, Daytonna

Dayvonne (African American) careful
Dave, Davey, Davonne, Dayvaughn

De (Chinese) virtuous

Deaborah (Spanish) form of Debora: prophetess

Deacon (Greek) joyful messenger
Deak, Deakon, Deecon, Deke

Dealba (Irish) Irish girl

Dean (English) practical
Deanie, Deanni

Deana (Latin) divine girl
Deane, Deanna

Deandea (English) form of
Deanne: divine woman; goddess
of hunt and fertility

Deandria (American) sweetheart
Deandreah, Deandriah

Deanie (English) feminine form
of Dean: leader
Deanee, Deaney, Deani

Deanna (Latin/English) divine
girl
Deana, Deanne, Dee

Deanne (Latin) form of Diana:
divine woman; goddess of hunt
and fertility
Deann, Dee, Deeann

Dearbhail (Welsh) held close

De-Armone (French) girl of the
army

Dearon (American) dear one
Dear, Dearan, Dearen, Deary

Dearoven (American) form of
Dearon: dear one
Derovan, Deroven

Deasa (Spanish) delightful

Deatra (English) form of Deitra:
goddesslike

DeAyn (Dutch) form of Deanne:
divine woman; goddess of hunt
and fertility

Debara (Spanish) form of
Deborah: prophetess

Debarath (Hebrew) bee; busy
Deborath, Daberath

Debbie (Hebrew) form of
Deborah: prophetess
*Deb, Debbee, Debbey, Debbi,
Debby, Debbye, Debee, Debi,
Debie*

Deborah (Hebrew) prophetess
*Debbie, Debbora, Debborah,
Debor, Deboreh, Deborrah, Debra*

Deboria (English) form of
Deborah: prophetess

Debra (Hebrew) prophetess
Debbra, Debbrah, Debrah

Debran (American) form of
Deborah: prophetess

Debrani (American) grace

Debray (American) form of
Deborah: prophetess
Dabrae, Deb, Debrae, Debraye

Debrean (Slavic) form of
Deborah: prophetess

Debreka (Slavic) form of
Deborah: prophetess

Dece (Spanish) tenth child

Decena (Latin) form of Decima:
tenth girl
Decia

Deceshia (American) tenth child

D'Echon (French) echo

Decima (Latin) tenth girl

Decole (French) form of Nicole:
winning

Decolia (American) form of
Nicole: winning

Decuma (Mythology) one of the
Roman Fates; measures

Dedra (American) spirited
*Dee, Deeddra, DeeDee, Deedra,
Deedrea, Deedrie, Deidra, Deirdre*

Dedranay (American) form of
Deidra: sparkling

Dee (English/Irish) lucky one
*Dea, Deah, DeeDee, Dee-Dee,
Dedee, Didee*

Deedee (American) form of D
names: vivacious
D.D., Dee Dee, DeeDee, Dee-Dee

Deen (English) form of Dean:
practical

Deena (American) soothes

Deepa (Hindi) light

DeErica (African American)
audacious
Dee-Erica

Deesha (American) dancing
*Dedee, Dee, Deesh, Deeshah,
Deisha*

Deianna (English) form of
Deanna: divine girl

Deidra (Irish) sparkling
Deedra, Deidre, Dierdra

Deighan (American) exciting
Daygan, Deigan

Deina (Spanish) soothes

Deiondra (Greek) feminine form
of Dionysis: joyous celebrant
*Deandrah, Deann, Deanndra, Dee,
Deean, Deeann, DeeDee, Deondra*

Deirdre (Irish) passionate
*Dedra, Dee, Deedee, Deedrah,
Deerdra, Deerdre, Didi*

Deissy (Greek) form of Desma:
oath
*Deisi, Deissey, Deissie, Desmee,
Desmer, Dessi*

Deitra (Greek) goddess-like
Deetra, Detria

Deittra (English) form of
Demetria: harvest goddess

Deja (French) already seen
Dejah, D'Ja

Dejan (Slavic) siren

Dejeane (French) born before

Dejoie (French) joy

Dejon (French) she came before
Daijon, Dajan, Dajona

Deka (African) a pleasure
Dekah, Dekka

Dekeidra (American) pleasant

Dela (English) dramatic

Delakate (American) delicate

Delana (German) protective
*Dalana, Dalanna, Dalayna,
Daleena, Dalena, Dalenna,
Dalina, Dalinna, Deedee, Delaina,
Delainah, Delena*

Delanah (American) wise
Delana, Delano, Dellana

Delandra (American) outgoing
Delan, Delande

Delaney (Irish) bouncy;
enthusiastic
*Dalanie, Delaine, Delainey,
Delane, DeLayney, Dellie, Dulaney*

Delaune (English) form of
Delaney: bouncy; enthusiastic

Delaura (American) prefix De
and Laura

Delcia (Latin) delightful

Delcine (Latin) a delight

Delcy (American) friendly
Del, Delcee, Delci

Dele (American) rash; noble
Del, Dell

Delene (French) dearest girl

Delfin (Spanish) of the dolphin

Delfina (Latin/Italian) flowering
Dellfina, Delphina

Delia (Greek) lovely; moon
goddess
*Dehlia, Deilyuh, Del, Delea, Deli,
Dellia, Dellya, Delya, Delyah*

Delicia (English) delights
*Delesha, Delice, Delisa, Delise,
Delisha, Delisiah, Delya, Delys,
Delyse, Delysia*

Delieca (Spanish) delight

Delight (French) wonderful

Delilah (Hebrew) beautiful
temptress
Dalia, Dalila, Delila, Lilah

Delina (French) dearest

Delinah (American) form of
Adeline: sweet

Delinda (American) form of
Melinda: honey; sweetheart
Delin, Delinde, Delynda

Delinde (French) dearest

Delise (Latin) delicious
Del, Delice, Delicia, Delisa, Delissa

Delite (American) a pleasure
Delight

Delja (Slavic) form of Deja:
already seen

Dell (Greek) kind
Del

Della (Greek) kind
Dee, Del, Dela, Dell, Delle, Delli, Dells

Dellana (Irish) form of Delaney: bouncy; enthusiastic
Delaine, Delana, Dell, Dellaina, Dellane, Dellann

Dellia (American) pretty

Delmee (American) star
Del, Delmey, Delmi, Delmy

Delmys (American) incredible
Del, Delmas, Delmis

Delo (Slavic) form of Delos: beautiful brunette; a small Aegean isle; stunning

Deloise (Italian) combative

Delon (American) musical
Delonn, Delonne

Delora (Spanish) form of Delores: woman of sorrowful leaning
Dellora, Delorita

Delores (Spanish) woman of sorrowful leaning
Del, Delora, Delore, Deloria, Delories, Deloris, Delorise, Dolores

Delos (Greek) beautiful brunette; a small Aegean isle; stunning
Delas

Delpha (Greek) form of Delphine: calmness
Delfa

Delphina (Greek) dolphin; smart

Delphine (Latin) calmness
Delfina, Delfine, Delpha, Delphe, Delphene, Delphi, Delphia, Delphina, Delphinia, Delvina

Delphy (Biblical) place name
Delphia, Delphi

Delta (Greek) fourth letter of the Greek alphabet
Del, Dell, Dellta, Delte, Deltra

Deltrese (African American) jubilant
Del, Delltrese, Delt, Delta, Deltreese, Deltrice

Delwyn (English/Welsh) friend from the valley; neat and fair
Delwen, Delwenne, Delwin

Demareas (Biblical) calf

Demetia (Greek) harvest goddess

Demetress (Greek) form of Demetria: harvest goddess
Deme, Demetra, Demetres, Demetri, Dimi, Tress, Tressie, Tressy

Demetria (Greek) harvest goddess
Deitra, Demeta, Demeteria, Demetra, Demetrice, Demetris, Demetrish, Demetrius, Demi, Demita, Demitra

Demetriase (Greek) harvest goddess

Demi (French) half
Demiah, Demie

Demtrialle (American) regal

Dena (English) laid back; valley
Deane, Deena, Deeyn, Denae, Denah, Dene, Denea, Deney, Denna

Denada (American) calm

Denae (Hebrew) form of Dena: shows the truth
Danay, Denee

Dencie (English) form of Denise: wine-lover

Denda (American) form of Dena: laid back; valley

Deneane (English) form of Denise: wine-lover

Denedra (American) lively; natural
Den, Dene, Denney

Denee (French) robust

Deneen (American) absolved
Denean, Denene

Deneka (Slavic) star

Denes (English) nature-lover
Denis, Denne, Denny

Denesha (American) rowdy

Denetria (Greek) from God
Denitria, Denny, Dentria

Denetrice (African American) optimistic
Denetrise, Denitrise, Denny

Denezia (Turkish) of the sea
Denizia, Deniz

Denise (French) wine-lover
Danice, Daniece, Danise, Denese,
Deni, Denica, Deniece, Denni,
Denny

Denisha (American) jubilant
Danisha, Deneesha, Denesha,
Deneshea, Deniesha, Denishia

Denna (American) lively

Dennice (American) festive

Denovia (American) reveler

Den'tessa (American) form of
Contessa: pretty

Denton (Place name) town in
Texas; from a holy town
Dent, Dentun, Denty, Dentyn

Denver (English) born in a green
valley
Denv, Denvie

Denyse (American) form of
Denise: wine-lover

Denz (Invented) lively
Dens

Denza (American) fun-loving

Deo (Scottish) God's grace

Deoniece (African American)
feminine
Dee, DeeDee, Deo, Deone,
Deoneece, Deoneese

Deonsha (American) form of
Deoniece: feminine

Deonta (American) calm valley

Deora (English) adored

Deoran (American) adored

Dephoine (American) form of
Delphine: calmness

Dera (Slavic) ocean's child

Derbe (Biblical) place name

Dericka (American) dancer
Derica, Dericca, D'ericka, Derika,
Derrica, Derricka, Derrika

Derie (Hebrew) form of Derorah:
free
Derey, Drora, Drorah

Derline (American) from land
of deer
Derlini

Derneeka (Slavic) of the ocean

Dernise (American) form of
Denise: wine-lover

Deronique (African American)
unique girl
Deron, Deroneek

Derorah (Hebrew) free
Derora

Derrinda (Spanish) form of
Dorinda: loved

Derrisa (American) form of
Merissa: ocean-loving

Derrona (American) natural
Derona, Derone, Derry

Derry (Irish) red-haired woman
Deri, Derrie

Deryn (Welsh) birdlike; small
Derren, Derrin, Derrine, Deryne

Desai (African) desired

Desba (African) desired

Desbiene (American) desired

Desdemona (Greek) tragic
figure; destined
Des, Desde, Dez

Desena (American) desired

Deshawna (African American)
vivacious
Dashawna, Deshan, Deshanda,
Deshandra, Deshane, Deshaun,
Deshauna, Deshaundra,
Deshaune, Deshawn, Deshawndra,
Deshawnna, Desheania, Deshona,
Deshonda, Deshonna

Deshette (African American)
dishy
Deshett

Deshondra (African American)
vivacious
Deshaundra, Deshondrah,
Deshondria

Desi (French) form of Desiree:
desired
Dezi, Dezzie

Desiah (French) form of Desiree: desired

Desire (English) desired
Dezire

Desiree (French) desired
Desairee, Desarae, Desaray, Desaraye, Desaree, Desarhea, Desary, Deseri, Des'ree, Desree, Des-Ree, Dezaray, Deziree, Dezray

Desireenah (American) desirable

Desirette (American) desires

Desislav (Slavic) glory girl

Deslin (American) tenth

Desma (Greek) oath

Desna (Hindi) giving

Despina (Greek) ladylike

Desreta (Spanish) desires

Dess (Slavic) tenth

Desta (Slavic) joyful

Destin (American) destiny
Destinn, Destyn

Destina (Spanish) destiny
Desteena, Desteenah

Destiny ❂ (French) fated
Destanee, Destanie, Desteney, Destinay, Destinee, Destinei, Destini, Destinyi, Destnay, Destney, Destonie, Destony, Destyni

Destry (American) well-fated; western feel
Destrey, Destri, Destrie

Deterrion (Latin) form of Detra: blessed
Deterr, Deterreyon, Detrae

Detra (Latin) blessed
Detraye

Deva (Hindi) moon goddess; wielder of power
Devi

Devahuti (Hindi) in mythology, daughter of Manu

Devaki (Indian) revered mother of Krishna

Devalca (Spanish) generous
Deval

Devan (Irish) poetic
Devana, Devn

Devashka (Hebrew) honey

Deven (English) dark

Devendra (Indian) dark skin

Devera (Jewish) form of Devorah: heroine

Devette (American) form of Devera: heroine

Devi (Hindi) beloved goddess
Devia, Devian, Deviann, Devie, Devri

Devin (Irish) poetic
Devan, Devane, Devanie, Devany, Deven, Devena, Deveny, Deveyn, Devine, Devinne, Devn, Devyn, Devynne

Devina (Irish) divine; creative
Davena, Devie, Devine, Devy, Divine

Devon (English) poetic
Dev, Devaughan, Devaughn, Devie, Devonne, Devy

Devonna (English) girl from Devonshire; happy
Davonna, Devon, Devona, Devonda, Devondra

Devorah (American) heroine
Devora, Devore, Devra, Devrah

Devy (American) poetic

Devyn (English) poetic

Dew (Word as name) misty; fresh
Dewi, Dewie

Dewanna (African American) clingy
Dewana, Dewanne, D'Wana

Dexhiana (Origin Unknown) nimble

Dexter (English) spunky; dexterous
Dex, Dexee, Dexey, Dexie, Dext, Dextar, Dextur, Dexy

Dextra (Latin) skilled

Deyanira (Spanish) aggressor
Deyan, Deyann, Dianira, Nira

Dezelia (American) desired

Dezena (American) desired

Dezra (American) desirable

Dezral (American) desirable

Dharcia (American) sparkler
Darch, Darsha, Dharsha

Dharika (American) sad
Darica, Darika

Dharini (Indian) earth

Dharma (Hindi) morality; beliefs
Darma, Darmah

Dhazalai (African) sweet
Dhaze, Dhazie

Dhelal (Arabic) coy

Dhessie (American) glowing
Dhessee, Dhessey, Dhessi, Dhessy

Dhira (Indian) flow

Dhivia (Indian) heavenly

Dhumma (Hebrew) form of
Dumia: quiet

Di (Latin) form of Diane: goddess-
like; divine; or form of Diana:
divine woman; goddess of hunt
and fertility
Didi, Dy

Di Anna (American) form of
Diana: divine woman; goddess of
hunt and fertility

Dia (Greek) shining
Deah

Diaelza (Spanish) divine; pretty
Diael, Dialza, Elza

Diah (American) pretty
Dia

Diamantina (Spanish) sparkling
Diama, Diamante, Mantina

Diamond (Latin) precious
gemstone
*Diamin, Diamon, Diamonda,
Diamonds, Diamonte, Diamun,
Diamyn, Diamynd, Dyamond*

Diamondah (African American)
glowing
Diamonda, Diamonde

Diamondique (African
American) sparkling
Diamondik

Diamony (American) gem
*Diamonee, Diamoney, Diamoni,
Diamonie*

Diamrose (Spanish) diamond
rose

Diana (Latin) divine woman;
goddess of hunt and fertility
*Dee, Di, Diahana, Diahna,
Dianah, Diannah, Didi, Dihanna,
Dyanna, Dyannah, Dyhana*

Diandro (American) special
Diandra, Diandrea, Diandroh

Diane (Latin) goddess-like; divine
*Deane, Deanne, Deeann, Deeanne,
Deedee, Di, Diahann, Dian,
Diann, Dianne, Didi*

Dianelle (American) divine

Diange (American) form of
Diane: goddess-like; divine

Dianita (Spanish) divine

Diannie (American) divine girl

Diantha (Greek) flower; heavenly
Dianth

Diarah (American) pretty
Dearah, Di, Diara, Diarra, Dierra

Diathe (Biblical) place name

Diathema (Greek) divine

Diavonne (African American)
jovial
Diavone, Diavonna, Diavonni

Dica (Slavic) cautious

Dicey (American) impulsive
*Di, Dice, Dicee, Dicy, Dycee,
Dycey*

Dicia (American) wild
Desha, Dicy

Didah (Biblical) of love

Diedre (Irish) form of Deidre:
sparkling
Diedra, Diedré

Diella (Latin) worships
Dielle

Diesha (African American) zany
Diecia, Dieshah, Dieshay, Dieshie

Diethild (German) believer

Difanee (American) form of
Daphne: pretty nymph

Diggs (American) tomboyish
Digs, Dyggs

Dihana (American) natural
Dihanna

Dijan (Slavic) divine goddess

Dijana (Slavic) form of Diana:
divine woman; goddess of hunt
and fertility

Dijonnay (American) fun-loving
Dijon, Dijonae, Dijonay,
Dijonnae, Dijonnaie

Dilan (American) form of Dylan:
creative; from the sea
Dillan, Dilon

Dilcia (Spanish) loved

Dileone (Spanish) worships

Dilia (Spanish) worships

Dilly (Welsh) loyal

Dillyana (English) worshipful
Diliann, Dilli, Dillianna, Dilly

Dilsey (American) dependable;
one who endures

Dilva (Slavic) loyal

Dilynn (American) form of
Dylan: creative; from the sea
Di, Dilenn, Dilinn, Dilyn, Lynn

Dilys (Welsh) of the truth

Dima (American) high-spirited
Deemah, Dema

Dimond (American) form of
Diamond: precious gemstone

Dina (Hebrew/Scottish) right;
royal

Dinah (Hebrew) fair judge
Dina, Dinna, Dyna, Dynah

Dinavia (American) form of
Dinah: fair judge

Dinesha (American) happy
Dineisha, Dineshe, Diniesha

Dini (American) joyful
Dinee, Diney, Dinie

Dinora (Spanish) judged by God
Dina, Dino, Nora

Dinorah (Spanish) light

Dinorot (American) form of
Dinah: fair judge

Dioma (Greek) form of Diona:
divine woman

Diona (Greek) divine woman
Dee, Di, Dion, Dionah, Dionuh

Dioneece (American) daring
Dee, DeeDee, Deon, Deone,
Deonece, Deoneece, Dioniece,
Neece, Neecey

Dionicia (Spanish) vixen
Di, Dione, Dionice, Dionise,
Nicia, Nise, Nisee

Dionis (English) feminine form
of Dion: joyous celebrant

Dionise (English) feminine form
of Dion: joyous celebrant

Dionish (American) feminine
form of Dion: joyous celebrant

Dionndra (American) loving
Diondra, Diondrah, Diondruh

Dionne (Greek) love goddess
Deona, Deondra, Deonia, Deonna,
Deonne, Dion, Dione, Dionna

Dionnesha (American) feminine
form of Dion: joyous celebrant

Dior (French) stylish
Diora, Diorah, Diore, Diorra,
Diorre

Diotima (Latin) in the time of
God

Dira (Arabic) soft-spoken

Direll (American) svelte
Di, Direl, Direlle

Dirisha (African American)
outgoing
Di, Diresha, Direshe

Dirkae (Scandinavian) feminine
form of Dirk: leader

Disa (Scandinavian) goddess

Disano (Italian) wise

Disha (American) fine
Dishae, Dishuh

Dishawna (African American)
special
Dishana, Dishauna, Dishawnah,
Dishona, Dishonna

Dishi (Indian) the right way

Divina (American) divine being

Divine (Italian) divine soul
Divin, Divina

Divinity (American) sweet; devout
Divinitee, Diviniti, Divinitie

Divora (Indian) divine

Divya (Indian) celestial

Divyanah (Hindi) divine

Dix (French) live wire

Dixie (English/French) from the South in the United States
Dixee, Dixi, Dixy

Diya (Indian) divine

Diyanne (Slavic) form of Diane: goddess-like; divine

Dizian (American) joyful

Dnisha (African American) rejoicing
Dnisa, Dnish, D'Nisha, Dnishay, Dnishe

Dobie (American) cowgirl
Dobee, Dobey, Dobi

Dobra (Polish) kindness

Docia (Latin) form of Docilla: docile
Docie

Docilla (Latin) docile
Docila, Docile

Dodie (Greek/Hebrew) gift of God
Doda, Dodee, Dodi, Dody

Dodona (Greek) ancient city in Greece

Doe (Polish) kind

Doherty (American) ambitious
Dhoertey, Dohertee, Dohertie

Doina (Slavic) lady *Dojna*

Doka (Slavic) dependable

Dolah (Hindi) loved

Dolas (American) sorrows

Dolchil (American) docile

Dolcy (American) a vision
Dolcee, Dolcie, Dolsee

Dollis (American) doleful

Dolly (American) toylike
Dol, Doll, Dollee, Dolli, Dollie

Doloarea (Spanish) sorrows

Dolores (Spanish) woman of sorrowful leaning
Delores

Dolory (Slavic) form of Dolores: woman of sorrowful leaning

Domel (American) steadfast; faithful
Domela, Domella

Dometria (American) form of Demetria: harvest goddess
Dome, Dometrea, Domi, Domini, Domitra

Domina (Latin) ladylike

Dominga (Spanish) her dominion

Domini (Latin) feminine form of Dominic: child of the Lord; saint
Dom, Dominee, Domineke, Dominey, Dominie, Dominika, Domino, Dominy

Dominica (Latin) follower of God
Dom, Domenica, Domenika, Domineca, Domineka, Domini, Dominika, Domonica, Domonika

Dominique (French) bright; masterful
Dom, Domanique, Domeneque, Domenique, Domino, Domonik

Domitila (Spanish) home-loving

Dona (Latin) always giving
Donail, Donalea, Donalisa, Donay, Donelle, Donetta, Doni, Donia, Donice, Donie, Donise, Donisha, Donishia, Donita, Donitrae

Donalda (Scottish) loves all
Donaldina, Donaleen, Donelda, Donella, Donellia, Donette, Doni, Donita, Donnella, Donnelle

Donalie (American) lady

Donata (Italian) celebrating
Donada, Donatah, Donatha, Donatta, Donni, Donnie, Donny

Donatella (Latin/Italian) gift
Don, Donnie, Donny

Donatilde (Spanish) gift

Donava (African) jubilant
Donavah

Dondra (American) ladylike

Dondranea (Invented) ladylike

Donela (Italian) leader
Donella

Donelda (Spanish) giving

Donia (American) form of
Donna: ladylike and genteel

Donicia (Spanish) feminine

Donika (African American) form
of Donna: ladylike and genteel
Donica

Donisha (African American)
laughing; cozy
Daneesha, Danisha, Doneesha

Donna (Italian) ladylike and
genteel
*Dom, Don, Dona, Dondi, Donnie,
Donya*

Donnata (Latin) giving
Dona, Donata, Donni

Donnelly (Italian) lush
*Donally, Donelly, Donnell,
Donnelli, Donnellie, Donni,
Donnie, Donny*

Donnettella (Italian) giving

Donnis (American) pleasant;
giving
Donnice

Donserena (American) dancer;
giving
*Donce, Doncie, Dons, Donse,
Donsee, Donser, Donsey*

Dontilan (American) donates

Donya (Italian) feminine

Donyale (African American) form
of Danielle: judged by God; spiritual
Donyelle

Donyan (English) feminine

Donyellan (African) upbeat

Dora (Greek) gift from God
*Dorah, Dori, Dorie, Dorra,
Dorrah*

Dorant (American) gifted

Dorat (French) a gift
Doratt, Dorey, Dorie

Dorby (Spanish) devout

Dorcea (Greek) sea girl
Dorcia

Dorcelline (English) fast

Dordea (English) heritage

Dore (Irish) form of Dora: gift
from God

Doree (Hebrew) heritage

Doreen (Greek/Irish) capricious
Dorene, Dorine, Dory

Dorei (American) form of Doris:
sea-loving; sea nymph

Dorekka (Slavic) form of Dorika:
God's gift

Dorel (Spanish) adored

Dorenda (American) adored

Dorende (American) adored

Doreneah (American) adored

Dorenee (American) form of
Doreen: capricious

Dorentia (American) adored

Doreth (American) form of
Dorit: God's gift; shy

Doretha (American) form of
Dorit: God's gift; shy

Dori (French) adorned
*Dore, Dorey, Dorie, Dorree, Dorri,
Dorrie, Dorry, Dory*

Doria (Greek) form of Dorian:
happy
*Dori, Doriana, Doriann,
Dorianna, Dorianne*

Dorial (American) form of
Dorit: God's gift; shy

Dorian (Greek) happy
*Dorean, Doreane, Doree, Doriane,
Dorri, Dorry*

Dorianna (Greek) of the sea
Dorianne

Dorie (American) faithful

Dorika (Greek) God's gift
Doreek, Dorike, Dory

Dorin (Greek) form of Dorian:
happy

Dorina (Hawaiian) loved

Dorind (American) form of Doreen: capricious

Dorinda (Spanish) loved

Dorinta (American) gift

Doris (Greek) sea-loving; sea nymph
Dor, Dori, Dorice, Dorise, Doriss, Dorris, Dorrise, Dorrys, Dory

Doriscus (Biblical) place name

Dorisette (American) form of Doris: sea-loving; sea nymph

Dorit (Greek) God's gift; shy
Dooritt

Dorita (Greek) empress

Dorle (Greek) empress

Dorly (Greek) empress

Dor-Lyn (Invented) combo of Dor and Lyn; empress

Dornay (American) involved
Dorn, Dornae, Dornee, Dorny

Dorothea (Greek) gift from God
Dorethea, Dorotha, Dorothia, Dorotthea, Dorthea, Dorthia

Dorothy (Greek) gift of God
Dorathy, Dorthy

Dorren (Irish) sad-faced
Doren

Dorte (Scandinavian) God's gift

Dortha (Greek) God's gift; studious
Dorth, Dorthee, Dorthey, Dorthy

Dorthe (Scandinavian) God's gift

Dorum (American) God's gift

Dory (French) gilded; gold hair
Dora, Dore, Dorie

Doshene (American) shares

Dosia (Russian) happy

Dossey (Last name as first name) rambunctious
Dosse, Dossi, Dossie, Dossy, Dozze

Dot (Greek) spunky
Dottee, Dottie, Dotty

Dottie (Greek) form of Dorothy: gift of God

Dottye (English) gift

Dottylene (English) gift

Doubta (Slavic) doubtful

Douce (French) sweet
Doucia, Dulce, Dulci, Dulcie

Douet (French) dew

Dove (Greek) dreamy

Dovie (English) dove of peace

Doxey (American) variant of Moxie and Dottie

Doxie (Greek) fine
Doxy

Dragana (Slavic) dragon lady

Drahomira (Czech) dearest

Drake (English) dragon

Draleen (American) dragon

Drancine (French) dragon lady

Draven (American) loyal
Dravan, Dravin, Dravine

Draxy (American) faithful
Drax, Draxee, Draxey, Draxi

Draya (Slavic) form of Drake: dragon

Drea (American) adorable

Dream (American) dream girl; misty
Dreama, Dreamee, Dreamey, Dreami, Dreamie, Dreamy

Dreana (Spanish) spiritual

Dreda (Anglo-Saxon) thoughtful
Drida

Dree (American) soft-spoken

Dreena (American) cautious
Dreenah, Drina

Drelan (Origin Unknown) watches

Drena (Spanish) form of Adriana: rich; exotic

Drenda (American) form of Dorinda: loved

Drenea (American) spiritual

Drestell (American) new

Drew (Greek) woman of valor
Dru, Drue

Driana (American) form of Adriana: rich; exotic

Dricea (American) form of Adriana: rich; exotic

Drina (American) form of Adriana: rich; exotic

Drinda (Spanish) form of Dorinda: loved

Drisena (Spanish) strong

Dristi (Indian) insightful

Drover (American) surprising
Drovah, Drovar

Dru (American) bright
Drew, Drue

Druanna (American) bold
Drewann, Drewanne, Druanah, Druannah

Drucelle (American) smart
Druce, Drucee, Drucel, Drucell, Drucey, Druci, Drucy

Druella (Latin) form of Drusilla: strong

Drummond (Last name used as first name) drummer's mountain

Druna (English) leader

Drusa (Latin) form of Drusilla: strong
Drucie, Drusie

Drusi (Latin) strong girl
Drucey, Drucie, Drucy, Drusey, Drusie, Drusy

Drusilla (Latin) strong
Dru, Drucilla

Dryden (Last name as first name) special
Dydie

Duana (Irish) dark
Dwana

Dubethza (Invented) sad
Dubeth

Duchess (American) fancy
Duc, Duchesse, Ducy, Dutch, Dutchey, Dutchie, Dutchy

Ducy (Slavic) purest

Duena (Spanish) chaperones; guards

Duffy (Irish) spunky

Dufvenius (Swedish) lovely
Duf, Duff

Duhnell (Hebrew) kindhearted
Danee, Danny, Nell

Duiene (Spanish) accompanies

Dulce-Maria (Spanish) sweet Mary
Dulce, Dulcey

Dulceria (Spanish) sweet

Dulcibella (Italian) sweet beauty

Dulcie (Latin/Spanish) sweet one
Dulce, Dulcey, Dulcy

Dulcinea (Latin) sweet nature

Dulvio (Italian) helpful

Duma (African) quiet help
Dumah

Dumia (Hebrew) quiet
Dumi

Duna (Spanish) protects

Dune (American) summery
Doone, Dunah, Dunie

Dunesha (African American) warm
Dunisha

Dunning (Last name used as first name) alive

Dupre (American) soft-spoken
Dupray, Duprey

Dura (Biblical) place name

Dureene (Latin) endures

Durice (American) out of reach

Durrah (Hindi) heroine

Dusanka (Slavic) soulful
Dusan, Dusana, Dusank, Sanka

Duscha (Russian) happy
Dusa, Duschah, Dusha, Dushenka

Duse (Slavic) happy

Dusky (Invented) dreamy

Dusky-Dream (Invented) dreamy
Duskee-Dream

Dustine (German) go-getter
Dustee, Dusteen, Dustene, Dusti, Dustie, Dustina, Dusty

Dusty (American) southern
Dustee, Dustey, Dusti, Dustie

Dwanda (American) athletic
Dwana, Dwayna, Dwunda

Dwayna (American) feminine form of Dwayne: swarthy

Dwyn (Welsh) fairhaired

Dyan (Latin) form of Diane: goddess-like; divine
Dian, Dyana, Dyane, Dyani, Dyann, Dyanna, Dyanne

Dyandra (Latin) sleek
Diandra, Dianndrah, Dyan, Dyandruh

Dylan (Welsh) creative; from the sea
Dilann, Dyl, Dylane, Dylann, Dylanne, Dylen, Dylin, Dyllan, Dylynn

Dylana (Welsh) sea-loving

Dymea (American) crazed

Dymond (American) form of Diamond: precious gemstone
Dymahn, Dymon, Dymonn, Dymund

Dymphia (Irish) poetic
Dimphia

Dynasty (Word as name) substantial; rich

Dynet (American) curious

Dyney (American) consoling others
Diney, DiNey, Dy

Dyonne (American) marvelous
Dyonn, Dyonna, Dyonnae

Dyronisha (African American) fine
Dyron

Dyshaunna (African American) dedicated
Dyshaune, Dyshawn, Dyshawna

Dyshay (American) healthy

Dywon (American) bubbly
Diwon, Dywan, Dywann, Dywaughn, Dywonne

Dzidzo (African) universal child

Eadrianne (American) standout
Eddey, Eddi, Eddy, Edreiann, Edrian, Edrie

Eamina (American) curious

E'ann (Irish) sunny

Eanna (Irish) sunny

Earla (English) leader
Earlah, Erla, Erlene, Erletta, Erlette

Earlean (Irish) dedicated
Earla, Earlecia, Earleen, Earlena, Earlene, Earlina, Earlinda, Earline, Erla, Erlana, Erlene, Erlenne, Erlina, Erlinda, Erline, Erlisha

Earlette (American) dedicated

Earlinetta (American) dedicated

Early (American) bright
Earlee, Earlie, Earlye, Erly

Earlyne (American) dedicated

Earnesia (Spanish) sincere

Earth (English) earth child

Eartha (English) earth mother

Earthelen (American) earthy

Earthine (American) of the earth

Easter (American) born on Easter; springlike

Easton (American) wholesome
Eastan, Easten, Eastun, Eeston, Estynn

Eavan (Irish) beautiful
Eevonne, Evaughn

Ebba (English/Scandinavian) strong
Eb, Eba, Ebbah

Ebban (American) pretty; affluent
Ebann, Ebbayn

Ebbie (English) blessed child

Ebony (Greek) hard and dark
Eb, Ebanie, Ebbeny, Ebbie, Ebonea, Ebonee, Eboney, Eboni, Ebonie, Ebonni

Ebonyishia (American) black

Eboyn (English) form of Ebony: hard and dark

Ebrel (Cornish) from the month April
Ebby, Ebrelle, Ebrie, Ebrielle

Echo (Greek) smitten; echo
Eko

Ecia (Slavic) royal

Ecstasy (American) joyful
Ecstasey, Ecstasie, Stase

Eda (Irish) form of Edith: a blessed girl who is a gift to mankind

Edaena (Irish) fiery; energetic
Ed, Eda, Edae, Edana, Edanah, Edaneah, Eddi

Edalene (German) refined
Eda, Edalyne, Edeline, Ediline, Lena, Lene

Edana (Irish) flaming energy
Eda, Edan, Edanna

Eddi (English) form of Edwina: prospering female
Eddie, Eddy, Edy

Edel (German) clever; noble
Edell, Eddi

Eden (Hebrew) paradise of delights
Ede, Edena, Edene, Edin, Edyn

Edessa (Biblical) place name; flourishes

Edia (Hebrew) special

Edie (English) form of Edith: a blessed girl who is a gift to mankind
Eadie, Edee, Edi, Edy, Edye, Eydie

Edieh (American) gifted

Edina (Slavic) affluent

Edith (English) a blessed girl who is a gift to mankind
Eadith, Ede, Edetta, Edette, Edie, Edithe, Editta, Ediva, Edy, Edyth, Edythe, Eydie

Editha (Spanish) blessed

Edithanette (American) blessed

Edju (Origin unknown) giving
Eddju

Edlin (German) noble; sophisticated
Eddi, Eddy, Edlan, Edland, Edlen

Edmea (Scottish) form of Edme: beloved

Edmee (American) spontaneous
Edmey, Edmi, Edmy, Edmye

Edmonda (English) feminine form of Edmond: protective
Edmon, Edmond, Edmund, Edmunda, Monda

Edna (Hebrew) youthful
Eddie, Ednah, Edneisha, Ednita, Eydie

Edreanna (American) merry
Edrean, Edreana, Edreanne, Edrianna

Edrika (Scandinavian) forever

Edrina (American) old-fashioned
Ed, Eddi, Eddrina, Edrena, Edrinah

Edsel (American) plain
Eds, Edsell, Edzel

Edshone (American) wealthy
Ed, Eds, Edshun

Edwina (English) prospering female
Eddi, Eddy, Edina, Edweena, Edwena, Edwenna, Edwine, Edwyna, Edwynna

Efanye (African) respected

Effemy (Greek/German) form of Euphemia: well-spoken
Efemie, Efemy, Effee, Effemie, Effey, Effie, Effy

Effen (English) eloquent

Effie (Greek) form of Euphemia: well-spoken
Effi, Effia, Effy, Ephie

Efigenia (Spanish) form of Eugenia: high-born

Efrat (Hebrew) bountiful
Efrata

Egan (American) wholesome
Egen, Egun

Eglantyne (French) flower

Egypt (Place name) country; exotic
Egypt

Egzanth (Invented) form of
Xanthe: beautiful blonde; yellow

Ehrone (Slavic) peaceful

Eileen (Irish) bright and spirited
Eilean, Eilee, Eileena, Eileene,
Eilena, Eilene, Eiley, Eilleen,
Eillen, Eilyn, Elene, Ellie

Eireen (Scandinavian) peacemaker
Eirena, Erene, Ireen, Irene

Eires (Greek) peaceful
Eiress, Eres, Heris

Eirianne (English) peaceful
Eirian, Eriann

Ekaja (Hindi) only child

Ekanta (Hindi) loyalty

Ekaterina (Slavic) respected

Ekaterini (Slavic) form of
Katherine: pure

Eko (American) form of Echo:
smitten; echo

Eks (Slavic) gleans

Ekta (Indian) together

Elaine (French) dependable girl
Elain, Elaina, Elainia, Elainna,
Elan, Elana, Elane, Elania, Elanie,
Elanna, Elayn, Elayna, Elayne,
Ellaine

Elana (Greek) pretty
Ela, Elan, Elani, Elanie, Lainie

Elanja (Slavic) gleeful girl

Elasa (Biblical) place name

Elata (Latin) bright; well-
positioned
Ela, Elate, Elatt, Elle, Elota

Elcida (Spanish) elucidate

Elda (Italian) protective

Eldee (American) light
El, Eldah, Elde

Eldora (Spanish) golden girl;
golden spirit
Eldoree, Eldorey, Eldori, Eldoria,
Eldorie, Eldory

Eldulita (Spanish) protective

Eleacie (American) forthright
Acey, Elea, Eleasie

Eleanor (Greek) light-hearted
Elana, Elanor, Elanore, Eleanora,
Elenor, Elenorah, Eleonor, Eleonore,
Elinor, Elinore, Ellie, Ellinor,
Ellinore, Elynor, Elynore, Lenore

Eleanora (Greek) light
Elenora, Eleonora, Eleora, Ella
nora, Ellenora, Ellenorah, Ellora,
Elnora, Elora, Elynora

Eleatrice (Greek) free girl

Electra (Greek) shining; brilliant
Elec, Elek, Elektra

Elegy (American) lasting
Elegee, Eleggee, Elegie, Eligey

Elek (American) star-like
Elec, Ellie, Elly

Elelvina (Spanish) resilient

Elena (Greek/Russian/Spanish)
form of Helen: beautiful; light
Elana, Eleana, Eleen, Eleena, Elen,
Elene, Eleni, Ilena, Ilene, Lena,
Leni, Lennie, Lina, Nina

Eleni (Greek) sweet
Elenee

Eleonore (French) form of
Helen: beautiful; light
Elenore, Elle, Elnore

Eleovina (Spanish) bright way

Eleri (Welsh) smooth
Elere, Eleree

Elettra (Latin/Italian) form of
Electra: shining; brilliant

Elfin (American) small girl
El, Elf, Elfan, Elfee, Elfey, Elfie,
Elfun, Els

Elfreda (English) elf strength;
good counselor

Elfrida (German) peaceful spirit
Elfie, Elfrea, Elfredda, Elfreeda,
Elfreyda, Elfryda

Elgie (Spanish) chosen elegy

Eliana (Hebrew) the Lord
answers
Eliane, Elianna, Elianne, Elliana,
Ellianne, Ellie, Liana, Liane

Eliane (French) cheerful; sunny

Elicabeth (American) form of Elizabeth: God's promise

Elicia (Hebrew) dedicated
Ellicia

Eliki (Hawaiian) abundant

Elisa (Spanish) dedicated to God
Elecea, Eleesa, Elesa, Elesia, Elisia, Elissa, Elisse, Elisya, Ellisa, Ellisia, Ellissa, Ellissia, Ellissya, Ellisya, Elysa, Elysia, Elyssia, Elyssya, Elysya, Leese, Leesie, Lisa

Elisabet (Hebrew/Scandinavian) form of Elizabeth: God's promise
Bet, Elisa, Elsa, Else

Elisabeth (Hebrew/French/German) form of Elizabeth: God's promise
Bett, Bettina, Elisa, Elise, Els, Elsa, Elsie, Ilsa, Ilyse, Liesa, Liese, Lisbeth, Lise

Elise (French) consecrated to God
Elice, Elisse, Elle, Ellyse, Lisie

Eliseu (Biblical) abundance in God

Elisha (Greek) God-loving
Eleacia, Eleasha, Elecia, Eleesha, Eleisha, Elesha, Eleshia, Elicia, Eliesha, Ellie, Lisha

Elishama (American) loves God

Elishca (American) form of Elizabeth: God's promise

Elisheba (Biblical) form of Elizabeth: God's promise

Elissa (Greek) from the blessed isles
Ellissa, Ellyssa, Elyssa, Ilissa, Ilyssa

Elita (French) selected one
Elida, Elitia, Elitie, Ellita, Ellitia, Ellitie, Ilida, Ilita, Litia

Elite (Latin) best
Elita

Eliza (Irish) sworn to God
Aliza, Elieza, Elize, Elyza

Elizabeth ✿ ❶ (Hebrew) God's promise
Beth, Betsy, Elisabeth, Elizebeth, Lissie, Liza

Elizeth (American) form of Elizabeth: God's promise

Elke (Dutch) distinguished
Elki, Ilki

Elken (American) believer

Elkie (Dutch) form of Elke: distinguished
Elk, Elka

Ella ✿ ❶ (Greek) beautiful and fanciful
Ellamae, Elle, Ellia, Ellie, Elly

Ellaina (American) sincere
Elaina, Ellana, Ellanuh

Ellan (American) coy
Elan, Ellane, Ellyn

Elle (Scandinavian) woman
Ele

Ellen (English) open-minded
El, Elen, Elenee, Eleny, Elin, Ellene, Ellie, Ellyn, Ellynn, Elyn

Ellender (American) decisive
Elender, Ellander, Elle, Ellie

Elli (Scandinavian) aged
Ell, Elle, Ellie

Ellice (English) loves God
Ellecia, Ellyce, Elyce

Ellie (English) candid
Ele, Elie, Elly

Ellina (Scandinavian) valuable

Ells (Scandinavian) patient
Els

Ellyce (French) abundance in God

Elm (Botanical) tree

Elma (Turkish) sweet
El

Elmas (Armenian) diamondlike
Elmaz, Elmes, Elmis

Elna (American) light

Elnora (American) sturdy
Ellie, Elnor, Elnorah

Elocile (Spanish) easy child

Elodia (Spanish) flowering
Elodi

Elodie (French) melody

Eloina (Spanish) fulfills destiny

Eloisa (Italian) sun girl

Eloise (German) high-spirited
Eluise, Luise

Elora (American) fresh-faced
Elorah, Flory, Floree

Eloyse (English) form of Eloise:
high-spirited

Eloysee (American) form of
Eloise: high-spirited

Elpidia (Spanish) shining
El, Elpey, Elpi, Elpie

Elrica (German) leader
Elrick, Elrika, Elrike, Rica, Rika

Elsa (German) form of Elizabeth:
God's promise
Ellsa, Ellse, Ellsey, Els, Elsah,
Elseh, Elsie, Ellsee

Elsie (German) hard-working
Elsee, Elsi, Elsy

Elsiy (Spanish) God-loving
El, Els, Elsa, Elsee, Elsi, Elsy

Elspeth (Scottish) loved by God
El, Elle, Els

Elspie (Scottish) regal

Elsy (Spanish) form of Elizabeth:
God's promise

Elton (American) spontaneous
Elt, Elten, Eltone, Eltun

Eluvia (Spanish) happy

Elva (English) tiny
Elvah, Elvenea, Elvia, Elvie,
Elvina, Elvinea, Elvineah

Elverna (American) form of
Elvire: truest of all

Elvetta (American) form of Elva:
tiny

Elvia (Latin) sunny
Elvea, Elviah, Elvie

Elvira (Latin/German) truth
Elva, Elvie, Elvina, Elwire, Vira

Elvire (French) truest of all

Elyana (Spanish) friend

Elyanna (American) good friend
Elyana, Elyannah, Elyunna

Elyse (English) soft-mannered
Elice, Elle, Elysee, Elysia, Ilysha,
Ilysia

Elysia (Latin) joyful
Elyse, Elysee, Elysha, Elyshia

Elyssa (Greek) form of Elissa:
from the blessed isles
Elisa, Elysa, Illysa, Lyssa

Elysse (French) God's abundance

Elzada (Polish) form of Elizabeth:
God's promise

Emalee (German) thoughtful
Emalea, Emaleigh, Emaley,
Emaline, Emally, Emaly,
Emmalynn, Emmeline, Emmelyne

Emann (American) soft-spoken
Eman

Emaunuela (Spanish) believes
in God

Ember (American) temperamental
Embere, Embre

Emberatriz (Spanish) respected
Emb, Ember, Embera,
Emberatrice, Emberatryce,
Embertrice, Embertrise

Emberli (American) pretty
Em, Emb, Ember, Emberlee,
Emberley, Emberly

Embray (American) form of
Emily: industrious; eager

Eme (Hawaiian) loved; (German)
form of Emma: universal: all-
embracing
Em, Emee, Emm, Emme, Emmee,
Emmie, Emmy

Emea (Dutch) competes

Emelle (American) kind
Emell

Emelsa (Spanish) emulates

Emely (German) go-getter
Emel, Emelee, Emelie

Emena (Latin) of fortunate birth
Em, Emen, Emene, Emina, Emine

Emera (Irish) talented

Emerald (French) bright as a gemstone
Em, Emmie

Emerenciana (Spanish) experienced

Emerene (Spanish) experienced

Emerita (Spanish) experienced

Emesa (Biblical) place name; reserved

Emestina (American) form of Ernestine: sincere spirit
Emee, Emes, Emest, Tina

Emigdea (Spanish) enigmatic

Emika (Slavic) charming

Emilee (American) form of Emily: industrious; eager

Emilia (Italian) soft-spirited
Emalia, Emelia, Emila

Emilie (French) charmer

Emily ○ ❶ (Latin) industrious; eager
Em, Emalie, Emilee, Emili, Emilie, Emmi, Emmie

Emma ○ ❶ (German) universal; all-embracing
Em, Emmah, Emme, Emmie, Emmi, Emmot, Emmy, Emmye, Emott

Emmaline (French/German) form of Emily: industrious; eager
Em, Emaline, Emalyne, Emiline, Emmie

Emmanuelle (Hebrew/French) believer
Em, Emmi, Emmie, Emmy

Emmatha (Biblical) place name; dedicated

Emme (German) feminine
Em

Emmi (German) pretty
Emmee, Emmey, Emmy

Emoke (Asian) charms

Emperatriz (Spanish) empress

Emroy (American) elegant royal

Emsky (American) fun

Ena (Hawaiian) intense
Eana, En, Enna, Ina

Encetta (Spanish) starts

Enchantay (American) enchanting
Enchantee

Endah (Irish) flighty
Ena, End, Enda

Endia (American) form of India: woman of India
Endee, Endey, Endie, Endy, Ndia

Endriss (Slavic) endears

Enedelia (Spanish) praiseworthy

Enedina (Spanish) praised; spirited
Dina, Ened

Enesha (American) warmth

Enette (American) warmth

Engracia (Spanish) ingratiates

Enid (Welsh) lively
Eneid

Enideen (American) vibrant

Enka (Scandinavian) gem

Enna (Greek) ninth child

Ennis (Irish) dignity

Enore (English) careful
Enoor, Enora

Enrichetta (French) enriches the home

Enslie (American) emotional
Ens, Enslee, Ensley, Ensly, Enz

Enya (Irish) fiery; musician
Enyah, Nya

Epatha (African) empathy

Epifania (Spanish) proof
Epi, Epifaina, Epifanea, Eppie, Pifanie, Piffy

Epiphania (Biblical) place name; religious epiphany

Eppy (Greek) lively
Ep, Eppee, Eppey, Eppi, Eps

Equoia (African American) great equalizer
Ekowya

Era (Slavic) from the windy place

Eranth (Greek) spring bloomer
Erantha, Eranthae, Eranthe

Erasema (Spanish) happy
Eraseme

Erathine (American) earth child

Erato (Mythology) pretty poet

Erba (Spanish) feminine

Ercella (Spanish) earnest

Ercie (Spanish) sincere

Ercilia (American) frank
Erci, Ercilya

Erdell (American) of the earth

Erendia (Spanish) calm

Erendira (Spanish) peaceful

Erene (Irish) Irish child

Eres (Greek) goddess of chaos
Era, Ere, Eris

Eridania (Spanish) rules

Erika (Scandinavian) honorable;
leading others
*Erica, Ericah, Ericca, Ericha,
Ericka, Erikka, Errica, Errika,
Eryka, Erykka*

Erin (Irish) peace-making
*Eran, Eren, Erena, Erene, Ereni,
Eri, Erian, Erine, Erinn, Erinne,
Eryn, Erynn, Erynne*

Erina (American) peaceful
*Era, Erinna, Erinne, Eryna,
Erynne*

Eriqueta (Spanish) ruling

Erla (Spanish) loyal; (Irish) playful

Erlen (Spanish) loyal

Erlina (Spanish) loyal

Erlind (Hebrew) form of Erlinda:
loyal
Erlinde

Erlinda (Spanish) loyal

Erma (Latin) wealthy
Erm, Irma

Ermelinda (Spanish) fresh-faced
Ermalinda, Ermelind, Ermelynda

Ermine (Latin) rich
*Erma, Ermeen, Ermie, Ermin,
Ermina, Erminda, Erminia,
Erminie*

Erminette (Italian) noble

Erna (English) form of Ernestine:
sincere spirit
Emae, Ernea, Ernie

Ernelle (German) earnest

Ernestine (English) sincere spirit
*Erna, Ernaline, Ernesia, Ernesta,
Ernestina, Ernestyne*

Ernme (Scandinavian) sincere

Erona (Welsh) form of Erin:
peacemaking

Ersemi (Scandinavian) gem

Ertha (English) form of Eartha;
also form of Bertha: earth mother

Erwen (Welsh) blessing

Eryn (Irish) calm

Erynea (English) earnest

Erzsebet (French) form of
Elizabeth: God's promise

Es (American) form of Estella:
radiant star
Esa, Essie

Esbelda (Spanish) black-haired
beauty
Es, Esbilda, Ezbelda

Esdey (American) warmhearted
Esdee, Esdy, Essdey

Esenzia (Spanish) essence

Esha (Slavic) vibrant

Eshah (African) exuberant
Esha

Eshe (African) life
Eshay

Eshey (American) life
Es, Esh, Eshae, Eshay

Esiquio (Spanish) child of
Sunday

Esmee (French) much loved
Esma, Esme, Esmie

Esmeralda (Spanish) emerald;
shiny and bright
*Emelda, Es, Esmerelda, Esmerilda,
Esmie, Esmiralda, Esmirilda,
Ezmerelda, Ezmirilda*

Esmirna (Spanish) noble

Esne (English) happy
Es, Esnee, Esney, Esny, Essie

Esperanza (Spanish) hopeful
*Es, Espe, Esperance, Esperans,
Esperanta, Esperanz*

Essence (American) ingenious
Esence, Essens, Essense

Essene (Slavic) girl of the wind
Essen

Essica (American) form of
Jessica: rich

Essie (English) shining; queenly
Es, Essa, Essey, Essy

Esta (Hebrew) bright star
Es, Estah

Estalyn (English) noble girl

Estana (Slavic) form of Esther:
myrtle leaf

Estee (English) brightest
Esti

Estefani (Spanish) crowned

Estefania (Spanish) crowned

Estelita (Spanish) little queen

Estella (French) radiant star
Es, Estel, Estell, Estelle, Estie, Stell, Stella

Estelle (French) glowing star
Es, Essie, Estee, Estel, Estele, Estell, Estie

Esterlea (Scandinavian) star
queen

Estevina (Spanish) adorned;
wreathed
Estafania, Este, Estebana, Estefania, Estevan, Estevana

Esth (French) star

Esthelia (Spanish) shining
Esthe, Esthel, Esthele, Esthelya

Esther (Persian) myrtle leaf
Es, Essie, Estee, Ester, Esthur

Estherelda (Spanish) form of
Esther: myrtle leaf

Estherita (Spanish) bright
Estereta

Estime (French) esteemed
Es

Estine (German) sweet child

Estrella (Latin) shining star
Estrell, Estrelle, Estrilla

Eta (German) form of Henrietta:
home-ruler
Etah

Etaney (Hebrew) focused
Eta, Etana, Etanah, Etanee

Ethel (English) noble
Ethelda, Ethelin, Etheline, Ethelle, Ethelyn, Ethelynn, Ethelynne, Ethyl

Ethelen (English) strong

Ethelene (American) form of
Ethel: noble
Ethe, Etheline

Ethne (Irish) blueblood
Eth, Ethnee, Ethnie, Ethny

Ethnea (Irish) kernel; piece of the
puzzle
Ethna, Ethnia

Etosha (African) energetic

Etta (German/English) form of
Henrietta: home-ruler
Etti, Ettie, Etty

Eudlina (Slavic) generous; affluent
Eudie, Eudlyna, Udie, Udlina

Eudocia (Greek) fine
Eude, Eudocea, Eudosia

Eudora (Greek) cherished

Eudore (Greek) treasured

Eudoxia (Spanish) fine

Eufrocina (Spanish) happiness

Eugenia (Greek) regal and
polished
Eugeneia, Eugenie, Eugenina, Eugina, Gee, Gina

Eula (Greek) specific
Eulia

Eulala (Greek) spoken sweetly
Eulalah

Eulalia (Greek/Italian) well-
spoken
Eula, Eulia, Eulie

Eulanda (American) fair
Eudlande, Eulee, Eulie

Eunice (Greek) joyful; winning
Euna, Euniece, Eunique, Eunise, Euniss

Eunja (Asian) silver

Eupheme (Greek) form of
Euphemia: well-spoken
Eu, Euphemee, Euphemi, Euphemie

Euphemia (Greek) well-spoken
Effam, Eufemia, Euphan, Euphie,
Uphie

Euphrosyne (Greek) one of the
three Graces; joy

Eureka (Word as name) surpise

Eurydice (Greek) adventurous
Euridice, Euridyce, Eurydyce

Eustacia (Greek) industrious
Eustace, Stacey, Stacy

Eustolia (Spanish) tenacious;
moves well

Euvenia (American) hardworking
Euvene, Euvenea

Eva ⊙ (Hebrew/Scandinavian)
life
Evah, Evalea, Evalee

Evadne (Greek) pleasing; lucky
Eva, Evad, Evadnee, Evadny

Evaline (French) form of Evelyn:
optimistic
Evalyn, Eveleen

Evan (American) bright;
precocious
Evann, Evin

Evana (Greek) lovely woman
Evania, Eve, Ivana, Ivanna

Evangelina (Greek) bringing joy
Eva, Evangelia, Evangelica,
Evangeline, Evania, Eve, Lina

Evania (Irish) spirited
Ev, Evana, Evanea, Evann,
Evanna, Evanne, Evany, Eve,
Eveania, Evvanne, Evyan

Evanka (Slavic) form of Ivanka:
gracious gift from God

Evanthie (Greek) flowering well
Evanthe, Evanthee, Evanthi

Eve (Hebrew) life
Eva, Evie, Evvy

Evegelina (Spanish) lively

Evelina (Russian) lively
Evalina, Evalinna

Evelyn ⊙ (English) optimistic
Aveline, Ev, Evaleen, Evalene,
Evalenne, Evaline, Evalyn,
Evalynn, Evalynne, Eveleen,
Eveline, Evelyne, Evelynn,
Evelynne, Evline

Evelyna (Scandinavian) form of
Evelyn: optimistic

Ever (Word as name) eternal
Ev

Everilda (Spanish) forever

Everilde (Origin unknown)
hunter

Everla (English) ever

Everleen (American) evergreen

Everlin (American) forever

Evette (French) dainty
Evett, Ivette

Evgenia (Slavic) form of
Eugenia: regal and polished

Evie (English) vibrant life

Evine (English) alive

Evlesin (American) lives large

Evline (French) nature girl
Evleen, Evlene, Evlin, Evlina,
Evlyn, Evlynn, Evlynne

Evolia (Slavic) form of Evelyn:
optimistic

Evonne (French) form of
Yvonne: athletic
Evanne, Eve, Evie, Yvonne

Evonnette (American) form of
Evelyn: optimistic

Ewelina (Polish) life
Eva, Lina

Exee (American) form of Lexie:
helpful; sparkling

Exelda (Spanish) excels

Eydie (American) endearing
Eidey, Eydee

Eyote (Native American) great
Eyotee

Ezra (Hebrew) happy; helpful
Ezrah, Ezruh

Ezza (American) healthy
Eza

Faba (Latin) bean; thin
Fabah, Fava

Fabette (Italian) fabulous little
girl

Fabi (Italian) generous

Fabia (Latin) fabulous; special
Fabiann, Fabianna, Fabianne

Fabienne (French) fabulous;
farming beans

Fabio (Latin) fabulous
Fabeeo, Fabeo, Fabeoh

Fabiola (Spanish) royalty

Fabrizia (Italian) manual worker
*Fabrice, Fabricia, Fabrienne,
Fabriqua, Fabritzia*

Fadia (Arabic) saved

Fae (English) form of Faye: light-
spirited

Fael (English) of the fairies

Faffa (American) frivolity

Fahimah (Arabic) form of
Fatima: wise woman

Faida (Arabic) bountiful
Fayda

Faillace (French) delicate beauty
Faill, Faillaise, Faillase, Falace

Faine (English) happy
Fai, Fainne, Fay, Fayne

Fairlee (English) lovely
Fair, Fairlea, Fairley, Fairly

Faith ○ ⊕ (English) loyal woman
Fay, Fayth

Faithette (American) trustworthy

Falesyia (Hispanic) exotic
Falesyiah, Falisyia

Faline (Latin/French) lively
Faleen, Falene

Fall (Word as name) changeable
Falle

Fallon (Irish) fetching; from the
ruling class
Falan, Fallen, Fallyn, Falyn

Falsette (American) fanciful
Falcette

Famke (Polish) little girl

Fanchon (French) form of France
*Fan, Fanchee, Fanchie, Fanny,
Fran, Frannie, Franny*

Fancine (French) fancy

Fancy (English) fanciful
Fanci, Fancie

Fandila (Spanish) dancer

Fane (American) strict
Fain, Faine

Fanfara (Last name as first name)
fanfare; excitement
Fann, Fanny

Fang (Chinese) pleasantly scented

Fanny (Latin) from France
Fan, Fani, Fannie

Fantasia (American) inventive
*Fantasha, Fantasiah, Fantasya,
Fantazia*

Fantazee (American) fantasy

Fantazie (American) fantasy

Fanteen (English) clever
*Fan, Fannee, Fanney, Fanny,
Fantene, Fantine*

Farah (English) lovely
Farrah

Faray (Arabic) form of Farrah:
good-looking; happy

Faredah (Arabic) special
Farida

Farhanah (Arabic) lovely

Farica (German) leader
Faricka, Fericka, Flicka

Farida (Arabic) wanders far

Farina (Latin) flour
Fareena

Faris (American) forgiving
Fair, Farris, Pharis, Pharris

Farrah (English/Arabic) good-
looking; happy
Fara, Farah

Farren (American) fair
Faren, Farin

Farrow (American) narrow-
minded
Farow, Farro

Faryl (American) inspiring
Farel, Farelle

Farzana (American) wanders

Fashion (American) stylish
Fashon, Fashy, Fashyun

Fatie (Arabic) winning

Fatima (Arabic) wise woman
Fatema, Fatimah, Fatime

Faulk (American) respected
Falk

Fauna (Roman mythology)
goddess of nature
Faunah, Fawna, Fawnah

Faunee (Latin) nature-loving
*Fauney, Fauneye, Fawnae, Fawni,
Fawny*

Fausta (French) desired; (Italian)
lucky

Faustene (French/American)
envied
*Fausteen, Faustine, Fausty,
Fawsteen*

Faustiana (Spanish) good
fortune
Faust, Fausti, Faustia, Faustina

Faustina (Italian) lucky
*Fausta, Faustine, Fawsteena,
Fostina, Fostynna*

Favela (Spanish) favored

Favianna (Italian) confident
Faviana

Faviolia (Indian) lucky

Fawn (French) gentle
Faun, Fawne

Fawna (French) soft-spoken
Fawnna, Fawnah, Fawnuh

Fawntae (English) fawn girl

Fawntay (American) fawn girl

Faye (English/French) light-
spirited
Fae, Fay, Fey

Fayette (American) southern
Fayet, Fayett, Fayetta, Fayitte

Fayleen (American) quiet
*Faylene, Fayline, Falyn, Falynn,
Faye, Fayla*

Fayrale (American) wins

Fayth (American) form of Faith:
loyal woman
Faithe, Faythe

Fe (Latin) believer

Feather (Native American) svelte
Feathyr

Febe (Polish/Greek) bright
Febee

February (Latin) icy
Feb

Fedora (Greek) God's gift

Fedyle (American) loyal

Felda (German) field girl

Felder (Last name as first name)
bright
Felde, Feldy

Felice (Latin) form of Felicia:
happy
Felece, Felise

Felicia (Latin) happy
Faleshia, Falesia, Felecia, Felisha

Felicie (Latin) form of Felicia:
happy
Feliccie, Felicee, Felicy, Felisie

Felicita (Spanish) gracious
Felice, Felicitas, Felicitee, Felisita

Felicity (Latin) form of Felicia:
happy
Felice, Felicite, Felicitee, Felisitee

Felisa (Spanish) form of Felicia:
happy

Felise (German) joyful
Felis

Felixae (Slavic) good fortune

Feliza (Spanish) good fortune

Felyn (Spanish) lucky

Femay (American) classy
Femae

Femi (African) love-seeking
Femmi

Femise (African American)
asking for love
Femeese, Femmis

Fena (Scottish) pale

Fenella (Irish) white
Fionola, Fionnuala

Fenia (Scandinavian) gold worker
Fenja, Fenya

Fenn (American) bright
Fen, Fynn

Fennell (Scottish) pale

Feo (Greek) given by God
Fee, Feeo

Feodora (Greek) God-given girl
Fedora

Feodossia (Slavic) influences

Fereda (Spanish) vigorous

Feride (Hawaiian) calm

Ferilen (American) dares

Fern (German/English) fern
Ferne

Fernanda (German) bold
Ferdie, Fernnande

Fernandaline (French) dares

Fernilia (American) successful
Fern, Fernelia, Ferny, Fyrnilia

Fernley (English) from the fern
meadow; nature girl

Feven (American) shy
Fevan, Fevun

Ffion (Irish) pale face
Fi

Fia (Scandinavian) perky

Fiamma (Italian) fiery spirit
*Feamma, Fee, Fia, Fiama,
Fiammette, Fifi*

Fiammetta (Italian) fiery

Fiby (Spanish) bright

Fidela (Spanish) loyal
Fidele, Fidella, Fidelle

Fidelia (Italian) faithful
Fidele

Fidelity (Latin) loyal
Fidele, Fidelia

Fidelma (Irish) loyal

Fife (American) dancing eyes;
musical
Fifer, Fifey, Fyfe

Fifer (Last name used as first
name) fife-player

Fifi (French) jazzy
Fifee

Fifia (African) Friday's child
FeeFee, Fifeea

Filia (Greek) devoted
Feleah, Filea, Filiah

Filipa (Italian) loves horses

Fillis (Greek) form of Phyllis:
beautiful; leafy bough; articulate;
smitten
Filis, Fill, Fillees, Filly, Fillys, Fylis

Filma (Greek) loved

Filomena (Polish) beloved

Fimy (English) form of Femy:
regal and polished

Fina (Spanish) blessed by God

Finch (English) bird; sings

Finelle (Irish) fair-faced
Fee, Finell, Finn, Finny, Fynelle

Finesse (American) smooth
Fin, Finese, Finess

Finette (Scottish) pale

Finley (English) fair

Finn (Irish) cool

Finnian (English) fiery

Finny (Irish) blonde

Finola (Italian) white

Fion (Irish) blonde

Fiona (Irish) fair-haired
Fi, Fionna

Fionnuala (Irish) white
Nuala

Fiorella (Irish) spirited
Fee, Feorella, Rella

Fire (American) feisty
Firey, Fyre

Flair (English) stylish
Flaire, Flairey, Flare

Flame (Word as name) fiery

Flaminia (Latin) flaming spirit

Flana (Irish) red-haired
*Flanagh, Flanna, Flannerey,
Flannery*

Flanders (Place name) region of
Belgium; creative
Fland, Flann

Flannery (Irish) warm; red-haired
Flann

Flavey (French) fun-filled

Flavia (Latin) light-haired
Flavie

Flaviana (Spanish) pale

Flavine (French) fun

Flax (Botanical) plant with blue
flowers
Flacks, Flaxx

Fleming (Last name as first
name) adorable
*Flemma, Flemmie, Flemming,
Flyming*

Flemmi (Italian) pretty
Flemmy

Fleur (French) flower
Fleura, Fleuretta, Fleurette, Fleuronne

Flicky (American) vivacious

Flirt (Word as name) flirtatious
Flyrtt

Flis (Polish) form of Felicity: happy

Flo (American) form of Florence:
flowering

Flor (Spanish) blooming
*Flo, Flora, Floralia, Florencia,
Florencita, Florens, Florensia, Flores,
Floria, Floriole, Florita, Florite*

Flora (Latin/Spanish) flowering
Floria, Florie

Floraba (Spanish) flowering

Florangel (Spanish) angel flower

Florcina (Spanish) flowering

Flordeperla (Spanish) pearly
blooms

Florella (Latin) girl from
Florence; blooming

Florence (Latin) flowering
*Flo, Flora, Florencia, Florense,
Florenze, Florie, Florina, Florrie,
Flos, Flossie, Floy*

Florenina (Spanish) flowering

Florens (Polish) blooming;
(Latin) thrives
Floren

Florent (French) flowering
Flor, Floren, Florentine, Florin

Florette (French) flowering

Florian (Dutch) flower-like

Florica (Spanish) flowers

Florida (Place name) U.S. state;
flowered
Flora, Flory

Florienna (Italian) flowering

Florin (English) floral

Florinda (English) flower of
spring

Florine (American) blooming
Flo, Flora, Floren, Floryne, Florynne

Floris (Latin) flowers

Florizel (Literature)
Shakespearean name; in bloom
Flora, Flori, Florisel

Florrie (English) blooms

Flossie (English) grows
beautifully

Flower (American) blossoming
beauty
Flo

Floy (English) blooms

Floya (Slavic) quick

Fluffy (American) fun-loving
Fluff, Fluffi, Fluffie

Flynn (Irish) red-haired
Flenn, Flinn, Flyn

Fog (American) dreamy
Fogg, Foggee, Foggy

Fola (African) honored
Folah

Folfeen (American) direct

Fonda (American) risk-taker
Fond

Fondee (American) fond

Fondice (American) fond of
friends
Fondeese, Fondie

Fontaine (French) fountaining
bounty
Fontane, Fontanna, Fontanne

Fontella (American) small fountain

Fontenot (French) special girl; fountain of beauty
Fonny, Fontay, Fonte, Fonteno

Ford (Last name as first name) confident
Forde

Forsythia (Botanical) flower girl

Fortney (Latin) strength
Fortnea, Fortnee, Fortneigh, Fortnie, Fortny

Fortuna (Latin) good fortune
Fortunata

Fortune (Latin) excellent fate; prized

Fotine (Greek) light-hearted
Foty, Fotyne

Fowler (Last name as first name) stylish
Fowla, Fowlar, Fowlir

Foxyn (American) perceptive

Foynt (English) fount

Fozyne (American) fortunate

Fracesca (American) form of Francesca: country; French girl

Frachette (French) fresh

Fran (Latin) form of France: country; French girl
Frann, Franni, Frannie

Franca (Italian) free spirit

France (Place name) country; French girl
Frans, Franse

Francena (English) form of France: country; French girl

Francene (French) free
Francine

Frances (Latin) form of France: country; French girl
Fanny, Fran, Francey, Franci, Francie, Franse

Francesca (Italian) form of France: country; French girl
Fran, Francessca, Franchesca, Francie, Frankie, Frannie

Franchelle (French) form of France: country; French girl
Franchelle, Franchey, Franshell

Franchesca (Italian) form of Francesca: country; French girl
Cheka, Chekkie, Francheska, Franchessca

Francina (Italian) form of France: country; French girl

Francine (French) form of France: country; French girl
Fran, Franceen, Francene, Francie

Françoise (French) free

Franicine (American) form of Francine: country; French girl

Franisbel (Spanish) beautiful French girl
Franisbella, Franisbelle

Frankie (American) a form of France: country; French girl
Franki, Franky

Frannie (English) friendly
Franni, Franny

Fransabelle (Latin) form of France: country; French girl
Fransabella, Franzabelle

Fraya (Scandinavian) highborn
Freya

Frayda (Scandinavian) fertile woman
Frayde, Fraydel, Freyda, Freyde, Freydel

Frea (Scandinavian) noble; hearty
Fray, Freas, Freya

Fred (English) form of Elfreda: elf strength; good counselor

Freda (German) serene

Freddie (English) form of Frederica: peacemaking
Fredi, Freddy

Frederica (German) peacemaking
Federica, Fred, Freda, Freddie, Freida, Frida, Fritze, Rica

Frederique (German) serene

Fredesminda (English) girl of peaceful mind

Fredna (American) strength of character

Fredy (American) strong

Free (Word as name) liberated spirit

Freesia (Botanical) fragrant flower

Freida (German) form of Frederica: peacemaking; form of Alfreda: wise advisor
Freda, Frida, Frieda

Frelecia (Slavic) form of Felicia: happy

Frenchie (American) saucy
French, Frenchee, Frenchi, Frenchy

Frenda (Asian) fern

Fresnay (American) place name

Fressia (American) form of the flower freesia

Freya (Scandinavian) goddess; beautiful
Freja, Freyja

Frida (Scandinavian) lovely

Frieda (German) happy
Freda

Friedelinde (German) gentle girl
Friedalinda

Frigg (Scandinavian) loved one

Frigga (Scandinavian) beloved
Fri, Friga, Frigg

Fristell (Last name used as first name) stiff

Fritzi (German) leads in peace

Frona (English) practical

Frond (Botanical) growing

Frosty (Word as name) crisp and cool
Frostie

Fructuose (Latin) bountiful
Fru, Fructuosa, Fruta

Frula (German) hardworking

Fruma (Hebrew) devout

Frythe (English) calm
Frith, Fryth

Fuchsia (Botanical) blossoming pink
Fuesha

Fudge (American) stubborn
Fudgey

Fuensanta (Spanish) holy fountain
Fuenta

Fulgencia (Latin) glowing

Fulki (Hindi) sparks

Fullan (Hindi) flourishing

Fuller (English) clothier

Fulmala (Hindi) wreath

Fulvia (Latin) blonde

Fulvy (Latin) blonde
Full, Fulvee, Fulvie

Fury (Latin) raging anger
Furee, Furey, Furie

Fushy (American) animated; vivid
Fooshy, Fueshy, Fushee

Gable (German) farming woman
Gabbie, Gabby, Gabe, Gabel, Gabell, Gabl

Gabor (French) conflicted
Gaber, Gabi

Gabriella ○ ① (Italian/Spanish) God is her strength
Caby, Gabela, Gabi, Gabrela, Gabriela, Gabryela, Gabryella

Gabrielle ○ (French/Hebrew) strong
Gabi, Gabraelle, Gabreelle, Gabreille, Gabriele, Gabriella, Gabrilla, Gabrille, Gabryele, Gabryelle, Gaby, Gaebriell, Gaebrielle, Garbreal

Gaby (French) form of Gabrielle: strong
Gabey, Gabi, Gabie

Gada (Hebrew) fortune

Gadar (Armenian) perfect girl
Gad, Gadahr, Gaddie, Gaddy

Gadara (Biblical) place name

Gae (Greek) form of Gaea: earth goddess
Gay, Gaye

Gaea (Greek) earth goddess
Gaia

Gaegae (Greek) form of Gaea: earth goddess
Gae, Gaege, Gaegie

Gaelle (American) of the earth

Gaenor (Welsh) beautiful

Gaetane (Italian) form of Gaeta, Italy

Gagane (American) sky

Gage (American) happy

Gaia (Greek) goddess of earth
Gaea, Gaya

Gail (Hebrew) form of Abigail: joyful
Gaelle, Gale, Gayle

Gaillen (American) joyful

Gaily (American) fun-loving
Gailai, Galhy

Gailya (Russian) serene
Galya

Gailyn (English) form of Galen: decisive

Gaines (Last name used as first name) gainful

Gaitlynn (American) hopeful
Gaitlin, Gaitline, Gaitlinn, Gaitlyn, Gaytlyn

Gala (French) merrymaking; festivity
Gaila, Gailah, Galaa, Galuh, Gayla

Galatea (Greek) sea nymph in mythology
Gal, Gala

Galatia (Biblical) place name; dramatic

Galaxy (American) universal
Gal, Galaxee, Galaxi

Galen (American) decisive
Galin, Galine, Galyn, Gaye, Gaylen, Gaylin, Gaylyn

Galena (Latin) metal; tough
Galyna, Galynna

Galenza (American) calming girl

Galia (Jewish) flows

Galiana (German) vaulted
Galiyana, Galli, Galliana

Galienna (Russian) steady
Galiena, Galyena, Galyenna

Galina (Russian) deserving
Gailina, Gailinna, Galyna, Galynna

Galise (American) joyful
Galeece, Galeese, Galice, Galyce

Gallaine (Last name used as first name) attractive

Galya (Hebrew) redeemed; merry
Galia

Galyan (Hebrew) saved

Gamala (Biblical) place name; lithe; Lovely

Gamin (American) gamine

Ganisia (American) gains

Garcelle (French) flowered
Garcel, Garsell, Garselle

Gardenia (Botanical) sweet flower baby

Gardner (Last name used as first name) gardens

Garetta (American) form of the name Garrett: bashful

Garim (Hindi) warm

Garima (Hindi) sincere

Garland (American) fancy
Garlan, Garlande, Garlinn, Garlynn

Garlanda (French) flowered wreath; pretty girl
Gar, Garl, Garlynd, Garlynda

Garlin (French) form of Garland: fancy
Garlinn, Garlyn, Garlynn

Garner (American) style-setter
Garnar, Garnir

Garnet (English) pretty; semi-precious stone

Garnett (English) red gemstone; valued

Garnetta (French) gemstone; precious
Garna, Garnet, Garnie, Garny

Garrett (Last name as first name) bashful
Garret, Gerrett

Garri (American) energetic
Garree, Garrey, Garry, Garrye

Garrielle (American) competent
Gariele, Garielle, Garriella

Garrison (American) sturdy
Garisen, Garisun, Garrisen, Garrisun

Garrity (American) smiling
Garety, Garrety, Garity, Garritee, Garritie

Gartha (American) feminine form of Garth: sunny; gardener

Garvin (Last name used as first name) craftsperson

Garyn (American) svelte
Garen, Garin, Garinne, Garun, Garynn, Garynne

Gates (Last name as first name) careful
Gate

Gauri (Hindi) golden goddess

Gavin (American) smart
Gave, Gaven, Gavey, Gavun

Gavion (American) daring
Gaveon, Gavionne

Gaviotte (French) graceful
Gaveott, Gaviot, Gaviott

Gavit (French) form of Gabrielle: strong
Gavitt, Gavyt, Gavytt

Gavotte (French) dancer
Gav, Gavott

Gavrielle (French) form of Gabrielle: strong
Gavriele, Gavryele, Gavryelle

Gay (French) jolly
Gae, Gaye

Gayathri (Indian) happy

Gayla (American) planner
Gaila, Gailah, Gala, Gaye, Gaylah, Gayluh

Gayle (Hebrew) rejoicing

Gaylene (English) delighted

Gaynor (American) precocious
Ganor, Gayner, Gaynorre

Gayor (Hebrew) sunny

Gazee (Hebrew) sturdy

Geanna (American) ostentatious
Geannah, Gianna

Geary (Hebrew) form of Jerry: hopeful
Gearee, Gearey, Geari, Gearie, Geeree, Geerey, Geeri, Geery

Gebra (Greek) graceful

Gederah (Biblical) place name

Geena (Italian) form of Gena: wellborn
Gina, Ginah

Geeta (Italian) pearl

Gelacia (Spanish) treasure
Gela, Gelasha, Gelasia

Gelda (American) gloomy
Geilda, Geldah, Gelduh

Gelil (American) smiling

Gem (American) shining
Gemmy, Gim, Jim

Gemesha (African American) dramatic
Gemeisha, Gemiesha, Gemme, Gemmy, Gimesha

Gemilie (American) gem

Gemini (Greek) twin
Gem, Gemelle, Gemmy

Gemma (Latin) gem; jewel
Gem, Gema, Gemmie, Gemmy

Gemmalis (American) gem

Gemmy (Italian) gem
Gemmee, Gemmi, Gimmy

Gems (American) shining gem
Gem, Gemmie, Gemmy

Gemze (American) gem

Gena (French) form of Gina: wellborn
Geena, Gen, Genah, Geni, Genia

Genay (American) form of Gena: wellborn

Genell (American) form of Janelle: exuberant
Genill

Genera (Greek) highborn
Gen, Genere

Generosa (Spanish) generous
Generosah, Generossa

Genesis ○ (Latin) fast starter; beginning
Gen, Gena, Genesys, Geney, Genisis, Genisys, Genysis, Genysys, Jenesis

Geneva (French) city in Switzerland; flourishing; like juniper
Gena, Geneeva, Genyva, Janeva, Jeneva

Genevera (Spanish) highborn

Genevieve (German/French) high-minded
Gen, Gena, Genavieve, Geneveeve, Geniveeve, Genivieve, Genna, Genovieve, Genyveeve, Genyvieve

Genica (American) intelligent
Gen, Genicah, Genicuh, Genika, Gennica, Jen, Jenika, Jennika

Genie (Greek) of high birth; tricky
Geenee, Geeney, Geeni, Geenie, Geeny, Genee, Geney, Geni, Geny

Genna (English) womanly
Gen, Genny, Jenna

Gennesaret (Biblical) place name

Gennese (American) helpful
Gen, Geneece, Geniece, Genny, Ginece, Gineese

Gennette (American) form of Jeannette: lively

Gennifer (American) form of Jennifer: white wave
Genefer, Genephur, Genifer

Genny (Greek) of high birth; loving
Genney, Genni, Gennie

Genoa (Italian) playful
Geenoa, Genoah, Jenoa

Genova (Place name)

Genovesia (Place name)

Genoveva (American) form of Genevieve: high-minded
Genny, Geno

Gentle (American) kind
Gen, Gentil, Gentille, Gentlle

Gentry (American) sweet
Gen, Gentree, Gentrie, Jentrie, Jentry

Geoma (American) outstanding
Gee, GeeGee, Geo, Geomah, Geome, Gigi, Jeoma, Oma, Omah

Geonna (American) sparkling
Gee, Geionna, Geone, Geonne, Geonnuh

Georgann (English) bright-eyed
Georganne, Jorgann, Joryann

Georganna (English) form of Georgia: farmer
Georgana, Georgeana, Georgeanna

Georgene (English) wandering
Georgeene, Georgena, Georgyne, Jorgeen, Jorjene

Georgenia (Dutch) farm girl

Georgette (French) lively and little
Georgett, Georgitt, Georgitte, Jorgette

Georgia (Greek) farmer
Georgi, Georgie, Georgina, Georgya, Giorgi, Jorga, Jorgia, Jorja

Georgianna (English) gracious farmer
Georganna, Georgeanna, Georgianne, Jorjeana, Jorgianna

Georgie (English) form of
Georgia: farmer
Georgee, Georgey, Georgi, Georgy

Georgina (Latin) feminine form
of George: land-loving; farmer

Geowanna (African) earthy

Geraldine (German) strong
Geraldyne, Geri, Gerri, Gerry

Geralena (French) leader
*Gera, Geraleen, Geralen, Geralene,
Gerre, Gerrilyn, Gerry, Jerrileena,
Lena*

Gerarda (Spanish) feminine form
of Gerard: brave

Gerardette (American) feminine
form of Gerard: brave

Gerasa (Biblical) place name

Gerda (Scandinavian) fertility
goddess

Gerdelle (American) fertile

Gerdellyne (American) form of
Geraldine: strong

Gerdi (Scandinavian) guards

Gerdina (Scandinavian) guarded

Gerdnan (German) guards

Gerisa (English) form of
Geraldine: strong
Gerry

Gerldine (American) form of
Geraldine: strong

Gerly (English) form of
Geraldine: strong

Gerlynne (German) tenderness
Gerlind

Germaine (French/German)
important
*Germain, Germane, Germayne,
Jermaine*

Gerol (English) rules

Geroldine (American) form of
Geraldine: strong

Gerritta (American) strong

Gerry (German) form of
Geraldine: strong

Gertrude (German) beloved
Gerdie, Gerti, Gertie

Gertudis (Slavic) form of
Gertrude: beloved

Gervaise (French) strong
Gerva, Gervaisa

Gessalin (American) loving
*Gessilin, Gessalyn, Gessalynn,
Jessalin, Jessalyn*

Gessica (American) form of
Jessica: rich
Gesica, Gesika, Gessika

Gethsemane (Biblical) peaceful
*Geth, Gethse, Gethsemanee,
Gethsemaney, Gethsemanie, Gethy*

Geynille (American) womanly
Geynel

Gezelle (American) lithe
Gezzelle, Gizele, Gizelle

Gezzi (Asian) believer

Ggana (African) place name

Ghada (Arabic) graceful
Ghad, Ghadah

Ghadeah (Arabic) graceful
Gadea, Gadeah

Ghaeda (Arabic) graceful

Ghandia (African) able
*Gandia, Ghanda, Ghandee,
Ghandy, Gondia, Gondiah*

Ghea (American) confident
Ghia, Jeah, Jeeah

Gherlan (American) forgiving;
joyful
Gerlan, Gherli

Ghislaine (French) loyal

Ghita (Italian) pearl
Gita, Gite

Gia (Italian) lovely

Giacinte (Italian) hyacinth;
flowering
Gia, Giacin, Giacinta

Giada (Italian) precious jade

Giani (Italian) feminine form of
John: God is gracious

Gianina (Italian) believer
*Gia, Giane, Giannina, Gianyna,
Janeena, Janina, Jeanina*

Gianine (American) feminine form of John: God is gracious

Gianna ⚬ (Italian) forgiving
Geonna, Giana, Gianne, Gianni, Giannie, Gianny, Ginny, Gyana, Gyanna

Giannelle (American) hearty
Geanelle, Gianella, Gianelle, Gianne

Giannesha (African American) friendly
Geannesha, Gianesha, Giannesh, Gianneshah, Gianneshuh

Giara (Italian) sensual
Gee, Geara, Gia, Giarah

Gidget (American) cute
Gidge, Gidgett, Gidgette, Gydget

Gift (American) blessed
Gifte, Gyft

Gigi (French) small; spunky
Geegee, Giggi

Gila (Hebrew) joyful
Gilla, Gyla, Gylla

Gilala (Jewish) happy
Gila, Gilah

Gilberta (German) smart
Bertie, Gill

Gilberte (German) shining

Gilda (English) gold-encrusted
Gildi, Gildie, Gill

Gilead (Biblical) place name

Gill (American) intelligent

Gillaine (Latin) young

Gilleese (American) funny
Gill, Gillee, Gilleece, Gillie, Gilly

Gillen (American) humorous
Gill, Gilly, Gillyn, Gyllen

Gilli (American) joyful
Gill, Gillee, Gilly

Gillian (Latin) youthful
Gila, Gili, Gilian, Giliana, Gilien, Gilliana, Gilliane, Gillie, Gillien, Gilly, Gillyan, Gillyen, Gilyan, Gilyen, Jillian

Gillis (Last name as first name) conservative
Gilise, Gillice, Gylis, Gyllis

Gillyle (American) smart

Gilma (American) form of Wilma: sturdy
Gee, Gilly

Gilmore (Last name as first name) striking
Gilmoor, Gill, Gillmore, Gylmore

Gina (Italian) wellborn
Geena, Gena, Gin, Ginah, Ginny, Gyna, Gynah, Jenah

Ginae (Biblical) place name

Ginane (French) wellborn
Gigi, Gina, Gine, Jeanan, Jeanine

Ginate (Italian) precious

Giner (English) ginger

Ginet (French) of the earth

Ginette (Italian) flower

Ginevieve (Irish) form of Genevieve: high-minded
Gineveeve, Giniveeve, Ginivieve, Ginyveeve, Ginyvieve

Ginge (English) feminine form of George: land-loving; farmer

Ginger (Botanical) ginger plant
Gin, Ginny, Jinger

Gingerly (American) careful

Ginnifer (American) form of Jennifer: white wave
Gini, Ginifer, Giniferr, Ginifir, Ginn

Ginny (English) form of Virginia: pure female
Ginnee, Ginney, Ginni, Ginnie

Gioconda (Italian) pleasing
Gio, Giocona

Giolla (Italian) helper

Giono (Last name as first name) delight; friendly
Gio, Gionna, Gionno

Giorgio (Italian) feminine form of George: land-loving; farmer
Giorgi, Giorgie, Jorgio

Giovanna (Italian) gracious believer; great entertainer
Geo, Geovanna, Gio, Giovahna, Giovana

Giovanne (Italian) form of Giovanna: gracious believer; great entertainer

Giovannina (Italian) little Giovanna; believes in God

Giritha (Sri Lankan) melodic
Giri, Girith

Girty (English) form of Gertie: graceful; gracious

Gisbelle (American) lovely girl
Gisbel

Gisella (German) pledged for service
Gisela

Giselle (French) a promise
Gis, Gisel, Gisela, Gisele, Gisell, Gissel, Gissell, Gissella, Gisselle, Gissie, Jizele

Gita (Sanskrit) song
Geta, Gete, Git, Gitah

Gitaleen (German) held in high esteem

Gitana (Spanish) gypsy

Gitele (Hebrew) good
Gitel

Githa (Slavic) form of Gita: song
Gytha

Gitika (Sanskrit) little singer
Getika, Gita, Giti, Gitikah

Gitka (Indian) singing

Gitta (German) highly regarded

Giuletta (Italian) tiny girl

Giulia (Italian) little girl

Giva (Sanskrit) form of Gita: song
Givah, Gyva, Gyvah

Givonnah (Italian) loyal; believer
Gevonna, Gevonnuh, Givonn, Givonna, Givonne, Jevonah, Jevonna, Jivonnah, Juvona

Gizela (Polish) dedicated
Giz, Gizele, Gizella, Gizzy

Gizelle (German) pledged to serve
Giselle, Gizel, Gizele, Gizell

Gizmo (American) tricky
Gis, Gismo, Giz

Glad (Welsh) form of Gladys: flower; princess

Gladdies (American) form of Gladys: flower; princess

Gladiola (Botanical) blooming; flower
Glad, Gladdee, Gladdy

Gladyce (Spanish) princess

Gladys (Welsh) flower; princess
Glad, Gladdie, Gladice, Gladis, Gladise, Gladiss

Glafira (Spanish) giving
Glafee, Glafera, Glafi

Glasira (Spanish) uncanny

Gleam (American) bright girl
Glee, Gleem

Glease (American) gleeful

Glee (American) gleeful

Glenda (Welsh) bright; good
Glinda, Glynda, Glynn, Glynnie

Glendora (English) form of Glenda: good; bright

Glenn (Irish) glen; from a sylvan setting
Glen

Glenna (Irish) valley-living
Glena, Glenah, Glenuh, Glyn, Glynna

Glennesha (African American) special
Glenesha, Gleneshuh, Gleniesha, Glenn, Glenneshah, Glenny, Glinnesha

Glennice (American) top notch
Glenis, Glennis, Glenys, Glenysse, Glynnece, Glynnice

Glennish (American) unique

Glensheen (French) from the home by the glen

Glenys (Welsh) holy
Glenice, Glenis, Gleniss, Glenyss

Glikeria (Slavic) cheerful

Gliselda (American) loyal

Glorene (American) form of Gloria: glorious

Gloria (Latin) glorious
Glorea, Glorey, Glori, Gloriah,
Glorrie, Glory

Glorielle (American) generous
Gloree, Glori, Gloriel, Gloriele,
Glory,

Gloris (American) glorious
Gloreeca, Glores, Gloresa, Glorisa,
Glorus, Gloryssa

Glory (Latin) shining
Gloree, Glorey, Glori, Glorie

Gloss (American) showy
Glosse, Glossee, Glossie, Glossy

Glow (American) glowing

Glyde (American) smooth

Glynis (Welsh) from the glen
Glyniss, Glynys, Glynyss

Glynisha (African American)
vibrant
Glynesh, Glynn, Glynnecia,
Glynnesha, Glynnie, Glynnisha

Glynn (Welsh) from the glen
Glin, Glinn, Glyn

Glynnis (Welsh) vivacious; glen
Glenice, Glenis, Glennis, Glinice,
Glinnis, Glynn, Glynnie, Glynny

Goala (American) goal-oriented
Go, GoGo, Gola

Gobnat (Irish) cuddly

Goddess (American) gorgeous
Godess, Goddesse

Godiva (English) God's gift;
brazen
Godeva, Godivah

Golda (English) golden
Goldi, Goldie

Golden (American) shining
Goldene, Goldon, Goldun, Goldy

Goldie (English) bright and
golden girl
Goldee, Goldey, Goldi, Goldy

Goliad (Spanish) goal-oriented
Goleade, Goliade

Gomery (Biblical) all there

Gomti (Hindi) river

Goneril (Literature)
Shakespearean name; ruthless
Gonarell, Gonarille, Gonereal

Gordie (American) girl who is
watchful

Gordyene (Biblical) place name

Gormie (Scottish) lady

Govindi (Sanskrit) devout; faithful

Grable (American) handsome
woman
Gray, Graybell

Grace ⊙ ❶ (Latin) graceful
Graci, Gracie, Gracy, Graice,
Gray, Grayce

Graceann (American) girl of grace
Gracean, Grace-Ann, Graceanna,
Graceanne, Gracee, Gracy

Gracell (American) graceful girl

Gracia (Spanish) gracious

Gracie (Latin) graceful
Gracee, Gracey, Graci, Gracy,
Graecie, Gray

Graciela (Spanish) pleasant; full
of grace
Chita, Gracee, Gracella, Gracey,
Gracie, Graciella, Gracilla,
Grasiela, Graziela

Gracilia (Latin) graceful girl
Gracillia, Gracillya, Gracilya

Grady (Irish) hardworking;
diligent

Graham (American) sweet
Graehm, Grayhm

Graichen (American) pearl-like

Grainne (Irish) loving girl
Graine, Grayne, Graynne

Grana (Irish) form of Grania:
love

Grania (Irish) love
Grainee, Graini

Grant (Last name used as first
name) good values

Grantyne (American) generous

Granya (Russian) breech baby

Gratia (Scandinavian) graceful;
gracious
Gart, Gert, Gertie, Grasha, Gratea,
Grateah, Gratie

Gray (Last name as first name) quiet
Graye, Grey

Graysha (American) gray hair

Grayson (Last name as first) child of quiet one
Graison, Grasen, Greyson

Grazie (Italian) graceful; pleasant
Grasie, Grazee, Grazy

Grazyna (Polish) graceful; pleasant

Grecian (Place name) form of Greece

Greer (Scottish) aware
Grear, Greare, Greere, Grier

Gregory (American) scholarly
Gregge, Greggy, Gregoree, Gregoria, Gregorie

Greshawn (African American) lively
Greeshawn, Greshaun, Greshawna, Greshonn, Greshun

Gresia (American) compelling
Grasea, Graysea, Grayshea, Grecia

Greta (German) pearl
Gretah, Grete, Gretie, Grette, Grytta

Gretchen (German) pearl
Grechen, Grechin, Grechyn, Gretch, Gretchin, Gretchun, Gretchyn, Grethyn

Grete (Dutch) pearl girl

Gretel (German) pearl; fanciful; (Dutch) manipulative
Gretal, Gretell, Gretelle, Grettel

Grethel (Dutch) form of Gretel: manipulative or pearl; fanciful

Grewn (American) supporter

Greyland (American) focused
Grey, Greylin, Greylyn, Greylynne

Gricie (Spanish) form of Griselda: patient

Griffie (Welsh) royal
Griff, Griffee, Griffey, Griffi, Gryffie

Griffin (Welsh) royal
Griff

Griffith (Last name used as first name) confident

Grindelle (American) live wire
Dell, Delle, Grenn, Grin, Grindee, Grindell, Grindy, Renny

Griselda (German) patient
Grezelda, Grisel, Grissy, Grizel, Grizelda, Grizzie

Griselia (Spanish) gray; patient
Grise, Grisele, Grissy, Seley, Selia

Grisham (Last name as first name) ambitious
Grish

Gritta (German) pearl

Grittith (American) form of Griffith: confident

Grizel (Spanish) long-suffering
Griz, Grizelda, Grizelle, Grizzy

Grove (Botanical) child of the outdoors

Grushenka (Russian) desirable

Guadalupe (Spanish) patron saint; easygoing
Guadelupe, Guadylupe, Lupe, Lupeta, Lupita

Guadarrama (Spanish) river of saints

Gubby (Irish) cuddly
Gub, Gubee, Gubbie

Gudrun (Scandinavian) wise
Gudren, Gudrenne, Gudrin, Gudrinne

Guendolen (Welsh) fair born

Guenevere (Welsh) soft; white

Guenna (Welsh) soft
Guena

Guessa (American) kind

Guinevere (Welsh) queen; white
Guenevere, Guenyveere, Guin, Gwen

Gulab (Hindi) darken

Gulanara (Spanish) needy

Gulenia (Spanish) wanted

Gullermina (Spanish) willful protector

Gumercindo (Spanish) famed

Gunda (German) combative

Gunilla (Scandinavian) warlike
Gun, Gunn

Gunta (German) form of Gunda:
combative

Gunun (German) lively
Gunan, Gunen

Gurlene (American) smart
Gurl, Gurleen, Gurleene, Gurline

Gurshawn (American) talkative
Gurdie, Gurshauna, Gurshaune,
Gurshawna, Gurty

Gussie (Latin) form of Augusta:
revered
Gus, Gussy, Gustie

Gusta (German) form of Gustava:
royal
Gussy, Gustana, Gusty

Gustava (Scandinavian) royal

Guy (French) guiding; assertive
Guye

Guyette (French) ambitious

Guyla (French) asserts

Guyna (American) aggressor

Gwen (Welsh) form of
Gwendolyn: mystery goddess;
bright
Gweni, Gwenn, Gwenna, Gwyn

Gwenda (Welsh) beautiful
Guenda

Gwendolyn (Welsh) mystery
goddess; bright
Gwenda, Gwendalinne,
Gwendalyn, Gwendelynn,
Gwendolen, Gwendolin,
Gwendoline, Gwendolynn,
Gwennie, Gywnne

Gwenless (Invented) fair
Gwen, Gwenles, Gwenny

Gwenllian (Welsh) lovely

Gwenna (Welsh) beautiful
Gwena

Gwitira (American) fair

Gwladys (Welsh) form of
Gladys: flower; princess

Gwyn (Welsh) form of Gwyneth:
blessed
Gwenn, Gwinn, Gwynn, Gwynne

Gwynedd (Welsh) blessed

Gwyneth (Welsh) blessed
Gwennie, Gwinith, Gwynethe,
Gwynith, Gwynithe, Gwynne,
Gwynneth, Win, Winnie

Gyanll (African) genuine

Gyda (Scandinavian) celestine

Gygi (French) form of GiGi:
small; spunky

Gylla (Spanish) feminine form of
Guillermo: attentive
Guilla, Gye, Gyla, Jilla

Gynette (American) form of
Jeanette: lively
Gyn, Gynett, Gynnee, Gynnie

Gypsy (English) adventurer
Gippie, Gipsie, Gypsie

Gyselle (German) form of
Giselle: a promise
Gysel, Gysele

Gyta (American) young

Gythae (English) feisty
Gith, Gyth, Gythay

Ha (Vietnamese) happy

Haafizah (Arabic) librarian
Hafeezah

Haalah (Arabic) librarian

Haarisah (Hindi) sun girl

Haarithah (Arabic) angel

Habbai (Arabic) well-loved

Habiba (Arabic) well-loved
Habeebah, Habibah

Habika (Arabic) loved and
cherished

Hadassah (Hebrew) myrtle tree
Hadasa, Hadasah, Hadaseh,
Hadassa, Haddasah, Haddee,
Haddi, Haddy

Hadil (Arabic) cooing

Hadlee (English) girl in heather
Hadlea, Hadley, Hadli, Hadly

Hady (Greek) soulful
Haddie, Hadee, Hadie, Haidee,
Haidie

Hadyn (American) smart
Haden

Haelee (English) form of Hailey:
natural; hay meadow

Hagai (Hebrew) abandoned;
alone
Haggai, Haggi, Hagi

Hagar (Hebrew) stranger
Hager, Haggar, Hagur

Hagen (Last name used as first
name) defender

Hagir (Arabic) wanderer
Hajar

Haidee (Greek) humble
Haydee

Hailey ○ ❶ (English) natural;
hay meadow
Haile, Hailea, Hailee, Hailie,
Haily, Halee, Haley, Halie, Hallie

Haiti (Place name)

Halalah (Slavic) serenity

Halcyone (Greek) calm
Halceonne, Halcyon

Halda (Scandinavian) half-Danish
Haldaine, Haldana, Haldane,
Haldayne

Halden (Scandinavian) half-
Danish girl
Haldin, Haldyn

Haldi (Scandinavian) form of
Halda: half-Danish
Haldie, Haldis

Halea (Hawaiian) halo

Haleemah (Arabic) speaks
quietly

Halena (Russian) form of Helen:
beautiful; light
Haleena, Halyna

Halene (Russian) staunch
Haleen, Halyne

Haletta (Greek) little country girl
from the meadow
Hale, Halette, Hallee, Halletta,
Halley, Hallie, Hally, Letta, Lettie,
Letty

Halfrida (German) peaceful

Hali (English) heroic

Halia (Hawaiian) remembering

Halima (Arabic) gentle

Halimeda (Greek) sea-loving
Hallie, Hally, Meda

Halina (Russian) faithful
Haleena, Halyna

Hall (Last name as first name)
distinguished
Haul

Halle (German) home ruler

Hallela (Hebrew) praiseworthy

Hallie (German) high-spirited
Haleigh, Hali, Halie, Halle,
Hallee, Hally, Hallye

Halona (Native American) lucky
baby
Halonna

Halsey (American) playful
Halcie, Halsea, Halsee, Halsie

Halston (American) stylish
Hall, Halls, Halsten

Halzey (American) leader
Hals, Halsee, Halsi, Halsy, Halze,
Halzee

Hameedah (Arabic) grateful

Hamilton (American) wishful
Hamil, Hamilten, Hamiltun,
Hamma, Hamme

Hamony (Latin) form of
Harmony: in synchrony

Hana (Arabic) delight

Haneefah (Arabic) true believer

Hanh (Vietnamese) moral

Hani (Hawaiian) sways

Hanifa (Arabic) righteous

Hanna (Polish) grace

Hannabelle (German) feminine form Hannibal: happy; beauty
Hannabell, Hannahbell, Hannahbelle

Hannah ○ ❶ (Hebrew) merciful; God-blessed
Hanae, Hanah, Hanan, Hannaa, Hanne, Hanni

Hanne (Scandinavian) girl of grace

Hannelore (American) form of Hannah: merciful; God-blessed

Hannette (American) form of Jannette: lovely
Hanett, Hann, Hannett

Hannia (Polish) graceful

Hannie (German) believer

Hansa (Indian) swanlike
Hans, Hansah, Hansey, Hanz

Happy (English) joyful
Hap, Happee, Happi

Haralda (Scandinavian) rules the army
Hallie, Hally, Harelda, Harilda

Hardin (Last name used as first name) keeps rabbits

Harla (English) country girl from the fields
Harlah, Harlea, Harlee, Harlen, Harlie, Harlun

Harlan (English) athletic
Harlen, Harlon, Harlun

Harlene (French) energetic

Harlequine (Invented) romantic
Harlequinne, Harley

Harley (English) wild thing
Harlea, Harlee, Harleey, Harli, Harlie, Harly

Harlie (English) in the field; dreamy

Harlinne (American) vivacious
Harleen, Harleene, Harline, Harly

Harlow (American) brash
Harlo, Harly

Harmon (Last name as first name) attuned
Harmen, Harmone, Harmun, Harmyn

Harmonita (Greek) in harmony

Harmony (Latin) in synchrony
Harmonee, Harmoni, Harmonia, Harmonie

Harolyn (American) form of Carolyn: womanly

Harper (English) musician; writer
Harp

Harrah (English) rejoicing; merriment
Hara, Harah, Harra

Harrell (American) leader
Harell, Harill, Harryl, Haryl

Harriet (French) homebody
Harri, Harrie, Harriett, Harriette, Harrott, Hat, Hatti, Hattie, Hatty

Harrisah (Indian) happy

Harsha (Indian) joyful

Harshita (English) form of Harriet: homebody

Hart (American) romantic
Harte, Hartee, Hartie, Harty, Heart

Hartley (Last name as first name) having heart
Hartlee, Hartleigh, Hartli, Hartlie, Hartly

Hasina (African) beauty

Hassaanah (African) first girl born

Hattie (English) home-loving
Hatti, Hatty, Hettie, Hetty

Hattina (Biblical) place name; homebody

Haute (French) high
Hautie

Hava (Hebrew) life; lively
Chaba, Chaya, Haya

Havana (Cuban) loyal
Havanah, Havane, Havanna, Havanuh, Havvanah

Haven (American) safe place; open
Havin, Havun

Havilah (Hebrew) beloved

Haviland (American) lively; talented
Havilan, Havilynd

Hawkins (American) wily
Hawk, Hawkens, Hawkey, Hawkuns

Hawlee (American) negotiator
Hawlea, Hawleigh, Hawlie, Hawley, Hawly

Haydee (American) capable
Hady, Hadye, Haydie

Haydeeline (English) sweet

Haydell (Last name used as first name) hill child

Hayden (Last name used as first name) hill child

Haydon (American) knowing
Hayden, Hadyn

Hayfa (Arabic) slim

Hayla (Arabic) moon's halo

Hayley ❶ (English) natural; hay meadow
*Hailey, Haley, **Haylee**, Hayleigh, Hayli, Haylie*

Haze (American) word as a name; spontaneous
Haise, Hay, Hays, Hazee, Hazey, Hazy

Hazel (English) powerful
Hazell, Hazelle, Hazie, Hazyl, Hazzell

Hazen (Hindi) joyful

Healy (Last name used as first name) healthy

Heart (American) romantic
Hart, Hearte

Heath (English) open; healthy
Heathe

Heather (Scottish) flowering
Heath, Heathar, Heathor, Heathur

Heaven ❶ (English) happy and beautiful
Heavyn, Hevin

Heavenly (American) spiritual
Heaven, Heavenlee, Heavenley, Heavynlie, Hevin

Heba (Greek) child; goddess of youth
Hebe

Hecate (Greek) goddess of witchcraft

Hedda (German) capricious; warring
Heda, Heddi, Heddie, Hedi, Hedy, Hetta

Heddalin (Scandinavian) contender

Hedley (Greek) sweet; (German) excites
Hedlee, Hedleigh, Hedli, Hedlie, Hedly

Hedviga (Scandinavian) excites

Hedy (German) mercurial
Hedi

Hedya (Hebrew) joy girl
Hedia, Hedva

Hedy-Marie (German) capricious

Heidi (German) noble; watchful; perky
Heide, Heidee, Heidie, Heidy, Hidi

Heidrun (German) form of Heidi: noble; watchful; perky

Heija (Korean) bright
Hia, Hya

Heilala (Asian) sun child

Heirnine (Greek) form of Helen: beautiful; light

Heirrierte (English) form of Harriet: homebody

Hela (Biblical) olden

Helaine (French) ray of light; gorgeous
Helainne, Helle, Hellyn, Helyna

Helanna (Greek) lovely
Helahna, Helana, Helani, Heley, Hella

Helayne (American) pretty girl

Helbon (Greek) form of Helen: beautiful; light
Helbona, Helbonia, Helbonna, Helbonnah

Held (Welsh) light

Helen (Greek) beautiful; light
Hela, Hele, Helena, Helyn, Lena, Lenore

Helena (Greek) beautiful; ingenious
Helana, Helayna, Heleana, Helene, Hellena, Helyena, Lena

Helene (French) form of Helen: beautiful; light
Helaine, Heleen, Heline

Helenore (Greek) form of Helen: beautiful; light
Hele, Helenoor, Helenor, Helia, Helie, Hellena, Lena, Lennore, Lenora, Lenore, Lenory, Lina, Nora, Norey, Norie

Helfine (Scandinavian) blessed

Helga (Anglo-Saxon) pious
Helg

Helia (Greek) sun
Heleah, Helya, Helyah

Helice (Greek) form of Helen: beautiful; light

Helie (Greek) sunny
Heley, Heli

Helina (Greek) delightful
Helinah, Helinna, Helinnuh

Heliodora (Spanish) loves sun

Helki (Native American) tender
Helkie, Helky

Hella (Greek) form of Helen: beautiful; light
Helle

Helma (German) helmet; well-protected

Helmina (German) form of Wilhelmina: staunch protector

Heloise (German) hearty
Hale, Haley, Heley, Heloese, Heloyse

Helsa (Scandinavian) God-loving
Helse, Helsie

Helynne (French) moon

Hema (Indian) gold child

Henda (English) form of Henna: mehndi
Hende, Hendel, Heneh

Hender (American) embraced
Hendere

Henia (English) form of Henrietta: home-ruler; (Spanish) well-groomed
Henie, Henna, Henye

Henley (American) sociable
Hendlee, Hendly, Henli, Henlie, Hinlie, Hynlie

Henna (Hindi) mehndi
Hena, Hennah, Hennuh, Henny

Henrietta (English/German) home-ruler
Harriet, Hattie, Henny, Hetta, Hettie

Henriette (French) leads the home

Hensley (American) ambitious
Henslee, Henslie, Hensly

Henton (Last name used as first name) open arms

Hera (Greek) wife of Zeus; radiant

Heraclea (Biblical) place name; of Hercules

Herdis (Scandinavian) army woman

Herendira (Invented) tender and dear
Heren

Herise (Invented) warm
Heree, Hereese, Herice

Herleen (American) quiet
Herlee, Herlene, Herley, Herline, Herly, Hurleen

Herliza (Spanish) sweet

Hermaina (Spanish) speedy

Hermelinda (Spanish) earthy

Hermilla (Spanish) fighter
Herm, Hermila, Hermille

Hermina (Greek) of the earth
Hermine

Hermione (Greek) sensual
Hermina, Hermine

Hermosa (Spanish) beautiful
Ermosa

Hernanda (Spanish) feminine
form of Hernando: daring

Herra (Greek) earth girl
Herrah, Hera

Hersala (Spanish) lithe and
lovely
Hers, Hersila, Hersilia, Hersy

Hersilia (Spanish) delicate

Hertha (English) earth
Eartha, Erda, Erta, Ertha, Herta

Hertnia (English) earth
Herrntia

Herwena (Slavic) winner

Hesna (Arabic) star

Hesper (Greek) night star
Hespera, Hespira

Hest (Greek) form of Hester:
starlike; literary
Hessie, Hesta, Hetty

Hesta (Greek) starlike
Hestia

Hester (American) starlike;
literary
*Esther, Hestar, Hesther, Hett,
Hettie, Hetty*

Hestia (Greek) hearth

Heti (English) form of Henrietta:
home-ruler

Hetta (German) ruler
Hedda, Heta, Hettie, Hetty

Hetty (English) form of
Henrietta: home-ruler

Heven (American) pretty
*Hevan, Hevin, Hevon, Hevun,
Hevven*

Hewaida (Indian) gift

Heydee (German) form of Heidi:
noble; watchful; perky

Heyzell (American) form of
Hazel: powerful
Hayzale, Heyzel, Heyzelle

Hezekiah (Biblical) pleases

Hiah (Korean) form of Heija:
bright
Hia, Hy, Hya, Hye

Hiatt (English) form of Hyatt:
high gate; worthwhile
Hi, Hye

Hibernia (Place name) Latin
word for Ireland

Hibiscus (Botanical) pretty

Hicks (Last name as first name)
saucy
Hicksee, Hicksie

Hidee (American) form of Heidi:
noble; watchful; perky
Hidey, Hidie, Hidy, Hydee, Hydeey

Hideko (Japanese) excellence

Hidie (German) lively

Hila (Hebrew) angelic

Hilan (Greek) happy

Hilaria (Latin/Polish)
merrymaker
Hilarea, Hilareeah, Hilariah

Hilary (Latin) cheerful and
outgoing
*Hilaire, Hilaree, Hilari, Hilaria,
Hillarree, Hillary, Hillerie, Hillery*

Hilda (German) protector
Hild, Hilde, Hildi, Hildie, Hildy

Hildar (Scandinavian) feisty

Hildebrand (German) strong

Hildegard (German) battle
*Hilda, Hildagarde, Hildegarde,
Hildred, Hillie*

Hildegunde (Last name as first
name) princess

Hildemar (German) strong

Hildreth (German) struggles

Hilina (Hawaiian) celestial

Hilja (Finnish) silence

Hilma (German) helmet; protects
herself
Helma

Hilmah (Scandinavian) form of Hilja: silence

Hilton (American) wealthy
Hillie, Hilltawn, Hillton, Hilly

Himalaya (Place name) mountain range; upwardly mobile
Hima

Hina (Scandinavian) leads the home

Hinda (Hebrew) held high

Hindal (Hebrew) form of Hinda: held high

Hinton (American) affluent
Hintan, Hinten, Hintun, Hynton

Hirani (Indian) gold child

Hiroko (Japanese) giving; wise

Hisa (Japanese) forever
Hissa, Hysa, Hyssa

Hisaye (Japanese) longlasting

Hoa (Southeast Asian) flowers

Hodalla (Jewish) queenly

Hodel (German) stern
Hodi

Hodge (Last name as first name) confident
Hodj

Hoku (Hawaiian) starlike

Holda (German) secretive

Holden (English) willing
Holdan, Holdun

Holder (English) beautiful voice
Holdar, Holdur

Holiday (American) jazzy
Holidae, Holidaye, Holladay, Holliday, Holly

Holine (American) special
Hauline, Holinn, Holli, Holyne

Hollah (German) hides much

Holland (Place name) expressive
Hollan, Hollyn, Holyn

Hollander (Dutch) form of Holland: expressive
Holander, Holender, Hollender, Hollynder, Holynder

Hollis (English) smart; girl by the holly
Hollice, Hollyce

Hollisha (English) ingenious; Christmas-born; holly
Holicha, Hollice, Hollichia, Hollise

Holly (Anglo-Saxon) Christmas-born; holly tree
Hollee, Holleigh, Holley, Holli, Hollie, Hollye

Holsey (American) laidback
Holsee, Holsie

Holton (American) whimsical
Holt, Holten, Holtun

Holyn (American) fresh-faced
Holan, Holen, Holland, Hollee, Hollen, Holley, Hollie, Holly, Hollyn

Homer (American) tomboyish
Homar, Home, Homera, Homie, Homir, Homma

Honesty (American) truthful
Honeste, Honestee, Honesti, Honestie, Honestye

Honey (Latin) sweet-hearted
Honie, Hunnie

Honeyblossom (American) sweet

Honeylee (American) sweet

Honor (Latin) ethical
Honer, Honora, Honour

Honora (Latin) honorable
Honorah, Honoree, Honoria, Honoura

Honorata (Polish) respected woman

Honoreen (American) has honor

Honoria (Spanish) of high integrity; a saint
Honoreah

Honorina (Spanish) honored
Honor, Honora, Honoryna

Hope ☉ (Anglo-Saxon) optimistic

Hopkins (American) perky
Hopkin

Hopsey (American) lively

Horatia (Latin) keeps time; careful
Horacia

Horiya (Japanese) gardens

Hortencia (Spanish) green thumb
Hartencia, Hartense, Hartensia,
Hortence, Hortense, Hortensia

Hortense (Latin) caretaking the
garden
Hortence, Hortensia, Hortinse

Hosanna (Greek) time to pray;
worshipping
Hosana, Hosanah, Hosannah

Hoshi (Japanese) shines

Houston (Place name) leader
Houst, Houstie, Huston

Hoyden (Last name as first name)
having high spirits
Hoydin, Hoydyn

Huberta (German) brilliant

Hud (American) tomboyish
Hudd

Huda (Arabic) the right way
Hoda

Hudalia (Spanish) leads

Hudel (Scandinavian) lovable

Hudi (Arabic) the right way

Hudson (English) explorer;
adventuresome
Hud, Huds

Hueline (German) smart
Hue, Huee, Huel, Huela, Huelene,
Huelette, Huelyne, Huey, Hughee,
Hughie

Huella (American) joyous
Huela, Huelle

Hueretta (American) smart

Huette (German) intellectual
Huetta, Hugette, Hughette

Hulda (Scandinavian) sweetheart
Huldah, Huldie, Huldy,

Hum (Indian) togetherness

Humairaa (Asian) generous

Humla (Polish) humble

Hun (American) form of Honey:
sweet-hearted
Hon

Hunni (American) form of
Honey: sweet-hearted

Hunter (English) searching;
jubilant
Hun, Huner, Hunner, Hunt,
Huntar, Huntter

Hunting (English) hunts

Hurd (Last name used as first
name) herds cattle

Hurley (English) fit
Hurlee, Hurlie, Hurly

Hutton (English) right
Hutten, Huttun

Huxlee (American) creative
Hux, Huxleigh, Huxley, Huxly

Hyacinth (Greek) flower
Hy, Hyacinthe, Hycinth

Hyatt (English) high gate;
worthwhile
Hyat

Hyde (American) tough-willed
Hide, Hydie

Hydia (German) form of Heidi:
noble; watchful; perky

Hydie (American) spirited
Hidi, Hydee, Hydey, Hydi

Hylaine (American) form of
Elaine: dependable girl

Hypatia (Greek) tops

Iadanna (Biblical) place name

Iana (Greek) form of Iantha:
flowering
Iann

Ianeke (Hawaiian) believer in a
gracious God
Ianete, Iani

Ianthe (Greek) flowering
Ian, Iantha, Ianthina, Ianthiria

Ibeth (Spanish) form of Elizabeth:
God's promise

Ibleam (Biblical) place name

Ibsen (Scandinavian) scholarly

Ida (German) heroine; warrior
Idah, Iduh

Idaa (Hindi) earth woman

Idahlia (Greek) sweet
*Idali, Idalia, Idalina, Idaline,
Idalis*

Idalia (Italian) sweet

Idam (American) feminine form
of Adam: original

Idarah (American) social
Idara, Idare, Idareah

Idasia (English) joyful

Ide (Irish) thirsty

Ideh (German) form of Ida:
heroine; warrior
Idit

Idelle (Celtic) generous
Idele

Idetta (German) serious worker
Ideta, Idettah, Idette

Idil (Latin) pleasant
Idee, Idey, Idi, Idie, Idyll

Idola (German) worker
Idolah, Idolia

Idolina (American) idolizes
Idol, Idolena

Idolyne (Spanish) idolizes

Idoma (American) form of Idona:
fresh

Idona (Scandinavian) fresh
*Idonah, Idonea, Idonia, Idonna,
Iduna*

Idonie (Scandinavian) loving

Idony (Scandinavian) reborn

Idoris (Greek) adores

Idowu (African) baby after twins

Idra (Aramaic) rich; fig tree;
flourishes

Idriya (Hebrew) duck; rich
Idria

Idumea (Biblical) place name

Iduna (Scandinavian) fresh
Idun

Iduvina (Spanish) dedicated
Iduvine, Iduvynna, Vina

Ieesh (Arabic) feminine
Ieasha, Ieesha, Iesha, Yesha

Ierne (Irish) form of Ireland:
vibrant

Iesha (Arabic) feminine

Ieshia (English) form of Iesha:
feminine

Ifama (African) well-being

Ife (African) loving

Ifigenia (Spanish) form of Effie:
well-spoken

Ignacia (Latin) passionate
Ignacy, Ignatia, Ignatzia

Ihab (Arabic) gift

Iheoma (Hawaiian) lifted by the
Lord

Ihsan (Arabic) good will
Ihsana, Ihsanah

Iianena (Slavic) form of Ileana:
soaring

Iilia (English) form of Ileana:
soaring

Ijada (Spanish) jade; beauty

Ikabela (Hawaiian) form of
Isabella: consecrated to God
Ikapela

Ikea (Scandinavian) smooth
Ikeah, Ikee, Ikie

Ikeida (Invented) spontaneous
Ikae, Ikay

Iku (Japanese) nurturing

Ila (Hindi) of the earth; lovely

Ilaisaane (Asian) bright

Ilamay (French) sweet; from an
island
Ilamae, Ila May, Ila-May, Ilamaye

Ilana (Hebrew) tree; gorgeous
*Elana, Ilaina, Ilane, Ilani, Illana,
Lainie, Lanie*

Ilaria (Greek) girl with a good
attitude

Ilda (German) warring; feisty

Ildiko (Hungarian) contentious;
warrior

Ileana (American) soaring•
Ileanna, Ileannah, Ilene, Iliana,
Ilianna, Illeana, Illiana

Ilena (Greek) regal
Ileena, Ilina

Ilene (American) svelte
Ileen, Ilenia

Ilesha (Hindi) loves the Lord of
the earth

Ilfa (American) ecstatic

Ilia (Greek) from ancient city
Ilion; traditional

Iliana (Greek) woman of Troy
Ileanai, Illeana

Ilima (Hawaiian) oahu flower

Ilka (Hungarian) beauty

Ilkee (Slavic) form of Ilka: beauty

Ilkka (Slavic) form of Ilka: beauty

Illana (Hebrew) tree

Illiana (Spanish) form of Helen:
beautiful; light

Ilma (American) stubborn

Ilon (Biblical) place name

Ilona (Hungarian) form of Helen:
beautiful; light

Ilonka (Slavic) lovely

Ilsa (Scottish) glowing
Elyssa, Illisa, Illysa, Ilsah, Ilse,
Lissie

Ilse (German) form of Elizabeth:
God's promise

Ilyse (English) charms

Ilyssa (English) form of Alyssa:
flourishing

Ima (Japanese) now; the present
Imah

Imagine (Word as name)
imaginative

Imaine (Arabic) form of Iman:
living in the present
Imain, Imane

Imala (Native American)
strongwilled

Iman (Arabic/African) living in
the present
Imen

Imana (Arabic) faithful; true

Imani (Arabic) faithful

Imanuela (Spanish) faithful

Imara (Hungarian) ruler

Imari (Japanese) today's girl

Imelda (German) contentious
Imalda

Imena (African) dreamy

Imin (Arabic) loyal

Immaculada (Spanish) spotless

Imogen (Gaelic) maiden
Emogen, Imogene

Imperia (Latin) imperial; stately

In (Arabic) generous

Ina (Latin) small
Inah

Inaki (Asian) generous spirit

Inam (Arabic) generous

Inanna (Mythology) goddess

Inas (Arabic) friendly

Inca (Indian) adventurer
Incah

Inda (Place name) lady

India (Place name) woman of
India
Indeah, Indee, Indie, Indy, Indya

Indiana (Place name) salt-of-the-
earth; U.S. state
Inda, India

Indiece (American) capable
Indeece, Indeese

Indigo (Latin) eyes of deep blue
Indego, Indigoh

Indira (Hindi) ethereal; God of
heaven and thunderstorms
Indra

Indra (Hindi) god of thunder and
rain; powerful
Indee, Indi, Indira, Indre

Indranee (Hindi) sky God's wife

Indrani (Indian) wife of Indra;
excellent

Indray (American) outspoken
Indee, Indrae, Indree

Indre (Hindi) splendor

Indya (Place name) form of India:
woman of India

Ineesha (African American) sparkling
Inesha, Ineshah, Inisha

Ineke (Japanese) nurtures

Ines (Spanish) chaste
Inez, Innez, Ynez

Inessa (Russian) pure
Inesa, Nessa

Inessae (Spanish) form of Ines: chaste

Inetha (Slavic) pure

Inez (Spanish) lovely
Ines

Infinity (American) lasting
Infinitee, Infinitey, Infiniti, Infinitie

Inga (Scandinavian) hero's daughter

Ingalill (Scandinavian) fertile

Ingalls (American) peaceful

Inge (Scandinavian) fertile
Inga

Ingeborg (Scandinavian) fertile

Ingegerd (Scandinavian) form of Ingrid: beautiful

Inger (Scandinavian) lovely

Inglesa (Spanish) English girl

Ingrad (American) form of Ingrid: beautiful
Inger, Ingr

Ingrid (Scandinavian) beautiful
Inga, Inge, Inger, Ingred

Ingrida (Scandinavian) form of Ingrid: beautiful

Iniguez (Spanish) good
Ina, Ini, Niqui

Inka (Scandinavian) abundant

Inna (Slavic) little girl

Innocence (American) pure
Innoce, Innocents, Inocence, Inocencia, Inocents

Inoa (Hawaiian) named

Inocencia (Spanish) innocent
Inocenta, Inocentia

Inola (Greek) form of Iola: dawn

Integrity (American) truthful
Integritee, Integritie

Ioannis (Greek) believer

Iola (Greek) dawn
Iole

Iolana (Hawaiian) violet; pretty

Iolanthe (English) violet; delicate
Iole, Iola

Iona (Place name) for the Isle of Iona in Scotland
Ione, Ionia

Ioni (English) place name; innocent

Ionica (Biblical) place name

Iosepine (Hawaiian) form of Josephine: blessed

Ira (Hebrew) contented; watchful
Irah

Ireland (Place name) vibrant
Irelan, Irelande, Irelyn, Irelynn

Irene (Greek) peace-loving; goddess of peace
Irine

Ireta (Greek) serene
Iretta, Irette

Irina (Greek/Russian) comforting
Ireena, Irena, Irenah, Irene, Irenia, Irenya

Iris (Greek) bright; goddess of the rainbow

Irisal (Greek) form of Iris: bright; goddess of the rainbow

Iriseene (American) iris flower; rainbow

Irish (American) Irish girl

Irma (Latin) realistic
Irmah

Irmaletta (Spanish) noble; complete

Irmgard (Latin) form of Irma: realistic

Irnee (Scandinavian) growth

Irodell (Invented) peaceful
Irodel, Irodelle

Irra (Greek) serene

Irvette (English) friend of the sea

Isa (Spanish) dark-eyed
Isah

Isabel (Spanish) God-loving
Isabela, Isabella, Isabelle, Issie, Iza

Isabella ○ ❶ (Spanish/Italian) consecrated to God
Isabela, Izabella

Isadora (Greek) beautiful; gift of Isis; fertile
Dora, Dori, Dory, Isidora

Isairis (Spanish) lively
Isa, Isaire

Isamu (Japanese) high-energy

Isandra (Spanish) form of Sandra: helpful; protective

Isatas (Native American) snow
Istas

Isaura (Greek) Asian country

Isela (American) giving
Iselah

Iselderine (Invented) loyal

Iseult (Irish) lovely

Isha (Hindi) protected

Ishana (Hindi) sheltered

Ishi (Japanese) rock; safe
Ishie

Ishiko (Japanese) rock; dependable

Ishtar (Biblical) mother-goddess; faithful

Isis (Egyptian) goddess supreme of moon and fertility

Isla (Place name) river in Scotland; flows

Isleana (Latin) sun girl; jolly
Isaeileen, Islean, Isleen

Ismaela (Hebrew) feminine form of Ishmael: God hears
Isma, Mael, Maella

Ismat (Arabic) protective

Ismene (French) form of the name Esme: much loved
Isme, Ismyne

Ismenia (Place name) region of Mars; loyal

Ismey (French) form of Esme: much loved

Isobelette (American) believes in God

Isoka (African) given by God
Isoke, Soka

Isoke (African) God's gift

Isola (Spanish) lovely

Isolde (Welsh) beautiful
Iseult, Isolda, Isolt, Izette, Yseult

Isotta (Irish) princess

Isra (Arabic) night mover

Issa (English) form of Isabel: God-loving
Isa

Issus (Biblical) place name; wise

Istvan (Hungarian) crowned

Ita (Irish) thirsts for knowledge

Italia (Italian) girl from Italy

Iti (Irish) form of Ita: thirsts for knowledge

Itiah (Hebrew) God comforts her
Itia, Itiya

Itica (Spanish) eloquent
Itaca, Iticah

Itidal (Arabic) cautious

Itinsa (Hawaiian) waterfall

Itka (Irish) form of Ita: thirsts for knowledge

Ito (Japanese) thread; delicate

Ituha (Native American) sturdy oak; white stone

Itzel (Spanish) form of Isabel: God-loving
Itz

Itzelle (Native American) earth goddess

Itzy (American) lively
Itsee, Itzee, Itzie

Iuana (Welsh) believes in gracious God

Iudita (Hawaiian) praises; affectionate

Iuginia (Hawaiian) highborn
Iugina

Iulaua (Hawaiian) eloquent

Iulia (Irish) form of Juliana: youthful; Jove's child

Iunia (Hawaiian) good victory

Iusitina (Hawaiian) justice

Iva (Slavic) dedicated
Ivah

Ivania (Russian) feminine form of Ivan: believer in a gracious God; reliable one

Ivaniah (Russian) feminine form of Ivan: believer in a gracious God; reliable one

Ivanna (Russian) gracious gift from God
Iva, Ivana, Ivanka, Ivie, Ivy

Iverem (African) lucky girl

Ives (French) form of Yves: clever

Ivet (Spanish) athletic

Iveta (French) athletic

Ivette (French) clever and athletic
Ivet, Ivett

Ivey (English/American) a climbing evergreen ornamental plant
Ivee, Ivie, Ivy

Iviannah (American) adorned
Iviana, Ivianna, Ivie, Ivy

Ivisse (American) graceful
Ivice, Iviece, Ivis, Ivise

Ivnia (Russian) feminine form of Ivan: believer in a gracious God; reliable one

Ivon (Spanish) light
Ivonie, Ivonne

Ivona (Slavic) gift
Ivana, Ivanna, Ivannah, Ivonah, Ivone, Ivonne

Ivonne (French) athlete
Ivonn

Ivory (Latin) white
Ivoree, Ivori, Ivorie

Ivria (Hebrew) from Abraham's country
Ivriah, Ivrit

Ivrie (English) form of Ivory: white

Ivy (English) growing
Iv, Ivee, Ivey, Ivie

Iwa (Japanese) strong character

Iwalani (Hebrew) heavenly girl

Iwilla (African American) I will rise

Iwona (Polish) archer; athletic; gift
Iwonna

Iyabo (African) her mother is home

Iyana (Hebrew) sincere

Izabella (American) form of Isabella: consecrated to God
Iza, Izabela, Izabell, Izabelle

Izanne (American) calming
Iza, Izan, Izann, Izanna, Ize

Izdihar (Arabic) blossoming

Izebe (African) staunch supporter

Izegbe (African) baby who was wanted

Izena (Slavic) gracious

Izene (Slavic) gracious

Izolde (Greek) philosophical
Izo, Izolade, Izold

Izusa (Native American) white rock; unique

Izzy (American) zany
Izzee, Izzie

Jaala (Arabic) seeks clarity

Jabinea (Biblical) sees

Jacalyn (American) form of Jacqueline: supplanter; substitute
Jacelyn, Jacelyne, Jacelynn, Jacilyn, Jacilyne, Jacilynn, Jacolyn, Jacolyne, Jacolynn, Jacylyn, Jacylyne, Jacylynn

Jacey (Greek) sparkling
J.C., Jace, Jacee, Jaci, Jacie, Jacy

Jacinda (Greek) attractive girl
Jacenda, Jacey, Jaci, Jacinta

Jacinta (Spanish) hyacinth; sweet
Jace, Jacee, Jacey, Jacinda, Jacinna,
Jacintae, Jacinth, Jacinthia, Jacy,
Jacynth

Jacinth (Greek) beauty

Jackalyn (American) form of
Jacqueline: supplanter; substitute
Jackalene, Jackalin, Jackaline,
Jackalynn, Jackalynne, Jackelin,
Jackeline, Jackelyn, Jackelynn,
Jackelynne, Jackilin, Jackilyn,
Jackilynn, Jackilynne, Jackolin,
Jackoline, Jackolyn, Jackolynn,
Jackolynne

Jackie (French) form of
Jacqueline: supplanter; substitute
Jackee, Jacki, Jacky, Jaki, Jaky

Jacklyn (American) careful
Jacklin, Jackline, Jacklyne,
Jacklynn, Jacklynne

Jackquel (French) watchful
Jackquelin, Jackqueline,
Jackquelyn, Jackquelynn,
Jackquilin, Jackquiline, Jackquilyn,
Jackquilynn, Jackquilynne

Jackson (Last name as first
name) swaggering
Jacksen, Jaksin, Jakson

Jaclyn (French) form of
Jacqueline: supplanter; substitute
Jacalyn, Jackalene, Jackalin,
Jackalyn, Jackeline, Jackolynne,
Jacleen, Jaclin, Jacline, Jaclyne,
Jaclynn

Jacoba (Hebrew) replaces

Jacobi (Hebrew) stand-in
Cobie, Coby

Jacomine (Dutch) best girl

Jacoy (French) form of Jackie:
supplanter; substitute

Jacqua (American) replacement

Jacqueline (French) supplanter;
substitute
Jacki, Jackie, Jacklin, Jacklyn,
Jaclyn, Jacqualin, Jacqualine,
Jacqualyn, Jacqualyne, Jacquel,
Jacquelyn, Jacquelynn, Jacqui,
Jacquie, Jakie, Jakline, Jaklinn,
Jaklynn, Jaqueline, Jaquie

Jacquelyn (French) form of
Jacqueline: supplanter; substitute
Jacquelyne, Jacquelynn

Jacquet (Invented) form of
Jacqueline: supplanter; substitute
Jackett, Jackwet, Jacquee, Jacquie,
Jakkett

Jacquetta (American)
replacement

Jacqui (French) form of
Jacqueline: supplanter; substitute
Jacquay, Jacque, Jacquee, Jacquie,
Jaki, Jakki, Jaquay, Jaqui, Jaquie

Jacynth (Spanish) hyacinth;
flower

Jada ○ ◑ (Spanish) personable;
precious
*Jadah, **Jayda***

Jade ◑ (Spanish) green
gemstone; courageous; adoring
Jada, Jadah, Jadda, Jadea,
Jadeann, Jadee, Jaden, Jadera,
Jadi, Jadie, Jadielyn, Jadienne,
Jady, Jadzia, Jadziah, Jaeda,
Jaedra, Jaida, Jaide, Jaiden, Jaiyde

Jaden (Hebrew) God has heard
Jadan, Jadi, Jadie, Jadin, Jadyn,
Jaeden, Jaiden

Jadie (Spanish) jade stone

Jadine (Spanish) jade stone

Jadran (American) jade stone

Jadwiga (Polish) religious
Jad, Jadwig, Wiga

Jadwin (American) friend of Jade

Jadza (Spanish) jade

Jae (Latin) small; jaybird
Jaea, Jay, Jayjay

Jael (Hebrew) high-climbing
Jaela, Jaelee, Jaeli, Jaelie, Jaelle

Jaela (Hebrew) bright
Jael, Jaell, Jayla

Jaelyn (African American) ambitious
Jaela, Jaelynne, Jala, Jalyn, Jaylyn

Jaenesha (African American) spirited
Jacey, Jae, Jaeneisha, Jaeniesha, Janesha, Jaynesha, Nesha

Jae-Sun (Japanese) sun's bird

Jaffa (Hebrew) lovely

Jagan (American) form of Jaden: God has heard
Jag, Jagann, Jagen, Jagun

Jagger (English) cutter
Jaeger, Jag, Jager

Jagodah (Slavic) little berry
Jaga, Jagada, Jago, Jagoda

Jaguar (American) runner
Jag, Jaggy, Jagwar, Jagwor

Jahel (Hebrew) moves upward

Jahnea (Scandinavian) feminine form of John: God is gracious

Jahnika (Scandinavian) believes in God

Jahnny (American) feminine form of Johnny: God is gracious
Jahnae, Jahnay, Jahnie, Jahnnee, Jahnney, Jahnnie, Jahny

Jaidan (American) golden child
Jaedan, Jai, Jaide, Jaidee, Jaidi, Jaidon, Jaidun, Jaidy, Jaidyn, Jaydan, Jaydyn

Jaime (French) girl who loves
Jaeme, Jaemee, Jaima, Jaimee, Jaimey, Jaimi, Jaimie, Jaimy, Jamie, Jaymee

Jaime-Day (American) loving

Jaimela (Spanish) lovely

Jainil (English) form of Janel: exuberent

Jairia (Spanish) taught by God's lessons

Jakira (Arabic) warmth

Jakisha (African American) favored
Jakishe

Jakki (American) form of Jackie: supplanter; substitute
Jakea, Jakia, Jakkia

Jalalynne (Combo of Jala and Lynne) important

Jalila (Arabic) excellent
Jalile

Jalit (American) sparkling
Jal, Jalitt, Jalitte, Jallit

Jalona (Spanish) excellence

Jalou (Scandinavian) form of Jaela: bright

Jamaica (Place name) Caribbean island
Jama, Jamaika, Jamaka, Jamake, Jamana, Jamea, Jameca, Jameka, Jamica, Jamika, Jamiqua, Jamoka, Jemaica, Jemika, Jemyka

Jamais (French) ever
Jamay, Jamaye

Jamalita (Invented) feminine form of James: supplanter
Jama

Jamar (African American) strong
Jam, Jamara, Jamareah, Jamaree, Jamarr, Jamarra, Jammy

Jamashia (African American) soulful
Jamash, Jamashea

Jame (Hebrew) feminine form of James: supplanter

Jameah (African American) bold
Jamea, Jameea, Jamiah

Jamecka (African American) studious
Jamecca, Jameeka, Jameka, Jameke, Jamekka, Jamie, Jamiea, Jamieka

Jameelah (Arabic) lovely

Jameia (Arabic) lovely

Jamelae (American) smart

Jamesetta (American) feminine form of James: supplanter
Jamesette

Jamesha (African American) outgoing
Jamece, Jamecia, Jameciah, Jameisha, James, Jamese, Jameshia, Jameshyia, Jamesia, Jamesica, Jamesika, Jamesina, Jamessa, Jamie, Jamisha, Jay

Jami (Hebrew) replacement
Jamay, Jamia, Jamie, Jamy

Jamie (Hebrew) supplants; fun-loving
Jamee, James, Jami, Jaymee

J'Amie (French) friend; form of Jamie: supplants; fun-loving

Jamika (African American) buoyant
Jameeka, Jamey, Jamica, Jamicka, Jamie

Jamila (Arabic) beautiful female
Jahmela, Jahmilla, Jam, Jameela, Jami, Jamie, Jamil, Jamilah, Jamile, Jamilla, Jamille, Jamilya, Jammell, Jammie

Jan (English) form of Janet: small; forgiving
Jani, Jania, Jandy, Jannie, Janny

JaNa (American) form of Jane: believer in a gracious God

Jana (Slavic/Scandinavian) God's gracious gift
Janna, Janne

Janae (American) giving
Janea, Jannah, Jannay, Jennae, Jennay

Janaina (Arabic) soulful

Janaki (Indian) seeta

Janalyn (American) giving
Jan, Janalynn, Janelyn, Janilyn, Jannalyn, Jannnie, Janny

Janan (Arabic) soulful
Jananee, Janani, Jananie, Janann, Jannani

Janara (American) generous
Janarah, Janerah, Janira, Janirah

Janay (American) forgiving
Janae, Janah, Janai

Janaya (American) form of Janae: giving

Jancy (American) risk-taker
Jan, Jance, Jancee, Jancey, Janci, Jancie, Janny

Jandy (American) fun
Jandee, Jandey, Jandi

Jane (Hebrew) believer in a gracious God
Jaine, Jan, Janelle, Janene, Janeth, Janett, Janetta, Janey, Janica, Janie, Jannie, Jayne, Jaynie

Janeana (American) sweet
Janea, Janean, Janeanah, Janine

Janeer (American) heartfelt

Janel (French) form of Janelle: exuberant
Janell, Jannel, Jaynel, Jaynell

Janelle (French) exuberant
Janel, Janell, Jannel, Jenelle, J'Nel, J'nell, Nell

Janene (American) form of Jane: believer in a gracious God
Janeen, Janine, Jenean, Jenine

Janessa (American) forgiving
Janesha, Janeska, Janessah, Janie, Janiesa, Janiesha, Janisha, Janissa, Jannesa, Jannesha, Jannessa, Jannisa, Jannisha, Jannissa, Janyssa

Janet (English) small; forgiving
Jan, Janett, Janetta, Janette, Jannet, Jannett, Janot, Jessie, Jinett, Johnette, Jonetta, Jonette

Janeth (American) fascinating
Janith

Jania (American) heart's delight

Janice (Hebrew) knowing God's grace
Genese, Jan, Janece, Janecia, Janeese, Janeice, Janiece, Jannice, Janyce, Jynice

Janida (Spanish) gracious

Janie (English) form of Jane: believer in a gracious God
Janey, Jani, Jany

Janiece (American) devout; enthusiastic
Janece, Janecia, Janeese, Janese, Janesea, Janesse, Janneece, Jeneece, Jeneese

Janiecia (African American) sporty
Jan, Janeisha, Janesha, Janeshah, Janisha, Jannes, Jannesa

Janielle (English) form of Janelle: exuberant

Janier (French) gracious

Janika (Scandinavian) form of Jane: believer in a gracious God
Janica, Janicah, Janik, Janikka, Jannike

Janina (Scandinavian) devout

Janine (American) kind
Janean, Janeen, Janene, Janey, Janie, Jannine, Jannyne, Janyne, Jenine

Janineata (American) form of Janine: kind

Janique (Scandinavian) believer; smart

Janis (English) form of Jane: believer in a gracious God
Janees, Janeesa, Janes, Janise, Jenice, Jenis

Janisse (American) elegant

Janitza (American) form of Juanita: believer in a gracious God; forgiving

Janiya (American) believer

Janiyah (American) believer

Janiyal (American) pious

Janjan (Last name as first) sweet; believer
Jan Jan, Jange, Janja, Jan-Jan, Janje, Janni, Jannie, Janny

Janke (Scandinavian) believer in God
Jankee, Jankey, Jankie

Janna (Hebrew) form of Johana: believer in gracious God

Janneke (Scandinavian) smart; believer

Jannette (American) lovely
Jan, Janette, Jannett, Jannie, Janny

Jannie (English) form of Jane: believer in a gracious God; form of Jan: small; forgiving
Janney, Janny, Jannye

Janoah (Biblical) place name

Jansen (Scandinavian) smooth
Jan, Jannsen, Jans, Jansie, Janson, Jansun, Jansy

Janteya (Dutch) form of Jantine: giving

Jantine (Dutch) giving
Jantee, Janteen, Jantene, Jantie, Janty

Jantje (Scandinavian) believer

Japana (American) form of Japan

Japha (Biblical) place name

Jaqueline (French) form of Jacquelyn: supplanter; substitute
Jaqlinn, Jaqlyn, Jaqlynn, Jaqua, Jaquaeline, Jaqualine, Jaqualyn, Jaquelina, Jaquelyn, Jaquelynne, Jaquie, Jaqulene

Jaquonna (African American) spoiled
Jakwona, Jakwonda, Jakwonna, Jaqui, Jaquie, Jaquon, Jaquona, Jaquonne

Jaranescia (Scandinavian) magnificent

Jardana (American) gardener
Jarde, Jardee, Jardy

Jardena (French) gardens
Jardan, Jardane, Jarden, Jardenia, Jardine, Jardyne

Jarenda (American) lovely

Jarene (American) bright
Jare, Jaree, Jareen, Jaren, Jareni, Jarine, Jarry, Jaryne, Jerry

Jariesha (India) clear-headed

Jarita (Arabic) carries water; befriends
Jara, Jari, Jaria, Jarica, Jarida, Jarietta, Jarika, Jarina, Jaritta, Jaritza

Jariya (Arabic) form of Jarita: carries water; befriends

Jarmila (Czech) beautiful spring

Jarone (American) optimistic
Jaron, Jaroyne, Jerone, Jurone

Jaroslava (Czech) glorious
spring

Jarren (American) lovable
Jaren, Jarran, Jarre

Jas (American) form of Jasmine:
fragrant; sweet
Jass, Jaz, Jazz, Jazze, Jazzi

Jasalin (American) devoted
*Jasalinne, Jasalyn, Jasalynn,
Jaselyn, Jasleen, Jaslene, Jass,
Jassalyn, Jassy, Jazz, Jazzy*

Jasia (Slavic) hopeful

Jasira (Polish) form of Jane:
believer in a gracious God

Jasmine ✿ (Persian/Spanish)
fragrant; sweet
*Jasamine, Jasime, Jasimen, Jasimin,
Jasimine, Jasmaine, Jasman,
Jasme, Jasmie, Jasmina, Jasminah,
Jas'mine, Jasminen, Jasminne,
Jasmon, Jasmond, Jasmone,
Jasmyn, Jasmynn, Jasmynne, Jazie,
Jazmaine, Jazman, Jazmeen,
Jazmein, Jazmen, Jazmin,
Jazmine, Jazmon, Jazmond,
Jazmyn, Jazmyne, Jazs, Jazsmen,
Jazz, Jazza, Jazzamine, Jazzee,
Jazzi, Jazzmeen, Jazzmin, Jazz-
Mine, Jazzmun, Jazzy*

Jasna (American) talented
Jas, Jazna, Jazz

Jasper (French) gemstone

Jaspreet (Punjabi) pure
*Jas, Jaspar, Jasparit, Jasparita,
Jasper, Jasprit, Jasprita, Jasprite*

Jasvina (Spanish) form of
Jasmine: fragrant; sweet

Ja-Tawn (African American) tawny
Ja Tawn, Jatawn, J'Tawn

Jatsue (Spanish) lively
Jat, Jatsey

Jatumn (American) form of
Autumn: joy of changing seasons

Jautanza (American) creative

Javalin (American) thrower

Javana (Asian) girl from Java;
dancer
*Javanna, Javanne, Javon, Javonda,
Javonna, Javonne, Javonya,
Jawana, Jawanna, Jawn*

Javette (American) lively

Javiera (Spanish) owns a home
Javeera, Viera

Jawanda (African) bejeweled

Jawara (Arabic) true gem

Jaya (Hindi) winning
Jaea, Jaia, Jay, Jayah

Jayal (Sanskrit) special

Jayanti (Indian) winning

Jayare (African) winner

Jayatissa (Indian) wins

Jayci (American) vivacious
*Jacee, Jacey, Jaci, Jacie, Jacy,
Jaycee, Jaycey, Jaycie*

Jayden (American) enthusiastic
*Jaden, Jay, Jaydeen, Jaydon,
Jaydyn, Jaye*

Jaydie (American) lively
Jadie, Jady, Jay-Dee, Jaydeye

Jaydra (Spanish) treasured jewel;
jade
Jadra, Jay, Jaydrah

Jaye (Latin) small as a jaybird
Jae, Jay

Jayla ☺ (American) smiling
Jaila, Jaylah, Jayle, Jaylee

Jayleena (English) wins
Jaylena, Jaylenna

Jaylen ☺ (English) wins

Jaylene (American) feminine
form of Jay: colorful
*Jayelene, Jayla, Jaylah, Jaylan,
Jayleana, Jaylee, Jayleen*

Jaylynn (American) feminine
form of Jay: colorful
*Jaelin, Jaeline, Jaelyn, Jaelyne,
Jaelynn, Jaelynne, Jalin, Jaline,
Jalyn, Jalyne, Jalynn, Jalynne,
Jaylin, Jayline, Jaylyn, Jaylyne,
Jaylynne*

Jayma (English) dedicated

Jayme (English) feminine form of James: supplanter
Jami, Jamie, Jaymee, Jaymi, Jaymia, Jaymie

Jayna (Hindi) winner
Jaynae

Jayne (Hindi) victorious
Jane, Janey, Jani, Jayn, Jaynee, Jayni, Jaynie, Jaynita, Jaynne

Jaynille (American) form of Janelle: exuberent

Jayrette (American) dear

Jazael (American) form of Giselle: a promise

Jazel (American) form of Giselle: a promise

Jazl (American) zany

Jazz (American) rhythmic
Jas, Jassie, Jaz, Jazzi, Jazzie, Jazzle, Jazzy

Jazza (American) quirky

Jazzell (American) spontaneous
Jazel, Jazell, Jazz, Jazzee, Jazzie

Jean (Scottish) God-loving and gracious
Jeana, Jeanie, Jeanne, Jeannie, Jeanny, Jena, Jenay, Jenna

Jeana (American) form of Gina: wellborn
Jeanna

Jeanane (French) religious

Jeanetta (American) impish
Janetta, Jeannet, Jeannette, Jeanney, Jen, Jenett, Jennita

Jeanette (French) lively
Janette, Jeannete, Jeanett, Jeanetta, Jeanita, Jeannete, Jeannett, Jeannetta, Jeannette, Jeannita, Jenet, Jenett, Jenette, Jennett, Jennetta, Jennette, Jennita, Jinetta, Jinette

Jeanie (Scottish) devout; outspoken
Jeani, Jeannie, Jeanny, Jeany

Jeanine (Scottish) peace-loving
Jeanene, Jeanina, Jeannina, Jeannine, Jenine, Jennine

Jeanisha (African American) pretty
Jean, Jeaneesh, Jeanise, Jeanna, Jeannie, Jenisha

Jearlean (American) vibrant
Jearlee, Jearlene, Jearley, Jearli, Jearline, Jearly, Jerline

Jebel (Origin unknown) form of Jezebel: wanton woman

Jeca (Slavic) untainted
Jeka

Jecelyn (Invented) form of Jocelyn: joyful
Jece, Jecee, Jeselyn, Jess

Jedid (Biblical) loving

Jeena (American) bold

Jeffrey (German) peaceful; sparkling personality
Jef, Jeff, Jeffa, Jefferi, Jeffery, Jeffie, Jeffre, Jeffrie, Jeffy, Jefry

Jefjun (Scandinavian) rich

Jekemea (Slavic) my Jeka

Jelana (Russian) form of Helen: beautiful; light

Jelane (Russian) light heart
Jelaina, Jelaine, Jelanne, Jilane, Julane

Jelani (American) pretty sky
Jelainy, Jelaney, Jelanie, Jelanni

Jele (Slavic) light

Jelee (Slavic) moon child

Jelena (Slavic) moon child

Jelene (Slavic) moon

Jelka (Slavic) sturdy

Jelline (French) robust

Jemiccia (Italian) treasured

Jemima (Hebrew) dove-like
Jamima, Jem, Jemi, Jemimah, Jemm, Jemma, Jemmi, Jemmia, Jemmiah, Jemmy, Jemora

Jemine (American) treasured
Jem, Jemmy, Jemyne

Jemma (Hebrew) form of Gemma: gem; jewel
Jem

Jems (American) treasured
Gemas, Jemma, Jemmey, Jemmi, Jemmy

Jena (Arabic) small
Janae, Jenaa, Jenaeh, Jenah, Jenai, Jenal, Jenay, Jenna

Jenaseth (English) bird

Jenavieve (American) form of Genevieve: generous

Jenaya (African) hospitable

Jene (English) form of Jane: believer in a gracious God

Jenea (English) form of Jane: believer in a gracious God

Jenell (American) form of Janelle: exuberant
Janele, Jen, Jenaile, Jenalle, Jenel, Jenella, Jennelle, Jenny

Jenesia (Latin) newcomer

Jenette (English) form of Jeanette: lively

Jeniece (American) form of Janice: knowing God's grace

Jenifer (Welsh) form of Jennifer: white wave
Gennefer, Gennifer, Ginnifur, Ginniphur, Jay, Jenefer, Jenjen, Jenna, Jenni, Jenny

Jenika (English) blonde

Jenille (English) believes in gracious God

Jenis (Hebrew) the start
Jenesis

Jenna (English) form of Jean: God-loving and gracious
Jena, Jennah, Jennat, Jennay, Jhenna, Jynna

Jennah (English) form of Jennifer: white wave
Genna, Jena, Jenna

Jennell (English) form of Janelle: exuberant

Jennelle (English) form of Janelle: exuberant

Jenni (Welsh) form of Jennifer: white wave
Jeni, Jenica, Jenie, Jenisa, Jenka, Jenne, Jennee, Jenney, Jennia, Jennier, Jennita, Jennora, Jensine

Jennifer (Celtic) white wave
Gennefur, Ginnifer, Jen, Jenefer, Jenife, Jenifer, Jeniferr, Jeniffer, Jenipher, Jenn, Jenna, Jennae, Jennafer, Jennefer, Jenni, Jenniffe, Jenniffer, Jenniffier, Jennifier, Jenniphe, Jennipher, Jenniphur, Jenny, Jennyfer, Jennypher

Jennings (Last name as first name) pretty
Jen, Jenny

Jennis (American) white; patient
J, Jay, Jen, Jenace, Jenice, Jenis, Jenn, Jennice

Jennison (American) form of Jennifer: white wave
Gennison, Jenison, Jennisyn, Jenson

Jenny (English) form of Jennifer: white wave
Jen, Jenae, Jeni, Jenjen, Jenney, Jenni, Jennie, Jennye, Jeny, Jinny

Jennys (American) white

Jeno (Greek) heavenly

Jenova (Italian) form of Genoa: playful

Jensen (Scandinavian) athletic

Jenvie (American) lovely
Jennvey, Jenvee, Jenvy

Jenz (Scandinavian) feminine form of Johannes: God is gracious
Jen, Jens

Jeolle (American) fair

Jerdin (English) grows a garden

Jeredine (English) grows a garden

Jerett (English) rules well

Jergen (Dutch) earthy

Jeri (American) hopeful
Geri, Jere, Jerhie, Jerree, Jerri, Jerry, Jerrye

Jeriesha (Biblical) owned

Jerikah (American) sparkling
Jereca, Jerecka, Jeree, Jeri, Jerica, Jerik, Jeriko, Jerrica, Jerry

Jerin (American) daring
Jere, Jeren, Jeron, Jerinn, Jerun

Jerina (Slavic) loyal

Jermaina (American) form of
Germaine: important

Jermaine (French) form of
Germaine: important
Jermain, Jerman, Jermane, Jermanee, Jermani, Jermany, Jermayne

Jernina (English) form of
Jemima: dove-like

Jeroen (Scandinavian) strong

Jerrett (American) spirited
Jerett, Jeriette, Jerre, Jerret, Jerrette, Jerrie, Jerry

Jerrica (American) free spirit
Jerrika

Jerusha (Hebrew) wealthy

Jesa (Indian) flowers

Jesaren (English) form of Jessie:
casual

Jesenia (Spanish) witty
Jesene, Jess, Jessenia, Jessie, Jisenia, Yesenia

Jessa (American) spontaneous
Jessah

Jessamine (French) form of
Jasmine: fragrant; sweet
Jesamyn, Jess, Jessamin, Jessamon, Jessamy, Jessamyn, Jessemin, Jessemine, Jessie, Jessmine, Jessmon, Jessmy, Jessmyn

Jesse (Hebrew) friendly
Jesie, Jessey, Jessi, Jessy

Jessenia (Arabic) flowering
Jescenia, Jesenia

Jessica ✪ (Hebrew) rich
Jesica, Jess, Jessa, Jessie, Jessika, Jessy, Jezika

Jessie (Scottish) casual
Jescie, Jesey, Jess, Jesse, Jessee, Jessi, Jessye

Jessika (Hebrew) rich
Jesika, Jessieka, Jessyka, Jezika

Jesusa (Spanish) loves Jesus;
feminine form of Jesus: saved by
God

Jesusita (Spanish) little Jesus

Jett (American) high-flying
Jettie, Jetty

Jetta (English) black gem;
knowing
Jette, Jettie

Jette (Dutch) black as coal
Jet, Jeta, Jetia, Jetta, Jette, Jettee, Jettie

Jeudi (French) born on Thursday

Jeune-Fille (French) young girl

Jevae (Spanish) desired
Jevaie, Jevay

Jevonne (African American) kind
Jev, Jevaughan, Jevaughn, Jevie, Jevon, Jevona, Jevonn, Jevvy

Jewel (French) pretty
Jeul, Jewelia, Jewelie, Jewell, Jewelle, Jewels, Juel, Jule

Jewelina (Spanish) jewel

Jezana (Slavic) womanly

Jezbelline (Spanish) form of
Jezebel: wanton woman

Jeze (Biblical) form of Jezebel:
wanton woman

Jezebel (Hebrew) wanton
woman
Jessabel, Jessebel, Jessebelle, Jez, Jezabel, Jezabella, Jezabelle, Jeze, Jezebell, Jezel, Jezell, Jezybel, Jezzie

Jezenya (American) flowering
Jesenya, Jeze, Jezey

Jhamesha (African American)
lovely; soft
Jamesha, Jmesha

Jharna (Hindi) springtime

Jhonsi (Scandinavian) feminine
form of John: God is gracious

Jianna (Italian) trusts in God
Jiana, Jianina, Jianine

Jigna (Hindi) intellectual

Jignasa (Hindi) curious

Jila (American) energetic; young

Jilan (American) mover
Jillan, Jillyn, Jilyn, Jylan, Jylann

Jilana (Slavic) moon child

Jilen (American) young girl

Jill (English) form of Jillian:
youthful
Jil, Jilee, Jilli, Jillie, Jilly

Jillaine (Latin) young-hearted
*Jilaine, Jilane, Jilayne, Jillana,
Jillane, Jillann, Jillanne, Jillayne*

Jilleen (American) energetic
*Jil, Jileen, Jilene, Jiline, Jill, Jillain,
Jilline, Jlynn*

Jillian (Latin) youthful
*Giliana, Jill, Jillaine, Jillana,
Jillena, Jilliane, Jilliann, Jillie,
Jillion, Jillione, Jilly, Jilyan*

Jillit (English) form of Jillian:
youthful

Jills (Scandinavian) young

Jillyn (American) high-energy;
young

Jimi (Hebrew) replaces; reliable
Jimae

Jimmi (American) assured
Jayjay, Jim, Jimi, Jimice

Jimmye (English) replaces; in
pain

Jimye (English) replaces; in pain

Jin (Chinese) golden; gem
Jinn, Jinny

Jina (Italian) form of Gina:
wellborn
*Jena, Jinae, Jinan, Jinda, Jinna,
Jinnae*

Jinger (American) form of
Ginger: ginger plant
Jin, Jinge

Jini (American) form of Jenny:
white wave

Jinkie (American) bouncy
Jinkee, Jinky, Jynki

Jinny (Scottish) form of Jenny:
white wave
*Jin, Jina, Jinae, Jinelle, Jinessa,
Jinna, Jinnae, Jinnalee, Jinnee,
Jinney, Jinni, Jinnie*

Jinte (Hindi) patient

Jinx (Latin) a spell
Jin, Jinks, Jinxie, Jinxy, Jynx

Jinxia (Latin) form of Jinx: a
spell
Jynx, Jynxia

Jirina (Czech) works the earth

Jisola (African) affluent

Jitendea (Indian) good

Jnae (American) darling
Jenae, J'Nay, Jnay, Jnaye

J'Neane (American) form of
Jeannine: peace-loving

J'Netta (American) form of
Jeanetta: impish
J'netta, J'Nette, Janetta, Janny

J-Nyl (American) flirtatious

Jo (American) form of Josephine:
blessed
Joey, Jojo

Joan (Hebrew) heroine; God-
loving
*Joane, Joane, Joani, Joanie, Joanni,
Joannie, Jonie*

Joana (Hebrew) kind
Joanah, Joanna, Joannah, Jonah

Joanie (Hebrew) kind
*Joanney, Joanni, Joannie, Joanny,
Joany, Joni*

Jo-Ann (French) believer;
gregarious
*Joahnn, JoAn, JoAnn, Joann,
Joanna, Joanne, Jo-Anne, Joannie*

Joanna (English) kind
*Jo, Joana, Joananna, Joananne,
Joandra, Joannah, Joeanna,
Johannah, Josie*

Joanne (English) form of Joan:
heroine; God-loving
*JoAnn, Joann, Jo-Ann, JoAnne,
Joeanne*

Joannie (Hebrew) forgiving
Joani, Joanney, Joanni, Joany

Joappa (Origin unknown) noisy

Joaquina (Spanish) form of Joaquin: God helps

Jobi (Hebrew) misunderstood; inventive
Jobee, Jobey, Jobie, Joby

Jobina (Hebrew) hurting
Jobey, Jobie, Joby, Jobye, Jobyna

Jobine (Biblical) friend

Jocasta (Italian) light

Jocelyn ✪ (Latin) joyful
Jocelie, Jocelin, Jocelle, Jocelyne, Jocelynn, Joci, Joclyn, Joclynn, Jocylan, Jocylen, Joycelyn

Jochebal (Biblical) glory to God

Joci (Latin) happy
Jocee, Jocey, Jocie, Jocy, Josi

Jocosa (Latin) laughs; jokes

Jocquice (French) blessed

Jodase (American) brilliant
Jo, Jodace, Jodasse, Jodie, Jody

Jode (American) form of Jodie: happy girl

Jodie (American) happy girl
Jo, Jodee, Jodey, Jodi, Jody

Joedy (American) jolly
Joedey, Joedi, Joedie

Joelle (Hebrew) willing
Jo, Joel, Joela, Joele, Joelee, Joeleen, Joelene, Joeli, Joeline, Joell, Joella, Joelle, Joellen, Joelly

Joelly (American) kindhearted
Joelee, Joeli, Joely

Joely (Hebrew) believer; lively
Jo, Joe, Joey

Joey (American) easygoing
Joe, Joeye

Joezee (American) form of Josey: blessed
Jo, Joe, Joes, Joezey, Joezy

Johanna (German) believer in a gracious God
Johana, Johanah, Jonna

Johnay (American) steadfast
Johnae, Jonay, Jonaye, Jonnay

Johnette (Hebrew) feminine form of John: God is gracious

Johnica (American) feminine form of John: God is gracious
Jonica

Johnna (American) upright
Jahna, John, Johna, Johnae, Jonna, Jonnie

Johnnell (American) happy
Johnelle, Jonell, Jonnel

Johnnetta (American) joyful
Johneta, Johnete, Johnetta, Johnette, Jonetta, Jonette, Jonietta

Johnnisha (African American) steady
Johnisha, Johnnita, Johnny, Jonnisha

Johnson (Last name as first name) confident
Johns

Johntell (African American) sweet
Johna, Johntal, Johntel, Johntelle, Jontell

Johntria (Hebrew) believer

Johppa (Origin unknown) different
Johppah

Joi (Latin) joyful
Joicy, Joie, Jojo, Joy

Joice (American) form of Joyce: joyous

Joji (English) form of JoJo: joyful

Jo-Kiesha (African American) vibrant
Joekiesha

Jola (Greek) violet flower

Jolan (Latin) violet

Jolanda (Italian) a violet flower
Jola, Jolan, Jolana, Jolande, Jolander, Jolane, Jolanka, Jolantha, Jolanthe, Joli

Jolanta (Greek) lovely girl

Jolene (American) jolly
Jo, Joeleane, Joeleen, Joelene, Joelynn, Joleen, Joleene, Jolen, Jolena, Joley, Jolie, Joline, Jolyn, Jolynn

Joletta (American) happy-go-lucky
Jaletta, Jolette, Joley, Joli, Jolie, Jolitta

Jolia (English) joyful girl

Jolie (French) pretty
Jo, Jole, Jolea, Jolee, Joleigh, Joley, Joli, Jollee, Jollie, Jolly, Joly

Jolienne (American) pretty
Joliane, Jolianne, Jolien, Jolina, Joline

Jolina (English) joyful girl

Joline (English) blessed

Jolivette (French) jubilant

Jolly (English) jolly

Jolyane (American) sweetheart
Joliane, Jollyane, Jolyan, Jolyann, Jolyanne

Jomonia (American) loyal

Jona (English) peaceful

JonBenet (French) with God's benediction

Jones (American) saucy

Jonette (American) peaceful

Joni (American) form of Joan: heroine; God-loving
Joanie, Jonie, Jony

Jonica (American) sweet soul

Jonice (American) casual
Joneece, Joneese, Jonise, Jonni

Jonille (English) believer

Jonina (Hebrew) sweetheart
Jona, Jonika, Joniqua, Jonita, Jonnina

Jonita (Hebrew) pretty little one
Janita, Jonati, Jonit, Jonite, Jonta, Jontae

Jonna (Scandinavian) believer
Johnna

Jonquill (American) flower
Jonn, Jonque, Jonquie, Jonquil, Jonquille

Jontelle (American) musical
Jahntelle, Jontaya, Jontel, Jontell, Jontia, Jontlyl

Joone (American) form of June: born in June
Joon

Jophery (American) feminine form of Christopher: the bearer of Christ

Joplin (Last name as first name) wild girl

Jorah (Hebrew) fresh as rain
Jora

Jordan ⚬ ❶ (Hebrew) excellent descendant
Johrdon, Jordaine, Jordane, Jorden, Jordenne, Jordeyn, Jordi, Jordie, Jordin, Jordon, Jordyn, Jordynne, Joudane, Jourdan

Jordana (Hebrew) smart; departs; lonely
Giordanna, Jordain, Jordane, Jordann, Jordanna, Jordanne, Jordannuh, Jorden, Jordenne, Jordi, Jordin, Jordine, Jordon, Jordona, Jordonna, Jordyn, Jordyne, Jori, Jorie, Jourdana, Jourdann, Jourdanna, Jourdanne

Jordy (American) quick
Jordee, Jordey, Jordi, Jordie, Jorey

Jorene (American) wanted

Joretta (English) wanted; pretty girl

Jorgina (Spanish) nurturing
Georgeena, Georgina, Jorge, Jorgi, Jorgie, Jorgine, Jorgy

Jorie (Hebrew) form of Jordan: excellent descendant
Joree, Jorey, Jorhee, Jorhie, Jori, Jorre, Jorrey, Jorri, Jory

Jorja (American) smart
Georgia, Jorge, Jorgia, Jorgie, Jorgy

Jorunn (American) loved by God

Josany (American) joyful girl

Joscelin (Latin) happy girl
Josceline, Joscelyn, Joscelyne, Joscelynn, Joscelynne, Joselin, Joseline, Joselyn, Joselyne, Joselynn, Joselynne, Joshlyn

Josee (American) delights
Joesee, Joesell, Joesette, Joselle, Josette, Josey, Josi, Josiane, Josiann, Josianne, Josielina, Josina, Josy, Jozee, Jozelle, Jozette, Jozie

Josefat (Spanish) feminine form of Joseph: he will add
Fata, Fina, Josef, Josefa, Josefana, Josefenna, Josefita, Joseva, Josey, Josie

Josefina (Hebrew) fertile
Jose, Josephina, Josey, Josie

Joselita (Spanish) joyful girl

Joselito (Spanish) joyful girl

Joselyn (German) pretty
Josalene, Joselene, Joseline, Josey, Josiline, Josilyn, Joslyn, Josselen, Josseline, Josselyne, Josslyn, Josslynn, Josylynn

Josephine (French) blessed
Fena, Fifi, Fina, Jo, Joes, Josefina, Josephene, Josie, Jozaphine

Josetta (French) she trusts in God

Josette (French) little Josephine

Josey (American) form of Josephine: blessed
Josee, Josi, Josie, Jozie

Josezaldy (Spanish) joyful girl

Joshi (Hebrew) God loves

Joshlyn (Latin) saved by God
Joshalin, Joshalyn, Joshalynn, Joshalynne, Joshann, Joshanna, Joshanne, Joshleen, Joshlene, Joshlin, Joshline, Joshlyne, Joshlynn, Joshlynne

Josie (American) thrills
Josee, Josey, Josi, Josy, Josye

Josien (American) joy

Josilin (Latin) form of Jocelyn: joyful
Josielina, Josiline, Josilyn, Josilyne, Josilynn, Josilynne, Joslin, Josline, Joslyn, Joslyne, Joslynn, Joslynne

Joslyn (Latin) jocular
Joclyn, Joslene, Joslinn, Josslin, Josslyn, Josslynn

Jossalin (Latin) form of Jocelyn: joyful
Jossaline, Jossalyn, Jossalynn, Jossalynne, Josseline, Jossellen, Jossellin, Jossellyn, Josselyn, Josselyne, Josselynn, Josselynne, Jossie, Josslin, Jossline, Josslyn, Josslyne, Josslynn, Josslynne

Jostin (American) adorable
Josten, Jostun, Josty, Jostyn

Joubyne (American) joy

Joudn (American) diplomatic
Joy

Jour (French) day

Jourbine (French) doer

Journey (Word as name) adventurer

Jovan (Slavic) feminine form of John: God is gracious

Jovana (Slavic) feminine form of John: God is gracious

Jovannah (Latin) regal
Jeovana, Jeovanna, Jouvan, Jouvanna, Jovan, Jovana, Jovanee, Jovani, Jovanie, Jovann, Jovanna, Jovanne, Jovannie, Jovena, Jovon, Jovonna, Jovonne, Jowanna

Joverne (Slavic) challenges

Jovernita (Slavic) challenges

Jovi (Latin) jovial

Jovita (Latin) glad
Joveeda, Joveeta, Jovena, Joveta, Jovetta, Jovi, Jovida, Jovie, Jovina, Jo-Vita, Jovitta, Jovy

Jowannah (American) happy
Jowanna, Jowanne, Jowonna

Joy (Latin) joyful
Joi, Joie, Joya, Joye

Joyalle (American) joy

Joyce (Latin) joyous
Joice, Joy, Joycey, Joyci, Joycie, Joysel

Joyceen (American) form of Joyce: joyous

Joycela (American) form of
Joyce: joyous
Joycey (American) form of Joyce:
joyous
Joyous (American) joyful
Joy, Joyus
Joyria (American) of the Lord
Joyslyn (American) form of
Jocelyn: joyful
Joycelyn, Joyslin, Joyslinn
Joysteen (American) joy
Jozel (American) joy
Jualle (American) young girl
Juandali (African) believer
Juanisha (African American)
delightful
Juanesha, Juaneshia, Juannisha
Juanita (Spanish) believer in a
gracious God; forgiving
*Juan, Juana, Juaneta, Juanika,
Juanna, Juanne, Juannie, Juanny,
Wanita*
Juanitra (Spanish) ill-fated
Juba (Hebrew) ram; strong-willed
Jubal (Biblical) flowing
Jubilant
Jubelka (African American)
jubilant
Jube, Jubi, Jubie
Jubilee (Hebrew) jubilant
Jubalie

Jubini (American) grateful;
jubilant
Jubi, Jubine
Jucinda (American) relishing life
Jucin, Jucindah, Jucinde
Judalon (Hebrew) merry
Judalonn, Juddalone, Judelon
Jude (French) confident
Judde, Judea, Judee
Judit (Hebrew) Jewish
Jude, Judi, Juditt
Judith (Hebrew) woman worthy
of praise
*Judana, Jude, Judi, Judie, Judine,
Juditha, Judy, Judyth, Judythe*
Judy (Hebrew) form of Judith:
woman worthy of praise
Joodie, Jude, Judi, Judie, Judye
Juel (American) dependable
Jewel, Juelle, Juels, Juile, Jule
Jueta (Scandinavian) form of
Judith: woman worthy of praise
Juetta, Juta
Juiby (Asian) flower girl
Juirl (American) careful
Ju, Juirll
Jula (American) form of Julia:
forever young
Juleen (American) sensual
Jule, Julene, Jules

Julenett (American) form of
Julia: forever young
Jules (American) brooding
Jewels, Juels
Juleva (Spanish) young
Julia ○ ● (Latin) forever young
*Jula, Juliann, Julica, Julina,
Juline, Julisa, Julissa, Julya, Julyssa*
Julian (Latin) effervescent
*Jewelian, Julean, Juliann, Julien,
Juliene, Julienn, Julyun*
Juliana (Latin) youthful; Jove's
child
*Juleanna, Julianna, Juliannah,
Julie-Anna, Jullyana*
Julice (American) feminine form
of Julius: attractive
Julie (English) young and vocal
*Juel, Jule, Julee, Juli, Juliene,
Jullie, July, Julye*
Juliet (Italian) loving
Juliette (French) romantic
Julie, Jules, Juliet, Julietta
Juling (American) form of Julia:
forever young
Julisan (American) young
Julissa (Latin) universally loved
Jula, Julessa, Julisa, Julisha
Julita (Spanish) adorable; young
Juli, Julitte

Juliza (Latin) form of Julia: forever young

Julo (American) form of Julia: forever young

Juluette (American) adorable; young
Jule, Jules, Julett, Julette, Julie, Julu, Julue, Juluett, Julu-Ette, LuLu

July (Latin) month; warm

Jumoke (African) most popular

Jun (Chinese) honest

Jundt (Scandinavian) hopeful

June (Latin) born in June
Juneth, Juney, Junie, Junieth, Juny

Junelle (American) form of June: born in June

Junia (Biblical) warm

Junieth (Latin) from the month June; heavenly
Juney, Juni, Junie, Juniethe

Junko (American) form of June: born in June

Juno (Latin) queenly
Juna, June

Juntese (American) form of June: born in June

Juokaka (Asian) pure

Juqwanza (African American) bouncy
Jukwanza, Juqwann, Qwanza

Juraj (American) moves fast

Jurgan (Scandinavian)

Jus (American) fair

Justice (Latin) fair-minded
Just, Justise, Justy

Justika (American) dancing-girl
Justeeka, Justica, Justie, Justy

Justille (American) fair

Justina (Latin) honest
Jestena, Jestina, Justeena, Justena, Justinna, Justyna

Justinan (American) fair

Justine (Latin) fair; upright
Jestine, Justa, Juste, Justean, Justeen, Justena, Justene, Justi, Justie, Justina, Justinn, Justinna, Justy, Justyne, Justynn, Justynne, Juzteen

Jutta (American) ebullient
Juta

Juttah (Biblical) place name

Juturna (Mythology) trickling water

Juvelia (Spanish) young
Juvee, Juvelle, Juvelya, Juvie, Juvilia, Velia, Velya

Juven (Mythology) young girl

Juwanne (African American) lively
Juwan, Juwann, Juwanna, Juwon, Jwanna, Jwanne

Jyneice (American) form of Janeese: devout; enthusiastic

Jyneisce (American) form of Janeese: devout; enthusiastic

Jynx (American) form of Jinx: a spell

Jyoti (Indian) bright light

Jyotsna (Indian) moonlight

Jzquelyn (Slavic) form of Jacqueline: supplanter; substitute

Kacey (Irish) daring
Casey, Casie, K.C., K.Cee, Kace, Kacee, Kaci, Kacy, Kasey, Kasie, Kaycee, Kaycie, Kaysie

Kachina (Native American) sacred dancer; doll-like
Cachina, Kachena, Kachine

Kacia (Greek) form of Acacia: everlasting; tree
Kaycia, Kaysia

Kacondra (African American) bold
Condra, Connie, Conny, Kacon, Kacond, Kaecondra, Kakondra, Kaycondra

Kaden (American) charismatic
Caden, Kadenn

Kadenza (Latin) cadence; dances
Cadenza, Kadena, Kadence

Kadie (American) virtuous
Kadee

Kady (English) sassy
Cady, K.D., Kadee, Kadie, Kaydie,
Kaydy

Kaela (Arabic) sweet
Kaelah, Kayla, Kaylah, Keyla,
Keylah

Kaelin (Irish) pure; impetuous
Kaelan, Kaelen, Kaelinn, Kaelyn,
Kaelynn, Kaelynne, Kaylin

Kagan (American) form of
Keagan: melodious

Kai (Hawaiian) the sea
Kaia

Kailah (Greek) virtuous
Kail, Kala, Kalae, Kalah

Kaileen (American) sweet

Kailey (American) spunky
Kaili, Kailie, Kaylee, Kaylei

Kaimi (American) form of
Cammy: wonderful

Kairen (French) pure heart

Kaitlin ⚙ (Irish) purehearted
Caitlin, Caitlyn, Kaitlan,
Kaitland, Kaitlinn, Kaitlyn,
Kaitlynn, Kalyn, Katelyn,
Katelynn, Katelynne, Kathlin,
Kathlinne, Kathlyn

Kaiulania (Hawaiian) sea and
heavens

Kajasa (Asian) forgiving

Kakay (American) pure

Kakiesta (Hawaiian) unblemished

Kala (Hindi) black; royal

Kalan (American) celestial

Kalani (Hawaiian) leader
Kalauni, Kaloni, Kaylanie

Kalavati (Indian) creates

Kalb (German) willful

Kalea (Arabic) sweet
Kahlea, Kahleah, Kailea, Kaileah,
Kallea, Kalleah, Kaylea, Kayleah,
Khalea, Khaleah

Kalei (American) sweetheart
Kahlei, Kailei, Kallei, Kaylei,
Khalei

Kaleigh (Sanskrit) energetic; dark
Kalea

Kalele (Hawaiian) pure

Kalena (Hawaiian) chaste
Kaleena

Kalet (French) beautiful energy
Kalay, Kalaye

Kaley (Sanskrit) energetic
Kalee, Kaleigh, Kalleigh

Kali (Greek) beauty
Kala, Kalli

Kalidas (Greek) most beautiful
Kaleedus, Kali

Kalila (Arabic) sweet; lovable
Cailey, Cailie, Caylie, Kailey,
Kaililah, Kaleah, Kalela, Kalie,
Kalilah, Kaly, Kay, Kaykay, Kaylee,
Kayllie, Kyle, Kylila, Kylilah

Kalina (Hawaiian) unblemished
Kalinna, Kalynna

Kalinda (Hindi) mythical
mountains; goal-oriented
Kaleenda, Kalindi, Kalynda,
Kalyndi

Kalindee (Indian) river
Kalindi

Kaliyan (Southeast Asian)
excellent

Kallan (American) loving
Kall, Kallen, Kallun

Kallie (Greek) beautiful
Callie, Kali, Kalie, Kalley, Kally

Kalliope (Greek) beautiful voice
Calli, Calliope, Kalli, Kallyope

Kallista (Greek) pretty; bright-eyed
Cala, Calesta, Calista, Callie, Callista, Cally, Kala, Kalesta, Kalista, Kalli, Kallie, Kally, Kallysta, Kalysta

Kalota (Hawaiian) vivacious

Kalpana (Indian) dream

Kalyana (Indian) lucky

Kalyani (Indian) lucky
Kalni

Kalyn (Arabic) loved
Calynn, Calynne, Kaelyn, Kaelynn, Kalen, Kalin, Kalinn, Kallyn

Kama (Sanskrit) beloved; Hindu god of love
Kam, Kamie

Kamala (American) interesting; (Arabic) perfection
Camala, Kam, Kamalah, Kamali, Kamilla, Kammy

Kamaria (African) moonlike
Kamara, Kamaarie

Kambria (Latin) girl from Wales
Kambra, Kambrie, Kambriea, Kambry

Kambrin (American) form of Cambria: the people

Kamea (Hawaiian) precious darling; adored
Cammi, Kam, Kameo, Kammie

Kameko (Japanese) turtle girl; hides

Kamela (Italian) form of Camilla: wonderful
Kam, Kamila, Kammy

Kameron (American) form of Cameron: popular; crooked nose
Cam, Cami, Cammie, Kamreen, Kamrin, Kamren, Kamron

Kamethia (American) divine

Kami (Italian) spiritual little one; (Japanese) perfect aura
Cami, Cammie, Cammy, Kammie, Kammy

Kamiah (Slavic) form of Kamila: desires

Kamilah (Hindi) desires; (North African) perfect
Kamila, Kamilla, Kamillah

Kamilia (Polish) perfect character; pure
Kam, Kamila, Kammy, Milla

Kamini (Indian) woman

Kamna (Indian) desired

Kamoya (Asian) focused

Kamyra (American) light
Kamera

Kanaka (Indian) golden child

Kanara (Hebrew) tiny bird; lithe
Kanarit, Kanarra

Kanda (Native American) magical

Kandace (Greek) charming; glowing
Candace, Candie, Candy, Dacie, Kandi, Kandice, Kandiss, Kandy

Kandi (American) form of Kandace: charming; glowing
Candi, Kandie, Kandy

Kandra (American) light
Candra

Kanear (American) talented

Kaneesha (American) dark-skinned
Caneesha, Kaneesh, Kaneice, Kaneisha, Kanesha, Kaneshia, Kaney, Kanish, Nesha

Kanel (Spanish) yellow hair

Kanesha (African American) spontaneous
Kaneesha, Kaneeshia, Kaneisha, Kanisha, Kannesha

Kanga (Australian) form of kangaroo: jumpy

Kanik (Egyptian) darkness

Kanisha (American) pretty
Kaneesha, Kanicia, Kenisha, Kinicia, Kinisha, Koneesha

Kannitha (Vietnamese) angelic

Kanoa (Hawaiian) freedom

Kansas (Place name) U.S. state
Kanny

Kanthi (Asian) angelic

Kanti (Indian) lovely

Kanya (Hindi) virginal
Kania

Kaori (Asian) free

Kaprece (American) capricious
Caprice, Kapp, Kappy, Kapreece,
Kapri, Kaprise, Kapryce, Karpreese

Kapuki (African) first girl in the
family

Kara (Danish) form of Cara:
beloved friend
Carina, Carita, Kar, Karah, Kari,
Karie, Karina, Karine, Karita,
Karrah, Karrie, Kera

Karbie (American) energetic
Karbi, Karby

Karelle (French) joyful singer
Carel, Carelle, Karel

Karen (Greek/Irish) purehearted
Caren, Carin, Caron, Caronn,
Carren, Carrin, Carron, Carryn,
Caryn, Carynn, Carynne, Kare,
Kareen, Karenna, Kari, Karin,
Karina, Karna, Karon, Karron,
Karryn, Karyn, Keren, Kerran,
Kerrin, Kerron, Kerrynn, Keryn,
Kerynne, Taran, Taren, Taryn

Karenina (Literature) purest

Karenz (English) form of
Kerensa: lovable
Karence, Karens, Karense

Karhime (Arabic) giving

Kari (Scandinavian) pure
Cari, Karri, Karrie, Karry

Kariah (American) form of
Mariah: sorrowful singer

Karian (American) daring
Kerian

Karianne (Scandinavian) pure
Kariane, Kariann, Kari-Ann,
Karianna, Kerianne

Karida (Arabic) pure
Kareeda, Karita

Karima (Arabic) giving
Kareema, Kareemah, Kareima,
Kareimah, Karimah

Karin (Scandinavian) kindhearted
Karen, Karine, Karinne

Karina (Russian) form of Karen:
purehearted
Kare, Karinda, Karine, Karinna,
Karrie, Karrina, Karyna

Karine (Russian) pure
Kaarrine, Karryne, Karyne

Karineh (Italian) form of
Chiarina: clear

Karise (Greek) graceful woman
Karis, Karisse, Karyce

Karissa (Greek) longsuffering
Carissa, Karessa, Karisa

Karitina (Spanish) pure

Karizma (African) hopeful
Karisma

Karla (German) well-loved
Carla, Karlah, Karlie, Karlla,
Karrla

Karlea (German) form of Karla:
well-loved

Karlee (Slavic) form of Karla:
well-loved

Karlin (American) winning;
daring

Karlotta (German) form of
Charlotte: little woman
Karlota, Karlotte, Lotta, Lottee,
Lottey, Lottie

Karly (German) womanly;
strength
Carly, Karlee, Karlie, Karlye

Karma (Hindi) destined for good
things
Karm, Karmie, Karmy

Karmel (Hebrew) garden
Carmel, Karmela, Karmelle

Karmen (Hebrew) loving songs
Carmen, Karmin, Karmine

Karmiaso (Italian) garden girl

Karmilita (Spanish) form of
Carmelita: in the garden

Karmille (Spanish) form of
Carmel: garden

Karmit (Native American) nature

Karnesha (American) spicy
Carnesha, Karnisha, Karny

Karnit (American) gem

Karolina (Polish) form of
Caroline: little; womanly
*Karaline, Karalyn, Karalynna,
Karalynne, Karla, Karleen,
Karlen, Karlena, Karlene, Karli,
Karlie, Karlina, Karlinka, Karo,
Karolinka, Karolline, Karolyn,
Karolyna, Karolyne, Karolynn,
Karolynne, Leena, Lina, Lyna*

Karoline (German) feminine
form of Karl: forceful
*Kare, Karola, Karolah, Karolina,
Lina*

Karolyn (American) friendly
*Carolyn, Kara, Karal, Karalyn,
Karilynne, Karolynn*

Karre (English) form of Carrie:
womanly; little

Karri (American) form of Karen:
purehearetd
Kari, Karie, Karrie, Karry

Karrington (Last name as first
name) admired
Carrington, Kare, Karring

Karryoun (American) form of
Caroline: little; womanly

Karuenne (American) sweetness

Karwa (African) independent

Karwanna (African) independent

Karwey (African) independent

Karyn (American) sweet
Caren, Karen

Karynn (English) pure

Kasalya (Indian) clever

Kasandrae (English) shines

Kasandrah (English) shines

Kascade (Italian) water

Kasey (American) spirited
Casey, Kacey, Kasie, Kaysie

Kasha (Greek) form of Katherine:
pure

Kashmir (Place name) a region
near India and Pakistan; fertile
*Cashmere, Cashmir, Kash,
Kashmere*

Kashonda (African American)
dramatic
Kashanda, Kashawnda, Koshonda

Kashondra (African American)
bright
*Kachanne, Kachaundra, Kachee,
Kashandra, Kashawndra, Kashee,
Kashon, Kashondrah, Kashondre,
Kashun*

Kasi (American) form of Cassie:
insightful
Kass, Kassi, Kassie

Kasia (Polish) form of Katarzyna:
creative

Kasmira (Slavic) peacemaker

Kassandra (Greek) capricious
*Cassandra, Kass, Kasandra,
Kassandrah, Kassie*

Kassidy (Irish) clever
*Cassidy, Cassir, Kasadee, Kass,
Kassie, Kassy, Kassydi*

Kassie (American) clever
Kassee, Kassi, Kassy

Kat (American) outrageous
Cat

Katalin (American) pure heart;
smart

Katana (English) form of Catina:
pure

Kataniya (Hebrew) little girl

Katarina (Greek) pure
*Katareena, Katarena, Katarinna,
Kataryna, Katerina, Katryna*

Katarzyna (Origin unknown)
creative
Katarzina

Katchen (Greek) virtuous
Kat, Katshen

Katchi (American) sassy
*Catshy, Cotchy, Kat, Kata, Katchie,
Kati, Katshi, Katshie, Katshy,
Katty, Kotchee, Kotchi, Kotchie*

Kate (Greek) form of Katherine: pure
Cait, Caitie, Cate, Catee, Catey, Catie, Kait, Kaite, Kaitlin, Katee, Katey, Kathe, Kati, Katie, Katy, Kay-Kay

Katelyn ○ (Irish) purehearted
Caitlin, Kaitlyn, Kaitlynne, Kat, Katelin, Katelynn, Kate-Lynn, Katline, Katy

Katera (Origin unknown) celebrant
Katara, Katura

Katherine ○ (Greek) pure
Kat, Katharin, Katharine, Katherin, Kathy, Kathyrn, Katwin, Kaykay

Kathlaya (American) fashionable

Kathleen (Irish) brilliant; unflawed
Cathaleen, Cathaline, Cathleen, Kathaleen, Kathaleya, Kathaleyna, Kathaline, Kathelina, Katheline, Kathie, Kathlene, Kathlin, Kathline, Kathlyn, Kathlynn, Kathy

Kathryn (English) powerful and pure
Kathreena, Kathren, Kathrene, Kathrin, Kathrine, Kathryne

Kathy (English/Irish) form of Katherine: pure
Cathie, Cathy, Kath, Kathe, Kathee, Kathey, Kathi, Kathie

Katia (French) stylish
Kateeya, Kati, Katya

Katie (English) lively
Kat, Kate, Katy, Kay, Kaykay, Kaytie

Katina (American) form of Katrina: melodious
Kat, Kateen, Kateena

Katlynn (Greek) pure
Kat, Katlinn, Katlyn

Katrice (American) graceful
Katreese, Katrese, Katrie, Katrisse, Katry

Katrina (German) melodious
Catreena, Catreina, Catrina, Kaitrina, Katreena, Katreina, Katryna, Kay, Ketreina, Ketrina, Ketryna

Katrine (German/Polish) form of Kate: pure
Catrene, Kati, Katrene, Katrinna

Katy (English) lively
Cady, Katie, Kattee, Kattie, Kaytee

Kau (Indian) princess
Kaur

Kaulana (Hawaiian) well-known girl
Kaula, Kauna, Kahuna

Kaulene (American) famed

Kavinli (American) feminine form of Kevin: pretty; gentle
Cavin, Kaven, Kavin, Kavinlee, Kavinley, Kavinly

Kavita (Hindi) poem
Kaveta, Kavitah

Kavitha (Indian) poetic
Kavita

Kawana (African) certain

Kay (Latin/Welsh) happy; rejoicing
Cay, Caye, Kaye, Kaykay

Kaya (Native American) intelligent
Kaja, Kayia

Kaycie (American) merrymaker
CayCee, K.C., Kaycee, Kayci, Kaysie

Kaydence (American) in cadence

Kayla ○ ◑ (Greek) pure
Cala, Cayla, Caylie, Kala, Kaela, Kaila, Kaylah, Kaylyn, Keyla

Kaylan (Irish) form of Caitlin: virginal

Kaylee ○ ◑ (American) open
Cayley, Kaelie, Kaylea, Kaylie, Kayleigh

Kayleen (Hebrew/American) sweet
Kaileen, Kalene, Kay, Kaykay, Kaylean, Kayleene

Kayley (Irish) form of Kaylee: open
Caleigh, Cayleigh, Cayley, Kaeleigh, Kailee, Kaileigh, Kailey, Kaili, Kaleigh, Kaley, Kaylea, Kaylee, Kaylie, Kaylleigh, Kaylley

Kaylin (American) form of Kaylee: open
Kailyn, Kaylan, Kaylanne, Kaylen, Kaylinn, Kaylyn, Kaylynn, Kaylynne

Kaylina (English) slim girl

Kaylon (Hebrew) crowned
Kalonn, Kaylan, Kaylen, Kayln, Kaylond, Kaylun

Kayterly (American) delightful

Kazuya (Asian) lovely

Keahs (Unknown) optimist

Keane (American) keen
Kanee, Keanie, Keany, Keen

Keani (Asian) bold

Keanna (American) curious
Keana, Keannah

Keara (Irish) darkness
Kearia, Kearra, Keera, Keerra, Keira, Keirra, Kera, Kiara, Kiarra, Kiera, Kierra

Kearney (Irish) winning
Kearne, Kearni, KeKe, Kerney

Keatha (American) feminine form of Keith: witty

Kechia (African) determined

Kecia (American) focused

Keekee (American) dancing
Keakea, Kee-Kee

Keeley (Irish) noisy
Kealey, Kealy, Keeley, Keeli, Keelia, Keelie, Keely, Keighley, Keighly, Keili, Keilie, Keylee, Keyley, Keylie, Keylley, Keyllie

Keelian (Irish) pretty

Keena (Irish) courageous
Keenya, Kina

Keenan (Irish) small
Keanan, Keen, Keeny

Keesee (American) joyous

Kefira (Hebrew) lioness
Kefeera, Kefeira, Kefirah, Kefirra

Kehohtee (Invented) alternate spelling for Quixote

Kei (Japanese) respectful

Keidra (American) form of Kendra: ingenious
Kedra, Keydra

Keija (Slavic) rapport

Keiki (Hawaiian) child

Keiko (Hawaiian) child of joy
Kei

Keila (Hebrew) crowned
Keilah

Keilani (Hawaiian) graceful leader
Kei, Lani, Lanie

Keira (Irish) dark-skinned
Keera, Kera

Keisha (American) dark-eyed
Keasha, Keesha, Keeshah, Keicia, Keishah, Keshia, Keysha, Kicia

Keishla (American) dark

Keishonna (English) form of Keisha: dark-eyed

Keita (Scottish) lives in the forest
Keiti

Keitha (Scottish) from the forest
Keithana

Kekoa (Hawaiian) happy

Kelby (English) lives in a farmhouse
Kelbea, Kelbeigh, Kelbey, Kellbie

Kelda (Scandinavian) spring of youth
Kellda

Keledi (African) sorrows

Kelila (Hebrew) regal woman
Kayla, Kayle, Kaylee, Kelula, Kelulah, Kelulla, Kelylah, Kyla, Kyle

Kelinda (American) form of Melinda: honey; sweetheart

Keller (Irish) daring
Kellers
Kellia (American) form of Kelly:
brave
Kelly (Irish) brave
Keli, Kellie, Kelley, Kellye
Kellyn (Irish) brave heart
Kelleen, Kellen, Kellene, Kellina,
Kelline, Kellynn, Kellynne
Kelsey (Scottish) opinionated
Kelcey, Kelcie, Kelcy, Kellsey,
Kellsie, Kelsea, Kelsee, Kelseigh,
Kelsi, Kelsie, Kelsy
Keltoriah (American) brave
Kember (American) zany
Kem, Kemmie, Kimber
Kemeel (American) form of
Camille: swift runner; great
innocence
Kemeelah (American) form
of Camille: swift runner; great
innocence
Kemelah (American) form of
Camille: swift runner; great
innocence
Kemella (American) self-assured
Kemele, Kemellah, Kemelle
Kemicia (American) form of
Kim: sharp

Kempley (English) from a
meadowland: rascal
Kemplea, Kempleigh, Kemplie,
Kemply
Kenda (English) aware
Kendi, Kendie, Kendy, Kennda,
Kenndi, Kenndie, Kenndy
Kendall (English) quiet
Kendahl, Kendal, Kendell,
Kendelle, Kendie, Kendylle
Kendella (English) form of
Kendall: quiet
Kendra (American) ingenious
Ken, Kendrah, Kenna, Kennie,
Kindra, Kinna, Kyndra
Kendrelle (English) rules quiet
place
Kendry (English) rules quiet
place
Kenia (African) giving; from the
place name Kenya
Ken, Keneah
Kenichi (American) feminine
form of Kenneth: good-looking
Kenine (Scottish) pretty
Kenith (American) feminine form
of Kenneth: good-looking
Kenna (English) brilliant;
(Scottish) creative
Kenina, Kennah, Kennette,
Kennina, Kynna

Kennae (Irish) feminine form of
Ken: good-looking
Kenae, Kenah
Kennedy (Irish) formidable
Kennedie, Kenny
Kenner (Scottish) feminine form
of Kenneth: good-looking
Kennice (English) beauty
Kanice, Keneese, Kenese, Kennise
Kensington (English) brash
Kensingtyn
Kenta (English) feminine form of
Kent: fair-skinned
Kentucky (Place name) U.S.
state
Kentuckie
Kenya (Place name) country in
Africa
Kenia, Kennya
Kenyatta (African) form of
Kenya: country in Africa
Kenyetta (Place name) form of
Kenya: country in Africa
Kenyie (Place name) form of
Kenya: country in Africa
Kenzie (Scottish) pretty
Kensey, Kinsey
Keoshawn (African American)
clever
Keosh, Keoshaun

Kerdonna (African American) loquacious
Donna, Kerdy, Kirdonna, Kyrdonna

Kerensa (English) lovable
Karensa, Karenza, Kerenza

Keri-Gee (English) awesome

Kerla (American) curly-haired

Kern (Irish) darkness

Kerra (American) bright
Cara, Carrah, Kara, Kerrah

Kerry (Irish) dark-haired
*Carrie, Kari, Kera, Keree, Keri,
Kerrey, Kerri, Kerria, Kerridana,
Kerrie*

Kerst (American) form of Kerstin:
a Christian

Kerstin (Scandinavian) a
Christian
Kersten, Kerston, Kerstyn

Kerthia (American) giving
Kerth, Kerthea, Kerthi, Kerthy

Kesha (American) laughing
Kecia, Kesa, Keshah

Keshia (American) bouncy
*Kecia, Keishia, Keschia, Kesia,
Kesiah, Kessiah*

Keshon (African American) happy
*Keshann, Keshaun, Keshawn,
Keshonn, Keshun*

Keshondra (African American)
joy-filled
*Keshaundra, Keshondrah,
Keshundra, Keshundrea,
Keshundria, Keshy*

Keshonna (African American)
happy
*Keshanna, Keshauna, Keshaunna,
Keshawna, Keshona*

Kesi (African) baby born in hard
times

Kessie (African) fat baby cheeks
*Kess, Kessa, Kesse, Kessey, Kessi,
Kessia, Kessiah*

Ketrina (German) musical

Keturah (African) long-suffering
Katura, Ketura

Kevine (Irish) lively
*Kevina, Kevinne, Kevyn, Kevynn,
Kevynne*

Kevyn (Irish) form of Kevin:
lovely face
*Keva, Kevan, Kevina, Kevone,
Kevonna, Kevynn*

Kew (English) form of Cumale:
open-hearted

Keydy (American) knowing
Keydee, Keydi, Keydie

Keyla (Irish) form of Kelia:
crowned

Keynny (American) feminine
form of Kenneth: good-looking

Keynshalli (Invented) form of
Keisha: dark-eyed

Keyonna (African American)
energetic

Keyshawn (American) lively
*Keyshan, Keyshann, Keyshaun,
Keyshaunna, Keyshon, Keyshona,
Keshonna, Keykey, Kiki*

Kezettea (African) form of Kezia:
confident

Kezia (Hebrew) form of Cassis:
confident
*Kazia, Kessie, Kessy, Ketzia,
Ketziah, Keziah, Kezzie, Kissie,
Kizzie, Kizzy*

Keziane (African) form of Kezia:
confident
Kezi, Kezian

Khadijah (Arabic) sweetheart
Kadija, Kadiya, Khadiya, Khadyja

Khai (American) unusual
Ki, Kie

Khaki (American) personality-
plus
*Kakee, Kaki, Kakie, Khakee,
Khakie*

Khali (Origin unknown) lively
Khalee, Khalie, Koli, Kollie

Khalida (Hindi) eternal
Khali, Khalia, Khalita

Khalilah (Arabic) friendly

Khalique (African) lasting

Kharol (American) form of Carol:
feminine; joyful song

Khasha (American) brash

Khawaja (American) excitable

Khawla (African) enthusiastic

Khiana (American) different
*Kheana, Khianah, Khianna, Ki,
Kianah, Kianna, Kiannah*

Khloe ✪ (English) form of
Chloe: flowering

Khonesa (Indian) able

Khorus (Greek) musical

Khyra (English) form of Kira:
sunny; lighthearted

Ki (Korean) born again

Kia (American) form of Kiana:
graceful
Keeah, Kiah

Kiana (American) graceful
*Kia, Kiah, Kianna, Kiannah,
Quiana, Quianna*

Kiani (Hawaiian) form of Kiana:
graceful

Kiantyne (Invented) laughs

Kiara (Irish) dark-skinned
*Chiara, Chiarra, Keearah, Keearra,
Kiarra*

Kibibi (African) small girl

Kidre (American) loyal
Kidrea, Kidrey, Kidri

Kiele (Hawaiian) aromatic flower;
gardenia
Kiela, Kieley, Kieli, Kielli, Kielly

Kienalle (American) light
Kieana, Kienall, Kieny

Kienna (Origin unknown) brash
Kiennah, Kienne

Kiera (Irish) dark-skinned
Keara, Keera, Kierra

Kiersten (Greek) blessed
*Kerston, Kierstin, Kierstn,
Kierstynn, Kirst, Kirsten, Kirstie,
Kirstin, Kirsty*

Kiersty (American) spiritual

Kihae (Asian) fragrant

Kijana (American) form of Kiana:
graceful

Kiki (Spanish/American) form
of names beginning with K:
vivacious
Keiki, Ki, Kiekie, Kikee

Kiko (Japanese) lively
Kiki, Kikoh

Kiku (Japanese) flower mum
Kiko

Kilday (American) pretty

Kiley (Irish) pretty
*Kilea, Kilee, Kili, Kylee, Kyley,
Kylie*

Kiliki (Mythology) feminine

Killie (English) returns

Kim (Vietnamese) sharp
Kimey, Kimmi, Kimmy, Kym

Kima (American) bright

Kimalida (Spanish) hopes

Kimana (American) form of
Kim: sharp

Kimaya (Asian) golden child

Kimberly ✪ (English) leader
*Kim, Kimber-Lea, Kimberlee,
Kimberleigh, Kimberley, Kimberli,
Kimberlie, Kimmy, Kimmie,
Kymberly*

Kimbra (English) fortified

Kimbrell (African American)
smiling
*Kim, Kimbree, Kimbrel, Kimbrele,
Kimby, Kimmy*

Kimeo (American) form of Kim:
sharp
Kim, Kime, Kimi

Kimetha (American) form of
Kimberly: leader
Kimeth

Kimi (Japanese) spiritual

Kimo (Asian) strong

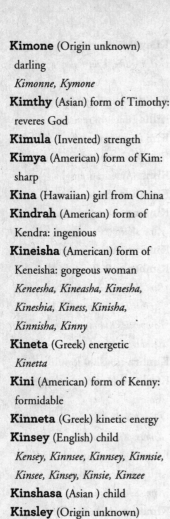

Kimone (Origin unknown) darling
Kimonne, Kymone

Kimthy (Asian) form of Timothy: reveres God

Kimula (Invented) strength

Kimya (American) form of Kim: sharp

Kina (Hawaiian) girl from China

Kindrah (American) form of Kendra: ingenious

Kineisha (American) form of Keneisha: gorgeous woman
Keneesha, Kineasha, Kinesha, Kineshia, Kiness, Kinisha, Kinnisha, Kinny

Kineta (Greek) energetic
Kinetta

Kini (American) form of Kenny: formidable

Kinneta (Greek) kinetic energy

Kinsey (English) child
Kensey, Kinnsee, Kinnsey, Kinnsie, Kinsee, Kinsey, Kinsie, Kinzee

Kinshasa (Asian) child

Kinsley (Origin unknown) familiar
Kingslea, Kingslee, Kingslie, Kinslea, Kinslee, Kinslie, Kinsly, Kinzlea, Kinzlee, Kinzley, Kinzly

Kintra (American) joyous
Kentra, Kint, Kintrey

Kinza (American) relative

Kioko (Japanese) happy baby
Kiyo, Kiyoko

Kiona (Native American) girl from the hill

Kionea (Native American) interesting

Kip (Literature) naive

Kipling (Last name as first name) energetic
Kiplin

Kippareen (American) humorous; young

Kipple (American) form of Kipling: energetic

Kira (Russian) sunny; light-hearted
Keera, Kera, Kiera, Kierra, Kiria, Kiriah, Kirra, Kirya

Kiran (Irish) pretty; (Indian) light
Kiara, Kiaran, Kira, Kiri

Kirby (Anglo-Saxon) right
Kirbee, Kirbey, Kirbie

Kiriath (Biblical) place name

Kirima (Eskimo) hill child; high aspirations

Kirsta (Scandinavian) Christian

Kirsten (Scandinavian) form of Christine: follower of Christ
Karsten, Keerstin, Keirstin, Kersten, Kerstin, Kiersten, Kierstin, Kierstynn, Kirsteen, Kirstene, Kirsti, Kirstie, Kirstin, Kirston, Kirsty, Kirstynn, Kristen, Kristin, Kristyn, Krystene, Krystin

Kirstie (Scandinavian) irrepressible
Kerstie, Kirstee, Kirsty

Kirti (Indian) famous

Kirtrina (American) form of Katrina: melodious

Kischchan (American) tries hard

Kisha (Russian) ingenious
Keshah

Kishala (English) form of Kisha: ingenious

Kishi (Japanese) eternal

Kishori (Indian) young

Kismet (Hindi) destiny; fate
Kismat, Kismete, Kismett

Kissa (African) a baby born after twins

Kit (American) strong
Kitt

Kita (Japanese) northerner

Kithos (Greek) worthy

Kitten (English) form of Katherine: pure

Kitty (Greek) form of Katherine: pure
Kit, Kittee, Kittey, Kitti, Kittie

Kiva (Origin unknown) bright
Keva

Kiwa (Origin unknown) lively
Kiewah, Kiwah

Kiya (Australian) form of Kylie: graceful
Kya

Kizzie (African) energetic
Kissee, Kissie, Kiz, Kizzee, Kizzi, Kizzy

Klara (Hungarian) bright
Klari, Klarice, Klarika, Klarissa, Klarisza, Klaryssa

Klarissa (German) bright-minded
Clarissa, Klarisa, Klarise

Klarybel (Polish) beauty
Klaribel, Klaribelle

Klaudia (Polish) lame

Klea (American) bold
Clea, Kleah, Kleea, Kleeah

Klementina (Polish) forgiving
Clemence, Clementine, Klementine, Klementyna

Kleta (Greek) form of Cleopatra: Egyptian queen
Cleta

Klotild (Hungarian) famous
Klothild, Klothilda, Klothilde, Klotilda, Klotilde

Klyra (Slavic) noble

Knoi (American) annoys

Koa (Hawaiian) seaside

Kobi (American) California girl
Cobi, Kobe

Kobra (Indian) form of cobra

Koche (American) bright

Koffi (African) Friday-born
Kaffe, Kaffi, Koffe, Koffie

Kogan (Last name as first name) self-assured
Kogann, Kogen, Kogey, Kogi

Koichi (Asian)

Kokan (American) real

Kokkie (Dutch) horn

Koko (Japanese) the stork comes

Kolleen (Irish) form of Colleen: young girl

Kona (Hawaiian) feminine
Koni, Konia

Konia (Hawaiian) bright light

Konki (American) constant

Konstance (Latin) loyal
Constance, Kon, Konnie, Konstanze, Stanze

Kora (Greek) practical
Cora, Koko, Korey, Kori

Koren (English) form of Corinne: maiden; protective

Kori (Greek) little girl; popular
Cori, Corrie, Koree, Korey, Kory

Korina (Greek) maiden
Corinna, Koreena, Korena, Korinna, Koryna

Kornelia (Latin) straight-laced
Cornelia, Kornelya, Korney, Korni, Kornie

Kortney (American) form of Courtney: domain of Curtis
Kortnee, Kortni, Kourtney, Kourtnie

Koshatta (Native American) diligent
Coushatta, Kosha, Koshat, Koshatte, Koshee, Koshi, Koshie, Koushatta

Koska (American) loose cannon

Kosta (Latin) form of Constance: loyal
Kostia, Kostusha, Kostya

Koto (Japanese) harp; musical

Koverne (Last name used as first name) homebody

Krenie (American) capable
Kren, Kreni, Krenn, Krennie, Kreny

Kresenz (German) crescent

Kris (American) form of Kristina: follower of Christ
Kaykay, Krissie, Krissy

Krishen (American) talkative
Crishen, Kris, Krish, Krishon

Krissa (German) form of Krista: follower of Christ

Krissen (American) feminine form of Christian: follower of Christ

Krissy (American) friendly
Kris, Krisie, Krissey, Krissi

Krista (German) form of Christina: follower of Christ
Khrista, Krysta

Kristanie (American) Christian

Kristeen (German) form of Christine: follower of Christ

Kristeenea (English) form of Christina: follower of Christ

Kristen (Greek) form of Christine: follower of Christ
Christen, Cristen, Kristin, Kristyn

Kristian (Greek) Christian woman
Kristiana, Kristianne, Kristyanna

Kristie (American) saucy
Christi, Christy, Kristi

Kristin (Scandinavian) high-energy
Kristen, Kristyne

Kristina (Scandinavian) form of Christina: follower of Christ
Krista, Kristie, Krysteena, Tina

Kristine (Swedish) form of Christine: follower of Christ
Kristee, Kristene, Kristi, Kristy

Kristy (American) form of Kristine: follower of Christ
Kristi, Kristie

Krysta (Polish) clear
Chrsta, Krista

Krystal (American) clear and brilliant
Cristalle, Cristel, Crysta, Crystal, Crystalle, Khristalle, Khristel, Khrystalle, Khrystle, Kristel, Kristle, Krys, Krystalle, Krystalline, Krystelle, Krystie, Krystle, Krystylle

Krystyna (Polish) Christian

Kuawanna (African) fragrant

Kubbae (American) wanderer

Kue (Biblical) place name

Kukan (Scandinavian) blossoms

Kumiko (Japanese) long hair in braids
Kumi

Kumud (Indian) lotus flower; Bright

Kundany (Indian) golden child

Kunday (Invented) form of Sunday: day of the week; sunny

Kurara (Japanese) peaceful

Kurene (American) monied

Kwanita (African) form of Juanita: believer in a gracious God; forgiving

Kyan (American) lively

Kyatana (American) vivacious

Kyishia (American) form of Keisha: dark-eyed

Kyla (Irish) pretty
Kiela, Kila, Ky

Kyle (Irish) pretty
Kyall, Kyel, Kylee, Kylie, Kyll

Kylee (Irish) form of Kylie: graceful
Kielie, Kiely, Kiley, Kye, Kyky, Kyleigh

Kyleighan (English) form of Kylie: graceful

Kylene (American) cute
Kyline

Kylera (English) feminine form of Kyler: peaceful

Kylern (English) feminine form of Kyler: peaceful

Kylie ✪ ❶ (Irish) graceful
Keyely, Kilea, Kiley, Kylee, Kyley

Kylynne (American) fashionable
Kilenne, Kilynn, Kyly

Kym (American) favorite
Kim, Kymm, Kymmi, Kymmie,
Kymy

Kyna (African) diamond

Kynci (American) form of Kinsey:
child

Kynthia (Greek) goddess of the
moon
Cinthia, Cynthia

Kyoko (Japanese) sees herself in
a mirror

Kyra (Greek) feminine
Kaira, Keera, Keira, Kira, Kyrah,
Kyreena, Kyrene, Kyrha, Kyria,
Kyrie, Kyrina, Kyrra, Kyry

Kyria (Greek) form of Kyra:
feminine
Kyrea, Kyree, Kyrie, Kyry

Laarni (American) honest

Labe (American) slow-moving
Labie

Lace (American) delicate
Lacee, Lacey, Laci, Lacie, Lase

Lacey (Greek) cheery
Lacee, Laci, Lacie, Lacy

Lachelle (African American)
sweetheart
Lachel, Lachell, Laschell, Lashelle

Lachesis (Mythological) one of
the Greek Fates; the measurer

Lachina (African American)
fragile

Lacole (American) sly
Lucole

Lacreta (Spanish) form of
Lacretia: efficient
Lacrete, LaLa

Lacretia (Latin) efficient
Lacracia, Lacrecia, Lacrisha, Lacy

LaDaune (African American) the
dawn
Ladaune, LaDawn

Ladda (American) open
Lada

Ladey (American) form of Lady:
feminine

LaDorna (Spanish) adorned

Ladrenaan (Invented) likeable

Ladrenda (African American)
cagy
Ladee, Ladey, Ladren, Ladrende,
Lady

Lady (American) feminine
Ladee, Ladie

Laela (Hebrew) form of Leila:
beauty of the night

Laetitia (Latin) joy
Lateaciah, Lateacya, Latycia,
Leticia, Letisia, Letyziah

Laheelah (American) gifted

Laila (Scandinavian) dark beauty
Laili, Laleh, Layla, Laylah, Leila

Lainil (American) softhearted
Lainie, Lanel, Lanelle

Laitalin (American) secure

Laith (Scottish) princess

Lajean (French) soothing;
steadfast
LaJean, Lajeanne, L'Jean

LaJoyce (English) combo of La
and Joyce

Lakanel (American) hurt

Lake (Astrology) graceful dancer

Lakeisha (African American) the
favorite; combo of La and Keisha

Lakeita (American) caring

Lakela (Hawaiian) feminine
Lakla

Lakendrae (American) great
hopes

Lakeny (American) superb

Lakesha (African American)
favored
Keishia, Lakaisha, Lakeesha,
Lakeishah, Lakezia, Lakisha,
LaKisha

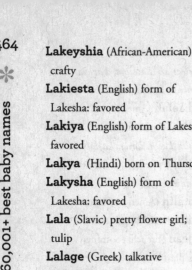

Lakeyshia (African-American) crafty

Lakiesta (English) form of Lakesha: favored

Lakiya (English) form of Lakesha: favored

Lakya (Hindi) born on Thursday

Lakysha (English) form of Lakesha: favored

Lala (Slavic) pretty flower girl; tulip

Lalage (Greek) talkative
Lal, Lallie, Lally

Lalaney (American) form of Leilani: heavenly girl
Lala, Lalanee, Lalani

Laleema (Spanish) devoted
Lalema, Lalima

Lalena (Indian) girlish
Lalana

Lalita (Sanskrit) charmer
Lai, Lala, Lali, Lalitah, Lalite, Lalitte

Lalitha (Spanish) form of Lalita: charmer

Lally (English) babbling
Lalli

Lalmani (American) sociable

Lalya (Latin) eloquent
Lalia, Lall, Lalyah

Lama (Muslim) dark lips

Lamarian (American) conflicted
Lamare, Lamarean

Lambda (Greek)

Lamercie (French) forgiving

Lamia (Egyptian) calm
Lami

Lamiena (Spanish) calming

Lamika (African American) form of Tamika: lively

L'Amour (French) love
Amor, Amour, Lamore, Lamour, Lamoura

Lana (Latin) pretty; peacemaker
Lan, Lanna, Lanny

Lanai (Hawaiian) heavenly
Lenai

Lanalee (Invented) combo of Lana and Lee

Land (American) word as name; confident
Landd

Landa (American) blonde beauty
Landah

Landra (American) form of Landa: blonde beauty

Landry (American) leader
Landa, Landree

Landy (American) confident
Land, Landee, Landey, Landi

Lane (Last name as first name) precocious
Laine, Lainey, Laney, Lanie, Layne, Laynie

Lanee (Asian) graceful

Laneedy (English) form of Laney: precocious

Lanette (American) healthy
La-Net, LaNett, LaNette

Langley (American) special
Langlee, Langli, Langlie, Langly

Lani (Hawaiian) form of Leilani: heavenly girl
Lannie

LaNiece (Invented) form of Lenice: delightful

Lanigill (American) happy

Lanilee (American) heaven

Lanitia (Slavic) unique

Lanle (African) enriched

Lannea (American) mobile

Lannette (American) form of Lynette: small and fresh

Lanola (American) generous

Lanonre (American) of the sea

Lanora (Italian) form of Leonora: bright light

Lansing (Place name) hopeful
Lanseng

Lantana (Botanical) flowering
Lantanna

Laperonita (Spanish) upward

Laquanna (African American) outspoken
Kwanna, LaQuanna, LaQwana, Quanna

Lara (Russian) lovely

Larae (Slavic) form of Lara: lovely

Laraine (Latin) pretty
Lareine, Larene, Loraine

Larante (Last name used as first name) shares

Laray (American) form of Lara: lovely

Larby (American) form of Darby: a free woman
Larbee, Larbey, Larbi, Larbie

Larch (American) full of life

Lareina (Greek) seagull; flies over water
Larayna, Larayne, Lareine, Larena, Larrayna, Larreina

Larenya (English) form of Laraine: pretty

Laressia (English) form of Larissa: giving cheer

Lariesha (English) form of Larissa: giving cheer

Larinda (American) smart
Lare, Larin, Larine, Lorinda

Larissa (Latin) giving cheer
Laressa, Larisse, Laryssa

Lark (American) pretty
Larke

Larkin (American) pretty
Larken, Larkun

Larklee (Invented) combo of Lark and Lee; birdlike

Larkly (American) form of Larklee: birdlike

Larkspur (Botanical) tall and stately

Larla (American) deserving

Larlett (American) winner

Larni (American) form of Marni: storyteller

LaRobin (English) combo of La and Robin

Larrie (American) tomboyish
Larry

Larsa (Biblical) place name

Larsen (Scandinavian) laurel-crowned
Larson, Larssen, Larsson

Laruthenne (American) combo of La and Ruthenne

Lasa (American) complex

Lasalle (French) explorer

Lasea (Biblical) place name

Lasha (Spanish) forlorn
Lash, Lass

Lashanda (American) brassy
Lala, Lasha, LaShanda, LaShounda

Lashauna (American) happy
Lashona, Lashawna, Leshauna

LaShea (American) sparkling
Lashay, La-Shea, Lashea

Lashoun (African American) content
Lashaun, Lashawn, Lashown

Lassie (American) lass
Lass

Lastashtia (American) form of Latasha: born on Christmas

Lastenia (Spanish) lovely Christian girl

Lata (Hindi) lovely vine; entwines

Latash (American) form of Latasha: born on Christmas

Latasha (American) born on Christmas
Latacha, LaTasha, Latayshah, Latisha

LaTeasa (Spanish) tease
Latea, Lateasa, LaTease, LaTeese

Lateefah (African) gentle; pleasant
Lateefa, Latifa, Latifah, Lotifah, Tifa, Tifah

Latesha (American) form of Letitia: joy
Lateesha, Lateisha, Lateshah, Laticia, Latisha

Lathenia (American) verbose
Lathene, Lathey

Latice (American) form of Letitia: joy

Latifah (Muslim) gentle
Lateefa, Latifa, Latiffe, Latifuh

Latiki (Indian) small
Latika

Latina (Spanish) Spanish girl

Latisa (English) form of Latasha: born on Christmas

Latisehsha (African American) happy; talkative
Lati, Latise, Latiseh, Latisha

Latochia (English) form of Latasha: born on Christmas

Latona (Latin) goddess

Latonia (African American) rich
Latone, Latonea

Latosha (African American) happy

Latoyia (English) watchful

Latoyra (American) circumspect

Latreece (American) go-getter
Latreese, Latrice, Letrice, Lettie, Letty

Latrelia (Spanish) of the trellis

Latrelle (American) laughing
Lettie, Letrel, Letrelle, Litrelle

Latrice (Latin) noble
Latreece, Latreese

Latricia (American) happy
Latrecia, Latreesha, Latrisha, Latrishah

Latrisha (African American) prissy
Latrishe

Latroa (American) athletic

Latunga (African) athletic

Latunya (American) form of Latonya: birdlike

Latyffanie (American) combo of La and Tyffanie

Lauda (Latin) praised

Laudette (American) lauded

Laudomia (Italian) praiseworthy

Laufeia (Scandinavian) thriving

Launa (American) ideal

Launie (American) heavenly

Laura (Latin) laurel-crowned; joyous
Lara, Lora

Laurain (English) graceful

Laurdina (American) form of Laurinda: the laurel plant

Laureen (American) old-fashioned
Laurie, Laurine, Loreen

Laureens (Scandinavian) wins laurels

Laurel (Latin) the laurel plant
Laural, Laurell, Laurella, Laurelle, Lorel, Lorell, Lorella, Lourelle

Lauren ○ (Latin) laurel-crowned
Laren, Laurene, Lauryn, Laryn, Loren

Laurencia (Latin) laurel-crowned
Laurenciah, Laurens, Laurentana

Laurenne (Scandinavian) wins laurels

Laurent (French) graceful
Laurente, Lorent

Laurentine (French) bright

Lauretta (American) graceful
Laureta, Laurettah, Lauritta, Lauritte, Loretta

Laurette (American) form of Laura: laurel-crowned; joyous; (English) form of Laurita: victorious
Etta, Ette, Laure, Laurett, Lorette

Laurettean (English) form of Laurita: victorious

Laurid (Welsh) form of Laura: laurel-crowned; joyous

Laurie (English) careful
Lari, Lauri, Lori

Laurima (Spanish) form of Laura: laurel-crowned; joyous

Laurinda (Spanish) the laurel plant

Laurissaa (Greek) pleased

Laurita (Spanish) victorious

Lavanda (Spanish) pure

Laveda (Latin) pure
Lavella, Lavelle, Laveta, Lavetta, Lavette

LaVeeda (Spanish) alive

Lavena (Celtic) joy
Lavi, Lavie, Lavina

Lavender (Latin) pale purple flowers; peaceful

Laverne (Latin) breath of spring
Lavern, Lavirne, Verna, Verne

La Verta (American) truth

Laveta (American) vibrant

Lavette (Latin) pure; natural
Laveda, Lavede, Lavete, Lavett

Lavigne (French) vineyard

Lavilla (Spanish) gathers

Lavina (Latin) woman of Rome

Lavinia (Latin) cleansed; (Greek) ladylike
Lavenia, Vin, Vina, Vinnie, Vinny

Lavita (American) charmer
Laveta, Lavitta, Lavitte

Lawanda (American) sassy
LaWanda, Lawonda

Lawenna form of Lawan: lovely

Lawrencetta (American) feminine form of Lawrence: honored

Layce (American) spunky

Layine (Scandinavian) loves the sea

Layla ✪ (Arabic) dark
Laela, Laila, Lala, Laya, Laylah, Laylie, Leila

Layli (American) form of Layla: dark

Layne (French) from the meadow
Laine, Lainee, Lainey

Laynn (American) form of Lane: precocious

Layoce (American) form of Loyce: delightful

Layouce (American) form of Loyce: delightful

Laysha (American) form of Letitia: joy

Lazette (American) form of Lizette: lively

Lazine (Dutch) joyful
Lazina, Lazee

Lea (Hawaiian) goddess-like

Leacille (American) form of Lucille: bright-eyed

Leaf (Botanical) hip

Leah ✪ (Hebrew) tired and burdened
Lea, Lee, Leeah, Leia, Lia

Leala (French) steadfast

Leandra (Greek) leonine
Leandrea, Leanndra, Leeandra, Leedie

Leanette (English) form of Lynnette: small and fresh

Leanna (English) leaning
Leana, Leelee, Liana

Leanne (English) sweet
Lean, Leann, Lee, Leelee, Lianne

Leanona (English) form of Leona: bravehearted

Leanora (Greek) light
Lanora, Lanoriah, Lenora

Leanore (Greek) form of Eleanor: lighthearted
Lanore

Leatha (English) form of Alethea: truthful

Leatrice (American) charming
Leatrise

Leatricea (English) leader

Lebonah (Biblical) place name

Lecia (Latin) form of Letitia: joy
Leecia, Leesha, Lesha, Lesia

Lectricia (English) form of Leatrice: charming

Leda (Greek) feminine
Ledah, Lida, Lita

Lee (English/American/Chinese) light-footed
Lea, Leelee, Leigh

Leeannette (Greek) form of Leandra: leonine
Leann, Leeanett, Lee Annette, Lee-Annette, Leiandra

Leelee (American/Slavic) form of Leanne: sweet
Lee-Lee, Lele, Lelee

Leena (Latin) temptress
Lena, Lina

Leene (Scandinavian) form of Lena: siren

Leeo (American) sunny
Leo

Leesha (English) form of Lisha: God-loving

Le Etta (American) small

Leeuwen (Dutch) dear friend

Leeza (American) gorgeous
Leesa, Leeze, Liza, Lize

Legend (American) memorable
Legen, Legende, Legund

Legia (Spanish) bright
Legea

Lehava (Hebrew) flaming

Lei (Hawaiian) form of Leilani: heavenly girl
Leilei

Léi (Chinese) open; truthful

Leigh (English) light-footed
Lee, Leelee

Leila (Arabic) beauty of the night
Layla, Leela, Leilah, Lelah, Leyla, Lila

Leilani (Hawaiian) heavenly girl
Lanie

Leisa (English) form of Lisa: dedicated and spiritual

Leith (Scottish) from the river; nature-loving
Leithe, Lethe

Lejoi (French) joy
Joy, Lejoy

Leka (Indian) graphic proof
Lehka

Leland (American) special
Lelan, Lelande

Lelann (Greek) faithful

Lelia (Greek) articulate
Lee, Leelee

Lemetria (American) perfection

Leminda (American) mindful

Lemon (Botanical) zany

Lemtraia (American) sporty

Lemuela (Hebrew) loyal
Lemuelah, Lemuella, Lemuellah

Lena (Latin) siren
Leena, Lenette, Lina

Lendez (Spanish) form of Linda: pretty girl

Lendorah (English) form of Linda: pretty girl

Lendtra (English) form of Linda: pretty girl

Lenesha (African American) smiling
Leneisha, Lenisha, Lenni, Lennie, Neshie

Lenetta (English) form of Lynette: small and fresh

Lenice (American) delightful
Lenisa, Lenise

Lenikka (American) roving

Lenita (Latin) gentle spirit
Leneeta, Leneta, Lineta

Lenka (Slavic) cleansed

Lenkan (Slavic) excellent

Lenna (Hebrew) shy

Lenoa (Greek) form of Lenore: lighthearted
Len, Lenor, Lenora

Lenore (Greek) form of Eleanor: lighthearted

Leoda (German) popular
Leota

Leola (Latin) fierce; leonine
Lee, Leo, Leole

Leolan (Last name used as first name) lionlike

Leolia (English) form of Leola: leonine

Leoma (American) form of Leona: bravehearted

Leona (Greek/American) bravehearted
Liona

Leonarda (German) lionhearted
Lenarda, Lenda, Lennarda, Leonarde

Leondrea (Greek) strong
Leondreah, Leondria

Leonetta (English) feminine form of Leon: tenacious

Leonie (Latin) lionlike; fierce
Leola, Leonee, Leoney, Leoni, Leontine, Leony

Leonila (Spanish) lioness

Leonora (English) bright light
Leanor, Leanora, Leanore, Lenora, Lenore, Leonore

Leonore (Greek) glowing light
Lenore, Leonor, Leonora

Leonsio (Spanish) feminine form of Leon: tenacious
Leo, Leonsee, Leonsi

Leopoldina (Invented) feminine form of Leopold: brave
Dina, Leo, Leopolde, Leopoldyna

Leora (Greek) lighthearted
Leorah, Liora

Leoycey (Invented) sassy

Lequita (Spanish) bright; clear

Lera (Russian) strong
Lerae, Lerie, Lira

Leretta (American) form of Loretta: large-eyed beauty
Lere, Lerie

Leria (Italian) brave

Lerita (Spanish) gives joy

Leritha (Spanish) gives joy

Lesha (Italian) kind

Leshia (Italian) feminine

Leslie (Scottish) fiesty; beautiful; smart
Les, Lesli, Lesley

Leslin (American) form of Leslie: feisty; beautiful; smart

Lessie (Scottish) form of Leslie: feisty; beautiful; smart

Lesstene (American) form of Leslie: feisty; beautiful; smart

Lesvia (Slavic) spiritual

Leszlee (American) form of Leslie: fiesty; beautiful; smart

Leta (Latin) happy
Leeta, Lita

Letai (Latin) glad

Letha (Greek) ladylike
Litha

Letian (Latin) glad

Letichel (American) happy; important
Chel, Chelle, Leti, Letichell, Letishell, Lettichelle, Lettychel

Leticia (Spanish) form of Letitia: joy
Letecia, Letisha, Lettice, Lettie, Letty, Tiesha

Letina (Spanish) Latina

Letitia (Latin) joy

Leto (Greek) mother of Apollo

Letricia (Spanish) happy

Letsey (American) form of Lettie: happy
Letsee, Letsy

Lettice (American) sweet
Letty

Lettie (Latin/Spanish) happy
Lettee, Letti, Letty, Lettye

Letycee (Invented) insightful

Leutricia (Spanish) form of Letricia: happy

Leutu (Asian)

Levana (Hebrew) fair
Lev, Liv, Livana

Leverah (American) form of Deborah: prophetess

Leverne (French) grove of trees

Levina (Latin) lightning

Levitt (American) straightforward
Levit

Levity (American) humorous

Levora (American) home-loving
*Levorah, Levore, Livee, Livie,
Livora, Livore*

Lewana (Hebrew) moon bright

Lexa (American) cheerful
Lex, Lexah

Lexandra (Slavic) bold

Lexi (Greek) helpful; sparkling
Lex, Lexie, Lexsey, Lexsie, Lexy

Lexine (Scottish) helper

Lexus (American) rich
*Lexi, Lexorus, Lexsis, Lexuss,
Lexxus*

Lexy (Scottish) helper

Leya (Spanish) true blue

Leysa (Spanish) loyal

Lez (American) form of Leslie:
feisty; beautiful; smart

Lezena (American) smiling
Lezene, Lezina, Lyzena

Lez'lee (American) form of
Leslie: feisty; beautiful; smart

Li (Chinese) plum; strong

Lia (Greek/Russian/Italian)
singular
Li, Liah

Liadin (Irish) sad

Lial (Italian) form of Leah: tired
and burdened

Lialeh (Italian) form of Leah:
tired and burdened

Lian (Latin/Chinese) graceful
Leane, Leanne, Liane

Liana (Greek) flowering;
complicated
Leanna, Lee, Liane

Liani (Hawaiian) caressed

Lianna (Italian) sunny

Lianne (English) light
Leann, Leanne, Leeann

Libba (Biblical) place name;
desired

Libby (Hebrew) form of
Elizabeth: God's promise
Lib, Libbi, Libbie

Liber (American) from the word
liberty; free
Lib, Libby, Lyber

Liberty (Latin) free and open
Lib, Libbie

Libnah (Biblical) place name;
white

Librada (Spanish) free
Libra, Libradah

Libva (Biblical) place name; white

Liceth (American) form of Lysett:
pretty little one

Licia (Greek) outdoorsy
Lisha

Licona (Spanish)

Lida (Greek) beloved girl
Leedah, Lyda

Liddan (Irish) form of Liadin: sad

Lidia (Greek) pleasant spirit
Lydia

Lidiya (Russian) form of Lydia:
musical, unusual

Liese (German) given to God

Liesel (German) pretty
Leesel, Leezel

Lieselotte (Hebrew/French)
charming woman

Light (American) light-hearted
Li, Lite

Ligia (Greek) talented musician
Ligea, Lygia, Lygy

Lignon (French) clarity

Liguria (Greek) music lover

Likiana (Invented) likeable
Like, Likia

Lila (Arabic) playful
Lilah, Lyla, Lylah

Lilac (Botanical) tiny blossom
Lila

Lilah (Sanskrit) playful

Lila-Lee (American) lily

Lilavati (Hindi) goddess

Lileah (Latin) lily-like
Lili, Liliah, Lill, Lily, Lilya

Lilette (Latin) little lily; delicate
Lill, Lillette, Lillith, Lilly

Lilia (American) flowing
Lileah, Lyleah, Lylia

Lilian (Latin) pure beauty

Liliana (Italian) pretty
Lilianah, Lylianah

Lilias (Hebrew) night
Lilas, Lillas, Lillias

Liliash (Spanish) lily; innocent
Lil, Lileah, Liliosa, Lilya, Lyliase, Lylish

Lilith (Arabic) nocturnal
Lilis, Lilita, Lill, Lilli, Lillie, Lillith, Lilly, Lilyth, Lilythe

Lillian ☺ ❶ (Latin) pretty as a lily
Lila, Lileane, Lilian, Liliane, Lill, Lilla, Lillah, Lillie, Lillyan, Lillyann, Lilyanne, Liyan

Lillias (Hebrew) night

Lily ☺ ❶ (Latin/Chinese) elegant
Lil, Lili, Lilie

Limor (Hebrew) myrrh; treasured
Leemor

Lin (English/Chinese) beautiful
Linn, Lynn

Lina (Greek/Latin/Scottish) light
of spirit; lake calm
Lena, Lin, Linah, Lynn

Linda (Spanish) pretty girl
Lind, Lindy, Lynda

Linden (American) harmonious
Lindan, Lindun, Lynden, Lynnden

Lindsay (English/Scottish)
calming; bright and shining
Lindsee, Lindsey, Lindsi, Lindz, Lyndsie, Lyndzee, Lynz

Lindse (Spanish) form of
Lindsay: calming; bright and
shining
Linds, Lindz, Lindze, Lyndzy

Lindy (American) music-lover
Lind, Lindee, Lindi, Lindie, Linney, Linnie, Linse, Linz, Linze

Linette (French/English/
American) graceful and airy
Lanette, Linet, Linnet, Lynette

Ling (Chinese) delicate

Linga (American) form of Ling:
delicate

Lingga (Scandinavian)

Linji (English) form of Linsey:
bright spirit

Lin-Lin (Chinese) beauty of a
tinkling bell
Lin, Lin Lin

Linna (Scandinavian) flower

Linnea (Swedish) statuesque
Lin, Linayah, Linea, Linnay, Linny, Lynnea

Linnesh (American) form of
Lindsay: calming; bright and
shining

Linnz (American) form of
Lindsay: calming; bright and
shining

Lino (American) form of Lindsay:
calming; bright and shining

Linsey (English) bright spirit
Linsie, Linsy, Linzi, Linzie

Linsley (English) form of
Lindsay: calming; bright and
shining

Linzetta (American) form of
Linzey: calming; bright and
shining
Linze, Linzette

Linzey (American) form of
Lindsay: calming; bright and
shining

Lio (Jewish) form of Liora: light

Liora (Hebrew) light
Leeor, Leeora, Lior, Liorit

Lioren (Jewish) form of Liora:
light

Liotta (Italian) of the bay

Lioudmila (Slavic) loved

Lisa (Hebrew/American)
dedicated and spiritual
Lee, Leelee, Leesa, Leesah, Leeza, Leisa, Lesa, Lysa

Lisanne (English/Dutch) God is my oath; favor; grace

Lisbet (Scandinavian) sweet

Lisbeth (Hebrew) form of Elizabeth: God's promise

Lise (German) form of Lisa: dedicated and spiritual
Lesa

Lisen (Dutch) form of Lisanne;: God is my oath; favor; grace

Lisette (French) little Elizabeth
Lise, Lisete, Lissette, Liz

Lisha (Hebrew) form of Elisha: God-loving
Lish, Lishie

Lissa (Greek) sweet
Lyssa

Lissandra (Greek) defends others

Lisset (French) form of Elizabeth: God's promise

Lisseth (Hebrew) form of Elizabeth: God's promise
Liseta, Liseth, Lisette, Lisith, Liss, Lisse, Lissi

Lissie (American) form of Elise: concecrated to God
Lis, Lissi, Lissey, Lissy

Liszt (Hungarian) musical

Lita (Latin) life-giving
Leta

Lithyia (Mythology) prepared

Litisha (Spanish) form of Letitia: joy

Litzy (Spanish) form of Letitia: joy

Liv (Latin/Scandinavian) lively
Leev

Livia (Hebrew) lively
Levia, Livya

Liviu (Spanish) lively

Livona (Hebrew) vibrant
Levona, Liv, Livvie, Livvy

Liya (Russian) lily; lovely
Leeya

Liz (English) form of Elizabeth: God's promise
Lis, Lissy, Lizy, Lizzi, Lizzie

Liza (American) smiling
Leeza, Liz, Lizah, Lizzie, Lizzy, Lyza

Lizabeth (English) abundant in God

Lizeth (Hebrew) ebullient
Liseth, Lizethe

Lizette (Hebrew) lively
Lizet, Lizett

Lizset (Spanish) form of Lysett: pretty little one

Lizzie (American) devout
Liz, Liza, Lizae, Lizette, Lizzee, Lizzey, Lizzi, Lizzy

Lizzine (American) form of Elizabeth: God's promise

Llewwllyn (Welsh) shines brightly

Lo (American) spunky
Loe

Loa (English) form of Louise: hardworking and brave

Loelia (Arabic) nocturnal
Leila

Loen (Spanish) lovely

Loey (Mythology) kind
Louhi

Logan (English) climbing
Lo, Logun

Logana (Scottish) form of Logan: climbing

Loganah (Scottish) form of Logan: climbing

Logred (Welsh) dedication

Loicy (American) delightful
Loice, Loisee, Loisey, Loisi, Loy, Loyce, Loycy, Loyse, Loysie

Loire (Place name) river in France; lovely wonder
Loir, Loirane

Lois (Greek) good
Lo, Loes

Loise (English) form of Louise: hardworking and brave

Lola (Spanish) pensive
Lo, Lolah, Lolita
Loleatha (Spanish) sad
Loleen (American) jubilant
Lolene
Loleta (Spanish) sad
Lo-Lin (Asian) sure
Lolita (Spanish) sad
Lo, Lola, Loleta, Lita
Lolly (English) candy; sweet
Loma (Spanish) lucky
Lomita (Spanish) good
Lona (Latin) lionlike; (Indian) lovely
Lonee, Lonie, Lonna, Lonnie
Londa (American) shy
Londah, Londe, Londy
London ♂ (Place name) calming
Londen, Londun, Londy, Loney, Lony
Loni (American) beauty
Loney, Lonie, Lonnie
Lonise (American) form of Denise: wine-lover
Lonjeana (Spanish) tall
Lonnecke (American) lone
Lonnette (American) pretty
Lonett, Lonette, Lonn, Lonnie
Lonzine (French) alone
Lopa (Spanish)
Loperena (Spanish)

Lora (Latin) regal
Laura, Lorah, Lorea, Loria
Lorain (English) sad
Loranden (American) ingenious
Lorandyn, Lorannden, Luranden
Lordena (Spanish) form of Lourdes: a girl from Lourdes, France; hallowed
Lordyn (American) enchanting
Lorden, Lordin, Lordine, Lordun, Lordynn
Loreen (American) variation on Lauren: laurel-crowned
Lorene
Lorel (German) tempting
Loreal
Lorela (German) attracts
Lorelei (German) siren
Loralee, LoraLee, Lorilie, Lurleen, Lurlene
Lorelle (American) lovely
Lore, Loreee, Lorel, Lorey, Lori, Lorie, Lorille
Loren (American) form of Lauren: laurel-crowned
Lorren, Lorri, Lorrie, Lorron, Lorryn, Lory, Loryn, Lourie
Lorena (English) form of Loren: laurel-crowned
Loreen, Lorene, Lorrie, Lorrine

Lorenia (English) form of Lorena: laurel-crowned
Loreniana (English) given laurels
Lorenza (Latin) form of Laura: laurel-crowned; joyous
Laurenza
Loreto (Italian) miraculous; honored
Loretta (English) large-eyed beauty
Lauretta
Lori (Latin) laurel-crowned and nature-loving
Laurie, Loree, Lorie, Lory
Lorinthe (American) form of Laura: laurel-crowned; joyous
Loris (Greek/Latin) fun-loving
Lorice, Lauris
Loriz (American) form of Loris: fun-loving
Lorna (Latin) laurel-crowned; natural
Lorenah
Lorola (Origin unknown) family
Lorraine (Latin/French) sad-eyed
Laraine, Lauraine, Lorain, Loraine, Lorrie, Lors
Lorril (American) praise-worthy
Lorya (American) form of Laura: laurel-crowned; joyous
Lotta (Swedish) sweet

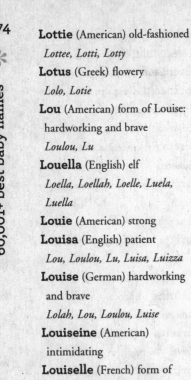

Lottie (American) old-fashioned
Lottee, Lotti, Lotty

Lotus (Greek) flowery
Lolo, Lotie

Lou (American) form of Louise:
hardworking and brave
Loulou, Lu

Louella (English) elf
Loella, Loellah, Loelle, Luela, Luella

Louie (American) strong

Louisa (English) patient
Lou, Loulou, Lu, Luisa, Luizza

Louise (German) hardworking
and brave
Lolah, Lou, Loulou, Luise

Louiseine (American)
intimidating

Louiselle (French) form of
Louise: hardworking and brave

Loura (Catalan) laurels

Louray (English) enchants

Lourdes (French) girl from
Lourdes, France; hallowed
Lordes, Lordez, Lourd

Louria (American) form of Laura:
laurel-crowned; joyous

Loutan (English) released

Love (English/American) loving
Lovey, Lovi, Luv

Loveada (Spanish) loving
Lova, Lovada

Lovella (Native American) soft
spirit
Lovela

Lovely (American) loving
Lovelee, Loveley, Loveli, Lovey

Lovie (American) warm
Lovee, Lovey, Lovi, Lovy

Lovina (American) warm
Lovena, Lovey, Lovinah, Lovinnah

Lovisa (Scandinavian) aggressor

Loway (Last name used as first
name) wolf; free

Lowe (English) sly; pretty

Lowell (American) lovely
Lowel

Lowena (American) form of
Louise: hardworking and brave
Lowenek, Lowenna

Loy (English) adoring

Loyalty (American) loyal
Loyaltie

Loycie (English) adoring

Loydia (Spanish) form of Lydia:
musical; unusual

Ltanya (American) form of
Latonya: birdlike

Ltaya (American) form of Latonya

Lualla (American) adoring;
graceful

Luba (Yiddish) dear
Liba, Lubah, Lyuba

Luberda (Spanish) light; dear
Luberdia

Luberta (Slavic) form of Luba:
dear

Lubica (Slavic) form of Luba: dear

Lublain (Slavic) form of Luba:
dear

Luca (Italian) light
Luka

Lucasta (Spanish) bringer of
light

Luceil (French) light; lucky
Luce, Lucee, Lucy

Lucelle (French) sheds light

Lucellene (French) sheds light

Lucerne (Latin) born into the
light
Lucerna

Lucero (Italian) light-hearted
Lucee, Lucey, Lucy

Lucetta (English) radiating joy

Lucette (French) pale light

Lucia (Italian/Greek/Spanish)
light; lucky in love
Chia, Luceah, Lucey, Luci

Luciana (Italian) fortunate
Louciana, Luceana, Lucianah

Lucie (French/American) lucky girl
Lucy

Lucienne (French) lucky
Lucianne, Lucien, Lucienn, Lucy-Ann

Lucilla (English) form of Lucille: bright-eyed
Loucilah, Loucilla, Lucilah, Lucylla, Lusyla, Luzela

Lucille (English) bright-eyed
Loucil, Loucile, Loucille, Lucyl, Lucie, Lucile, Lucy

Lucillea (French) sheds light

Lucillet (French) sheds light

Lucina (American) happy
Lucena, Lucie, Lucinah, Lucy, Lucyna

Lucinda (Latin) prissy
Cinda, Cindie, Lu, Luceenda, Lucynda, Lulu

Lucindia (English) form of Lucinda: prissy

Lucine (Scandinavian) lucid

Lucinea (Spanish) lucid

Lucita (Spanish) light
Lusita, Luzita

Lucja (Polish) light
Luscia

Luckette (Invented) lucky
Luckett

Lucretia (Latin) wealthy woman
Lu, Lucrecia, Lucreesha, Lucritia

Lucy ☉ (Latin/Scottish/Spanish) lighthearted
Lu, Luca, Luce, Luci, Lucie

Ludivina (Slavic) loved

Ludmilla (Slavic) beloved one
Lu, Ludie, Ludmila, Ludmylla, Lule, Lulu

Ludne (French) loved

Ludora (Spanish) loved

Lue (English) cheering

Lue-Ella (English) form of Ella: beautiful and fanciful
Louel, Luella, Luelle

Luella (German) conniving
Loella, Louella, Lu, Lula, Lulah, Lulu

Luenetter (American) egotistical
Lou, Lu, Luene, Luenette

Lugene (American) form of Eugene: blue-blood

Luicia (Spanish) light

Luisa (Spanish) smiling
Louisa

Luisana (Place name) from Louisiana
Luisanna, Luisanne, Luisiana

Luisito (Spanish) light

Luke (American) bouncy
Luc, Luka, Lukey, Lukie

Lula (German) all-encompassing
Lulu

Lulani (Polynesian) heaven-sent
Lula, Lani, Lanie

Lular (English) bounty of heaven

Lulu (German/English) kind
Lou, Loulou, Lu, Lulie

Lulua (English) comforts

Lulunena (German) comforts

Luminosa (Spanish) luminous

Luna (Latin) moonstruck
Loona

Luna-Coco (American) coconut moon

Lunan (Latin) moon

Lund (German) genius
Lun, Lunde

Lundria (Slavic) smart; from the grove

Lundy (Scottish) grove by an island
Lundea, Lundee, Lundi

Lundyn (American) different
Lundan, Lunden, Lundon

Luned (Welsh) moonlike

Lunell (American) luminous

Lunette (French) of the moon

Lunwonda (African) moon child

Lupe (Spanish) enthusiastic
Loopy, Loopey, Lupeta, Lupey, Lupie, Lupita

Luquitha (African American) fond
Luquetha, Luquith

Lur (Spanish) earth

Lura (American) loquacious
Loora, Lur, Lurah, Lurie

Luree (German) lures

Luretta (German) lures

Lurissa (American) beguiling
Luresa, Luressa, Luris, Lurisa, Lurissah, Lurly

Lurlaine (German) alluring

Lurlene (German) tempting
Lura, Lurleen, Lurlie, Lurline

Lushea (American) form of Lucia: light; lucky in love

Lutee (German) of the people

Lutherene (American) feminine form of Luther: reformer

Luticha (Spanish) form of Letitia: joy

Luvelle (American) light
Luvee, Luvell, Luvey, Luvy

Lu Verna (English) form of Laverne: breath of spring

Luvy (American) spontaneous
Lovey, Luv

Lux (Latin) light
Luxe, Luxee, Luxi, Luxy

Luz (Spanish) lighthearted
Lusa, Luzana, Luzi

Luzille (Spanish) light
Luz, Luzell

Lyanna (English) fierce

Lyanne (Greek) melodious
Liann, Lianne, Lyan, Lyana, Lyaneth, Lyann

Lyawonda (African American) friend
Lyawunda, Lywanda, Lywonda

Lycia (Biblical) place name

Lycoris (Greek) twilight

Lyda (American) unique

Lydda (Biblical) place name

Lydia (Greek) musical; unusual
Lidia, Lidya, Lyddie, Lydie, Lydy

Lydie (Slavic) girl of Lydia

Lyfe (American) life

Lyla (French) island girl
Lila, Lilah, Lile

Lyle (English) strident
Lile

Lymekia (Greek) form of Lydia: musical; unusual
Lymekea

Lynda (Spanish) form of Linda: pretty girl
Lindi, Lynde, Lyndie, Lynn

Lyndsay (Scottish) bright and shining
Lindsay, Lindsey

Lynelle (English) pretty girl; bright as sunshine
Linelle, Lynel, Lynie, Lynn

Lynette (French) small and fresh
Lyn, Lynet, Lynnet, Lynnie

Lynita (English) form of Lynette: small and fresh

Lynn (English) fresh as spring water
Lin, Linn, Linnie, Lyn, Lynne

Lynna (English) by the lake

Lynnaia (English) lake girl

Lynona (American) form of Wynona: firstborn girl

Lynsey (American) form of Lindsay: calming; bright and shining
Linzie, Lyndsey, Lynze, Lynzy

Lynzeen (American) form of Lindsay: calming; bright and shining

Lyonda (American) form of Lynda: pretty girl

Lyra (Greek) musical
Lyre

Lyric (Greek) musical
Lyrec

Lyrics (English) lyrical

Lyris (Greek) plays the lyre
Liris, Lirisa, Lirise

Lys (German) form of Elizabeth: God's promise

Lysa (Hebrew) God-loving
Leesa, Lisa

Lysalette (English) form of Lisette: little Elizabeth

Lysandra (Greek) liberator; she frees others
Lyse, Lysie

Lysanne (Greek) helpful
Lysann

Lysbeth (English) form of Elizabeth: God's promise

Lysett (American) pretty little one
Lyse, Lysette

Lysle (Spanish) pretty

Lyssan (Greek) form of Alexandra: defender of mankind
Liss, Lissan, Lissana, Lissandra, Lyss

Lyssette (English) form of Lisette: little Elizabeth

Lystra (Biblical) place name

Lytanisha (African American) scintillating
Litanisha, Lyta, Lytanis, Lytanish, Lytanishia, Nisa, Nisha

Lyttle (Last name used as first name) small

Lyudmilea (Slavic) beloved

Maacah (Biblical) place name

Maarath (Biblical) place name

Mab (Literature) Shakespearean queen of fairies

Mabel (Latin) well-loved
Mabbel, Mabil, Mable, Mabyl, Maybel, Maybie

Mabellee (Asian) beauty

Maben (Welsh) child

Mablee (Welsh) pretty

Macallister (Irish) confident

Macander (Biblical) place name

Macarena (Spanish) name of a dance; blessed
Macarene, Macaria, Macarria, Rena

Macaria (Spanish) blessed
Maca, Macarea, Macarie, Maka

Macey (American) upbeat; happy
Mace, Macie, Macy

Machelle (Hebrew) thinks of God

Mackenzie ✿ ❶ (Irish) leader
Mac, Mackenzee, Mackenzey, Mackenzi, Mackenzy, Mackie, Mackinsey, Mckenzie, McKinsey, McKinzie, MaKenzie

Macress (American) thankful

Mada (American) helpful
Madah, Maida

Madai (Biblical) place name

Madalena (Greek) form of Madeline: strength-giving
Madalayna, Madaleyna, Madalayna, Madelena, Madeleyna, Madelyna

Madalyn ✿ (Greek) high goals
Madelyn

Madchen (German) girl
Madchan, Madchin, Maddchen

Maddie (English) form of Madeline: strength-giving
Mad, Maddee, Maddey, Maddi, Maddy, Mady

Maddox (English) giving
Maddax, Maddee, Maddey, Maddie, Maddux, Maddy

Maddye (English) form of Madeleine: high-minded

Madeleine (French) high-minded
Madelon

Madeleinea (English) form of Madeleine: high-minded

Madeline ✿ (Greek) strength-giving
Madaleine, Maddie, Maddy, Madelene, Madi

Madelyn (Greek) strong woman
Madalyn, Madlynne, Madolyn

Madge (Greek/American) spunky
Madgie, Madg

Madgie (English) form of Madge: spunky; form of Margaret: treasured pearl; pure-spirited

Madhur (Hindi) sweet girl

Madina (Greek) form of Madeline: strength-giving
Mada, Maddelina, Maddi, Maddy, Madele, Madena, Madlin

Madine (American) form of Nadine: dancer

Madis (English) form of Madison: good-hearted

Madison ✿ ♂ (English) good-hearted
Maddie, Maddison, Maddy, Madisen, Madysin

Madlyina (English) form of Madeleine: high-minded

Madonna (Latin) my lady; spirited

Madora (Place name) from Madeira, Spain: volcanic
Madorra

Madrigal (Word as name)

Madrina (Spanish) godmother
Madra, Madreena, Madrine

Madrona (Spanish) mother; maternal
Madrena

Mae (English) bright flower
May

Maegan (Irish) a gem of a woman
Megan

MaElena (Spanish) light
Elena, Lena

Maeli (English) great
Maelee, Maeley, Maelie, Maely, Maylee, Mayley, Mayli, Maylie, Mayly

Maeve (Irish) queen
Maive, Mave, Mayve

Maevey (Irish) exciting

Mafe (Italian) strong

Magadan (Biblical) place name

Magali (French) treasured pearl

Magan (Greek) heavy-hearted
Mag, Magen, Maggie

Magany (Greek) doleful

Magda (Scandinavian) believer
Mag, Maggie

Magdala (Greek) girl in the tower
Magdalla

Magdalene (Greek/Scandinavian) spiritual
Mag, Magda, Magdalena, Magdaline, Magdalyn, Magdelin, Magdylena, Maggie

Magella (Slavic) starry-eyed

Maggie (Greek/English/Irish) priceless pearl
Mag, Maggee, Maggi

Magina (Russian) hardworking
Mageena, Maginah

Magli (French) treasured pearl

Maglie (French) treasured pearl

Magnolia (Latin) flowering and flourishing
Mag, Maggi, Maggie, Maggy, Magnole, Nolie

Magryta (Slavic) desired

Mahal (Filipino) loving woman
Mah, Maha

Mahala (Hebre/Native American) tender female
Mah, Mahalah, Mahalia, Mahla, Mahlie

Mahelia (Arabic) form of Mahala: tender female
Maheelia, Maheelya, Mahelya

Mahina (Hawaiian) moonbeam

Mahira (Hebrew) vibrant

Mahogany (Spanish) rich as
wood
Mahagonie, Mahogony

Mahoney (American) high
energy
Mahhony, Mahonay, Mahonie,
Mahony

Mai (Scandinavian/Japanese)
treasure; flower; singular
Mae, May

Maia (Greek) fertile; earth goddess
Maya, Mya

Maida (Greek) shy girl
Mady, Maidie, May, Mayda

Maidie (Scottish) maiden; virgin
Maidee, Maydee, Maydie

Maija (Scandinavian) form of
Mary: star of the sea; sea of
bitterness

Maike (German) form of Maria:
desired child

Mailanna (Hawaiian) lei of Anna

Maileen (Hawaiian) lei

Mailene (Hawaiian) lei

Mailie (Scottish) virtuous

Mainan (American) guesses

Mair (Irish) form of Mary: star of
the sea; sea of bitterness
Maire

Maira (Hebrew) bitter; saved
Mara, Marah

Maired (Irish) pearl; treasured
Mairead, Mared

Mairin (Irish) form of Mary: star
of the sea; sea of bitterness

Maisha (Arabic) proud

Maisie (Scottish) treasure
Maesee, Maesey, Maesi, Maesie,
Maesy, Maisee, Maisey, Maisi,
Maisy, Maizie, Mazee

Maitland (American) form of
Maitlyn: kind
Maitlande, Mateland, Matelande,
Maytland, Maytlande

Maitlin (American) form of
Maitlyn: kind
Matelin, Matelyn, Maytlin,
Maytlyn

Maj (Slavic) star

Maja (Scandinavian) fertile

Majella (Slavic) star

Majidah (Arabic) slendid

Majula (Slavic) star

Maka (Hawaiian) face

Makala (Hawaiian) natural
outdoors
Makal, Makie

Makani (Hawaiian) in the wind

Makay (American) charming

Makayla ○ ❶ (American)
magical
Makaila, Makala, Michaela,
Mikaela, Mikayla, Mikaylah

Makeda (African) excellent

Makena (African) wisdom's child

Makkedah (African) lovely

Makula (American) exacting

Makyll (American) innovative
Makell

Makynna (American) friendly
Makenna, Makinna

Malah (Indian) garland
Mala

Malak (Arabic) angelic

Malatha (Biblical) place name

Malati (Indian) jasmine flower

Malay (Place name) from
Malaysia; softspoken
Malae

Malaya (Filipino) free and open
Malea

Maleah (Hawaiian) sad

Malendita (Spanish) royal

Malene (Scandinavian) in the
tower
Maleen, Maleene, Malyne

Malha (Hebrew) queenlike and
regal

Mali (Thai) flowering beauty
Malee, Maley, Malie, Malley,
Mallie, Maly

Malia (Hawaiian) thoughtful
Maylia

Maliaval (Hawaiian) peaceful

Malika (Hungarian) hardworking
and punctual
Maleeka

Malikian (Hawaiian) of the
queen

Malin (Native American)
comfort-giver
Malen, Maline, Mallie

Malina (Scandinavian) in the
tower
Maleena, Maleenah, Malinah,
Malyna, Malynah

Malinda (Greek/American)
honey
Melinda

Malinee (American) sweet

Malini (Indian) river

Malisa (English) loyal

Malissa (Greek) honey bee
Melissa

Maliyah (Hawaiian) form of
Malia: thoughtful

Malla (Indian) adorned with
necklace

Mallika (Indian) watchful;
tending the garden
Malika

Mallory (French/German/
American) tough-minded; spunky
Mal, Malery, Mallari, Mallery,
Mallie, Mallorey, Mallori,
Mallorie, Maloree, Malorey,
Malori, Malorie, Malory

Malu (Hawaiian) peaceful
Maloo

Malvika (Slavic) darkness

Malvina (Scottish) romantic
Malv, Malva, Malvie, Melvina

Mame (American) form of
Margaret: treasured pearl; pure-
spirited
Maime, Mayme

Mamie (American) form of
Margaret: treasured pearl; pure-
spirited
Mamee, Mamey, Mami, Mamy

Manasa (Asian) lovely

Mancie (American) hopeful
Manci, Mansey, Mansie

Manda (American) form of
Amanda: fit to be loved
Amand, Mandee, Mandi, Mandy

Mandana (African) combative

Mandeece (African) loved

Mandeen (American) form of
Amanda: fit to be loved

Mandia (Indian) beloved

Mandisa (African) kind

Mandy (Latin) lovable
Manda, Mandee, Mandey, Mandi,
Mandie

Mane (American) top
Main, Manie

Manee (Korean) peace giving
Mani, Manie

Manessa (Sanskrit) wise

Manilow (Last name as first
name) musical

Manisha (Hindi) sharp intellect

Manju (Hindi) sweetheart

Manna (Hawaiian) perceptive
Mana, Manah, Mannah

Manolita (Spanish) girl who lives
in God

Manon (French) exciting

Mantae (Slavic) form of Maria:
desired child

Mantill (American) guarded
Mant, Mantell, Mantie

Manuela (Spanish) sophisticated
girl
Manuella

Manya (Spanish) form of Maria:
desired child

Manzie (Native American) flower
Mansi

Mappie (American) zany

Maquila (Spanish) stubborn

Mara (Greek) thoughtful believer
Marah, Marra

Maralys (American) devout

Maranda (Latin) wonderful
Marandah, Miranda

Marat (American) form of Merit:
deserving

Marbell (American) pretty

Marbella (Spanish) pretty
Marb, Marbela, Marbelle

Marbury (American) substantial
Mar, Marbary

Marcelina (Latin) form of
Marcella: dedicated to Mars
*Marceleena, Marcelyna,
Marcileena, Marcilina, Marcilyna,
Marcyleena*

Marceline (Latin) form of
Marcella: dedicated to Mars
*Marceleene, Marcelline, Marcelyne,
Marcileene, Marcilyne, Marcyleene*

Marcella (Latin) dedicated to
Mars
*Marce, Marcela, Marci, Marcie,
Marse, Marsella*

Marcellette (French) staunch

Marcellita (Spanish) desired;
feisty
*Marcel, Marcelita, Marcelite,
Marcelle, Marcelli, Marcey, Marci*

Marcellyn (English) form of
Marceline: dedicated to Mars

Marcena (Latin/American)
spirited
Marce, Marceen, Marcene, Marcie

March (American) month of
March; spring girl

Marcia (Latin/American)
dedicated to Mars
Marcie, Marsha

Marciana (Spanish) warring

Marcie (English) chummy
*Marcee, Marcey, Marci, Marcy,
Marsi, Marsie*

Marcine (American) bright
Marceen, Marceene

Marconi (Italian) creates

Marcy (English/American)
opinionated
Marci, Marsie, Marsy

Mardi (French) Tuesday

Mardjaneh (Indian) of the
meadow

Mardonia (American) approving
*Mardee, Mardi, Mardone,
Mardonne, Mardy*

Mare (American) living by the
ocean

Mareane (Irish) form of Mary:
star of the sea; sea of bitterness

Marelly (French) form of Mary:
star of the sea; sea of bitterness

Maren (American) ocean-lover
Marin, Marren, Marrin

Marenz (Slavic) of the sea

Maret (English) form of Mary:
star of the sea; sea of bitterness
*Marett, Marit, Maritt, Maryt,
Marytt*

Marete (English) pearl girl

Marfelia (Spanish) form of
Martha: lady

Marfo (Russian) form of Martha:
lady

Marg (American) tenacious
Mar

Margaret (Greek/Scottish/
English) treasured pearl; pure-
spirited
*Mag, Maggie, Marg, Margerite,
Margie, Margo, Margret, Meg,
Meggie*

Margaretta (Spanish) pearl

Margarita (Italian/Spanish)
winning
*Marg, Margarit, Margarite,
Margie, Margrita, Marguerita*

Margarite (Greek/German) form of Margaret: treasured pearl; pure-spirited
Gretal, Marga, Margareeta, Margaryta, Margereeta, Margerita, Margeryta, Margit, Margot

Margaux (French) form of Margaret: treasured pearl; pure-spirited

Marge (English/American) form of Marjorie: bittersweet; pearl
Marg, Margie

Margery (English) form of Marjorie: bittersweet; pearl
Marge, Margie

Marghanita (Spanish) pearl

Margherita (Italian/Greek) form of Margaret: treasured pearl; pure-spirited
Marg

Margia (American) form of Margie: friendly
Marge, Margea, Margy

Margie (English) friendly
Margey, Margy, Marjie

Margina (American) centered

Margoletta (French) little Margo; spunky

Margot (French) lively
Margaux, Margo

Margrit (Spanish) treasured

Margrita (Spanish) treasure
Margreeta, Margrytaa

Margrite (Dutch) form of Margaret: treasured pearl; pure-spirited

Margrune (Slavic) form of Margaret: treasured pearl; pure-spirited

Marguerite (French) stuffy
Maggie, Marg, Margerite, Margie, Margina, Margurite

Margyd (Welsh) pearl-like

Mari (Japanese) ball; round

Maria ☉ (Latin/French/German/Italian/Polish/Spanish) desired child
Maja, Malita, Mareea, Marica, Marike, Marucha, Mezi, Mitzi

Mariah ☉ (Hebrew) God is my teacher
Marayah, Mariahe, Marriah, Meriah, Moriah

Marial (Spanish) embittered

Mariama (Hebrew) form of Mariam: bitter

Mariamne (French) form of Miriam: living with sadness
Mariam, Marianne

Marian (English) thoughtful
Mariane, Marianne, Maryann, Maryanne

Mariana (Spanish) quiet girl
Maryanna

Marianda (Invented) combo of Mari and Rianda

Maribel (French/English/American) star of the sea; beautiful
EmBee, Marabel, Maribela, Merrybelle

Maricruz (Spanish) Maria of the cross

Marid (English) form of Maria: desired child

Marie (French) form of Mary: star of the sea; sea of bitterness
Maree, Marye

Mariea (English) form of Maria: desired child

Mariel (German) spiritual
Mari, Mariele, Marielle

Mariella (Italian) form of Maria: desired child

Marielos (Spanish) form of Mariel: spiritual

Mariene (Spanish) devout
Mari, Marienne

Mariet (French) form of Marie: star of the sea; sea of bitterness
Mariett, Mariette, Maryet, Maryett, Maryette

Marigene (Dutch) embittered

Marigold (Botanical) sunny
Maragold, Marigolde, Marigole,
Marrigold, Marygold, Marygolde

Marijana (Slavic) aggressive

Marijonna (Slavic) aggressive

Marika (Slavic/American)
thoughtful and brooding
Mareeca, Mareecka, Mareeka,
Marica, Maricka, Maryca,
Marycka, Maryka, Merica,
Merika, Merk, Merkie

Marikae (Slavic) bitter

Marilan (American) form of
Marilyn: fond-spirited

Marilyn (Hebrew) fond-spirited
Maralynne, Mare, Marilin,
Mariline, Marilinn, Marilynn,
Marrie, Marrilyn, Marylyn,
Marylynn, Merilyn, Merrilyn

Marin (Latin) sea-loving
Mare, Maren

Marina (Latin) lover of the ocean
Mareena, Marena, Maryna

Marinaea (American) form of
Marin: sea-loving

Marinalla (American) of the sea

Marine (French) of the sea

Marinen (Mythology) sea

Marineuza (Spanish) sea child

Marioara (Indian) delicate

Marion (French) form of Mary:
star of the sea; sea of bitterness
Mare, Marien, Marrion, Maryen,
Maryian, Maryon

Mariposa (Spanish) butterfly
Mari, Mariposah, Maryposa

Mariquita (Spanish) form of
Margaret: treasured pearl; pure-
spirited
Marikita, Marrikita, Marriquita

Maris (Latin) sea-loving
Mere, Meris, Marys

Marisa (Latin) sea-loving
Marce, Maressa, Marissa, Marisse,
Mariza, Marsie, Marysa, Maryssa,
Merisa

Marisela (Spanish) hearty
Marisella, Marysela

Mariska (American) endearing
Mareska, Marisca, Mariskah

Marisol (Spanish) stunning
Mare, Mari, Marizol, Marrisol,
Marzol, Merizol

Marisse (French) beloved

Maritala (Scandinavian) pearl

Maritel (Scandinavian) pearl

Maritza (Place name) for St.
Moritz, Switzerland

Marixa (Spanish) endearing

Marixbel (Spanish) pretty
Marix

Marizu (Spanish) blessed

Marjetta (Slavic) form of
Margaret: treasured pearl; pure-
spirited

Marjie (Scottish) form of
Marjorie: bittersweet; pearl
Marji, Marjy

Marjolein (Dutch) spice

Marjorie (Greek/English/
Scottish) bittersweet; pearl
Marg, Marge, Margerie, Margery,
Margorie, Marjie, Marjori

Marketa (Slavic) form of
Margaret: treasured pearl; pure-
spirited
Marketta

Marky (American) mischievous
Marki, Markie

Marla (German) believer; easygoing
Marlah, Marlla

Marlaina (American) form of
Marlene: child of light; bitter
Marlaine, Marlane

Marlake (Slavic) of the lake

Marlam (American) wanted

Marlana (Hebrew/Greek) vamp
Marlanna

Marleal (American) form of
Mary: star of the sea; sea of
bitterness
Marle, Marleel, Marly

Marlee (Greek) guarded
Marleigh, Marley, Marli, Marlie, Marly

Marlen (American) desired
Marl, Marla, Marlin

Marlena (German) pretty; bittersweet
Marla, Marlaina, Marleena, Marlina, Marlyna, Marlynne, Marnie

Marlene (German) child of light; bitter
Marlean, Marlee, Marleen, Marleene, Marley, Marline, Marly, Marlyne

Marlette (English) form of Merlette: magical

Marley (English) form of Marlene: child of light; bitter
Mar, Marlee, Marlie, Marly

Marliece (Spanish) desirable

Marlinn (German) form of Mary: star of the sea; sea of bitterness

Marlise (English) considerate
Marlice, Marlis, Marlys

Marlo (American) vivacious
Marloe, Marloh, Marlow, Marlowe

Marlona (German) form of Mary: star of the sea; sea of bitterness

Marlonene (German) form of Mary: star of the sea; sea of bitterness

Marluce (German) form of Marlis: religious

Marlycia (Spanish) desired
Lycia, Marly, Marlysia

Marlys (English) form of Marlis: religious

Marna (French) form of Marlene: child of light; bitter

Marnelle (Hebrew) form of Marnie: storyteller

Marnie (Hebrew) storyteller
Marn, Marnee, Marney, Marni, Marny

Marnina (French) form of Marlene: child of light; bitter
Marneena, Marnyna

Marnita (American) worrier
Marneta, Marni, Marnite, Marnitta, Marny

Marolyn (Invented) form of Marilyn: fond-spirited
Maro, Marolin, Marolinne

Marqeen (American) form of Marquise: noble-spirited

Marquetisha (Spanish) form of Marquita: happy girl

Marquise (French) noble-spirited
Markeese, Marquees, Marquisa, Mars

Marquisha (African American) form of Marquise: noble-spirited
Marquish

Marquista (Spanish) form of Marquita: happy girl

Marquita (Spanish) happy girl
Marqueda, Marquitta, Marrie

Marquittaian (Spanish) form of Marquita: happy girl

Marrea (American) form of Maria: desired child

Marri (American) form of Mary: star of the sea; sea of bitterness

Marrie (American) form of Mary: star of the sea; sea of bitterness
Marry

Mars (Roman) warring

Marsala (Italian) seaport in Sicily
Marse, Marsela, Marsie

Marschelle (Scottish) form of Marsail: happy

Marselle (Spanish) happy

Marsha (Latin) form of Marcia: dedicated to Mars
Mars, Marsie

Marshay (American) exuberant
Marshae, Marshaya

Marshaye (French) difficult

Marshette (French) difficult

Marta (Danish) treasure
Mart, Marte, Marty, Merta

Martcia (Spanish) unmanageable

Marterrell (American) changeable
Marte, Marterill, Martrell

Martha (Aramaic) lady
Marta, Marth, Marti, Marty,
Mattie

Marthe (Aramaic) ladylike

Marti (English) form of Martha:
lady
Martee, Martey, Martie, Marty

Martijn (Dutch) unmanageable

Martina (Latin/German)
combative
Marteena, Martene, Marti,
Martinna, Martyna, Tina

Martine (French) combative

Martivanio (Italian) form of
Martina: combative
Mart, Marti, Tivanio

Martonette (American) feminine
form of Martin: warlike
Martanette, Martinette, Martonett

Martreece (American)
unmanageable

Marty (English) form of Martha:
lady
Marti

Maruja (Slavic) soft heart

Marusya (Slavic) softhearted

Marvel (French) astounding;
marvelous

Marvella (French) marvelous
woman
Marva, Marvelle, Marvie, Mavela

Marvis (American) form of
Mavis: singing bird

Marwyn (Welsh) beautiful

Mary (Latin/Hebrew) star of the
sea; sea of bitterness
Maire, Mara, Mare, Maree, Mari,
Marie, Mariel, Marlo, Marye,
Merree, Merry, Mitzie

Marya (Arabic) white and bright
Marja

Maryam (Arabic) form of
Miriam: living with sadness

Maryann (English) form of
Mary: star of the sea; sea of
bitterness
Mariann, Marianne, Maryan,
Maryanne

Maryina (Spanish) little Mary

Maryke (Dutch) kind; desired
Mairek, Marika, Maryk, Maryky

Mary-Marg (American) dramatic
Marimarg

Maryon (American) form of
Marian: thoughtful

Marzel (Italian) form of Marzia:
star of the sea; sea of bitterness

Marzia (Italian) form of Mary:
star of the sea; sea of bitterness

Marzol (Spanish) form of
Marisol: stunning

Masailda (American) supportive

Masha (Russian) child who was
desired

Mashayl (Slavic) form of Mary:
star of the sea; sea of bitterness;
form of Masha: child who was
desired

Mashella (Slavic) form of Mary:
star of the sea; sea of bitterness;
form of Masha: child who was
desired

Mashonda (African American)
believer
Masho, Mashonde

Masi (African) star

Masina (Last name as first)
charming; delightful

Mason (French) diligent; reliable

Massey (German) confident
Massi, Massie

Massiel (American) giving
Masie, Masiel, Massey, Massielle

Massim (Latin) great
Massima, Maxim, Maxima

Matia (Hebrew) a God-given gift
Matea, Mattea, Mattie

Matild (Hungarian) strong

Matilda (German) powerful
fighter
Mat, Mathilda, Mattie, Tilda,
Tillie, Tilly

Matina (Scandinavian) morning child

Matney (American) born in the morning

Mattanah (Biblical) place name; God's child

Mattie (English) most honored
Matt, Matte, Mattey, Matti, Matty

Matus (Slavic) essential

Matusea (Slavic) essential

Matylda (Polish) strong fighter
Matyld

Maude (English) old-fashioned
Maud, Maudie

Maudeen (American) countrified
Maudie, Mawdeen, Mawdine

Maudella (English) mighty

Maudest (French) modest

Maudette (English) mighty

Maudisa (African) sweet
Maudesa, Maudesah

Mauline (English) strong

Mauna (American) attractive
Maune, Mawna, Mon

Maupassant (French) writes

Maura (Latin/Irish) dark
Moira, Maurie

Mauree (Spanish) dark

Maureen (Irish/French) night-loving
Maura, Maurene, Maurine, Moreen, Morene

Maureena (Irish) form of Mary: star of the sea; sea of bitterness

Maurelle (French) petite
Maure, Maurie, Maurielle

Mauricea (Spanish) form of Mary: star of the sea; sea of bitterness

Maurilia (Spanish) dark beauty

Maurise (French) dark
Maurice, Morise

Maurshia (Slavic) form of Marsha: dedicated to Mars

Mauve (French) gentle
Mauvey, Mauvie

Mave (French) bird; melodic

Mavi (French) sings

Mavis (French) singing bird
Mauvis, Mav, Mave

Maxcie (English) best

Maxcien (English) best

Maxeeme (Latin) form of Maxime: maximum

Maxence (English) best

Maxie (Latin) fine
Maxee, Maxey, Maxy

Maxien (English) best

Maxilla (English) best

Maxime (Latin) maximum
Maxey, Maxi, Maxim

Maxine (Latin) greatest of all
Max, Maxeen, Maxene, Maxie, Maxy

May (English) the fifth month
Mae, Maye

Maya ✪ (Spanish/Hindi/Russian) industrious; one of a kind; bitter
Maia, Maiya, Mayah, Mya, Myah, Mye

Mayada (English) form of May: the fifth month

Maybelline (Latin) variation of Mabel: well-loved
Mabie, May, Maybeline, Maybie, Maybleene

Maybelyn (Spanish) form of Mabel: well-lovedl

Mayeta (Native American) fruitful

Mayghaen (American) fortunate

Mayim (Origin unknown) special
Mayum

Maykaylee (American) ingenious
Maykayli, Maykaylie, Maykayly

Mayo (Place name) a county in Ireland; vibrant
Mayoh

Mayphous (American) imaginative

Mayra (Spanish) flourishing; creative
Mayrah

Mayrallea (Spanish) form of May: the fifth month

Mayrant (Spanish) industrious
Maya, Mayrynt

Maytra (English) form of Myra: fragrant

Mayuri (Indian) hen

Mayya (Slavic) lovely

Mazeka (Slavic) form of May: the fifth month

Mazel (Hebrew) luck
Masel, Mazil, Mazal

Mazella (English) form of May: the fifth month

Mazen (English) form of May: the fifth month

Mazie (Scottish) form of Maisie: treasure

Mazu (Chinese) goddess of the sea

McCanna (American) ebullient
Maccanna, McCannah

McCauley (Irish) feisty
Mac, McCauly, McCawlie

McCay (Irish) creative
Mackaylee, McCaylee

McCormick (Irish) last name as first name
MacCormack, Mackey

McGown (Irish) sensible
Mac, MacGowen, Mackie, McGowen

McKenna (American) able
Mackenna, Makenna

McKenzie ❶ (Scottish) form of Mackenzie: leader
Mackie, McKinzie, Mickey

McMurtry (Irish) last name as first name
Mac, McMurt

Mead (Greek) honey-wine-loving
Meade, Meed, Meede

Meadhoh (Irish) joyful

Meador (Irish) righteous; form of the meadow

Meadow (English) open land; calm
Meadoh

Meagan (Irish) joyous; precious
Maegan, Meaghan, Meegan, Meg, Meganne, Meggie, Meggye, Meghan

Meagara (Mythology) first

Meanda (Invented) models

Meanne (American) models

Meara (Irish) happy girl

Meashley (American) charmer
Meash, Meashlee

Meatah (American) athletic
Mea, Mia, Miata, Miatah

Meatra (American) models

Meave (Irish) sings

Mecjhelle (Slavic) form of Michelle: like the Lord

Mecoline (American) form of Nicole: winning

Medal (Word as name)

Medalla (Spanish) lovely

Medalle (American) pretty
Medahl, Medoll

Medardo (Spanish) pretty

Medea (Greek) ruling; cruel
Medeia

Medeba (Biblical) place name

Medes (Biblical) place name

Media (Greek) form of Medea: ruling; cruel

Mediatrix (Greek) ingenious

Medilyn (American) gift

Medina (Place name)

Medisyn (American) gift

Medusa (Greek) contriver; temptress

Medy (American) gift

Meeleen (Irish) excites

Meena (Hindi) fish

Meeno (Sanskrit) form of Meena: fish

Meera (Hindi) rich

Meg (Greek) able; lovable
Megs

Megan ☉ (Irish) precious; joyful
*Meagan, Meaghen, Meggi,
Meghan, Meghann*

Meggie (Greek) best
Meggey, Meggi, Meggy

Megha (Indian) cloudy; (Welsh)
pearl

Meghan (Welsh) pearl
Meghen, Meghyn

Mehetabel (Hebrew) won by faith
Mehitabel

Mehul (Hindi) rain girl

Meirion (Hebrew) light

Meissa (Hindi) form of Mesha:
born in lunar month; moon-
loving
Meisa, Meysa, Meyssa

Mejia (Slavic) flowers

Mekeba (Invented) jubilant

Mel (Greek) sporty
Mell

Melada (Greek) form of Melanie:
dark; sweet
Mel, Melli

Melaina (Greek) dark; generous

Melana (Greek) giving; dark

Melancon (French) dark beauty;
sweet
*Mel, Melance, Melaney, Melanie,
Melanse, Melanson, Melonce,
Melonceson*

Melangel (Welsh) darling angel

Melania (Italian) giving;
philanthropic
Mel, Melly

Melanie ☉ (Greek) dark; sweet
*Melanee, Melaney, Melani,
Melany, Meleni, Melenie, Meleny*

Melanna (Greek) dark

Melantha (Greek) dark-skinned;
sweet
Melanthah

Melaynee (Greek) dark; sweet

Melb (Greek) mellow

Melba (Australian) talented; lighthearted
Melbah

Melbal (Greek) mellow

Melea (German) diligent

Melecio (Spanish) mild

Meleda (Spanish) sweet
Meleeda, Melida, Melyda

Melete (Greek) effective

Melezio (Spanish) mild

Melia (German) dedicated
Meelia, Meleea, Melya, Melyah

Melicent (English) form of
Millicent: soft-hearted
Melisent

Melina (Greek) honey; sweet
*Meleena, Melena, Melinah,
Melyna*

Melinane (Greek) honey
sweetness

Melinda (Latin) honey;
sweetheart
*Linda, Linnie, Linny, Lynda,
Mellie, Melynda, Milinda, Mindy,
Mylinde*

Melisande (French) strong
Melisenda

Meliss (American) honey bee

Melissa (Greek) honey
Melisa, Melysa, Melyssa, Melyssuh

Melita (Biblical) place name

Melitene (Biblical) place name

Melize (English) nymph; bee

Melizza (English) form of
Melissa: honey

Mellicent (German) form of
Millicent: soft-hearted
Melicent, Mellycent, Melycent

Mellie (Greek) bee; busy

Mellony (English) form of
Melanie: dark; sweet

Melnie (English) dark

Melody (Greek) song; musical
*Mel, Mellie, Melodee, Melodey,
Melodie*

Melona (English) dark

Meloney (American) form of
Melanie: dark; sweet
Mel, Melone, Meloni

Melora (Latin) good
Meliora, Melorah, Melourah

Melosa (Greek) form of Melissa: honey
Melossa

Melotta (English) form of Melissa: honey

Melrose (English) honey of roses; sweet girl
Mellrose, Melrosie

Melua (Unknown) rising

Melusine (Mythology) honey bee

Melvia (American) leader; dark
Mel, Mell, Melvea

Melvina (Irish) prepared to lead
Malvina

Mena (Egyptian) pretty
Meenah, Menah

Menaka (Indian) heavenly girl

Mencina (Place name) serious

Mendee (American) form of Melinda: honey; sweetheart

Meng (Asian) shines

Mengline (Asian) shines

Menon (French) form of Mariel: spiritual

Menzalah (Biblical) place name

Meosha (African American) talented
Meeosha, Meoshe, Miosha

Merah (Biblical) abundant

Merary (American) merry
Marary, Meraree, Merarie

Mercadel (Spanish) mirth

Merce (Asian) merciful

Mercedes (Spanish) merciful; rewarded
Mercedez, Mercides, Mersadez, Mersaydes

Mercer (English) mercy

Mercia (English) form of Marcia: dedicated to Mars

Mercilite (American) mercy

Mercy (English) forgiving
Merce, Mercee, Mercey, Merci, Mercie

Meredith (Welsh) protector
Mer, Meredithe, Meredyth, Merridith, Merry, Merydith, Merydithe

Meredythe (English) excellent

Merel (Scandinavian) sea

Meri (Irish) by the sea
Merrie

Meria (Scandinavian) sea

Meribah (Biblical) place name

Meridian (American) perfect posture
Meredian, Meridiane

Merie (French) secretive; blackbird
Mer, Meri, Myrie

Meriel (Irish) girl who shines like the sea
Meri, Merial, Merri, Merriyl, Merry

Meris (Latin) form of Merissa: ocean-loving
Meriss, Merris, Merrys, Merys

Merissa (Latin) ocean-loving
Merisa, Meryssa

Merit (American) deserving
Merite, Meritt, Meritte, Meryt, Merytt, Mirit

Merithian (American) sea girl

Merka (Slavic) connives

Merle (Irish) shining girl
Merl, Murl, Murle

Merlette (English) magical

Merlin (English) magical

Merlina (English) magical

Merlyn (Spanish) sea child

Merney (American) form of Marnie: storyteller

Merolina (American) form of Carolina: well-loved

Merom (Biblical) place name

Meroth (Biblical) place name

Merribeth (English) cheerful
Merri-Beth, Merrybeth

Merridy (American) form of Meredith: protector

Merrience (American) merry child

Merrill (Irish) shines
Merril

Merry (English) cheerful
Mer, Meri, Merie, Merree, Merrey, Merri, Merrie, Mery

Mersaydes (Invented) form of Mercedes: merciful; rewarded
Mercy, Mersa, Mersy

Mersey (English) river Mersey; rich
Merce, Merse

Mersia (Hebrew) princess
Mercy, Mers, Mersea, Mersy

Mertha (American) joyful

Mertie (American) famed

Meryl (Irish) shining sea
Mer, Merel, Merri, Merrill, Merryl, Meryll

Meryletta (American) form of Mary: star of the sea; sea of bitterness

Merylette (American) form of Mary: star of the sea; sea of bitterness

Merynda (American) form of Marin: sea-loving

Merzi (American) mercy

Mesa (Place name) earthy
Mase, Maysa, Mesah

Mesembria (Biblical) place name

Mesha (Hindi) born in lunar month; moon-loving
Meshah

Meshalle (French) leader

Meshawnda (Invented) oblivious

Meshelle (French) leader

Messana (Biblical) place name

Meta (Scandinavian) form of Margaret: treasured pearl; pure-spirited

Metchie (Scandinavian) odd

Metta (Scandinavian) unique

Meverly (American) form of Beverly: beavers by the stream; friendly

Mexill (Invented) self-involved

Mhari (Scottish) form of Mary: star of the sea; sea of bitterness
Mhairi

Mi (Chinese) obsessive
My, Mye

Mia ○ ⊕ (Scandinavian/Italian) blessed; girl of mine
Me, Mea, Meah, Meea, Meya, Mya

Miaka (Japanese) influential

Mialinda (Italian) my sweet beauty

Miami (Place name)

Miano (Italian) my sweet

Micaela (Italian) form of Michael: like the Lord

Micah (Hebrew) religious
Mica, Mika, My, Myca

Micala (Hebrew) form of Michaela: God-loving
Micalah, Michala, Michalah, Mikala, Mikalah, Mycala, Mycalah, Mychala, Mychalah, Mykala, Mykalah

Michaela (Hebrew) God-loving
Meeca, Micaela, Micela, Michael, Michal, Michala, Michalla, Michela, Mikaela, Mikala, Mikela, Mycaela, Mycela, Mychaela, Mychela, Mykaela, Mykela

Michaele (Hebrew) loving God

Michaeleen (Italian) feminine form of Michael: like the Lord

Michaelena (Italian) feminine form of Michael: like the Lord

Michelin (American) lovable
Michalynn, Mish, Mishelin

Micheline (French) form of Michelle: like the Lord
Mishelinne

Michelle ○ ⊕ (Italian/French/American) feminine form of Michael: like the Lord
Machele, Machelle, Mechele, Mia, Michell, Michele, Mischel, Mischell, Mischelle, Mish, Mishell, Mishelle

Mickellette (Slavic) feminine
form of Michael: like the Lord
Mickey (American) quirky
*Mick, Mickee, Micki, Micky, Miki,
Mikie, Mycki*
Mickley (American) form of
Mickey: quirky
*Mick, Mickaella, Micklee, Mickli,
Miklea, Miklee, Mikleigh, Mikley,
Myk, Mykkie*
Mid (American) middle child
Middi, Middy
Middy (American) middle
Midge (English) form of Margaret:
treasured pearl; pure-spirited
Midian (Biblical) place name
Mie (Dutch) form of Mary: star of
the sea; sea of bitterness
Mienna (Dutch) form of Mary:
star of the sea; sea of bitterness
Migdaluy (Spanish) form of
Miguel; form of Michael: like the
Lord
Mignon (French) cute
*Migonette, Mim, Mimi, Minyon,
Minyonne*
Migon (American) precious
*Mignonne, Migonette, Migonn,
Migonne*
Mika (Hebrew) wise and pious
Micah, Mikah, Mikie

Mikaela (Hebrew) God-loving
*Mik, Mikayla, Mike, Mikhaila,
Miki*
Mikan (Slavic) child of God
Mikelle (Slavic) loves God
Mikenzi (American) form of
Mackenzie: leader
Mila (Russian; Italian) form of
Camilla: wonderful
Milah, Milla, Millah, Mimi
Milagros (Spanish) miracle
Mila, Milagro
Milana (Slavic) hospitable
Milandi (Italian) form of Milan:
city in Italy; smooth
Milantia (Panamanian) calm
Mila
Milcah (Biblical) direct
Milda (Slavic) love goddess
Mildred (English) gentle
*Mil, Mildread, Mildrid, Millie,
Milly*
Mildredena (Slavic) favorite
Milena (Greek) loving girl
Mela, Mili, Milina
Miley (Invented) form of Smiley:
radiant
Miliani (Hawaiian) one who
caresses
Mil, Mila
Milind (Slavic) favorite

Milinea (Slavic) favorite
Milissa (Greek) softspoken
Melissa, Missy
Miliulva (Slavic) loved
Milla (Polish) gentle; pure
Mila, Millah
Millay (Literature) for poet Edna
St. Vincent Millay; soft
Millea (English) mild
Millice (French) favored
Millicent (Greek/German)
softhearted
*Melicent, Melly, Milicent, Millie,
Millisent, Milly, Millycent,
Milycent, Missy*
Millie (English) form of Mildred:
gentle and Millicent: soft-hearted
*Mil, Mili, Millee, Milley, Milli,
Milly*
Millimaci (Spanish) softhearted
Milu (Asian) lovely
Mim (American) form of Miriam:
living with sadness
Mimm, Mym, Mymm
Mima (Burmese) feminine
Mimi (French) form of Camilla:
wonderful
Meemee, Mim, Mims, Mimsie
Mimosa (Botanical) sensitive; tree
Min (Chinese) sensitive;
softhearted

Mina (German/Polish) resolute
protector; willful
*Meena, Mena, Min, Minah,
Myna, Mynah*

Minal (German) kind

Minda (American) form of
Melinda: honey; sweetheart;
(Hindi) wise

Minden (American) form of
Melinda: honey; sweetheart

Mindy (Greek) form of Melinda:
honey; sweetheart
*Mindee, Mindey, Mindi, Mindie,
Myndee, Myndi*

Minelle (English) pretty

Minerv (English) form of
Minerva: bright; strong

Minerva (Latin/Greek) bright;
strong
Menerva, Min, Minnie, Myn

Minette (French) loyal woman
Min, Minnette, Minnie

Mineya (American) form of
Minerva: bright; strong

Ming (Chinese) shiny; hope of
tomorrow

Minhtu (Asian) light and clear

Mini (Scandinavian) mine

Miniver (English) assertive
Meniver, Minever, Miniverr

Minn (German) form of Minnie:
bright; strong

Minna (German) sturdy
Mina, Minnie, Mynna

Minnae (American) form of
Minnie: bright; strong

Minnie (German) form of
Minerva: bright; strong
Mini, Minni, Minny

Minnifer (American) form of
Jennifer: white wave

Minstie (American) amiable

Minsue (Asian) paradise

Minta (English) memorable
Minty

Mira (Latin/Spanish) wonderful girl
Meara, Mirror

Mirabel (Latin) marvelous;
beautiful reflection
*Marabelle, Mira, Mirabell,
Mirabelle*

Mirabella (Italian) marvelous
*Mira, Mirabell, Mirabellah,
Mirabelle, Myrabell, Myrabelle*

Miracle (American) miracle baby
Merry, Mira, Mirakle, Mirry

Miraflor (Spanish) flower girl

Miranda (Latin) unique and
amazing
*Maranda, Meranda, Mira, Mirrie,
Myranda*

Mirella (Spanish) wonderful
*Mira, Mirel, Mirela, Mirell,
Mirelle, Myrela, Myrella*

Mirelle (Latin) wonder
Mirell, Myrell, Myrelle

Mireya (Hebrew) form of
Miriam: living with sadness

Mireyli (Spanish) wondrous;
admirable
Mire, Mirey

Miri (Gypsy) bittersweet
Meeri, Miree, Mirey, Mirie, Miry

Miriam (Hebrew) living with
sadness
*Mariam, Maryam, Meriam, Miri,
Miriame, Miriem, Mirriam,
Miryam, Miryem, Mitzi, Myriam,
Myriem, Myryam, Myryem*

Mirinse (American) form of
Marin: sea-loving

Mirit (English) form of Merit:
deserving
Miritt, Miryt, Mirytt

Mirka (Polish) glorious
Mira, Mirk

Mirtha (Greek) burdened
Meert, Meerta, Mirt, Mirta

Mirthe (Dutch) mirth

Miryana (American) form of
Mariana: quiet girl

Mischanna (Hebrew) form of Miriam: living with sadness
Misch, Mischana, Mish, Mishanna, Mishke

Miselsa (Spanish) form of Michael: like the Lord

Misha (Russian) feminine form of Michael: like the Lord
Mischa

Mishelene (French) form of Micheline: like the Lord
Mish, Mishlene

Mishna (Slavic) form of Misha; like the Lord

Missy (English) form of Melissa: honey
Miss, Missee, Missey, Missi, Missie

Misty (English) dreamy
Miss, Missy, Mistee, Mistey, Misti, Mistie, Mysti

Misty-Kyd (American) child in the mist

Mistyne (American) form of Misty: dreamy

Mita (Slavic) the day

Mitola (American) hopeful

Mitri (American) feminine form of Dimitri: fertile; flourishing

Mitten (American) cuddly
Mitt, Mittun, Mitty

Mittie (American) form of Matilda: fighter and Mitten: cuddly
Mittee, Mittey, Mitti, Myttie

Mitylene (Biblical) place name

Mitzi (German) dancer
Mitsee, Mitzee, Mitzie, Mitzy

Miya (Japanese) peaceful as a temple
Miyah

Mizpah (Biblical) place name

Mnemosyne (Greek) goddess of memory

Mo (Irish) form of Maureen: night-loving

Moana (Hawaiian) from the ocean

Mobley (Last name as first name) beauty queen
Moblee, Mobli, Moblie, Mobly

Mocha (Arabic) coffee with chocolate
Mo, Moka, Mokka

Modena (American) modest

Modesty (Latin) modest
Modesti, Modestie

Modestyne (French) modest
Modestine, Modie

Moema (Native American) sweetness

Moeshea (African American) talented
Moesha, Moeesha, Moeshia, Moisha, Mosha, Moysha

Mohana (Hindi) enchants; siren

Mohini (Indian) bewitches

Moina (Hawaiian) ocean-loving
Moyna

Moira (English/Irish) pure; great one
Maura, Moir, Moirah, Moire, Moyrah

Moire (Irish) great girl

Moirin (Irish) excellent

Mokysha (African American) dramatic
Kisha, Kysha, Mokesha, Mokey

Moladah (Biblical) place name

Moll (Literature) for Daniel Defoe's Moll Flanders; outgoing
Mol, Molly

Mollo (Italian) form of Molly: jovial

Molly ✿ (Irish) jovial
Moli, Moll, Molley, Molli, Mollie

Momo (Japanese) peaches

Mona (Greek) form of Ramona: beautiful protector
Monah, Mone

Monael (American) form of Monet: artistic

Moncita (Spanish) alone

Monday (American) born on Monday; hopeful
Mondae

Mondra (American) of the world

Monecha (English) alone

Moneek (Invented) form of Monique: saucy; advisor
Moneeke

Monet (French) artistic
Mon, Monae, Monay

Monge (Spanish) thoughtful

Monica (Greek) seeking company of others
Mon, Mona, Monicka, Monika, Monike, Monique

Monicke (Spanish) form of Monique: saucy; advisor

Monika (Polish) advisor

Monina (American) alone

Monique (French) saucy; advisor
Mon, Mone, Monee, Moneeqe, Moneeque, Moni, Moniqe

Monita (Spanish) regal

Monroe (Last name as first) orderly
Monro, Monrow, Monrowe

Monserrat (Latin) tall
Monserat

Montana (Place name) U.S. state
Montayna, Montie, Monty

Montenia (Spanish) climber
Monte, Montenea, Montynia

Montoyia (Spanish) of the mountain

Monya (American) confident
Mon, Monyeh

Monyka (American) moon

Moon (American) dreamy
Monnie, Moone, Moonee, Mooney, Moonny, Moonnye

Moon Unit (Invented) universal appeal
Moon-Unit

Moonbeam (American) moon child

Moonbee (American) moon bee

Moonstone (American) gemstone

Mor (Irish) sweet

Mora (Spanish) sweet as a blueberry

Morag (Scottish) goddess
Morrag

Moraima (Spanish) forgiving
Mora, Morama

Moran (French) dark

Morayma (Spanish) lovely; forgiving

More (American) bonus
Moore, Morie

Moreen (English) good friend

Moreh (Biblical) place name

Morena (Irish) dark

Moreshath (Biblical) place name

Morettlia (American) royal

Morgan ○ ❶ (Welsh) girl on the seashore
Mor, Morey, Morgane, Morgannna, Morgen, Morgyn

Morgander (American) soft-spoken; divine

Moriah (French/Hebrew) dark girl; God-taught
Mareyeh, Mariah, Moorea, More, Moria, Morie, Morria, Morya

Morigan (Mythology) queenly

Morimasa (Asian) mermaid

Morimosa (Spanish) mermaid

Morine (American) form of Maureen: night-loving
Morri

Morinette (Irish) lush mane

Moritza (Place name) St. Moritz, Switzerland

Morla (American) form of Marla: believer; easygoing
Morley, Morly

Morna (French) dark

Morta (Mythological) one of the Roman Fates; the cutter

Morteza (Spanish) mortal

Morven (American) magical
Morvee, Morvey, Morvi

Morwenna (Welsh) seamaiden
Mo, Morwen

Morwyn (Welsh) maiden
Morwen, Morwenn, Morwynn,
Morwynna

Moselle (Hebrew) uplifted
Mose, Mozelle, Mozie

Motumia (African) desirable

Mouna (Arabic) wanted

Moxie (American) determined

Moya (Scandinavian) mother
Moiya, Moy

Moyra (Irish) excellent

Mrina (Indian) lotus girl

Muadhnait (Irish) little noble
girl

Mudeana (Spanish) glowing

Mudiwa (African) beloved
Mudewa

Muirne (Irish) affectionate

Muna (Arabic) hopes
Moona

Munashe (African) believer

Mundee (Irish) in demand

Munder (American) in demand

Mundy (Irish) in demand

Munira (Irish) wishful

Murali (Irish) seagoing

Murdina (Slavic) dark spirit
Murdi, Murdine

Mureann (Irish) pale

Mureen (Irish) form of Muriel:
shining

Muriel (Celtic) shining
Meriel, Mur, Murial, Muriele,
Muriell, Murielle, Muryel,
Muryell, Muryelle

Murieliette (Irish) little Muriel;
of the sea

Murieline (French) form of
Muriel: shining

Murla (American) form of Merle:
shining girl

Murle (American) form of Merle:
shining girl

Murleance (American)
blackbird; secretive

Murma (American) whispers

Murphy (Irish) spirited
Murphee, Murphey, Murphi,
Murphie

Murray (Last name as first name)
brisk
Muray, Murraye

Musa (African) child; muse

Musetta (French) instrument;
musical
Museta

Musette (French) instrument;
musical
Musett

Musique (French) musical
Museek, Museke, Musik

Mussie (American) musical
Muss, Mussi, Mussy

Muthanna (Biblical) gifted

Muyka (American) form of
Michael: like the Lord

Mwazi (Israeli) type of fig

My (Scandinavian) dear

Myalinda (American) my beauty

Myana (American) my Ana

Myeshande (American) my
Shande

Myeshia (African American)
giving
Meyeshia, Mye, Myesha

Myfanwy (Welsh) water baby

Myisha (American) form of
Moesha: talented

Mykala (Scandinavian) giving
Mykaela, Mykela, Mykie

Mykelle (American) generous
Mykell

Mykenya (American) form of
Michaela: like the Lord

Myla (English) forgiving
Miela, Mylah

Mylee (American) forgives

Mylene (Greek) dark-skinned girl
Myleen

Mylie (German) forgiving
Miley, Mylee, Myli

Myliki (Mythology) changeable

Myna (English) talkative
Mina, Minah

Myndee (American) form of
Melinda: honey; sweetheart

Mynola (Invented) smart
Minola, Monoa, Mynolla, Mynolle

Myra (Latin) fragrant
Mira, Myrah

Myralette (American) form of
Myra: fragrant

Myreka (American) form of
Myra: fragrant

Myriam (French) bittersweet life

Myrisa (Spanish) fragrant

Myrischa (African American)
fragrant doll
*Myresha, Myri, Myrish, Myrisha,
Rischa*

Myrna (Irish) loved
Merna, Mirna, Murna

Myrnatte (Irish) adored

Myrtle (Greek) loving
Mertle, Mirtle, Myrt, Myrtie

Mysha (Russian) form of Misha:
like the Lord
Mischa, Mish, Mysh

Mysta (Invented) mysterious
Mista, Mystah

Mystique (French) intriguing
woman
*Mistie, Mistik, Mistique, Misty,
Mystica*

Myteen (American) girl

Mythi (American) loved

Mythiah (American) loved

Mythili (Slavic) most

Naama (Hebrew) sweet
Naamah, Naamit

Naamah (Biblical) sweet
Nanay, Nayamah, Naynay

Naarah (Aramaic) bright light
Naara

Naava (Hebrew) delightful girl
Naavah, N'Ava

Nabiha (Arabic) noble
Naihah

Nabila (Arabic) noble
Nabeela, Nabilah, Nabilia

Nabulungi (African) of nobility

Nacarena (Spanish) reborn

Nacey (Spanish) born

Nachaka (African) born leader

Naci (Spanish) born

Nada (Arabic) morning dew; giving

Nadaka (American) gives

Nadara (American) gives

Nadasen (American) gives

Nadelie (American) form of
Natalie: born on Christmas
Nadey

Nadeline (Invented) born on
Christmas
Nad, Nadelyne

Nadera (Indian) gives

Nadette (French) darling girl

Nadezda (Russian) hopeful
Nadeia

Nadia (Slavic) hopeful
*Nada, Nadea, Nadeen, Nadene,
Nadi, Nadie, Nadina, Nadine,
Nady*

Nadidaa (Slavic) hopes
Nadidah

Nadine (Russian/French) dancer
*Nadeen, Nadene, Nadie, Nadyne,
Naidyne*

Nadinia (Slavic) optimist

Nadira (Arabic) precious gem
Nadirah, Nadra

Nadya (Russian) optimistic; life's
beginnings

Nadyan (Hebrew) pond; reflective
Nadian

Nadzieja (Greek) water nymph
Nadzia, Nata, Natia, Natka

Naeemah (African) breathtaking

Nafisa (Arabic) treasure

Nafshiya (Persian) precious girl

Nagara (Indian) flourishes

Nagida (Hebrew) thrives
Nagia, Nagiah, Nagiya, Najiah,
Najiya, Najiyah, Negida

Nagisa (Japanese) from the shore

Nahara (Aramaic) light
Nehara, Nehora

Nahida (Hebrew) rich
Nahid

Nahla (Arabic) succeeds

Nahtanha (African) warm

Nai (Japanese) intelligent
Nayah

Naia (Hawaiian) water nymph

Naida (Greek) nymph-like
Naiad, Naya, Nayad, Nyad

Nailah (African) successful
Naila

Naimah (Arabic) happy
Naeemah, Naima

Naimaina (American) sweet

Naja (Greek) form of Nadia:
hopeful

Najat (Arabic) safe
Nagat

Najiba (Arabic) safe
Nagiba, Nagibah, Najibah

Najla (Arabic) large-eyed

Najwa (Arabic) confidante
Nagwa

Nakecia (American) pure

Nakeya (Arabic) pure

Nakeylia (American) pure

Nakia (Arabic) purest girl
Nakea

Nakita (Russian) precocious
Nakeeta, Nakeita, Nakya,
Naquita, Nikita

Nala (African) loved
Nalah, Nalo

Nalani (Hawaiian) calming
Nalanie, Nalany

Nalin (Native American) serene
maiden

Nalinee (Indian) lotus girl
Nalini

Nalini (American) form of
Nalani: calming

Nallely (Spanish) friend
Nalelee, Naleley, Nallel

Nalukea (Hawaiian) sky girl

Nami (Japanese) rides a wave
Namiko

Namisha (African) content with
life

Namono (African) twin

Nampeyo (Native American)
female snake; sly
Nampayo, Nampayu

Namrata (Indian) demure

Nan (German/Scottish/English)
bold; graceful
Na, Nana, Nannie, Nanny

Nana (Hebrew) form of Ann:
loving; hospitable

Nanabah (Hebrew) form of Ann:
loving; hospitable

Nanala (Hebrew) form of Ann:
loving; hospitable

Nanalie (American) form of
Natalie: born on Christmas
Nan, Nana, Nanalee

Nance (American) giving
Nans

Nancy (English/Irish) generous
woman
Nan, Nancee, Nanci, Nancie,
Nansee, Nonie

Nandana (Hindi) delightful;
challenges
Nandini, Nandita

Nandini (Indian) gives happiness

Nanek (Hebrew) form of Nancy:
generous woman
Naneka, Naneki, Naneta

Nanette (French) giving and
gracious
Nanet

Nani (Greek) charming beauty
Nan, Nannie

Nanice (American) open-hearted
Nan, Naneece, Naneese, Naniece

Nanie (Hawaiian) charismatic
beauty

Nanise (American) form of Nan:
bold; graceful

Nanna (Scandinavian) brave
Nana

Nanon (French) slow to anger
Nan, Nanen

Nanvah (African) God's gift; an
infant

Nao (Japanese) truthful; pleasing

Naola (American) form of
Naomi: beautiful woman

Naoma (Hebrew) lovely

Naomi ✪ ❶ (Hebrew) beautiful
woman
*Naoma, Naomia, Naomie, Naomy,
Naynay, Nene, Neoma, Noami,
Noemi, Noemie, Noma, Nomah,
Nomi*

Naone (Hawaiian) fragrant

Naora (Native American) happy

Naoya (Asian) happy

Nara (Greek/Japanese) happy;
dreamy
Narah, Nera

Narbata (Biblical) place name

Narbona (Spanish) place name

Narcedalia (Spanish) dark flower

Narcisista (Spanish) self-absorbed

Narcissa (Greek) narcissistic
Narcisa, Narcisse, Narkissa, Nars

Narcisse (French) self-absorbed

Narcissie (Greek) conceited;
daffodil
*Narci, Narcis, Narcissa, Narcisse,
Narcissey, Narsee, Narsey, Narsis*

Narcy (French) self-absorbed

Narda (Latin) fragrant

Narelle (Australian) of the sea

Narendara (Indian) form of
Narendra, man of Indra: god of
thunder and rain; powerful

Naresha (Hindi) ruler; wise

Nari (Japanese) thunders loudly

Narilla (Gypsy) boisterous
Narrila, Narrilla

Naroline (American) form of
Caroline: little; womanly

Narses (American) self-absorbed

Nartlyn (American) self-conscious

Nasaria (Spanish) miracle

Nascha (Native American) owl;
watchful

Naseem (Hindi) breezy

Nasha (Spanish) miracle

Nashae (American) miracle

Nashan (Origin unknown)
miracle child

Nashota (Native American)
second twin

Nasia (Hebrew) miraculous child
*Naseea, Naseeah, Nasiah, Nasya,
Nasyah*

Nasnan (Native American)
miracle child; mystical

Naspa (Hebrew) form of Nasia:
miraculous child
Nasya

Nasrin (Hindi) wild rose
Nasreen

Nastasia (Greek/Russian)
gorgeous girl
Nas, Nastasha, Natasie

Nasya (Hebrew) God's miracle
Nasia

Nat (American) form of Natalie:
born on Christmas
Natt

Nata (Latin) saving

Natalia ✪ (Russian) form of
Natalie: born on Christmas
*Nat, Nata, Natala, Natalea,
Natalee, Natalya, Nati, Nattie,
Nattlee, Natty*

Natalie ✿ ❶ (Latin) born on
Christmas
*Natala, Natalee, Natalene,
Natalia, Natalina, Nataline,
Natalka, Natalya, Natelie,
Nathalia, Nathalie*

Natane (Native American)
daughter; giving

Nataniah (Hebrew) God's gift
*Natania, Nataniela, Nataniella,
Natanielle, Natanya, Nathania,
Nathaniella, Nathanielle, Netana,
Netanela, Netania, Netaniah,
Netaniela, Netaniella, Netanya,
Nethania, Nethanisah, Netina*

Natarsha (American) splendid
Natarsh, Natarshah

Natasha (Russian) form of
Natalie: born on Christmas
*Nastasia, Nastassia, Nastassja,
Nastassya, Nastasya, Natacha,
Natashah, Natashia, Natassia,
Nitasha, Tashi, Tashia, Tasis,
Tassa, Tassie*

Natesa (Hindi) goddess

Nathadria (Hebrew) feminine
form of Nathan: God's gift to
mankind
*Natania, Nath, Nathe, Nathed,
Nathedrea, Natty, Thedria*

Nathalie (French) form of
Natalie: born on Christmas

Nathitfa (Arabic) unflawed
Nathifa, Nathifah, Natifa, Natifah

Nation (American) spirited;
patriotic
Nashon, Nayshun

Natividad (Spanish) Christmas
baby

Natka (Polish) hope for
tomorrow; (Russian) wonders

Natosha (African American)
form of Natasha: born on
Christmas
Nat, Natosh, Natoshe, Natty

Natsu (Japanese) summer's child
Natsuko, Natsuyo

Nauasia (Latin) kind princess in
The Odyssey

Navaira (Spanish) lovely girl

Naveen (Spanish) snowing

Navita (Hindi) new
Nava, Navite

Navy (American) daughter of a
member of the Navy; dark blue

Nawal (Arabic) gifted

Nayana (Irish) form of Neala:
spirited

Nayeli (African) of beginnings

Nayo (African) joy baby

Nazihah (Arabic) truthful

Nazira (Arabic) equality
Nazirah

Nazly (American) idealistic
Nazlee, Nazli, Nazlie

Neal (Irish) spirited
Neale, Neel, Neil

Neala (Irish) spirited
*Neal, Nealie, Nealy, Neeli, Neelie,
Neely, Neila, Neile, Neilla, Neille*

Nealy (Irish) winner
Nealee, Nealey, Neali, Nealie

Neapolis (Biblical) place name

Neary (English) form of Nerissa:
snail; movves slowly
*Nearee, Nearey, Neari, Nearie,
Neeree, Neerey, Neeri, Neerie,
Neery*

Neasa (Irish) sweet

Neata (Russian) born on
Christmas
Neeta

Neba (Latin) misty
Neeba, Niba, Nyba

Necati (Spanish) sad

Necedah (Native American)
yellow hair

Nechama (Hebrew) comforts
others
Nachmi, Necha, Neche, Nehama

Neche (Spanish) pure

Nechona (Spanish) pure

Neci (Hungarian) intense

Necie (Hungarian) intense
Neci

Necolae (Spanish) form of
Nicole: winning

Necole (French) winning

Neda (Slavic) Sunday baby
Nedda, Neddie, Nedi

Nedaviah (Hebrew) generous girl
Nedavia, Nedavya, Nediva

Nedda (English) born to money
Ned, Neddy

Nedra (English) secretive
Ned, Nedre

Nedwyn (American) Ned's friend

Nedya (American) flourishes

Neeka (American) flourishes

Neelima (Indian) flourishes;
sapphire
Neelam, Neela

Neely (Irish) sparkling smile
Nealy, Neelee, Neilie, Nelie

Neema (Hebrew) melodious

Neenah (Native American)
flowing water

Neevay (American) gives

Nefertari (Egyptian) beautiful
queen

Nefris (Spanish) glamorous
Nef, Neff, Neffy, Nefras, Nefres

Neh (Hebrew) form of Nehara:
light

Neha (Hindi) loves; rainy
Nehali, Nehi

Nehanda (Hebrew) comforter

Neia (African) promising

Neiana (Slavic) winning

Neidy (Spanish) winning

Neiley (Irish) winner
*Neelee, Neeley, Neeli, Neelie,
Neely, Neilee, Neili, Neilie, Neily*

Neilytta (American) winning

Neima (Hindi) growing; tree

Neith (Egyptian) feminine
Neit, Neithe

Neka (Native American) wild

Nekeisha (African American)
bold spirit
*Nek, Nekeishah, Nekesha, Nekisha,
Nekkie*

Nekia (Arabic) unblemished

Nekoma (Native American)
uninhibited; new moon

Neld (American) blonde

Nelda (American) friend
Neldah, Nell, Nellda, Nellie

Nelemita (Spanish) honest

Nelia (Spanish) form of Cornelia:
practical
Neelia, Neely, Nela, Nelie, Nene

Nelida (Spanish) honest

Nelka (Spanish) yellow hair
Nela

Nell (English) sweet charmer
Nelle, Nellie

Nellena (American) honest

Nellie (English) form of Cornelia:
practical; form of Eleanor:
lighthearted
Nel, Nela, Nell, Nelle, Nelli, Nelly

Nelliene (American) form of
Nellie: practical; lighthearted
Nell, Nelli, Nellienne

Nelvia (Greek) brash
Nell, Nelvea

Nelwynette (American) Nell's
friend

Nemera (Hebrew) leopard; exotic

Nemesis (Mythological) goddess
of justice and retribution

Nemoria (American) crafty
Nemorea

Nenan (American) sea child

Nenet (Egyptian) sea goddess

Nenita (Spanish) of the sea

Neola (Greek) new baby
Neolah

Nepa (Arabic) talented

Nera (Hebrew) candlelight
Neria, Neriah, Neriya

Nereida (Spanish) sea nymph
Nere, Nereide, Nereyda, Neri,
Nireida

Neressa (Greek) coming from
the sea
Narissa, Nene, Nerissa, Nerisse

Nerida (Greek) sea nymph
Nerice, Nerina, Nerine, Nerisse,
Neryssa, Rissa

Nerissa (English) snail; moves
slowly
Nerisa, Nerise

Nerizza (Spanish) slow

Nerthus (Scandinavian)
masterful

Nerys (Welsh) ladylike
Neris, Neriss, Nerisse

Neshalinda (Spanish) peak of
beauty

Nesiah (Greek) lamb; meek
Nesia, Nessia, Nesya, Nisia,
Nisiah, Nisva

Nessa (Irish) devout
Nessah

Nessie (Greek) form of Vanessa:
flighty
Nese, Nesi, Ness

Nest (Welsh) pure
Nesta

Nestora (Spanish) she is leaving
Nesto, Nestor

Neta (Hebrew) growing and
flourishing

Netania (Hebrew) form of
Nathaniel: God's gift

Netia (Hebrew) form of Neta:
growing and flourishing

Netira (Spanish) flourishing

Netis (Native American)
worthwhile

Netra (American) maturing well
Net, Netrah, Netrya, Nettie

Netta (Scottish) champion
Nett, Nettie

Nettie (French) gentle
Net, Neta, Netta, Netti, Nettia,
Netty

Neva (Russian/English) the
newest; snow
Neeva, Neve, Niv

Nevada (Spanish) girl who loves
snow
Nev, Nevadah

Nevaeh ✪ ✆ (American) heaven
spelled backward

Neve (Irish) promising princess

Neviah (Irish) form of Nevina:
she worships God
Nevia

Nevina (Irish) she worships God
Nev, Niv, Nivena, Nivina

Newlin (Last name as first name)
healing
Newlinn, Newlinne, Newlyn,
Newlynn

Neya (Spanish) wishful

Neyda (Spanish) pure
Ney

Neza (Slavic) form of Agnes: pure
Neysa

Ngabile (African) aware; knowing

Ngozi (African) fortunate

Ngu (African) peaceful

Nguyet (Vietnamese) moon child

Nia (Greek) priceless
Niah

Niabi (Native American) fawn;
docile

Niamh (Irish) promising

Niandrea (Invented) form of
Diandro: special
Andrea, Nia, Niand, Niandre

Niani (Spanish) icon

Nibal (Arabic) completed

Nibedita (Spanish) nubile

Nicaea (Biblical) place name

Nicelda (American) industrious
Niceld, Nicelde, Nicey

Nichole (French) light and lively
Nichol

Nichols (Last name as first name) smart

Nick, Nickee, Nickels, Nickey, Nicki, Nickie, Nicky, Nikels

Nick (American) form of Nicole: winning

Nik

Nicki (French) form of Nicole: winning

Nick, Nickey, Nicky, Niki

Nicks (American) fashionable

Nickee, Nickie, Nicksie, Nicky, Nix

Nico (Italian) victorious

Nicco, Nicko, Nikko, Niko

Nicola (Italian) lovely singer

Nekola, Nick, Nikkie, Nikola

Nicolasa (Spanish) spontaneous; winning

Nico, Nicole

Nicole ☺ (French) winning

Nacole, Nichole, Nick, Nickie, Nikki, Nikol, Nikole

Nicolette (French) a tiny Nicole; little beauty

Nettie, Nick, Nickie, Nicoline, Nikkolette, Nikolet

Nicolie (French) sweet

Nichollie, Nikolie

Nicomedia (Biblical) place name

Nicopolis (Biblical) place name

Nida (Greek) sweet girl

Nidhi (Indian) beloved gift

Nidia (Latin) home-loving

Nidie, Nidya

Niecy (Spanish) pure

Niemi (Origin unknown) beauty

Nyemi

Niesha (African American) virginal

Neisha, Nesha, Nesia, Nessie

Nieves (Spanish) snows; snow maiden

Neaves, Ni, Nievez, Nievis

Nihal (Greek) form of Nicole: winning

Nika (Scandinavian) God's child

Nike (Greek) goddess of victory; fleet of foot; a winner

Nikeesha (American) form of Nikita: daring

Niceesha, Nickeesha, Nickisha, Nicquisha, Nykesha

Niki (American) form of Nicole: winning and Nikita: daring

Nick, Nicki, Nicky, Nik, Nikki, Nikky

Nikita (Russian) daring

Nakeeta, Niki, Nikki, Niquitta

Nikithia (African American) winning; frank

Kithi, Kithia, Nikethia, Niki

Niko (Greek) form of Nikola: lovely singer

Neeko, Nyko

Nikole (Greek) winning

Nik, Niki

Nilana (Invented) combo of Nila and Lana

Nilanjana (Indian) girl of Nile

Nile (Biblical) place name; form of the Nile River

Niles (American) of the Nile River

Nili (Hebrew) plant; flourishes

Nilima (Indian) blue

Nilsine (Scandinavian) wine; ages well

Nima (Arabic) blessed

Neema, Neemah, Nema, Nimah

Nimfa (Spanish) blessed

Nina (Russian/Hebrew/Spanish) bold girl

Neena, Nena, Ninah

Ninel (Spanish) girlish

Ninelle (Spanish) girlish

Ninetta (American) form of Nanette: giving and gracious

Nineta

Ninette (American) form of Nanette: giving and gracious

Nineveh (Biblical) place name

Nini (Hungarian) forgiving
Ninee, Niney, Ninie, Ninnee,
Ninney, Ninni, Ninnie, Niny

Ninon (French) feminine
Ninen

Ninoska (Russian) form of Nina:
bold girl

Niobe (Greek) vain

Nipa (Hindi) stream

Nira (Hindi) night
Neera, Nyra

Niranjana (Hindi) full moon

Nirel (Hebrew) light of
knowledge

Nirvana (Hindi) completion;
oneness with God
Nirvahna, Nirvanah

Nirveli (Hindi) water babe

Nisha (Hindi) nighttime
Nishi

Nishi (Japanese) from the west;
sincere
Nishie, Nishiko, Nishiyo

Nisibis (Biblical) place name;
feminine

Nissa (Hebrew) symbolic
Nisa, Niss, Nissah, Nissie

Nissie (Scandinavian) pretty; elf
Nisse, Nissee

Nita (Hebrew) form of Juanita:
believer in gracious God; forgiving
Neeta, Nitali, Nite, Nittie

Nitalooma (American) moral

Nitara (Hindi) well-grounded

Niteen (American) growing

Nitsa (Greek) form of Helen:
beautiful; light

Nituna (Native American) sweet
daughter

Niu (Chinese) girlish; confident

Niva (Spanish) form of Neva: the
newest; snow

Nivaeh (Spanish) form of Nieves:
snow maiden

Nivea (Spanish) reborn

Nixi (German) mystical
Nixee, Nixie

Niy (American) lively
Nye

Nizana (Hebrew) form of
Nitzana: budding beauty
Nitza, Zana

Noa (Hebrew) chosen
Noah

Noami (Hebrew) form of Naomi:
beautiful woman
Noamee, Noamey, Noamie, Noamy

Nobantu (African) able

Noel (Latin) born on Christmas
Noela, Noelle, Noellie, Noli

Noelan (Hawaiian) Christmas girl

Noelani (Hawaiian) Christmas
child

Noelle (French) Christmas baby
Noel, Noell

Noemian (Spanish) pleases

Noga (Hebrew) light of day

Noheali (Hawaiian) Christmas

Nohelia (Hispanic) kind
Nohelya

Noicha (African) light heart
Nolcha

Noirin (Irish) form of Norin:
acknowledging others

Nokomis (Native American)
moon child

Noksu (African) princess

Nola (Latin) sensual
Nolah, Nolana, Nole, Nolie

Nolan (Latin) bell; form of Nola:
sensual
Nolen, Nolyn

Noleen (Irish) known

Noleta (Latin) reluctant
Nolita

Nolia (American) known

Nolina (Spanish) reticent

Nomalanga (Hawaiian) lingers

Nombeko (African) honored
child

Nombese (African) wonder girl

Nomble (African) beautiful
Nombi

Nomita (Spanish) wins

Nomusa (African) goodhearted

Nona (Latin) ninth; knowing
Nonah, Noni, Nonie, Nonn,
Nonna, Nonnah

Noni (Latin) ninth child

Nonie (Spanish) ninth child

Noor (Hindi) lights the world
Noora

Nora (Greek/Scandinavian/
Scottish) light
Norah, Noreh

Norazah (Malaysian) light

Norberta (German) famous girl
from the north

Noreen (Latin) acknowledging
others
Noreena, Norene, Noire, Norin,
Norine, Norinne, Nureen

Norell (Scandinavian) northern
girl
Narelle, Norelle

Norena (American) leads

Nori (Japanese) normal

Norika (Japanese) athletic
Nori, Norike

Noriko (Japanese) follows
tradition

Norita (Spanish) form of Nora:
light

Norlaili (Asian) northern

Norlita (Spanish) knowing

Norma (Latin) gold standard
Noey, Nomah, Norm, Normah,
Normie

Norna (Scandinavian) time
goddess

Norrie (Asian) traditional
Nori

Norris (English) serious
Nore, Norrus

Nota (American) negative
Na, Nada, Not

Notaku (Asian) dealing with grief

Noula (Irish) form of Nuala:
white
Noulah

Noura (Arabic) light girl
Nourah

Nourbese (African) wonderful

Nouvel (French) new

Nova (Latin) energetic; new
Noova, Novah, Novella, Novie

Novak (Last name as first name)
emphatic
Novac

Novella (Latin) new

Novena (Latin) blessing; prayerful
Noveena, Novina, Novyna

Novia (Spanish) sweetheart;
girlfriend
Nov, Novie, Nuvia

Nowell (American) form of
Noelle: Christmas baby
Nowel, Nowele, Nowelle

Noyola (Spanish) knowing

Nu (Vietnamese) confident
Niu

Nuala (Irish) white

Nubia (Egyptian) white

Nudar (Arabic) golden girl

Nueva (Spanish) new; fresh
Nue, Nuey

Nuha (Arabic) great mind

Numa (Spanish) delightful
Num

Nuna (Native American) girl of
the land

Nunia (Native American) girl of
the land

Nunu (Vietnamese) friendly

Nur (Arabic) bright light
Nura, Nuri, Nurya

Nura (Aramaic) light-footed
Noora, Noura, Nurrie

Nuria (Arabic) light
Noor, Noura, Nur, Nuriah, Nuriel

Nurit (Hebrew) form of Nurita:
flower
Nurice

Nurlene (American) boisterous
Nerlene, Nurleen
Nuru (African) light of day
Nusi (Hungarian) form of
Hannah: merciful; God-blessed
Nutan (Native American) heart
Nuvia (American) new
Nuvea
Nyasia (Greek) starts life
Nyckillan (American) form of
Nicky: smart
Nydia (Latin) nest-loving; home
and hearth woman
Nidia, Nidiah, Ny, Nydiah,
Nydie, Nydya
Nyla (Arabic) successful;
astounding
Nila
Nylee (American) girl of Nile
Nylene (American) shy
Nyle, Nylean, Nyleen, Nyles,
Nyline
Nyque (American) sea child
Nyra (American) sea child
Nyree (Asian) seagoing
Nysa (Greek) life-starting
Nisa, Nissa, Nissie, Nyssa
Nyura (African) light
Nyx (Greek) lively
Nix

Oak (Botanical) sturdy
Oakene (Botanical) sturdy
Oanna (Hawaiian) oceanic
Oba (Mythology) river goddess
Obala (African) form of Oba:
river goddess
Oballa, Obla, Obola
Obdulia (Spanish) comforts
Obede (English) obedient
Obead
Obedience (American) obedient
Obey
Obelia (Greek) needle; cautious
Obel, Obellia, Obiel
Obey (American) obedient
Obioma (African) kind
Oceana (Greek) ocean-loving;
name given to those with
astrological signs that have to do
with water
Oceonne, Ocie, Oh
Ocin (Origin unknown) comes
into life

Octavia (Latin) eighth child;
born on eighth day of the month;
musical
Octave, Octavie, Octivia, Octtavia,
Ottavia, Tave, Tavi, Tavia, Tavie
Oda (Hebrew) praises the Lord
Odalis (Spanish) humorous
Odales, Odallis, Odalous, Odalus
Oddrun (Scandinavian) secret
love
Oda, Odd, Oddr
Oddveig (Scandinavian) woman
with spears
Ode (African) born on a road
Odeda (Hebrew) strength of
character
Odeen (Hebrew) praises
Odele (Hebrew/Greek) melodious
Odela, Odelle, Odie
Odelette (Greek) melodic; rich
Odelet, Odette
Odelia (Hebrew/Greek) singer of
spiritual songs
Odele, Odelle, Odie, Odila, Odile,
Othelia
Odelimpia (Spanish) melodic;
wealthy
Odelinda (Hebrew) praises
Odelita (Spanish) vocalist
Odelite
Odera (Hebrew) works the soil

Odessa (English) traveler on an odyssey
Odessah, Odie, Odissa

Odette (French) good girl
Oddette, Odet, Odetta

Odhairnait (Irish) little and green; elfin-like

Odile (French) sensuous
Odyll

Odilia (Spanish) wealthy
Eudalia, Odalia, Odella, Odylia, Othilia

Odina (Native American) mountain girl

Odine (Scandinavian) rules

Odiya (Hebrew) God's song

Odra (English) affluent

Odrenne (American) rich

Ofa (Polynesian) loving

Ofira (Hebrew) golden girl

Ogin (Native American) rose

Ohara (Japanese) meditative
Oh

Ohela (Hebrew) tent; nature-loving

Oheo (Native American) beauty

Oira (Latin) form of Ora: glowing

Okalani (Hawaiian) heavenly child

Okei (Japanese) form of Oki: born mid-ocean; loves the water

Oki (Japanese) born mid-ocean; loves the water

Oksana (Russian) praise to God
Oksanah, Oksie

Ola (Scandinavian) bold
Olah

Olabisi (African) joy

Olaide (American) lovely; thoughtful
Olai, Olay, Olayde

Olaug (Scandinavian) loves her ancestors; loyal

Olda (Spanish) snow child

Oldriska (Czech) ruling noble
Olda, Oldra, Oldrina, Olina, Oluse

Oleda (Spanish) audacious

Oleia (Greek) smooth

Olena (Russian) generous
Olenya

Olenka (Russian) form of Helen: beautiful; light

Olenta (Origin unknown) sweet

Olesia (Greek) regal

Oleta (Greek) true
Oletta

Olga (Russian) holy woman
Ola, Olgah, Ollie

Olgicia (Scandinavian) holy child

Oliana (Polynesian) oleander; beautiful

Olida (Spanish) lighthearted
Oleda

Olidie (Spanish) light
Oli, Olidee, Olydie

Olina (Hawaiian) joy
Oleen, Oline

Olinda (Latin) fragrant

Oline (Hawaiian) happy
Olina

Olino (Spanish) scented
Olina, Oline

Olisa (African) loves God

Olive (Latin) subtle
Olyve

Olivia ○ ⊕ (English) flourishing
Alivia, Olive, Olivea, Oliveah, Oliviah, Ollie

Olubayo (African) resplendent

Olufemi (African) God loves her

Olva (Latin) form of Olivia: flourishing

Olvyen (Welsh) footprint in white; lasting impression

Olwen (Welsh) magical; white
Olwynn

Olwyn (Welsh) holy friend

Olya (Latin) perfect
Olyah

Olympia (Greek) heavenly woman
Olimpia, Ollie, Olympe, Olympie

Olynda (Invented) form of
Lynda: pretty girl
Lyn, Olin, Olinda, Olynde

Oma (Hebrew) reverant
Omah

Omana (Hindi) womanly

Omani (African) devout

Omanie (Origin unknown)
exuberant
Omanee

Omari (African) believer

Omayra (Latin) fragrant
Oma, Omyra

Omega (Greek) last is best

Omemee (Native American)
dove; peaceful

Omesha (African American)
splendid
Omesh, Omie, Omisha

Omie (Italian) homebody
Omee

Ominotago (Native American)
sweet sound

Omolara (African) birth timed
well; welcome baby

Omora (Arabic) red-haired

Omorose (African) lovely

Omri (Arabic) red-haired

Omusa (African) adored

Omusupe (African) precious
baby

Ona (Latin) the one
Oona

Onamwa (Native American)
from the river

Onatah (Native American) earth
child

Onawa (Native American) alert

Ondina (Latin) water spirit
Ondi, Ondine, Onyda

Ondrea (Czech) form of Andrea:
feminine
Ondra

Ondreja (Czech) form of Andrea:
feminine

Oneida (Native American)
anticipated
*Ona, Oneeda, Onida, Onie,
Onyda*

Oni (African) desired child

Onia (Latin) one and only

Onie (Latin) flamboyant
Oh, Oona, Oonie, Una

Onita (American) holy

Onora (Latin) honorable
Onoria, Onorine

Ontina (Origin unknown) an
open mind
Ontine

Onyx (Latin) pretty shine

Oona (Latin) one alone
Oonagh, Oonah

Opa (Native American) owl; stares

Opal (Hindi) the opal; precious
Opale, Opalle, Opie

Opalina (Sanskrit) gem
Opaline

Ophelia (Greek) helpful woman;
character from Shakespeare's
Hamlet
*Ofelia, Ofilia, Ophela, Ophelie,
Ophlie, Phelia, Phelie*

Ophira (Hebrew) fawn; lovable
Ofira

Ophrah (Biblical) place name;
helpful

Opportina (Italian) sees
opportunity; successful
Opportuna

Oprah (Hebrew) one who soars;
excellent
*Ophie, Ophrie, Opra, Oprie,
Orpah*

Ora (Greek) glowing
Orah, Orie

Orabel (Latin) believes in prayer
Orabelle, Oribel, Oribella, Oribelle

Oraleyda (Spanish) light of
dawn
Ora, Oraleydea, Oralida

Oralie (Hebrew) light of dawn
Oralee, Orali, Orla

Orange (English) warm

Oranna (Australian) sought after

Orbelina (American) excited;
dawn
*Lina, Orbe, Orbee, Orbeline,
Orbey, Orbi, Orby*

Orchard (American) fruitful

Ordan (American) form of
Jordan: excellent descendant

Ordella (Latin) form of Ora:
glowing

Orea (Latin) form of Ora:
glowing

Oreille (Latin) form of Oriole:
golden light

Orela (Latin) form of Oriole:
golden light

Orella (Latin) golden girl
Oralla

Orelle (Italian) feminine

Orenda (Place name) Orinda,
California; lovely gold

Orene (French) nurturing
Orane, Orynne

Oresty (Greek) feminine form of
Orestes: leader

Orestynna (Greek) feminine
form of Orestes: leader

Oreun (Greek) star

Orfelinda (Spanish) pretty dawn
Orfelinde, Orfelynda

Orgina (Greek) origins

Orianettea (Italian) form of
Orianna: sunny; dawn

Orianna (Latin) sunny; dawn
*Oria, Orian, Oriana, Oriane,
Oriannah, Orie*

Orin (Irish) dark-haired
Oren, Orinn

Oringa (Invented) golden

Orino (Japanese) works outside
Ori

Oriole (Latin) golden light
*Oreilda, Oreole, Oriel, Oriella,
Oriol, Oriola*

Orit (Spanish) dawn

Orita (Spanish) dawn

Oritha (Greek) motherly

Orithna (Greek) natural

Orla (Irish) gold

Orlain (French) famed

Orlaith (Irish) golden lady

Orlanda (German) celebrity

Orlena (Russian) sharp-eyed

Orlenda (Russian) eagle-eyed
Orlinda

Orly (French) busy
Orlee

Ormanda (Latin) noble
Ormie

Ormey (German) sea child

Orna (Irish) dark-haired
Ornah, Ornas, Ornie

Ornice (Irish) pale face

Oropeza (Spanish) peaceful

Orpah (Hebrew) escapes; fawn
*Ophra, Ophrah, Orpa, Orpha,
Orphy*

Orrilla (Spanish) gold

Orrine (French) golden

Orsa (Greek) form of Ursula:
little female bear

Orseline (Latin) bearlike

Orshan (American) of stars

Ortega (Spanish) nettles

Ortensia (Italian) form of
Hortense: caretaking the garden

Orthia (Greek) straightforward

Ortia (Spanish) golden child

Ortrud (Scandinavian) form of
Gertrude: beloved
Ortrude

Orva (French) golden girl
Or, Orvah, Orvan

Orwenn (Welsh) waves

Orya (Origin unknown)
forthcoming

Osa (American) praises God

Osana (Latin) praises the Lord

Osarma (Origin unknown) sleek

Osbely (Spanish) lovely you

Osen (Japanese) one in a
thousand

Oseye (African) happy

Osithe (Place name) form of Ostia, Italy: together
Osyth

Osni (Spanish) bearlike

Osroene (Biblical) place name

Ostia (Biblical) place name

Osyka (Native American) eagle-eyed

Otellia (Spanish) form of Othelia: singer of spiritual songs

Otha (Spanish) form of Othelia: singer of spiritual songs; (German) excels

Otilia (Slavic) fortunate

Otilie (Czech) fortunate girl

Otina (Origin unknown) fortunate

Ottavia (English) form of Octavia: eighth child; born on the eighth day of the month; musical

Otthild (German) prospers
Ottila, Ottilia, Ottilie, Otylia

Ottilie (Czech) lucky omen

Otylia (Polish) rich
Oteelya

Ouida (Literature) for the Victorian author Ouida; romantic

Ourania (Greek) heavenly

Ovalia (Spanish) helpful
Ova, Ove, Ovelia

Ovanna (Italian) feminine form of Ivan: believer in a gracious God; reliable one

Ovida (Hebrew) worships

Ovidea (German) sheep herder; believer

Ovyena (Spanish) helps

Owen (Welsh) wellborn

Owena (Welsh) feisty
Oweina, Owina, Owinne

Oya (Africa) invited to earth

Oyama (African) called out

Oza (African) strong

Ozara (Hebrew) treasured
Ozarah

Ozelina (Spanish) strong

Ozera (Hebrew) of merit

Ozioma (Origin unknown) strength of character

Ozmeen (American) prepared

Ozora (Hebrew) rich

Paavani (Hindi) purity of the river

Paavna (Hindi) pure

Pabiola (Spanish) small girl
Pabby, Pabi, Pabiole

Paca (Spanish) free girl

Pace (Last name as first name) charismatic
Pase

Pacifica (Spanish) peaceful
Pacifika

Pacita (Spanish) free; peaceful

Paden (American) pious

Padgett (French) growing and learning; lovely-haired
Padge, Padget, Paget, Pagett, Pagette

Padilla (Spanish) loving

Padma (Hindi) lotus blossom

Page ♀ ⚦ (French) sharp; eager
*Pagie, **Paige**, Paje, Payge*

Pageant (American) theatrical
Padg, Padge, Padgeant, Padgent, Pagent

Paigene (American) youth

Paili (Irish) wished-for child

Paisha (Slavic) wise

Paisley (Scottish) patterned
Paislee, Pazley

Paiton (English) from a warring town; sad

Paiva (Scandinavian) sun goddess

Paiz (Spanish) peaceful

Paka (African) kitty cat

Pal (American) friend; buddy

Pala (Native American) water

Palacia (Spanish) palace

Palakika (Hawaiian) much loved

Palanis (American) water child

Palcey (American) wise

Palemon (Spanish) kind
  Palem, Palemond

Paley (Last name as first name) wise
  Palee, Palie

Palila (Polynesian) bird; free flight

Palla (Greek) form of Pallas: wise woman

Pallas (Greek) wise woman
  Palace, Palas

Pallavi (Indian) new growth

Palma (Latin) successful
  Palmah, Palmeda, Palmedah

Palmer (Latin) palm tree; balmy

Palmira (Spanish) palm-tree girl
  Palmyra

Palom (Spanish) dove

Paloma (Spanish) dove
  Palloma, Palometa, Palomita, Peloma

Palomaelle (Spanish) dove

Palomares (Spanish) dove

Pamela (Greek) sweet as honey
  Pam, Pamala, Pamalia, Pamalla, Pamee, Pamelia, Pamelina, Pamelinn, Pamella, Pamelyn, Pamilla, Pammee, Pammela, Pammi, Pammie, Pammy, Pamyla, Pamylla

Pana (Native American) partridge; small

Panchett (American) freedom

Panda (Greek) all-knowing

Pandita (Hindi) learned

Pandora (Greek) a gift; curious
  Pan, Pand, Panda, Pandie, Pandorah, Pandorra, Panndora

Panea (Biblical) place name; open

Panfila (Greek) befriends all

Pang (Chinese) innovative

Panga (Native American) nature

Pangiota (Greek) all is holy

Panna (Hindi) emerald; knowing

Pannonia (Biblical) place name; friend of all

Panola (Greek) all

Panphila (Greek) all loving
  Panfila, Panfyla, Panphyla

Panse (Greek) pansy flower

Pansee (Greek) pansy flower

Pansy (Greek) fragrant
  Pan, Pansey, Pansie, Panze, Panzee, Panzie

Pantea (Indian) all-loving of gods

Pantelis (Greek) happy with all

Panthea (Greek) loves all gods

Panther (Greek) wild; all gods
  Panthar, Panthea, Panthur, Panth

Panya (Greek) she is crowned

Panyin (African) the older twin

Paola (Italian) firebrand

Paolabella (Italian) lovely firebrand

Papina (African) vine; clings

Paradise (Word as name) dream girl

Parenth (American)

Parima (Indian) perfection

Paris (French) capital of France; graceful woman
  Pareece, Parice, Parie, Parisa, Parris, Parrish

Parissa (Spanish) form of Paris: capital of France; graceful woman

Pariste (American) of Paris

Paristeen (American) of Paris

Park (Last name as first name) of the park

Parker (English) noticed; in the park
  Park, Parke, Parkie

Parminder (Hindi) attractive

Parnelle (French) small stone
  Parn, Parnel, Parnell, Parney

Paronda (Indian) good

Parslee (Botanical) complementary
Pars, Parse, Parsley, Parsli

Partha (Greek) pure; full

Parthenia (Greek) from the
Parthenon; virtuous
*Parthania, Parthe, Parthee,
Parthena, Parthene, Parthenie,
Parthina, Parthine, Pathania,
Pathena, Pathenia, Pathina,
Thenia*

Parthenope (Greek) siren

Parthia (Biblical) place name;
pure; full

Parvani (Hindi) full moon
Parvina

Parvati (Hindi) mountain child

Parvin (Hindi) star
Parveen

Pascale (French) born on a
religious holiday
*Pascal, Pascalette, Pascaline,
Pascalle, Paschale, Paskel, Paskil*

Pascasia (French) born on Easter
Paschasia

Pascha (Slavic) Easter baby

Paschel (African) spiritual
Paschell

Pash (French) clever
Pasch

Pasha (Greek) lady by the sea
Passha

Pasionne (Spanish) passion

Pasqualina (Spanish) Easter baby

Passion (American) sensual
Pashun, Pass, Passyun, Pasyun

Pasua (French) Easter child

Pat (Latin) form of Patricia:
woman of nobility; unbending
Patt, Patty

Patara (Biblical) place name

Paterekia (Hawaiian) patrician
Pakelekia

Pati (African) gathers fish

Patia (Latin) form of Patricia:
woman of nobility; unbending

Patience (English) woman of
patience
Pacience, Paciencia, Pat, Pattie

Patric (American) form of Patricia:
woman of nobility; unbending

Patrice (French) form of Patricia:
woman of nobility; unbending
*Pat, Patreas, Patreece, Pattie,
Pattrice, Trece, Treece*

Patricia (Latin) woman of
nobility; unbending
*Pat, Patreece, Patreice, Patria, Patric,
Patrica, Patrice, Patricka, Patrisha,
Patrizia, Patsie, Patsy, Patti, Pattie,
Patty, Tricia, Trish, Trisha*

Patriena (Slavic) form of Patrice:
woman of nobility; unbending

Patrika (Slavic) form of Patrice:
woman of nobility; unbending

Patrina (American) noble;
patrician
Patryna, Patrynna, Tryna, Trynnie

Patriz (Italian) noble

Patsy (Latin) form of Patricia:
woman of nobility; unbending
*Pat, Patsey, Patsi, Patsie, Patti,
Patty*

Patty (English) form of Patricia:
woman of nobility; unbending
Pat, Pati, Patti, Pattie

Paula (Latin) small and feminine
*Paola, Paolina, Paulah, Paule,
Pauleen, Paulene, Pauletta,
Paulette, Paulie, Paulina, Pauline,
Paulita, Pauly, Paulyn, Pavla,
Pavlina, Pavlinka, Pawlah,
Pawlina, Pola*

Paulee (American) small

Paulette (French) form of Paula:
small and feminine
Paula, Paulett, Paulie, Paullette

Paulina (Latin/Italian) small;
lovely
Paula, Paulena, Paulie

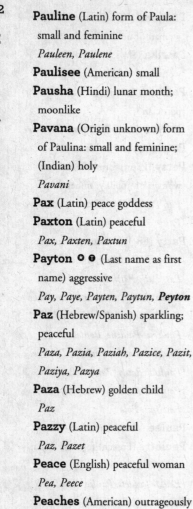

Pauline (Latin) form of Paula: small and feminine
Pauleen, Paulene

Paulisee (American) small

Pausha (Hindi) lunar month; moonlike

Pavana (Origin unknown) form of Paulina: small and feminine; (Indian) holy
Pavani

Pax (Latin) peace goddess

Paxton (Latin) peaceful
Pax, Paxten, Paxtun

Payton ♀ ♂ (Last name as first name) aggressive
*Pay, Paye, Payten, Paytun, **Peyton***

Paz (Hebrew/Spanish) sparkling; peaceful
Paza, Pazia, Paziah, Pazice, Pazit, Paziya, Pazya

Paza (Hebrew) golden child
Paz

Pazzy (Latin) peaceful
Paz, Pazet

Peace (English) peaceful woman
Pea, Peece

Peaches (American) outrageously sweet
Peach, Peachy

Peakalika (Hawaiian) happiness

Pearl (Latin) jewel from the sea
Pearla, Pearle, Pearaleen, Pearlena, Pearlette, Pearley, Pearlie, Pearline, Pearly, Perl, Perla, Perle, Perlette, Perley, Perlie, Perly

Pearlette (American) treasured pearl

Pearline (American) treasured pearl

Pecola (American) brash
Pekola

Pedzi (Origin unknown) gold

Pefilia (Spanish) profile

Pega (Greek) form of Peggy: pearl; princess

Peggy (Greek) pearl; priceless
Peg, Peggi, Peggie

Pegma (Greek) happy

Pehel (Biblical) place name

Pei (Place name) village; from Tang Pei, China

Peigi (Scottish) pearl; priceless

Peigo (American) athletic

Peisha (American) lovely

Peke (Hawaiian) form of Bertha: bright

Pela (Polish) loves the sea; special

Pelagia (Polish) sea girl
Pelage, Pelageia, Pelagie, Pelegia, Pelgia, Pellagia

Pelagla (Greek) girl of the sea
Pelagie, Pelagi, Pelagia, Pelagias, Pelaga

Pele (Hawaiian) volcano; conflicted; (Polish) weaves dreams

Peleka (Hawaiian) strong; marvel

Pelham (English) thoughtful
Pelhim, Pellam, Pellham, Pellie

Pelia (Hebrew) marvelous
Peliah, Pelya, Pelyia

Pelika (Hawaiian) strong

Pelipa (African) loves horses
Phillipa

Pella (Biblical) place name; weaves dreams

Pelulio (Hawaiian) sea treasure

Pelusium (Biblical) place name

Pemba (African) powerful

Pemelia (American) form of Pamela: sweet as honey

Penda (African) beloved

Pendant (French) necklace; adorned
Pendan, Pendanyt

Penelope (Greek) patient; weaver of dreams
Pela, Pelcia, Pen, Penalope, Penelopa, Penina, Penine, Penna, Pennelope, Penni, Pennie, Penny, Pinelopi, Popi

Peni (Greek) thinker

Peninah (Hebrew) pearl; lovely
Peni, Penie, Penina, Penini,
Peninit, Penny

Peninia (Biblical) precious girl

Penn (Last name as first name)
loyal

Pennelle (American) loyal

Penny (Greek) form of Penelope:
patient; weaver of dreams
Pen, Penee, Penni, Pennie

Penthea (Spanish) orchid; lovely
Fentheam, Fentheas, Pentha,
Pentheam, Pentheas

Peony (Greek) flowering; giving
praise
Pea, Peoni, Peonie

Peoria (Place name) city in
Illinois; poised

Pepita (Spanish) high-energy
Pepa, Peppita, Peta

Pepper (Latin) spicy
Pep, Peppie, Peppyr

Peppy (American) cheerful
Pep, Peppey, Peppi, Peps

Pequita (Spanish) form of Pepita:
high-energy

Perach (Hebrew) flowering
Perah, Pericha, Pircha, Pirchia,
Pirchit, Pirchiya, Pirha

Perano (Spanish) wanders

Perciella (Greek) great excess

Perdita (Latin) wanders away

Perea (Biblical) place name

Perel (Latin) tested
Perele

Perfecta (Spanish) perfection
Perfekta

Perga (Biblical) place name

Peridot (Arabic) green gem;
treasured
Peri

Peril (Latin) victor

Perita (Spanish) treasure

Periwinkle (Botanical) blue-
eyed; flower girl

Perla (Latin) substantial
Perlah

Perlace (Spanish) small pearl
Perl, Perlahse, Perlase, Perly

Perlette (French) pearl; treasured
Pearl, Pearline, Peraline, Perl,
Perle, Perlett

Perlie (Latin) form of Pearl: jewel
from the sea
Perli, Perly, Purlie

Perlina (American) small pearl
Pearl, Perl, Perlinna, Perlyna

Pernella (Scandinavian) rock;
dependable
Parnella, Pernelle, Pernilla

Pernille (Scandinavian) rock; safe

Peron (Latin) travels

Perouze (Armenian) turquoise
gemstone
Perou, Perous, Perouz, Perry

Perpetua (Spanish) lasting

Perri (Greek/Latin) outdoorsy;
(English) wanderer
Peri, Perr, Perrie, Perry

Perrinada (American) generous

Persephone (Greek) breath of
spring
Pers, Perse, Persefone, Persey

Persevera (Spanish) persevers

Pershella (American)
philanthropic
Pershe, Pershel, Pershelle, Pershey,
Persie, Persy

Persia (Place name) colorful
Persha, Perzha

Persis (Latin) form of Persia:
colorful
Perssis

Perusia (Biblical) place name

Pesha (Hebrew) flourishing
Peshah, Peshia

Peshe (Hebrew) saved

Pessim (Native American)

Peta (English) saucy
Pet, Petra, Petrice, Petrina,
Petrona, Petty

Petila (Slavic) adored

Petra (Slavic) glamorous; capable
Pet, Peti, Petrah, Pett, Petti, Pietra

Petri (Scandinavian) feminine
form of Peter: dependable; rock

Petrine (Scandinavian) rock

Petrona (Italian) reliable

Petronilla (Greek) feminine
form of Peter: dependable; rock
*Petria, Petrina, Petrine, Petro,
Petrone, Petronela, Petronella, Pett*

Petru (Slavic) able

Petula (Latin) petulant song
Pet, Petulah, Petulia

Petunia (American) flower; perky
Pet, Petune

Pfeiffer (Last name as first name)
lovely blonde; talented

Phaedra (Greek) bright
*Faydra, Faydrah, Padra, Phae,
Phedra*

Phalba (American) offspring

Phalin (Asian) sapphire

Phan (Asian) shares

Phaselis (Biblical) place name

Phashestha (American)
decorative
Phashey, Shesta

Pheakkley (Vietnamese) faithful

Pheba (Greek) smiling
Phibba

Phedella (American) lasting;
loyal

Phedra (Greek) bright child
*Faydra, Fedra, Phadra, Phaedra,
Phedre*

Phelisa (American) form of
Felicity: friendly; happy

Phemia (Greek) language

Phenice (Origin unknown)
enjoys life
Pheni, Phenica, Phenicia, Venice

Pheodora (Greek) God's gift to
mankind

Pheresa (Spanish) form of
Theresa: gardener

Phernita (American) articulate
Ferney, Phern

Phia (Irish) saint

Phila (Greek) loving
Phil, Philly

Philadelphia (Greek) loving
one's fellow man
Fill, Phil, Philly

Philana (Greek) loving
Filana, Filly, Philly

Philantha (Greek) loves flowers

Philberta (English) intellectual

Philene (Greek) loving others

Philenet (American) loving

Philia (American) loving

Philida (Greek) loving others
Philina, Phillada, Phillida

Philippa (Greek) horse lover
*Feefee, Felipa, Phil, Philipa,
Philippe, Phillie, Phillipina,
Phillippah, Pippa, Pippy*

Philippitta (American) loves
horses

Philise (Greek) loving
Felece, Felice, Philese

Philistia (Biblical) place name

Philly (Place name) from
Philadelphia, Pennsylvania: loving
one's fellow man
Filly, Philee, Phillie

Philma (Greek) loves others

Philomena (Greek) beloved
*Filomena, Filomina, Mena,
Phil, Phillomenah, Philomen,
Philomene, Philomina*

Philoteria (Biblical) place name

Philtherian (Greek) loving

Phiona (Scottish) form of Fiona:
fair-haired
Phionna

Phira (Greek) loves music

Phoebe (Greek) bringing light
*Febe, Fee, Feebe, Feebs, Pheabe,
Phebe, Phebee, Pheby, Phobe,
Phoeb, Phoebey, Phoebie, Phoebs*

Phoenicia (Biblical) place name

Phoenix (Greek) rebirth
Fee, Fenix, Fenny, Phenix, Phoe

Phonsa (Origin unknown)
jubilant

Phosa (Biblical) delicate girl

Photina (Origin unknown)
fashionable

Phrgia (Biblical) place name

Phylicia (Greek) fortunate girl
Felicia, Phillie, Phyl, Phylecia

Phyllida (Greek) lovely; leafy
bough
Filida, Phyll, Phyllyda

Phyllis (Greek) beautiful; leafy
bough; articulate; smitten
Fillice, Fillis, Phil, Philis, Phillis,
Philliss, Phillisse, Phyl, Phylis,
Phyllys

Phynise (American)

Phyrus (Greek) form of
Zephyrus: breezy

Pia (Latin) devout
Peah, Piah

Picabo (Place name) city in
Idaho; swift
Peekaboo

Piedad (Spanish) devout

Pier (Greek) feminine form of
Peter: dependable; rock
Peer

Pierette (Greek) reliable
Perett, Perette, Piere

Pierina (Greek) dependable
Peir, Per, Perina, Perine, Pieryna

Pierrette (French) little rock

Piers (French) little rock

Piki (Hindi) little cuckoo

Pilar (Spanish) worthwhile; pillar
of strength

Pili (Spanish) pillar; strength

Pililani (Hawaiian) strong one

Pilisi (Hawaiian) simple life

Piluki (Hawaiian) little leaf; small

Pilvi (Italian) cheerful
Pilvee

Pineki (Hawaiian) peanut; tiny girl

Pinga (Hindi) dark

Pingjarje (Native American) shy;
little doe

Pingla (Hindi) goddess

Pink (American) blushing
Pinkee, Pinkie, Pinky, Pinkye,
Pynk

Pinquana (Native American)
fragrant girl

Piper (English) player of a pipe;
musical

Pippa (English) ebullient; horse-
lover
Pip, Pipa

Pippi (English/French) blushing;
loving horses
Pip, Pippie, Pippy

Pirene (French) rock; dependable

Pirouette (French) ballet term
Piro, Pirouet, Pirouetta

Pisidia (Biblical) place name; of
the water

Pita (English) comforting

Pitana (Origin unknown)
accented

Pitarra (American) interesting
Pitarr, Peta, Petah

Pity (American) sad
Pitee, Pitey, Pitie

Pixie (American) small; perky;
(English) zany
Pixee, Pixey, Pixi

Placida (Latin) serenity
Plasida

Platinum (English) from the
Spanish platinal; fine metal
Plati, Platnum

Platona (Spanish) good friend
Pleasance, Pleasant, Pleasants,
Pleasence

Playla (Place name)

Pleshette (American) plush
Plesh

Pleun (Origin unknown)
wordsmith

Plina (Spanish) full

Plum (Botanical) fruit; healthy

Po (Italian) effervescent
Poe

Pocahontas (Native American)
joyful
Poca, Poka

Poe (Last name as first name)
mysterious

Poetry (Word as name) romantic
Poe, Poesy, Poet

Polete (Hawaiian) small; kind
Poleke, Polina

Policia (Spanish) guards

Polina (Russian) small
Po, Pola, Polya

Poliquin (Last name as first
name) all-encompassing

Polishia (Slavic) smooth

Polly (Irish) devout; joyous
*Pauleigh, Paulie, Pol, Pollee,
Polley, Polli, Pollie*

Pollyanna (English) heroine of
Eleanor Porter's novel
*Polianna, Polliana, Pollie-anna,
Polly*

Polymnea (Mythology)
songstress for all

Polyxena (Mythology) very
hospitable

Pomona (Latin) apple of my eye;
(Mythology) bears fruit
Pomonah

Pompa (Last name as first name)
pompous
Pompy

Pompey (Place name) lavish
Pomp, Pompee, Pompei, Pompy

Poni (African) second daughter

Ponise (Spanish) sets aside
Pomice

Pony (American) wild west girl
Poney, Ponie

Poodle (American) sweet; curly-
haired
Poo, Pood, Poodly

Poonam (Hindi) kind soul

Poppy (Latin) flower; bouncy girl
Pop, Poppi, Poppie

Poppy-Honey (American) sweet
girl

Pora (Hebrew) fertile

Porsche (Latin) giving; high-
minded
*Porsh, Porsha, Porshe, Porshie,
Portia*

Porsha (German) giving
Porshea

Portia (Latin) a giving woman
*Porcha, Porscha, Porsh, Porsha,
Porshuh*

Posala (Native American) good-
bye to spring

Posh (American) fancy girl
Posha

Posy (American) sweet
Posee, Posey, Posie

Poupée (French) doll
Pou

Powder (American) gentle; light
*Pow, Powd, Powdy, Powdyr,
PowPow*

Poweline (American) ready

Pragyata (Hindi) knowledgeable

Prancey (American)
rambunctious

Prancine (American) form of
Francine: beautiful

Prarthana (Hindi) prays

Prasanna (Indian) unswerving

Pratibha (Hindi) understanding

Precia (Latin) important
Preciah, Presha, Presheah, Preshuh

Preciliano (Spanish) precious

Precious (English) beloved
*Precia, Preciosa, Preshie, Preshuce,
Preshus*

Predenita (Spanish) pretentious

Prema (Hindi) love

Premlata (Hindi) loving

Prentice (Last name as first name) learns
Prentiss

Prescilian (Hispanic) fashionable
Pres, Priss

Prescilline (Spanish) form of Priscilla: wisdom of the ages

Presencia (Spanish) presents well

Presley (English) talented
Preslee, Preslie, Presly, Prezlee, Prezley, Prezly

Prestha (Hindi) dearest girl

Pretice (American) form of Prentice: learns

Pribislava (Polish) glorifed; helpful
Pribena, Pribka, Pribuska

Price (Welsh) loving
Pri, Prise, Pry, Pryce, Pryse

Prima (Latin) first; fresh
Primalia, Primetta, Primia, Primie, Primina, Priminia, Primma, Primula

Primalia (Spanish) prime; first

Primavera (Italian) spring child

Primola (Botanical) flower; from primrose; first
Prim, Prym, Prymola

Primrose (English) rosy; fragrant
Prim, Primie, Rosie, Rosy

Princelle (American) princess

Princess (English) precious
Prin, Prince, Princesa, Princessa, Princie, Prinsess

Princy (American) form of Princess: precious

Prisca (Latin) old spirit

Prisciliana (Spanish) wise; old
Cissy, Priscili, Priss, Prissy

Priscilla (Latin) wisdom of the ages
Cilla, Precilla, Prescilla, Pricilla, Pris, Priscella, Priscila, Prisilla, Priss, Prissie, Prissilla, Prissy, Prysilla

Prisisima (Spanish) wise and feminine
Priss, Prissy, Sima

Prisma (Hindi) cherished baby

Prissy (Latin) form of Priscilla: wisdom of the ages
Prisi, Priss, Prissie

Pristina (Latin) pristine

Priti (Hindi) lovely

Priya (Hindi) sweetheart
Preeya, Preya, Priyah

Prizela (Spanish) form of Priscilla: wisdom of the ages

Prochora (Latin) leads

Promise (American) sincere
Promis

Proserpine (Mythology) queen of the underworld; secretive

Prospera (Latin) does well

Protima (Hindi) dancing girl

Prova (Place name) Provence, France
Pro, Proa, Provah

Pru (Latin) form of Prudence: wise; careful
Prudie, Prue

Prudence (Latin) wise; careful
Perd, Pru, Prudencia, Prudie, Prudince, Pruds, Prudu, Prudy, Prue

Prunella (Latin) shy
Pru, Prue, Prune, Prunie

Pryor (Last name as first name) wealthy
Prieyer, Pryar, Prye, Pryer

Psyche (Greek) soulful
Sye, Sykie

Pua (Hawaiian) flower

Pulcheria (Italian) chubby; curvy
Pulchia

Puma (American) cougar; wild spirit
Poom, Pooma, Poomah, Pumah, Pume

Punita (Indian) unblemished

Punsey (American) form of Pansy: fragrant

Purity (English) virginal
Puretee, Puritie

Purnima (Hindi) full moon baby

Pyera (Italian) sturdy; formidable;
rock
Pyer, Pyerah

Pyllyon (English) enthusiastic
Pillion, Pillyon, Pillyun

Pyrena (Greek) fiery temper

Pyria (Origin unknown)
cherished
Pyra, Pyrea

Pyrrha (Latin) fire

Pythia (Greek) prophet

Qadira (Arabic) wields power
Kadira

Qamra (Arabic) moon girl
Kamra

Qing (Origin unknown) quick

Qitarah (Arabic) aromatic

Qiturah (Arabic) aromatic
Qeturah, Quetura, Queturah

Q-Malee (American) form of
Cumale: open-hearted
*Cue, Q, Quemalee, Quemali,
Quemalie*

Quan (Chinese) goddess of
compassion

Quanda (English) queenly
*Kwanda, Kwandah, Quandah,
Qwanda*

Quanella (African American)
sparkling
Kwannie, Quanela

Quanesha (African American)
singing
*Kwaeesha, Kwannie, Quaneisha,
Quanisha*

Quantina (American) brave
queen
*Kwantina, Kwantynna,
Quantinna, Quantyna, Tina*

Qubilah (Arabic) easygoing

Queen (English) regal; special
*Quanda, Queena, Queenette,
Queenie*

Queendiosa (American) queenly

Queenie (English) royal and
dignified
Kweenie, Quee, Queen, Queeny

Queisha (American) contented
child
Queshia, Queysha

Quenby (Swedish) feminine
*Quenbee, Quenbey, Quenbi,
Quenbie, Quinbee, Quinbie, Quinby*

Quenna (English) feminine
Kwenna

Queosha (American) soulful

Querida (Spanish) dear one

Questa (French) looking for love
Kesta

Queta (Spanish) head of the house
Keta

Quiana (Origin unknown) form
of Hannah: merciful; God-blessed
Qiana, Qianna, Quianna, Quiyanna

Quilla (English) writer
*Kwila, Kwilla, Quila, Quillah,
Quyla, Quylla*

Quillee (Spanish) high spirits

Quina (African) fifth baby

Quinby (Scandinavian) living like
royalty
Quenby, Quin, Quinbie, Quinnie

Quinceanos (Spanish) fifteenth
child
Quin, Quince, Quincy

Quincy (French) fifth
*Quince, Quincey, Quinci, Quincie,
Quinsy*

Quincylla (American) popular;
fifth child
Cylla, Quince, Quincy

Quindelin (American) form of Gwendolyn: mystery goddess; bright

Quinella (Latin) a girl who is as pretty as two
Quinn

Quinetra (American) fifth baby

Quinise (American) fifth baby

Quinitka (American) fifth baby

Quinn (English/Irish) smart
Quin, Quinnie

Quinta (Latin) fifth day of the month

Quintana (Latin) fifth; lovely girl
Quentana, Quinn

Quintessa (Latin) essential goodness

Quintessen (American) fifth baby

Quintilla (Latin) fifth girl
Quintina

Quintina (Latin) fifth child
Quentina, Quintana, Quintessa, Quintona, Quintonette, Quintonice

Quintona (Latin) fifth

Quintwana (American) fifth girl in the family
Quintuana

Quinyette (American) likeable; fifth child
Kwenyette, Quiny

Quirina (Latin) contentious

Quisagna (Slavic) sister

Quisha (African American) beautiful mind
Keisha, Kesha, Key

Quita (Latin) peaceful
Keeta, Keetah

Raah (Greek) saved

Rabab (Origin unknown) different

Rabbah (Biblical) place name

Rabbit (American) lively; energetic
Rabit

Rabia (Arabic) wind

Rabiah (Arabic) breezy

Rachael (Hebrew) form of Rachel: peaceful as a lamb
Rach, Rachaele, Rachal, Rachel, Rachie, Rae, Raechal, Rasch, Ray, Raye

Rache (American) form of Rachel: peaceful as a lamb

Rachel ✿ (Hebrew) peaceful as a lamb

Rachelle (French) calm
Rach, Rachell, Rashell, Rashelle, Rochelle

Rachen (Slavic) peaceful

Rachene (French) peaceful

Rachna (Indian) organized

Racinda (Slavic) peaceful

Racquel (French) friendly
Racquelle, Raquel

Rada (Polish) glad

Radha (Hindi) successful; excels
Radhika

Radia (Slavic) happy

Radmilla (Slavic) glad; hardworking

Rae (English) raving beauty
Raedie, Raena, Ray, Raye

Raegan (French) delicate
Reagan, Regan, Regun

Raelan (American) simple beauty

Rafa (Arabic) joyful girl
Rafah

Rafaela (Hebrew) spiritual
Rafayela

Rafeline (French) happy

Raffaella (French) happy

Rafferty (Irish) prospering
Raferty, Raff, Raffarty, Rafty

Rageana (Spanish) form of
Regina: queen

Ragnild (Scandinavian) goddess
of war
Ragnhild, Ragnhilda, Ragnhilde,
Ragnilda, Ranillda, Reinheld,
Renilda, Renilde, Reynilda,
Reynilde

Raheel (Hebrew) form of Rachel:
peaceful as a lamb
Raheela

Rahela (Hawaiian) lamb

Rahil (Hebrew) form of Rachel:
peaceful as a lamb

Rahima (Pakistani) loving
Raheema, Raheema

Rain (English) falling water
Rainie, Reign

Raina (German) dramatic
Raine, Rainna, Rayna

Rainbow (American) bright
Rain, Rainbeau, Rainbo, Rainie

Raine (Latin) helpful friend
Raina, Rainie, Rana, Rane, Rayne

Rainey (Last name as first name)
giving
Rainee, Rainie, Raney

Raisa (Russian) embraced
Rasa

Raissa (Russian) form of Rose:
rose; blushing beauty

Raja (Arabic) optimist

Rajani (Hindi) dark; hopeful

Rajata (Indian) silver; queen

Rajeana (Slavic) form of Regina:
queen

Raji (Hindi) royal

Rajni (Hindi) dark night

Raka (Hindi) royal

Raleigh (Irish) admirable
Raileigh, Railey, Raley, Rawleigh,
Rawley

Ralphenne (American) feminine
form of Ralph: advisor to all

Ralphina (American) feminine
form of Ralph: advisor to all
Ralphine

Rama (Hindi) godlike; good

Ramah (Biblical) place name

Ramani (Indian) lovely

Ramba (African) high goals

Ramilia (Slavic) strong

Ramina (German) lovely

Ramona (Teutonic) beautiful
protector
Rae, Ramonah, Ramonna,
Raymona

Ramonda (American) form of
Ramona: beautiful protector

Ramsay (English) from the isle of
rams; country girl
Ramsey

Ramsee (English) from the rams'
land

Ramsie (English) from the rams'
land

Rana (Hindi) royal

Ranchel (American) range girl

Randa (Latin) admired
Ran, Randah

Randall (English) protective of
her own
Rand, Randal, Randi, Randy

Randella (American) sheltered

Randelle (American) wary
Randee, Randele

Randi (English) audacious
Randee, Randie, Randy

Rane (Scandinavian) queen-like
Rain, Raine, Ranie

Rani (Sanskrit) a queen
Rainie, Ranie

Rania (Sanskrit) regal
Ranea, Raneah, Raney, Ranie

Ranielle (French) royal; frank

Ranita (Hebrew) musical
Ranit, Ranite, Ranitra, Ranitta

Raoule (Spanish) feminine form
of Raoul: wild heart
Raoula, Raula

Rapa (Hawaiian) lovely by
moonlight

Raphaela (Hebrew) helping to heal
Rafaela, Rafe

Raphenn (American) dreamy

Raphia (Biblical) place name

Raphina (German) exciting

Raquel (Spanish) sensual
Racuell, Raquelle, Raqwel

Raquita (Spanish) aggressive

Rasa (Slavic) morning dew

Rasheeda (Hindi) pious
Rashee, Rashida, Rashie, Rashy

Rashidah (Arabic) on the right path
Rashida

Rashinique (African American) rash
Rash, Rashy

Ratna (Indian) beauty

Raula (French) advises

Ravada (Spanish) raven

Raven (English) blackbird
Ravan, Rave, Ravin

Ravenna (English) blackbird

Ravette (English) special

Ravistene (American) raven

Rawn (American) ambitious

Rawnie (Slavic) ladylike
Rawani, Rawn, Rawnee

Ray (American) simplistic approach
Rae, Raymonde

Rayleen (American) popular
Raylene, Raylie, Rayly

Rayna (Scandinavian) strong girl

Raynee (Scandinavian) strong

Raynekka (Slavic) raven

Raynelle (American) giving hope; combo of Ray and Nelle
Nellie, Rae, Raenel, Raenelle

Raynette (American) ray of hope; dancer
Raenette, Raynet

Rayola (Spanish) hopeful

Razia (Hebrew) secretive
Razeah, Raziah

Raziella (Italian) graceful

Razina (African) nice

Rea (Polish) flowing
Raya

Reagan ❶ (Last name as first name) strong
Regan, Reganne, Reggie

Reanika (American) happy

Reanne (American) happy
Reann, Rennie, Rere, Rianne

Reason (Word as name)

Reba (Hebrew) fourth-born
Rebah, Ree, Reeba

Rebazar (Spanish) fourth child

Rebecca (Hebrew) loyal
Becca, Becki, Beckie, Becky, Rebeca, Rebeka, Rebekah

Rebi (Hebrew) friend who is steadfast
Reby, Ree, Ribi

Rebop (American) zany
Reebop

Redettea (American) righteous

Redita (Slavic) peaceful

Redonna (American) peaceful

Ree (Asian) mannered

Reed (English) red-haired
Read, Reade, Reid, Reida

Reem (Arabic) antelope; graceful

Reena (Arabic) antelope

Reenie (Greek) peace-loving
Reena, Reeni, Reeny, Ren, Rena

Reese (American) style-setting
Ree, Reece, Rees, Rere

Reeve (Last name as first name) strong

Regan (Irish) queenly
Reagan

Reganean (American) form of Regan: queenly

Regeana (American) form of Regina: queen
Rege, Regeanah, Regeane

Regene (Latin) queen

Regina (English/Latin) queen
Gina, Rege, Regena, Reggie, Regine

Regine (Latin) royal
Regene, Rejean

Reginia (American) queen

Regne (Slavic) leader

Rehema (African) well-grounded
Rehemah, Rehemma, Rehima

Reidee (American) red hair

Reidnilda (German) form of
Reynalda: wise

Reiko (Japanese) appreciative

Rein (German) advises

Reina (Spanish) a thinker
Rein, Reinie, Rina

Reine (Spanish) form of Reina: a
thinker

Reith (American) shy
Ree, Reeth

Rejena (Slavic) queen

Rejunda (Slavic) queen

Rekha (Hindi) focuses

Rela (German) everything
Reila, Rella

Relin (German) kind

Rella (Origin unknown) rogue

Remah (Hebrew) pale beauty
*Rema, Remme, Remmie, Rima,
Ryma*

Remaliah (American) helps

Remata (German) helps

Remedios (Spanish) helpful

Remember (American)
memorable
Remi, Remmi, Remmie, Remmy

Remi (French) woman of Rheims;
jaded
Remee, Remie, Remy

Remille (French) helps

Remolda (Slavic) strong

Remonia (Slavic) strong

Ren (Asian) flower

Rena (Hebrew) joyful singer
Reena, Rinah, Rinne

Renae (French) form of Renee:
born again
Renay, Rennie, Rere

Renard (French) fox; sly
Ren, Renarde, Rynard, Rynn

Renata (French) reaching out
Renie, Renita, Rennie, Rinata

Renatha (Slavic) born again

Rene (Greek) hopeful
Reen, Reenie, Reney

Renea (French) form of Renee:
born again
Renny

Renee (French) born again
Rene, Rennie, Rere

Renetta (French) reborn
Ranetta, Renette

Renie (Latin) renewal

Renis (American) welcomed

Renita (Latin) poised
Ren, Renetta, Rennie

Renite (Latin) stubborn
Reneta, Renita

Reniti (English) upward

Renna (English) reborn

Rennyll (French) form of Renee:
born again
Renelle

Renshaw (Last name as first
name) directed

Renuka (Slavic) calm

Renzia (Greek) form of Renee:
born again
Renze

Reonne (Welsh) maiden

Resa (Greek) productive; laughing
Reesa, Reese, Risa

Reseda (Latin) healing
Res, Reseta

Reseme (American) fragrant

Resenetta (Spanish) fragrant
flower

Reshea (American) girlish

Reshma (African) compassionate;
(Indian) sun

Reshma (Indian) sun

Resie (German) form of Theresa:
gardener

Reta (African) shakes up
Reda, Reeda, Reeta, Rheta, Rhetta

Retanica (American) chaotic

Retha (German) form of Aretha:
virtuous; vocalist

Retrola (American) retrospective

Reva (Hebrew) rainmaker
Ree, Reeva, Rere

Revada (American) revival

Reveca (Spanish) form of
Rebecca: loyal
Reba, Rebeca, Reva

Revelina (American) revival

Reveriana (Spanish) of the river

Rew (Australian) of the spring

Rexie (American) confident
Rex, Rexi, Rexy

Reyna (Filipino) queen
Raina, Rayna, Rey

Reynalda (German) wise
Raynalda, Rey, Reyrey

Reynee (English) peaceful

Reynolds (Scottish) wispy
Rey, Reye, Reynells, Reynold

Reza (Czech) form of Theresa:
gardenerl
Rezi, Rezka, Riza

Rezeda (Spanish) prayerful

Rhea (Greek) earthy; mother of
gods; strong
Ria

Rheta (American) form of Rita:
precious pearl

Rhiall (Welsh) nymph

Rhianna (Welsh) pure
Rheanna

Rhiannon (Welsh) goddess;
intuitive
*Rhian, Rhiane, Rhianen, Rhiann,
Rhianon, Rhyan, Rhye, Riannon*

Rhilla (Slavic) nymph

Rhoda (Greek) rosy
*Rhodie, Roda, Rodi, Rodie, Rody,
Roe*

Rhodanthe (Greek) form of
Rhodes: lovely
Rhodante

Rhodette (American) rose girl

Rhodora (Spanish) rose girl

Rhogean (French) form of
Regine: royal

Rhola (Slavic) form of Rachel:
peaceful as a lamb

Rhon (Welsh) blessing

Rhona (Scottish) power-wielding
Rona, Ronne

Rhonda (Welsh) vocal;
quintessential
Rhon, Ron, Ronda, Ronnie

Rhondie (American) perfect
Rond, Rondie, Rondy

Rhonella (American) feminine
form of Ronald: kind

Rhonetta (American) maximum

Rhonni (American) form of
Ronnie: energetic

Rhonwen (Welsh) lovely
Rhonwenne, Rhonwin, Ronwen

Rhuenette (American) great

Rhyan (Welsh) magical

Rhyannah (Greek) nymph

Ria (Spanish) water-loving; river
Reah, Riah

Riah (Biblical) river

Riana (Irish) frisky
Reana, Rere, Rianna, Rinnie

Rianda (American) river

Riane (American) attractive
Reann, Reanne

Riannah (Irish) sweet

Riannon (Irish) free spirit
Rianna

Rica (Spanish) celestial
*Ric, Ricca, Rickie, Rieka, Rika,
Ryka*

Ricarda (German) has power

Richelle (French) strong and
artistic
*Chelle, Chellie, Rich, Richel,
Richele, Richie*

Richenda (German) rules

Richesse (French) wealthy
Richess

Richilda (American) sainted

Ricielle (African) beauty

Ricki (American) sporty
Rici, Rick, Rickie, Ricky, Rik,
Riki, Rikki

Rickiann (Combo of Ricki and
Ann) sporty

Rickma (Hindi) golden

Rico (Italian) sexy
Reko, Ricco

Rida (Arabic) satisfied
Ridah

Rierla (Scandinavian) helpful

Rieshanda (American) nymph

Rihana (Irish) pretty

Rihanna (Scandinavian) nymph

Rijana (Slavic) nymph

Rikina (Hawaiian) Christian

Rilena (English) lively

Riley ✪ (Irish) courageous; lively
Reilly, Rylee, Ryleigh, Ryley, Rylie

Rilla (German) lives by the brook

Rima (Arabic) graceful; antelope
Rema, Remmee, Remmy, Rimmy,
Ryma

Rimona (Hebrew) pomegranate;
small

Rina (Hebrew) joy
Renah

Rinda (Scandinavian) loyal
Rindah

Ring (American) magical
Ringe, Ryng

Riona (Irish) regal
Rina, Rine, Rionn, Rionna, Rionne

Ripley (American) unique
Riplee, Ripli, Riplie

Riquette (French) feminine form
of Richard: wealthy leader

Risen (Last name as first name)
rysen
Ryzenne

Rish (American) born in religion

Risingsun (Native American)
sun child

Rissa (Latin) laughing
Resa, Risa, Riss, Rissah, Rissie

Rita (Greek) precious pearl
Reda, Reita, Rida

Ritsa (Greek) form of Alexandra:
defender of mankind

Ritz (American) rich
Rits

Riva (Hebrew) joining; sparkling
Reva, Revi, Revvy

River (Latin) woman by the stream
Riv

Rivernne (American) water child

Rivers (American) trendy

Riya (American) excited

Riza (Greek) dignified
Reza, Rize

Rizalin (American) form of
Theresa: gardener

Rizalina (American) form of
Theresa: gardener

Rizalinne (American) form of
Theresa: gardener

Rizalyne (American) form of
Theresa: gardener

Roanna (Spanish) brown skin
Ranna, Roanne, Ronni, Ronnie,
Ronny

Roberta (English) brilliant mind
Robbie, Robby, Robertah, Robi

Robertia (English) feminine form
of Robert: brilliant; renowned

Robertz (French) feminine form
of Robert: brilliant; renowned

Robin (English) taken by the
wind; bird
Robbie, Robby, Robinn, Robinne,
Robyn

Robina (Scottish) birdlike; robin
Robena

Robitaille (French) girl of grace

Rocheen (French) sturdy

Rochelle (French/Hebrew) small
and strong-willed; dreamlike beauty
Roch, Roche, Rochel, Rochi, Rochie,
Rochy, Roshelle

Rockella (Invented) rocker
Rockell, Rockelle

Rocky (American) tomboy
Rock, Rockee, Rockey, Rockie

Roda (Polish) intelligent

Roddy (German) well-known
Rod, Roddee, Roddey, Roddi, Roddie

Roderica (German) princess
Rica, Roda, Roddie, Rodericka, Rodrika

Roelina (German) famous

Rogelim (Biblical) place name

Rogeria (American) feminine form of Roger: famed warrior

Rogertha (American) feminine form of Roger: famed warrior
Rodge

Rohan (Hindi) sandalwood; pretty

Rohana (Hindi) sandalwood; textured
Rohanna

Roi Anne (American) royal

Roisin (Irish) rose

Roksana (Polish) dawn
Roksanna, Roksona

Rolanda (German) rich woman
Rolane, Rollande, Rollie

Rolandan (German) feminine form of Roland: renowned
Roland, Rolanden, Rollie, Rolly

Roldyn (Spanish) famed

Roline (German) destined for fame
Roelene, Roeline, Rolene, Rollene, Rolleen, Rollina, Rolline, Rolyne

Rolleen (Italian) famed

Rollettea (Italian) rolling

Roma (Italian) girl from Rome; adventurous
Romy

Romaine (French) daredevil
Romain, Romane, Romayne, Romi

Romalice (American) form of Rome: city in Italy

Roman (Italian) adventurous
Romi, Romie, Rommie, Rommye, Romyn

Romana (Italian) distinct; Roman

Romey (Latin) sea-loving
Romy

Romilda (Latin) striking
Romelda, Romey, Romie, Romy

Romilla (Latin) form of Rome: city in Italy
Romella, Romi, Romie, Romila

Romilly (Latin) wanderer
Romillee, Romillie, Romily

Romina (Spanish) form of Rome: city in Italy

Romney (Welsh) winding river

Romola (Latin) form of Rome: city in Italy

Romona (Spanish) form of Ramona: beautiful protector
Mona, Rome, Romie, Romy

Romy (French) form of Romaine: daredevil
Roe. Romi, Romie

Rona (Scandinavian/Scottish) powerful
Rhona, Ronne, Ronni

Ronallia (Scottish) smart

Ronat (Scandinavian) form of Rhona: power-wielding

Ronda (Welsh) form of Rhonda: vocal; quintessential
Ronni

Rondra (American) form of Rhonda: vocal; quintessential

Ronea (American) form of Rona: powerful

Roneathea (American) good face

Ronelle (English) winner
Ronnie

Ronette (English) form of Rona: powerful

Roney (Scandinavian) form of
Rona: powerful
Roneye, Roni

Ronia (Scandinavian) lake

Ronis (English) image of beauty

Ronna (Slavic) image of beauty

Ronneta (English) go-getter
Roneda, Ronnete, Ronnette, Ronnie

Ronni (American) energetic
Ron, Ronee, Roni, Ronnie, Ronny

Rooki (American) sharp novice

Roopa (Hindi) beauty

Roquia (Spanish) royal

Rori (Irish) spirited; brilliant
Rory

Ros (English) form of Rosalind:
lovely rose
Roz

Rosa (Italian/German) rose;
blushing beauty
Rose, Rossah, Roza

Rosa-Adriana (Spanish) exotic
rose

Rosaire (French) rosary

Rosalba (Latin) glorious as a rose
Rosalbah, Rosey, Rosi, Rosie, Rosy

Rosalia (Italian) hanging roses
*Rosa, Rosalea, Rosaleah, Rosaliah,
Roselia, Rosey, Rosi, Rosie,
Rossalia, Rosy*

Rosalie (English) striking dark
beauty
*Leelee, Rosa, Rosalee, RosaLee,
Rosa-Lee, Rosie, Rossalie, Roz,
Rozalee, Rozalie*

Rosalind (Spanish) lovely rose
*Lind, Ros, Rosa, Rosalyn,
Rosalynde, Rosie, Roslyn, Roslynn,
Roz*

Rosalinda (Spanish) lovely rose
Rosa-Linda, Rosalynda

Rosaline (Spanish) a rose
Rosalyn, Rosalynne, Roslyn

Rosallie (Italian) fair rose

Rosalvo (Spanish) rosy-faced
Rosa, Rosey

Rosamond (English) beauty
*Rosa, Rosamun, Rosamund, Rose,
Rosemond, Rosie, Roz*

Rosanna (English) lovely
Rosannah

Rosau (Spanish) rosary

Rosaura (Spanish) rosary

Rose (Latin) rose; blushing beauty
*Rosa, Rosey, Rosi, Rosie, Rosy, Roze,
Rozee*

Rosebud (Latin) flowering

Roselle (Latin) rose

Rosellen (English) pretty
Roselinn, Roselyn

Rosena (American) form of Rose:
rose; blushing beauty
Roze, Rozena, Rozenna

Rosenda (Spanish) rosy
*Rose, Rosend, Rosende, Rosey, Rosie,
Senda*

Rosetta (Italian) longlasting
beauty
Rose, Rosy, Rozetta

Rosette (Latin) flowering; rosy
Rosett, Rosetta

Roshall (African American) form
of Rochelle: small and strong-
willed; dreamlike beauty
Rochalle, Roshalle

Rosheen (Latin) rose

Roshell (French) form of
Rochelle: small and strong-willed;
dreamlike beauty
Roshelle

Roshi (Indian) bright
Roshni

Roshni (Sanskrit) light

Roshumba (African American)
gorgeous
Rosh, Roshumbah

Roshunda (African American)
flamboyant
Rosey, Roshun, Roshund, Rosie, Roz

Rosie (English) bright-cheeked
Rose, Rosi, Rosy

Rosina (English) rose

Rosita (Spanish) pretty

Roseta, Rosey, Rosie, Rositta

Ross (Scottish) peninsula is home

Rosse

Rossana (Italian) rose

Rosshalde (Welsh) rosary

Rossian (American) rosary

Roszl (Scottish) rose

Rotella (American) smart

Rotel, Rotela

Roth (American) studious

Rothe

Rotnei (American) bright

Rotnay

Roula (Scandinavian) secret

Rowan (Welsh) blonde

Rowanne

Rowena (Scottish) blissful; beloved friend

Roe, Roenna, Rowina

Rowenta (Slavic) highborn

Roxanna (Persian) bright

Roxana, Roxie

Roxanne (Persian) lovely as the sun

Roxane, Roxann, Roxie, Roxy

Roxy (American) sunny

Rox, Roxi, Roxie

Royal (English) royal

Royale (English) of royal family

Royalla, Royalene, Roayalina, Royall, Royalle, Royalyn, Royalynne

Royce (English) king's child

Roice

Roynale (American) motivated

Roy, Royna, Roynal

Roysee (English) royal

Roz (French) form of Rosalind: lovely rose

Ros, Rozz, Rozzie

Rozanne (Slavic) rose

Rozen (Native American) rose

Rozettaline (American) rose

Rozina (Indian) pretty rose

Rozonda (American) pretty

Rosonde, Rozon, Rozond

Rubaina (Hindi) bright

Rube (Hawaiian) ruby; gem

Rubena (Hebrew) sassy

Rubyn, Rubyna, Rueben

Rubicela (Spanish) ruby

Rubina (Pakistani) gem

Rubi

Rubra (French) form of Ruby: precious jewel

Rube, Rue

Ruby (French) precious jewel

Rubi, Rubie, Rue

Ruchi (German) brash

Rudelle (English) ruddy skin

Rudella

Rudy (German) sly

Rudee, Rudell, Rudie

Rue (English/German) looking back

Ru

Rufaro (African) happy

Rufina (Italian) red-haired

Rufeena, Rufeine, Ruffina, Ruphyna

Rujona (Slavic) form of Regina: queen

Rujula (Indian) rich

Rujuta (Hindi) truthful

Rula (American) wild-spirited

Rue, Rulah, Rewela

Rulia (English) ruler

Rumah (Biblical) place name

Rumer (English) unique

Ru, Rumor

Rumiko (Asian)

Runa (Scandinavian) secret

Rupli (Hindi) beautiful

Ruri (Japanese) emerald

Rure, Rurrie, RuRu

Rusbel (Spanish) beautiful girl with reddish hair

Rusbell, Rusbella

Ruselle (French) red hair

Rushenda (Slavic) red hair

Russine (French) red hair

Russo (American) happy
Russoh

Rusty (English) red-haired girl
Rustee, Rusti

Ruta (Lithuanian) practical
Rue, Rudah, Rutah

Rutanya (Slavic) friend

Ruth (Hebrew) loyal friend
Rue, Ruthie, Ruthy

Rutha (Hebrew) friend

Ruthian (American) friend

Ruthie (Hebrew) friendly and
young
Ruth, Ruthey, Ruthi, Ruthy

Ryan (Irish) royal; assertive
Rian, Ryann, Ryen, Ryunn

Ryanna (Irish) leader
*Rianna, Rianne, Ryana, Ryanne,
Rynn*

Ryba (Hebrew) traditional
Reba, Ree, Riba, Ribah

Ryenline (American) ruler

Ryenni (American) ruler

Rylee (Irish) brave
Rilee, Rili, Ryelee, Ryley, Ryli, Ryly

Ryleen (American) brave

Ryn (American) form of Wren:
flighty girl; bird
Ren, Rynn

Ryne (Irish) form of Ryan: royal;
assertive
Rynea, Ryni, Rynie

Rynie (American) loves the woods
Rinnie, Ryn

Rynn (American) outdoorsy
woman
Rin, Rynna, Rynnie, Wren

Rynnea (American) sun-lover
Rynnee, Rynni, Rynnia

Saba (Arabic) morning star
Sabah

Sabella (English) spiritual
*Bella, Belle, Sabela, Sabell, Sabelle,
Sebelle*

Sabeth (American) form of
Elisabeth: God's promise

Sabina (Latin) desirable
*Sabeena, Sabine, Sabinna, Sabyna,
Say*

Sabine (Latin) tribe in ancient
Italy
Sabeen, Sabienne, Sabin, Sabyne

Sabirah (Arabic) young

Sabla (Arabic) young

Sable (English) chic
Sabelle, Sabie

Sablette (American) luxurious
Sable, Sablet

Sabra (Hebrew) substantial
Sabe, Sabera, Sabrah

Sabrina (Latin) passionate
*Breena, Brina, Brinna, Sabe,
Sabreena, Sabrinna*

Sabrinus (English) princess

Sabry (American) worthwhile

Sacha (Greek) helpful girl
Sachie, Sachy

Sachen (Slavic) lucky

Sachi (Japanese) girl
*Sachee, Sachey, Sachie, Sachy,
Sashi, Shashie*

Sachika (Japanese) happy

Sachin (Slavic) lucky

Sadawn (American) pure

Sadhana (Hindi) loyal

Sadiah (Arabic) good omen

Sadie (Hebrew) charmer; princess
Sade, Sadee, Sady, Sadye, Shaday

Safe (Word as name)

Safeenah (Muslim) ship at sea

Saffron (Indian) spice
Saffrone, Safron

Safia (Arabic) pure

Saga (Scandinavian) sensual
Sagah

Sagal (American) action-oriented
Sagall, Segalle

Sagartia (Biblical) place name

Sage (Latin) wise
Saige

Sahara (Place name) desert;
wilderness
Saharra

Sahare (American) loner

Sahila (Hindi) guides others

Sahri (Arabic) giving

Saiby (American) gifted

Saida (Hebrew) happy girl
Sada, Sadie

Saige (English) wise

Sailor (American) outdoorsy
Sail, Saile, Sailer, Saylor

Sairsha (Indian) defends

Sajah (Hindi) meritorious
Sajie, Sayah

Sajida (Arabic) lady

Sakura (Japanese) wealthy

Sal (Spanish) savior

Salacia (Mythology) earthy

Salama (African) safe

Salamis (Biblical) place name

Salecah (Biblical) place name

Salena (Latin) needed; basic
Salene, Sally

Saletta (American) earthy

Salia (American) esoteric

Salih (Arabic) virtuous

Saliha (Arabic) correct

Salila (Indian) water child

Salima (Arabic) healthy; safety
Salma

Salina (French) quiet and deep
Sale, Salena

Sally (Hebrew) princess
Sal, Salli, Sallie

Salma (Hebrew; Spanish)
peaceful; ingenious
*Sal, Sali, Sallee, Salley, Salli, Sally,
Salmah, Salwah*

Salmone (Biblical) place name

Salome (Hebrew) sensual;
peaceful
Sal, Salohme, Salomey, Salomi

Salonae (Biblical) place name

Saloni (Indian) peaceful

Salonna (American) peaceful

Salowmee (Invented) form of
Salome: peaceful; sensual
*Sal, Salomee, Salomie, Salomy,
Slowmee*

Salvadora (Spanish) saved
Sal, Salvadorah

Salvia (Spanish) healthy

Salwa (Indian) healthy

Sam (Hebrew) God leads

Samalyn (American) God-loving

Samantha (Hebrew) good
listener
Sam, Samath, Sammi, Sammie

Samara (Hebrew) God-led;
watchful
Sam, Samora

Samaria (Biblical) place name

Samatha (American) form of
Samantha: good listener

Sami (Hebrew) insightful
Sam, Sammie, Sammy

Samia (Hindi) joyful
*Sameah, Samee, Sameea, Samina,
Sammy*

Samimah (Hebrew) praised

Samine (Hindi) happy

Samira (Arabic) charismatic

Samona (Hebrew) form of
Simone: wise and thoughtful

Samosata (Biblical) place name

Samothrace (Biblical) place
name

Samuela (Hebrew) selected
Samm, Sammi, Sammy, Samula

Samyrah (African American)
music-loving
Samirah, Samyra

Sana (Arabic) quintessential
beauty

Sanaa (Arabic) excellent

Sancha (Spanish) sacred child
Sanchia

Sanchine (Italian) aware

Sandal (Word as name)

Sandhya (Indian) night

Sandhyn (Indian) night

Sandi (Greek) defends others
Sand, Sanda, Sandee, Sandie, Sandy

Sandip (Hindi) knowing

Sandra (Greek) helpful; protective
Sandrah, Sandy

Sandrea (Greek) selfless
Sandreea, Sandie, Sanndria

Sandreen (American) great
Sandrene, Sandrin, Sandrine

Sandy (American) playful
Sandee, Sandey, Sandi, Sandie

Sanella (Indian) golden

Saniata (Spanish) praised

Sanika (Spanish) old

Sanila (Indian) full of praise
Sanilla

Sanimora (Asian) good health

Sanita (Spanish) twilight

Saniyya (Hindi) a special moment in time

Sanjuana (Spanish) God-loving
Sanwanna

Sanjuanita (Spanish) form of San Juan; combo of San Juan and Juanita: believer
Juanita, Sanjuan

Sanna (Scandinavian) truthful
Sana

Sanne (Persian) regal

Sanqueneta (Spanish) saint

Santa (Latin) saint

Santana (Spanish) saintly
San, Santanne, Santie, Santina

Sante (Spanish) healthy

Santeene (Spanish) passionate
Santeena, Santene, Santie, Santina, Santine, Satana

Santi (Spanish) saint

Santia (African) lovable
Santea

Santina (Italian) loves life

Santine (Italian) loves life

Santonina (Spanish) ardent

Sanya (Slavic) dreamer

Sanyu (African) joy

Saper (American) dancer

Sapphira (Greek) blue gem

Sapphire (Greek) precious gem
Safire, Saphire, Sapphie, Sapphyre

Sapphireen (Greek) blue gem

Sappho (Greek) blue

Saqqarah (Biblical) place name

Sarafina (Hebrew) angelic
Seraphina

Sarah ✪ ❶ (Hebrew) God's princess
Sae, Sara, Saree, Sarrie

Sarai (Hebrew) contentious
Sari

Saraid (Irish) best

Saralyn (American) combo of Sara and Lyn

Saree (Hebrew) woman of value
Sarie, Sary

Sarepta (Biblical) place name

Saretta (Indian) river
Sarita

Sari (Hebrew; Arabic) noble
Saree, Sarey, Sarie, Sarree, Sarrey, Sarri

Sariah (English) form of Sarah: God's princess

Sarika (Hindi) thrush; sings

Sarilla (Spanish) princess
Sarella, Sarill, Sarille

Sarina (Hebrew) strong
Sareena, Sarena, Sarrie

Sarit (Hebrew) form of Sarah: God's princess
Saritt, Saryt, Sarytt

Sarita (Spanish) regal
Sareeta, Sarie, Saritah

Sarmila (Indian) comforts

Sarolyn (English) form of Sharilyn: dear

Sarria (Arabic) superb

Sarun (Indian) valued

Sarva (Indian) river

Sash (Indian) moon child
Sashhi

Sasha (Russian) beautiful courtesan; helpful
Sacha, Sachie, Sascha, Sasheen, Sashy

Sashay (American) defends

Sasi-Ann (American) dramatic

Sasily (American) form of Cecile: blind

Saskia (Dutch) dramatic; armed with a knife
Saskiah

Saskie (Dutch) Saxon girl

Sasmita (Hindi) laughter

Sassy (Irish) Saxon girl; flirtatious
Sass, Sassi, Sassie

Sata (Spanish) princess

Satchel (American) unusual
Satchal

Satha (Hindi) untruthful

Satin (French) shiny
Saten

Satomi (Indian) sweet

Saturine (American) from planet Saturn; melancholy
Saturenne, Saturinne, Saturn, Saturyne

Satya (Arabic) lucky

Sauda (African) darkness

Saumet (French) good advisor

Saundra (Greek) defender
Sandi, Sandra, Sandrah

Saundrall (American) form of Saundra: defender

Sauni (Arabic) genius
Sani

Sauri (Hebrew) princess

Savannah (Spanish) open heart
Sava, Savana, Savanah, Savanna, Seven

Savarne (Indian) ocean

Savea (Scandinavian) global view

Savedra (Indian) sun love

Saveen (Indian) morning

Savina (Latin) form of Sabina: desirable
Saveena, Savyna

Savone (Italian) morning

Savonna (American) morning

Savy (American) morning

Sawyer (Last name as first name) industrious
Sawya, Sawyar, Sawyhr, Sawyie, Sawyur

Say (Asian) night

Sayde (American) form of Sadie: charmer; princess
Saydey, Saydie

Sayleem (Arabic) safe haven

Saylem (Arabic) safe haven

Sayo (Japanese) born at night
Saio, Sao

Sayuri (Hindi) blooms

Sazana (African) princess

Scally (Last name as first) introspective
Scalley, Scalli

Scarlett (English) red
Scarlet, Scarletta, Scarlette

Schae (Irish) variation of Shea: soft beauty
Schay

Scharissea (American) form of Cherise: cherry

Schelunda (American) invented

Schemika (African American) form of Shameka: loving
Schemi, Schemike

Scheree (American) form of Sherry: outgoing

Scherry (American) form of Sherry: outgoing
Scherri, Scherrie

Schmoopie (American) baby; sweetie
Schmoopee, Schmoopey, Schmoopy, Shmoopi

Schulyer (Dutch) form of Skyler: protective; sheltering
Schulyar, Sky, Skye

Schunetta (American) invented

Schylar (Dutch) sheltering
Schylarr, Schyler, Schylerr, Schylur, Schylurr

Scodra (Biblical) place name

Scooter (American) wild-spirit
Scooder, Scoot

Scottia (Scottish) form of Scotland

Scotty (Scottish) girl from Scotland
Scota, Scotti, Scottie

Scout (French) precocious
Scouts

Scully (Irish) strong
Scullee, Sculleigh, Sculley, Sculli, Scullie

Scupi (Biblical) place name

Scylla (Greek mythology) monstrous

Scyllaea (Greek) mythological monster; menace
Cilla, Scylla, Silla

Scythian (Biblical) place name

Sea (American) sea-loving; flowing
Cee, See

Sealy (Last name as first name) fun-loving
Celie, Seal, Sealie

Sean (Hebrew/Irish) God is giving

Seana (Irish) giving
Seane, Seanna, Suannea

Seandra (American) form of Deandra: divine
Seandre, Seandreah, Seanne

Season (Latin) special; change
Seas, Seasee, Seasen, Seasie, Seasun, Seazun, Seezun

Seaton (English) from the coast
Seaten, Seeten, Seeton, Seten, Seton

Sebaste (Biblical) place name

Sebastiana (French) respected

Sebastiane (Latin) respected female
Sebastian, Sebbie

Seely (English) bright
Sealee, Sealey, Seali, Sealie, Sealy, Seelee, Seeley, Seeli, Seelie

Seema (Hebrew) treasured; softhearted
Seem

Sehba (Indian) form of Shobha: smart and pretty

Sehria (American) form of Sarah: God's princess

Seine (French) river; flowing
Sane

Seire (Irish) form of Sierra: peaks; outdoorsy

Sejal (Hindi) good character; together

Sela (Hebrew) form of Cecilia: blind
Cela, Celia, Selah, Selia

Selahkiyah (Indian) girl of mountain

Selame (Biblical) place name

Selanne (American) of the moon

Selannotta (American) of the moon

Selda (German) sure-footed
Seda, Seldah, Selde, Seldee, Seldey, Seldi, Seldie

Selena (Greek) like the moon; shapely
Celina, Sela, Seleene, Selene, Selina, Sylena

Selene (Greek) goddess of the moon
Seleene, Seline, Selyne

Seleucia (Biblical) place name

Selfina (Spanish) moon child

Selima (Hebrew) peacemaker
Selema, Selemmah

Selin (Turkish) calm

Selina (Greek) moon
Celina

Sella (English) form of Selena: like the moon; shapely
Sela

Selma (German) fair-minded female
Selle, Sellma, Selmah, Zele, Zelma

Selona (Greek) form of Selena: like the moon; shapely
Celona, Sela, Seli, Selo, Selone

Selsa (Hispanic) enthusiastic
Sel, Sels

Sema (Greek) earthy
Semah, Semale, Semele

Semane (Biblical)

Semele (Mythology) needs proof; (Latin) number one

Semilia (Latin) number one

Semilla (Spanish) earth mother
Samilla, Sem, Semila, Semillah, Semmie, Semmy, Sumilla

Semira (Indian) divine

Semiramis (African) meets goals

Semone (American) sentimental
Semonne

Semora (English) form of Samara: God-led; watchful

Semra (Arabic) earthy

Senay (Italian) happy

Sendy (American) form of Cindy: moon goddess
Sendee, Sendie

Seneca (Native American) name of a tribe that is part of the Iroquois confederacy
Seneka

Senell (American) serene

Sennabis (Biblical) place name

Senone (Spanish) energetic

Senora (Spanish) old soul

Senorah (Spanish) old soul

Senovian (American) high-energy

Senta (German) crescent

Senza (Spanish) sensation

Senzala (Spanish) sensation

Seone (Scottish) sweet

Sephene (American) form of Stephanie: regal

Sepphoris (Biblical) place name

September (Latin) serious; month
Seppie, Sept

Septima (Latin) seventh child
Septimma, Septyma

Sequoia (Cherokee) giant redwood; formidable
Sekwoya

Serafina (Hebrew) ardent
Serafeena, Serafeenah, Serafinah, Serafyna, Serafynah, Seraphina, Seraphine, Serifina

Seraphina (Latin) angel
Serapheena, Serapheenah, Seraphinah, Seraphyna, Serphynah

Seraphine (French) treasure

Seren (Latin) serene
Ceren, Seran

Serena (Latin) calm
Sarina, Sereena, Serenah, Serina

Serendipity (Invented) mercurial; lucky
Sere, Seren, Serendipitee, Serin

Serene (American) word as name; calm

Serenity ✪ ❶ (American) serene
Sera, Serenitee, Serenitie

Seriah (Spanish) smooth

Serida (Spanish) aggressive

Serpina (Mythology) form of Proserpine: queen of the underworld; secretive

Sesame (American) inventive
Sesamee, Sezamee

Sesha (Hindi) snake

Sesiti (Italian) sixth sextus

Seta (Hindi) form of Sita: divine

Seth (Hebrew) set; appointed; gentle
Sethe

Severia (Spanish) severe

Seville (Place name) from Seville, Spain
Sevill, Sevyll, Sevylle

Sevrea (American) severe

Sexton (English) church worker

Seymoura (Invented) feminine form of Seymour: prayerful
Seymora

Shade (English) cool
Shadee, Shadi, Shady

Shadi (Iranian) happy

Shadow (English) mysterious
Shado, Shadoh

Shady (English) in shade

Shae (Hebrew) shy
Shay

Shaela (Irish) pretty
Shae, Shaelie, Shala

Shaelin (Irish) pretty
Shae, Shaelyn, Shaelynn, Shalyn

Shaeterral (African American) well-shaped
Shatey, Shatrell, Shayterral

Shafiqa (Arabic) loves fellow man

Shahira (Arabic) famed

Shahla (Afghani) pretty girl

Shail (American) pretty
Shale

Shaila (Indian) laughter

Shailendra (Jewish) lovely

Shailesh (Jewish) lovely

Shaina (Hebrew) beauty

Shaine (Hebrew) pretty girl
Shanie, Shay, Shayne

Shainel (African American) animated
Shainell, Shainelle, Shaynel

Shajara (Muslim) tree

Shajee (Muslim) brave

Shakila (Arabic) beauty

Shakira (Arabic/Spanish) grateful
Shak, Shakeera, Shakeerah, Shakeira, Shakie, Shakyra, Skakarah

Shakonda (African American) lovely

Shalanda (African American) vivid
Shalande, Shally, Shalunda

Shaleah (Hebrew) weary
Shalea, Shalee, Shaleeah

Shaleina (Turkish) humorist
Shalina, Shalyna, Shalyne

Shalene (Hindi) giving

Shalimar (Polish) peace and glory

Shalina (Indian) form of Selena: like the moon; shapely

Shalini (Indian) modest

Shallan (American) humorous

Shalonda (African American) enthusiastic
Shalie, Shalondah, Shalonna, Shelonda

Shamara (Arabic) assertive
Shamarah, Shemera

Shamarie (American) form of Shamara: assertive

Shameccah (American) form of Shameka: loving

Shameena (Arabic) beautiful
Shamee, Shameenah, Shamina, Shaminna

Shameka (African American) loving
Shameika, Shamekah, Shamika, Shemeca

Shamica (American) form of Shameka: loving

Shamilia (American) form of Shameka: loving

Shamine (Hindi) pretty

Shamiyk (African) believer

Shamsa (Pakistani) adorable

Shan (Chinese) coral

Shana (Hebrew) pretty girl
Shaina, Shan, Shanah, Shane, Shannah, Shanni, Shannie, Shanny, Shayna, Shayne

Shanae (Irish) generous
Shan, Shanea, Shanee

Shanan (American) believes in a gracious God

Shanasita (Spanish) wishful

Shanaye (American) form of Shay: fairy place

Shanda (American)

Shandee (English) hopeful
Shandi, Shandie, Shandy

Shandel (American)

Shandilyn (American) not forsaken
Shandi, Shandy

Shandon (American)

Shandra (American) fun-loving
Chandra, Shan, Shandrie

Shane (Irish) soft-spoken
Shain, Shaine, Shanee, Shanie, Shayne

Shaneka (African American) perky; pretty
Chaneka, Shan, Shanekah, Shanie, Shanika

Shanelle (African American) form of Chanel: fashionable; designer name
Shanel, Shannel, Shannell, Shanny

Shaney (African) fabulous

Shani (African) great

Shania (African) ambitious; bright-eyed
Shane, Shaniah, Shanie, Shaniya, Shanya

Shanian (American) form of Shania: ambitious; bright-eyed

Shanice (African American) bright-eyed
Chaniece, Shaneese, Shani, Shaniece

Shaniga (American) believer

Shanigan (Last name used as first name)

Shaniger (Last name as first name)

Shanika (African American) pretty; optimistic
Shan, Shane, Shanee, Shaneeka, Shaneika, Shaneikah, Shanequa, Shaney, Shaneyka

Shaniqua (African American) outgoing
Shane, Shaneekwa, Shaneequa, Shanequa, Shanie, Shanikwa, Shaniquah, Shanneequa

Shanique (African American) pretty; optimistic

Shanisha (African American) bright
Chaneisha, Chanisha, Shan, Shanecia, Shaneisha, Shanie

Shaniya (American) form of Shania: ambitious; bright-eyed

Shaniyer (American)

Shanna (Irish) lovely
Shanah, Shanea, Shannah

Shannon (Irish) smart
Shann, Shanna, Shannen, Shannyn, Shanon

Shanny (Irish) bubbly
Shannee, Shanni, Shannie

Shanta (French) singing; (Indian) peace
Shantah, Shante, Shantie

Shantara (French) bright-eyed
Shantay, Shantera, Shantie

Shante (French) form of Chantal: singer of songs
Shantae, Shantay

Shantell (American) bright singer
Chantel, Shantal, Shantel

Shanti (Hindi) calm

Shantinel (American) form of Shantell: bright singer

Shaphane (American)

Shaqi (American) form of Shaquan: fine

Shaquan (American) fine
Shak, Shaq, Shaquanda, Shaquanna, Shaquie, Shaquonda

Shaquita (African American) delight
Shaq, Shaqueita, Shaqueta, Shaquie

Shara (Hebrew) form of Sharon: open heart; desert plain
Sharah, Sharra, Sherah

Sharada (Indian) knowledge

Sharath (Slavic) protects

Shardae (Arabic) wanderer
Chardae, Sade, Shaday, Sharday, SharDay

Shar-Dae (African) generous

Sharee (American) dear
Sharie

Sharel (Spanish) princess

Shari (French) beloved girl
Shar, Sharee, Sharree, Sher, Sherri

Sharice (French) graceful
Cherise, Shar, Shareese, Shares

Sharif (Russian) mysterious
Shar, Shareef, Sharey, Shari, Sharrey, Shary

Sharil (American) form of Cheryl: beloved

Sharine (Hebrew) form of Sharon: open heart; desert plain
Shareen, Shareene, Sharyne

Sharissa (Hebrew) flat plain; quiet

Sharita (French) charitable
Shar, Shareetah, Shareta

Sharla (American) friendly
Sharlah

Sharlena (French) strong

Sharlene (German) form of Charlene: petite and beautiful
Charleen, Shar, Sharl, Sharleen, Sharline, Sharlyne

Sharlette (American) form of Charlotte: little woman

Sharlott (American) form of Charlotte: little woman

Sharmaine (American) form of Charmaine: bountiful orchard

Sharmanah (American) form of Sharmaine: bountiful orchard

Sharmeal (African American) exhilarating
Sharm, Sharma, Sharme, Sharmele

Sharna (Hebrew) broad-minded
Sharn, Sharnah

Sharnam (American) form of Sharmaine: bountiful orchard

Sharnea (American) quiet
Sharnay, Sharnee, Sharney

Sharnelle (African American) spiritual
Sharnel, Sharnie, Sharny

Sharnette (American) fighter
Chanet, Charnette, Shanet, Sharn, Sharnett, Sharney

Sharon (Hebrew) open heart; desert plain
Shar, Sharen, Shari, Sharin, Sharren, Sharron, Sharry, Sharyn, Sheron, Sherron

Sharona (Hebrew) form of Sharon: open heart; desert plain
Sharonah, Sharonna, Sharonnah

Sharonda (African American) open
Sharondah, Sheronda

Sharonett (American) form of Sharon: open heart; desert plain

Sharonetta (American) form of Sharon: open heart; desert plain

Sharr (Hebrew) vigilant

Sharrona (Hebrew) open
Sharona, Sharonne, Sherona, Shironah

Sharterica (African American) beloved
Sharter, Sharterika, Shartrica, Sharty

Sharuhen (Biblical) place name

Shashee (Hindi) luminous

Shashi (Indian) giving

Shasta (American) majestic mind
Shastah

Shatoya (African American) spirited
Shatoye, Shay, Shaytoya, Toya

Shauhna (Irish) form of Shauna: giving heart

Shauna (Hebrew/Irish) giving heart
Shauhna, Shaunie, Shaunna, Shawna

Shaundra (American) giving

Shaune (American) wide smile
Shaun, Shaunie, Shawn

Shauneice (American) excitable

Shaunelle (American) excitable

Shaunta (American) sings

Shauntee (Irish) dancing eyes
Shaun, Shawntey, Shawntie, Shawnty

Shauntrie (American) sings

Shavon (Irish) devout; energetic
Chavon, Chavonne, Shavaun, Shavon, Shavonne

Shawana (African American) dramatic
Shavaun, Shawahna, Shawanna, Shawnie

Shawandreka (African American) gutsy
Shawan, Shawand, Shawandrika, Shawann, Shawuan

Shawn (American) smiling
Shawne, Shawnee, Shawnie, Shawny

Shawna (Hebrew/Irish) feminine form of Sean: God is gracious
Shawnna

Shawnda (Irish) helpful friend
Shaunda, Shaundah, Shona

Shawneequa (African American) loquacious
Shauneequa, Shawneekwa

Shawnel (African American) audacious
Shaune, Shaunel, Shaunelle, Shawn, Shawnee, Shawnelle, Shawney, Shawni

Shawnet (American) feminine form of Sean: God is gracious

Shawnie (American) playful
Shaunie, Shawni

Shawyne (American) feminine form of Sean: God is gracious

Shay (Irish) fairy place
Shaye

Shayla (Irish) fairy palace

Shayleen (Greek) moon

Shaylie (Latin) playful
Shaleigh, Shaylea, Shaylee, Shealee

Shayna (Hebrew) beauty

Shayne (Hebrew) form of Shane: soft-spoken
Shaine, Shay, Sheyne

Shayni (Hebrew) beauty

Shayonda (African American) regal
Shay, Shaya, Shayon, Shayonde, Sheyonda, Yona, Yonda

Shayter (American) friend of fairies

Shea (Irish) soft beauty
Shae, Shay

Sheaden (French) lovely

Sheba (Hebrew) form of Bathsheba: beautiful; daughter of Sheba
Chebah, Sheeba, Sheebah

Sheconna (American) of fairies

Sheddreka (African American) dynamo
Shedd, Sheddrik, Shedreke

Shedy (American) of fairies

Sheela (Hindi) gentle spirit
Sheelah, Sheeli, Sheila

Sheelyah (Irish) form of Shelia: woman; gorgeous
Sheel, Sheil

Sheem (Native American) believer

Sheena (Hebrew) shining
Sheen, Sheenah, Shena

Shefalia (American)

Shehagh (Irish)

Sheila (Irish) vivacious; divine
woman
*Shaylah, Sheela, Sheilia, Sheilya,
Shel*

Shelagh (Irish) fairy princess

Shelby (English) dignified
*Chelby, Shel, Shelbee, Shelbi,
Shelbie*

Sheldon (English) farm on the
ledge
Shelden

Sheleatha (American) shy

Shelia (Irish) woman; gorgeous
Shelya, Shelyah, Shillya

Shelita (Spanish) little girl
Chelita, Shelite, Shelitta

Shell (English) meadow
Shel

Shelley (English) outdoorsy;
meadow
Shelee, Shelli, Shelly

Shelline (French) form of
Shelley: outdoorsy; meadow

Shelton (English) farm on a ledge
Shelten

Shemari (American) sheltered

Shemelia (American) sheltered

Shemina (American) sheltered

Shemira (American) sheltered

Shena (Irish) shining
Shenae, Shenea, Shenna

Shenease (Hebrew) believer

Sheneda (Hebrew) believer

Sheneeka (African American)
easygoing
*Shaneeka, Shaneka, Sheneecah,
Sheneka*

Shepard (English) vigilant
Shep, Sheperd, Shepherd, Sheppie

Shephelah (Biblical) place name

Shera (Hebrew) lighthearted
Sheera, Sheerah, Sherah

Sherael (American) form of
Sherry: outgoing
Sheraelle, Sherelle, Sherryelle

Sheray (French) saucy
Cheray, Sherayah

Sheree (French) dearest girl
Sheeree, Sher, Shere

Shereen (Indian) sheen

Shereitta (Spanish) effervescent

Sherele (French) bouncy
Sher, Sherell, Sherrie

Sheresa (American) dancer
Sher, Sherisa, Sherissa, Sherri

Shereth (American) loved

Sheretta (American) sparkling
Shere, Sherette

Sheri (French) sparkling eyes
Sher, Sherri, Sherrie

Sherice (French) artistic
Cherise, Sher, Shereece, Sherisse

Sheridan (Irish) free spirit;
outstanding
*Cheridan, Cheridyn, Sheridyn,
Sherridan*

Sherika (Arabic)

Sherine (American) shines

Sherita (French) stylish
Cherita, Sheretta

Sheritt (French) form of Sherry:
outgoing

Sherleen (American) easygoing
*Sherl, Sherlene, Sherline, Sherlyn,
Shirline*

Sherlie (English) form of Shirley:
bright meadow; cheerful girl

Sherlitha (Spanish) feminine
Sherl, Sherli

Sherlotta (American) form of
Charlotte: little woman

Sherolynna (American) lovely
*Cherolina, Sher, Sheralina,
Sherrilina*

Sherrill (English) bright
*Cheril, Cherrill, Sherelle, Sheril,
Sherrell, Sheryl*

Sherrone (Hebrew) form of
Sharon: open heart; desert plain

Sherrunda (African American) free spirit
Sharun, Sharunda, Sherr, Sherrunde, Sherunda

Sherry (French) outgoing
Sher, Sheri, Sherreye, Sherri, Sherrie, Sherye

Sheryl (French) beloved woman
Cheryl, Sharal, Sher, Sheral, Sheril, Sherill

Shevonne (Gaelic) ambitious
Shavon, Shevaune, Shevon

Sheyenne (Native American) form of Cheyenne: Native American tribe
Shey, Shianne, Shyann, Shyanne, Shyenne

Sheyn (Hebrew) beauty

Shiaray (Native American)

Shibhan (Irish) variation of Siobhan: believer; lovely
Shiban, Shibann, Shibhann

Shiela (Irish) blind

Shiffawn (American) pretty

Shifra (Hebrew) beautiful woman
Sheefra, Shifrah

Shikendra (African American) spirited
Shiki, Shikie, Skikend

Shiloh (Hebrew) gifted by God
Shilo, Shy

Shilpa (Indian) in synch; rock

Shimchi (Asian) good

Shinae (American) shines

Shine (American) shining example
Shena, Shina

Shinea (Asian) good

Shinetta (American) shines

Shiney (American) glowing
Shine, Shiny

Shinikee (African American) glorious
Shinakee, Shinikey, Shynikee

Shira (Hebrew) song; singer
Shirah, Shiree

Shireen (English) charmer
Shareen, Shiree, Shireene, Shirene, Shiri, Shiry, Shoreen, Shureen, Shurene

Shirenzio (American) form of Sharon: open heart; desert plain

Shirince (American) form of Sharon: open heart; desert plain

Shirleen (American) nature-loving
Shirlene, Shirline

Shirlei (English) form of Shirley: bright meadow; cheerful girl

Shirleth (American) form of Shirley: bright meadow; cheerful girl

Shirley (English) bright meadow; cheerful girl
Sherlee, Sherley, Sherly, Shir, Shirl, Shirly

Shiyama (African) believer in God

Shlomith (Jewish) peaceful

Shlonda (African American) bright
Londa, Schlonda, Shodie

Shobby (American) smart

Shobha (Indian) smart and pretty

Shola (Hebrew) spirited
Sholah

Sholia (American) form of Salih: virtuous

Shon (Irish) form of Shona: open-hearted
Shonn

Shona (Irish) open-hearted
Shonah, Shonie

Shonda (Irish) runner
Shondah, Shonday, Shondie, Shounda, Shoundah

Shondra (Irish) pretty

Shonta (Irish) fearless
Shauntah, Shawnta, Shon, Shontie

Shony (Irish) shining
Shona, Shonee, Shoni, Shonie

Shoshana (Hebrew) beautiful; lily
Shoshanna, Shoshannah, Shoshauna

Shreya (Indian) good fortune

Shrill (American) word as name; ingenious

Shrilla (Hindi) beauty
Shrila

Shryl (American) ingenious

Shu Jane (Asian) kind

Shuchi (Hindi) pure

Shue (Asian) kind

Shula (Arabic) flaming

Shulamit (Hebrew) serene

Shulondia (African American) dynamic
Shulee, Shuley, Shuli, Shulonde, Shulondea, Shulondiah

Shumay (Muslim) eloquent

Shun (Irish) form of Jane: believer in a gracious God

Shuna (Irish) form of Jane: believer in a gracious God

Shunta (Irish) form of Jane: believer in a gracious God

Shuntay (African American; Irish) form of Shonta: fearless
Shuntae

Shuntele (Irish) energetic

Shura (Greek) protective

Shuranda (American) kind

Shurkela (American) kind

Shurla (American) fun

Shushan (Biblical) place name

Shyama (Native American) form of Cheyenne: Native American tribe

Shyanne (Native American) form of Cheyenne: Native American tribe
Shy

Shyla (English) creative
Shila, Shy, Shylah

Shyne (American) standout
Shine

Shyree (Native American) form of Cheyenne: Native American tribe

Sia (Welsh) calm; believer
Cia, Seea

Sian (Welsh) believer

Siana (Welsh) ebullient
Sian, Siane

Sianoee (Welsh) believer

Sib (Anglo-Saxon) form of Sibley: related
Sibb

Sibila (Greek) form of Sybil: future-gazing

Sibley (Anglo-Saxon) related
Siblee, Sibly

Sibmah (Biblical) place name

Sibyl (Greek) intuitive
Cibyl, Cyb, Cybil, Cybill, Cybyl, Sib, Sibbi, Sibbie, Sibby, Sibella, Sibil, Sibill, Sibyll, Sibylla, Sybela, Sybil, Sybyl

Sicily (Biblical) place name

Sid (Place name) form of Sidney: from Saint-Denis, France
Sidd

Sidelia (Spanish) stars

Sidhi (Indian) excels

Sidnah (American) form of Sidney: from Saint-Denis, France

Sidney (Place name) from Saint-Denis, France
Sidnee, Sidni, Sidny

Sidonia (French) spiritual
Sid, Sidoneah, Sydonya

Sidonie (French) appealing
Sidonee, Sidony, Sydoni

Sidra (Latin) star
Cidra, Siddey, Siddie, Siddy, Sidi, Sidrie, Sydra

Siely (American) form of Sealy: fun-loving

Sienna (English) delicate; reddish-brown
Siena, Siene

Sierra (Place name) peaks;
outdoorsy
*Cierra, Searah, Searrah, Siera,
Sierrah, Sierre*

Sigfrid (German) peacemaker
Sig, Sigfred, Sigfreid, Siggy

Signe (Latin) symbol
Sig, Signie, Signy

Signet (Scandinavian) form of
Signe: symbol

Sigourney (English) leader who
conquers
*Sig, Siggie, Signe, Signy, Sigournay,
Sygourny*

Sigrid (Scandinavian) lovely
Segred, Sig, Siggy, Sigrede

Sigrun (Scandinavian) winning
Cigrun, Segrun

Sikita (American) active
Sikite

Sila (Native American) flowers

Sile (Turkish) misses home

Silenceia (Spanish) quiet

Siline (Greek) form of Selene:
like the moon; shapely
Sileen, Sileene, Silyne

Silke (German) divine spirituality

Silvanna (Spanish) nature-lover
*Sil, Silva, Silvana, Silvane,
Silvanne, Silver*

Silver (Anglo-Saxon) light-haired
Silva, Silvar, Sylver

Silvia (Latin) deep; woods-loving
Sill, Silvy, Siviah, Sylvia

Sima (Indian) wise

Simcha (Hebrew) joyful
Simchah

Simi (Lebanese) soft
Sim

Simica (American) tender
Sim, Simika, Simmy

Simoli (American) energy

Simona (American) form of
Simone: wise and thoughtful
Sim, Simon, Sims

Simone (French) wise and
thoughtful
Sim, Simonie, Symone

Simonetta (French) feminine
form of Simon: good listener;
thoughtful

Simonias (Biblical) place name

Sinaflor (Spanish) flowers

Sinai (Place name) Mt. Sinai

Sinclair (French) person from St.
Clair; admired
*Cinclair, Sinclare, Synclair,
Synclare*

Sinden (English) form of Cindy:
moon goddess

Sindy (American) left behind
Cindy

Sine (Irish) God's gift

Sinead (Irish) singer; believer in a
gracious God
Shanade

Sinforosa (Spanish) bad luck

Singrid (Scandinavian) form of
Sigrid: lovely

Sinope (Biblical) place name

Sinue (Spanish)

Siobhan (Irish) believer; lovely
*Chevon, Chevonne, Chivon,
Shavonne, Shevon*

Siphronia (Greek) sensible
*Ciphronia, Sifronea, Sifronia,
Syfronia*

Sippar (Biblical) place name

Sirbonis (Biblical) place name

Siren (Greek) enchantress
Syren

Sirena (Greek) temptress
*Sireena, Sirenah, Sirine, Sisi, Sissy,
Syrena*

Sirene (Greek) enchantress
Sireen, Sireene, Siryne

Siri (Scandinavian) lovely

Siriny (Greek) spellbinding

Sirmium (Biblical) place name

Sirneicsa (Sanskrit) immortal

Siscia (Biblical) place name

Sisely (American) form of Cicely: clever

Sisley (Last name as first name) able

Sissy (Latin) little sister; immature; ingenue
Cissee, Cissey, Cissy, Sis, Sissi, Sissie

Sistene (Italian) spiritual
Sisteen, Sisteene

Sita (Hindi) divine
Seeta, Seetha

Sitiveni (Slavic) high esteem

Siv (Scandinavian) kinship; wife of Thor
Sive

Sivana (Irish) form of Sivney: satisfied
Sivanah

Siwa (Biblical) place name

Siyona (Hindi) graceful

Sjanie (Scandinavian) energetic

Skayla (Slavic) smart

Skudra (Biblical) place name

Skye (Scottish) high-minded; head in the clouds

Skyler (Dutch) protective; sheltering
Schuyler, Skieler, Skilar, Skiler, Skye, Skyla, Skylar, Skylie, Skylor

Slane (Irish) form of Sloane: strong
Slaine

Slaney (Last name as first name) selective

Slava (Russian) glory

Sloane (Irish) strong
Sloan, Slone

Sloni (Latin) clarity

Sly (American) form of Slyvestra: forest-dweller; heavy duty

Slyvestra (American) feminine form of Slyvester: forest-dweller; heavy duty

Smera (Hindi) smiles

Smiley (American) radiant
Smile, Smilee, Smiles, Smili, Smily

Smirna (American) refined

Smisha (American) feminine form of Smith: crafty; blacksmith

Smita (Indian) grinning

Smyrna (Biblical) place name

Snooks (American) sweetie
Snookee, Snookie

Snow (American) quiet
Sno, Snowy

Snowdrop (Botanical) white flower

Sochia (American) form of Sasha: beautiful courtesan; helpful

Socoh (Biblical) place name

Socorro (Spanish) helpful
Socoro

Socra (Greek) feminine form of Socrates: philosophical; brilliant

Sofie (Greek) wise

Sofina (Spanish) form of Sophia: wise one

Sofonias (Greek) form of Sophia: wise one

Sofya (Russian) wise
Sofi, Sofie, Sofiya

Sohanne (Hindi) lovely

Soheila (Indian) sun

Sohella (Arabic) form of Saliha: correct

Sohni (Hindi) lovely

Sokan (Native American)

Solada (Asian) attentive

Solana (Spanish) sunny
Solanah, Soley, Solie

Solange (French) sophisticated
Solie

Soledad (Spanish) solitary woman
Saleda, Solada, Solay, Sole, Solee, Solie, Solita

Soleil (French) sun

Soli (Biblical) place name

Solida (Spanish) alone

Soline (French) solemn
Solen, Solenne, Souline

Solita (Latin) alone
Soleeta, Solyta

Soloma (Hindi) lunar

Somansh (Hindi) half-moon

Somayeh (Indian) moon

Somers (Last name as first name) summer girl

Somilla (Hindi) calm

Sommai (American) summer

Sommer (English) warm
Sommie, Summer, Summi

Sona (Hindi) form of Sonal: golden girl of the sun

Sonal (Hindi) golden girl of the sun

Sonali (Hindi) golden

Sonay (Asian) bright-eyed
Sonnae

Sondra (Greek) defender of mankind

Sonel (Hindi) form of Sonal: golden girl of the sun
Sonell

Sonesse (American) sings

Song (Chinese) independent

Songsira (American) sings

Sonia (Slavic) effervescent
Soni, Sonnie, Sonny, Sonya

Sonja (Scandinavian) bright woman

Sonnet (American) poetic
Sonnett, Sonni, Sonny

Sonnie (Slavic) wise

Sonoe (Asian) bright

Sonoma (Place name) city in California; wine-loving
Sonomah

Sonora (English) easygoing
Sonorah

Sonova (Spanish) nice

Sonseria (American) giving
Seria, Sonsere, Sonsey

Sonya (Greek) wise
Sonia, Sonje

Soo (Korean) gentle spirit

Soon-Yi (Chinese) delightful; assertive

Soozi (American) form of Suzy: lily; pretty flower
Soos, Sooz, Souz, Souze, Souzi, Soozy

Sophath (American) form of Sophie: wise one

Sophia ✿ ❶ (Greek) wise one
Sofeea, Sofi, Sofia, Sofie, Sophea, Sopheea, Sophie, Sophy

Sophia-Loren (Italian) namesake of movie star

Sophie ✿ (Greek) form of Sophia: wise one
Sophee, Sophey, Sophi, Sophy

Sophorn (American) form of Sophie: wise one

Sora (Native American) chirping bird
Sorra

Sorangel (Spanish) heavenly
Sorange

Soraya (Persian) royal

Sorayal (Russian) princess

Sorayalle (Russian) princess

Sorcha (Irish) bright
Shorshi, Sorsha, Sorshie

Sorek (Biblical) place name

Sorel (French) reddish-brown

Sorele (French) reddish-brown hair

Sorphal (Asian) speaks well

Sorrel (English) delicate
Sorel, Sorell, Sorie, Sorree, Sorrell, Sorri, Sorrie

Sosamma (Hindi) pretty

Sosannah (Hebrew) form of Susannah: gentle
Sosana, Sosanah, Sosanna

Soshana (Hebrew) lily
Soshanah

Sosy (Indian) health

Sotee (Greek) saved

Soulah (American) afire

Souza (Persian) fiery

Sowanna (Hindi) peaceful

Soynia (American) form of Sonya: wise

Sozos (Hindi) clingy
Sosos

Spaulding (English) divided field
Spalding

Spencer (English) sophisticate
Spence, Spenser

Spirit (American) lively; spirited
Spirite, Spyrit

Sprague (American) respected
Sprage

Sprandee (Invented) spry

Spring (English) springtime; fresh
Spryng

Sri (Hindi) glorious
Shree, Shri, Sree

Srikantha (Hindi) goddess

Srini (Hindi) feminine

Srinivas (Hindi) goddess

Srividya (Hindi) praised

Stacey (Greek) hopeful and
spiritual
Stace, Staci, Stacie, Stacy, Staycee

Stacha (English) form of
Anastasia: resurrection

Stacia (English) form of
Anastasia: resurrection
Stace, Stacie, Stasia, Stayshah

Stahsha (Slavic) form of Stacia:
resurrection

Stana (American) form of Stacia:
resurrection

Stancie (American) adored

Stanise (American) darling
*Stanee, Staneese, Stani, Stanice,
Staniece*

Star (English) a star
Starr

Starla (American) shining
Starlah, Starlie

Starlene (American) star

Starling (English) glossy bird

Starlite (American) extraordinary
Starlight, Starr

Starne (American) star

Stasia (Greek/Russian)
ressurection
Stacie, Stasie, Stasya

Stefanie (Greek) form of
Stephanie: regal
*Stafanie, Stefannye, Stefany, Steff,
Steffany, Steffie*

Stefee (Greek) crowned

Steff (Greek) form of Stephanie:
regal

Steffi (Greek) form of Stephanie:
regal
Steffie, Steffy, Stefi

Stefnee (American) form of
Stephanie: regal
Stef, Steffy

Stelanie (American) crowned

Stella ✪ (Latin) bright star
Stele, Stelie

Stephanie ✪ (Greek) regal
*Stefanie, Steff, Steffie, Stephenie,
Stephney*

Stephel (American) crowned

Stephene (French/Greek)
dignified
Steph, Stephie, Stephine

Stephine (French) crowned

Stephney (Greek) crowned
Stef, Steph, Stephie, Stephnie

Sterla (American) quality
Sterl, Sterlie, Stirla

Sterry (Dutch) star child
Sterree

Stevie (Greek/American) jovial
Steve, Stevee, Stevey, Stevi

Stevina (Slavic) crowned

Stina (Scandinavian) believer

Stockard (English) stockyard;
sturdy
Stockerd, Stockyrd

Storelle (Invented) legend
Storee, Storell, Storey, Stori

Storm (English) powerful

Stormy (American) impulsive
Storm, Stormi, Stormie

Story (American) creative
Stori, Storie, Storee, Storey

Stuti (Hindi) goddess

Sua (Spanish) loved

Suazo (Spanish) loved

Subha (Indian) lucky

Sublime (Word as name)

Suchi (Indian) lovely

Sudha (Indian) nectar

Sue (Hebrew) form of Susan: lily;
pretty flower

Suelita (Spanish) comforts

Suez (Place name)

Suganda (Slavic) cedar

Sugar (American) sweet
Shug

Sugy (Spanish) form of Sugar:
sweet
Sug, Sugey, Sugie

Suha (Indian) nectar
Sudha

Suhas (Hindi) jovial

Sujata (Indian) wellborn

Sujey (Asian) loved

Sukanya (Hindi) lovely

Sukhee (Asian) wise

Suki (Japanese) beloved
Suke, Sukie, Suky

Sula (Greek) sea-going
Soola, Sue, Suze

Sulafah (Muslim) best

Sulanie (American) sea

Sulay (Arabic) pleased

Sulema (Spanish) pleasant

Sullivan (Last name as first
name) bravehearted
Sulli, Sullie, Sullivin, Sully

Sumati (Indian) strong mind

Sumayah (Indian) good
temperament
Sumana, Sumaaya

Sumi (Asian) distinguished

Summer (English) summery;
fresh
Somer, Sommer, Sum, Summie

Summerly (American) vivid
summer

Sumona (Hindi) calm

Sun (Korean) obedient girl
Suna, Suni, Sunnie

Sunanda (American) sunny

Sunda (Slavic) form of Sandra:
helpful; protective

Sundancer (American) easygoing
Sunndance

Sunday (Latin) day of the week;
sunny
*Sun, Sundae, Sundaye, Sundee,
Sunney, Sunni, Sunnie, Sunny,
Sunnye*

Sunil (American) sunny

Sunila (Hindi) blue sky

Sunita (Hindi) Dharma's child
Suniti

Sunna (American) sunny
Sun, Suna

Sunny (English) bright attitude
Sonny, Sun, Sunni, Sunnye

Sunshine (American) sunny

Supree (Indian) loved
Supriya

Suprema (Hindi) affectionate

Suprina (American) supreme
Suprinna

Suprita (Hindi) pleasant

Surbhi (Indian) sweet smelling

Surekha (Indian) fragrant

Suren (American) delivers

Surene (American) delivers

Suri (Hebrew) princess

Surina (Hindi) wise

Surrender (Word as name)
dramatic
Surren

Suruchi (Hindi) pleasant

Surupa (Hindi) beauty

Surya (Indian) sun

Susa (Biblical) place name

Susan (Hebrew) lily; pretty
flower
*Soozan, Sue, Susahn, Susanne,
Susehn, Susie, Suzan*

Susaneca (Hebrew) lily

Susannah (Hebrew) gentle
Sue, Susah, Susanna, Susie, Suzannah

Susene (French) pretty girl

Susette (French) form of Susan: lily; pretty flower
Susett

Susha (Hindi) beauty

Sushma (Hindi) gorgeous

Sushmita (Indian) pretty smile

Susiana (Biblical) place name

Susie (American) form of Susan: lily; pretty flower
Susey, Susi, Susy, Suze, Suzi, Suzie, Suzy

Susila (Hindi) sensual

Susita (Hindi) white

Susithah (Biblical) place name

Suszane (Slavic) form of Susan: lily; pretty flower

Sutanu (Hindi) pretty

Sutapa (Hindi) follows God

Sutton (Last name as first name) southern town
Suten, Sutten, Suton

Suvi (Hindi) excels

Suz (American) form of Susan; lily; pretty flower
Suze

Suzan (American) form of Susan: lily; pretty flower
Suzen

Suzanne (English) fragrant
Susanne, Suzan, Suzane, Suzann, Suze

Suzette (French) pretty little one
Sue, Susette, Suze

Suzy (French) form of Susan: lily; pretty flower
Susy, Suze

Svana (Hindi) noisy

Svea (Swedish) patriotic
Svay

Svetlana (Russian) star bright
Sveta, Svete

Swaga (Hindi) gracious

Swan (Scandinavian) swan-like

Swanhildda (Teutonic) swan-like; graceful
Swan, Swanhild, Swann, Swanney, Swanni, Swannie, Swanny

Swarna (Hindi) lustrous

Swaru (Hindi) honest

Sweeney (Irish) young and rambunctious
Sweenee, Sweeny

Sweetpea (American) sweet
Sweetie, Sweet-Pea

Swell (Invented) good
Swelle

Sweta (Hindi) fair

Swetha (Indian) light

Swift (word as name) bold
Swiftie, Swifty

Swoosie (American) unique
Swoose, Swoozie

Syama (Sanskrit) dark

Syantha (American) form of Cynthia: moon goddess

Syb (Greek) form of Sybil: future-gazing
Sybb

Sybil (Greek) future-gazing
Sibel, Sibyl, Syb, Sybill, Sybille, Sybyl

Syble (American) foresees

Syd (French) form of Sydney: enthusiastic
Sydd

Sydel (Hebrew) princess

Sydlyn (American) quiet
Sidlyn, Sydlin, Sydlinne

Sydne (French) enthusiastic

Sydney ❂ (French) enthusiastic
Sidney, Syd, Sydnee, Sydnie

Syene (Biblical) place name

Syfronia (Slavic) serious

Syka (Slavic) studious

Syl (Latin) loves the woods
Sill

Sylvah (Slavic) form of Sylvia:
sylvan; girl of the forest
Sylvan (Latin) from the forest
Silvan, Silven, Silvyn, Sylven,
Sylvyn
Sylvana (Latin) forest; natural
woman
Silvanna, Syl, Sylvie
Sylvenita (Spanish) sylvan
Sylvestra (English) lives in the
woods
Sylvia (Latin) sylvan; girl of the
forest
Syl, Sylvea
Sylvie (Latin) sylvan; peacefulness
Sil, Silvie, Silvy, Syl, Sylvey, Sylvi,
Sylvy
Sylwia (Polish) serene; in the woods
Silwia
Sylwia (Latin) form of Sylvia:
sylvan; girl of the forest
Symira (American) enthusiastic
Sym, Symra, Syms, Symyra
Symone (Hebrew) good listener
Sym
Symphony (American) musical
Simphony, Symfonie, Symfony,
Symphonee, Symphonie
Syna (Invented) sweet
Sina

Synde (American) form of
Sydney: enthusiastic
Cindy
Synora (American) languid
Cinora, Sinora, Synee, Syni, Synor,
Synore
Synov (Scandinavian) sun girl
Synpha (American) capable
Sinfa, Sinpha, Synfa
Syntiche (Biblical) shared goal
Syreeta (Hindi) orderly
Syreta (American) assertive
Sireta

Tabbath (Greek) gazelle
Tabea (German) lithe
Tabeen (American) pretty
Tabel (Biblical) happy
Tabia (African) talented girl
Tabina (Arabic) follower of
Muhammed
Tabitha (Greek) graceful; gazelle
Tabatha, Tabbatha, Tabbi, Tabytha
Tabla (Native American) wears a
tiara; regal

Tacey (American) precious
Tace, Tacita
Tacha (American) form of Tasha:
born on Christmas
Tach
Tacho (American) form of Tasha:
born on Christmas
Taci (American) strong
Tacie (American) healthy
Tace, Taci, Tacy
Tadewi (Native American) wind
Tadi (Native American) variation
of Tadewi: wind
Tadit (Native American) fast
Tadita (Native American) runner
Tadeta
Taesha (American) sterling
character
Tahisha, Taisha, Tisha
Taffese (Welsh) loved
Taffeta (American) shiny
Tafeta, Taffetah, Taffi, Taffy
Taffy (Welsh) sweet and beloved
Taffee, Taffey, Taffi
Tafin (American) loved
Taft (English) loved
Tafie
Tafta (American) loved
Taghrid (Arabic) singing bird
Tahcawin (Native American) doe

Tahira (Arabic) pure
Tahirah

Tahiyya (Arabic) welcome
Tahiyyah

Tahmeena (Arabic) form of
Tamina: palms

Tahnee (English) little one

Tai (American) fond
Tie, Tye

Taima (Native American) thunder
Taimah, Taiomah

Tain (Native American) new moon

Taina (Spanish) form of Taima:
thunder

Taipa (Native American) quail

Tairra (Irish) towers high

Taisha (American) form of
Tasha: born on Christmas

Taiwo (African) firstborn of twins

Tajanan (American) regal bearing

Tajarah (Hindi) crowned

Tajie (American) highborn

Tajudeen (Spanish) clingy
Taj, Tajjy, Taju

Taka (Japanese) honorable

Takala (Native American) cornstalk
Takalah

Takara (Japanese) beloved gem
Taka, Taki

Takayren (Native American)
commotion

Takeko (Japanese) child of the
bamboo

Takenya (Native American)
falcon in flight

Takeya (African American)
knowing
Takeyah

Taki (Japanese) waterfall

Takia (Arabic) spiritual
Taki, Tikia, Tykia

Takiyah (Arabic) devout
Takeya, Takiya

Takona (American) special

Taku (Asian) worshipful

Takuhi (Armenian) queen

Tala (Native American) wolf

Talal (Hebrew) dew

Talasi (Native American)
cornflower

Tale (African) green

Taleen (American) golden

Talent (American) self-assured
Talynt

Talesha (African American)
friendly
*Tal, Taleesh, Taleisha, Talisha,
Tallie, Telesha*

Tali (Hebrew) confident

Talia (Greek) golden; dew from
heaven
*Tahlia, Tali, Tallie, Tally, Talya,
Talyah*

Talian (American) golden girl

Talibah (African) intellectual
Tali, Talib, Taliba

Talila (Hebrew) dew

Talisa (African American) variation
of Lisa: dedicated and spiritual
Telisa

Talise (Native American)
beautiful creek

Talitha (African American)
inventive
*Taleetha, Taleta, Taletha, Talith,
Tally*

Taliyah (American) blooms

Tallis (English) forest

Tallulah (Native American)
leaping water; sparkling girl
*Talie, Talley, Tallula, Talula,
Talulah*

Talluse (American) bold
Talloose, Tallu, Taluce

Tally (Native American) heroine
Tallee, Talley, Talli, Taly

Talma (Hebrew) hill

Talou (American) saucy
Talli, Tallou, Tally

Talutah (Native American) red

Talya (Hebrew) lamb
Talia

Tam (Japanese) decorative
Tama

Tamah (Hebrew) marvel
Tama

Tamajer (American) palms

Tamaka (Japanese) bracelet;
adorned female

Tamaki (Japanese) bracelet

Tamala (American) kind
Tam, Tama, Tamela, Tammie,
Tammy

Tamani (Hindi) desirable

Tamanna (Hindu) desire

Tamar (Hebrew) palm; breezy
Tama, Tamarr

Tamara (Hebrew) royal female
Tamera, Tammy, Tamora, Tamra

Tamas (Hindu) palm tree
Tamasa, Tamasi, Tamasvini

Tamasailau (Hawaiian) gem

Tamasine (English) twin;
feminine of Thomas
Tamasin, Tamsin, Tamsyn,
Tamzen, Tamzin

Tamatha (American) palms

Tamaura (American) palms

Tamay (American) form of
Tammy: sweetheart
Tamae, Tamaye

Tamaya (Native American)
grounded

Tambara (American) high-energy
Tam, Tamb, Tambra, Tamby,
Tammy

Tambra (American) palms

Tambre (American) high energy

Tambusi (African) frank
Tam, Tambussey, Tammy

Tame (American) calm

Tamefa (African American) form
of Tamika: lively
Tamefah, Tamifa

Tameria (Hebrew) palms

Tamesha (African American)
open face
Tamesh, Tamisha, Tammie, Tammy

Tamesis (Spanish) name for the
Thames River
Tam, Tamey

Tami (Japanese) people
Tamie, Tamiko

Tamia (Japanese) little gem
Tameea, Tamya

Tamiah (Hebrew) palms

Tamika (African American) lively
Tameca, Tameeka, Tameka,
Tamieka, Tamikah, Tammi,
Tammie, Tammy, Temeka

Tamiko (Japanese) the people's
child
Tami, Tamico, Tamika

Tamina (Hebrew) palms

Tamirisa (Indian) night; dark
Risa, Tami, Tamirysa, Tamrisa,
Tamyrisa

Tammy (American) sweetheart
Tam, Tammie, Tammi, Tammye

Tamohara (Hindu) the sun

Tamony (Hebrew) form of
Tamara: royal female
Tamanee, Tamaney, Tamani,
Tamanie, Tamany, Tamonee,
Tamoney, Tamoni, Tamonie

Tamra (Hebrew) sweet girl
Tammie, Tamora, Tamrah

Tamrika (African) newly created
Tamreeka

Tamsin (English) benevolent
Tam, Tami, Tammee, Tammey,
Tammy, Tammye, Tamsa,
Tamsan, Tamsen

Tamsinn (English) form of
Thomasina: twin

Tamula (American) giving

Tamyrah (African American)
vocalist
Tamirah

Tamyren (Hebrew) form of
Tamyrah: vocalist

Tamzin (American) palms

Tana (Slavic) petite princess
Taina, Tan, Tanah, Tanie

Tanaga (American) form of
Tanya: queenly bearing

Tanai (American) thorough

Tanaka (Japanese) swamp dweller

Tanay (African American) new
Tanee

Tanaya (Hindu) daughter

Tanda (English) altogether

Tanden (English) altogether

Tandra (English) altogether

Tandria (English) altogether

Tandy (English) team player
Tanda, Tandi, Tandie

Tane (Polynesian) fertile

Tanesha (African) strong
Tanish, Tanisha, Tannesha, Tannie

Tangelia (Greek) angel
Gelia, Tange, Tangey

Tangenika (American) form of
former country Tanganyika
Tange, Tangi, Tangy

Tangerla (American) of the fairies

Tangi (American) tangerine
Tangee

Tango (Spanish) dance
Tangoh

Tangyla (Invented) form of
Tangela: combo of Tan and Angela
Tange, Tangy

Tani (Slavic) glorious
Tahnie, Tanee, Tanie

Tania (Russian/Slavic) queenly
Tannie, Tanny, Tanya

Tanikella (American) of the
fairies

Tanimu (American) of the fairies

Tanina (American) bold
*Tan, Tana, Tanena, Taninah,
Tanney, Tanni, Tannie, Tanny,
Tanye, Tanyna*

Tanis (Slavic) form of Tania:
queenly
Taniss, Tanys, Tanyss

Tanise (American) unique
Tanes, Tanis

Tanish (Greek) eternal
Tan, Tanesh, Tanny

Tanisha (African American)
talkative
*Taniesha, Tannie, Tenisha,
Tinishah*

Tanit (American) goddess

Tanith (Irish) estate
Tanita, Tanitha

Taniyah (Slavic) form of Tanya:
queenly bearing

Taniyen (Slavic) form of Tanya:
queenly bearing

Tanja (American) queen of fairies

Tanjiela (American) queen of
fairies

Tannelle (English) tans leather

Tanra (English) tans leather

Tanrik (Hindi) flowers

Tansy (Latin) pretty
Tan, Tancy, Tansee, Tanzi

Tanuneka (African American)
gracious
Nuneka, Tanueka, Tanun

Tanvi (Hindu) young woman;
fragile

Tanya (Russian) queenly bearing
*Tahnya, Tan, Tanyie, Tawnyah,
Tonya*

Tanyav (Slavic) regal
Tanyev

Tanyette (Italian) talkative
Tanye, Tanyee, Tanyett

Tanze (Greek) form of Tansy:
pretty
*Tans, Tansee, Tanz, Tanzee,
Tanzey, Tanzi*

Tanzy (Greek) eternal

Tao (Vietnamese) apple

Tapa (Spanish) little snack
Tapas

Tapasya (Hindu) bitter

Tapia (Spanish) small
Tapice (Spanish) covered
Tapeece, Tapeese, Tapese, Tapiece,
Tapp, Tappy
Tappuah (Biblical) place name
Tapus (Sanskrit) deliberate
Taquanna (African American)
noisy
Takki, Takwana, Taquana,
Taque, Taquie
Taquesha (African American)
joyful
Takie, Takwesha
Taquilla (American) from the
Spanish word tequila; lively
Takela, Takelah, Taque, Taquella,
Taqui, Taquile, Taquille
Tara (Gaelic) towering
Tarah, Tari, Tarra
Tarafena (Biblical) gentle
Tarakini (Hindi) nighttime with
stars
Taral (Hindu) rippling
Taralah (Biblical) place name
Taran (American) earthy
Taren, Tarran, Tarren, Tarryn,
Taryn
Tarani (Hindu) light
Taree (Japanese) tree branch
Tarena (Slavic) melodic
Taricheae (Biblical) place name

Tarika (Hindu) star
Tarina (Slavic) kind
Tarita (American) starry
Tarla (American) flamboyant
Tarlam (Hindu) flowering
Tarlease (American) flamboyant
Tarleen (American) flamboyant
Tarmica (American) flamboyant
Tarnettia (American) from the
lake
Taro (Invented) card name;
farsighted
Tarona (American) form of Tara:
towering
Tarracina (Biblical) place name
Tarub (Arabic) cheerful
Taryn (English) county in
Northern Ireland
Taran, Taren, Tarran, Tarrin,
Tarron
Tasha (Russian) form of Natasha:
born on Christmas
Tacha, Tahshah, Tash, Tashie,
Tasia, Tasie, Tasy, Tasya
Tashanah (African American)
spunky
Tash, Tashana
Tashanee (African American)
lively
Tashaunie

Tashawndra (African American)
bright smiling
Tasha, Tashaundra, Tashie
Tashel (African American)
studious
Tasha, Tashelle, Tochelle
Tashina (African American)
sparkles
Tasheena, Tasheenah, Tashinah
Tashka (Russian) together
Tashca, Tashcka
Tashua (American) cherishes
Tashza (African American) form
of Tasha: born on Christmas
Tashi, Tashy, Tashzah
Tasia (American) Christmas baby
Tasida (Native American) rides
a horse
Taska (American) Christmas baby
Tasma (American) twin
Tasmah
Tasmin (Pakistani) twin
Tasmind (American) twin
Tasmine (English) twin
Tasmin
Tasni (Arabic) spring
Tassi (Slavic) bold
Tassee, Tassey, Tassy
Tassie (English) twin
Tatanika (Slavic) fairy queen
Tataren (Slavic) fairy queen

Tate (English) short

Tateeahna (Invented) form of Tatiana: snow queen

Tatenda (Indian) fanciful

Tatiana (Russian) snow queen
Tanya, Tatania, Tatia, Tatianna, Tatiannia, Tatie, Tattianna, Tatyana, Tatyanna

Tatiyama (Asian) joyful

Tatjana (Slavic) vibrant

Tatrika (American) playful

Tatsu (Japanese) dragon

Tatum (English) cheery; high-spirited
Tata, Tate, Tatie, Tayte

Tauni (American) tawny; little

Taunja (American) form of Tonya: queenly

Taunya (American) form of Tonya: queenly

Taura (Latin) bull-like; stubborn

Tauvia (American) form of Octavia: eighth child; born on the eighth day of the month; musical

Tavia (Latin) form of Octavia: eighth child; born on the eighth day of the month; musical
Tava, Taveah, Tavi

Tavina (American) form of Tavia; form of Octavia: eighth child

Tavishi (Hindi) brave

Tavonia (American) form of Tavia; form of Octavia: eighth child

Tawannah (African American) talkative
Tawana, Tawanda, Tawanna, Tawona

Tawanner (American) loquacious
Tawanne, Twanner

Tawanta (African American) smart
Tawan, Tawante

Tawia (African) born after twins

Tawn (English) small girl

Tawnida (American) small

Tawny (American) tan-skinned
Tawn, Tawnee, Tawni, Tawnie

Tawnya (American) form of Tanya: queenly bearing
Tawnie, Tawnyah, Tonya, Tonyah

Tawyn (American) reliable; tan
Tawenne, Tawin, Tawynne

Taya (English) tailor

Tayanita (Native American) beaver

Tayla (American) doll-like
Taila, Taylah

Taylor ○ ❶ (English) tailor by trade; style-setter
Tailor, Talor, Tay, Taye, Taylar, Tayler

Tazmin (American) form of Jasmine: fragrant; sweet
Tazminn, Tazmyn, Tazmynn

Tazmind (American) form of Jasmine: fragrant; sweet

Tazu (Japanese) stork

Teagan (Irish) worldly; creative
Teague, Teegan, Tegan

Teague (Irish) creative
Tee, Teegue, Tegue

Teah (Greek) goddess
Tea

Teale (English) blue-green; bird
Teal, Teala

Tealisha (American) good heart
Tee

Teamhair (Irish) hill

Teamikka (African American) form of Tamika: lively
Teamika

Teana (American) form of Tina: little and lively
Teanah, Teane

Teasa (Slavic) calm

Techa (Greek) of God

Tecoa (American) precocious
Tekoa

Teddi (Greek) cuddly
Ted, Teddie, Teddy

Tedra (Greek) outgoing
Teddra, Tedrah

Teen (Spanish) form of Tina: little and lively

Tegin (Welsh) pretty

Tegvyen (Welsh) lovely

Tehara (Native American) darling
Tihara, Tyhara

Teishya (American) joyful

Tejuana (Place name) Tijuana, Mexico
Tijuana, T'Juana

Tekira (American) legendary
Tekera, Teki

Tekla (Greek) legend; divine glory
Tekk, Teklah, Thekla, Tikla, Tiklah

Tela (Greek) wise
Tella

Teleri (Welsh) variation of Eleri: smooth

Telery (Welsh) delight

Teletha (American) loving child

Teleza (African) slippery

Telina (American) storyteller
Teline, Telyna, Telyne, Tilina

Telma (Greek) ambitious

Telmah (American) capable

Telsa (American) form of Tessa: reaping a harvest
Telly

Tema (Biblical) place name; orderly

Temetris (African American) respected
Teme, Temi, Temitris, Temmy

Temika (American) form of Tamika: lively

Temike (American) form of Tamika: lively

Temira (Hebrew) tall
Temora, Timora

Temperance (Latin) moderation

Tempest (French) tempestuous; stormy
Tempeste, Tempie, Tempyst

Templa (Latin) spiritual; moderate
Temp, Templah

Tenay (American) praised
Tendai

Tenday (African) praiseworthy

Tenesha (African American) clever
Tenesia, Tenicha, Tenisha, Tennie

Tenia (Spanish) tenuous

Tenika (American) cautious

Tennie (American) cautious

Tennille (American) innovative
Tanielle, Tanile, Ten, Teneal, Tenile, Tenneal, Tennelle, Tennie

Tenuvah (Hebrew) fruit and vegetables

Teo (Spanish) form of masculine name Teodoro: God's gift
Teeo, Teoh

Teodomira (Spanish) important

Teodora (Scandinavian) God's gift
Teo, Teodore

Teodula (Spanish) gives

Tequila (Spanish) intoxicating
Tequela, Tequilla, Tiki, Tiquilia

Terah (Latin) earth's child

Tereena (American) earth

Terena (English) feminine version of Terence
Tereena, Terenia, Terina, Terrena, Terrina, Teryna

Teresa (Greek) gardener
Taresa, Terese, Terhesa, Teri, Terre, Tess, Tessie, Treece, Tressa, Tressae

Terese (Greek) nurturing
Tarese, Therese, Treece

Teresille (American) earth

Teresita (Spanish) form of Teresa: gardener

Tereso (Spanish) reaper
Tere, Terese

Teressa (English) reaps what she sows

Teri (Greek) reaper
Terre, Terri, Terrie

Terlah (Arabic) of the earth

Teronica (American) form of Veronica: girl's image; real

Terra (Latin) earthy; name for someone born under an astrological earth sign
Tera, Terrie

Terrea (Spanish) earth

Terrell (Greek) hardy
Ter, Teral, Terell, Terrelle, Terrie, Teryl

Terrena (Latin) smooth-talking
Terina, Terrina, Terry

Ter-Ri (American) form of Terri: reaper

Terrian (American) earth

Terry (Greek) form of Theresa: gardener
Teri, Terre, Terrey, Terri, Tery

Terson (Last name used as first name) child of earth

Tertia (Latin) third
Ters, Tersh, Tersha, Tersia

Teshuah (Hebrew) reprieve
Teshua, Teshura

Tess (Greek) harvesting life
Tesse

Tessa (Greek) reaping a harvest
Tesa, Tessie, Teza

Tessella (Italian) countess
Tesela, Tesella, Tessela

Tessica (American) form of Jessica: rich
Tesica, Tess, Tessa, Tessie, Tessika

Tessie (Greek) form of Theresa: gardener
Tessey, Tessi, Tezi

Tetsu (Japanese) iron

Teuila (Spanish) young

Tevy (Cambodian) angel

Texie (American) form of Texas: U.S. state; cowboy

Tezuma (Spanish) form of the word Montezuma

Thada (Greek) appreciative
Thadda, Thaddeah

Thadyne (Hebrew) worthy of praise
Thadee, Thadine, Thady

Thalassa (Greek) sensitive
Talassa, Thalassah, Thalasse

Thalia (Greek) joyful; fun
Thalya

Thana (Arabic) happy; thanksgiving

Thandiwe (African) affectionate

Thanh (Vietnamese) brilliant

Thao (Vietnamese) respect

Tharamel (Invented) form of the word caramel: dedicated
Thara

The (Vietnamese) pledged

Thea (Greek) goddess
Teah, Teeah, Theah, Theeah, Theo, Tiah

Theadora (Greek) God's gift

Theadra (Greek) goddess

Thebes (Biblical) place name

Theda (American) confident
Thada, Thedah

Theia (Greek) divine one

Thekia (Greek) famous

Thekla (Greek) famous; divine
Tecla, Tekla, Thecla

Thel (American) opinionated

Thelia (Greek) form of Thalia: joyful; fun

Thelina (American) musical

Thelma (Greek) giver
Thel

Thema (African) queen

Themba (African) trusted

Themis (Greek) just

Themla (Greek) just

Theodora (Greek) sweetheart; God's gift
Dora, Teddi, Teddie, Teddy, Tedi, Tedra, Tedrah, Theda, Theo, Theodorah, Theodrah

Theola (Greek) excellent
Theo, Theolah, Thie

Theone (Greek) serene
Theona, Theonne

Theoni (Greek) God's child
Theonus (American) calm
Theophania (Greek) God's
features
Theophanie
Theophila (Greek) loved by God
Theofila
Theora (Greek) God's gift
Theorah, Theorra, Theorrah
Theres (Greek) reaps what she
sows
Theresa (Greek) gardener
Reza, Teresa, Terri, Terrie, Terry
Therese (Greek) bountiful
harvest
Tereece, Terese, Terise, Terry
Theresia (Spanish) harvests
Theressa (Spanish) harvests
Therna (Greek) wild
Thera
Thersa (Hebrew) pleases
Therza, Thirza
Thesina (American) creates
Thessalonica (Biblical) place
name
Thessaly (Biblical) place name
Theta (Greek) letter in Greek
alphabet; substantial
Thayta, Thetah
Thetis (Greek) mother of Achilles
Theya (American) pleases

Thi (Vietnamese) poem
Thia (Greek) goddess
Thim (Thai) ice cream; sweet
Thirzah (Hebrew) pleasant
Thirza, Thursa, Thurza
Thoa (Asian) hopeful
Thocmetony (Native American)
flower
Tocmetone
Thomasina (Hebrew) twin
Tom, Toma, Tomasa, Tomasina,
Tomina, Tommie, Toto
Thomia (Hebrew) twin
Thonie (American) prepared
Thonne (American) prepared
Thora (Scandinavian) like
thunder
Thorah
Thrixia (American) kindness
Thu (Vietnamese) autumn
Thuy (Vietnamese) gentle
Thyatira (Biblical) place name
Tiamat, Tiam, Tya
Thyra (Scandinavian) loud
Thira
Tia (Greek/Spanish) princess; aunt
Teah, Tee, Teia, Tiah
Tiama (Mythology) ocean-loving
Tian (Greek) lovely
Ti, Tiane, Tiann, Tianne, Tyan,
Tyann, Tyanne, Tye

Tiana (Greek) highest beauty
Tana, Teeana, Tiane, Tiona
Tiandye (American) princess
Tianth (American) pretty and
impetuous
Teanth, Tia, Tian, Tianeth
Tiara (Latin) crowned goddess
Teara, Tearra, Tee, Teeearah,
Tierah, Tira
Tiare (French) ornamented
Tiaret (French) wears a crown
Tiarna (American) tiara
Tiaura (American) form of Tiara:
crowned goddess
Tibby (American) frisky
Tib, Tibb, Tybbee
Tiberia (Latin) majestic
Tibbie, Tibby
Tibisay (American) uniter
Tibi, Tibisae
Tichanda (African American)
stylish
Tichaunda, Tishanda
Tiena (Spanish) earthy
Teena
Tierah (Latin) jeweled; ornament
Tia, Tiarra, Tiera
Tiernan (English) lord
Tierney (Irish) wealthy
Teern, Teerney, Teerny, Tiern
Tierra (Latin) tiara

Tifara (Hebrew) festive
Tiferet, Tifhara

Tifaya (Greek) form of Tiffany: lasting love
Tifayane, Tiff, Tiffy

Tiffa (American) holy trinity

Tiffany (Greek) lasting love
Tifanie, Tiff, Tiffanie, Tiffenie, Tiffi, Tiffie, Tiffy, Tiphanie, Tyfannie

Tiffin (American) form of Tiffany: lasting love

Tig (American) tigress

Tigerlilly (American) flower

Tigress (Latin) wild
Tigris, Tye, Tygris

Tigris (Biblical) place name; (Irish) tiger

Tija (Spanish) form of Tijuana, Mexico

Tijana (American) form of Tijuana, Mexico

Tiki (Polynesian) ancestor; image
Tekee

Tikoletta (American) frivolous

Til (American) form of Matilda: powerful fighter

Tilana (Spanish) truth

Tilda (German) form of Matilda: powerful fighter
Telda, Tildie, Till, Tylda

Tiliera (American) strong

Tilira (American) strong

Tilla (German) industrious
Tila

Tilly (German) cute; strong
Till, Tillee, Tillie

Timerra (American) timid

Timia (American) timid

Timmie (Greek) form of Timothie: honorable
Tim, Timi, Timmy

Timna (Biblical) Anah's sister

Timothea (Greek) honoring God
Timaula, Timi, Timie, Timmi, Timmie

Timothie (Greek) honorable
Tim, Timmie, Timothea, Timothy

Timsuh (Biblical) place name

Tina (Latin/Spanish) little and lively
Teena, Teenie, Tena, Tiny

Tinker (American) animated

Tinkette (American) form of Tinker: animated

Tinna (American) form of Tina: little and lively

Tinsia (American) form of Tina: little and lively

Tiofila (Spanish) friend

Tionne (American) hopeful
Tionn

Tiphanie (Spanish) form of Tiffany: lasting love

Tiphsuh (Biblical) place name

Tiponya (Native American) owl; watchful

Tippah (Hindi) form of Tipo: tiger; ferocious

Tipper (Irish) pourer of water; nurturing
Tip, Tippy, Typper

Tippett (American) giving

Tippie (American) generous
Tippi, Tippy

Tira (Hebrew) camp

Tirathana (Biblical) place name

Tiri (Welsh) sweet

Tirica (American) form of Erica: honorable; leading others

Tirion (Welsh) gentle

Tirrza (Hebrew) sweet; precious
Thirza, Thirzah, Tirza, Tirzah

Tirtha (Hindu) ford

Tirza (Hebrew) kindness
Thirza, Tirzah

Tisa (African) ninth child
Tesa, Tesah, Tisah

Tish (Latin) happy
Tysh

Tisha (Latin) joyful
Tesha, Ticia, Tishah, Tishie

Tishbe (Biblical) place name

Tishema (American) joyful

Tishka (American) joyful

Tishra (African American)
original
Tishrah

Tishunette (African American)
happy girl
Tish, Tisunette

Tita (Greek) giant; large

Titania (Greek) giant

Tivona (Hebrew) lover of nature

Tiwa (Native American) onion

Tobago (Place name) West Indies
island; islander
Bago, ToTo

Tobarista (American) believer

Tobi (Hebrew) good
Tobie, Toby

Toblene (American) believer

Toffey (American) spirited
Toff, Toffee, Toffi, Toffie, Toffy

Tohuia (Polynesian) flower

Toinette (Latin) wonderful
Toin, Toinett, Toney, Tony,
Toynet

Toireasa (Irish) strong
Treise

Toki (Japanese) chance

Tokiwa (Japanese) steady

Tolice (American) creative

Tolikna (Native American)
coyote ears

Tollie (Hebrew) confident
Toll, Tollee, Tolli, Tolly, Tollye

Toloisi (French) ingenious

Tomazja (Polish) twin

Tomea (American) twin

Tomeka (African American) form
of Tamika: lively
Tomeke

Tomiko (Japanese) wealthy
Miko, Tamiko, Tomi

Tomitria (African American)
form of Tommie: sassy
Tomi

Tommie (Hebrew) sassy
Tom, Tomi, Tommy

Tomo (Japanese) intelligence

Tonaya (American) valuable
Tona, Tone

Tonesa (Greek) thriving

Tonet (French) form of Tony:
meritorious

Tonetta (American) thriving

Toney (American) form of Tony:
meritorious

Toni (Latin) form of Tony:
meritorious
Tone, Tonee, Tonie

Tonia (Latin) a wonder
Toneah, Tonya, Tonyah, Toyiah

Tonia (Latin) daring
Tonni, Tonnie, Tony, Tonya

Tonicia (American) form of
Tony: meritorious

Tonisha (African American)
lively
Nisha, Tona, Toneisha, Tonesha,
Tonie, Tonish

Tonla (American) form of Tonya:
queenly

Tonna (American) form of Tony:
meritorious

Tooka (Japanese) ten days

Topaz (Latin) gemstone; sparkling
Tophaz

Topher (Greek) feminine form of
Christopher: the bearer of Christ

Tophery (Greek) form of
Topher: the bearer of Christ

Tophie (Greek) form of Sophie:
wise one

Topsy (English) topnotch
Toppie, Toppsy, Topsey, Topsi,
Topsie

Tora (Scandinavian) thunder

Toranda (American) wins

Torborg (Scandinavian) thunder
Thorborg, Torbjorg

Tordis (Scandinavian) Thor's
goddess

Tori (Scottish) rich and winning
Toree, Torri, Torrie, Torry, Tory

Torill (Scandinavian) loud
Toril, Torille

Torrance (Place name) town in California; confident
Torr, Torri

Torsha (American) wins

Torta (American) wins

Torunn (Scandinavian) loved by Thor

Toscha (Slavic) prepared

Tosha (Slavic) priceless
Tosh, Toshia

Toshala (Hindu) satisfied

Toshio (Japanese) year-old child
Toshi, Toshie, Toshiko, Toshikyo

Toski (Native American) bug

Tossia (Slavic) prepared

Toti (English) form of Charlotte: little woman

Totsi (Native American) moccasins

Toula (American) athletic

Tova (Hebrew) good woman
Tovah

Toxie (American) athletic

Toy (American) playful
Toia, Toya, Toye

Tozie (American) friendly

Trace (French) takes the right path
Traice, Trayce

Tracey (Gaelic) aggressive
Trace, Tracee, Traci, Tracie, Tracy

Tracinal (American) form of Tracy: summer

Tracy (English) summer
Trace, Tracee, Tracey, Traci, Tracie, Trasey, Treacy, Treesy

Traina (American) thinker

Trana (American) thoughtful

Trancine (American) form of Francine: beautiful

Tranell (American) confident
Tranel, Tranelle, Traney, Trani

Trang (Vietnamese) smart

Trangera (American) smart

Traniqua (African American) hopeful
Tranaqua, Tranekwa, Tranequa, Trani, Tranikwa, Tranney, Tranniqua, Tranny

Trava (Czech) grass

Traviata (Italian) woman who wanders

Travistene (American) feminine form of Travis: conflicted

Tray (American) feminine form of Trey: third-born; creatively brilliant

Trayceez (American) form of Tracy: summer

Traysha (American) form of Tricia: humorous

Trazanna (African American) talented
Traz, Trazannah, Traze

Treana (American) pure

Treann (American) pure

Treasah (American) pure

Treat (Word as name)

Trecia (American) form of Tricia: humorous

Tree (American) sturdy

Treece (American) form of Terese: nurturing
Treese, Trice

Treena (American) form of Trina: perfect; scintillating
Treen

Treesjie (American) distinctive

Trella (Spanish) star; sparkles
Trela

Tremira (African American) anxious
Tremera, Tremmi

Treneth (American) smiling
Trenith, Trenny

Trenia (American) form of Trina: perfect; scintillating

Trenica (African American) smiling
Trenika, Trinika

Trenise (African American) songbird
Tranese, Tranise, Trannise, Treenie, Treneese, Treni, Trenniece, Trenny

Trenllita (Spanish) form of Trina: perfect; scintillating

Trentine (American) pure

Trenyce (American) smiling
Trienyse, Trinyce

Tres (Greek) form of Theresa: gardener

Tresca (American) form of Theresa: gardener

Treseme (American) form of Theresa: gardener

Tressa (Greek) reaping life's harvest
Tresa, Tresah, Tress, Trisa

Tressel (American) form of Theresa: gardener

Tressem (American) form of Theresa: gardener

Tressie (American) successful
Tress, Tressa, Tressee, Tressey, Tressi, Tressy

Tressy (American) form of Theresa: gardener

Tresure (Invented) giving
Treasure, Tress

Treva (English) homestead by the sea

Trevei (American) wise

Trevina (English) variation of Treva: homestead by the sea

Treyvin (American) form of Trevin: strong

Tricia (Latin) humorous
Treasha, Tresha, Trich, Tricha, Trish, Trisha

Trido (American) threefold

Trilby (English) literary
Trilbie

Trill (American) excitable

Trin (American) pure

Trina (Greek) perfect; scintillating
Tina, Treena, Trine, Trinie

Trinda (American) pure

Trinesse (American) pure

Trinh (Vietnamese) virgin

Trinida (Spanish) trinity

Trinidad (Place name) island off of Venezuela; spiritual person
Trini, Trinny

Trinity ✿ ❶ (Latin) triad
Trini, Trinita

Trinka (American) ideal

Trinlee (American) genuine
Trinley, Trinli, Trinly

Trionelle (Scottish) pure

Tripti (Hindi) content

Tris (American) form of Patricia: woman of nobility; unbending

Trish (American) form of Patricia: woman of nobility; unbending
Trysh

Trisha (American) form of Patricia: woman of nobility; unbending
Tricia

Trishelle (African American) humorous girl
Trichelle, Trichillem, Trish, Trishel, Trishie

Trishna (Indian) desired

Trissy (American) tall
Triss, Trissi, Trissie

Trista (Latin) pensive; sparkling love
Tresta, Trist, Tristie, Trysta

Tristen (Latin) bold
Tristan, Tristie, Tristin, Trysten

Tristica (Spanish) form of Trista: pensive; sparkling love
Trist, Tristi, Tristika

Trixie (Latin) personable
Trix, Trixi, Trixy

Tru (English) form of Truly: honest
True

Truc (Vietnamese) desire

Trudin (American) form of
Trudy: hopeful

Trudis (German) optimist

Trudy (German) hopeful
Trude, Trudi, Trudie

True (American) truthful
Truee, Truie, Truth

Truette (American) truthful
Tru, True, Truett

Truffle (French) delicacy
Truff, Truffy

Trulea (American) honest

Trulencia (Spanish) honest
Lencia, Tru, Trulence, Trulens,
Trulense

Truly (American) honest
True, Trulee, Truley

Trusteen (American) trusting
Trustean, Trustee, Trustine,
Trusty, Trusyne

Truth (American) honest
Truthe

Try (American) earnest
Tri, Trie

Tryna (Greek) form of Trina:
perfect; scintillating
Trine, Tryne, Trynna

Tsifira (Hebrew) crown

Tsomah (Native American) rose

Tsonka (American) capricious
Sonky, Tesonka, Tisonka, Tsonk

Tsuhgi (Japanese) second
daughter

Tsula (Native American) fox

Tteirrah (American) form of
Tara: towering

Tua (Polynesian) outdoors

Tualau (Polynesian) outdoors

Tucker (English) tailor
Tukker

Tuenchit (Thai) mysterious

Tuesday (English) weekday

Tuhina (Hindu) snow

Tuki (Japanese) moon

Tula (Native American) moon

Tulasi (Indian) basil sacred

Tulia (Spanish) glorious
Tuli, Tuliana, Tulie, Tuliea, Tuly

Tuliki (Mythology) of the wind

Tully (Irish) powerful; dark spirit
Tull, Tulle, Tulli, Tullie

Tulse (Hindi) growing

Tulsi (Hindu) basil

Tunishua (American) place name
Tunisia

Tunisia (Place name)

Turin (American) creative
Turan, Turen, Turrin, Turun

Turney (Latin) wood worker
Turnee, Turni, Turnie, Turny

Turquoise (French) blue-green
Turkoise, Turquie, Turrkoise

Tursha (Slavic) warm
Tersha

Turush (Biblical) place name

Turya (Hindi) spiritual

Tusa (Native American) prairie
dog

Tusti (Indian) peace

Tuwa (Native American) earth

Tuyen (Vietnamese) angel
Tuyet

Twaina (English) divided
Twayna

Twanda (African) dual

Tweetie (American) vivacious
Tweetee, Tweetey, Tweeti

Twiggy (English) slim
Twiggee, Twiggie, Twiggey

Twyla (English) creative
Twila, Twilia

Twynceola (African American)
bold
Twin, Twyn, Twynce

Tyana (African American) new

Tyberia (Place name)

Tyce (American) Ty's child

Tye (American) talented

Tyeoka (African American)
rhythmic
Tioka, Tyeo, Tyeoke

Tyesha (African American) duplicitous
Tesha, Tisha, Tyeisha, Tyiesha, Tyisha

Tyisha (African American) sweet
Isha, Tisha, Ty, Tyeisha, Tyish

Tyla (American) form of Tyler: stylish; tailor

Tyler (American) stylish; tailor
Tielyr, Tye

Tymitha (African American) kind
Timitha, Tymi, Tymie, Tymith, Tymy, Tymytha

Tyndall (Irish) dark
Tyndal, Tyndel, Tyndell, Tyndyl, Tyndyll

Tyne (American/English) dramatic; sylvan
Tie, Tine, Tye

Tynisha (African American) fertile
Tinisha, Tynesha, Tynie

Tyonia (American) of the river

Tyra (Scandinavian) assertive woman
Tye, Tyrah, Tyre, Tyrie

Tyrea (African American) form of Thora: like thunder
Tyree, Tyria

Tyredda (American) form of Tyra: assertive woman

Tyrina (American) ball of fire
Tierinna, Tye, Tyreena, Tyrinah

Tyrra (Scandinavian) aggressive

Tyson (French) son of Ty
Ty, Tysen

Tyzna (American) ingenious; assertive
Tyze, Tyzie

Tzadika (Hebrew) loyal
Zadika

Tzafra (Hebrew) morning
Tzefira, Zafra, Zefira

Tzahala (Hebrew) happy
Zahala

Tzeira (Hebrew) young

Tzemicha (Hebrew) in bloom
Zemicha

Tzeviya (Hebrew) gazelle
Civia, Tzevia, Tzivia, Tzivya, Zibiah, Zivia

Tzigane (Hungarian) gypsy
Tsigana, Tsigane

Tzila (Hebrew) darkness
Tzili, Zila, Zili

Tzina (Hebrew) shelter
Zina

Tzipiya (Hebrew) hope
Tzipia, Zipia

Tziyona (Hebrew) hill
Zeona, Ziona

Tzofi (Hebrew) scout
Tzofia, Tzofit, Tzofiya, Zofi, Zofia, Zofit

Tzuriya (Hebrew) God is powerful
Tzuria, Zuria

Uberta (Italian) bright

Uchechi (African) God's will

Udavine (American) thriving
Uda

Udele (English) prospering woman
Uda, Udela, Udell, Udella, Udelle

Uela (Unknown) dedicated to God
Uella

Ufrosinne (Mythology) jovial
Euphrosyne

Uganda (Place name) African nation

Ujhala (Hindi) shines

Ula (Celtic) jewel-like beauty
Eula, Ulah, Ule, Ulla, Ylla

Ulanda (American) confident
Uland, Ulandah, Ulande

Ulani (Hawaiian/Polynesian) happy
Ulanee

Ulatha (Biblical) place name; happy

Ulda (Unknown origin) prophetess

Ule (Unknown origin) burdens

Ulielmi (Unknown origin) intelligent

Ulima (Unknown origin) smart

Ulla (German) powerful and rich

Ulphi (Unknown origin) lovely
Ulphia, Ulphiah

Ulrika (Teutonic) leader
Rica, Ulree, Ulric, Ulrica, Ulrie, Ulry, Urik

Ultima (Latin) aloof

Ulupi (Hindi) pretty

Ulva (German) wolf; courage

Ulyssia (Invented) feminine form of Ulysses: forceful
Lyss, Lyssia, Uls, Ulsy, Ulsyia

Uma (Hebrew) nation; worldview
Umah

Umberlina (Unknown origin) feminine form of Umberto: earthy

Umeko (Unknown origin) blossom

Umma (Hindi) mother
Uma, Umah

Umnia (Arabic) desirable
Umniah, Umniya, Umniyah

Una (Latin) unique
Ona, Oona, Unah

Unda (Scandinavian) water child

Undine (Latin) from the ocean
Ondine, Undene, Undyne

Undra (American) one; long-suffering

Unet (French) the one

Unette (American) the one

Unice (English) sensible
Eunice, Uniss

Unika (Slavic) different

Unique (Latin) singular
Uneek

Unity (English) unity of spirit
Unitee

Unn (Scandinavian) loving
Un

Ural (Place name) Ural Mountains
Ura, Uralle, Urine, Uris

Urania (Greek) universal beauty
Ranie, Uraine, Urana, Uraneah, Uranie

Urbai (Unknown origin) gentle

Urbana (Latin) born in the city
Urbani, Urbanna, Urbannai

Urbi (Egyptian) princess

Urena (Slavic) lights the way

Urgita (Hindi) energetic

Uria (Hebrew) God is my flame
Ria, Uri, Uriah, Urial, Urissa

Uridia (Slavic) light

Uriela (Hebrew) God's light
Uriella, Uriyella

Urit (Hebrew) candle

Urith (Hebrew) bright
Urit

Urmia (Biblical) place name

Ursa (Greek/Latin) star; bearlike
Urs, Ursah, Ursie

Ursula (Latin) little female bear
Ursa, Urse, Ursela, Ursila

Urta (Latin) spiny plant

Usha (Indian) dawn; awakening

Usher (Word as name) helpful
Ush, Ushar, Ushur

Usiana (Biblical) place name

Uta (Teutonic) battle heroine

Utas (Unknown origin) glorious

Ute (German) rich and powerful

Utica (Native American)
Uticas, Uttica

Utopia (American) idealistic
Uta, Utopiah

Uttasta (Unknown origin) from the homeland

Uzbek (Place name) for Uzbekistan
Usbek

Uzetta (American) serious
Uzette

Uzia (Hebrew) God is my
strength
Uzial, Uzzia, Uzzial

Uzma (Spanish) capable
Usma, Uz, Uzmah

Uzoma (African) the right way

Vacla (Origin unknown) vain

Vaclava (Origin unknown)
conceited

Vada (German) form of Valda:
high spirits
Vaida, Vay

Vadnee (Origin unknown) gives

Vairie (Spanish) versatile child

Val (Latin) form of Valerie: robust

Vala (German) chosen one

Valaida (German) chosen

Valaine (French) chooses

Valarie (Latin) strong
Val, Valaria, Valerie

Valda (German) high spirits
Val, Valdah, Valida, Velda

Vale (English) valley; natural
Vail, Vaylie

Valecia (Spanish) form of
Valencia: city in Spain; strong-
willed

Valeda (Latin) strong woman
Val, Valayda, Valedah

Valencia (Place name) city in
Spain; strong-willed
*Val, Valecia, Valence, Valenica,
Valensha, Valentia, Valenzia,
Valincia*

Valene (Latin) strong girl
*Valaine, Valean, Valeda, Valeen,
Valen, Valena, Valeney, Valina,
Valine, Vallan, Vallen*

Valensia (Spanish) strong

Valenteen (American) strong

Valentina ❶ (Latin) romantic
*Val, Vala, Valantina, Vale,
Valentin, Valentine, Valiaka,
Valtina, Valyn, Valynn*

Valeny (American) hard
Val, Valenie

Valera (American) form of
Valerie: robust

Valeria ❶ ❶ (Spanish) having
valor
Valeri, Valerie, Valery

Valerie (Latin) robust
*Vairy, Val, Valarae, Valaree,
Valarey, Valari, Valarie, Vale,
Valeree, Valeri, Valeriane, Valery,
Vallarie, Valleree, Valleri, Vallerie,
Vallery, Valli, Vallie, Vallirie,
Valora, Valry, Veleria, Velerie*

Valerta (Invented) form of
Valerie: robust
Valer, Valert

Valesca (Slavic) rules

Valeska (Polish) joyous leader
*Valese, Valeshia, Valeske, Valezka,
Valisha*

Valetta (Italian) feminine
Valettah, Valita, Valitta

Valida (Spanish) right

Valince (American) valiant

Valinda (American) valiant

Valindae (American) valiant

Valkie (Scandinavian) fantastic
Val, Valkee, Valki, Valkry, Valky

Valley (Word as name)

Vallie (Latin) natural
Val, Valli, Vally

Vallie-Mae (Latin) form of
Valentina and Mae: romantic
Valliemae, Vallimae, Vallimay

Valluri (Slavic) form of Valerie:
robust

Valma (Scandinavian) loyal

Valmay (American) spring

Valonia (Scandinavian) loyal
Vallon, Valona

Valora (Latin) intimidating
*Val, Valorah, Valori, Valoria,
Valorie, Valory, Valorya*

Valore (Latin) courageous
Val, Valour

Valoria (Spanish) brave
Vallee, Valora, Valore

Valrie (American) form of
Valerie: robust

Value (Word as name) valued
Valu, Valyou

Valyn (American) perky
Valind, Valinn, Valynn

Vamia (Hispanic) energetic
Vamee, Vamie

Vanay (American) honor

Vanda (German) smiling beauty
*Vandah, Vandana, Vandelia,
Vandetta, Vandi, Vannda*

Vandan (American) honors

Vandana (Hindi) honor
Vandani

Vandeen (Sanskrit) prayerful

Vandyke (Dutch) lives by the
water

Vaneecai (Slavic) form of
Vanessa: flighty

Vanessa ☺ (Greek) flighty
*Nessa, Van, Vanassa, Vanesa,
Vanesah, Vanesha, Vaneshia,
Vanesia, Vanessah, Vanesse,
Vanessia, Vanessica, Vaniece,
Vaniessa, Vanisa, Vanissa, Vanita,
Vanna, Vannessa, Vanneza, Vanni,
Vannie, Vanny, Varnessa, Venesa,
Venessa, Veneza*

Vani (Russian) form of Vania:
gifted

Vania (Hebrew) gifted
Vaneah, Vanya

Vanille (American) simplistic
*Vana, Vani, Vanila, Vanile,
Vanna*

Vanity (English) vain girl
Vanita, Vaniti

Vanna (Greek) golden girl
*Van, Vana, Vanae, Vannah,
Vannalee, Vannaleigh*

Vanniea (American) capricious

Vanora (Welsh) wave; mercurial
Vannora

Vantha (Greek) yellow hair

Vanthe (Greek) form of Xanthe:
beautiful blonde

Vantje (Scandinavian) blonde

Vanya (American) form of
Vanna: golden girl
Vani, Vanja, Vanni, Vanyuh

Vara (Greek) strange
Varah, Vare

Varaina (Invented) form of
Lorraine: sad-eyed

Varda (Hebrew) rosy
*Vadit, Vardah, Vardia, Vardice,
Vardina, Vardis, Vardit*

Varetta (American) methodical

Varina (Czech) form of Barbara:
traveler from a foreign land

Varna (Origin unknown) no trace
of vanity

Vasa (Slavic) pretty

Vashi (Slavic) pretty

Vashti (Persian) beauty
Vashtee, Vashtie

Vasta (Persian) pretty
Vastah

Vasteen (American) capable
Vas, Vastene, Vastine, Vasty

Vateyo (American) pious

Vatima (Slavic) form of Fatima:
wise woman

Vaughan (Last name as first
name) smooth talker
Vaughn, Vawn, Vawne

Veanetta (American) knowing

Veanu (American) knowing

Veata (Cambodian) smart;
organized
Veatah

Veaunarda (Slavic) vineyard

Veda (Sanskrit) wise woman
*Vedad, Vedah, Vedis, Veeda,
Veida, Vida, Vita*

Veddy (Slavic) jubilant

Vedea (Slavic) spirited child

Vedette (French) watchful
Veda, Vedett, Vedetta

Vedi (Sanskrit) wisdom

Vedis (Slavic) lively

Vedrana (Slavic) pleasant

Veena (Indian) musical
instrument

Veera (Spanish) form of Vera:
faithful friend

Vega (Scandinavian) star
Vay, Vayga, Vegah, Veguh

Velacy (Origin unknown)
delicate

Velda (German) famous leader
Valeda, Veleda

Veleda (German) intelligent
Vel, Veladah, Velayda

Veletta (American) secretive

Velia (American) secretive

Velika (Slavic) wonder

Velina (American) secretive

Velinda (American) form of
Melinda: honey; sweetheart
*Vel, Velin, Velind, Vell, Velly,
Velynda*

Vell (American) form of Velma:
hardworking
Vel, Velly, Vels

Vellamo (Mythology) attractive

Velma (German) hardworking
*Valma, Vel, Vellma, Velmah,
Vilma, Vilna*

Velonne (Spanish) capable

Velore (Origin unknown) poised

Veltria (American) secretive

Velvet (French) luxurious
Vel, Vell, Velvete, Velvett

Vendy (American) respects

Venecia (Italian) girl from
Venice; sparkles
*Vanecia, Vanetia, Veneise, Venesa,
Venesha, Venesher, Venesse,
Venessia, Venetia, Venette,
Venezia, Venice, Venicia, Veniece,
Veniesa, Venise, Venisha, Venishia,
Venita, Venitia, Venize, Vennesa,
Vennice, Vennisa, Vennise,
Vonitia, Vonizia*

Veneradah (Spanish) honored;
venerable
Ven, Venera, Venerada

Veneranda (Spanish) venerated;
respected

Venetia (Latin) girl from Venice

Veney (American) respects

Venice (Place name) city in Italy;
coming of age
Vanice, Vaniece, Veneece, Veneese

Venitia (Italian) forgiving
*Esha, Venesha, Venn, Venney,
Venni, Vennie, Venny*

Venka (Indian) hunter

Venkata (Indian) hunter

Venke (Polish) form of Venice:
city in Italy; coming of age

Vennita (Italian) form of Venice:
city in Italy; coming of age
*Nita, Vanecia, Ven, Venesha,
Venetia, Venita, Vennie, Vinetia*

Ventura (Spanish) fortunate

Venus (Latin) loving; goddess of
love
*Venis, Venise, Vennie, Venusa,
Vinny*

Veola (American) form of Viola:
violet; lovely lady
Violet

Veoline (American) violet

Veonia (American) form of
Venus: loving; goddess of love

Veonialle (American) form of
Venus: loving; goddess of love

Vera (Russian) faithful friend
*Vara, Veera, Veira, Veradis,
Verah, Vere, Verie, Vira*

Verbena (Latin) natural beauty

Verchema (American) honest

Verda (Latin) breath of spring
Ver, Vera, Verdah, Verde, Verdi, Verdie, Viridiana, Viridis

Verdad (Spanish) verdant; honest
Verda, Verdade, Verdie, Verdine, Verdite

Verdelina (American) verdant

Verdia (American) verdant

Verdie (Latin) fresh as springtime
Verd, Verda, Verdee, Verdi, Verdy

Verena (English) honest
Veren, Verenah, Verene, Verenis, Vereniz, Verina, Verine, Virena, Virna

Verenase (Swiss) flourishing; truthful
Ver, Verenese, Verennase, Vy, Vyrenase, Vyrennace

Verity (French) truthful
Verety, Verita, Veritee, Veriti, Veritie

Verla (Latin) truthful

Verlene (Latin) vivacious
Verleen, Verlena, Verlie, Verlin, Verlina, Verlinda, Verline, Verlyn, Verlynne

Verlita (Spanish) growing

Vermekia (African American) natural
Meki, Mekia, Verme, Vermekea, Vermy, Vermye

Verna (Latin) springlike
Vernah, Verne, Vernese, Vernesha, Verneshia, Vernessa, Vernetia, Vernetta, Vernette, Vernia, Vernice, Vernis, Vernisha, Vernishela, Vernita, Verusya, Viera, Virida, Virna, Virnell

Verneake (American) spring

Verneta (Latin) verdant
Verna, Vernita, Virena, Virna

Vernice (American) natural
Verna, Vernica, Vernicca, Vernie, Verniece, Vernique

Vernicia (Spanish) form of Vernice: natural
Vern, Verni, Vernisia

Vernita (Latin) of the spring

Verona (Place name) city in Italy; flourishes; honest

Veronica (Latin) girl's image; real
Nica, Ronica, Varonica, Veron, Verhonica, Verinica, Verohnica, Veron, Verone, Veronic, Veronice, Veronika, Veronne, Veronnica, Vironica, Von, Vonni, Vonnie, Vonny, Vron, Vronica

Veronican (American) form of Veronica: girl's image; real

Veronique (French) form of Veronica: girl's image; real
Veroneek, Veroneese, Veroniece

Veroniquea (French) form of Veronica: girl's image; real
Vesna, Vezna

Versperah (Latin) evening star
Vesp, Vespa, Vespera

Vertrelle (African American) organized
Vertey, Verti, Vertrel, Vetrell

Vesela (Origin unknown) open
Vess

Vesnah (Slavic) spring goddess

Vespera (Latin) evening star

Vesta (Latin) home-loving; goddess of the home
Vess, Vessie, Vessy, Vest, Vestah, Vesteria

Veste (Latin) keeps home fires burning
Esta, Vesta

Vetaria (Slavic) regal woman

Vevay (Latin) form of Vivian: bubbling with life
Vevah, Vi, Viv, Vivay, Vivi, Vivie

Vevila (Irish) vivacious

Vevina (Latin) sweetheart

Vi (Latin) form of Viola: violet; lovely lady
Vy, Vye

Viana (Italian) vital

Vianca (American) form of Bianca: white

Vianey (Spanish) form of Vivian: bubbling with life
Via, Viana, Viane, Viani, Vianne, Vianney, Viany

Vianne (French) striking
Vi, Viane, Viann

Viara (American) vibrant

Vibeke (Hindi) vibrant

Vickay (American) form of Vicky: winner

Vicky (Latin) form of Victoria: winner
Vic, Viccy, Vick, Vickee, Vickey, Vicki, Vickie, Vikkey, Vikki, Viky

Victoria ○ ① (Latin) winner
Vic, Vicki, Vicky, Victoriah, Victoriana, Victorie, Victorina, Victorine, Victory, Vikki, Viktoria, Vyctoria

Victorine (French) winner

Victory (Latin) a winning woman
Vic, Viktorie

Vida (Hebrew) form of Davida: beloved one
Veeda

Vidella (Spanish) life
Veda, Vida, Videline, Vydell

Vidette (Hebrew) loved
Viddey, Viddi, Viddie, Vidett, Videy

Vidonia (Portuguese) vine; winding

Vidrine (Last name as first name) life

Vie (American) competitor

Vienna (Place name) a city in Austria
Veena, Vena, Venna, Viena, Vienette, Viennah, Vienne, Vina

Viennese (Place name) form of Vienna: a city in Austria
Vee, Viena, Vienne

Viera (Spanish) smart; alive

Vieyra (Spanish) lively

Vigdis (Scandinavian) war goddess

Vigilia (Latin) vigilant

Vignette (American) special scene

Vijaya (Indian) wins

Vilhelmina (Scandinavian) form of Wilhelmina: able protector
Velma, Vilhelmine, Vilma

Villa (American) of the village

Villette (French) little village girl
Vietta

Villian (American) form of Lillian: pretty as a lilly

Villoria (Spanish) valor

Vilma (Spanish) form of Velma: hardworking
Vi, Vil

Vilmean (American) form of Velma: hardworking

Vimala (Hindi) attractive

Vina (Hindi) musical instrument
Veena, Vena, Vin, Vinah, Vinesha, Vinessa, Vinia, Viniece, Vinique, Vinisha, Vinita, Vinna, Vinni, Vinnie, Vinny, Vinora, Vyna

Vinah (American) up-and-coming
Vi, Vyna

Vincentia (Latin) winner
Vicenta, Vin, Vincenta, Vincentena, Vincentina, Vincentine, Vincenza, Vincy, Vinnie

Vinci (Spanish) wins

Vincia (Spanish) forthright; winning
Vincenta, Vincey, Vinci

Vinee (Spanish) welcomed

Vineeta (Indian) modest

Vinefrida (Scandinavian) bold

Vinelle (English) wine

Vineta (Indian) modest
Vinata

Vinetae (English) wine

Vinia (Spanish) vineyard woman

Vinishia (English) wine

Vinita (Hindi) she comes home

Vinital (Indian) asks

Vinne (American) from the vineyard

Vinuela (Spanish) longsuffering

Viola (Latin) violet; lovely lady
Vi, Violah, Violaine, Violanta, Viole, Violeine

Violanth (Latin) from the purple flower violet
Vi, Viol, Viola, Violanta, Violante

Violet (English/French) purple flower
Vi, Viole, Violette, Vylolet, Vyoletta, Vyolette

Violeta (Spanish) form of Violet: purple flower

Violia (Italian) form of Violet: purple flower

Violin (American) instrument

Violyne (Latin) form of Violet: purple flower
Vi, Vio, Viola, Violene, Violine

Viorica (Spanish) views

Virendra (Spanish) alive

Virethal (American) vibrant

Virgilia (Latin) bears all; stoic
Virgillia

Virginia (Latin) pure female
Giniah, Verginia, Verginya, Virge, Virgen, Virgenia, Virgenya, Virgie, Virgine, Virginio, Virginnia, Virginya, Virgy, Virjeana

Viridas (Latin) green; growing
Viridis

Viridis (Latin) green and verdant
Virdis, Virida, Viridia, Viridiana

Virjean (American) virginal

Virtue (Latin) strong; pure

Virzie (American) virginal

Visala (Indian) heavenly

Visidora (Spanish) clear view; strong

Vision (Word as name) visionary

Visitacion (Spanish) a visit

Vita (Latin) animated; lively; life
Veda, Veeta, Veta, Vete, Vitaliana, Vitalina, Vitel, Vitella, Vitia, Vitka, Vitke

Viv (Latin) form of Vivian: bubbling with life

Viva (Latin) alive; lively
Veeva, Vivan, Vivva

Vivadell (Combo of Viva and Dell) lively

Vivecca (Scandinavian) lively; energetic
Viv, Viveca, Vivecka, Viveka, Vivica, Vivie, Vyveca

Vivi (Hindi) vital
Viv

Vivian (Latin) bubbling with life
Viv, Viva, Vive, Vivee, Vivi, Vivia, Viviana, Viviane, Vivie, Vivien, Vivienne, Vivina, Vivion, Vivyan, Vyvyan

Vivianeth (American) form of Vivian: bubbling with life

Vivianetta (American) form of Vivian: bubbling with life

Vivianna (American) inventive
Viviannah, Vivianne

Vivilyn (American) vital
Viv, Vivi

Vivka (Slavic) form of Vivian: bubbling with life

Vix (American) form of Vixen: flirt
Vixa, Vixie, Vyx

Vixen (American) flirt
Vix, Vixee, Vixie

Vlada (Slavic) admired

Vladmirea (Slavic) admired

Vlasta (Slavic) likeable

Voila (French) attention; seen
Vwala

Volante (Italian) veiled

Voletta (French) mysterious
Volette, Volettie

Volette (Greek) hidden; veiled

Volina (American) form of Violin: instrument

Vona (French) pretty woman

Vonceil (Spanish) form of
Yvonne: athletic

Voncille (American) form of
Yvonne: athletic; form of Vonna:
graceful

Vonda (Czech) loving; talented
Vondah, Vondi

Vondrah (Czech) loving
*Vond, Vonda, Vondie, Vondra,
Vondrea*

Vonese (American) form of
Vanessa: flighty
*Vonesa, Vonise, Vonne, Vonnesa,
Vonny*

Voni (Slavic) affectionate
Vonee, Vonie

Vonna (French) graceful
*Vona, Vonah, Vonne, Vonni,
Vonnie, Vonny*

Vonnala (American) sweet
Von, Vonala, Vonnalah, Vonnie

Vonzetta (American) form of
Yvonne: athletic

Voula (Greek) sly

Voyage (Word as name) trip;
wanderer
Voy

Vrant (American) truth

Vrenean (American) truth

Vyera (Spanish) form of Viera:
alive

Wade (American) campy

Wafa (Arabic) loyal

Wakana (Japanese) plant;
thriving

Wakanda (Native American)
magical
Wakenda

Wakebia (African) strong

Wakeen (American) spunky
Wakeene, Wakey, Wakine

Wakeishah (African American)
happy
Wake, Wakeisha, Wakesha

Walburga (German) protective
Walberga, Wallburga, Walpurgis

Walda (German) powerful
woman
*Waldah, Waldena, Waldette,
Waldina, Wallda, Wally, Welda,
Wellda*

Waldeen (American) strong

Waleria (Polish) sweet

Waleska (Last name as first
name) effervescent
Wal, Walesk, Wally

Walker (English) active; mover
Wallker

Walkiria (Mythology) fantastic

Wallis (English) open-minded
*Walis, Wallace, Walless, Wallie,
Walliss, Wally, Wallys*

Walsie (American) form of
Waltz: graceful

Waltz (American) graceful

Wana (American) wandering

Wanakee (Native American)
innovative

Wanda (Polish) wild; wandering
*Vanda, Wahnda, Wandah,
Wandie, Wandis, Wandy,
Wannda, Wenda, Wendaline,
Wendall, Wendeline, Wendy,
Wohnda, Wonda, Wonnda*

Wandelka (Slavic) praised

Wanetta (English) fair
Waneta, Wanette, Wanita

Wanicka (American) form of
Juanita: believer in a gracious
God; forgiving

Wanita (American) form of
Juanita: believer in a gracious
God; forgiving

Warda (German) guards her own
Wardia, Wardine

Warma (American) warmth-filled
Warm

Warna (German) defends her own

Warner (German) outgoing; fighter
Warna, Warnar, Warnir

Wasana (Native American) good health

Washina (Native American) good health

Waun (Native American) vocal

Wauneta (American) form of Juanita: believer in a gracious God; forgiving

Waverly (English) wavers in the meadow of swaying aspens
Waverley

Wayla (African) young child

Waynette (English) makes wagons; crafts wood
Waynel, Waynelle, Waynlyn

Waywan (Native American) little girl

Weeko (Native American) pretty

Wehilani (Hawaiian) heaven

Weinsia (American) of the heavens

Wenda (German) adventurer
Wend, Wendah, Wendy

Wendell (English) has wanderlust
Wendaline, Wendall, Wendelle

Wendy (English) friendly; childlike
Wenda, Wendaline, Wende, Wendee, Wendeline, Wendey, Wendi, Wendie, Wendye

Weneta (American) of the heavens

Wenetta (American) of the heavens

Weslee (English) girl from meadows of the west
Weslea, Weslene, Wesley, Weslia, Weslie, Weslyn

Weslia (English) meadow in the west
Wesleya, Weslie

Weslie (English) woman in the meadow
Wes, Weslee, Wesli

Wheeler (English) inventive
Wheelah, Wheelar

Whitley (English) outdoorsy
Whitelea, Whitlea, Whitlee, Whitly, Whittley, Witlee

Whitman (English) white-haired
Whit, Wittman

Whitney (English) white; fresh
Whit, Whiteney, Whitne, Whitnea, Whitnee, Whitneigh, Whitni, Whitnie, Whitny, Whittaney, Whittany, Whittney, Whytnie

Whitson (Last name as first name) white
Whits, Whitty, Witte, Witty

Whittier (Literature) for the poet John Greenleaf Whittier; distinguished
Whitt

Whoopi (English) excitable
Whoopee, Whoopie, Whoopy

Whynesha (African American) kindhearted
Whynesa, Wynes, Wynesa, Wynesha

Wibeke (Scandinavian) vibrant
Wiebke, Wiweca

Wiktoria (Polish) victor
Wikta

Wilda (English) wild-haired girl
Willda, Willie, Wylda, Wyle

Wildress (American) form of the wilderness

Wile (American) coy; wily
Wiles, Wyle

Wilemma (English) determined

Wilene (English) determined

Wilfreda (English) goal-oriented
Wilfridda, Wilfrieda

Wilfrid (Spanish) willful

Wilhelmina (German) feminine form of William: staunch protector
Willa, Willhelmena, Willie, Wilma

Willa (English) desirable
Will, Willah

Willette (American) open
Wilet, Wilett, Will, Willett

Willima (Spanish) protective

Willine (American) form of will:
willowy
Will, Willene, Willy, Willyne

Willis (American) sparkling
Wilice, Will, Willice

Willistine (French) form of
Willis: sparkling

Willough (American) form of
Willow: free spirit; willow tree

Willow (American) free spirit;
willow tree
Willo

Willsie (American) form of
Willow: free spirit; willow tree

Wilma (German) sturdy
*Willma, Wilmah, Wilmina, Wylm,
Wylma*

Wilmot (English) feminine form
of William: staunch protector

Wilona (English) desirable;
desired child
*Willone, Willonoa, Wilo, Wiloh,
Wilonah, Wilone, Wylona*

Win (German) flirty
Winnie, Wyn, Wynne

Winata (American) form of
Juanita: believer in a gracious
God; forgiving

Wind (American) breezy
*Winde, Windee, Windey, Windi,
Windy, Wynd*

Winda (African) hunts for prey

Windy (English) likes the wind
*Windee, Windey, Windi, Windie,
Wyndee, Wyndy*

Winella (American) form of
Juanita: believer in a gracious
God; forgiving

Winema (Native American)
leader

Winesa (American) winning

Winetta (American) peaceful;
country girl
Winette, Winietta, Wyna, Wynette

Winifred (German) peaceful
woman
*Win, Wina, Winafred, Windy,
Winefred, Winefride, Winefried,
Winfreda, Winfrieda, Winifryd,
Winne, Winnie, Winniefred,
Winnifreed, Wynafred, Wynifred,
Wynn, Wynne, Wynnifred*

Winkie (American) vital
Winkee, Winky

Winna (African) friendly
Winnah

Winner (American) outstanding

Winnie (English) winning
Wini, Winny, Wynnie

Winnielle (African) victorious
female
Winielle, Winniele, Wynnielle

Winnien (American) saintly

Winola (German) vivacious

Winona (Native American)
firstborn girl
*Wenona, Wenonah, Winnie,
Winnona, Winoena, Winonah,
Wye, Wynnona, Wynona,
Wynonah, Wynonna*

Winonia (American) oldest girl

Winsome (English) nice; beauty
Wynsome

Winter (English) child born in
winter
Wynter

Wisdom (English) discerning

Wistar (German) respected
Wistarr, Wister

Wisteria (Botanical) vine;
entangles
Wistaria

Witera (American) dramatic

Wonder (American) filled with
wonder
*Wander, Wonda, Wondee, Wondy,
Wunder*

Wonila (African American) swaying
Waunila, Woṇilla, Wonny

Wood (American) smooth talker
Woode, Woodee, Woodie, Woody, Woodye

Woodett (English) of the woods

Woodine (English) of the woods

Worship (Word as name) religious

Wova (American) brassy
Whova, Wovah

Wowena (American) form of Rowena: blissful; beloved friend

Wren (English) flighty girl; bird
Renn, Wrin, Wryn, Wrynne

Wrenny (American) wren

Wurei (American) combative

Wyanda (American) form of Wanda: wild; wandering
Wyan

Wyanet (Native American) lovely
Wyanetta, Wyonet, Wyonetta

Wyetta (French) feisty
Wyette

Wyld (American) spirited

Wyldanen (American) spirited

Wyleen (American) spirit

Wylie (American) wily
Wylee, Wyley, Wyli

Wymette (American) vocalist
Wimet, Wimette, Wymet, Wynette

Wyna (American) oldest

Wynell (American) oldest

Wynelle (American) oldest

Wynndi (American) friend
Wendy

Wynne (Welsh) fair-haired
Win, Winne, Winnie, Winny, Winwin, Wyn, Wynee, Wynn, Wynnie

Wynnika (American) friend

Wynstelle (Latin) chaste; star
Winstella, Winstelle, Wynnestella, Wynnestelle

Wyntress (American) friend

Wyomie (Native American) horse-rider on the plains
Why, Wyome, Wyomee, Wyomeh, Wyomia

Wyoming (Native American) U.S. state; cowgirl
Wy, Wye, Wyoh, Wyomia

Wyrene (American) helps

Wysandra (Greek) fair; protects

Wyss (Welsh) spontaneous; fair
Whyse

Xandra (Greek) protective
Xandrae, Zan, Zandie, Zandra

Xanthe (Greek) beautiful blonde; yellow
X, Xanth, X-Anth, Xantha, Xanthie, Xes, Zane, Zanthie

Xanthippe (Greek) form of Xanthe: beautiful blonde; yellow

Xara (Hebrew) form of Sarah: God's princess

Xavia (Origin unknown) feminine form of Xavier: familiar

Xaviera (French) smart
Zavey, Zavie, Zaviera, Zavierah, Zavy

Xena (Greek) girl from afar
Xenia, Zen, Zena, Zennie

Xeniah (Greek) gracious entertainer
Xen, Xenia, Zenia, Zeniah

Xianona (American) fragrant

Ximena (Greek) greets

Ximenia (Spanish) form of Serena: calm

Xiomara (Spanish) congenial

Xloie (American) form of Chloe: flowering

Xylene (Greek) outdoorsy
Leen, Lene, Xyleen, Xyline, Zylee, Zyleen, Zylie

Xylia (Greek) woods-loving
Zylea, Zylia

Xylophila (Greek) lover of nature

Yacoa (American) form of Coco: coconut

Yadavendra (Indian) friendly

Yadira (Hindi) dearest

Yael (Hebrew) strength of God
Yaele, Yayl, Yayle

Yaffa (Hebrew) beautiful girl
Yafa, Yafah, Yaffah, Yapha

Yagna (Slavic) giving

Yahaira (Hebrew) precious
Yajaira

Yahnnie (Greek) giving
Yahn, Yanni, Yannie, Yannis

Yahsah (American) dear one

Yajaira (Spanish) dear one

Yaki (Japanese) tenacious
Yakee

Yakira (Hebrew) adored baby

Yalcin (American) violet

Yale (English) fertile moor
Yaile, Yayle

Yalonda (American) form of Yolanda: pretty as a violet flower

Yamayo (Asian) lovely

Yamileth (American) form of Yamila: beautiful

Yamilla (Arabic) form of Jamila: beautiful female; form of Camilla: wonderful
Yamila, Yamyla, Yamylla

Yamille (Arabic) beautiful
Yamill, Yamyl, Yamyle, Yamylle

Yamin (Hebrew) near to God

Yamini (Indian) nighttime

Yamya (Hindi) nighttime

Yan (Slavic) forgiving

Yana (Slavic) lovely
Yanah, Yanna, Yanni, Yannie, Yanny

Yancy (Native American) Yankee; sassy
Yancee, Yancey, Yanci, Yancie

Yanessa (American) form of Vanessa: flighty
Yanesa, Yanisa, Yanissa, Yanysa, Yanyssa

Yanet (Spanish) form of Janet: small; forgiving

Yaney (American) form of Janey: believer in a gracious God

Yanine (American) form of Janine: kind

Yanni (Australian) peaceful

Yaquelin (Spanish) form of Jacqueline: supplanter; substitute
Yackie, Yacque, Yacquelyn, Yaki, Yakie, Yaque, Yaquelinn, Yaquelinne

Yara (Spanish) expansive; princess
Yarah, Yare, Yarey

Yarai (African) modest
Nyarai

Yardena (Hebrew) flows naturally

Yardley (English) open-minded
Yardlee, Yardleigh, Yardli, Yardlie, Yardly

Yareli (American) grateful

Yarine (Russian) peaceful
Yari, Yarina

Yarita (Spanish) flashy

Yarkona (Hebrew) growing

Yas (Hindi) scented

Yasha (Indian) maternal

Yashita (Indian) famous

Yashona (Hindi) rich
Yaseana, Yashauna, Yashawna,
Yeseana, Yeshauna, Yeshawna,
Yeshona

Yasmina (Hindi) form of
Jasmine: fragrant; sweet
Yasmeena, Yasmyna

Yasmine (Arabic) pretty
Yasmeen, Yasmen, Yasmin,
Yasminn, Yasmyn, Yasmynn

Yati (Indian) careful

Yaura (American) desirous
Yara, Yaur, YaYa

YaVonne (Indian) beautiful girl

Yazith (Biblical) place name

Yazmin (Persian) pretty flower
Yazmen, Yazminn, Yazmyn,
Yazmynn

Yeardley (English) home
enclosed in meadow
Yeardlee, Yeardleigh, Yeardli,
Yeardlie, Yeardly

Yebenette (American) little
Yebe, Yebey, Yebi

Yechiel (Spanish) helps

Yelba (Spanish) form of
Melba: talented; light-hearted

Yelena (Russian) friendly

Yelisabeta (Russian) form of
Elizabeth: God's promise
Yelizabet

Yemaya (African) smart; quirky
Yemye

Yenisey (French) spellbound

Yepa (Native American)
traditional

Yeriel (Hebrew) God's child

Yesica (Hebrew) form of Jessica:
rich

Yeskia (Spanish) yesida
Yesika

Yesmin (Spanish) jasmine flower

Yessenia (Spanish) devout
Jesenia, Yesenia

Yessi (Hebrew) God-loving

Yesun (Turkish) jade
Jesin, Yesim

Yetta (English) head of home

Yeva (Russian) lively; loving
Yevka

Yevettea (Slavic) form of Yvette:
lively archer

Yevgeniya (Slavic) highborn

Yildiz (Spanish) star

Yilma (Spanish) form of Wilma:
sturdy

Yilmalla (Spanish) form of
Wilma: sturdy

Yina (Spanish) winning
Yena

Yinyin (Asian) silver hair

Yitta (Hebrew) lightness

Ynez (Spanish) form of Inez:
lovely

Yoanna (Hebrew) feminine form
of John: God is gracious
Yoana, Yoanah, Yoannah

Yochana (Indian) thoughtful

Yodelle (American) old-fashioned
Yode, Yodell, Yodelly, Yodette,
Yodey

Yoella (Hebrew) loves Jehovah
Yoela, Yoelah, Yoellah

Yogee (American) bright

Yogeta (American) bright

Yogini (Indian) centered

Yogita (Indian) smart

Yohanna (Greek) violet; textured
Yohana, Yohanah, Yohannah

Yoka (Native American) bird song

Yokasta (Greek) form of Jocasta:
light

Yoko (Japanese) good; striving
Yokoh

Yola (Spanish) form of Yolanda:
pretty as a violet flower
Yolanda, Yoli

Yolada (Spanish) form of
Yolanda: pretty as a violet flower

Yolanda (Greek) pretty as a violet
flower
Yola, Yolana, Yolandah, Yolie,
Yoyly

Yolia (Spanish) form of Julia: forever young

Yolie (Greek) violet; flower
Yolee, Yoley, Yoli, Yoly

Yomi (Spanish) sun child

Yon (Korean) lotus; lovely
Yonn

Yona (Hebrew) dove; calm
Yonah, Yonna, Yonnah

Yonaide (American)
Yonade, Yonaid

Yonina (Hebrew) dove; calm
Yonyna

Yonit (Hebrew) passive
Yonitt, Yonyt, Yonytt

Yorba (Place name)

Yordaine (French) form of Jordan: excellent descendant
Yordane, Yordayne

Yordan (Hebrew) form of Jordan: excellent descendant
Yorden, Yordyn

Yordana (Hebrew) humble
Yordanah, Yordanna, Yordannah

Yoreni (Place name)

Yori (Japanese) dependable
Yoree, Yorey, Yorie, Yory

York (English) forthright
Yorkie, Yorkke

Yoselin (Spanish) form of Joselin: happy girl

Yosepha (Hebrew) form of Josephine: blessed

Yoshe (Japanese) form of Yoshi: good girl
Yoshee, Yoshey, Yoshi, Yoshie, Yoshy

Youhanna (Slavic) form of Johanna: believer in a gracious God

Young (Korean) forever

Yousha (Indian) girl

Yousheika (Slavic) joyful

Youvet (French) form of Yvette: lively archer

Youvone (American) form of Yvonne: athletic

Yovana (Slavic) joy

Yovelle (Hebrew) joy

Yovona (African American) form of Yvonne: athletic
Yovaana, Yovanna, Yovhana, Yovhanna, Yoviana, Yovianna

Ysabel (Spanish) form of Isabel: clever
Ysabell, Ysabelle, Ysebel, Ysebell, Ysebelle, Ysybel, Ysybell, Ysybelle

Ysabella (Spanish) smart and witty
Ysabela, Ysebela, Ysebella, Ysybela, Ysybella

Ysanne (English) graceful
Esan, Esanne, Essan, Ysan, Ysann

Yseult (Irish) prettiness
Yseulte

Yu (Asian) jade; a gem

Yue (Asian) happy

Yuette (American) capable
Yue, Yuete, Yuetta

Yuki (Japanese) snow child

Yukolina (Slavic) form of Julia: forever young

Yulan (Spanish) splendid

Yuldene (Slavic) form of Juliana: youthful; Jove's child

Yule (Spanish) competitive

Yulondita (Spanish) form of Juliana: youthful; Jove's child

Yuna (African) gorgeous
Yunah

Yuri (Chinese) lily

Yuridia (American) lily

Yuta (American) dramatic
Uta

Yutaca (Spanish) dramatic

Yuti (Indian) united as one

Yuvati (Indian) girl

Yuventia (Spanish) archer

Yuvette (English) petite archer

Yuvrani (Indian) princess

Yves (French) clever

Yvette (French) lively archer
Yavet, Yevette, Yvete, Yvett

Yvonnda (American) form of Yvonne: athetic

Yvonne (French) athletic
Vonne, Vonnie, Yavonne, Yvone, Yvonna

Yvonnig (Invented) athlete

Yzabel (Hebrew) form of Isabel: God-loving
Yzabell, Yzabelle, Yzebel, Yzebell, Yzebelle, Yzybel, Yzybell, Yzybelle

Z

Zabrina (American) form of Sabrina: passionate
Zabreena, Zabryna

Zac (American) God remembers her

Zachah (Hebrew) lord remembered; bravehearted
Zach, Zacha, Zachie, Zachrie

Zachree (Hebrew) loves God

Zada (Arabic) fortunate
Zaida, Zayda

Zadie (American) form of Sadie: charmer; princess

Zafira (Arabic) successful
Zafirah

Zahara (African) flower
Zahari, Zaharit

Zahavah (Hebrew) golden girl
Zahava, Zeheva, Zev

Zahidee (Arabic) white

Zahira (African) flower
Zahara, Zahirah, Zahrah, Zara, Zuhra

Zahra (African) blossoming
Zara, Zarah

Zaibunissa (Spanish) peaceful

Zaida (Spanish) peacemaker
Zada, Zai

Zaina (Arabic) lovely; beautiful girl

Zainab (Arabic) brave

Zaira (Arabic) flower
Zara, Zarah, Zaria, Zayeera

Zaire (Place name) country in Africa
Zai, Zay, Zayaire

Zakah (African) smart
Zaka, Zakia, Zakiah

Zakiya (Arabic) chaste
Zakiyah

Zakiyyah (Hebrew) pure

Zakria (Hebrew) pure

Zaky (Hebrew) pure

Zakya (Hebrew) chaste

Zale (Greek) strong force of the sea
Zaile, Zayle

Zalika (African) born to royalty

Zaltana (Native American) high mountain

Zaltene (American) highborn

Zambee (Place name) form of Zambia
Zambi, Zambie, Zamby

Zamilla (Greek) strong force of the sea
Zamila, Zamyla, Zamylla

Zamir (Hebrew) intelligent leader
Zameer, Zamyr

Zan (Greek/Chinese) supportive; praiseworthy
Zander, Zann

Zana (Greek) defender; energetic
Zanah

Zanabria (Greek) defends

Zandile (American) pure

Zandra (Greek) shy; helpful
Zan, Zondra

Zane (Scandinavian) bold girl
Zain

Zaneta (Spanish) God is good

Zanita (American) gifted
Zaneta, Zanetta, Zanette, Zanitt, Zeneta

Zanna (Hebrew) lily
Zana, Zanah, Zannah

Zanoah (Biblical) place name

Zanth (Greek) leader
Zanthe, Zanthi, Zanthie, Zanthy

Zara (Hebrew) dawn; glorious
Zahra, Zarah, Zaree

Zaray (Arabic) going strong

Zareen (Hebrew) form of Sareen:
strong

Zarena (Hebrew) dawn
Zareena, Zarina, Zaryna

Zarephath (Biblical) place name

Zaria (Hebrew) form of Zara:
dawn; glorious

Zarieh (Hebrew) form of Zara:
dawn; glorious

Zarifa (Arabic) successful

Zarina (Hebrew) form of Sarika:
thrush; sings

Zarita (Hebrew) form of Sarah:
God's princess

Zarmina (Origin unknown)
bright
Zar, Zarmynna

Zarney (American) progressive

Zarni (American) direct

Zarreta (American) form of
Zara: dawn; glorious

Zarria (Arabic) splendid

Zavina (Spanish) flower

Zawadi (African) gift

Zayba (Muslim) lovely

Zayit (Hebrew) olive

Zaylee (English) heavenly
Zay, Zayle, Zayley, Zayli, Zaylie

Zayna (Arabic) wonderful; pretty
girl
Zayne

Zaynab (Iranian) child of Ali
Zainab

Zaza (Hebrew) golden

Zazalesha (African American)
zany
Lesha, Zaza, Zazalese, Zazalesh

Zazula (Polish) outstanding

Zdenka (Czech) one from Sidon;
winding sheet
Zdena, Zdenicka, Zdenina,
Zdeninka, Zdenuska

Zdeslava (Czech) present glory
Zdevsa, Zdisa, Zdiska, Zdislava

Zea (Latin) grain
Zia

Zeandrea (American) form of
Deandra: divine
Zeandraea, Zeandraya, Zeandria,
Zeandrya

Zeb (Hebrew) Jehovah's gift

Zebrine (American) form of
Sabrina: passionate

Zecua (American) loyal

Zeezee (American) sunny

Zef (Polish) moves with the wind
Zeff

Zeffa (Origin unknown) breezy

Zefiryn (Polish) form of Zephyr:
the west wind; wandering girl

Zehara (Hebrew) light

Zehava (Hebrew) gold
Zahava, Zehovit, Zehuva, Zehuvit

Zehira (Hebrew) careful

Zel (Persian) cymbal

Zela (Greek) blessed; smiling

Zelana (American) sunny

Zelda (German) practical
Zell, Zellie

Zeldia (Spanish) form of Zelda:
practical

Zelenka (Czech) fresh

Zelfa (African American) in
control

Zelia (Spanish) sunshine
Zeleah

Zella (German) resistant

Zelma (German) divine

Zelpha (American) confident

Zemira (Hebrew) song

Zemorah (Hebrew) tree branch
Zemora

Zena (Greek) holy

Zenae (Greek) helpful
Zen, Zenah, Zennie

Zenaida (Greek) daughter of Zeus

Zenana (Hebrew) woman
Zena, Zenia

Zenda (Hebrew) holy

Zeni (Slavic) gracious

Zenia (Greek) open
Zeniah, Zenney, Zenni, Zennie, Zenny, Zenya

Zenobia (Greek) strength of Zeus

Zenobietta (Spanish) form of Zenobia: strength of Zeus

Zenorina (Spanish) holy

Zenov (Slavic) gracious

Zenzi (German) crescent

Zephirin (English) form of Zephyr: the west wind; wandering girl

Zephirinia (English) form of Zephyr: the west wind; wandering girl

Zephyr (Greek) the west wind; wandering girl
Zefir, Zeph, Zephie, Zephir, Zephira, Zephyra

Zeppelina (English) beautiful storm

Zera (Hebrew) seeds

Zerafina (Greek) the west wind; zephyr
Zerafeena, Zerafyna

Zeraldina (Polish) spear ruler

Zerdali (Turkish) wild apricot

Zeredah (Biblical) place name

Zerel (Hindi) brave

Zerena (Turkish) golden woman
Zereena, Zerina, Zeryna

Zerlinda (Hebrew) dawn
Zerlina

Zerly (Hebrew) morning

Zerren (English) flower

Zesiro (African) first of twins

Zesta (American) zestful
Zestah, Zestie, Zesty

Zeta (Greek) born last
Zetah, Zetta

Zett (Hebrew) olive; flourishing
Zeta, Zetta

Zetulio (Spanish) from the rose

Zevida (Hebrew) current
Zevuda

Zezziska (Slavic) form of Jessica: rich

Zhane (African American) feminine of Shane

Zhanna (Slavic) form of Janet: small; forgiving

Zhen (Chinese) pure

Zhenia (Latin) bright
Zennia, Zhen, Zhenie

Zhi (Chinese) of high character; ethical

Zho (Chinese) character

Zhong (Chinese) honorable

Zhuo (Chinese) smart; wonderful
Zuo

Zi (Chinese) flourishing; giving

Zia (Latin) textured
Zea, Ziah

Zibah (Biblical) delights

Zibute (Lithuanian) shines

Zigana (Hungarian) gypsy

Zihna (Native American) spinning

Zila (Hebrew) shadowy
Zilah, Zilla, Zillah, Zylla

Zildjian (Slavic) God judges her

Zilias (Hebrew) shadow
Zillia, Zillya, Zilya

Zillah (Biblical) in the shade

Zilpah (Hebrew) dignity
Zillpha, Zilpha, Zulpha, Zylpha

Zilu (Biblical) place name

Zilvinas (Spanish) hidden

Zimbab (Place name) form of Zimbabwe
Zimbob

Zimriah (Hebrew) songs
Zimria, Zimriya

Zina (Greek) hospitable woman
Zena, Zinah, Zine, Zinnie

Zindi (Spanish) form of Cindy: moon goddess

Ziniah (Muslim) prepared

Zinnia (Botanical) flower
Zenia, Zinia, Zinny, Zinnya,
Zinya

Zinzi (American) flower

Zinzida (African) gracious

Ziona (Hebrew) symbol of good
Zionah, Zyona, Zyonah

Zipory (Hebrew) bird

Zipporah (Hebrew) bird in flight
Ziporah, Zippi, Zippie, Zippora,
Zippy

Ziracuny (Native American)
water

Zirah (Hebrew) coliseum
Zira

Zisla (Slavic) rose

Zita (Greek) seeker; (Spanish)
rose girl
Zeeta, Zitah

Ziv (Hebrew) radiant

Ziva (Hebrew) brilliant
Zeeva, Ziv

Ziz (Hungarian) dedicated
Zizz, Zyz, Zyzz

Zlata (Czech) golden

Zoa (Greek) life; vibrant

Zocha (Polish) wisdom

Zoe ✿ ❶ (Greek) lively; vibrant
Zoee, Zoey, Zoie, Zooey

Zoelle (Spanish) form of Noelle:
Christmas baby

Zofia (Polish) skilled

Zofie (Czech) wise

Zoheret (Hebrew) shining

Zohreh (Hebrew) shines

Zoila (Italian) earthy

Zola (French) earthy
Zolah

Zolema (American) confessor
Zolem

Zona (Latin) funny; brash
Zonah, Zonia, Zonna

Zonia (English) flower

Zonice (American) form of Zona:
funny; brash

Zonta (Native American) honest

Zooey (Greek) life

Zoom (American) energetic
Zoomi, Zoomy, Zoom-Zoom

Zora (Slavic) beauty of dawn
Zara, Zorah, Zorrah, Zorre, Zorrie

Zoralle (Slavic) ethereal
Zoral, Zoralye, Zorre, Zorrie

Zore (Slavic) dawn of day

Zorina (Slavic) golden
Zorana

Zorka (Slavic) dawn
Zorke, Zorky

Zorna (Slavic) golden

Zorrie (American) gold

Zosa (Greek) lively
Zosah

Zosima (Greek) vibrant

Zowie (Irish) vibrant
Zowee, Zowey, Zowi, Zowy

ZsaZsa (Hungarian) wild-spirited
Zsa, Zsaey

Zuba (English) musical

Zubaida (Arabic) laborer
Zubaidah, Zubeda

Zubeen (American) excellent

Zubida (Spanish) singer

Zubinelle (Spanish) vocal

Zudora (Sanskrit) laborer

Zulah (African) country-loving
Zoola, Zoolah, Zula

Zulaila (African) smart

Zyan (Native American)
everlasting

Zydeco (French) musical

Bibliography

20,000+ Names Page. "20,000+ Names from Around the World." 1 Nov. 2002 www.20000-names.com.

"America's 40 Richest Under 40." Fortune Online. 16 Sept. 2002 www.fortune.com.

American Girl Catalog.

"The American States." Collin, P.H., ed. *Webster's Concise Desk Dictionary.* New York: Barnes & Noble Books, 2001.

"The Animal Kingdom." Collin, P.H., ed. *Webster's Concise Desk Dictionary.* New York: Barnes & Noble Books, 2001.

Baby Center Baby Name Finder Page. 1 Dec. 2002 www.babycenter.com/babyname.

Baby Chatter Page. 1 Dec. 2002 www.babychatter.com.

Baby Names/Birth Announcements Page. 1 Oct. 2002 www.princessprints.com.

Baby Names Page. 1 Dec. 2002 www.yourbabysname.com.

Baby Names Page. 1 Nov. 2002 www.babynames.com.

Baby Names Page. 1 Oct. 2002 www.babyshere.com.

Baby Names World Page. 15 Jan. 2003 www.babynameworld.com.

Baby Zone Page. "Around-the-World Names." 15 Jan. 2003 www.babyzone.com/babynames.

"Biographical Names." Collin, P.H., ed. *Webster's Concise Desk Dictionary.* New York: Barnes & Noble Books, 2001.

"Biographical Names." *The Merriam-Webster Dictionary.* Springfield, MA: Merriam-Webster, Inc., 1998.

"Books of the Bible." Collin, P.H., ed. *Webster's Concise Desk Dictionary.* New York: Barnes & Noble Books, 2001.

Celebrity Names Page. 1 Nov. 2002 www.celebnames.8m.com.

"Common English Given Names." *The Merriam-Webster Dictionary.* Springfield, MA: Merriam-Webster, Inc., 1998.

Death Penalty Info Page. 1 Feb. 2003 "Current Female Death Row Inmates." www.deathpenaltyinfo.org/womencases.html.

Dunkling, Leslie. *The Guinness Book of Names.* Enfield, UK: Guinness Publishing, 1993.

eBusinessRevolution Page. 1 Nov. 2002 www.ebusinessrevolution.com/babynames/a.html.

ePregnancy Page. 1 Dec. 2002 www.Epregnancy.com/directory/Baby_Names.

"Fifty Important Stars." Gove, Philip Babcock, ed. *Webster's Third New International Dictionary of the English Language Unabridged.* Springfield, MA: Merriam-Webster, Inc., 1981.

"Gambino Capos Held in 1989 Mob Hit." Jerry Capeci. This Week in Gangland, The Online Column Page. 1 Aug. 2002 www.ganglandnews.com/column289.htm.

Gooch, Anthony, and Garcia de Paredes, Angel. *Cassell's Spanish-English Dictionary*. New York: Macmillan Publishing, Inc., 1982.

Guinagh, Kevin. *Dictionary of Foreign Phrases*. New York: H.W. Wilson Company, 1965.

Hanks, Patrick, and Flavia Hodges. *A Dictionary of First Names*. Oxford: Oxford University Press, 1992.

Hanley, Kate and the Parents of Parent Soup. *The Parent Soup Baby Name Finder: Real Advice from Real Parents Who Have Named Their Babies and Lived To Tell About It—with More Than 15,000 Names*. Lincolnwood, IL: Contemporary Books, 1998.

Harrison, G.B., ed. *Major British Writers*. New York: Harcourt, Brace &World, Inc., 1959.

HypoBirthing Page. "Baby Names." 1 Oct. 2002 www.hypobirthing.com.

Indian Baby Names Page. 1 Nov. 2002 www.indiaexpress.com/specials/babynames.

Irish Names Page. 15 Jan. 2003 www.hylit.com/info.

Jewish Baby Names Page. 15 Jan. 2003 www.jewishbabynames.net.

Kaplan, Justin, and Anne Bernays. *The Language of Names: What We Call Ourselves and Why It Matters*. New York: Simon & Schuster, 1997.

Lanigan, Catherine. *Writing the Great American Romance Novel*. New York: Allworth Press, 2006.

Lansky, Bruce. *The Mother of All Baby Name Books: Over 94,000 Baby Names Complete with Origins and Meanings*. New York: Meadowlark Press (Simon and Schuster), 2003.

"Months of the Principal Calendars." Gove, Philip Babcock, ed. *Webster's Third New International Dictionary of the English Language Unabridged*. Springfield, MA: Merriam-Webster Inc., 1981.

"Most Popular Names of the 1990s." Social Security Administration Online. 1 Nov. 2002 www.ssa.gov/OACT/babynames.

"Most Popular Names of the 1980s." Social Security Administration Online. 1 Nov. 2002 www.ssa.gov/OACT/babynames.

"Most Popular Names of the 1970s." Social Security Administration Online. 1 Nov. 2002 www.ssa.gov/OACT/babynames.

"Most Popular Names of the 1960s." Social Security Administration Online. 1 Nov. 2002 www.ssa.gov/OACT/babynames.

"Most Popular Names of the 1950s." Social Security Administration Online. 1 Nov. 2002 www.ssa.gov/OACT/babynames.

"Most Popular Names of 2001." Social Security Administration Online. 1 Nov. 2002 www.ssa.gov/OACT/babynames.

"Most Powerful Women in Business." Fortune Online. 14 Oct. 2002 www.fortune.com.

"Movie-Star Names." Internet Movie Database online. 1 Nov. 2002 www.imdb.com.

Nameberry. "Movie Character Names." 1 Feb. 2011. http://nameberry.com/list/225/movie-characters-names.

Norman, Teresa. *A World of Baby Names: A Rich and Diverse Collection of Names from Around the World*. New York: Perigee (Penguin Putnam), 1996.

Origins/Meanings of Baby Names from Around the World Page. 1 Nov. 2002 www.BabyNamesOrigins.com.

Oxygen Page. "Baby Names." 1 Nov. 2002 www.oxygen.com/babynamer.

Parenthood Page. 1 Nov. 2002 www.parenthood.com/parent_cfmfiles/babynames.cfm.

"The Plant Kingdom." Collin, P.H., ed. *Webster's Concise Desk Dictionary*. New York: Barnes & Noble Books, 2001.

Popular Baby Names Page. 1 Nov. 2002 www.popularbabynames.com.

"Presidents of the United States." Collin, P.H., ed. *Webster's Concise Desk Dictionary*. New York: Barnes & Noble Books, 2001.

"Prime Ministers of the U.K." Collin, P.H., ed. *Webster's Concise Desk Dictionary*. New York: Barnes & Noble Books, 2001.

Racketeering and Fraud Investigations Page. 4 Feb. 2003 www.oig.dol.gov/public/media/oi/mainz01.htm.

Rick Porelli's AmericanMafia.com Page. 21 June 2002 www.americanmafia.com/news/6-21-02_Feds_Bust.html.

Rosenkrantz, Linda, and Pamela Redmond Satran. *Baby Names Now*. New York: St. Martin's Press, 2002.

Rosenkrantz, Linda, and Pamela Redmond Satran. *Beyond Charles and Diana: An Anglophile's Guide to Baby Naming*. New York: St. Martin's Press, 1992.

Rosenkrantz, Linda, and Pamela Redmond Satran. *Beyond Jennifer and Jason*. New York: St. Martin's Press, 1994.

Roster of Attorneys, Orange County, California.

Ryan, Joal. *Puffy, Xena, Quentin, Uma: And 10,000 Other Names for Your New Millenium Baby*. New York: Plume (Penguin Putnam), 1999.

Schwegel, Janet. *The Baby Name Countdown*. New York: Marlowe & Company (Avalon), 2001.

Seger, Linda. *Creating Unforgettable Characters*. New York: Henry Holt and Company, Inc., 1990.

Shaw, Jessica. *The Everything Baby Names Book*. Massachusetts: Adams Media Corporation, 1996.

"Signs of the Zodiac." Gove, Philip Babcock, ed. *Webster's Third New International Dictionary of the English Language Unabridged*. Springfield, Mass: Merriam-Webster Inc. Publishers, 1981.

Star Magazine. American Media, Inc. New York.

Television-show credits. 1 Oct. 2002–25 Feb. 2003.

Texas Department of Criminal Justice Page. "Offenders on Death Row." 1 Feb. 2003 www.tdcj.state.tx.us/stat/offendersondrow.htm.

ThinkBabyNames. "Top 1000 Popular Baby Names for Boys." www.thinkbabynames.com. 1 Feb. 2011.

ThinkBaby Names. "Top 1000 Popular Baby Names for Girls." www.thinkbabynames.com. 1 Feb. 2011.

Trantino, Charlee. *Beautiful Baby Names from Your Favorite Soap Operas.* New York: Pinnacle Books, 1996.

United Kingdom Baby Name Page. 15 Jan. 2003 www.baby-names.co.uk.

US Weekly, February 11, 2011, Issue 836. US Weekly, New York.

US Weekly, February 7, 2011, Issue 834. US Weekly, New York.

Wallace, Carol McD. *The Greatest Baby Name Book Ever.* New York: Avon, 1998.

Writer's Digest Handbook of Novel Writing. Edited by Clark, Tom; Brohaugh, William; Woods, Bruce; Strickland, Bill; Blocksom, Peter. Cincinnati, Ohio: Writer's Digest Books, 1992.

About the Author

Diane Stafford

Author of the wildly popular books *40,001 Best Baby Names* and *50,001 Best Baby Names*, magazine editor (five times running) and book editor, Diane Stafford has twenty-five years of experience in writing and editing—but nothing has rivaled the indecent amount of fun involved in turning out a second edition of *60,001+ Best Baby Names*, with 10,000 more names for readers.

Adding names from numerous sources, including radio talk-show listeners who called in when Stafford did first edition interviews, this high-energy author gamely enlarged the scope of a book already filled with great names, fun anecdotes, and baby-naming tips.

"Today people are more creative than ever when it comes to naming their babies," notes Stafford. "Though it may be hard to believe, the fact is, every name in this book belongs to someone out there—even ones as off-the-wall as Dijonaise, Zero, and Oddrun. Although the traditional favorites like Isabella and Jacob still reign supreme, lots of people enjoy making up names for their kids, thus adding to the huge universe of options. While name inventing is controversial—people even talk about it at cocktail parties—my feeling is that you have every right to relish choosing a name for your baby. Sure, take it seriously, but not too seriously."

Stafford adds, "Having a baby is absolutely the most wonderful thing that can happen to a person, and I hope this book reflects my enormous respect for parents and my celebration of the special privilege of parenting."

Living with her husband, Superior Court judge Greg Munoz, in sunny Newport Beach, California, Stafford—a transplant from Houston, Texas—writes and edits books. Her published books include: *Migraines For Dummies*, *Potty Training For Dummies*, *The Encyclopedia of STDs*, *No More Panic Attacks*, *1000 Best Job-Hunting Secrets*, *The Vitamin D Cure* (with Jim Dowd, MD), and her latest, *60,001+ Best Baby Names*. Stafford coauthored four of these books with her daughter, Jennifer Shoquist, MD; her job-hunting book coauthor was Moritza Day.

Dad's Picks

Mom's Picks

Our Picks

Our Picks